THE GOVERNMENT PARTY:
ORGANIZING AND FINANCING THE LIBERAL PARTY
OF CANADA
1930–58

CANADIAN GOVERNMENT SERIES

General Editors

R. MACG. DAWSON, 1946–58 / J.A. CORRY, 1958–61
C.B. MACPHERSON, 1961–75 / S.J.R. NOEL, 1975–

REGINALD WHITAKER

The Government Party: Organizing and Financing the Liberal Party of Canada
1930–58

UNIVERSITY OF TORONTO PRESS
Toronto and Buffalo

©University of Toronto Press 1977
Toronto and Buffalo
Printed in Canada

Canadian Cataloguing in Publication Data

Whitaker, Reginald, 1943–
 The government party

(Canadian government series; 20 ISSN 0068-8835)

Originally presented as the author's thesis (Ph.D.),
University of Toronto.
Includes bibliographical references and index.
ISBN 0-8020-5401-3
ISBN 0-8020-6320-9 pa.

1. Liberal Party (Canada) – History. 2. Canada – Politics and government –
1930-1935.* 3. Canada – Politics and government – 1935-1957.* I. Title. II. Series.
JL197.L5W43   329.9'71   c77-001371-6

This book has been published during the
Sesquicentennial year of the University of Toronto

To Pam

CONTENTS

ACKNOWLEDGMENTS

No book of this magnitude could have been written without the assistance, advice, criticism, and encouragement of many people. The project began as a doctoral dissertation in the Department of Political Economy at the University of Toronto. Professor Donald Smiley, now of York University, presided over its initial stages and supervised it from afar after I left Toronto. His benign and judicious direction is gratefully acknowledged. I should also like to thank my own Department of Political Science at Carleton University for supporting me in the period of research and writing. Two of my Carleton colleagues in particular – Khayyam Paltiel, whose goading, encouragement, and inexhaustible knowledge of the intricacies of political organization and finance was of the utmost importance, and Leo Panitch, whose friendly and critical interest was much appreciated – deserve special mention. Robert Bothwell of the Toronto History Department read the manuscript with great care and offered many valuable criticisms. Stephen Clarkson and Joseph Wearing were also particularly helpful. Among others who have offered comments along the way are Guy Bourassa, R. Craig Brown, Jane Jenson, Ron Manzer, Jack McLeod, Sid Noel, Garth Stevenson, and Conrad Winn.

The Liberal party itself was fully co-operative in facilitating the project through its willingness to grant me access to the voluminous files of the National Liberal Federation. I should in particular like to thank Senator Richard Stanbury, former president of the Liberal party, and two successive national directors of the party, Torrence Wylie and Blair Williams. J.W. Pickersgill was kind enough to grant me access to the closed sections of the Mackenzie King papers, the Louis St Laurent papers, and the C.D. Howe papers, as well as offering generous encouragement to the project. Mention should also be made of W.P. Power, who gave me access to the papers of his late father, C.G. Power, and Mrs S.B. Ralston, who allowed me to use the J.L. Ralston papers. Special acknowledgment should be made to the staff of the Public Archives of Canada, especially Jean Dryden (now with the Provincial Archives of Alberta), Eldon Frost, and Lee McDonald, and to Ian Wilson and the staff of the Douglas Library at Queen's University. The unfailing courtesy and assistance offered by both these institutions makes the task of the researcher both easier and more pleasant than it would otherwise be.

The University of Toronto Press was most helpful from the first. R.I.K.

Davidson's infectious enthusiasm for the project was deeply appreciated, as was his skill at guiding it through to publication. Gerald Hallowell did a judicious editing of the text. I would also like to thank John Malcomson for assistance with the preparation of the index. Mrs Phyllis Wilson and Mrs Dulcie O'Neill, as well as a number of secretaries in the Carleton Political Science Department, contributed to the typing of what proved to be a voluminous manuscript.

I should like to acknowledge the financial assistance of the Canada Council, which supported me for two years of a doctoral fellowship while at Toronto and provided editorial support as well, and the C.D. Howe Memorial Foundation which offered me generous financial assistance for a year. Carleton University provided funds to assist typing and editorial work. This book has been published with the help of a grant from the Social Science Research Council of Canada, using funds provided by the Canada Council, and a grant from the Publications Fund of the University of Toronto Press.

Finally, but most importantly, I would like to thank Pam MacDonald, my wife, whose unfailing help and support throughout the long period of the research and writing of this book was, in the deepest sense, crucial to its completion.

R.W.

INTRODUCTION

In 1955 *Canadian Forum* noted the twentieth anniversary of uninterrupted Liberal rule at Ottawa with an article by Paul Fox, who drew attention to the *silence* which characterized not only the workings of Liberal government but also the intellectual and academic attitudes toward that goverment. 'How few of our politicians even bother to write their memoirs!' Fox lamented. 'The Liberal government aims at operating noiselessly, like a respectable mammoth business corporation which fears nothing more than making people aware that it is there. The shadows flit silently along the wall, as in Plato's cave, and the citizen is never sufficiently disturbed to turn his head.'[1]

Yet who could deny the crucial importance of this era to the development of the Canadian nation and the Canadian political system? It was, after all, the era in which Canada emerged from the Great Depression into the modern welfare state, when the basis for a new relationship between government and business was achieved, and when the economic and social foundations of a transformed federalism were built. And who could deny the importance of the Liberal party, that quintessential agent of political change in an era of apathy and political quiescence? And when one considers that after the brief 'Diefenbaker interlude' Canada has returned once again to uninterrupted Liberal domination of national government, the silence and obscurity within which the Liberal party of this earlier era has been wrapped becomes a matter of serious concern to those who wish to inquire into the present state of Canadian politics.

The urgency of an investigation of the Liberal party has been recently demonstrated by Alan Cairns in an article comparing Canadian and American political science: 'The dozens of books on the Democratic party highlight the absence of a single academic book on the Canadian Liberal party.'[2] The Symons Report on Canadian Studies, prepared for the Association of Universities and Colleges of Canada, recently cited this same gap in scholarship. There is a relatively wide literature on third parties in Canada and a scanty literature on the Conservatives. There are, of course, political biographies of leading Liberals, as well as studies of the political institutions which the Liberals have done much to shape, from cabinet to civil service. But on the subject of the Liberals as a *party*, there is indeed very little in print. Symons suggests that a 'rough rule of thumb appears to be that the less successful a political party is, the more scholars will wish to write about it. Conversely, the more successful a political party is, the less scholars will be willing to write about it.'[3] There is an unpublished doctoral thesis on the Liberals, of uncommonly high quality, by Peter Regenstreif.[4] But Regenstreif's work has gone unrevised and unpublished for over a decade, during which time much information to which he did not have access has become available. This study differs from Regenstreif's in being both less extensive and more intensive. No attempt has been made here to cover the Liberal party from its nineteenth-century origins to the Pearson and Trudeau eras, nor is there any attempt to cover as broad a spectrum of factors as Regenstreif, including party leadership, ideology, and voter support. Both in historical sweep and in analytic scope, then, this study is much more limited than Regenstreif's earlier work. On the other hand, it is much more intensive in its chosen area of examination – party organization and finance in the period from 1930 to 1958 – based on the enormous amount of evidence available in the collections of private papers of leading Liberal politicians which have become accessible to researchers within the past decade.

The methodology of this study is, perhaps, in this age of mathematical political 'science' and sophisticated theoretical models, rather strikingly old-fashioned. The point is made without any particular sense of apology, perhaps even with a touch of belligerence. The methodology is certainly *empirical*, although generally not *quantitative*, and rests on the use of historical evidence; it may be judged on the basis of the standards of historical description and interpretation. That a study of the Liberal party in Canada should rest on a historical-descriptive basis is not, at this point, merely an accident or a reflection of the personal tastes of the author. The very dearth of material in print on the Liberal party is itself one of the strongest arguments for beginning with description. As Cairns, in the paper cited previously, has argued, the relative scantiness of the basic descriptive literature available in Canada as compared to the much broader infrastructure available to behavioural scholars of American politics, suggests a warning about the replication of American-style quantitative studies in Canada to the exclusion of more traditional inquiries: 'Canadian research decisions pertaining to the Canadian polity should not be made in the light of American knowledge of the American political system. If decisions are made in the light of Canadian knowledge it is highly probable that traditional types of research will have a greater utility in the Canadian than in the American setting. Robert Dubin's admonition, that "we make progress slowly because we value description so lowly," probably has special application to the Canadian situation in which descriptive studies are still lacking.'[5] Nowhere is this latter condition more evident than in regard to the study of the Liberal party.

The two factors to be analysed, party organization and finance, do not, of course, offer comprehensive insight into the question of what the Liberal party was, or its impact on the Canadian political system. The failure to systematically examine voting support, party ideology, parliamentary behaviour, administrative performance, or the social and economic basis of recruitment into the Liberal party, does not arise from an indifference to these factors or to their importance, but simply from a need to specialize, given the vast amount of information now available to this narrow but, I think, significant question of party organization and finance. Other factors do enter into the picture at various points, but only tangentially, as they become relevant to the central focus. What is offered here is thus a contribution to an understanding of the Liberal party from a particular perspective.

There are, moreover, some very good reasons for concentrating on the question of party organization and finance, which emerge from the current state of the academic study of political parties, outside Canada as well as within. Max Weber broke down the study of political parties into the following categories of analysis: the party-in-itself (that is, the party as an organization), the party-in-office, the party-in-the-electorate, and the contributors of party funds.[6] The second and third of these categories, the party-in-office and the party-in-the-electorate, have been examined in much greater detail than the other two. The development of voting studies based on survey data has particularly mined the area of voting support for political parties. The organization of the legislature and the functioning of cabinet government under party discipline have also been extensively studied. Although this is generally true in Western political science, it is especially true with regard to the Liberal party of Canada. I have chosen to concentrate in this study on the least examined aspects of the Liberal party: party organization and party finance.

If there are particular intellectual antecedents to be found for the approach taken in this study, they are in an older, but recently rediscovered, European tradition of organizational analysis, founded in the late nineteenth and early twentieth centuries by Lord Bryce and by M. Ostrogorski, whose classic work on the growth of extra-parliamentary party organizations in Britain and the United States is only now returning to its rightful place as the foundation of the study of political parties. Ostrogorski in turn exercised considerable influence on Weber, and on Robert Michels, whose famous 'iron law of oligarchy' has overshadowed his more comprehensive organizational examination of socialist parties. After the Second World

War this tradition was revived once more by Maurice Duverger in a sweeping comparative framework.[7] This approach has, however, never been very popular in the United States, and in Canada it has had a very uneven history.[8] The neglect of the Ostrogorski tradition on this continent is beginning to change with the realization, as one leading American student of parties has concluded, that 'the major theoretical contributions to the study of political parties have come from that sector of the literature in which the party as an empirically observable organization dominates the work.'[9]

A renewed organizational focus also leads to a concern for another neglected area of research: the historical development of parties. A recent survey of voting studies for Western liberal democracies has concluded that the most striking feature of the electorates of these countries since the Second World War has been the lack of any observable long-term trends in voting: 'Whatever index of change is used ... the picture is the same: the electoral strength of most parties in Western nations since the war has changed very little from election to election, or within the life span of a generation ... [T]he first priority of social scientists concerned with the development of parties and party systems since 1945 is to explain the absence of change in a far from static period in political history.'[10]

As S.M. Lipset and Stein Rokkan have noted, the party alternatives, and in remarkably many cases the party organizations, are older than the majorities of the national electorates, 'reflecting the cleavage structures of the 1920s.'[11] In the Canadian case it is the 1930s which would seem to be the decisive period for the freezing of political alternatives. With the exception of gains made by the Social Credit party in British Columbia in the early 1950s and in Quebec in the early 1960s, and the rise of the Parti Québécois in the 1970s, no new parties have forced their way into local political systems. The New Democratic party, for instance, remains locked into four significant pockets of electoral support: rural Saskatchewan, working class British Columbia, and urban Manitoba and Ontario, all of which date from the early days of its predecessor, the Co-operative Commonwealth Federation. Areas of the country hospitable to third-party movements in the early part of the century remain hospitable to them; areas like the Maritimes which remained impervious then remain impervious now. Areas, such as municipal politics, which have been non-partisan, are highly resistant to the entry of any parties.

All this strongly suggests that to understand the basis of party support it is not enough to understand contemporary issues and contemporary social structure. Parties in a sense represent frozen elements of earlier alignments. It is becoming increasingly obvious that only a longer historical perspective can begin to make sense of party systems which in a static framework raise more questions than answers. There seems to be little hope of explaining why, for instance, anti-government resentment against strongly free enterprise administrations in Alberta and Saskatchewan in 1971 should take the form of the Conservative party in the former and the New Democratic party in the latter, without an examination of the freezing of party alternatives in the 1930s in divergent fashions in the two provinces, along with subsequent party histories.

This historical emphasis has in turn led to a renewal of interest in regionalism and conflicts between the cultures of the centre and the periphery. Although the supposedly homogeneous nations of Europe have been often considered exempt from regional cleavages, it would appear that party alignments do often divide along just such lines, even where the original conflict may by now be diminished or largely forgotten. Rokkan has shown that even in a country as ethnically and culturally integrated as Norway the party system reflects regional differences in the inherited socio-economic structure; the complex crosscutting of cleavage lines in the national system can be understood only against this background.[12] What seems to be involved here is the historical phenomenon of uneven modernization. The rate of social mobilization, to use Karl Deutsch's phrase,[13] has not proceeded at an equal pace for all sections of any nation; the level of integration into national political systems has consequently been quite variable. Party alignments based on these divisions become frozen even after these divisions have lost their initial force. Organization is thus a kind of dead hand which, having once solidified party structures around certain regional alignments, perpetuates these structures in the face of new challenges and conflicts.

This leads to the question of local entrenchment of political parties over time. The process by which parties build strong local organizational bases, most often founded on the distribution of the patronage which comes from control of municipal or regional offices, is a general phenomenon of party politics in Western liberal democracies and applies equally well to the mass Communist parties of Italy and France as to more traditional parties. This question, which has been little studied within a comparative framework until recently, has been relatively ignored in Canadian political science.[14]

In the Canadian case, national parties do not seem to have built bases on municipal political office, but rather on provincial office. To analyse local party entrenchment in Canada, then, is to look to provincial party organization. In a federal state as decentralized and regionalized as Canada, the parties themselves, especially the two older brokerage-type parties, exhibit internal party decentralization and organizational discontinuity to an extreme degree;[15] thus the analysis of local entrenchment can in no sense be understood to assume an organizational framework of central hierarchy. Indeed, organizational discontinuity between the federal and provincial levels of national parties in Canada has historically been so significant that cross-party alliances, either tacit or acknowledged, have sometimes been put into practical operation with a degree of effectiveness which, in the short run at least, calls into question the very concept of the collective identity of the party transcending federal-provincial lines. The relationship between the national party in Canada and its provincial entrenchments is thus one of extraordinary complexity, yet this complexity should not be allowed to obscure the significance of the relationship itself. However difficult the task, any study of national party organization in this country must include provincial party organizations as an essential element.

To recapitulate, the lessons drawn from the past and current literature on political parties are that the focus of study should be on party *organization*, on the party as a structure or institution; that it should be *historical* in nature; and that it should not rest on the national party alone but should include an analysis of *provincial* party organization.

Although parties are elected to govern, parties, as such, are less concerned with the organization of government than with the organization of the means of getting elected. In periods of one-party dominance the party-in-office does become closely identified with the party organization – but our analytical focus will be on the party as an electoral organization. Similarly, this study is not concerned with party policy or ideology, as such; although issues continually impinge upon party organization, we are interested in them only indirectly, as they affect organization. In short, the focus will be on the organizational apparatus linking the party-in-office in the legislature to the unorganized electorate, whether such linkage exists only at elections or has a more continuous life.

Two variables stand out in any analysis of the organization of this linkage. The first is the question of the organization's economic base, how it finances its activities and allocates its resources. Or, more succinctly, who owns the means of political production, and how are they controlled? The second is the nature of the political 'market' in which the party participates. What are the electoral *mores*, the political culture, the rules of the game within which it must operate?

The latter point is of great significance for the study of national parties in a country as diverse as Canada, especially when we wish to examine the historical development of the organizational freezing of party alternatives. A party like the Liberals which has found throughout the century significant bases of support in almost every section of the country cannot be a unified or monolithic organization employing the same strategy in a single common 'market.' Quite apart from the question of different ideological appeals to different sections, there is the more basic fact that the very electoral process is different in different sections. The 'rules of the game' vary considerably: an election in New Brunswick may in empirical terms bear little resemblance to the same process in Saskatchewan; it may be a quite different game being played, in which there may be little in common other than the desire to defeat the other side. The Committee on Election Expenses, for example, found a dramatic divergence in the use of money in elections between Canada east of the Ottawa River and that part to the west.[16] It would seem a reasonable hypothesis that such differences will lead to differences in the structure of party organization.

It was suggested earlier that a critical factor in the organizational solidification of party alternatives seems to be the differential regional rate of social mobilization. Samuel Hays has proposed a theoretical framework for the study of the development of American parties in the late nineteenth and early twentieth centuries along such lines. Seeing industrial development as shifting society further toward impersonal or functional relationships, Hays detects a conflict between 'locals' and 'cosmopolitans,' between local party organizations rooted in small, face-to-face communities and national organizations based on impersonal, functional interest relationships. In this view, the Progressive era in the United States with its 'reform' of the party machines becomes in retrospect a triumph of corporate capitalist 'efficiency' over local community control. Direct primaries, initiatives, referendums, recalls, and the like were attempts to weaken or destroy the political party organization in favour of new decision-making bodies such as corporations and bureaucratic boards or commissions.[17] This model offers some important clues.

If we may assume that politics is essentially concerned with the redistribution of resources – Lasswell's 'who gets what, when, how' – it can be seen that there are two polar models of redistribution in modern societies: *patronage* and *bureaucracy*. These models fit into the two cultures described by Hays, patronage relationships being rooted in the 'local' or less mobilized culture and bureaucratic relationships resting most easily on the 'cosmopolitan' or highly mobilized national culture. Bureaucratic relationships of redistribution imply universality and a reliance on the state as agent; redistribution takes the form of impersonal taxation and welfare policies (that is, one is taxed at a certain rate because one earns a certain income, and one receives certain transfer payments because of one's status as 'citizen,' 'old age pensioner,' 'parent,' etc.). Patronage relationships of redistribution imply personal specificity and a reliance on the politician as agent (that is, one advances the politician certain dues in labour or votes, and one receives a personalized payoff in money, goods, or jobs). In the former case there is an impersonal relationship between two abstract entities, citizen and state; in the latter a personal relationship between two individuals, client and patron. Each model has important implications for the electoral culture and the organization of political parties.

There is now a wealth of comparative literature available on the patron-client model in political development.[18] The major elements in the model may be identified as follows. It involves a relationship between actors of *unequal* wealth, power, or status, the relationship being one of *reciprocity* involving a mutual exchange, the patron providing protection and the client offering support. This exchange system is at base particularistic, typified by a personal, face-to-face relationship. In a democratic political system, with a mass franchise, the currency of the patron-client exchange involves the manipulation of indirect, office-based property, that is, the ability on the part of the patron to dispense rewards placed in his hands by a larger and more impersonal body, the political party, and the ability of the client to offer electoral support, in various forms. From the local level to the national level, the basic diadic relation extends upward in a pyramidal form as patrons become themselves clients of patrons more powerful, or with command over greater resources. Although it is essentially a *hierarchical* or *vertical* model of the distribution of political power – indeed one of the particular strengths of the model is that it helps to explain the lack of horizontal solidarity among people of equivalent status and the apparently deferential submission to higher status actors characteristic of many underdeveloped nations where class and ethnicity seem less important indicators of association than might be assumed – the model also allows for the existence of a high degree of discontinuity in the structure of power, and the possibility of intense competition and conflict between different, and shifting, patron-client clusters and pyramids. Where the bases of different clusters or pyramids are articulated with regional economies and regional political systems, as in a federal state, and these bases are persistent over time, the stage is set either for violent conflict or for *horizontal* accommodations between the leaderships of the various clusters and pyramids.

While the model of patron-client politics has most often been assumed to apply to underdeveloped nations with traditional elements persistent in their societies and political cultures, there are aspects of the model which seem to be appropriate to advanced industrial nations as well. Some writers have tried to extend the concept in this way, and while it might seem to be stretching a point there are certain patterns of political behaviour and certain types of political institutions in liberal democracies which are better explained along patron-client lines than in other, more orthodox, ways. The big city machines in urban America, the persistence of political patronage, the phenomenon of political corruption, all appear to fall within this category. There are also reasons to believe that the model may be of use in the specific Canadian context. It is generally recognized that traditional authority patterns have persisted much longer in rural Quebec than in the more urbanized parts of English Canada; patron-client politics have been fairly extensively employed by Quebec political scientists in recent years to analyse changes in the political culture of that province.[19] The Atlantic region has also presented a similar face of economic underdevelopment and persistence of pre-bureaucratic forms of political relations, as have some rural sections of Ontario and western Canada. The recent interest in the model of consociational democracy or élite accommodation to explain political stability in a culturally fragmented federal system like Canada would also seem to fit very well within the patron-client system of vertically unequal and horizontally accommodative relationships.[20] Finally, in the broadest historical context, Canada, as a nation whose political system derived from a clientage-type of colonial relationship to England, and whose economy today demonstrates an unparalleled dependency upon that of another nation, the United States, offers an international context conducive to the persistence within of patron-client patterns, as the literature on Latin American dependency and neo-colonialism in Africa and Asia has demonstrated in linking the power of local patron-élites to the external power of dominant foreign economies. National clientage rests more comfortably on a base of internal clientage; in turn, local clientage is reinforced by the fact that a portion of the resources derived from national clientage is channeled into the hands of the dependent internal élites, whose position vis-à-vis their own clients is thereby enhanced. Thus both the weakness of the Canadian élites in dealing with external challenges to Canadian national autonomy and their strength in dealing with any challenges from below within Canada may be viewed as part of a web of clientage relationships from the local to the international level.

Clearly patron-client politics is not an exhaustive explanation, and any attempt to apply this model in too narrow and relentless a fashion will miss the mark. There is above all the fact that Canada exhibits most of the attributes of a mass society and most of the political characteristics of mass liberal democracies, such as highly impersonal bureaucratic redistributive systems and the use of mass communication techniques to contest elections, which are every bit as widespread in Canada as in any other advanced industrial nation – and just as subversive, by definition, of strict patron-client politics. The modernizing factors of industrialization, urbanization, and technological development have cut severely into the traditional currency of clientage politics – political patronage.

Patronage is a form of economic redistribution which, at a certain level of economic development and social mobilization, fits readily and efficiently into the social structure. Take the example of rural Quebec. Lemieux's important work on kinship and politics on l'Ile d'Orléans have gone far toward demonstrating the rationale for resistance against the bureaucratization of redistribution on the part of the traditional Quebec society, and the tenacity with which the old patronage relationships are maintained. The 'pre-modern' social structure tends to reject the depersonalized, inhuman face of an abstract bureaucracy in favour of the greater human warmth of the patronage relationship: 'un rapport bureaucratique peut se définer comme une relation très extensive entre deux classes, et un rapport de patronage comme une relation très compréhensive entre deux individus.'[21]

The specific forms of patronage redistribution could involve the passing of sums of money, or goods such as alcohol, clothes, food, or fuel, at election time; assistance to the needy; the provision of local services, such as roads, bridges, or post offices; and the appointment of party supporters to government positions, from local construction jobs to judgeships. Large-scale economic development in the late ninteenth and early twentieth century created a new age of corporate capitalism in which there was a growing tendency to uproot patronage as being economically inefficient. As F.W. Gibson has pointed out, this change hardly implies any moral superiority, for all that is really involved is a transformation of the old 'staple' patronage into corporate patronage:

The controllers of corporate capitalism, though they were by no means shy about seeking governmental assistance where it would be useful, were not greatly interested in the petty jobs or minor contracts which the traditional varieties of staple patronage had to offer. They sought other and grander advantages: tariff adjustments and trade treaties to protect particular industries and firms; government guarantees for corporate bond issues; subsidies and subventions for iron and steel, for railways and shipbuilding; tax concessions; and preferential access to natural resources.[22]

In effect, redistribution as it affected the ordinary Canadian citizen was increasingly bureaucratized, while at the same time redistribution among the corporate élite retained a patronage form. There is thus a double complexity in the application of the model. On the one hand, we find a growing tension between patronage and bureaucracy as it affects the organization of political life at the local, or voter, level. The tension exists to some degree everywhere, from the constant complaints over the years from MPs and local party activists against the Civil Service Act and the merit system in the federal public service, to the equally persistent complaints of party leaders and cabinet ministers that they had neither time nor inclination to look after mundane local matters of patronage, when important policy issues and problems of administration claimed their attention. Obviously the balance of these two forces varied from region to region, and even within the same region between different classes, groups, or even parties. Moreover, the balance was a shifting one, varying with such external factors as the state of economic development and the relationship of the region to the national government. The second complexity rests with the relationship of the political parties to corporate economic power, and the question of whether this relationship, however much it rested on patronage, could be called a patron-client relationship, or whether it could be better termed an equal or horizontal exchange between accommodating élites.

In examining the national Liberal party from the period 1930 to 1958 the model remains highly suggestive and offers what seems to be the most useful framework for analysis – always bearing in mind, of course, its limitations as well. Important elements of the clientage relationship were a tenacious feature of Liberal party organization in this era, even though in constant tension with the tendency of bureaucracy to undermine the traditional relationships. No alternative hypothesis can explain the peculiar and distinctive features of the Liberal party as an organization in this era.

The Liberals were themselves very much aware of the precise nature of this arrangement. Explicit statements of what amounts to a recognition of the clientage basis of national party organization are not wanting. For example, the secretary of the National Liberal Federation wrote a memorandum to the president of the federation in 1946 to complain about the bureaucratic bent of the postwar Liberal government and the damage this tendency was doing to the very basis of party organization:

Support for the party is held and extended to a considerable degree through local leaders in each community who support Liberal principles. Their support can only be effective when the community leader's prestige is promoted through his connections with the party and the government in the handling of local problems. Failure to give fair and sympathetic consideration to his representations endangers his prestige and weakens his influence for Liberalism, indeed such action often drives the local community leader to the support of the opposition parties.[23]

At a party executive meeting in the 1950s, one official suggested that the cabinet ministers should 'pay particular attention to key men in the little towns. He thought the most urgent need was to build up lots of "foremen," straw bosses, because it was these men who were tremendously important in building grass roots organization.'[24] Examples could be multiplied, but the point should be obvious.

The basic outlines of the structure of the party began in the local community where the MP or the defeated candidate held the key to local patronage. The crucial organizational problem for the party at the local or constituency level was how to interest enough people in the party to put together the hundreds-strong organization needed for election day, ranging from returning officers to poll clerks to scrutineers, inside and outside, to drivers, and to the other odd jobs required. Direct cash payments were by no means unknown, but indirect promises of patronage or influence following success at the polls were also featured as commodities of exchange. Regional or provincial clusters of MPs and candidates would then in turn become clients to the regional or provincial cabinet minister who was the leading figure in the political organization of the area, and who controlled higher levels of government patronage as a rewards system for maintaining the allegiance of his MPs. Finally the cabinet ministers were themselves clients to the prime minister, who held such powers as that of appointment and firing over them, not to speak of the power of dissolution of Parliament. It must be remembered that the reciprocal nature of the exchange relationship in clientist systems meant that it was not a one-way street of influence. Secondly, at the national level, it always remained true that the relationship between the cabinet ministers, and thus between the leaders of the various regions within the party, were as much relations of mutual accommodation as hierarchical, involving horizontal rather than vertical patterns of interaction. This form of party organization will be called 'ministerialist.'

There are a number of cross-cutting problems which require some attention in delineating this model. First, there is the vexed question of the relationship of the top levels of the party to the corporate capitalist world of wealth, upon which the party was dependent in two senses: to finance its own electoral operations and to operate the national economy to the mutual benefit of party and shareholder. A considerable amount of attention will be paid to this question throughout this study. Second is the matter of the relationship of the national party and the provincial party, and the extent of dependence or domination between these two separate systems of power. Part II of this study is intended to examine this question at length. Third, there is the question of the relationship of the extra-parliamentary organization of the party to the ministerialist parliamentary organization. When the Liberal party was out of office, it became necessary to activate an extra-parliamentary party organization, since ministerialism only worked efficiently when the regional leaders were in fact cabinet ministers, with control of the resources which those positions gave them. It was also found that certain functions even when in power were best performed by a specialized body separate organizationally from the cabinet, although under its control. A constant theme of the first part of this study is the changing relationship between the parliamentary and the extra-parliamentary party.

Fourth, throughout most of the period, the Liberal party was the party in government. The identification of the Liberals with government, and the structural implications for party organization, is so important that the Liberals can be called 'the Government party' as a label indicating not only an electoral situation of success but, more significantly, a form of party organization in which the distinction between state and party becomes difficult to draw. Unlike the case of the one-party dominant system in patronage cultures, of which the Union Nationale in Quebec may best be used as an example, the long Liberal dominance in the national government did not develop in a purely patronage culture, but in an environment where patronage and bureaucratic forms rested in uneasy equilibrium, an equilibrium in which bureaucratic relations were generally displacing patronage relations, in the electoral sphere at least, if not in the area of government-business relations, where corporate patronage remained largely unchallenged. The paradox is that ministerialist organization of party and government, although in one sense resting firmly on a clientist system of power, also did much to undermine that system. Cabinet ministers played a dual role, one political and clientist, the other administrative and bureaucratic. The system of party organization left the cabinet ministers in an ambiguous position between these two quite different, and sometimes conflicting, roles. Long identification with office and the external constraints of dealing with problems, for which patronage politics simply offered no solutions – problems such as depressions, wars, the management of a modern economy, and the provision of social welfare measures – tended in the long run to atrophy the patronage side of the ministers' role and to enhance the bureaucratic forms of governmental and party organization. The decline of the private member of

Parliament as a factor in government is a reflection of this trend, and a symptom of a decline in clientist party organization. The implications of these changes in party structure for the relationship of the national party to its constituent provincial parties, whose own electoral cultures might not necessarily have developed apace with that of the national government, will be discussed in Part II. The strains and tensions caused within the national party itself will be examined throughout Part I.

The approach adopted for this study is not a rigorous application of a single model, but rather an attempt to examine the Liberal party in the light of a changing balance between two different systems, one slowly but very unevenly being displaced by the other. These systems did not interact in a vacuum, but were themselves the result of more significant underlying changes in the economy and society. While we cannot deal in any depth with these underlying factors, it is well to bear them in mind, to understand that a political party, in this case the Liberal party, is an adaptive mechanism, changing its structure to meet changing circumstances, its attempts at organizational survival thus adjusting and modifying the political system itself. A study of the Liberal party during the period of its greatest dominance of Canadian national politics ought to be of some significance for any understanding of the development of that system.

PART I

The national Liberal party, 1930-58

1

Background to the Liberal revival, 1930–2

The Liberal party of Canada had, like the Canadian nation itself, passed through some very profound changes in the first thirty years of the twentieth century. The first major signal of the tumult of the new century was the defeat of the Laurier government in 1911. Fifteen years of Liberal ascendancy marked by prosperity, industrialization, and national confidence – a late extension of the nineteenth-century certitudes, but under Liberal auspices rather than Conservative – had come to an end in the atmosphere of resurgent Tory nationalism and imperialism. The old tactics of 1836, 1878, and 1891 had once more succeeded in wrapping the Conservative party in the Union Jack and the reflected glory of the British Crown. Major defections from Liberal ranks during the reciprocity campaign and the adherence of significant sections of the Toronto business community to the Borden Conservatives were among the more public manifestations of internal party disintegration which was confirmed with the actual election results. But underlying the great issue of trade and its direction were signs of organizational malaise after a decade and a half of power. Indeed, it has been argued recently that the major cause of Liberal defeat was the aging and incompetent Liberal organization in the province of Ontario.[1] Moreover, the failure of the Liberals to hold the Bourassa *nationalistes* in Quebec, where Liberal organizational strength had given the first thrust to Liberal victory in the 1890s,[2] was another indication that the old formulas for political success could not hold up in the twentieth century. When great issues about national status swept the hustings and the old organizational structures proved inadequate, the combination was disastrous.

If 1911 was dispiriting to Liberals, the events of the Great War as they impinged on the Canadian political process were even more so. The spectre of conscription and the division of Canada into warring 'races' could only bode ill for a party which based its national strength upon its French-Canadian leader and its popularity in Quebec. The formation of a Union government in 1917 seemed to give concrete form to the fears of further Liberal decay. An English-Canadian coalition government versus a French-Canadian Liberal opposition was anything but a formula for Liberal victory. The wartime election of the same year produced exactly these results in stark relief.

Yet a strange dialectic of history was preparing a Liberal rebirth on the very ground of its catastrophe in 1917. The Union triumph was self-limiting and, as it turned out, self-defeating. The problem of the distribution of patronage, the lifeblood of political organization, proved practically insoluble. Indeed, a civil service commissioner wryly compared the administration of patronage by a Union government to the command of the ancient Egyptian Pharaoh that the Israelites make bricks without straw.[3] More serious yet was the impact of Union government on the political loyalties of English-speaking Canadians. The transformation of Canada from an agricultural to an industrial nation, accelerated by the demands of the war, was changing the economic basis of Canadian politics. Two social classes, the farmers and the industrial workers, were about to explode into the political arena at war's end. The farmers were, in historical perspective, a declining demographic factor, especially in the east, but they entered politics as a group pushed to the wall and ready to fight back with a doctrine that emphasized class as the basis of politics and de-emphasized traditional party loyalties. The organized working class was an ascending factor, but one which at the end of the war was not yet ready to take a decisive role. The astonishing victory in 1919 of the United Farmers party in the very heartland of industry, the province of Ontario, signalled the end of the traditional two-party system in Canada. The Winnipeg General Strike in the same year demonstrated that the more politically unfocused discontent of the workers could take serious form indeed. In the face of this seething political cauldron a Union government offered living proof of the arguments of the anti-party and third-party advocates: the old parties had no real differences.

If a farmer-worker alliance had been built at this time which was national in its organization and appeal, one of the two old parties might have disappeared. As it was, the election of 1921 left the Conservatives as the 'third' party in Parliament, although the anti-party ideology of the Progressives rendered them incapable of consolidating their partisan position, or even of maintaining it. But two other factors helped the two old parties to retain their hegemony over national power, and the Liberal party in particular to recapture its position as the dominant of the two. The first was the very liability of 1917: the profound identification, in the hour of greatest wartime crisis, of the Liberal party with French Quebec. When English Canada was flying off in various political directions, the solidity of *rouge* Quebec, fired by the passions of the conscription crisis, was the single most important political counter in a national electoral confrontation. The second factor was the traditional affinity with the Liberal party held by so many Progressives, never too far below the surface anywhere except perhaps in Alberta where the Liberal party would never fully recover from the farmers' victory of 1921. On both counts, then, the one immediate and the other delayed, the Liberals held a better hand than the Tories.

The better hand could not win, however, without a skilled and well-situated leader to play it. William Lyon Mackenzie King was such. One of the few prominent English-speaking Liberals who had not joined the Union government in 1917, the author of *Industry and Humanity*, and the 'brains trust' of the Rockefeller empire's labour relations operations, King was ideally suited to combine the allegiance of Catholic Quebec with the perspectives of a modern twentieth-century political technician. The death of Laurier and the coming of King do seem to mark a turning point in the development of the Liberal party, something more than a mere change of leaders would in itself indicate. With King in the leadership, the Liberal party in English Canada became somewhat more of a modern, urbanized political party, with Quebec forming a loyal but conservative rearguard – not altogether unlike the Democratic party under Franklin D. Roosevelt with its 'solid South.'

The qualities of Mackenzie King as party leader and prime minister are not here at issue. What is more pertinent to the study of Liberal party organization is the effect of the new political circumstances and the new party leadership on the organizational structures of the party. Here the changes were not very significant. The first decade or so of King's leadership saw little in the way of major innovations in the national organization. The Liberal party was in this sense not very different in 1930 from the Laurier Liberal party thirty years earlier. The party system had been recast into a new mould, the issues were significantly different, the nature of national election campaigns had evolved considerably – yet the organizational structure of the party was very much the same.

PARTY ORGANIZATION

The party which King took over in 1919 was obviously in an organizational mess as a result of the division between Unionist and Laurier Liberals, a division which extended from the highest levels of the party down to the constituencies.[4] The pulling away of agrarian Liberal elements in the Prairies and Ontario towards the farmers' movement was a further organizational problem. Added to this was the uncomfortable fact that the one solidly Liberal area, Quebec, was precisely the wing of the party dominated by high-tariff big business interests most inimical to the kind of policies required to attract the farmers back into the Liberal flock. The fledgling leader, who had yet to acquire the reputation for political genius which was to surround his activities in later life, thus faced a hazardous initiation under fire. His strategy, which is difficult to confute even with the benefit of hindsight, was to avoid organizational innovations and to concentrate his energies on the policy problems of which the organizational problems were reflections. A decade later he was to regret the resultant neglect of organization, but in the context of the setting of political priorities during the immediate postwar period this neglect is understandable.

The 1919 convention not only chose King as leader and passed policy resolutions considered to be to the left of the political spectrum of that era but also examined the problem of party organization. The weakness of the party structure was evident from the fact that the convention itself apparently was organized by two men: Charles Murphy, Liberal MP and organizer, and his secretary, Andrew Haydon.[5] Murphy, later to be one of the most venomous King-haters in the Liberal party, was especially interested in the question of more efficient party organization, believing as he did that it was the soft spot of the Laurier Liberals even when they had been winning elections – victories being due not to organization but to the popularity of the party's policies or the weakness of the opposition. An anonymous memorandum, which Peter Regenstreif identifies as coming from Murphy,[6] was circulated to the convention outlining a scheme for reorganization, stressing that a permanent national office to link the parliamentary wing with the local rank and file, not subject to change by the death or defection of a few men here or there, was necessary to mount a sustained political effort in the modern era. Murphy drew on an analogy to the business world:

If good business be good politics, it is submitted that to attain the objects for which it exists the Liberal party should be organized on the same basis as a joint stock company ... [T]he basis of a joint stock company is made up of its capital, its board of directors and its general manager. By analogy, the capital of the Liberal party is represented by its principles and its policy, its board of directors are the national leader and those associated with him ... and its general manager would be the official engaged by the board of directors to act as general organizer, to carry out the board's instructions and generally to supervise the detailed work of the party in all the provinces ...

This neat analogy, to be repeated in various forms in the years to come by Murphy's successors – more or less wistfully, depending upon the realism of the official in question – was a false and misleading comparison. One fallacy was in the substitution of the 'principles and policy' of the party for the capital with which a business financed its activities. Joseph Israel Tarte had long before coined his memorable phrase 'les élections ne se font pas avec des prières,' and principles or policies were as unlikely in themselves to pay for organization as prayers. Canadian parties had not been able to solve the problem of inter-election financing; since the Liberal party had from the reciprocity campaign of 1911 been suffering from a lack of funding even at election time, a permanent organizational superstructure without any economic base was merely an exercise in daydreaming. Principles and policy were important, but scarcely a substitute for this economic base.

A second problem in the Murphy scheme was an inherent contradiction between centralization and decentralization. After outlining the expansive plan for a central corporate-style structure indicated above, the memorandum quickly followed with the proviso that the new head office must not interfere with provincial autonomy: '... provincial rights ... must be absolute and must be carefully guarded; for it is the Liberal tradition.' Nor was this merely a ritual bow by an Ontario Liberal to the ghost of Oliver Mowat. Head office must be only a co-ordinating and liaison link between east and west, a 'general clearing house' passing on information, not sending out orders. Murphy knew that the Central Information Office set up after the election of 1911 had met with the open hostility of Quebec Liberals. Provincial autonomy was a given, not a problematic, factor. Yet at the same time Murphy also wanted the national organizer to be a competent man with business experience, commanding a respectable salary. Why such a man was needed to oversee a central 'clearing house' of information is not clear. In fact, there was what amounts to an irresolvable contradiction between centralism and decentralism, a contradiction which was in no way to lessen with the passing years. This contradiction would be manifest not only in regard to actual provincial and constituency organizations but more usually in regard to the regional power brokers of the cabinet when the party was in power, thus reinforcing a conflict between parliamentary and extra-parliamentary wings of the party, which existed even in such a relatively centralized nation as Britain, with a more specifically North American conflict between nation and province. All this was known and even familiar by the time of the 1919 convention. Murphy's best efforts certainly failed to indicate any way out of the dilemma of national party organization in a federal society.

The convention readily adopted Murphy's plan. A National Liberal Organization Committee was to be set up, headed by the national leader, nine vice-presidents, one from each province, and a national council of fifty-four, six from each province, including the Liberal provincial leader. A national office was to be set up in Ottawa under the direction of a national organizer, whose duties were to take charge of publicity and organization. The members of the council in each province were to constitute a finance committee for that province. The chairman of the convention's committee on party organization echoed the contradiction in the Murphy memorandum by reassuring delegates that the provincial parties would retain organizational autonomy while at the same time asserting that the new national organization committee would provide a 'united command' for the party.[7] The plan passed unanimously without debate. Perhaps the delegates understood that it was more bromide than blueprint.

An executive council was named, and Andrew Haydon was appointed executive secretary, a title which failed to encompass Haydon's real role as the effective one-man national organization throughout the 1920s. An office was set up which in the Canadian tradition functioned at election times but failed to achieve solvency between elections. A plan for annual $250 contributions from constituency associations provided little actual sustenance and in 1926 Murphy, tired of paying the rent personally, closed the office down, while remarking to Haydon that he could think of 'no reason why you or I should continue to make any further payments when nobody else connected to the Liberal party takes the slightest interest in the place.' The executive council failed to meet at all after 1922.

Haydon had emerged as an informal national organizer, an 'ambassador from the Liberal government in Ottawa to the provincial governments,' in Regenstreif's phrase.[8] A practising lawyer in the city of Ottawa and called to the Senate in 1924, Haydon was fairly comfortably situated to play the role assigned to him. His close relationship with Mackenzie King was another important factor.[9] Yet his role, it seems, had evolved in a remarkably haphazard fashion. In 1932, facing his fellow senators over the Beauharnois affair, Haydon recalled how he had reached the unenviable position of a central figure in a major scandal:

I was general organizer of the Liberal party ... until March, 1922, when I resigned. There was never any definite appointment of a successor, and just because I had

gone everywhere, I suppose, and seen everybody ... it was just ordinary organization, going here and there and trying to get men to come and make reports of situations in counties all over Canada ... There was never any definite successor; because
I have done that for two or three years men took it for granted – as they do in political life take much more for granted than they should – I got the job, and they came
from everywhere – 'See Haydon; he will do this; ask him about that,' and most of
my life was spent at that job for ten years. It came in the manner of ordinary devolution that I was expected to be treasurer for this campaign [1930] ...[10]

The reasons why national organization turned out to be such a small and
informal affair go beyond the inherent contradictions in the plan passed by
the 1919 convention. One special factor was the style and manner of the
new leader. King had a very strong personal dislike for any public airing of
'family' quarrels[11] and, considering the divergent crowds assembled under
the umbrella of the Liberal party, he had a justifiable fear of any permanent
structure which might give voice to divisive policy initiatives, not to speak
of challenges to his own leadership. In fact King would never call a national
convention until his own retirement almost thirty years later. A more general explanation is that offered by Regenstreif's model of the growth of extra-parliamentary organization when the party is out of power, followed by
its atrophy when the party returns to power and the cabinet once more as-
sumes responsibility for political organization in the regions. Since the party
had the good fortune to be in office throughout most of the 1920s, the domination of the party by the parliamentary leadership was the rule. A final cir-
cumstance which helps explain the informality of national organizing is the
delicate minority position in which King found himself after the 1921 election. Believing as he did that his most important job as Liberal leader was
to co-opt the Progressives into the Liberal ranks, King wanted a free hand
to bargain with the Progressives. Regular party organization, with a highly
partisan rank and file, might conceivably have provided some opposition to
this process if a national organization of some standing had offered a channel for such discontent.[12] By the time the danger had passed and a Liberal
majority had been consolidated in 1926, the pattern was already set and apparently successful. Mackenzie King never argued with success.

King faced his fourth election as party leader in 1930 with an air of confidence derived from a sense of accomplishment of nine years of Liberal administration and a lack of recognition of the meaning and depth of the
Great Depression which had already taken firm hold when King went to
the electorate.[13] His misplaced serenity also masked a fragile organizational
structure underlying the party. Defeat in the election and the relegation of

the party to the opposition benches during the worst and bleakest days of the Depression turned out to be a blessing in the long run, but few saw it that way in the first year or so out of office. To King the reason for defeat had little to do with Liberal policies and certainly almost nothing at all to do with the Depression and mass unemployment. Aside from some regret over the importation of New Zealand butter which had damaged the party in rural Canada, King was convinced that it was lack of organization alone which had led to defeat. Of course it is not uncommon for defeated politicians to seek rationales which absolve themselves (this was before the invention of the magic formula of the 'failure to communicate'), and to shift the blame onto the party organization was in this sense an easy out for King as prime minister and party leader. But there can be no doubt of King's insistence on this point; typical of his answers to correspondents suggesting reasons for the defeat was his reply to Senator W.A. Buchanan's belief that unemployment had something to do with it: 'I shall ... always believe that efficient organization on the part of our opponents, and its lack on our part, were even more responsible for the result ... Where we had any kind of organization in the constituencies we were successful.'[14]

Blair Neatby has commented penetratingly on King's organizational alibi for defeat in the following terms: 'Organizing a party is like stirring syrup; if the faithful are cool, no amount of effort will produce a whirlpool of activity.'[15] But being a party in office does present special problems, as well as special opportunities, in this process. After 1935 the Liberal party and its leaders were able to exploit successfully the opportunities of power, to the extent that they can be justly termed 'the Government party' in federal politics. But King in the 1920s had not yet become the master of circumstances. The chief problem was that in the absence of extensive extra-parliamentary organization the burden of organization had fallen naturally onto the shoulders of his cabinet ministers. Later this system was to perform very well indeed, but by 1930 King had yet to attract all the human resources necessary for the requisite level of efficiency. The Liberal party was still in part an inherited property and there was much in the inheritance about which King was less than enthusiastic. Many regions of the country were inadequately represented in the cabinet, including the two largest provinces, Ontario and Quebec. The Ontario situation proved to be particularly damaging just as it had proved to Laurier before.

The problems which weak cabinet representation posed for organization were later summed up by C.G. 'Chubby' Power who pointed out to King that even where the ministers were effective as administrators the organizational problem might remain unsolved: 'I pointed out to you ... that the difficulties of a Party in power were much greater than when in Opposition in that the Organization must be left in the hands of the Ministers since otherwise there would be an almost continual clash of interests. Unfortunately, it is not always possible to make a good Organizer out of a good Minister, and some of your best Colleagues in the Cabinet were utterly incapable of understanding anything whatsoever about practical Party Organization.'[16]

Two months before Parliament was dissolved in 1930, King found it necessary to lecture the Liberal caucus on the party's lack of preparedness:

I spoke of what the tories were doing, their office & staff of 15, the weekly paper they are about to issue, the franking of campaign material, the amounts of it being sent out, the organization in the ridings, etc. etc. I said we had none of these things, spoke of the need for publicity, pamphlets, distribution of literature, of organizing the women & the men, of the extent to which the tories were buying up the press ... There was a desultory sort of discussion, no one seemed in a position to offer ideas, the Whips were formed into a committee to look into the matter.

A month later King turned once again to his most trusted political adviser, Andrew Haydon, to take charge of the campaign organization. Haydon had already agreed to act as treasurer for English Canada, with Senator Donat Raymond acting in the equivalent capacity in Montreal. The assignment of collecting responsibilities in the latter city had presented problems, involving 'jealousy' between Senators Raymond and W.L. McDougald. The difficulties were apparently resolved with the latter agreeing to help and Raymond getting the 'recognition' he felt was lacking.[17] Haydon as both national organizer and fund-raiser was the key figure in co-ordinating the overall campaign effort, the main burden of which was supposed to be shouldered by the cabinet ministers.

The finance problem was the critical one in party organization as was evident from a memorandum which Haydon submitted to his leader on the general state of the party earlier in the year.[18] Haydon summarized the state of extra-parliamentary organization in the provinces mainly in terms of financial resources, or the lack thereof. Quebec took care of itself: 'I have no information,' Haydon commented on that province, 'they never look to Ottawa in matters of this kind.' Toronto was the centre of English-Canadian fund-raising, and was under the direction of Senator A.C. Hardy, the wealthy son of a former Ontario premier. In the rest of the country only British Columbia and Manitoba managed a precarious self-sufficiency. Elsewhere, the financial and organizational picture was hardly encouraging. Most striking of all, however, was Haydon's general lack of information.

The only man in Ottawa who could be expected to know the state of organization in the provinces had at best sketchy knowledge, and in the case of Quebec none at all. This ramshackle provincial autonomy came perhaps less from principle – except for Quebec – than from the financial incapacity of the national party to control the constituent units of the organization, with a consequent dependence of the federal party on the fortunes and favours of its provincial counterparts. 'So far as I know,' Haydon told King, 'we have never had anything' for continuing organization. Since not even a national publicity office could be maintained when the party was in power it is easy to see that the power of the purse over the provincial units was non-existent. The organization of Liberal women had to be put in the hands of a (male) senator who was willing to finance whatever activity he was able to organize: that kind of arrangement was the rule rather than the exception. Even when it came to funds for the election itself, Haydon was equally gloomy. Since 1911 he could not remember an election when the party had enough funds for the national campaign let alone any of the other needs already mentioned. When the time came, Haydon felt certain, 'there will not be as much as there ought to be and ... there will be many complaints and many tears when the election is declared.' The tears were beside the point, however, for in Haydon's mind 'it is perfectly useless to try to compete with the Tories. We have not got the kind of millionaires that they have ...' Instead, the Liberals must concentrate on making 'the best kind of publicity, which is by word of mouth' and to try informally to 'gather in some editors.'

Haydon's pessimism about finances turned out to be unfounded. Indeed, the day following the election Haydon confided to King that for once money had not been the problem: 'we were never as well of [sic] in financial assistance, or press assistance.'[19] The unexpected stroke of fortune which had intervened was in the shape of Mr R.O. Sweezey of the Beauharnois Power Corporation, the political philanthropist non pareil of the world of high finance, who in the Depression year of 1930 was able to dispense campaign funds to the Liberal party with a bountifulness almost breath-taking in its scope. The approximately $700,000 collected from this single source was more than the total amount which the party would be able to collect from all its sources on Bay Street in each of two subsequent elections,[20] and in the light of Haydon's previously quoted remarks to King there is little reason to believe that the party had ever uncovered such a bonanza before. But like the magic wishes of the fairy tales which somehow always rebound on their wealth-struck recipients, this remarkable Aladdin's Lamp proved to be doubly deceptive: the election was lost in any event and, in its aftermath, Beauharnois re-emerged as the ugliest scandal ever to involve the national Liberal party, leaving in the public mind an exaggerated idea of the largesse lavished by business on political parties and on the Liberal party in particular. The idea that this vast donation was in effect a bribe offered in exchange for a handsome power contract was to cloud the Liberal party's public image for some time to come. In fact, the Beauharnois affair was more notable by its contrast to the regular business-as-usual of party finance than by its example.

The Beauharnois Corporation's 'faerie gold' not only failed to win the election but also failed to solve the endemic organizational problems of the party. The cabinet ministers retained the real influence and legitimacy, for better or for worse. It was for worse in the crucial province of Ontario where the Liberals lost nine incumbents to the Conservatives. Following the vote, Haydon complained to King about the Ontario ministers, W.D. Euler, J.C. Elliot, and James Malcolm, 'each *demanding* financial help in large amounts for their own seats, before helping others.'[21] In Quebec, disaffection between King's Quebec lieutenant, Ernest Lapointe, and Premier L.-A. Taschereau harmed the Liberal cause. Twenty seats were lost here.

The election campaign was not organized to King's satisfaction. Literature was distributed late and speakers' itineraries were poorly organized. The Conservatives seemed to be ahead of the government at every turn, whether it was in securing halls or buying up radio time. There was, King complained in his diary, 'anything but the team work there should be, & a deplorable lack of organization. The latter is really heartbreaking.' Two days before the election, King reflected sadly that 'Haydon had fallen off much, not in loyalty, but in strength, had he been what he was ten years ago, our organization wd. have been much better.'[22]

Impressed, as were many Liberals, with the work of Brigadier General (later Senator) A.D. McRae as national organizer of the Conservative victory,[23] King's thoughts following the defeat turned to the possible organizational ability and the respect of financial donors. One possibility was W.H. Moore, who managed to be a lawyer, farmer, businessman, and somewhat of an intellectual at the same time. Moore's name was bruited about by various Liberals in the days following the election, and on 8 August King met with his ex-ministers and secured agreement on Moore as the Grit McRae. But Moore was a high tariff man closely connected to certain big business interests; it would appear that he had acted as a lobbyist for the Beauharnois syndicate in seeking the power contract while the previous King government was still in office. This latter affiliation entirely changed King's mind about Moore, once the scandal had become public, and the latter quickly faded both from prominence in the party and in the esteem of the leader.[24]

Another possibility was Charles Dunning, the ex-minister of finance whose budget had so pleased the business world earlier in the year. But Dunning, personally defeated in the election, was not an independently wealthy man at this time and was principally concerned with his own financial future. It was therefore determined that a fund be set up to permit him to continue in a political career as the party organizer. Dunning, who wished to remain in public life but feared being the object of 'charity,' finally decided to take a politically undesirable entry into the world of business through an affiliation with the CPR, for the purpose, as he put it to a friend, of making money in the short run so as to return to politics in a financially secure position later.[25] Dunning proved more than competent in making money and he did later return to politics, but this was in the future and was of no help in the party's hour of need in 1930-1.

Dunning's departure also left the party with the embarrassing dilemma of how to retain the money collected expressly for Dunning under the auspices of Vincent Massey and W.E. Rundle, general manager of the National Trust. This task fell to King personally, since, as he explained to Rundle, now that his former colleagues had scattered to all parts of the country he could no longer maintain his old prime ministerial practice of isolation from financial details. Despite Rundle's efforts to persuade the subscribers, they were unwilling to see their money go to the party as apart from Dunning himself, and the funds were returned. King not unnaturally began to feel 'real concern as to the party's future, if no one can be found who is prepared to subscribe to the work of organization and publicity, which are the essentials of a party's progress.'[26]

With Moore and Dunning out of the running as organizers, King's thoughts turned to Vincent Massey, who had the advantage of independent wealth and could afford the luxury of a few years of political uncertainty. Moreover, Massey had strong personal motives for wanting to see R.B. Bennett's defeat: he had been cheated out of fulfilment of his life's ambition when Bennett rescinded King's appointment of Massey as high commissioner in London. King's personal attitude toward Massey was, to say the very least, ambivalent, but early in 1931 he confided to his diary that despite all his faults (of which King was somewhat obsessively aware) Massey was 'the *only* one who had done anything since July last, the others have *all* disappeared.'[27] Massey was not, however, willing personally to undertake the funding of the Liberal party and remained uncertain about his course of action throughout 1931.

King was thus left with no respectable figure of any consequence to take charge of the party in a year when Liberal representation in the provinces fell to a single government, Quebec, and when the Beauharnois scandal led to the public humiliation of the federal party and many of its major figures, including to some extent King himself. During the dispiriting spring and summer of that year the party organization at Ottawa, or what passed for organization, was entrusted to Charles Stewart, a man whom King had tried to replace as Alberta minister in 1929. Stewart proved incapable of raising money and departed for the west at the end of the summer leaving King with a list of names of possible donors. By the end of the year he concluded that Stewart was 'a weak and broken reed, a smoking flax' and that Massey was the only possible answer.[28]

In the interim the problem of party finance came first. It is an indication of just how misleading the large sums involved in the Beauharnois affair were to an understanding of Liberal party finance that the two years following the election were characterized by the virtual bankruptcy of the party as a national organization and the personal burden imposed on Mackenzie King to act against all his instincts and beg money from wealthy Liberals and Liberal businessmen. Of course, the financial plight of a party just relegated to opposition in Ottawa and out of office in eight provinces could be expected to be bleaker than that endured by the party when in power. But coupled with what King rightly called the party's 'valley of humiliation' over Beauharnois and the inability to attract anyone of substance to head the party organization, the financial plight was symptomatic of a serious crisis in the party which might impair its future effectiveness as the major alternative to the Conservatives, especially in the light of moves being made in the early 1930s towards the formation of a broadly based social democratic party to the left of the Liberals – to King an ominous portent of the displacement of the centre reform party by a labour grouping as had happened already in England. But the securing of financing was the *sine qua non* of organizational revival. King constantly returned to this theme whenever suggestions were put to him about party organization. Typical of his insistence on solving the money problem first was his answer to one correspondent inquiring about the lack of party publicity: 'I can think of nothing I would welcome quite as much as an offer of financial assistance from any source towards publicity work for the Liberal party. If we could secure the financial end, there would, I believe, be little trouble in securing what is needed in other directions, for helpful educational work. It is the financial problem that is the troublesome one, and, with the party in opposition, it is a problem more difficult than ever.'[29]

Complicating the financial picture were the numerous debts from the past which would have to be cleared up before any secure future funding of the party could be undertaken. From all over the country – including King's own riding of Prince Albert – came pleas for national funds to make up local constitency deficits from the 1930 election, deficits which on occasion ran into thousands of dollars.[30] Since there was no national money as such, these pleas gained no tangible response from the Ottawa office of the party, but the burden fell on the former cabinet ministers with regional responsibilities and on the local organizers – which in turn made it yet more difficult for the national party to raise funds through these sources.[31] A prominent Quebec member wrote to King that his life was 'simply unbearable with all the letters I receive every day to pay election bills,' and the head of the federal Liberal organization in Quebec refused to help him out, citing his own precarious financial position.[32] A federal organizer hired under the auspices of Ontario cabinet ministers before the election claimed $10,000 in salary arrears against the party – a claim later reduced by almost half through negotiation. With legal action threatened, the party was desperately seeking ways to meet the demand. It was with this overall financial situation in mind that King wrote to Lucien Cannon early in 1931 that all election protests having been called off in Ontario, it would be wise for the same to be done in Quebec as well, 'because I do not know where the money is to be found to carry on the necessary litigation.' 'Discretion in some of these matters,' King added sadly 'may be the better part of valour.' The Ontario Liberal Association, which had been able to extract a mere $2000 from the Beauharnois Corporation, had managed to amass debts of $27,000 by the latter half of 1931, and had 'apparently no way of meeting them.'[33]

Worse yet were the debts that extended further back in time. One senator who had 'paid out of his own pocket the secretariat of the Western Ontario Liberal Association, from 1917 to 1930 – something over two thousand a year' was driven into near bankruptcy by the Depression and eventually had to be bailed out by his fellow Liberal senators.[34] Indeed, senators of means – men like A.C. Hardy, Raoul Dandurand, and Rodolphe Lemieux – were constantly called upon in such situations to kick back, in effect, part of their senatorial salary to the party which had appointed them. It would seem to have been a kind of unwritten understanding that senators ought to pay for their seats; unwritten understandings are, however, notoriously difficult to hold people to, and complaints of ingratitude were not infrequent.[35] Senator J.H. Spence, guarantor of the lease on the Toronto Liberal office, wanted someone to take it off his hands when the rent fell into arrears. Senator Hardy, a faithful party war-horse, was markedly unsympathetic: 'I gave him a good sharp letter today,' he reported to King, 'and asked why anyone should take it off his hands ... I told him he had received a Senatorship and that he had better pay for it like the rest of us.' Hardy's enmity toward his colleague later led to a most serious breach of party solidarity. A complicated affair arising out of old election debts from the 1920s culminated in Hardy suing Spence for a substantial sum of money which Spence claimed he could not repay. Two former ministers came to Spence's rescue but the suit had already been officially lodged and the case was publicized in the Tory press. Another possible legal action, involving a Liberal MP and Senator Haydon, was only narrowly averted.[36] Even Mackenzie King was named in legal actions over old election debts; only an out-of-court settlement avoided the awful publicity attendant on *that* possibility.[37]

A further complicating factor was the multiplicity of purposes which required funding, many of them quite separate and distinct. One was the maintenance of the national office in Ottawa, the future of which was in doubt. As Haydon announced three months after the election: 'I am not going to carry it, for the simple reason that I cannot do so, and if the men are not interested, I will just close it in the Spring ... I can see no way of getting any support for [*sic*] outside interests.'[38] The only thing to be done was to appeal to a few wealthy friends of the party, most of them being in the Senate. A small finance committee met and put it to King that he would personally have to make the appeal. The target was to gather $25,000 per year on a basis of sustaining donations of $1000 per donor pledged over at least two years and preferably over the four- to five-year period before the next election. About half was to be raised in Montreal and Quebec City, the rest mainly in Toronto. Although King 'disliked' this task, he realized that 'I shall have to take the initiative in all branches ...' Massey was enlisted to speak to a few of his Toronto friends, but King wrote to most of the names on the list, including such luminaries of Bay Street as J.H. Gundy, E.R. Wood, and A.E. Ames. King cited the precedent of Sir Wilfrid Laurier having raised the money to support the Liberal information office after the party's defeat in 1911, and spoke of the vital importance to the official opposition of sound extra-parliamentary organization: 'The parliamentary forces of themselves can effect but little unless their work is supplemented by the organization of the party's forces outside of parliament, and by much in the way of justifiable publicity. Without the latter, I fear the burden upon the shoulders of the few in parliament would soon become such as quickly to impair their capacity for effective service.'[39]

Yet, as he confided to one correspondent, 'I hope you realize how unpleasant it is to me, as the leader of the Party, to have to communicate with any of our friends with respect to its financial affairs but apparently that is expected of me ...' Less than half the target was reached from these sources. Five Quebec senators (Dandurand, Georges Parent, J.M. Wilson, Lemieux, and McDougald) and five Torontonians of means (Massey, Rundle of the National Trust, Ames of Dominion Securities, Gerald Larkin of Salada Tea, and Leighton McCarthy of Canadian Life), together with a personal friend of Massey, all contributed, McCarthy giving double the normal quota of $1000. But it was not enough.[40]

Yet another fund was also raised for the particular needs of King as leader of the opposition. Now that O.D. Skelton and other leading civil servants were no longer available to him as a 'brains trust,' King felt the need for help in research and speech-writing. With the demands of the party on his time coming in from all over the country, he felt that he had every right to financial assistance in the performance of his duties. Early in 1931 Senator Hardy promised to raise $4000 per year, and included $500 of his own as a starter. It is not clear what happened to this initiative, for two years the entire project was apparently getting underway again, once more under the benign direction of Senator Hardy.[41]

Despite King's protestations over money, he would seem to have constituted one of the least deserving of the various Liberal charities vying for attention. King had been launched in politics on a personal trust fund sponsored by the late P.C. Larkin of Salada Tea, whom King had honoured by an appointment as high commissioner in London, and some other wealthy Liberal businessmen. This fund had originally amounted to the sum of $225,000, and grew with interest. Lady Laurier had willed Laurier House to King as his Ottawa residence and Larkin and friends had renovated it and helped furnish it; his extensive summer property at Kingsmere had similarly begun with a Larkin gift. In addition, King had very considerable savings accumulated over the years, some of it from the Rockefeller Foundation, as well as his salary and expenses as leader of the opposition. All in all, King calculated his personal worth in 1930 at just over $500,000, exclusive of property which he estimated at a further quarter of a million dollars. His regular income from Parliament and investment income he put at about $35,000 per year. King was not suffering either from being in the opposition or from the Depression. This is of more than passing interest, for Liberal party backers have continued to look after the economic security of party leaders if they required it. P.C. Larkin began a tradition which was to be followed in the cases of both Louis St Laurent and Lester Pearson.[42]

Yet none of this prevented King from complaining about his financial 'sacrifices,' and since no one knew how much he really possessed his complaints often enough received sympathetic hearings. He was reluctant in the extreme to let a cent of his own money go for any political purposes; perhaps, considering the unhealthy dependency of the Conservatives on the personal support of R.B. Bennett, King had reason to avoid such commitments. King briefly toyed with the idea of donating $1000 to the national office in 1931 as an 'example' to 'shame some of the party into doing something,' but gave what was for him the still generous sum of $200 instead for fear of otherwise establishing a 'precedent – expecting me to give, wd. lead to impression I have considerable means etc. besides reversing the proper order of things.' It is little wonder that Senator Hardy, who did so much to relieve King of whatever financial burdens he could, should have expressed some astonishment years later when King died and his estate became public: '... I am amazed at the size of the estate because his subscriptions to the usual charity campaigns were always very small – around $50. or so.'[43]

Whatever the state of Mackenzie King's personal finances, those of the Liberal party were in genuine distress. The multiplicity of appeals to the small number of the party's moneyed friends could only create confusion and antagonism, and complaints began to come back to King. There were increasing doubts about who was in charge of the party's finances and of the legitimacy of some of the appeals. King became more and more convinced that it would be necessary to put financial matters on a more businesslike basis, '... to get party matters into such shape that all contributions from friends of the party can be made to one source and properly audited.'[44]

The final impetus toward a rationalization of the financial situation came with the Beauharnois investigation, to which reference has already been made. The details of the affair need not be entered into here except to note the effect on the Liberal party financial structures.[45] First of all, the scandal revealed the distance between the party treasurers and the party leader, or at least the distance which the party leader could publicly maintain so as to keep his own name uninvolved – a course of action impossible for John A. Macdonald to maintain at the time of the Pacific Scandal in 1873 when the underdeveloped state of Canadian political parties forced the leader to do his own collecting. Yet this distance might on closer examination appear problematic. Neatby notes that King could not possibly have remained ignorant either of the amount of funds available for a campaign or of the names of the most generous donors, however sincere his efforts to avoid such knowledge.[46] The other side of the coin was the paradox of ignorance: if the fund-raisers resorted to dubious sources, was the leader's ignorance then not itself a fault? Ought he not to be responsible for controlling and directing his officials? Yet how could he do this without knowing the details? King's justification of his position in the scandal was ingeniously worked out to serve his own immediate interests, but it concealed a serious contradiction which both R.B. Bennett and J.S. Woodsworth were intelligent enough to detect. Moreover, there were those, even some close to King, who did not take his protestations of innocence too literally. Such suspicions have continued down to the present day.[47] Faced with such a dilemma King unhesitatingly chose the plea of ignorance as the lesser of the evils. But as he confided to his diary later, 'I can well afford to look at my own relations with Haydon, and my willingness to allow him to collect funds from sources that were corrupting public life even if as I knew and believe the funds were in no way used or intended to be used for corrupt but only for legitimate purposes.'[48]

The one public link with Beauharnois which did ensnare King was the famous Bermuda trip paid for in part indirectly out of Beauharnois funds. This proved to be a weak link, however, and King emerged relatively unscathed. The same could not be said for the Liberal party as an organization. It quickly became clear as the investigation unfolded that the Beauharnois Corporation had built up a symbiotic relationship with the Liberal party, establishing firm links at numerous points to Liberal figures of various ranks and stations. Senator W.L. McDougald, a very prominent Liberal senator and contributor to the party funds for a number of years, was the worst tarred of all. Forced to resign from the Senate, McDougald was virtually read out of the party by King.[49] Senators Haydon and Raymond were not so flagrantly in breach of ethics as McDougald, but both were strongly criticized for their conduct by the parliamentary committees of investigation. Other links with the Liberal party included a deputy minister (appointed by the King government) in the Department of Railways and Canals, and in the pay of Beauharnois; a former personal secretary to King; an Ottawa lawyer who had been secretary of the national Liberal office; a prominent Liberal in Montreal who acted as counsel for the corporation; and a former federal Liberal cabinet minister, now a Beauharnois stockholder. Many of these links were probably not corrupt in themselves. The point was that a broad picture was being created in the public mind of a thoroughgoing interrelationship of the Liberal party with a large corporation willing to dispense vast sums of money to corrupt the democratic process.[50] A close appraisal of the evidence suggests that it is more likely that R.O. Sweezey of the Beauharnois Corporation was naïve than that the Liberal party was corrupt. Certainly the incredible story of John Aird, Jr., who walked out of Sweezey's office $125,000 richer because of the latter's apparent willingness to believe that Aird represented the Ontario Conservative party, suggests a certain naïveté. It seems rather likely, in the words of one contemporary journalist, that 'Sweezey was played for an out-and-out sucker by the collection agents, ... that he was that amazing phenomenon which the mine-stock salesmen dignify by the term mooch. As I see it, Sweezey was a mooch for the Liberal Party.'[51]

King feared that his hard-won reputation as a social reformer was in jeopardy: 'It has seemed to me that all I have may be misunderstood, misinterpreted, or what is worse might lead to a sort of separation from the poor & simple & humble & honest folk of the world.' King's close friend and confidant, Professor Norman Rogers of Queen's University, was so shaken by the events that he wondered if money were not the real master so long as private property were the basis of society, and if wealth ought not to belong to all, 'down-right socialism – but I sometimes wonder if there is any alternative ...' Even to those not led so far by their consciences as Rogers, Beauharnois had clearly besmirched much of what went on under the name of party organization. It might be harder to enlist respectable figures to take part in organizational activities, especially fund-raising. King got a taste of this when he asked Senator H.H. Horsey in the fall of 1931 to act as treasurer for the national office fund. The next day Horsey rejected the post: 'The Senate's name had been brought in, etc etc.'[52] The role of 'bagman' was not an enviable one after Beauharnois. Yet what was the party to do? As Haydon had somewhat pathetically testified before his fellow senators sitting in judgment on him:

This whole matter of campaign funds is one on which the general public is liable to become very self-righteous. Everybody knows that elections cost money – and a lot of money – for perfectly legitimate expenses. The ordinary voter gives nothing. The practices referred to by Mr. Sweezey in his evidence of large contributions by wealthy men or corporations to political campaign funds was not invented either by Mr. Sweezey or by me. When I acted officially as the general party organizer ... I used to preach the doctrine at organization meetings that a man should give to his political party as he would to his church – but I never got any cheers.[53]

Haydon had concluded that elections could in fact be won on money and money alone, but he told this to his party leader in 'a sort of despairing way, as a man who feels that the end would justify the means.' Haydon himself was ruined by the process. When Senator McDougald came to see him on his deathbed, 'Haydon had turned over in bed and cried like a child with his face in the pillow.' When Haydon died in 1932, King noted in his diary – rather unctuously perhaps under the circumstances – that it has required this death to bring a proper 'sense of responsibility to others ... He was the lamb sacrificed for this achievement of party organization on lines he had hoped for ... and in which he believed and for which he strove.'[54]

It had become important in King's mind to establish a distinct extra-parliamentary office to undertake both organization and fund-raising so as to consolidate the distance between the leadership and organizational and financial functions. Moreover, even before the scandal had broken, King had become increasingly aware of the fact that his colleagues in the House and Senate who had undertaken organizational responsibilities in the past were falling victim one by one to sickness, death, or retirement from public life. When Senator Philippe Paradis of Quebec suffered a stroke, King wrote in his diary that 'It is hardly believable that one after the other should break up in this fashion ... the organizational "machine" is pretty well gone.' Thus the imperatives of Beauharnois reinforced the natural tendency of a party out of office to build up its extra-parliamentary organization – in this case accelerated by the disappearance of key parliamentary figures from the scene. But while the needs were tolerably clear, the means to satisfy those needs were not readily at hand. By November of 1931, King confessed to T.A. Crerar that 'I have grown nearly desperate over the matter of party organization ... I really do not know what I shall do.'[55]

The situation in the national office, which had maintained a precarious existence since the election, was one of chaos and confusion. Publicity was mainly handled by R.J. Deachman of the Consumers' League, who also published his own newsletter, but who devoted some of his time to research and writing on behalf of the party. There was one office secretary. Following the election King had persuaded a young man, R.A. MacDougall, who had just won a competition for a career in the foreign service, to take up instead the job of national secretary in the Liberal office. 'I shall always,' MacDougall wrote later, 'give Senator Haydon credit for trying to warn me that the post was not all my imagination pictured it as, but I was carried away by the prospect, and refused to listen to him.' MacDougall's main problems revolved around the lack of money and his own inexperience and lack of prestige in the party. As he explained later to King: 'You and other[s] prominent in the party were urging me to throw myself into the work and to move mountains. But those who were collecting the funds not only said, "Where is the money coming from?" but repeatedly intimated that it would be difficult even to find my own salary.' The fact of MacDougall's youth and inexperience further crippled his efforts to enlist the co-operation of prominent Liberals around the country, so much so that he later wondered if he had ever had the 'proverbial snowball's chance': 'The moral of all this seems to be that it is a mistake to pick out a young man with no previous general political experience, to drop him into an office in Ottawa, and to say to him: "You are it. We won't give you any advice or adequate training. We expect you to work out your own salvation. There is no money to work with, but throw yourself into the job, and remember, we expect results." ' The inevitable result was disillusion, and MacDougall reported that he 'soon became utterly discouraged and lost all confidence in myself and my fellow men.' Having thrown away his chance for a career in the diplomatic service, finished with politics, he then had to attempt to build up a law practice in a small Ontario town in the early years of the Depression.[56] Such personal tragedies were not merely accidental; they were the result of the chaotic and impoverished state of political organization. Political organization was like leprosy: no one coming in contact with it seemed able to emerge intact.

Mackenzie King was aware that, however distasteful it might be, organization was necessary to make the political world go round, although he prudently wished to avoid as much personal contact as he could with the problem. It was thus with a sense of deep chagrin that he realized that others could not be trusted to take care of the details. King was very strongly impressed with J.A. Spender's book on Sir Robert Hudson, secretary of the British National Liberal Federation, which had just appeared. King read and reread the book and recommended it as an 'immense help and inspiration' to those who would have to rebuild the Liberal party organization in Canada. He kept up a lengthy correspondence with Spender and sought his advice on many matters having to do with party structures; when Spender sent him a copy of the *Liberal Handbook* – a party publication of the British Liberals – King was both impressed and ashamed: 'It is a great reflection on myself and others of the party that nothing of the kind has yet come into being in Canada, and that we have as yet no publications Department or Association comparable to that of the British Federation of Liberal Associations.'[57]

There was a strong tendency among Canadians to romanticize the 'British way' of doing things, and to contrast this favourably with the venal and uncivilized manners of North American public life. Yet King was not unaware of the seamier side of British party politics, with its auctioning of peerages and other 'Honours' to the highest campaign fund bidders. Indeed, Spender had drawn attention to the existence of such practices in another book with which King was also familiar.[58] The ambiguity of the

British ideal was captured in King's attitude toward Vincent Massey, the man whom King believed to be the only eminent figure capable of heading a British-style federation in Canada. The Massey family was perhaps as close to an 'aristocratic' family as could be found in Canada, having passed through the stage of what Marx called 'primitive accumulation,' through corporate consolidation, to a third generation of philanthropy, art, and public service.[59] But King wanted Massey not only for his high-toned respectability, however important that was. He also wanted him for his money, and for his moneyed friends. When King tried to conjure up an enticing vision for Massey of what a Liberal federation under his leadership would look like, he rhapsodized as follows: 'I can see it all so clearly. A National Association from coast to coast. Dignified headquarters at the Capital. Study groups, speakers' committees, Liberal Clubs, scattered at regular intervals of space across the continent. Above all, a great body of public opinion slowly mobilizing itself – enlightened and increasingly powerful, restive until it has overthrown the powers that be.' Massey commented in his memoirs: 'I was also assured that the president of the proposed federation would not be charged with responsibility for raising money. About none of this did I cherish any illusions, especially about the last, and this was just as well.'[60]

King's personal relationship with Massey reflected this contradiction to an extreme degree. By mid-summer of 1931 King had become so irritated with Massey's hesitations over assuming the job that he took exception to Massey's suggestion that he might 'help' King. King was not grateful:

... I opened out straight from the shoulder, said ... that I was getting tired of others speaking of helping *me*. It was the party that needed help. Liberalism that needed help. I had been doing all in my power to that end but had been left very much alone, that I had made up my mind unless there were more in the way of divisions of labour, the party wd have to find a new leader. That I wd not & could not do the work of organization or publicity, and that means must be found to that end by the party itself ... I wd continue to do my best in prlt & the country if others wd co-operate, but wd not be the one around whom others were to hang their weight ...

Massey, who had been considering an offer to become lieutenant-governor of an Australian state, then touched on *his* major motive in getting involved in party politics: would his absence from Canada affect his chances of appointment as high commissioner in London following a Liberal election victory? King agreed: 'I said most decidedly so. That I felt that those who left the party in its time of need would get no recognition later on. That I intended to leave to those who did the party's organization and publicity, the naming of persons for positions my approval being necessary, that I felt if he were away it wd be impossible to appoint him to London later on.'

The cards were on the table. Ten days later Massey accepted his terms. 'I confess,' King wrote in his diary, 'I felt a mental relief & the dawn of a new day. Nothing has given me quite the same hope.' But Massey insisted on the condition that the new federation's finances be put on a sound basis before he would assume the presidency. He then departed for a prolonged visit to the Far East, leaving others to sort out the situation. As Senator Hardy acidly commented to King: 'He leaves us behind to do the work of preparing a place for him, if not in Heaven, at least in London.'[61]

Meanwhile, almost $2500 was owing in salaries at the skeletal national office still in existence, which had to be paid off before new plans could be laid. At this juncture it was decided to resurrect the defunct National Liberal Organization Committee established by the authority of the 1919 party convention but allowed to lapse after 1922. The first meeting took place without Massey, who was still junketing in the Orient, and was intended by King to confine itself entirely to the problem of finances in an attempt to resolve the money problem before Massey's return – 'Having in mind,' King explained to the latter by mail, 'what you said to me about not wishing to incur responsibility with respect to the financial side.' According to King, the other side of this bargain was Massey's 'promise' that if the money were found he would 'take the presidency and, more, that he will see that the Association finds ways and means of carrying on its work in future years, once provision is made for the year immediately ensuing.'[62] As later events were to prove, there was a certain failure of communication on this point.

King addressed the first meeting of the committee and spoke about the need for the non-parliamentary members of the party, including the women and young people, to take 'some real part in party management & framing of policies.' Having said that, King then noted sourly in his diary that there was subsequently 'quite a task keeping the discussion off of matters of policy.' The next day there was talk of calling a national party convention; King immediately took this to suggest a challenge to his leadership. 'They soon dropped the Convention talk,' he noted with evident satisfaction. An executive committee was struck to report on finances, on which women and young Liberals were to be represented. When the executive committee met the next day there appears to have been opposition to King's plans from elements which he identified as those 'trying to hold to old machine methods in politics.' He then 'spoke more than plainly from the shoulder' about the new order of things after Beauharnois:

... the open method, with publicity in all things, and the rank and file having more to do with finance and policy, also that it was to determine whether everything would come again on to my shoulders, to call meetings – take things in and when others gone – to be involved further in organizational matters, or separated from this business once and for all. I said very plainly, I would have nothing further to do with organization matters.

I told [Stewart] the old methods were responsible for wrecking Haydon's life – & for destroying in part young MacDougall ... [N]othing in all the world would cause me to risk again the injury of my name, and the kind of thing I had had to endure the last few months. Unless the party rose to the obligation to find ways & means for a proper organization, I wd call a Convention, tender my resignation as leader & let the party know the reasons why. I then said nothing short of 50,000 to be raised immediately – on a quota basis for provinces of 200 each constituency wd suffice for what is needed, and I asked the Committee to recommend that this be secured.

The committee did as it was told and passed the resolutions demanded of them. The committee members 'looked as if they had been subjected to rough treatment, but they have given themselves a name & place in the history of the party they cannot begin to estimate ... but it was a nasty fight, it is tragic that there has to be unpleasantness, heads have to be shoved into what becomes a yoke to get anything done.'[63] Thus the national Liberal party organization was dragged kicking and screaming into the hands of Vincent Massey.

Moreover, it quickly became apparent that the Liberal party was not ready to be made over in a new image, whether the image of King or of Massey. Despite the 'many expressions of delight' at the prospect of Massey assuming the presidency which had come in from all over the nation,[64] the constituency quota campaign was a failure. Only Nova Scotia, New Brunswick, and British Columbia appear to have come close to their provincial quotas. In the Prairies the ravages of the Depression and the dust bowl virtually eradicated any financial support whatsoever and central Canada fell far behind as well. Moreover, the dream of small contributions replacing the party's dependence on a few wealthy and influential donors proved to be a chimera. 'Most of the money came, as usual, from Senators and wealthy Liberals ...' Neatby states.[65] By the spring of 1932 only $20,000 had been collected out of the original target of $50,000. The money was coming in so slowly, and the burden of past debt was so heavy, that it seemed that the target would never get any closer. After a 'gloomy and depressing' dinner with the Masseys, King inspired the Liberal parliamentary caucus to petition the reluctant party benefactor to make a definite decision. The parliamentary delegation proved to be the 'stroke necessary,' and Massey and the French-language secretary accompanied King to the new office quarters, where Massey ' "began history" by sitting at an empty table in an empty room.' Massey formally agreed to become president pro tem of the National Liberal Federation and, in King's enthusiastic words, 'to get out after subscriptions, etc.' [66]

Another major stumbling block to the creation of the new organization was the persistent autonomy of that province 'pas comme les autres,' Quebec. Even before the 1930 election Quebec organizers had been protesting the attempts made by the national office to communicate with local constituency organizations in that province concerning the coming campaign. As Senator Paradis pointedly informed King, 'in Quebec we are conducting our organization in a way different to what is being done in other provinces and owing to the good results obtained in the past, I am inclined to let well enough alone.' Chubby Power took 'very energetic exception' to the attempt to organize Twentieth Century clubs of young Liberals in Quebec. Believing that his own Quebec South machine was the most efficient in all of Canada, he saw the attempt to impose new organizational structures as causing his people to 'bitterly resent the interference of outsiders.'[67] None of this autonomist feeling had changed by 1932. Even though the National Liberal Federation was intended to be a federation of provincial associations, Quebec was the only province which refused to set up a provincial body. Instead it was represented by the parliamentary and provincial leaders without any formal or constitutional basis – and continued in this fashion until the 1950s. Nor could it be said that Quebec ever entered wholeheartedly into the activities of the federation.

However shaky the infrastructure, the new federation was able to begin operation. The most important single decision was made in February 1932 when Massey suggested to King that Norman Lambert be appointed secretary. King readily accepted.[68] The man who more than anyone else was to constitute the real core of the national Liberal organization for the rest of the 1930s was then persuaded to come to Ottawa. With Lambert's appointment, a formal break with the remnants of the tattered organizational apparatus of the 1920s was made.

2

Organizing for victory, 1932–5

The year 1932 was the bleakest of the Great Depression, the year the New York stock exchange hit the lowest point in the long decline following the crash in 1929, the year that the hopelessness and despair of the unemployed reached an equivalent depth. But for Mackenzie King 1932 was a turning point on the road to political recovery. While staying at the Massey home in Port Hope in the late summer of that year, King had a dream of the future: 'Last night I dreamt that a fine Reform Club was in the process of construction, a very fine building, large interior walls, a sort of marble effect of green and gold, then it seemed to me that Wilfred Campbell was helping me to take hangings from some old temple for their new building ... I woke up to a glorious sunrise while in the midst of this wonderful revelation.'[1] King's vision was typically baroque, but the years ahead did in fact see the reconstruction of the Liberal party in preparation for R.B. Bennett's electoral Armageddon. There has been a tendency among Canadian political scientists and historians to attribute the Liberal victory in 1935 to Bennett's self-destruction and the lack of a clear alternative to the Liberals. There is no doubt much truth in the characterization of the Liberal return as simply a case of *faute de mieux*. Yet this is to beg the question in another, important, sense. The Depression years saw a major political realignment in Canada, with the emergence of two new parties as lasting participants in national elections. There was no mystical power inherent in the name 'Liberal' to insure that the party would not only survive the period of opposition but to go on to assume the role of one-party dominance for almost a generation following. That it did so cannot be wholly dissociated from its ability to regenerate itself organizationally so as to prevent any newer party from supplanting it as the 'inevitable' alternative to the discredited Conservatives. History, after all, does not merely happen, it is made. Following the nadir of electoral defeat, public humiliation over Beauharnois, organizational col-lapse, and near financial bankruptcy, the Liberal party showed a degree of vigour and dedication during the last three years of the Bennett régime which belied the belief on the left and right of the political spectrum that the age of traditional party politics was shattered by the events of the De-pression.

There were those within the party who would later look back on this pe-riod of reorganization as the party's golden age of youthful achievement. W.A. Fraser, an Ontario MP and organizer in this period, later a senator, reminisced in 1960 about an era which had by then taken on in his mind an heroic aura. During the early 1930s, he recalled, the party 'started an organ-ization in the House, made every member pay, hired a field organizer, picked candidates for the by-elections and were ready for the 1935 general election ... [W]e had the best organized House from the fighting standpoint that ever existed in opposition ... In those days chaps like Senator Hardy contributed generously to the fund and we travelled the highways and by-ways of the country in the interests of the Liberal party.'[2]

The reorganization of the party took a number of distinct phases, as Fraser's remarks indicate. On the extra-parliamentary side there was the creation of the National Liberal Federation, the organization of the numer-ous by-elections, the assignment of responsibility in the various regions, the sorting out of federal-provincial lines of authority, and the supreme prob-lem of party finance. All these will be analysed in this chapter. But another point raised by Fraser is of considerable significance as well, although it falls outside the terms of reference of this study. The parliamentary caucus of the Liberal party was a major area of weakness following the 1930 elec-tion. Not only had many Liberals been defeated in that election but many of the best had been lost through retirement, defeat, or illness and death fol-lowing the election. Mackenzie King felt the loss of talent around him in the House very acutely in the first year or two of opposition, as his diary tire-lessly reiterates. He began to realize that he was the only survivor of an ear-lier generation of politicians of the Laurier era. King personally made the transition into the era of Depression politics with the adaptability which characterized his entire career. But the younger and inexperienced Liberal caucus also proved under King's parliamentary leadership capable of grad-ually wearing away the self-confidence of the prime minister and his minis-ters in the face of the implacable economic catastrophe in the country. The creation of a credible alternative in the day-to-day business of Parliament did not happen by accident any more than the revivification of the party as an electoral organization. Here the guiding hand of Chubby Power, the convivial, much beloved, backroom boy from Quebec South, was of great importance. Power took it upon himself to suggest a detailed plan of caucus organization for the purpose of enhancing the effectiveness of the party in debate. King was grateful for this initiative, coming as it did when the leader was beginning to doubt that anyone else was willing to do anything, and was even more grateful when Power undertook to effect the plan himself among the members.[3] J.L. Ralston was also important in guiding this caucus organization. By the last year or two of the Bennett régime the rationalization of the operations of the opposition had begun to bear obvious fruit, much to King's satisfaction and the Liberal party's benefit.

THE NATIONAL LIBERAL FEDERATION

The major innovation in this period was in the extra-parliamentary side of party organization, in the development of the National Liberal Federation as an effective body. The federation which Vincent Massey and Norman Lambert took charge of in 1932 was a formless creature. Indeed, its protean nature was demonstrated by its history first under Massey's direction in the years of opposition, and its subsequent transformation into quite a different organization under Lambert's direction after the return to office in 1935. This plastic quality arose not only from the different tasks set by opposition and government but also, perhaps equally importantly, from the highly ambivalent and contradictory conceptions held by the party leader, Mackenzie King, about party organization and the role of the NLF. A close and careful perusal of King's papers and diaries on the subject of party organization reveals that the man with the reputation as the master of ambiguity in his public statements was, on this particular issue at least, fundamentally ambiguous in his own mind as well as in his public expression. Party organization did not occupy his thoughts to any great extent, if the amount of space devoted to the subject in his diaries is any indication. When he did turn his mind to organizational matters, more questions than answers seem to have been raised. Ideally, King would have preferred to delegate the responsibility onto others and be done with it. 'In every political party,' he explained to the party's former national secretary, 'there must be a division of labour, and the organizational end is one which others than those who have to do with matters of policy, etc. should handle.'[4] But King never made clear the relationship between the NLF on the one hand and the provincial organizations and constituency associations on the other, between the NLF and the parliamentary leaders of the party, the role of fund-raising and the place of the financial collectors, nor indeed whether the NLF was to be primarily a publicity body or a functioning electoral organization.

Sometimes King seemed to place the NLF at the highest level of importance; he wrote in his diary following the 1932 NLF meeting, for example, that the organization was a success, 'how great no one knows but myself. It realizes all that I have sought & worked & fought for for the last 13 years.' Yet at other times he seemed quite capable of forgetting the very existence of the federation. Just before the 1935 election, after the NLF had been in effective operation for almost three years, King could casually muse that he ought to have at least four personal secretaries, including one to 'handle wholly party matters of organizaton.' Since this off-handed negligence toward recognition of his extra-parliamentary organization was often publicly as well as privately expressed, tensions were always present. A major obstacle to co-operation was King's intense suspicion of any rivalry for control of the party and its policies. Early in 1933 he secured the parliamentary caucus' acceptance of his own position regarding the party's attitude toward the new Co-operative Commonwealth Federation, and noted with rather smug satisfaction in his diary that this was a 'better arrangement than issuing anything from the [NLF] Office.' There was jealousy of the latter body 'seeking to settle or to announce policy & rightly so. It is a great business to drive this pair together & keep them in the same harness, the parliamentary party & the party in the country.'5 Since it was the national leader alone who could presumably have delineated authoritative lines of responsibility in these matters, King's elusive conception of the NLF and its role was to become itself a complicating factor in the new organization's struggle for identity. When one adds to this King's penchant for blaming 'organization' when things did not work out, while taking full personal credit for political success, it becomes obvious why the party leader and the extra-parliamentary organization never achieved an easy accommodation.

There was little clue to these relations in the constitutional structure of the federation. The only relevant point enshrined in the constitution was the decidedly federal nature of the organization. The largest representative body in the federation, the advisory council, was composed of seven representatives from each province named by the provincial associations (or the MPs from the province in the case of Quebec), two representatives of the Liberal Women, two representatives of the Twentieth Century Liberal Association (later the Young Liberals), and the president and secretary of the federation. Or as Vincent Massey told the first meeting of the advisory council in 1933: 'The National Liberal Federation is a real federation in that it represents a central superstructure resting on provincial pillars. In accordance with this principle the contact between the National Liberal office and the rank and file of Liberalism throughout the country is established through the provincial offices and provincial organizations.' [6] The advisory council in itself proved to be less than crucial to the workings of the Liberal party in the years to come, other than providing the closest semblance of a national party meeting countenanced by Mackenzie King until the end of his twenty-nine-year reign as leader, but its structure mirrored the very real decentralization in the party's electoral operations. Liberals have continued to place great stock in the federal nature of the party organization. Over thirty years later, Jack Pickersgill – himself no stranger to party organization – in a tribute to Norman Lambert who had just died, reiterated that Lambert's success as an organizer rested squarely on his recognition that the 'organization of the party structure should correspond closely to the political organization of Canada itself' and that the NLF had to be based 'almost entirely' on the 'participation of strong provincial associations,' to act generally as a 'co-ordinating body' among these provincial units.[7] On the other hand, in his first presidential address Massey also noted that notwithstanding the provincial basis of the federation, 'it has been thought advisable that the office of your Federation should come in touch and maintain contact with individual Liberals, throughout the Dominion, through the establishment of what has been called an "associate membership." ' This individual membership was to serve the dual function of fund-raising (membership dues were set at $1.00 per year) and providing the national office with a mailing list for its publicity. Although Massey mentions the figure of 50,000 memberships, there is no evidence that there was anything remotely approaching that number of dues-paying supporters.[8]

The permanent officers of the federation were to be the honorary president (the party leader), the president, two vice-presidents, a secretary, and an honorary treasurer. Later (1938) a second secretary was added to the roster; this was a recognition of the role of the head of the office's French-speaking section, which had begun operations in 1933. An executive committee involving provincial representation was specified to supervise the operations of the office, but it was quickly realized that such a body could not meet on a regular basis and its role was in 1933 handed over to the finance committee as the 'working Executive Committee of the Federation'; this body was to have five members, one of which must be the president.[9] The original members of this committee, in addition to Massey, were Albert Matthews, a leading Bay Street financier and Liberal party fund-raiser; Senator H.H. Horsey, an Ottawa utilities executive and long-time party organizer; Pierre Casgrain, Liberal whip in the House of Commons; and Mme Grant de Rouen. The last seems to have been an honorary appointment only, but Messrs Matthews, Horsey, and Casgrain were of considerable significance in attempting to rouse the interest and support of the business world, the Senate, and the House, holding five meetings in 1933.[10]

The real core of the national organization was the permanent office under the direction of Norman Lambert. When the finance committee in late 1932 was able to guarantee Lambert a salary for three years, Mackenzie King correctly identified the importance of this action in his diary: 'That is the pivotal point in everything, around that everything will work and can be secured.' Although the overall finances of the NLF were in appalling decrepitude, King had no doubt that 'with Lambert in charge, nothing else matters.'[11] Lambert had a varied background including journalism (the *Globe* and the *Grain Growers' Guide*), political organization (with the United Farmers of Manitoba), and business (Manitoba Maple Leaf Milling Company). He possessed intimate knowledge of Manitoba politics, as well as having roots in Ontario. His connection with the Progressives was important to King, whose concern with the co-optation of western third-party sentiment was never very far from the surface. Yet Lambert also proved that he could get along very well indeed with the financiers of Bay Street and St James Street. It was an excellent combination for a centre party. But Lambert also demonstrated the soundest of political instincts and very considerable organizational sense. His cool-headed and tactful approach to party problems made him an ideal trouble-shooter.[12] In the years ahead he needed all the cool-headedness he could muster to deal with Mackenzie King. Finally the strain became too much even for a man of Lambert's moderate disposition and he retired from active party service in 1940, a decision in which the party leader played far more of a part than the party itself.

In 1943, when the Liberal party was undergoing a revitalization after a period of dormancy during the early war years, Lambert, by then a senator, told the advisory council of the NLF of his original conception of his role in the beginning:

It was the idea of the Prime Minister and the Honourable Vincent Massey, its first President, that the National Liberal Federation should develop along the lines of the National Liberal Federation in England. I remember when I became Secretary of the new Canadian body I was presented with a book written by a well known Liberal, Mr. J.A. Spender, memorializing the life of Sir Robert Hudson, who for forty years had been the moving spirit of that organization in the old land. Two things in that book have stuck in my mind. The first was what Mr. Spender had to say by way of introduction in the book about political organizations ...

'There will always be debate as to the part played by organization in party politics. When disasters happen, the organizer is the handiest scapegoat; when victories are won, there is not much left over for him after the political stars have taken their share of the honour and glory. The best organization will not save a party when it has made great mistakes or when for good cause or bad it is running counter to the main stream of public opinion. The best leadership and the greatest cause may also miss or fall short of their mark if not backed by good organization.'

The second thing that I remember about that book was that Sir Robert Hudson succeeded in his job because he constituted the most effective bridge between the Federation and the machinery of the Liberal party as it was represented in parliament and the government of his country ... The responsibility for party patronage, financing and the operations of the party's political organization rested with the parliamentary group. The work of promoting Liberal ideas and policies amongst the rank and file of the electorate was the job of Sir Robert Hudson and the National Liberal Federation.[13]

Lambert went on to note that after Massey's departure for London in 1935 'it fell to my lot as his successor to try to combine the educational and promotional features of that institution with the practical operations of the party's affairs,' a combination with which 'I was never satisfied.' While it was quite true that the NLF took on a very different colouration after 1935, the break with the early history was not as decisive as Lambert argued. From the very beginning Lambert was expected to take an interest in the 'practical operations' of the party, and the more flair he demonstrated for this kind of work, the more was offered him. The NLF was never simply an educational or promotional body. Although that function dominated in the first few years, the other side was always present as well.

Massey's report to the 1932 meeting of the NLF on the activities of the new body since the arrival of Lambert in July of that year gives an early indication of the varied duties involved. There was first of all the basic task of compiling a list of names and addresses of executives or responsible persons in the constituency associations – no easy or simple job, as it turned out. Then there were the routine publicity assignments, such as maintaining a clipping service, writing and distributing a newsletter, mailing out copies of speeches. There was also a policy and research aspect involving the federation in background work on the Imperial Economic Conference in relation to Liberal policies, and general assistance to members of Parliament in preparation of debates. Lambert had already been on a tour of the Maritimes and the West, for the purpose of establishing organizational contacts with important party people in those regions. Moreover, one member of the staff had been seconded to direct the organization of a successful Liberal by-election campaign in South Huron, Ontario. [14] The NLF dealt in nuts and bolts as well as words and phrases.

One of the central figures in the organization of publicity and research for the NLF was R.J. Deachman, a freelance journalist and publicity man for such organizations as the Consumers' League. Deachman published his own newsletter, *Basic Facts,* which had a small but influential subscription list, including a good number of small weekly newspapers across the country. He had been retained by the old national office under Andrew Haydon to provide Liberal publicity under the guise of non-partisan journalism, which was felt to be of some use in colouring local news reports with the proper point of view. This arrangement was continued after the creation of the new NLF. Deachman had the use of the NLF office, a stenographer, and equipment and supplies along with a regular retainer. He was expected to do direct party publicity as well as put out his newsletter. Deachman also was involved in electoral work as in the Huron South by-election victory of 1931, an involvement which led to his own successful candidacy in Huron North in the next general election, and his consequent departure from party publicity work.

The arrangement with Deachman was not a happy one. Norman Lambert was not an admirer of Deachman, and he thought the special arrangement the latter had worked out to be to the party's disadvantage. Indeed, early on in Lambert's career at the NLF, Deachman went to King to complain that Lambert was out to 'get him.' When the latter inquired of Lambert about the situation, Lambert 'explained that D[eachman] was working on his own and not as an N.L.F. employee; that he never advised with anybody; that he proceeded in an unbusinesslike way to exploit his Basic Facts service; & complained that his expenditures were more than he received from us.' Massey apparently felt that Deachman had a 'persecution complex,' and Lambert told King that Deachman would eventually either have to go it alone or become an NLF employee. In 1934 Lambert made an attempt to put the arrangement on a new footing; a few days later, however, Lambert indicated that nothing had changed: 'Had bad period with R.J.D. whose abrupt manner this morning finally caused a bad blow-out.'[15] Deachman's departure in 1935 from the NLF office thus settled one internal personal problem.

Another special feature of the NLF's publicity function was the French section. The Liberal national office from the beginning demonstrated a dual

English-French structure. In part this was simply a response to the fact of being the major party in Quebec and drawing a significant degree of support from French-language voters. The growth of a special, and semi-autonomous, French-Canadian section in the NLF was in this sense a positive response on the part of the federal party to Quebec provincialism, albeit a response which firmly rejected an equal Quebec share in the overall direction of the national organization. The French section of the NLF was in roughly the same relation to the national secretary as Ernest Lapointe was as Quebec lieutenant to Mackenzie King: in command with regard to Quebec matters but not given any special weight in regard to national matters.

As early as 1932 it was apparent that a special French-speaking input would be necessary. P.-F. Casgrain was given receipt books for financial collections for the NLF in Quebec which he discovered, to his 'great horror and dissatisfaction,' contained a number of unpardonable errors in French grammar.[16] However, it was not merely a question of proper translation, as Adjuter Savard, the man hired to run the French-language publicity, explained: 'The [mailing] lists are divided into French and English and the French publications are not simply a translation of the English since different types of arguments are needed to convince the two races – the English can be presented with statistics, with the French the statistics must be clothed with argument.' Moreover, Savard indicated that Deachman's newsletter was never translated into French because his low-tariff views 'would not appeal to protectionist Quebec.'[17]

One publicity venture was the launching of the so-called *Liberal Monthly*, a magazine to be distributed to the NLF mailing list throughout the country. The magazine was at this time a 'so-called' *Monthly* since it never appeared on a monthly basis. The major problem was the lack of money. The other problem was the lack of a party press tradition in Canada. In the past daily commercial newspapers had of course been highly partisan, although this partisanship was already waning by the time of the Depression. There was no tradition of party organs, owned and operated by the parties and devoted to party purposes alone. It was difficult to see just what gap was being filled by a party magazine, especially since it could be neither a *news* vehicle nor a lively source of party debate, given the tight control exercised over policy by the party leader and the parliamentary caucus. The project was a priority one, however, and early in 1934 Lambert was able to present a pilot copy to King. The latter, typically, 'suggested changes in appearance of front page, including the name, vol. and no.' On the whole, though, King 'thought it was good, and said it was like "a ray of light." ' A year later Lambert was still scrambling to find the money to allow the

Monthly to come out semi-monthly.[18] It was only in the late 1940s that the *Liberal Monthly* began appearing on a regular basis.

VINCENT MASSEY

The most extreme difficulty associated with the establishment of the NLF rested on the relationship between Mackenzie King and Vincent Massey. To say that this relationship was strained would be rather too mild; it would be more precise to call it poisonous. It is perhaps an interesting commentary on the process of élite accommodation in Canada that two men who disliked each other so thoroughly should have been able to work together for the common purpose of sending Mackenzie King back to the office of prime minister and Vincent Massey to his high commissionership in London. Massey's memoirs display a sustained bitterness toward King in no way dimmed by the passage of years and the death of his old antagonist, mitigated only by a certain Upper Canadian sense of social propriety.[19] In King's private record there is no such sense of constraint, only sustained distaste for Massey and all his works.

The explanation of King's attitude is undoubtedly complex, compounded of dislike for Massey's British imperialism and love of royalty and titles; of intense suspicion of Massey's attempts to put forward his personal views on Liberal policy; and of a general tendency to demand total personal loyalty and subordination in colleagues which Massey was quite unwilling or unable to fulfil. Most important of all perhaps was Massey's status as a man of wealth and social position. Such men were a source of profound ambivalence to Mackenzie King, who alternately raised the darkest suspicions about the role of capitalism and then romantically idealized those capitalists who were his personal financial benefactors, such as John D. Rockefeller, Jr., and P.C. Larkin. These contradictory impulses reflected the very profound contradiction between King's reformism and his conservatism, an ineradicable tension in his mind to which his diary bears interminable witness. Massey was unfortunate enough to stand somewhere in the twilight zone between the two contradictory images of wealth. On the one hand, he was a Liberal, and was willing to offer his services to the Liberal party. On the other hand, his assistance was not rendered personally to King – as in the case of P.C. Larkin – nor was it disinterested, since Massey obviously expected a *quid pro quo*. Massey gave promise of being a Larkin or Rockefeller, yet failed to deliver on the promise, which may account for the obsessive quality of King's dislike and suspicion. Nor was King without a certain jealous resentment against the social prestige of a Massey, a prestige which alternately repelled and lured him. On a stormy summer night in 1933 Massey came to visit King at his summer home at Kingsmere in the Gatineau Hills. King wrote rather pathetically in his diary after Massey had left: 'There was nothing very congenial about our conversation, nothing un-congenial but a sort of lack of sympathetic co-operation. The rain & cold-ness of the night may have played its part. What I feel most is being so much alone, & lacking some of the "solid" environment needed to interest a man like Massey.'

At times King's enmity knew no bounds, and Massey was subjected to the kind of invective in his diary that was normally reserved only for R.B. Bennett. After one meeting with Massey, in which King poured out what he himself described as his 'righteous indignation,' he concluded his personal record with the dire phrase: 'I could have spewed him out of my mouth.' Yet on other, more businesslike, occasions, King would recognize Massey's very real and tangible contributions to the Liberal party's fortunes. In writing to one very prominent Quebec backer of the party King went out of his way to report that Massey 'as you know, is a contributor of considerable amount, and all that he is doing by way of speaking and travelling is wholly at his own expense.'[20] The problem was that in King's Manichean universe it was the dark side of his image of Massey which seemed most often to win out. Massey, for his part, had definite problems coming to terms with what had necessarily to be a subordinate and instrumental role in the party. It was the common observation of many that Massey, not to put too fine a point upon it, was a snob.

One of the continuing sources of differences between the two men was Massey's attempt to act as a source of inspiration for a revision of Liberal policy. Convinced that the Depression called for Liberal rethinking, Massey seemed to see himself as a kind of enlightened patrician reformer, perhaps not unlike Franklin D. Roosevelt, with a special mandate to reorient the Liberal party along more progressive lines. There were a number of problems stemming from this conception of his role. The Liberal party in this era had no constitutional procedures for policy-making except for the passage of platform resolutions at national conventions and the 'advice' of the small advisory council meetings of the NLF. The latter lacked any real legitimacy and was in no way binding on the parliamentary leadership; the former would only follow the death or retirement of the national leader. Even at that, King had been notoriously loath to bind himself or his party to the resolutions passed at the 1919 convention which had chosen him as leader, declaring in a well-known phrase that the resolutions were no more than a 'chart on which is plotted the course desired by the people of the country.'[21]

A further complication was Mackenzie King's personal reaction to the Depression: a strongly liberal emphasis on recovery through business confidence rather than any reform adventures through illiberal state intervention and regulation. King was not impressed with the American trend under the New Deal toward central planning and national protection which he tended to identify with Bennett's 'Tory dictatorship' and even with European fascism. Hence he was deeply suspicious of elements within his own party who might attempt to move the party's policies in such directions from under his own protective and moderate wing. Since it was Massey, whom King mistrusted on other grounds already, who spearheaded the drive to modify Liberal policy in this period, King's tight-fisted control over the party platform was intensified. Yet despite this reflex response, King was in the end forced by the exigencies of the era to modify his thinking on a number of points.[22] It is altogether probable, however, that Massey's particular role impeded rather than hastened this process.

In his 1933 report to the NLF advisory council, Massey, in pointing to the useful work which the federation was accomplishing, took note of a number of 'research groups' formed 'under the auspices' of the NLF involving men of 'practical experience and expert knowledge' in Toronto, Montreal, Winnipeg, and Kingston, who had met to discuss such important economic questions as the establishment of a central bank, the railways problem, unemployment relief, and changes to the Companies Act. The results of these inquiries were on file in the NLF office for any Liberals who wished to make use of them. They had, Massey asserted, already served a 'very useful purpose.'[23] Massey had in fact organized a series of small meetings involving some of Canada's leading academics, a smaller number of businessmen, and some of the party's more thoughtful politicians, to discuss new directions in public policy. The introduction of academics was a rather new development in Canada which the intractable problems of the collapse of the old economic order was making increasingly necessary – and one toward which Mackenzie King, the graduate of Chicago and Harvard and the author of *Industry and Humanity* might have been favourable. Indeed, King did make good use of the ideas of academics and intellectuals, especially those who could be co-opted into the bureaucracy, like O.D. Skelton, or directly into politics, like Norman Rogers. But King was less favourable to such gatherings as Massey organized, which lay outside his direct personal supervision.

Some of the politicians who took part had their doubts as well. J.L. Ralston attended one such meeting at the Massey home in Port Hope which involved a number of professors of economics and a lesser number of MPs.

Ralston's report to a correspondent was mixed: 'As usual at these conferences, I am afraid we did not settle very much, but at least we did beat up some old straw and considerable new stuff. There was plenty of chaff to burn, but there were a few kernels of good grain.'[24]

Early in 1933 some of the results of these meetings went into a policy draft worked out in King's office with Massey and Lambert, along with twenty-five to thirty Liberal MPs. The draft then went to the full Liberal caucus, which divided sharply on the matter. Lambert noted in his diary that the caucus 'finally decided to leave whole matter in Mr. King's hands to express as he saw fit on the floor of the House.' Not surprisingly, King 'seemed quite happy; & left impression that he had got everything he wanted.' No less surprisingly, Massey appeared 'not overly keen about developments.'[25]

Matters were not furthered by Massey's penchant for public pronouncements on the nature of Liberalism. One speech on the 'new Liberalism' at Windsor in the spring of 1933 brought about the resignation of a Quebec member of the NLF. Another about the 'new nationalism' drew a stern private rebuke from Norman Lambert who suggested to his superior that 'on the basis of political philosophy, you and Mr. Keynes are presenting the best case possible for a fascist government for Canada.'[26] Later on, Lord Keynes would become an important mentor of the Liberal party in power; in the shorter run, the concept of a state-owned and state-controlled central bank to regulate monetary policy – an idea articulated in the Massey study sessions – would also become Liberal policy. But in the confused and bewildered atmosphere of the early 1930s many would see Massey's mild and often merely rhetorical invocations of 'planning' as a call to revolution. Mackenzie King no doubt knew better than that, but he was just as enraged at the stirring up of the demons of division as he was at the ideas themselves. Eventually King made it clear to Massey that he had best both put up *and* shut up. As he conveyed the matter forcefully to Lambert: 'he didn't want V.M[assey] to speak publicly; let him organize or not as he pleased: London was the stake.'

The major effort launched by Massey was the summer school in September 1933. The Conservatives also had a summer conference the same year. The fledgling CCF was gathering in the support of intellectuals through the League for Social Reconstruction in Montreal and Toronto.[27] The Liberal party obviously had to accommodate themselves to the new trend. But King suspected that Massey intended to use the summer school as a club to coerce the leader to give way on policy matters. Nor was this suspicion without foundation. Lambert recorded that Massey wished to reverse the decision of the caucus to give the leader a free hand with policy: ' ... he proposes to have summer school made the basis of a liberal program, evidently more definite & more radical than that issued by King on Feb. 23 [1933] on floor of Parliament.' The idea of the school became a contentious issue within the party caucus, which finally allowed Massey to go ahead 'on condition that it did not have anything to do with any Liberal party organizaton.' Massey angrily insisted to Lambert that the NLF office machinery be used and the costs absorbed in the NLF printing accounts, that 'unless the office of the Federation could do this, he would take steps to close it up.' When the financial condition of the NLF made it clear that it could not afford to absorb such special costs, Massey had a change of heart. It was, after all, he confessed to Lambert, 'unthinkable' that the office should be closed down, and he agreed to have the costs of the summer school sent on to him personally.[28] This was a considerable financial contribution to the party, but not one which Mackenzie King was apt to appreciate.

The summer school was held in Port Hope in the first week in September and included a number of invited guests, political figures and academics from Canada, the United States, and Britain. There were a number of Liberal party people, although conspicuously *not* including the parliamentary caucus from which there were only four representatives, including Mackenzie King. King himself was not happy to be in attendance. On the eve of travelling to Port Hope where he was to be the guest of Vincent and Alice Massey during the conference, he had what he took to be a prophetic dream: '... [C]uriously enough saw first one snake in grass come out of a marshy ground – a little one – and a little later a larger one. It is the first time I have ever dreamed of anything of the kind; concluded it was a warning to be careful – I wondered if it could mean that by any chance my hosts at Port Hope were not to be trusted.'

It is a bizarre commentary on the relationship of the party leader to policy-making in this era that one of the major effects of a policy conference was to make the party leader constipated for the duration, as duly noted on a daily basis in his diary. On a more serious plane, King was disgusted at the tendency of many of the speakers to stress planning and governmental controls. Indeed, the more he heard about the American New Deal, the less he liked it. Raymond Moley, from Roosevelt's 'brains trust,' made King's 'blood run cold.' He experienced a rising feeling of 'indignation' at 'university men, etc.' who 'fail to realize the price at which liberty has been achieved & what liberty means.' All in all, King was quite unimpressed with the 'amateurish' contribution of intellectuals to the political world.

'Everything is a new discovery,' he suggested in a revealing phrase, 'which fools proclaim from the housetops, & concerning which wise men have long known & been silent.'[29] In any event, a volume was published of selected speeches and discussions at the conference, entitled *The Liberal Way*, as the party's public contribution to the growing debate over the way out of the economic catastrophe.[30] It was the only such contribution from the Liberal party throughout the Depression.

Vincent Massey had hoped to establish a tradition of such summer conferences, and had indeed called it the 'First Liberal Summer Conference.' It was also the last. When Massey raised the matter of a second conference the following year, King – fully restored in political self-confidence and smelling the blood of R.B. Bennett – would have none of it. To the former secretary of the national office, King confided that 'personally, I feel that what would be of much greater service to the party than a discussion of public issues' would be 'an extension course on political organization.' He told Vincent Massey exactly the same thing when the conference idea was being advanced by the latter. When Massey rejected King's counter idea, King brought the interview to a close in a flurry of violent denunciations – and for good measure told Massey to call off a proposed speaking tour of the West.[31] It would seem that King felt strong enough by 1934 to get tough with Massey. The high commissionership in London was increasingly used as a crude but effective bludgeon to force Massey to concentrate on raising money rather than ideas. Lambert was told by King to convey to Massey that the erstwhile policy-maker 'would have to decide on organization, during next 6 months or forego London, need for finances emphasized.' Lambert brought this message to Massey a number of times. In the fall of the same year he visited the Masseys at Port Hope and put it bluntly: 'I told him and Mrs. M. that K[ing] expected him to attend to business end of things & in effect that this was to be the price of London appointment. Mrs. M. said she had been urging this on V.M.'[32] In the face of such pressures Massey capitulated. King was told that he was right, that there would be no summer school, no western trip, and that from then on the NLF would be used 'primarily for organization purposes' with Massey's own special attention given to this function.[33]

During the 1935 general election campaign Massey did give some aid in fund-raising, which will be discussed later. Despite his efforts, and his amazement at the 'prodigious sums' required which 'pressed heavily on a good many candidates despite the fact that everything is being done to meet the situation,' King was not particularly grateful as may be seen from Massey's account of their last meeting before the election:

On October 5, 1935, I saw Mackenzie King aboard his private car to report to the Leader, as chairman of the party organization, and to receive whatever instructions he cared to give me. I hadn't seen him for several weeks. My visit that morning was most unwelcome and gave rise to a conversation that was far from pleasant, and the atmosphere was not sweetened by the fact that King's valet had wakened him on my arrival. I was accused of invading his privacy on numerous occasions, even to the point of affecting his health, of making suggestions which were unacceptable; of being generally wrong in my views and not stressing sufficiently in the campaign publicity his own qualities as leader; of being moved in my work in the campaign by self-interest. After Mackenzie King's outburst on this occasion, I felt it better that we should not meet again for a while, and I didn't see him until after the election on October 14.[34]

Massey was not invited to spend election night at King's home at Laurier House. As one of King's secretaries told Lambert, Massey 'was not wanted.' Yet Massey had fulfilled his side of the bargain, however reluctantly, and King was once again prime minister of Canada following the election. Although he pointedly failed to thank the NLF office for its part in the victory on election night,[35] King did give Massey the reward for which he had been longing, the appointment in London. The Bible used for Massey's swearing-in was cryptically inscribed by King in the fly-leaf with a verse from *Chronicles*: 'Be ye strong therefore, and let not your hands be weak: for your work shall be rewarded.'[36]

NORMAN LAMBERT

One of the most damaging aspects of the King-Massey split for the party was that it inevitably drew Norman Lambert into the vortex of personal animosities. Lambert was in a precarious and delicate position, torn between his immediate superior, Massey as president of the NLF, and the party leader. Since Lambert and King eventually came to a personal parting of the ways, it is ironic to follow the progress of their relationship in their respective diaries. Their mutual first impressions were good. King, as noted earlier, thought highly enough of Lambert to believe that his hiring was the 'pivotal point' in establishing the NLF on a sound basis. Lambert's first meeting with King led to this positive assessment of the Liberal leader: 'His expressed views on organizations, & the outlook of the Liberal mind in Canada, were all that one could desire.' The impression became less positive, however, as soon as Massey began urging King to make a political trip to the West, a suggestion which King rejected as improper. When Lambert inquired about the leader's response to the western tour idea, King 'remonstrated very vigorously about being rushed, and resented any interference with his arrangements.' The following day King telephoned Lambert 'reemphasizing his point of view regarding interference or undue management of his affairs in connection with Parliament.' King had emerged, Lambert noted acutely, 'completely and extremely from his valley of humiliation.' Moreover, Lambert commented, 'his references to V.M[assey] were as much out of place as they were unflattering.'[37] Lambert began to entertain serious doubts about his party leader.

The curious aspect of Lambert's developing alienation from King is that King himself continued to hold a highly favourable image of Lambert. When King did go on a western tour the following year, Massey arranged to have Lambert accompany him, despite the lack of funds, in order, as Massey suggested to King, to 'save you a great deal of unnecessary worry and strain by being present as a buffer between you and the importunities of our good friends all through the West.' The two men had a number of prolonged conversations on the train, and King's comments in his diary were uniformly complimentary. 'He has,' King mused, 'a fine nature, kind, unselfish & big, has too[,] much knowledge of western conditions & economic matters generally.'[38]

The problem was that as King moved in 1934 to severely restrict Massey's freedom of action, Lambert was used as a cat's-paw by King, and was then in turn used by Massey in a similar manner. Early in that year Lambert was planning a trip to Manitoba to arrange a number of organizational matters for the next election, such as the selection of a finance chairman. King concluded that Lambert was preparing the way for a Massey speaking tour and suggested that he had better concentrate his efforts on organizing in Ontario, where an all-important provincial election was coming up. King put this quite bluntly to Lambert, telling him, in the latter's words, 'that I was indifferent to Ont., didn't seem to like it.' Lambert had to enumerate his contributions to Ontario organization, and plead truthfully that his Manitoba trip had nothing to do with Massey. Then King confronted Massey, who swore that Lambert was in favour of accompanying him on a western tour. King confided to his diary: 'Lambert is simply his man Friday, he [Massey] has sent him West to prepare the way for him; Lambert depending on him for salary, is in a very tight & difficult place. I think Lambert is perfectly straight & Massey simply using him ...' King thought it a clever strategy to pretend to Massey that Lambert had lied to himself, rather than that Massey had lied to him about Lambert, although he fully believed that the latter was the case. That Lambert would hear this from

Massey was of course inevitable. These Byzantine intrigues finally culminated a few months later in a meeting between King and Lambert in
which the latter was told by King 'frankly and completely my opinion of
Massey.' King concluded with evident satisfaction that he was 'glad to
get Lambert's confidence.'[39] He did get Lambert's undertaking to impress
upon Massey the necessity of organizing, raising money, and staying as
quiet as possible if he wanted to go to London. But things were past
the point where he could get Lambert's confidence. Lambert, as
his diary makes abundantly clear, was simply fed up with the entire
back-stabbing atmosphere and the petty Machiavellianism of the party
leader.

The final straw for Lambert was King's public indifference to the work of
the NLF. King was all for 'organization' so long as somebody else was doing
it, and so long as it was done silently, out of sight, out of mind, and out of
public notice. He himself would do as little as possible to draw attention to
it, but would be just as quick to take personal credit for electoral success.
The logical result of this attitude was that the Liberal organizers were made
to feel like plumbers allowed to use only the tradesmen's entrance. On election night King never called to thank Lambert for the considerable contribution that the NLF, and Lambert in particular, had made to King's re-election. Three days later King called to claim that he had called on election
night, 'late,' and 'wanted me to be the first he spoke to because he felt if it
hadn't been for me & my work that he wouldn't be in office.' There then followed some desultory 'consultation' about various cabinet candidates. King
told Vincent Massey that C.D. Howe, who had been brought to King's attention by Massey, was the NLF's 'contribution to the cabinet.' Massey replied that that was 'very kind.'[40]

BY-ELECTION CAMPAIGNS

In view of these internal divisions and the constraints imposed on the organization by the party leader, it is remarkable that the period from 1930 to
1935 was characterized by a steadily increasing success in one key area of
political activity – the winning of by-elections. There were fifteen by-elections held between the two general elections. Of these, the Liberal party
won ten, the Conservatives only three, one independent was elected, and
one 'labour' candidate who later turned out to be a Liberal supporter.
Moreover, the trend continued: in 1933 the Liberals won three out of three;
in 1934 five out of six. It was an enviable record, borne along without doubt
by the rising tide of revulsion against Bennett Toryism in the country, but

not accomplished without effective organizational efforts both at the constituency and at the national levels.

There were two by-elections within a year of the 1930 general election. The time was not auspicious and the results were not encouraging. One Quebec constituency which had elected a Liberal a year earlier turned Tory. In the other contest, Hamilton East, the Liberals gave up the field in advance. Or so it appeared. In fact, there was a more subtle game at work, which is quite revealing of the political shrewdness of Mackenzie King in the face of electoral adversity. Hamilton East was a traditionally Conservative seat which had voted almost two-to-one Tory over Liberal in 1930. Depleted by federal and provincial activities, a local Liberal official informed King that the constituency association was without funds and without prospect of raising enough to conduct a 'proper campaign.' In fact, King was actively working behind the scenes to ensure that the Hamilton Liberals did not contest the by-election in order to leave the field open to a Labour candidate, Humphrey Mitchell, who was opposing the Conservatives. Powerful local Liberals were favourable to a tacit alliance with labour which could work to the benefit of the Liberal cause in the long run. As one Hamilton Liberal of some consequence put it, they were only advocating 'giving Labour a fair representation in exchange for Labour support in the other City constituency or constituencies.'[41] To King it was not just a case of making a virtue out of necessity; he was acting on one of his lifelong principles: that labour was the proper area for Liberal advance through co-operation and co-optation. When the idea of the Labour candidacy came before the Liberal caucus in Ottawa, King wrote in his diary that he 'was sorry to see some of our men almost as bitter against Labour as against the Conservatives.' Or as he told the Hamilton Liberals, '… with no Liberal in the field, it is infinitely preferable that Labour rather than Conservatives should win in the forthcoming by-election.'[42]

Mitchell won a strong victory over the Tory candidate. A number of beneficial results flowed to the Liberal party beyond the simple defeat of a Conservative. The riding lost its traditional Tory cast and has since been a Liberal stronghold, where the party has drawn considerable support from the unionized working class electorate.[43] Mitchell himself was given a number of positions on boards and commissions dealing with labour relations during the Second World War, and was appointed minister of labour in the Liberal government in 1941, a position which he retained until his death in 1950. The Liberal party thus gained a labour base in a working class constituency which might otherwise have turned to the CCF, and drew in a representative of organized labour to the federal labour ministry. Thus when

King noted in his diary the night of Mitchell's victory in 1931 that he was 'not sorry to see the people come into their own,'[44] it was with a certain amount of well-founded faith in where the 'people' would go.

The most interesting of four by-election contests in 1932 from the standpoint of the national organization was Huron South, where a narrow Liberal victory in 1930 was strengthened in a by-election. Recognizing that Ontario would be the decisive battlefield in the next election, Ontario constituencies were given top priority. R.J. Deachman of the national office was despatched to direct operations and supervise the 'work of organization in detail.' As King later told Massey, 'too much credit for the victory cannot be given to Deachman. He was on the spot both day and night, seeing that the polls were properly organized and supplying the candidate and other speakers with arguments to refute those of the Administration.'[45] It was a successful example of what organizational services a national office could provide in a practical way, and King was momentarily grateful.

Three by-elections were scheduled for 23 October 1933, Restigouche-Madawaska in New Brunswick, Yamaska in Quebec, and the Saskatchewan riding of Mackenzie, where a Progressive member had resigned. This simple agenda of elections precipitated a tangled web of plots and counterplots within the Liberal party, the ultimately successful resolution of which casts some light on the nature of party organization in this era.

Mackenzie was the critical contest, for it was here that the new Co-operative Commonwealth Federation, fresh from its founding meeting in Regina in August of that year, would face its first electoral test. It was as good ground as the new party could expect to find under the circumstances; to the Liberals it was critical that they meet the CCF on its own territory and demonstrate that they could head off this new challenge on their left. There was the sinking feeling in Ottawa that not merely the Conservatives but the Liberals as well were in serious trouble in the West once again; as Escott Reid told the readers of the *American Political Science Review* early in the year, 'there were signs that the allegiance of most of the Prairie countryside to the two old parties was no longer merely doubtful – it was foresworn.'[46]

The chief problem was, of course, money. From the beginning, Norman Lambert in the NLF office was involved in the attempts to raise funds for the Mackenzie election. Since it seemed obvious that the business community would be dismayed at a signal success for a fledgling socialist party attempting to break into the two-party system, it might have been expected that Bay Street dollars would pour into the campaign chests of the major 'safe' alternative to an increasingly discredited Tory government. Lambert first heard encouraging notes about a 'prominent banking friend' who had 'promised to do all that was necessary.' A month later reports were 'discouraging,' and requests were also beginning to come to Lambert from Restigouche-Madawaska. Then the chief Liberal organizer in the Montreal district, Pierre Cardin, intimated that something was cooking behind the scenes involving a deal with the Conservatives to 'saw-off' the Yamaska and Restigouche-Madawaska contests. Cardin had been speaking to the Conservatives about the possibility of allowing the Tories an acclamation in Yamaska in return for a Liberal acclamation in the New Brunswick seat 'in order to save money.' Mackenzie King was apparently resigned to the notion, despite his instinctive distaste for dealing with Tories. As he noted in his diary: '... it all comes down to what those who have to raise the funds for a campaign are determined to do. No matter how good the cause, if men won't fight for it, one is helpless as a leader, & the Quebec and New Brunswick men will not fight without funds & seemingly unable to raise any. It is most disheartening.' Meanwhile, Lambert had arranged to have E.G. Long, an influential figure on Bay Street, handle the raising of money for the Mackenzie election. Long said he would talk to the loan companies and the banks. Things might thus fall neatly into place, with the Liberals freed to take on the CCF in the West with all the available funds directed into that fight. As Cardin summed up his case for a saw-off to Lambert, it was 'a case of funds on the one side and the CCF on the other.'[47]

Things were not so simple as that, however, as Lambert learned when he travelled to New Brunswick to assess the local situation, and discovered that the local Liberals were against any saw-offs in principle. On the other hand they also wanted funds from outside the province to defray the cost. Lambert estimated that perhaps $3000 might be raised locally. It was not enough. The problem was that New Brunswick was controlled financially by the Montreal treasury of the party, which was unwilling to put very much into the election. By this time the grumbling acquiescence of the party leader in the saw-off arrangement had abruptly changed. King, in Lambert's words, was 'on the rampage.' As soon as Lambert had informed the leader that the local people in Restigouche-Madawaska preferred to make a fight of it, King was transformed: 'I felt my heart filled with blood as the word came – trust the people – they are better than their leaders – I was delighted.' Moreover, King had increasing reason to suspect the motives of Cardin and Raymond and the Montreal Liberals in the whole affair. Cardin had told Lambert that the money to be raised in the Yamaska contest, just as in the Maisonneuve by-election in Montreal the year before, would come from the same source for both parties, the Simard contractors. The extension of certain contracts to the Simards was not criticized by either Liberals or Conservatives because to do so would be to 'spoil sources of help.' Since Cardin was willing to promise Lambert money for Mackenzie, once the Yamaska contest had been called off, suspicions about the inability of Montreal to finance the New Brunswick election were difficult to allay. King told Lambert bluntly that 'it looked as if a group of people in Montreal were trying to show him he couldn't do without them.' King noted in his diary that A. Duranleau, the Tory who had succeeded Cardin as minister of marine in 1930, drew his funds from the same source as Cardin: 'I do not place confidence in either.' King's suspicions of Cardin would later carry over into his cabinet selection in 1935; they were certainly strong enough in 1933 to make King very wary of any deals devised under the auspices of the Montreal organizer. King turned once again to the one man whom he trusted in the Quebec organization, Ernest Lapointe, and poured out his 'outrage' at the idea of a saw-off. Taking on all by-election contests, he asserted, 'at the moment, is the supreme task and duty of our party and we must not fail in it, even if you and I have to fight single-handed to achieve the desired end.'[48]

The initial hopes of raising a war chest from finance capital on Bay Street had proved insubstantial. The problem was that the corrosive effect of the Depression on the Canadian West had turned so many farmers into debtors that even the western Liberals were forced to turn to increasingly radical monetarist solutions, including deliberate inflation – solutions which were of course anathema to the creditor capitalists of the east. One highly placed loan company executive told Lambert that 'the mortgage & loan companies were fed up with the Liberals in the West as much as [with] the Conservatives & farmers.'[49]

One western Liberal who was trusted by the financiers was Jimmy Gardiner, who alone among western Liberals exhibited a consistent ability to gain a direct access to eastern big business which many of the regular party financial collectors lacked. Gardiner had contact with the National Trust and the Bank of Commerce, a financial institution with long-standing ties to the Liberal party, and with the all-powerful CPR and its president, Sir Edward Beatty. In light of the CPR's alienation from the Conservative party over the nationalization of private lines into the CNR,[50] the Liberals might have expected some help. But the CPR was a hard taskmaster. King informed Lambert that he had approached Beatty many times 're cooperation' but Beatty would do nothing. The trouble was, as Charles Dunning reported from St James Street, that Beatty had been 'distrubed over King's reference to "integrity of the CNR."' Beatty wanted nothing less than the removal of his publicly owned rival. In late August of 1933 King was a house-guest at Beatty's Westmount mansion. King appears to have made no promises but his visit does seem to have changed Beatty's attitude. Nevertheless, it was Gardiner who was sent to arrange CPR money for the Mackenzie election. It is not clear how much was raised in this effort, but it does appear that some CPR donations found their way into the Liberals' hands in this first electoral test of the new CCF. Gardiner's influence was also of some help in Toronto among the finance companies, which reluctantly gave in rather small amounts, and with J.S. McLean of Canada Packers who contributed $500. All in all, it appears that at least $6000 was raised in Toronto, with Cardin, peeved at the fact that his saw-off deal had fallen through, contributing another $500 for Mackenzie, while refusing to help in Restigouche-Madawaska, which lay under Montreal's financial jurisdiction.[51]

The Liberals won a comfortable victory over the CCF in Mackenzie, with the Conservatives able to muster a mere 12 per cent of the vote. As King put it, 'The result was significant of the whole West & the C.C.F. movement in relation to our party. Had they won there, the fire would have spread.'[52] In Restigouche-Madawaska, despite the lack of Montreal money, the Liberals won a two-to-one victory over the Conservatives. Even Yamaska, which Cardin had been so loath to contest, voted Liberal. These successes seemed to indicate an electoral tide shifting to the Liberals, if the party could be put in harness to seize its opportunities.

Thus it was that King experienced a renewed burst of indignation when he discovered that everything returned to square one as soon as the trio of by-elections was completed. A Liberal seat had been opened up in Oxford South by the death of the sitting member, and as King explained to Senator Rodolphe Lemieux:'Incredible as it may seem, for the month past I have been experiencing the same difficulty in getting our forces organized for the campaign in South Oxford as I had with respect to the other three campaigns.' He then added, in a rather unusual show of gratitude toward the NLF, 'without the Liberal office I should be like a captain on a ship, with crew aplenty, but without the necessary means of imparting or having orders carried out.' King was concerned that organizational responsibility for the election be firmly placed on his Ontario lieutenants along with the NLF. In early November 1933 he wrote letters to Massey, the ex-ministers from Ontario, the Ontario provincial leader Mitch Hepburn, and MPs with organizational responsibilities. 'It was,' he wrote in his diary, 'a sort of ultimatum to the lot to get busy and disclose whether they are deserving of any recognition should the party be returned to power.' In fact, King put it quite vividly to the hopeful ministers of a future Liberal government that 'it will not do for Members who wish to find a place in the Ministry to wait to display their capacity and qualifications for leadership until the party victory has been won.' At least one of King's Ontario MPs agreed with his leader's assessment: 'I can tell you quite frankly that it has been a big effort to get our Members and Ex-Ministers included, to take any interest in the Ontario situation, as they should.'[53] If Mackenzie King as party leader sometimes seemed to use his patronage stick both frequently and directly, it may well be that he was forced to. In any event, Oxford South was contested satisfactorily by the Liberals, who were able to add yet another victory to an impressive string of by-election successes.

The year 1934 was generally easier for Liberal electioneering. Between the South Oxford victory and a set of five by-elections, all in Ontario, scheduled for the same day in September (the Ontario 'miniature general election' as it was dubbed), the Liberal party had won a return to power in Saskatchewan with Jimmy Gardiner's supporters capturing 50 out of 55 seats, and, more important yet, an assumption of office in Ontario itself after a generation in opposition. As the Bennett government was being rent from within by the split between Bennett and H.H. Stevens, his crusading minister of trade and commerce, and beset from without by growing public hostility and rejection, the miniature general election promised to be a triumph for the Liberals. It was thus much less difficult to muster prominent Ontario Liberals to take charge of the campaign. Indeed, the real organizational problem was how to sort out the conflicting claims of those clamouring to get in on the spoils.

The Ontario provincial party, fresh from its victory, was ready and willing to take on the Tories federally as well as provincially. There was a difficult jurisdictional problem to sort out between Hepburn's provincial organization and the federal Liberal members for the province. As Massey informed King, the 'basic problem' in the by-elections was to maintain harmony between the provincial and federal factions. The problem was further complicated by the fact that the power of the purse was perceptibly passing to the provincial party. As Massey explained:

The Treasurer of the recent Provincial campaign as you of course know is Frank O'Connor who did a magnificent piece of work. It is very important to enlist his services in connection with the September by-elections. Lambert and I are spending a couple of days in Toronto this week with O'Connor and others on this important subject. Albert Matthews and E.G. Long will be meeting with us. The more clearly the responsibility for the elections can be placed on the Ontario Liberal Association Office the more likely we are to have the assistance of O'Connor and others who made possible the good work in the Provincial fight.[54]

O'Connor, the millionaire owner of Laura Secord Candy Shops, was a key figure in rallying the support of important business interests behind Mitch Hepburn's Liberals. What was particularly significant to the federal party, many of these financial interests were involved in areas of activity which fell much more under provincial rather than federal jurisdiction. Their connections were established primarily with the provincial Liberals, and the federal wing of the party had to reach them through the provincial organization. All this will be explored later in greater detail in Chapter 8.

King's former minister of public works, J.C. Elliott, as the only ex-minister from Ontario available for this duty, was put in official charge of the campaign. Hepburn himself took personal responsibility for Elgin West, his former seat, and the secretary of the Ontario Liberal Association, Harry Johnson, took charge of Toronto East. But responsibility for the distribution of funds and the supervision of their use was to rest with Lambert – 'all to work with him' as King put it. It appears that Elliott's overall command was in fact rather nominal. 'To all,' King wrote to his ex-minister, 'I have expressed the view that all threads should link up with Mr. Lambert as secretary of the National Liberal Federation, so that from that quarter there might be a complete supervision.' Almost $22,000 was raised by the Toronto finance committee and distributed among the five ridings according to Lambert's instructions.[55]

The NLF office and the newly affluent provincial machine worked in tandem with relative ease and efficiency. The Liberals took four out of five contests, including two former Tory seats. Overall, the Liberals averaged 57.9 per cent of the popular vote in this miniature general election, while the Conservatives managed only 38.2 per cent. The province which had given R.B. Bennett fifty-nine seats in 1930, almost half the government's total, seemed ready to desert him in enormous numbers once a general election were called. The organizational efficiency with which the Liberals had met the by-election challenge in 1934, in a province which had until then been rather disastrous for Liberalism, was a clear indication that the Liberal party was ready and able to seize the opportunities with which the disintegration of the Tory régime presented it. Particularly heartening was the high degree of federal-provincial intra-party co-operation which had been reached. That this harmony had been bought at the price of a growing provincial hegemony was little noted by the federal party at the time, for, after all, the provincial Liberals were now in power and the federal party were still in opposition. Later, the problem of co-operation would become acute.

PARTY FINANCE

Organizational problems were of course closely related to the endemic problem of party finances. Two of the major tasks facing the Liberal party in this period were the financing of the NLF and the building of viable structures to raise money for the 1935 election campaign. The first problem sometimes seemed insoluble; in fact, a truly satisfactory solution never was found, even after the party returned to power. The second task was fulfilled in a somewhat ramshackle and incomplete fashion.

It is an ironic commentary on just how very misleading the enormous sums involved in the Beauharnois affair are to any understanding of the day-to-day reality of financing the Liberal party in the 1930s that the party was hard put indeed to raise a mere 3 per cent of the Beauharnois contribution of 1930 for an entire year's operation of the national office – and this with the smallest staff and services possible and the NLF president paying for his own expenses personally. Table 2.1 gives some indication of the miniscule size of the NLF's operating budget in the early Depression years. Even more striking than the small size of the budgets is the provincial pattern of quota collections. Each province was supposed to contribute annually a sum equal to $200 times the federal constituencies in the province; Table 2.2 shows the quota figures set alongside the actual contributions.

By 1934 the growing disparity between the amounts raised in the provinces by quota and the total operating budget had to be met by voluntary levies on MPs and senators, by small amounts accruing from sales of subscriptions to the *Canadian Liberal Monthly* magazine, and by bank overdrafts – $3975 in all for this year. But the main significance of the quota figures is that the NLF fell far short – by about half – of what they expected to gain, and that the hinterland areas of Canada, the West and the Maritimes, were in no way prepared to finance a national party office out of local money during the worst rigours of the Great Depression. Quebec was somewhat volatile as a source of support, but always fell short of its quota. This left Ontario to shoulder an increasing share of the financial burden, rising from 39 per cent of the actual total raised in 1931-2 to 68 per cent in 1933-3. Ontario, of course, meant Toronto, and Toronto meant Bay Street. The growing dependence of the party on this source also meant an increasing dependence on the good will and interest of the provincial party which was securing a firm hold on major Bay Street donors. While the provincial machine was able to deliver by 1934, when the Liberals had achieved power in Queen's Park, this dependence on the provincial wing was also a cause for unease. Moreover, it surely belied the Liberal party's insistence that the NLF was a genuine federation of provincial associations, in so far as its

Table 2.1
Finances of the National Liberal Federation, 1931-4

	Receipts	Expenditures	Balance
1931-2	$24,063.50	$22,655.95	$1407.55
1932-3	25,703.35	26,755.43	−1052.08
1933-4	28,033.40	28,471.81	− 438.41

Source: JLR, v. 12, Massey statement to NLF, 25 Nov. 1932; NLF, v. 861, Massey statement to NLF, 1 Dec. 1933; NPL, v. 8, folder 9, Ryan and Gorman, CA, 'Financial Statement of the National Liberal Federation of Canada'

Table 2.2
Provincial contributions to the NLF, 1931-4

		Actual amounts raised		
	Quota	1931-2	1932-3	1933-4
Prince Edward Island	$ 800	$ 355.80	$ 22.00	
Nova Scotia	2800	2810.00	97.65	$ 1000.00
New Brunswick	2200	1600.00	130.55	25.00
Quebec	13,000	6101.00	8344.65	5200.00
Ontario	16,400	9474.48	13,658.70	16,393.63
Manitoba	3400		106.00	755.00
Saskatchewan	4200	500.00	181.35	51.03
Alberta	3200	865.00	153.50	255.00
British Columbia	2800	2417.25	346.55	305.00
Total	48,800	24,123.53	23,040.95	24,004.66

Note: slightly different figures appear in WLMK, Memoranda and Notes, v. 192, file 1755, which may be accounted for by a slightly different time period; the differences are not significant. Source: same as for Table 2.1

funding went. Like so many other institutions of Canadian life, the 'national' office of the Liberal party was in reality dominated by Toronto, not out of design but out of necessity.

Well over two-thirds of the operating budget was eaten up in salaries, with the rest going for the rent of office space, travel, the production of the party magazine, and repayment of the constant bank overdrafts. The original target of $50,000 a year was scaled down to $40,000 at a meeting of the finance committee in Montreal in December 1932 but even this was well beyond the actual capacity of the fund-raisers. Ways and means of reducing the costs of the national office were discussed, and in April 1933 the finance committee reduced the salaries of the staff and slashed R.J. Deachman's retainer from $500 to $300 per month – thus precipitating another confrontation between Lambert and the somewhat testy publicist. Lambert himself agreed to take on his own moving expenses as well as those of another employee, $1500 in all. By midsummer Massey was talking darkly of releasing everyone but Lambert and the one secretary. The plan to raise money by popular subscriptions was a flop. Indeed, according to Lambert the sharp drop in quota contributions from the Nova Scotia and New Brunswick associations, and from British Columbia as well, could be traced to a feeling that the popular appeal had replaced the quota system. Massey himself, who raised funds from only three sources, including Frank O'Connor, Gerald Larkin (the son of King's late benefactor), and a wealthy widow in Toronto, was loath to get too involved with the money business for fear of being drawn into campaign finances, which was of course exactly what Mackenzie King expected. At first Massey tried to keep the two areas of fund-raising separate. Lambert noted that Massey 'in discussing plans for this office ... does not want to know any details of election campaign finances.' Massey could not expect for long to maintain his political virginity, because King would not let him but also because in the real world of party finance the National Liberal Federation was nothing special but just another expense to be met in the same way as campaign funds, and by the same people. In short, viable financial structures had to be set up which would meet the needs of both the NLF and the party in elections. The finances of the NLF were, in Lambert's words, 'past joking about,' and 'there were too many people running around now, & ... it [that is, fund-raising] shd. be centralized.'[56]

In 1934 Charles Stewart, who had never proven effective in the past, was brought back into the finance picture, apparently at the insistence of King. Stewart's main task was to raise the funding necessary to put out the *Liberal Monthly* on a regular basis. This he failed to do. Toronto was too much involved in financing the five by-elections of that year, and in Montreal the man designated by Stewart could not find any money at all, due, Lambert wrote to Stewart, 'to the countermanding influence of your senatorial friend, who evidently, thinks that nothing worth while exists outside of Montreal and Quebec.' The 'senatorial friend' was Donat Raymond, whose lack of interest in the national office was a major financial obstacle to the NLF.[57]

By the time King had persuaded Massey in 1934 that the road to London ran through Bay Street, the NLF was in desperate financial condition. The conversion of Massey to a financial collector for the party campaign chest meant that Lambert had to put in a claim for a share in what was gathered. As he wrote to Massey:

In view of the fact that the regular Finance Committee of the Federation may now be said to be merged with a campaign Finance Committee; and that Mr. Matthews will now be having any contributions he can control, centered in Mr. Long's treasury, it becomes necessary immediately, to have a definite understanding about the needs of this office, and the systematic supplying of these needs.

In the first place, this office exists for the purpose of meeting certain demands for publicity ... and for organization purposes (devolving upon myself largely). Therefore, in the way finances are shaping themselves under our Finance Committee, my job, as I see it, should be confined to meeting the two demands I have mentioned. I should not have to be worrying and bothering about the flow of financial support to this office at all.[58]

Lambert cited the need for $2000 per month operating expenses and an additional $1500 if the *Liberal Monthly* were to be produced on a regular basis. He then went on: 'I am bringing this subject before you, as President of the National Liberal Federation, because you or Mr. Matthews, I think, should see that this financial provision is made ... [O]ne thing is certain, and that is that I, or no other person, can carry on the work that is to be done here, under the present uncertain and undefined financial support of our office.' A few months later the NLF was still living from day to day, and being saved by timely cheques when on the very verge of financial extinction.[59]

The most important task associated with fund-raising – indeed, one of the most important of all the tasks facing the Liberal party during the period of opposition – was to reconstitute the collection structures of campaign funds in Montreal and Toronto, as well as in smaller centres across the country. The Depression years were not a fertile time for gathering in large bundles of money from anyone, even from the capitalists of Bay Street and St James Street, and the notoriety attached to the Beauharnois scandal did little to make businessmen favourable to the call of party support. Despite Mackenzie King's disclaimers during the investigation, he was not and could not be ignorant of campaign finance. Most particularly he could not remain ignorant of the makeup of the finance committees of Montreal and Toronto, since, in the last analysis, the appointment of collectors had to be a responsibility of the party leader. And when, as was the case in the early

1930s, the composition of these committees was in a state of flux, the party leader had to assert his authority and exercise the final choice, since there was no one else with sufficient prestige in the party to make such important and binding decisions. On the other hand, the links established by the collectors with powerful sections of big business meant that they, for their part, had some leverage with the party leader as well. It was the bagmen who had primary access to the corporate boardrooms; this access gave them an independent base. The negotiations between these men and the party leader thus offers some interesting insights into the nature of government-business relations.

Since it was Montreal which had generated the Beauharnois scandal, it was inevitable that the repercussions generated by the scandal would be felt most directly in Montreal. The first casualty was of course Senator W.L. McDougald, whose resignation in disgrace from the Senate and ejection from the party by King has already been discussed. Since McDougald had been both a personal contributor of some consequence and a man of influence among his Westmount compatriots, his departure left a gap in the Montreal collection operation. The other major figure in Montreal Liberal finance, Senator Raymond, had not been censured by the Senate but, in Mackenzie King's mind, he remained under a cloud. Raymond was an example of the kind of French Canadian who made it into the world of Montreal big business. His links were with financial capital, including the Bank of Commerce, and he sat on the board of directors of a number of enterprises such as Canada Cement, International Paper, and Dominion Glass. While it could hardly be said that Raymond was at the highest level of economic power, he was a respectable enough figure in the boardrooms of Montreal to present all the necessary credentials as party collector. From Raymond's own point of view, his political connections were perhaps of some use in advancing his own progress in an élite not notable for its high proportion of Francophones. As a recent analyst of the Canadian corporate élite has argued, 'a major avenue for mobility for French-Canadians into the economic elite has been through connections with the state ... the French have been successful in using the state as a means for access to the economic elite and ... they have strong relations with the state after gaining access.'[60]

After Beauharnois, Raymond's future seemed in doubt. In contrast to his solicitude for Andrew Haydon, which King maintained, in private at least, right up to the senator's death, King never hastened to the defence of Raymond. Indeed he appears to have harboured certain suspicions about Raymond, as was his tendency with regard to all the Montreal party figures to

some degree. Raymond and Senator Marcellin Wilson, also a French Canadian moving in the higher circles of Montreal finance and a Liberal collector, were both 'put out' by King's failure to defend Raymond publicly during the investigation. Liberal MP Pierre Casgrain was sent to raise money in
Montreal, mainly it would seem for the NLF, about which Raymond was not
enthusiastic. The competition between Raymond and Casgrain was not
very functional from the party's point of view. Given the alternatives, King
recognized that Raymond was much more useful than Casgrain, whose
ability to raise large sums was doubtful. By the close of 1933 King was
ready to come to terms with Raymond for the sake of establishing a viable
finance committee in the city. A meeting was arranged and King spent an
afternoon with Raymond, speaking 'freely.' The outcome was satisfactory
and King later told Raymond that 'my only regret is that we did not have
the talk we did a couple of years ago.' King then arranged a further meeting
between himself, Massey, and Marcellin Wilson to formally draw the latter
back into active service.[61]

King in fact never did get over his suspicions of Raymond, despite the
apparent reconciliation. He sometimes hinted, when in a bad mood, that he
had proof of Raymond's complicity in Beauharnois. As he once angrily told
Lambert, he did not want Raymond coming to his house: 'He didn't want
Raymond there, he had documents which wd. smash Raymond if he
wanted to use them.'[62] Whether he actually had such proof or not, the
arm's-length attitude to Montreal was very characteristic of King. He
needed someone like Raymond, and Raymond knew King needed him.
Raymond in turn valued his Liberal connection. The need for the Raymond
type was discussed by King in an interesting conversation with Senator
Raoul Dandurand who agreed with King that 'it needed a millionaire to ask
millionaires for twenty five thousand or so, that he nor I could not go in to
ask for donations, it was only men of great wealth who knew what others
had & shld. give – I said there was a sort of Masonic interest among them.'
As King reflected, even Sir Wilfrid Laurier had allowed corruption to creep
into his party by leaving the 'necessary evil' to others, 'as I have left to campaign managers securing funds, without being sure that they might not
prove a greater evil than good.'[63]

Whatever basis King may have had for doubting Raymond's motives,
there is some evidence that Raymond was himself averse to accepting donations with conditions attached. On two occasions he reported to Lambert
that some of the most powerful interests in the country had intimated
strings-attached donations, which he had turned down. 'He was not
favorable,' he told Lambert, 'to helping CPR or Beatty at national expense.'

J.W. McConnell of the *Montreal Star* and St Lawrence Sugar, had approached him about advancing the old chestnut of 'national government' (a Liberal-Conservative grand coalition) but Raymond had said 'nothing doing.'[64]

One man whom King did trust was J.L. Ralson, who by the early 1930s was installed in a prominent legal office in Montreal. Ralson was lined up with Raymond, Wilson, and businessman Gordon Scott, a former Quebec provincial treasurer, in a loose committee. Casgrain was called off, but appears not to have heeded the call. In the summer of 1935 Raymond was again complaining about Casgrain competing with his committee for money. Lambert, who had explicitly told Casgrain to keep out of Raymond's jurisdiction, hastened to assure the latter that Casgrain's activities were wholly without the authority of the national party.[65]

The final problem with which the national party had to deal in regard to Montreal finance was the co-ordination of activities with Toronto. This was a very tough nut to crack, and they never seem to have satisfactorily solved the problem of Montreal's rather secretive autonomy. The effort to get Montreal to provide a fair share of the expenses of the NLF was a cause for which Montreal, and Raymond in particular, showed very little enthusiasm. The NLF never did get sustained support from that city on the scale which Toronto provided, although sporadic support was forthcoming. There was also the question of co-ordinated fund-raising for the election campaign. Montreal was still seen as the more lucrative of the two Canadian metropolises, so far as the Liberals were concerned. Hence there was a tendency for Toronto to seek its own sources in the other city, not to speak of independent operators like Jimmy Gardiner from Saskatchewan. If the Montreal committee were to be left a clear field, the rest of the party would have to have at least limited access to what they raised. This necessitated some coordinated structures so that the rules could be agreed upon and the various collectors would not work at cross-purposes. Raymond disliked working with large committes, but he told Lambert that he was sufficiently impressed with Albert Matthews in Toronto to agree to work with him. Raymond was equally impressed with Frank O'Connor, and Lambert was able on this basis to arrange co-operation between Toronto and Montreal.[66]

The financial structure in Toronto went through a rather more decisive transformation than was the case in Montreal, where indeed the final resolution looked suspiciously like the former arrangements. The financial structure of the Liberal party in Toronto both mirrored and helped give rise to an important shift in the balance between the federal and provincial wings of the party during this period. King's own role was much more personal in the settling of arrangements in Toronto than in Montreal, perhaps simply because King had deeper personal connections with Ontario but also because Montreal had established a traditional autonomy, a kind of independent baronial status, which Toronto had not yet achieved. Ironically, one of the results of King's personal intervention in the Toronto situation was to help establish Toronto in the same position as Montreal, although this no doubt also relates to Toronto's coming of age as an industrial and financial metropolis.

Toronto was in this era always known as 'Tory Toronto,' for the good reason that the Conservatives regularly took every seat in the city in every federal election in the twentieth century, until the victory of Liberal Sam Factor in Toronto West Centre in 1930. But what the traditional voting pattern of the city obscured was that a section of the Toronto bourgeoisie had established a long-standing affiliation with the Liberal party.[67] So important was this attachment of Toronto's financial, transportation, and industrial interests to the Liberal party's national vitality that the public defection of the Toronto Liberal capitalists to the Tories over reciprocity in 1911 was sufficient, along with the defection of the *nationalistes* in Quebec, to bring down the Laurier government. A few of the 'revolting Eighteen' of 1911, such as Sir Thomas White, stayed with the Tories, but others returned to their original loyalty. King himself, of course, was the beneficiary of the largesse of one prominent Toronto capitalist, P.C. Larkin of Salada Tea, and received consistent press and sometimes financial support from Joseph Atkinson's *Toronto Star*, along with less reliable support from the *Globe*. Finally there was Vincent Massey, brought in briefly as minister without portfolio in King's government in 1925 and now president of the NLF. The Liberal party was by no means without lines of credit in Tory Toronto.

In the early years of the Depression this Liberal link reasserted itself among Toronto businessmen. The first sign was the organization of a club of young Toronto businessmen and professionals in 1932 which later became known as the Toronto Mens' Liberal Association. The first president of this association was the son of the general manager of the Toronto General Trust and its membership included many of the 'best known young men in business and social circles,' as one of King's informants told him.[68] One of the founding members was C. George McCullagh, later to take on a certain notoriety as publisher of the *Globe and Mail* and spokesman for the mining interests to the Hepburn government. Such clubs were a useful reservoir of Liberal strength for the future, but they did not offer much substantial help in meeting the pressing financial needs of the moment. As Albert Matthews, president of Excelsior Life and a director of Toronto

General Trust, told Lambert in 1933, 'under present conditions it was impossible to get the young men together to make a popular canvass.' Matthews himself, who was angling for a cabinet post in a future Liberal government either at Queen's Park or at Ottawa, agreed to undertake supervision of collections in the city. Although neither King nor Hepburn would agree to making Matthews any specific promises, Matthews remained as a central figure in fund-raising through the federal election until his appointment by King as lieutenant-governor of Ontario in 1937.[69] In fact, his son, Bruce Matthews, who succeeded his father as the head of Excelsior Life, also followed in his footsteps as chief Toronto collector for the party, and later became president of the NLF after the fall of the St Laurent government in the late 1950s.

King was scarcely more trusting of the Toronto businessmen than he was of the Montreal variety. At one small joint meeting of federal and provincial party people at which King was present in late 1933, attempts were made to sort out the duties of the two wings with regard to financing, with Massey suggesting that the provincial organization collect most of the money while reporting on the sources to the national office. King's overall reaction was sour and suspicious, characterized by his description of one of the provincial people in his diary: '[Duncan] Marshall's whole manner was dour & hard & sinister, his gold teeth shining out like tusks on either side of his mouth.'[70] When Lambert, early in 1934, suggested to King that Senator A.C. Hardy, King's personal friend and the organizer of a special fund for King's expenses as leader of the opposition, might be appointed as 'financial manager of campaign funds,' King 'assented readily.' Unfortunately for King's peace of mind, Hardy refused to act in this capacity, fearing that his previous experience as Ontario provincial party treasurer, when he had been 'left high and dry' and expected to fund campaigns out of his own pocket, would be replicated on the federal scene.[71]

The victory of the Hepburn Liberals in the provincial election that year brightened the picture considerably. Hepburn had been able to mobilize significant financial support for his party from important business interests, especially the mining promoters who got along with the provincial leader very well indeed, on both a personal as well as on a business and political level. Hepburn as premier never swerved from his resolve to maintain the support of the mining interests through thick and thin. His success in this resolve, as well as his ability and that of Frank O'Connor as his party treasurer, to consolidate the support of other financially significant interests in the province, meant that Hepburn now had an important card to play with the federal party. Only a few days after the provincial victory, Hepburn consulted with his national leader and raised some immediate apprehension in the latter's mind. King worried that Hepburn's 'remark that he might be able to help us in an election suggested to my mind some thought he might have re campaign funds. I did not like that – we must get away from that curse now and altogether.'[72]

But King had no idea how to get away from that 'curse' and with the five Ontario by-elections coming up in September the sudden infusion of funds from Toronto was in fact more than welcome, as was the willingness of the Ontario organization to take charge of the canvass. At a meeting at the King Edward Hotel in Toronto early in August, King, Massey, and Lambert for the federal party and Matthews, O'Connor, and E.G. Long for the Toronto finance committee hammered out an agreement on the ground rules for federal-provincial party co-operation in fund-raising. The Toronto committee would raise the money, but Lambert was to be, in King's words, 'the centre through which all should operate, a link with Quebec & other provinces as well, with myself a court of last resort to approve or disapprove important steps.' Frank O'Connor, who was agreeing to solicit funds, wanted King to make a specific promise to the mining promoter, Sir Harry Oakes. King was opposed to this, and spoke frankly about Beauharnois and its lessons for the party leader not getting personally involved with donors. A few weeks later Lambert learned that O'Connor had put a man in charge of 'collecting federal funds in Toronto, from door to door amongst business offices.' Such action was gratifying, but Lambert was already worrying out loud to Massey about their money 'being concentrated too much in prov'l hands.'[73] But the fact was, as indicated earlier, that the Ontario organization was successful in directing the 'miniature general election' in that province, and in politics it is always difficult to argue with success.

In the fall of 1934 another important figure was added to the Toronto finance committee in the person of J.S. McLean, the head of Canada Packers. McLean was not only a leading businessman and Liberal contributor himself, but he also undertook to channel other significant sources of funding to the party, most notably the giant retail merchandising chains of Eaton's and Simpson's, which he claimed had donated $40,000 to the Conservative campaign in the previous election.[74] It is no accident that McLean's adhesion to the Liberals, and his promises on behalf of the chain stores, followed the Stevens inquiries into pricing and mass-buying in which Eaton's, Simpson's, and Canada Packers (which, it was revealed, paid farmers 1½ cents per pound for beef retailed at 19 cents) figured very prominently as corporate villains whose huge profits were matched by pitiful wages to their own employees and exploitation of both primary producers and consumers. McLean, an old opponent of Bennett's trade and commerce minister, had clashed publicly with Stevens before the parliamentary committee on price spreads. C.L. Burton, president of the Robert Simpson Company, was so enraged by statements made by Stevens in a pamphlet distributed across the country that he went to the prime minister and threatened to sue if Stevens did not apologize. Stevens' refusal led to Bennett's repudiation of his minister and Stevens' resignation from the cabinet.[75] Burton, who had once turned down an offer from Mackenzie King to join his cabinet in the 1920s,[76] was not content to simply bring down the offending minister; he wished to bring down the offending government as well. Burton was a personal friend of the Liberal leader, and had already been able to arrange a co-operative approach to the price spreads inquiry, moving King to write all the Liberal members of the committee to help protect the 'business interests of a perfectly honourable concern,' the Robert Simpson Company. Lambert had coached McLean on how to handle possible questions before the Stevens committee.[77]

The president of Canada Packers was important not only for the chain store donations but also for his influence with what the finance committee called the 'food group.' But the addition of McLean, for which Vincent Massey took full credit, had a special importance for the federal Liberals. McLean was not a Hepburn man, unlike O'Connor, and his eyes were turned to Ottawa. When McLean volunteered his services, Lambert explained the financial setup to him: 'Frank O'Connor & the prov'l-federal equation.' McLean was to be an additional weight on the federal side, which badly needed some ballast. Significantly, when Lambert informed O'Connor about McLean becoming an 'auxiliary' of the finance committee, O'Connor 'did not seem very keen.' Lambert, however, firmly suggested O'Connor's 'keeping off that ground ... until the next general election campaign came on.'[78] It was clear that Lambert was becoming very wary of the Hepburn influence and was doing what he could to protect the national party from a dangerous dependence on the volatile and unpredictable provincial people. When he was asked to speak to the Young Liberals in Toronto, Lambert told them plainly 'to forget about Queens Park, & devote themselves to federal matters.' The problem was that O'Connor had the best sources.

Near the end of 1934 Hepburn had told King that he could help him in financing the coming federal contest.[79] At a meeting of the finance committee in March the participants complained of the slowness of collections. O'Connor informed Lambert that the Ontario government had just made an agreement with a contractor which totalled $2.5 million, of which

$200,000 'had been left.' Hepburn had however stipulated that it could not be used for federal purposes. Lambert relayed this information to King as soon as possible.[80] It was a striking example of the power of a party in office, and the weight which it could bring against its supposedly 'senior' counterpart in federal politics.

Yet whatever his misgivings, Lambert knew that the federal party would have to come to terms with O'Connor, and hence with Hepburn, if they were to raise the kind of money necessary to finance a national campaign. By May Lambert felt it incumbent upon himself to gain Mackenzie King's personal intervention to get O'Connor seriously down to work. The results were unpromising: 'I asked him to speak to F.O'C. about finances, on account of the needs of the West, etc., but he said he did not want to put himself under any obligation to O'C.; that he had had a lesson from the Beauharnois affair & from MacDougall [sic], and never again wd. he put himself in the power of any man. He did not trust an Irish Catholic drinking man any too far anyhow.' O'Connor for his part told Lambert that he did not have time to collect for the federal party: 'He was looking after prov'l affairs preparing for another election 4 years hence; and desired to get a good fund of a million in hand.' Lambert suggested to Massey that, in the light of the prevalent attitude in Toronto, he and Massey should devote their own efforts to raising the money required for the campaign in the West and leave Ontario to the Toronto committee. Massey agreed with Lambert's plan and 'expressed doubts about intentions of O'C., Long & Matthews.' [81]

Neil McKenty comments that 'King's trust for "an Irish Catholic drinking man" seemed to deepen in almost direct proportion to the need for campaign money.'[82] It is true that King swallowed his Scots pride with regard to O'Connor – just as he did many times with that more notorious Irish Catholic drinking man, Chubby Power – and spoke to both O'Connor and Long to the effect that 'everything would be ready' for Lambert when the campaign really got under way in the fall.[83] The Toronto committee did raise money, but there were two catches. First, there was not an abundance of funds by any means, despite the almost sure victory and the disillusionment of Canadian capitalism with Bennett's 'New Deal.' Second, there was a great deal of difficulty experienced by Lambert in getting what he considered a reasonable proportion of the Toronto money transferred to the western provinces. These two problems concealed a much more devastating problem, which surfaced after the election: the mastery over Liberal party organization which the power of the purse gave to the provincial party. Hints of just what lay behind this provincial ascendancy did come to light during the campaign, as when Hepburn wrote King that an 'intimate friend of mine and a good supporter of the Party' would drop in to see him. This was none other than J.P. Bickell, described by McKenty as a 'rough-and-ready "Bay Street cowboy" and millionaire mining magnate,' and one of those entrepreneurs of northern Ontario gold mining who were claiming Mitch Hepburn as their very own man in Queen's Park.[84] Hepburn wanted King to make a joint policy announcement on the federal mining tax. King was suitably ambiguous and non-committal.

Charles Dunning informed a correspondent in August that the delay in calling an election – Bennett had not dissolved Parliament until slightly over five years had elapsed since taking office – had made things difficult for the Liberals: 'We are not any too well supplied with funds and you know what it takes to keep an organization on its tip-toes for any length of time.' Donat Raymond informed Lambert only three weeks before the election that he had been turned down on $100,000 in Montreal 'by those who tried to hold back on the ground of seeing which way things were going.' Things seemed to reach such a crisis in September that both Massey and Lambert were looking for ways out of responsibility. Lambert's diary for 9 September records the following events:

Massey came in here at 6:15 P.M. & went to K[ing]'s for dinner. Said he would suggest giving him a letter freeing himself of any responsibility, on account of poor financial response, said he had had letter from Hardy.

Told K. earlier that finances bad & should call together 3 or 4 of the comtee. He said that I should write a letter to the comtee, if worst came to worst, putting myself on record as to facts, & thus freeing myself of any responsibility.

King even tried to get Massey to make a national broadcast calling for small donations from interested citizens, which Massey was reluctant to do. Lambert thought such an appeal, while it might make some political mileage, would not result in any funds, but might equally discourage some of the party's substantial contributors. King agreed with his organizer, but added cynically that they could be told 'it was only a blind.'[85]

One of the problems encountered in the course of collecting was the reluctance of two major interests to commit their money. The first were the mining magnates of Bay Street. J.Y. Murdoch, already a mining entrepreneur of some significance, later to be a major figure in the Iron Ore Company of Canada of Ungava fame, was going from mining office to mining office in Toronto, and promising good results. But ten days before the election Massey reported 'nothing doing yet with mining co's,' despite their support of local candidates.[86] The mining entrepreneurs, especially the gold mining interests, did come through in the end, although not in the amounts which the federal Liberals might have wished for. The mining interests were first and foremost provincially oriented and Mitch Hepburn was their man in the Liberal party. They did give – indeed they were, as indicated below, the second largest identifiable interest contributing to the Toronto fund – but it appears that their contributions fell far short of what might have been expected from their provincial operations.

The second interest to disappoint the collectors were the banks and financial institutions – the real backbone of Canadian capitalism.[87] It has already been indicated that the Liberals had not raised the kind of money that they had expected from this source to fight the CCF in the Mackenzie by-election in 1933. It seems that the mistrust of the bankers for the Liberal party manifested on that occasion continued until the general election. Near the end of September J.S. McLean and E.G. Long were sent to canvass the head offices of the banks in Toronto. Four banks turned McLean down flat. Long got one contribution and promised to keep in touch with the situation.[88] The bankers had particular reason to remain cool to the Liberals. Bennett's 'banker's central bank,' controlled privately rather than publicly, was in sharp contrast to the Liberal policy, developed by King and his parliamentary caucus, of a publicly controlled central bank. The Liberal concept not only suggested government control of the financial sector but was interpreted (wrongly) in the West by some monetary enthusiasts as a policy of inflation – desired by the farmers but anathema to the bankers. Some of the closest banking friends of the party were understandably distressed by this turn. For example, W.E. Rundle of the National Trust, one of the few Toronto supporters who remained as a faithful donor in the year or two after the defeat of 1930, wrote letters and had private interviews with King to oppose a state-owned and state-controlled central bank.[89] There is no record of what transpired in their meetings, but it is a matter of public knowledge that King did not back down from the Liberal bank policy as originally specified. It seems that disgruntlement with Liberal monetary policy did tend to dry up banking and trust company contributions to the party in the 1935 election. Rundle himself contributed modestly in that campaign in the amount of $500. One could well conclude from this that being a known contributor could purchase access to the party leader – but with no guarantee of having advice on policy accepted.

The greatest difficulty experienced by Massey and Lambert in the funding of the campaign was in securing Toronto money for the western provinces, for which Lambert had taken major personal responsibility. Early in

September Lambert calculated that only $35,500 had been distributed to the West; there was an additional $35,000 on hand earmarked for these provinces; but that a total of $180,000 was needed. Thus a shortfall of $110,000 remained. A week later Lambert still had no idea how this balance was to be filled. Despite Mackenzie King's personal intervention with the Toronto committee and O'Connor in particular, the Toronto collectors remained obdurate about the West. Massey told Lambert a little over two weeks from the election that Long had stated that the West needed no more funds. Lambert 'objected strenuously:' 'Had heated argument with V. M[assey] over failure to turn funds to West as agreed, & compared situation to heavy artillery in rear under camouflage getting ammunition while the front line trenches being deprived of ammunition.' In the end only $115,900 was distributed to the West from Toronto, a marked reduction from Lambert's projected $180,000 in early September and an even more marked reduction from the first estimate of $200,000 made in March. [90] Very serious questions are thus raised as to the ability of the national party to direct its own finances.

Toronto and Montreal were not the only areas of the country where money could be raised. Manitoba had traditionally been a source of some money: the bourgeoisie of South Winnipeg had always taken an interest in politics, and the Liberal party had since the days of Sir Clifford Sifton been well attached to some of these interests. J.B. Coyne was the finance chairman in Winnipeg and he revealed to Lambert that some sources could be found which might be of significance outside of Manitoba as well. James Richardson and others associated with him on the Winnipeg grain exchange were disturbed over the establishment by the Conservative government of a national wheat board. This was clearly an attempt of the government to make a last desperate appeal to the wheat farmers, and the bill was introduced in the shadow of an impending election. The private grain merchants were highly displeased with many of the control features of the new legislation and concerted Liberal opposition in the committee stage in fact yielded significant modifications.[91] It was at this stage that the grain exchange interests made their views known to the highest levels of the Liberal party. J.R. Murray, who was to become the Liberal appointee to the chairmanship of the wheat board after the election, was shepherded into King's office by Lambert to confer about specific amendments. Lambert insured that members friendly to the grain exchange were placed on the committee. Richardson also felt it was in his interest to help speed a Liberal victory at the polls, and was ready to offer $20,000 to the campaign fund, which Lambert wished to be divided, half going to Saskatchewan, half remaining in

Manitoba. Massey and Lambert then tried to persuade King to meet with Richardson. King would do no such thing: '... I told him that I didn't want to be brought in touch with that group at all ... I told Massey it would be all right for him to interview Richardson himself, if he wished to do so ... Here again, we have an organization office and its desire to get financial support for a campaign, seeking the adoption of a course which might destroy a party politically. The question of campaign funds is the most baffling of all in connection with our electoral system.'[92] Since the money came through it is apparent that Richardson thought the investment worthwhile, although it must also be noted that the King government did not abolish the wheat board after 1935, although open market operations were allowed to continue until 1943 when the board was given exclusive rights over exports.

King was less hesitant about letting his party officials make arrangements than he was about getting his own office involved. It would seem that the distinction lay in the refusal to make direct policy commitments in return for donations. If the party leader could be kept out of direct contact, then there could be no question of such commitments. Yet there was a lingering ambiguity about such a rule, since party officials could always relay policy advice after the election. Indeed, at one meeting with the Toronto finance committee along with Massey and Lambert, King had spelled out just what he meant. In Lambert's record, King 'spoke about [Aimé] Geoffrion's Order-in-Council re Beauharnois, and Raymond's letter; about Percy Parker and W.H. Moore coming to see him re Beauharnois as evidence to support his own refusal to see some people when they want to see him. He said too that contact should be established between N.L.F. office & Gov't later in the matter of placing Gov't business.'

King's own account in his diary elaborates on this. On any contracts without tender, he argued, 'supporters of the government should get the preference, and between supporters those who had helped the most.'[93] There are two important points that may be made about this. First of all, there was a clear attempt on the part of the party leader to put the matter of patronage at one remove, although not out of the picture altogether. Second, King explicitly indicated that he was talking about contracts without tender. He was not suggesting that the Liberals, in the vernacular of politics, 'toll-gate' contractors, that is, demand campaign contributions before tenders are even considered. In fact the record of the party in office after 1935 indicates that 'toll-gating' was not the general practice, that contractors were more apt to be approached after tendered contracts had been let and asked to translate their gratitude at government largesse into a contribution to the government party. The latter practice is quite within the letter of the law. However, it does not cover the wide area of government business not given out by tender. Here there has never been any question: patronage is the rule, not the exception. The most spectacular example of this is advertising, which is discussed later in Chapter 6. King was in no way challenging this tradition; he simply wished to let others make the arrangements.

Of course, the day-to-day business of government contracts was one thing, the wider question of government policy and legislation as it affected powerful private interests was another. Here it was obviously more difficult for the party leader to maintain a condition of splendid isolation from the pressures of contributors. There was no doubt whatever that King knew that Rundle of the National Trust was a contributor and that he, along with other prominent bankers, disliked the Liberal central bank policy. Yet that policy was not changed. On the other hand, Liberal policy was very close to the views of J.S. McLean and C.L. Burton, both of whom were equally well known to King as party supporters. Perhaps Liberal policy toward the Stevens inquiry would have been the same without the money from Eaton's, Simpson's, and Canada Packers. Perhaps King's thinking was already attuned to their concerns. There is obviously no answer possible to this question. At some point one must graduate from simple mechanistic attempts to link policy to campaign funds to the much more subtle and complex analysis of the overlapping identities of interests and outlook of government and business in liberal democratic societies, if one is to make any real sense of the behaviour of politicians with respect to private economic power.[94]

In any event, it was not always possible for King to maintain his at-one-remove rule. Some interests were so big that only the personal contact of the party leader would be sufficiently dignified to be noticed. Such apparently was the case with the CPR and its magisterial president, Sir Edward Beatty. King's visit with Beatty in 1933 to discuss the question of the CNR has already been described, as well as the apparently successful outcome of the visit. King himself was quite aware of his personal role in furthering the connection between the party and the CPR. As he noted in his diary after a visit to Montreal in 1932: 'The reform club – the political – the Wedding – the University – the Colemans – The C.P.R. financial interests were all touched, and contacts formed which are helpful to one in public life. I can see that this is what I must do more & more.'[95]

PARTY PATRONAGE

The leader also took a personal interest in the party's financial supporters where appointments were being sought in exchange for donations. There is now good evidence that the practice of dispensing peerages and other titles for campaign funds was well established in the United Kingdom.[96] Oddly enough, despite the general view that Canadian politics were more venal than those of the mother country, it seems that such practices were less solidly established, at least on a regularized basis, in Canada. King was himself opposed to titles and put an end to the practice of granting them after his return to office in 1935, despite some evidence that money might be offered the party in return for such honours.[97] There were many areas which remained, of course, including the Senate, lieutenant-governorships, and various government appointments either to the foreign service or to the many boards and commissions at home. King was hardly above using these posts as clubs with which to beat contributions out of supporters – Vincent Massey being of course the most notable example. Since the government's patronage power in these appointments was unquestioned, it was an obvious weapon in the hand of the party leader. Yet, in the case of the Liberals at least, there never seems to have developed any regular schedule of prices for offices. It was taken for granted that persons would not be called to the Senate without contributing to the party's fortunes in some form or other, but the criteria for reward remained highly indefinite – perhaps, considering the regional constraints placed upon Senate appointments, such vagueness was necessary to avoid undue division arising from those who might have felt themselves better entitled through higher cash value of contributions.

The lack of coherent criteria for Senate candidacies is nowhere better shown than in the case of Frank O'Connor. In the late stages of the general election campaign in 1935 Donat Raymond saw O'Connor and Vincent Massey separately, and proposed that O'Connor put up $100,000 for the campaign in return for Massey's influence for a senatorship. O'Connor was unimpressed by the Montreal senator's proposition, and stated flatly that he had already put up $25,000 and 'that was all.'[98] One wonders just how much Vincent Massey's 'influence' with Mackenzie King was in fact worth – probably much less than $100,000. In any event, O'Connor stuck to his $25,000 and was awarded a Senate seat within two months of King's victory.

Nor could party supporters count on a senatorship just because they had offered help. At least that was the experience of A.J. Freiman, Jewish department store owner and leading Canadian Zionist, whose indefatigable support for the party never did get him into the Senate. The fact that a Jew had never been appointed to that body was both Freiman's reason for such persistence and the cause of his downfall. Freiman was described by Lambert as an annual contributor to the NLF, and was a dinner guest of King on

occasion, as well as a host to Lambert and Massey. The idea of a senatorship in return for contributions was discussed at these meetings. But the political significance of the first Jewish senatorship was such that considerable
contention was raised in the Jewish community itself. Sam Jacobs, the first
Jewish MP, was an opponent of Freiman and threw in his weight against the
latter with King, claiming that Freiman had supported Meighen in 1926 in
return for the promise of a Senate seat.[99] Freiman could buy a seat from
neither Tory nor Grit. It was not until 1955, after Mackenzie King had
passed from the scene, that the first Jewish Senate appointment was made,
in the person of David Croll.

Another aspect of the same phenomenon was the question of promises
given of future consideration in return for candidacies. King always tried to
be as cagey as possible on this score, greatly fearing, as any party leader no
doubt would, the possible entanglements arising from promises of cabinet
posts, judgeships, senatorships, etc. It was, moreover, quite clear that this
was an area of prime ministerial prerogative, and one in which the party organizers must steer clear. At the annual meeting of the NLF advisory council
in late 1934, King complained to Lambert that he was approached by
'several people ... all of whom wanted something' in return for offering
themselves as candidates in the next election. King told Lambert that he
must never make any commitments in King's name: 'He would not give
any promises; when people like Rogers were willing to take a chance on
election, he would *not* promise others definite appointments.' The reference
was to Norman McLeod Rogers, Queen's University professor and close
confidant and adviser of King, who had decided to resign his position to
run in Kingston. Lambert was impressed enough with this example to employ it against those seeking promises through his office. King was not being entirely ingenuous in this argument, however. As early as September
1934 he had written his good friend a word of advice as to whether he
should offer his candidacy. King suggested that he would very much like to
see Rogers as a member of the prime minister's office, but would not stand
in the way of his candidacy. 'I should be surprised,' he added slyly, 'if that
latter would not lead to an equally intimate association, but of that I cannot
write at the moment.'[100] It is obvious that King was capable of giving a virtual promise of a cabinet position to someone of the stature of Rogers.
Lesser mortals would have to take their chances.

These were some of the conditions of party finance and the power of patronage in the organization of an election campaign. The setting up of
finance committees in the two major centres of party funding; the shaky national liaison between the two money centres and the distribution of funds

through the NLF and the provincial organizations; and the delicate problem of the relationship between this party leader and the financial supporters; all were problems which involved persistent questions of the relationship between politics and business, the party leader and his officials, and the federal and provincial sections of the party organization. Generalizations are not easy, but it does seem fair to say that the hold of the national party over the finance committees was tenuous at most times, that this tenuousness was connected to the power of the provincial wings of the party, and that the provincial ascendancy was in turn related to the connections between the provincial parties and major business interests with a stake in provincial policies. On the other hand, the obverse of this was the stubborn refusal of the national leader to allow policy commitments to be made in return for campaign funds. The case of the Stevens inquiry and the Canada Packers, Simpson's, and Eaton's support might seem to be an exception to this rule, but, as previously suggested, that case is not without ambiguity. It would seem more likely that Mackenzie King, whose basic suspicion of the business world had been particularly deepened by the Beauharnois affair, was highly sensitive to the possibility of being entrapped in another scandal. This of course does not mean that King's overall policy orientation of making the corporate free enterprise system work had been altered. It meant in much more narrow and specific terms that he did not want campaign funds at the cost of corruption. The Liberal party organization at the national level had to play the game by these rules; if provincial Liberals might demonstrate fewer scruples with the reward of greater affluence, that was the price of respectability for the federal party.

CAMPAIGN SPENDING 1935

The sum of $626,000 had been raised in Montreal and $558,478 in Toronto – making for a combined national total of just over $1,184,000.[101] Of course, money was also raised in smaller metropolitan areas such as Winnipeg, Vancouver, Hamilton, and Ottawa, of which no record remains, and candidates raised their own funds in the constituencies.[102] Moreover, there were some intra-party transfers which do not show up in these totals, such as the occasional direct sally by central Canadian corporations into financing provincial efforts in the hinterlands, presumably when some specific interest was felt to be at stake. A spectacular example of this was the transmission of $50,000 from the Dominion Bridge Company of Montreal to the Vancouver Liberal machine and the provincial Liberal party of British Columbia, 'on a gamble' as Donat Raymond explained it.[103] But taking the amounts raised by the Montreal and Toronto finance committees it is clear that St James Street and Bay Street had not been overly generous to the Liberal party in 1935. A little over one million dollars raised in the two financial and industrial centres of the country was a less than staggering sum, considering that the Beauharnois Corporation alone had set aside almost that much in 1930 for its own political fund, of which almost $700,000 had gone to the Liberals – more than the total amount raised in either Montreal or Toronto five years later. Senator Raymond even claimed that he ended the election $4000 in debt personally.[104]

The breakdown of the amounts raised by distribution to provinces is shown in Table 2.3. Quebec still led the way in campaign expenditure, involving a small subsidy from Toronto in its total of almost $518,000. The widely differing amounts distributed to the various western provinces perhaps call for some explanation. Manitoba, with its Winnipeg base, was always expected to raise much of its own money. In fact, Manitoba Liberals expended $67,347 on a province-wide basis, which meant that about 87 per cent of the funds were raised locally. British Columbia, on the other hand, appears to have been a net importer of election funds, although the exact proportions are not clear from the available evidence. In fact, it has been the complaint of federal Liberals for at least two generations that British Columbia has never been financially self-sustaining to the extent that its own economic potential would seem to warrant.[105] Saskatchewan's very large transfer was also quite typical of a pattern which remains to this day. Very little money was ever raised in that province, yet the famous Liberal machine, especially under the guidance of Jimmy Gardiner, was notoriously profligate in expending Toronto and Montreal money. The low amount recorded for Alberta probably accounts for almost all the money spent in that province since it was unlikely very much could have been raised in that poverty-stricken jurisdiction in the middle of the Great Depression. The explanation for the very small federal grant is quite simple: Alberta was a write-off in the eyes of the national party, and any addition would have been seen as sending good money after bad.

One complication which arises from the available figures is the question of how much Montreal sent to the national campaign. Toronto did spend $37,500 on national purposes, of which $31,000 went directly to the national office. Since it is also on record that the national publicity campaign cost $107,344, there is a balance of just over $76,000 not accounted for. Yet two years later Lambert told a meeting of the executive committee of the NLF that 'there was a financial contribution from the Quebec organization, but that it amounted to only a small fraction of the total expenditure for

Table 2.3
Distribution of money raised for the Liberal party in Montreal and Toronto,
general election 1935

Montreal ($626,000)		Toronto ($558,478.10)	
Quebec	$513,000	Ontario ridings	$265,763.75
Nova Scotia	53,000	Ontario publicity	116,329.13
New Brunswick	45,000	Quebec	4900.00
Prince Edward Island	15,000	Manitoba	8500.00
		Saskatchewan	65,600.00
Total	626,000	Alberta	8300.00
		British Columbia	33,500.00
		National	37,500.00
		Miscellaneous	17,579.15
		Total	557,972.03
		Balance	506.07

Source: NPL, Diary, 1935; v. 13, file 3:1 and 2; v. 2, file '1938,' budget,
31 March 1936

dominion purposes.'[106] It is clear from Lambert's diary at the time that some
aid was given from Montreal to the national office, but certainly never anything like he expected. It is possible that some of this mysterious balance
may have been met by Vincent Massey's own sources in Toronto, but this
remains as conjecture only. In any event, the general lack of co-operation
by Montreal with the campaign outside Quebec and the Maritimes – its traditional financial hinterland – is quite evident.

Perhaps the most interesting aspect of the information available in Norman Lambert's papers concerning party finance is the very complete record
of the identity of contributors to the Liberal campaign in Toronto. Since it
has long been a complaint of students of party finance in this country that
only speculation about the actual names of contributors is possible, the
Lambert records offer a useful snapshot of the basis of party finance in one
of the two major centres of fund-raising.

In 1935 the five largest identifiable contributors were Labatt's Breweries
($29,000); Imperial Oil ($25,000); Laura Secord Candy Shops, that is,
Frank O'Connor ($25,000); Canadian General Electric ($25,000); and National Breweries ($20,000). The general breakdown by size of donation is
given in Table 2.4. It may be seen that just over three-quarters of the funds
collected in Toronto came from thirty-nine individuals or companies, and

Table 2.4
Contributions to the Toronto Liberal finance committee, 1935, by size of donation

	Number of donors	Percentage of total collected
$20,000 and over	5	25.7
$10,000 to $19,999	7	14.6
$5000 to $9999	27	36.4
$1000 to $4999	52	19.1
$100 to $999	70	3.9
Less than $100	25	0.3
Total	186	100.0

Source: NPL, Diary, 1935

40 per cent of the money (over $10,000 each) came from only twelve sources. Conversely, ninety-five sources which gave in amounts of less than $1000 accounted for a mere 4 per cent of the total collected.

Another way of looking at the financial picture of the party in Toronto is to examine the sources of funds in terms of the economic interests involved. Table 2.5 gives a percentage breakdown of the total contributions by the type of economic activity most significant to the contributors. This classification involves identifying the major activity of corporate or company donors, as well as designating the primary corporate interest of individual donors.[107] Liquor and gold mine interests were the most important single groups of contributors.[108] Both, it might be pointed out, were interests which were more closely tied to provincial political concerns than to federal, which offers further confirmation of the shift toward provincial control over party financing in this era. No other interests stand out as significantly as these two. The low percentages accounted for by certain major interests, such as textiles, may be explained by political reasons (the traditional identification of the Tories with high tariffs, of which the textile industry was adamantly in support), others perhaps by the concentration of certain spheres of activity in Montreal, for which, unfortunately, no detailed information is available.

The motives of the donors must have been quite mixed. Subsequent events following the Liberal victory in the election demonstrate that construction contractors and office equipment firms expected government business as a result of their support. Corporations in the steel and manufacturing

Table 2.5
Percentage breakdown of contributions to the Toronto
finance committee, 1935, by major economic activity of
donors

Breweries and distilleries	17.6
Mining (mainly gold mining)	16.0
Manufacturing	9.5
Food products and processing	8.9
Construction contractors	7.5
Banking and finance	7.4
Oil and chemical	7.2
Iron and steel	5.1
Retail merchandising	4.8
Entertainment	2.2
Power, pulp and paper	1.3
Textiles	1.1
Office equipment	0.7
Other and unidentified	10.6

Source: compiled from NPL, Diary, 1935; *Financial Post,
Directory of Directors,* 1935, for affiliation of individu-
als; *Financial Post, Survey of Industrials* and *Survey of
Mines,* appropriate years, for the activities of companies

industries may have been doing little more than attempting to purchase
access to the prospective prime minister. Some contributors were traditional
party supporters, such as Leighton McCarthy of Canada Life, a former Liberal MP and a veteran party financial backer who gave $10,000 to the 1935
campaign.[109] Political donations, it seems, were a tradition in the liquor
business. As N.W. Rowell, a strong prohibitionist, once indicated, where
the liquor companies gave money they tended to give to both parties, 'very
often but not always on an equal division.' Chubby Power was convinced
that the 'liquor interests were not so interested in good government as in
their particular interests,' and cited such concerns as the federal excise tax
as an example of their particular interest;[110] another might be federal import
duties on foreign brands.

The interests of the gold mining entrepreneurs was much more directly
obvious. Gold was a commodity peculiarly tied to a world price; gold producers were thus unable to pass on either tax or wage increases to their cus-
tomers. They therefore had a strong stake in attempting to head off such developments. And, as Viv Nelles has put it: 'The most annoying and painful
interference suffered by the mining community in what it considered to be
its private, provincial affairs came from the federal government, and against

this mutual enemy the miners called upon the provincial government to help with the defence.'[111] The bullion tax imposed by the Bennett government was the major source of complaint; in this sense the gold producers may have had a direct motive in financing a federal Liberal victory. If so, they were to be bitterly disappointed following the election, when the new King government refused to change the tax in question, despite the public support of the provincial Liberal government for its removal.

CAMPAIGN ORGANIZATION

If campaign finances were the toughest problem for the Liberal election effort, there were the regular tasks of organizing a campaign which had to be carried out as well. The campaign was essentially organized like most Liberal national campaigns before and since: a highly decentralized set of provincial organizations each under the general direction of regional leaders within the federal caucus operating very loosely under the co-ordination of a national campaign committee, which in the 1955 election was centred around the NLF office, and most particularly its secretary, Norman Lambert. As one astute Liberal politician said of the provincial situation in Nova Scotia: 'I am more convinced than ever that the chief and most important function of a central organization is to get the local organizations to work and show them how to carry on.'[112] This was just as true of the national campaign organization in Ottawa as it was of a provincial organization in Nova Scotia. There existed neither the funds nor the inclination in a country like Canada to run a monolithic, centralized campaign. It was a basic tenet of the conventional wisdom of politicians that if the local troops were not willing and able to do the local job, then the party was in local trouble – and no amount of artificial injections from Ottawa would change that basic malaise.

Of course, the high degree of decentralization and local autonomy which this entailed could lead to a variegated picture of the national strength of the party, ranging from a hopeless disaster area like Alberta to the bright promise of the Maritime provinces. Obviously, the degree to which provincial organizations had placed themselves in a state of readiness for the impending election varied considerably. This in turn also rested upon the degree of enthusiasm and initiative shown by the constituency associations. This could range from the type of riding where the Liberal association was nothing but a paper organization – and sometimes not even that – to the kind of traditional local Liberal machine which kept up-to-date lists of everyone in the constituency with their political preferences. Much depended upon the presence of an MP with a strong and sustained interest in the maintenance of good local organization. An authoritative voice to the right local people to keep the ball rolling was always of critical importance.

Following the 1930 election J.L. Ralston wrote to his association in Shelburne-Yarmouth to request that lists be prepared for all the polls in the riding based on the recent vote. These lists were to be 'carefully preserved' and to be revised annually, with 'Tories' removed, families which had moved noted along with deaths, and the names added of potential Liberal voters who turned twenty-one before the next election. Care should be taken, Ralston suggested, to watch the newspaper subscription lists to determine who received Liberal papers. Five years later, in response to an inquiry from Lambert at national headquarters, the president of the Nova Scotia Liberal Association wrote Ralston for advice on how to prepare for the coming election. The immediate job, Ralston advised, was to secure good candidates, then to burnish up the constitency organizations by revising lists of committee men in every district, 'deadwood being dropped and vacancies filled.' It was particularly important, he added, to compile lists of first-time voters sympathetic to the Liberal cause. A Young Liberal organization would be helpful here: 'it is a great thing to have people who are polling their first vote feel that an organization is interested in them.'[113] It is not surprising, given the watchful eye of Ralston, that this constituency in 1935 was able to greatly increase the Liberal vote despite the loss of Ralston as candidate and the entry of a third-party candidate.

One point emphasized by Ralston in his advice to his constituency was the importance of organizing the young Liberals. The years between the defeat of 1930 and the return to office in 1935 did witness a great resurgence in local Young Liberal – or Twentieth Century Liberal, as they were then known – clubs and associations. These seem often to have taken form in a local, spontaneous fashion. There is little record in the Lambert diaries, for example, of any sustained or detailed intervention of the national office in such projects. A national organization of Twentieth Century clubs was set up at the same time as the NLF, and had a loose association with the office, sometimes drawing small sums of money from the NLF treasury, such as it was, and sometimes using the office facilities, such as they were. The first president of the Twentieth Century association was, perhaps significantly, Duncan MacTavish, who was later to be a president of the NLF itself. The Young Liberals were seen as a training ground for future Liberal leaders as well as a useful electoral device. In western Ontario alone there were twenty-five to thirty local Twentieth Century clubs, 'actual clubs that worked,' in the years leading up to the 1935 election.[114] The Twentieth Century clubs were at this time divided into men's and women's sections. This sexual dichotomy only paralleled the much more significant sexual dichotomy at the national level of party organization. The Women's Liberal organization was little more than a ghetto for a group of Liberals whom the real party organizers wished to use but to keep at arm's length. Unlike the Twentieth Century Liberals, who were clearly seen as potential leaders of the party in the future, the women were generally treated as something of a nuisance. Lambert's laments at the importunities of the women were usually concurred in by other party figures who commiserated with him at the trouble caused by women who failed to recognize their proper place in the male world of politics. Both the Twentieth Century and the Liberal Women were constitutionally associated with the NLF, but the use to which they were put varied considerably.

One special problem of the maintenance of a balance between local autonomy and national party interests concerned the nomination of candidates. Since in this era it was still considered exceptional and even disgraceful to have a contest for a local nomination – an open contest that is, since there was often enough competition behind the scenes – there was considerable pressure sometimes exerted on the provincial associations or even the national organization to step in to settle differences over nominations which seemed irreconcilable without outside intervention. Considering the obvious dangers posed to the party in taking sides in a nasty local squabble, it is scarcely surprising that the larger organizations tended to resist these pressures wherever possible. But if the situation demanded some action, the tendency was to call in the regional party leader – the regional cabinet minister after the election victory – to sort out the problem. The party leader, as well as the national office, tried to avoid direct intervention as much as possible. King told Lambert, when the latter sought advice about a local problem in British Columbia, that 'we cd. not interfere from here in the regular choice of any candidate.'[115]

But as with all general rules there were exceptions. In this case the exceptions centred around Mackenzie King's principle of the Liberals taking a co-optive stance toward the labour and social democratic expression in politics. The Hamilton East case has already been noted, where the Liberals declined to contest a by-election against a Labour candidate. North Winnipeg was another case in point. The Liberals had not opposed either of the Labour candidates in the two constituencies in the working class north end of the city in 1930. One of these members, J.S. Woodsworth, was the leader of the new CCF, and it seemed unlikely that the Liberal party could afford not to oppose the leader of the new party in its first general election. But the other member, A.A. Heaps, although a founding member of the new party as well, was also a personal friend of the Liberal leader. In 1934 a local Liberal informed King that the Winnipeg North Liberal Association had been held together on paper but not as a 'live organizaton' 'on account of the fact that it has been your wish for at least the last two Federal elections that we as a party should not oppose Mr. Heaps ...' The decision was renewed by King in consultation with Charles Stewart and Heaps himself in the office of the leader of the opposition, 'in order,' as King explained to Lambert, 'that the Communists should receive full opposition from Heaps.'[116] If the moderate socialists could not be persuaded to join the Liberals, it was still preferable to King that they be supported to defeat more left-wing socialists if such a radical challenge existed. But in this case the local organization was not willing to abide by decisions based on such esoteric *raisons d'état*. A Liberal candidate was nominated by the local association and beaten by Heaps in the election. Also defeated was the national Communist leader, Tim Buck.

Another task which lay on the agenda of a national party preparing to contest an election was the complex and intricate matter of the Canada Elections Act and the setting up of electoral machinery by the government, which employed parties as unofficial agents in the state's business of setting up polls and preparing voting lists. Since the Liberals were out of office and their opponents in charge of the electoral machinery, the onus for ensuring that Liberals received a fair shake in the critical job of deciding who could vote rested with the party organizers. The appointment of returning officers, enumerators, poll clerks, etc., was also an important patronage plum, particularly in a depression; it was necessary for the party to ensure that these appointments were distributed efficiently and equitably. Here Chubby Power stepped in to fill a breach which the NLF was either unable or unwilling to fill itself. Power took the matter in hand in 1934, and continued into the election year.[117]

The major thrust of the national campaign, aside from ensuring that provincial campaigns were in running order and co-ordinating financial and organizational efforts across the country, was the national publicity effort, centred around the NLF. Here again the provinces were heavily involved in their local publicity drives, which in total were more significant than that mounted from national headquarters. The Ontario campaign committee, for instance, spent $116,329 on province-wide publicity in newspapers and on radio; the national publicity budget for the entire country in the same media came to only $107,343.[118] Figures for Quebec are not available, but it might be expected that they would be in a similar range. The general feeling in the party here as elsewhere was that local people knew best where election publicity should go, and how its message should be pitched. Even the relatively small national campaign sometimes drew criticism for lack of local knowledge, one example being complaints from Liberals in Nova Scotia that the newspapers chosen for national advertising were 'not very well chosen from the standpoint of their effectiveness in the campaign.'[119]

On the other hand, it was obviously necessary that some unification of the Liberal image across the nation be carried out by the national office, in the absence of which the Liberal face might lose all coherence in a welter of local issues. The day of the advertising image had not fully arrived, although ad agencies were being employed to some effect. But a campaign across the country which stressed 'King or Chaos' and 'Only King Can Win' made the point that the Liberals were the safe stable centre alternative to the débâcle of Toryism and the right- and left-wing adventurists entering the political picture for the first time. As Vincent Massey rather ironically suggested, the slogan 'King or Chaos' was 'perhaps not very flattering to the leader';[120] but that it well described the basic appeal of the distinctly unheroic Liberal party at this juncture of Canadian history there can be little doubt. The breakdown of the publicity budgets of the national campaign and that of Ontario is given in Table 2.6. It appears that the official publicity budget is in fact an underestimate of the amount of publicity actually generated at the national level since it fails to take into account free services offered by certain media and advertising persons. The most notable of these was N.L. Nathanson of Paramount Theatres, who not only donated $10,000 to the Toronto finance committee but assisted in the publicity drive to the extent of designing a billboard which he 'set up by the thousand and paid for himself.' In addition, a film about Mackenzie King was produced and shown in 221 Paramount cinemas across the country.[121] All in all, no less than 8,750,000 pieces of party literature were produced and distributed across the country, in both the English and French languages. A dozen Canada-wide radio broadcasts were given, and the central office planned national tour itineraries of the party leader and eight other leading Liberals.[122]

Free publicity was sometimes given by Joseph Atkinson's *Toronto Star* which in 1933, for instance, published without charge two to three thousand copies of a pamphlet. A series of laudatory articles on King's social policies penned by a Montreal Liberal, Bernard Rose, were published as a pamphlet, 10,000 of which were distributed, at the expense of the Montreal finance committee member, Gordon Scott, in early 1934. King wished copies to be sent to all members of Parliament, the 'key men' in the different

Table 2.6
Liberal publicity budgets, national and Ontario, general election 1935

	National	Ontario
Radio	$ 45,073.68	$ 46,696.53
Billboard posters	20,955.35	26,173.84
Daily newspapers	13,823.93	18,037.10
Farm papers	4859.45	4855.45
Magazines	2000.00	
One-sheet posters	6353.61	
Booklets and leaflets	7754.66	11,458.29
Halls and speakers		9107.92
Sundries	6522.36	
Total	107,343.04	116,329.13

Source: NPL, v.13; WLMK, Memoranda and Notes, v.162, 'Liberal Publicity Campaign' (116251-76)

constituencies, and to labour leaders 'in particular.'[123] Such freelance ventures obviously relieved the national office of some of the publicity burden.

Another facet of Liberal publicity was the recycling of King's 1918 classic, *Industry and Humanity*. The redoubtable old Liberal feminist, Nellie McClung, wrote to King early in 1935 suggesting that a shortened reprint of the book might be a useful electoral weapon: 'Something that the ministers will preach about and the young peoples' clubs discuss ... ' In March the Macmillan company agreed to publish an abridged version. The task of cutting down the lengthy original was passed on to King's private secretary, E.A. Pickering, who prepared a shortened manuscript which was rushed into print by July, just in time for the election campaign – 'the cause,' as King explained, 'which the book itself is intended to serve.'[124]

A final item in the national publicity campaign was the publication of a campaign biography of the party leader. This book, published by George Morang, and allegedly authored by Norman Rogers, was in fact an amalgam of an old campaign biography by Senator John Lewis, who had worked for the national office in the early 1920s, some revisions by Rogers, and extensive sections written by King himself. King in fact took the most minute and detailed interest in the project, down to the point of commenting on the quality of the paper and the texture of the cloth covers. While King obviously believed that the book was politically useful, it cost the party a fair sum of money in subsidy to the publisher – at least $6000 from the Toronto treasury. Senator Hardy also gave financial assistance to publicizing the volume, and the Ontario Liberal Association supervised the distribution of copies to all the public libraries in Canada.[125]

CONCLUSION

The results of the 1935 election were not unforeseen. As King noted in his diary in July, the Conservatives in the House of Commons already gave every indication of seeing the handwriting on the wall: '... a sort of sadness seemed to pervade the chambers. It was quite plain that the Tories recognized they were defeated, and that nothing could save them.' The extent of the Liberal victory was not foreseen by most. Norman Lambert's estimate based on the best intelligence from the provinces on the eve of the election was 148 to 158 seats. In fact, they won 173 ridings to pile up the most massive majority ever achieved by a party in federal politics up to that time. The Tories fell from 137 members elected in 1930 to a mere 40 five years later. Yet on closer examination the Liberal victory was not so inspiring. The Liberal share of the total popular vote actually declined from 45.5 per cent in 1930 to 44.9 per cent in 1935. In the Maritimes the Liberal vote rose sharply; central Canada gave little indication of change, with the Liberals going up very slightly in Quebec, and down slightly in Ontario; but in the provinces west of Manitoba the Liberal vote dropped significantly. The reason for the great disparity between popular vote and seats in this election was the combination of the collapse of the Tory vote and the entry of third-party candidates in profusion. A total of 892 candidates contested the 245 seats, which had in 1930 attracted only 546 aspirants. The quirks of the single-member plurality voting system in three-, four-, and five-way contests favoured the Liberals, whose vote at least held fairly steady. But in certain regions, new parties made their mark. In Alberta the Social Credit party easily led the field, more than doubling the Liberal vote. More surprising to the Liberals was British Columbia, where the CCF polled the highest party vote of any entrant.[126]

Canada had definitely entered into the era of multi-party politics. The Liberal party was just as capable as it had been in the early 1920s of benefiting from its centrist position. And King himself was particularly skilled at playing both sides to benefit the middle. As one of King's correspondents described the electoral situation in Vancouver in 1935, the splintering of political options put the Liberals in an especially ambiguous position: 'This cuts different ways in different constituencies. Ian on the waterfront has to court the Reds and has had some success. McGeer in Burrard is making the issue "Order versus Disorder," Manson stands to get a big vote in the West side of his riding under McGeer's wing and has to court working class support, sympathize with the protest vote in the East side of his riding.'[127] This was a veritable paradigm of the Liberal situation in the country. But as Mackenzie King was able to demonstrate, out of ambiguity can come political longevity.[128]

Thus the Liberals were able to turn the Great Depression and the political instability which resulted to their own long-term advantage. A great deal of plain luck was obviously involved in this good fortune, particularly the luck of losing in 1930 and the luck of having R.B. Bennett as prime minister. But the fact that Mackenzie King was able to offer himself to the electorate as the alternative to chaos in 1935 was a result of more than luck alone. Apart from the ability of King himself to maintain his political balance in the face of considerable pressures, there was the continued strength of the provincial Liberal parties which during the period of federal opposition were able to win a series of important victories in Ontario, British Columbia, Saskatchewan, Nova Scotia, New Brunswick, and Prince Edward Island. Equally important was the ability of the national party to meet the challenges which faced it during these years: to reconstitute its financial apparatus on a working basis after Beauharnois; to rebuild a national office after the collapse of the old office; to maintain a united and effective front in Parliament; to organize and win the string of by-elections which came up from year to year; to co-ordinate and supervise a national campaign when the call finally came; and, finally, and most subtly, to maintain an image of a viable and safe alternative ready to step into office when the electorate was given a chance to decide. It may be true, as J.M. Beck suggests, that in the 1935 election 'the voters had asked not so much to have Mackenzie King back in office as to be rid of R.B. Bennett.'[129] But that King was there to inherit the office did not just happen. The Liberals remained an *organizational* alternative, with an electoral machinery ready to be used. The new third parties lacked that national organizational presence, and however popular their radical policies might be with disaffected and discontented sections of the depression-wracked country, these did not add up to national organizations capable of inheriting the power left in Ottawa by Bennett's self-immolation. Only the Liberals had that capacity. They retained that capacity at least in part because they retained the will and the ability to regenerate themselves after defeat.

3

Building the Government party, 1935–40

The return of the Liberals to power in 1935 meant different things to different people. To the business community, badly shaken by the continuing economic slump and by the seemingly radical directions taken by the New Deal Democrats in Washington, Mackenzie King was accepted as a generally reassuring figure who could be trusted to keep within the well-trodden paths of fiscal convention. As Dominion Securities Corporation explained to its American shareholders a few days after the election results were in, the Liberal victory 'eliminates the possibility of the introduction of unorthodox and experimental policies of government which were advocated by certain minority parties ...'[1] To those on the political left, King's victory meant at least the end of R.B. Bennett's 'iron heel' and the development of a more conciliatory attitude toward trade union organization. The eight Liberal provincial administrations across the country no doubt expected a new era in federal-provincial co-operation with a national government of the same partisan stripe.

The inability of a political party in office to remain all things to all people after even a few days in power was nowhere more manifest than in the internal party organization. The scores of people around the country who had helped the party in the election, whether as candidates, party workers, or financial supporters, expected some recognition of their services – ranging from a cabinet post to a local road construction job. Power has its advantages in the provision of rewards, but it has its drawbacks as well, as ably summed up by Lord Melbourne's exclamation when faced with yet another exasperating problem of ecclesiastical patronage: 'Damn it, another bishop dead!'[2] Given the critical nature of the patronage relationship to party organization, it was imperative that the Liberal party sort out the lines of authority and responsibility now that they had returned to office. And this immediately raised the question of the relationship between the party in Parliament and the extra-parliamentary wing.

Faced with the electoral defeat of five years earlier, the disappearance from the active political scene of many of the old organizational figures, and the destructive effects of the Beauharnois affair, Mackenzie King had turned in the years of opposition to the National Liberal Federation and the idea of an extra-parliamentary organization as an essential, although ill-defined, element in the party structure. With Vincent Massey's departure in 1935 for his reward in London, there was a real possibility that the NLF might go the way of the national office set up after the 1919 convention, once the party had fallen into the comfortable exercise of power. Even with the best of intentions the NLF might simply wither away in the face of the power and influence wielded by the leading regional patronage and policy brokers of the newly appointed cabinet. And the good intentions of the prime minister and his colleagues toward the extra-parliamentary party were not altogether above question, as the early history of the NLF had already amply indicated.

The nub of the problem lay with the nature of a parliamentary system superimposed upon a federal society. The leading cabinet ministers not only held ministerial prerogatives over wide areas of appointments and issuing of contracts, but they represented the various regions of the country to the national government with the direct legitimacy of electoral support. Consequently there was never any real question that the locus of organizational responsibility would inevitably be located in the inner sanctum of the cabinet. Nobody, certainly not Norman Lambert, ever doubted that responsibility must rest here, in any ultimate sense.

Yet that recognition still left considerable room for organizational innovation by comparison to the strict traditionalism of King's first two governments in the 1920s. It was King's own belief that his organization had failed him in 1930. That failure might be attributed to the inadequate human resources in the cabinet, but such an explanation could be only partially convincing. The lack of some co-ordinating structure to link the individual cabinet minister's efforts to the vaguely defined but real conception of the party 'out there' – in the provinces, in the constituencies, and even in the electorate – was also seen by many as a weakness which would have to be remedied if the party were not to fall into another period of organizational sclerosis as the bureaucratic-state functions hardened around the vitally important partisan functions. Ministers were not only regional brokers within the party, they were ministers of large departments, staffed by senior civil servants of growing expertise and competence and growing impatience with old-fashioned party politics. As the Liberal party became 'the Government party,' one of its central problems was the relationship between 'government' and 'party.'

The party did not in fact return to the situation of the 1920s, and the new factor was the creation of a special role for Norman Lambert as an organizational link between the cabinet ministers and the external party, especially the financial backers. Until the Second World War changed the entire conditions of Canadian politics, the party in office did allow the growth of functional differentiation in its structure: the special role of Lambert as the party 'fixer' or middleman between the bureaucratic incarnation of the party and what he himself liked to call 'business' side of politics.[3] Lambert was the new Andrew Haydon, but it appears that he was something more than Haydon had ever been or at least had been allowed to become – although much less than Lambert himself would have liked to become.

THE POLITICAL ROLE OF THE CABINET

In choosing his new cabinet King had a much easier time of it than in the minority government circumstances of his first ministry fourteen years earlier. There were two reasons for this: the Liberal party of 1935 had much greater strength in almost all the regions of the country, and King himself had established a more decisive personal ascendancy within the party. The combination of these two factors enabled the prime minister to exercise his prerogatives in appointment with more long-term considerations in mind, both as to administrative ability and to political talent. The result was a cabinet with which King was generally well pleased – 'a good cabinet,' as he wrote in his diary a few months after taking office, 'it gives me an authority I did not feel so strongly before, with the experience I have had and men chosen by myself, not therein solely because of long service to Party, etc.'[4]

The process of cabinet selection was not, however, without constraints, especially in the case of Quebec, where King's initial doubts about certain appointments had perforce to be waived in the face of that province's considerable degree of autonomy. Both Ernest Lapointe's firm defence of Chubby Power – an Irish Catholic drinking man of whom King was apprehensive – and P.-J.-A. Cardin's tough negotiating stance on his own behalf in the face of King's suspicions of his involvement with the Simard family and the Beauharnois Corporation, were successful in changing the party leader's mind.[5] But then Quebec was always a law unto itself. There were some other constraints imposed upon the leader elsewhere. Jimmy Gardiner, premier of Saskatchewan, had been sounded out by King before the election as a potential prairie lieutenant; Gardiner's selection ran up against the influence of Charles Dunning, who was an old rival of Gardiner for the leadership of Saskatchewan Liberals. Dunning, who had by this time established himself in eastern financial circles, gradually was eased out of identification with the western agricultural interests which Gardiner represented. Gardiner was placed in agriculture and Dunning in finance, but the 'feud' between the two was a constant source of tension within the cabinet, which King noted 'keeps cropping out at different places.'[6] T.A. Crerar was chosen as the Manitoba representative, despite his own clear perception that King did not like him personally.[7] In Ontario, King had a large and youthful contingent from which to choose, and two newly elected members, C.D. Howe and Norman Rogers, were immediately brought into the cabinet as highly important and influential ministers – in Howe's case with significant organizational and party patronage responsibilities as well – but some other young and able men had to be kept out because of their apparent identification with the provincial Hepburn machine. Thus one weak and aging minister from the 1920s, J.C. Elliott, and another carry-over whose protectionism King disliked, W.D. Euler, had to be appointed. Finally, Alberta had ignored King's threat of no cabinet recognition and had returned only a single Liberal in a Social Credit landslide; King left that province to be represented by Jimmy Gardiner until such time as they could show cause for greater gratitude.

Despite these constraints, King had reason to be pleased with the overall quality of his cabinet, especially in an administrative sense. In political and organizational terms King turned out to be less pleased, although in fairness to his ministers it must be admitted that King was a chronic complainer about political organization. Quebec district was in the able, if at times erratic, hands of Chubby Power, with Lapointe exercising a general supervision. Montreal was in a more indeterminate state under Cardin and F. Rinfret, who was very weak. Yet despite the endemic factionalism of the Liberals on the Island of Montreal, the party never did seem to be in any real danger of losing its electoral hegemony. In a sense, Quebec was such a solid area for Liberals that they could afford the luxury of internal divisions and a certain amount of organizational laxity. Ontario, in the face of the brutal assaults launched against the federal Liberals by the Hepburn machine in the late 1930s, was a definite weak point in party organization, as it indeed had been for a very long time. C.D. Howe was to emerge as the most important figure in the Ontario party so far as organizational strength went; it was Howe, in tandem with the direct intervention of Lambert and the NLF into that province's internal political affairs, who was to be the main counterweight to the centrifugal force of the provincial breakaway. The Prairies were under the firm hand of Jimmy Gardiner who, despite misgivings about his judgement expressed from time to time by various party insiders, devoted very considerable attention to organizational matters. British Columbia was to be under the direction of Ian Mackenzie who, although not entirely a success as an administrator, proved reasonably competent as a political boss in the Pacific region. The Maritimes did not boast any strong organizational figures, but the strength of the Liberals in that area after 1935 did not lend any particular urgency to the task of finding politically energetic ministers.

In the inevitable conflicts between the administrative responsibilities and political tasks, the Liberal cabinet did seem to be weighted rather in the administrative direction. Some ministers, such as J.L. Ilsley, who were highly competent and successful administrators, proved to be rather impatient, or even intolerant, of political and organizational matters. Others were more aware of the less exalted side of politics, but showed a certain reluctance to devote any great proportion of their admittedly busy schedules to the prosaic details of partisan activity. A tendency toward concentration on the bureaucratic aspects of government, later to be greatly accelerated by the demands of the war on the Canadian state, was already a manifest tendency in the late 1930s. King sometimes grew very impatient at the readiness of his ministers to entrust themselves to their deputies in the permanent civil service, together with a concomitant insensitivity to the specifically political implications of policy. 'It is perfectly appalling,' he confided in his diary, 'how little many Ministers will exercise authority themselves and how completely they get into the hands of members of the permanent service.' Yet, on the other hand, the more old-fashioned politicians in the cabinet sometimes could go rather too far in the direction of naked political advantage. When Jimmy Gardiner wished to dismiss a number of employees of his agriculture department on the declaration of a local MP that they were Conservatives, King tried to draw the line, stating that such a practice bespoke 'great injustice' and that public opinion would no longer stand for it. Gardiner and the Quebec ministers argued that there was more to gain by the firings than to lose; most of the ministers from the rest of the country supported King. Nevertheless, King did not call for a vote, thinking it best under the circumstances not to 'conclude the discussion.'[8]

The point of these divergent tendencies would seem to be that the traditional patronage politics so characteristic of an earlier era of the Liberal party in office – Sir Wilfrid Laurier's biographer had written flatly that the 'distribution of patronage was the most important single function of the government'[9] – were losing ground to the newer, bureaucratic, policy-oriented politics of the era of depressions and world wars. The older patronage politics was not eliminated by the new order but was resting in sometimes uneasy coexistence with it. In one sense patronage simply took new and more elevated forms, in line with increasing state intervention in the private sphere of production and all the opportunities that such a development presaged for a profitable relationship between a government party and the business world. In another sense the old-fashioned type of patronage remained because it still fulfilled important functions for party organization, especially in certain sections of the country, and because nobody had either the will, the imagination, or the ability to transform the nature of the party in the light of changing conditions in the role of the state. The time was not yet ripe for daring experiments in party organization. Instead, the first Liberal administration after 1935 witnessed a number of piecemeal adaptations to changing conditions.

THE CABINET AND THE EXTRA-PARLIAMENTARY ORGANIZATION

The principal adaptation was the attempt to incorporate the extra-parliamentary organization, in the person of Norman Lambert and his small staff at the NLF office, into the workings of the cabinet as a political body. This attempt never reached the institutionalized stage of the 'political cabinet' inaugurated in the government of Pierre Elliott Trudeau in the late 1960s – and indeed, in Lambert's eyes, left a great deal to be desired – but it was a tentative attempt to establish some linkage between the parliamentary and extra-parliamentary parties. Although a cabinet liaison committee was established to provide a formal link, little substantial use was ever made of it. The real functioning link was between Lambert and C.D. Howe; the usefulness of that link revolved around their personal and political relations – sometimes for better, sometimes for worse.

Howe was one of those politicians who seemed born to rule. As Lambert had noted acutely almost two years before Howe's first election victory in the Liberal sweep of 1935, Howe's 'approach to running in Port Arthur seems to be a desire for a guaranteed cabinet position!'[10] While he got no prior commitment from King, it was inevitable that the dynamic and acerbic engineer would rise rapidly to prominence. Everyone, from fellow politicians to academic observers, has recognized Howe's dominating position in the Liberal party in the long period of Liberal rule under King and St Laurent. Yet there is a curious ambiguity about this image of power and influence, reflected in the sharply differing conceptions of Howe's role which have been put forward. Most curious of all is the image of Howe as simply a businessman in politics, a good administrator and 'doer' but not a politician. Of all the ministers in King's cabinet, Howe was in fact the most intimately connected to the practical details of the national party organization, and particularly to the day-to-day practice of party patronage and the delicate matter of relating government business to party financial support. Only Gardiner had as important a role in the party's affairs, but that was more strictly in a regional sense. To the national party organization, Gardiner always remained a bit of an outsider, while Howe was definitely an insider.

Howe's appointment was viewed by King as having special significance for the extra-parliamentary party. As indicated briefly in the previous chapter, Massey had 'discovered' Howe and King wished Massey to know that Howe's appointment constituted a recognition of the contribution of the NLF to the election victory. That this was not merely a sop to an already disillusioned Massey was indicated the next day when King told Howe himself the same thing. The portfolio given to the new minister was transport which incorporated the old ministries of marine and of railways and canals. It was a crucial area for government spending, particularly as related to large contracts to private business. King later advised Howe, in making appointments to the various boards and commissions which proliferated under his portfolio, to bear in mind the importance of representing such non-partisan interests as women, youth, labour, and other organized groups, but also to 'keep the party forces in mind ... keep the political point of view in mind, to cultivate it in addition to the business method ...' At the time of the cabinet's formation, Howe appeared to Lambert to be 'very much bewildered.' The conflicting advice and the somewhat divergent terms of reference were of little help in resolving his perplexity.[11]

Lambert had realized during the election campaign that if the extra-parliamentary organization were to be of any lasting value it would have to have some control over patronage. As Massey and Lambert told one local Liberal involved in a constituency squabble in the midst of the election, 'patronage in future ... should be in the hands of the organization, not the defeated candidate, or sitting member, who ordinarily wd. be consulted.' That eventually was highly unlikely, but Lambert was certain that at least some organizational role had to be given to the NLF if it were to retain any force within a party which had now come to office. Massey discussed the future of the federation with him just before receiving his London appointment, and suggested possible successors to the presidency. Lambert was adamant that he 'would not continue unless I controlled whole situation, finance & all.' He went on to suggest that 'the character of the organzn. had changed now that Libs in power & the job was to keep organizns. alive in each provce.'[12] As Lambert recalled a few years later, he had believed it necessary to recognize 'frankly and honestly that a political organization has a business side to it which does not have to be comcealed from the public as something unclean and untouchable.' There were thus two quite different conceptions of what an extra-parliamentary structure ought to be; an 'educational influence devoted to the extension of Liberal ideas among the rank and file of the electorate' as King had sometimes stated, or, in Lambert's succinct phrase, a 'party machine.' Under Lambert's guidance in the late 1930s the NLF tried to be a bit of both. The ultimate result was that by the election of 1940 the NLF offices 'were regarded throughout this country and in far too many quarters as the gateway to departmental favours from the Liberal party in power. I can assure you that few of the steady stream of people who passed through my door in those days gave evidence of appreciating the character of the National Liberal Federation as it had been conceived in the beginning.' Yet Lambert went on to note that many of the applicants, including the more deserving, often failed to gain the rewards they were seeking, which led him to conclude that 'possibly this conflict between the party's ideals and its actual administration cannot be settled for a long time to come. My own opinion is that it cannot be settled without a considerable measure of electoral reform.'[13]

At first Lambert had been more than willing to give up a job which he recognized as thankless. Expecting a reward for his service to the party since 1932, he looked to some reasonably respectable appointment. Howe undertook to find such a position, with the Harbour Commission being mentioned. The prime minister, however, appeared reluctant to grant the request, and instead emphasized Lambert's importance to the NLF. Lambert formally requested King to give him an 'administrative post' to free him from the NLF altogether; King made more plain than before that he wanted him for the organization. Then Howe, who had spoken of the chairmanship of the Harbour Commission at a salary of $15,000 to $16,000, 'without excuse or explanation' changed the terms to a mere $10,000 per year. Lambert, clearly angered, held out for $12,000.[14] But it was not to be. As subsequent events were to prove, King's motives in this were mixed. It was not merely that he wanted Lambert for the NLF; equally important was his aversion to giving a major appointment to a man who had been too closely associated with the party organization. Lambert was getting his first real taste of being a necessary evil.

However unsettling the attitude of the party leader may have been to his peace of mind, Lambert was not about to accept any terms offered. He told King that if he were to remain in the organization he would expect two conditions to be fulfilled: that he be given the presidency of the NLF, and that a future undertaking be given for a major appointment, the Senate being mentioned as first choice. Although he made clear that his preference was for the Harbour Commission, he would carry on if his conditions were met. King agreed, with the proviso that the Senate appointment would not come until the third year of the administration. After referring to the 'uncertainty' of Senate appointments, Lambert asked what he meant by the 'third year.' King somewhat ominously replied that 'earning it' would be part of the job. A few days later, King formally communicated to Lambert the information that the cabinet had agreed to place him in charge of the NLF as president, and that the ministers had agreed that Lambert's acceptance 'would be recognized as immediately placing the Party under an even greater obligation to yourself than that which at present is recognized by all.' King had in fact gone out of his way to placate his organizer since he had never previously made such a firm prior commitment concerning a Senate appointment. Lambert, who had wanted badly to get out of organizational work, did not treat it as any sort of victory. On the contrary, he told Howe that the Harbour position had obviously been out of the question from the beginning, that it 'cd. not have been otherwise,' and concluded philosophically by quoting Morley: 'one who had anything to do with public men should learn never to have disappointments.'[15]

Lambert's position as president was made official the following year at an advisory council meeting, the first since the party returned to power. The prime minister did not attend the meeting but he did tell Albert Matthews that he wished Lambert to be voted officially as federation president, which was duly accomplished.[16] The official position did not, however, resolve any of the problems associated with the exercise of the office. The differing conceptions mentioned earlier of the extra-parliamentary party organization as a propaganda outlet or party machine coexisted uneasily in Lambert's person. After his official election to the presidency, Lambert asked for a personal interview with the party leader to try to clear up the situation:

Saw P.M. & said that I was willing to make the best of executive setup, but was somewhat apprehensive of developments; and as a back-log of defence I should like confirmation of the distinction between the Presidency of the N.L.F. & the post of Dom. Organizer of the Party, responsible to him, the Govt. & members of Parlt., – as custodian of party funds etc. He agreed to this, saying 'quite right' as I defined my conception of the Federation as representing the electorate, while Dom. party organizer represented directly leaders & elected members of the Party. He agreed also that work of next two years should be quietly to build up financial reserves.[17]

To King, Lambert had taken a 'terrible time to say to me in a round about way' that he wished to pursue a course of action of 'which I strongly approve.'[18] Lambert was, in fact, trying to grapple with a very real problem which the party leader was too ready to dismiss. In effect, King had set Lambert a task which he did not have the requisite powers to accomplish. The crux of the problem lay with the relationship between Lambert as 'Dominion organizer' and the parliamentary caucus, particularly the cabinet. If a national organizer were to be effective, he must have the co-operation of the cabinet and the members; such co-operation was important not only in relation to regional and constituency affairs but also to the delicate question of the *quid pro quo* for the donation of funds or services to the party, the co-ordination of patronage through the departments – in short, the 'practical' or 'business' side of politics to which Lambert so often referred. Since King had expressly charged Lambert with building up the party funds, this question took on an urgency which the party leader seemingly failed to recognize.

An attempt was made to set up a formal link between the NLF and the cabinet in the form of a committee of ministers on which Lambert would be included to provide 'liaison.' Although the ministers involved were those most conscious of organizational affairs – Howe, Power, Gardiner, and Mackenzie – the committee appears to have been scarcely operative, except for assuming 'collective management' over the conduct of two federal by-elections in 1937. Indeed, so innocuous was this committee that when Norman Rogers and King complained about the reluctance of ministers to co-operate with the NLF by speaking on radio, even the members of the committee 'sat silent when Illesley [*sic*] said he did not know there was a committee.'[19]

According to Lambert's own testimony, there was only one occasion during his presidency of the NLF that he was 'invited to discuss practical matters of organization with the members of the Government.' This unique instance of co-operation in 1937 was for the sole purpose of naming party treasurers in the provinces with the approval of the respective ministers. King himself was aware of the lack of co-operation, and believed Lambert's complaints on this score to be only 'too true': 'it is shocking,' he wrote, 'the apathy & worse than apathy – the absolute indifference of practically all the ministers – excepting Gardiner – to organization.'[20] Even Howe, the minister with whom Lambert worked most closely, was prickly and independent and often pursued courses which Lambert believed to be at cross-purposes with the legitimate interests of the party organization. In late 1936 Lambert had grown so incensed at Howe's behaviour that he devoted an unusual diary entry to an enumeration of the transport minister's 'breaches of faith.' There were no less than a half dozen of these breaches, mainly involving patronage matters of government business to Liberal contractors, in which undertakings had been allegedly abandoned.[21] Nevertheless, Howe remained closer to Lambert than any other minister, and it was through Howe that much of Lambert's 'business' side of politics was transacted. The other ministers were, if anything, more difficult yet. In the disposition of government business, Howe's colleagues either tended to non-partisan propriety or jealously guarded their own patronage prerogatives against the incursion of the extra-parliamentary organization. Even in areas where there were no tenders and the patronage relationship with firms was on a widely recognized basis, such as advertising, Lambert was unable to control the departmental contracts – although in this case he did get the voluntary co-operation of Howe.[22] Yet it is an interesting reflection on the power of regionalism in Canadian parliamentary government that even so strong a prime minister as Mackenzie King could not always force or compel his own ministers to behave in a manner which they were reluctant to follow, particularly as regards those political or partisan matters which lay outside the scope of grand policy. Early in 1940, for example, the cabinet was considering a number of Senate appointments. King was not very impressed with some of the names being accepted. As if conscious of future political scientists looking over his shoulder, King wrote the following entry in his diary: 'One might say: why, then, appoint these men? The answer is: it wd. be impossible to keep one's colleagues together unless their collective will to some extent in matters of this kind was recognized.'[23]

Even though King might on rare occasions express sympathy for Lambert's difficult position, his own attitude toward his organizer scarcely helped the situation. The debilitating effect of being treated as 'dirty workers' in the field of politics was felt by all who were involved in the 'business' side. Frank O'Connor eased his way out of financial collections, both provincial and federal, after receiving his senatorship in 1935, citing his disgust at the attitude of the cabinet: 'we wanted to work with the ministers,' he asserted to Lambert's obvious agreement, 'but it was up to them. We were as good as they were, & we did not propose to be pointed to as undesirables because we were connected with the organization.' Lambert and the Toronto financial committee concluded that 'if we cd. not finance with co-operation of Gov't in business, we had better quit altogether.' Not only O'Connor but another key figure in the Toronto committee did just that.

Lambert's personal frustration at his position came to the surface one day when he went for a walk with Rod Finlayson, R.B. Bennett's organization man, and the nearest equivalent in the Tory party to Lambert himself. Finlayson had been passed over for a senatorship in the dying days of the Bennett régime, despite an apparent commitment by the then prime minister to reward his right hand man. The two men commiserated with one another on the fate of political organizers, and 'talked about following one road until you found a dead end; and then seeking another instead of remaining at the dead end forever.'[24] Lambert went on to say that 'rather than stay in one of these under-posts, as the intimate nonentity of famous men, I should prefer doing another kind of work. I also said that my work was interesting only in the team work it developed, and referred to the fact that I now had pivotal men in each prov'ce, with the hope that when an election came along, they would be ready to go on a self-sufficient basis.'

Even when King fulfilled his undertaking to appoint Lambert to the Senate early in 1938, the latter's pride was not assuaged. Although the senatorship relieved the party of a financial burden in allowing it to reduce Lambert's NLF salary, it did not place him in any more enviable a position with regard to the cabinet. Lambert, who by this time had become convinced that the 'lack of co-operative interest in the business aspect of party organization' was a closely related and aggravating factor in the deepening strains between the federal party and the provincial wings in Ontario and Quebec, decided to bring matters to a head in early 1939, when an Ontario cabinet vacancy presented itself to the government. Lambert went to the prime minister's office and laid his cards on the table: 'suggested he take me into Gov't as Ontario minister. I said I was not applying, but was available, senatorship & all, if could be of service. Gave reason that gap between organizn. & Gov't too wide. He mentioned they didn't want to lose me from NLF, etc., but I pointed out it would help organzn, that NLF should be identified more & more as an educational body. I said that constituency and acclamation could be got.' King countered with the suggestion of Norman McLarty, who eventually was given the appointment. Lambert summed up his relationship to the party leader in answer to a local Liberal organizer who wished to use Lambert to gain influence with King: 'I told him that I had nothing to offer ... that the prevailing idea about my closeness to the P.M. was an illusion, and anything but true to fact. He expressed great surprise & said that if people generally knew that it would suggest disintegration of party.'[25]

Since the functions of the extra-parliamentary organization were divided in this period between the NLF as an educational or publicity office and the president's role as organizer and fund-raiser, it is convenient to examine the two functions separately. We may begin with the publicity area, which was rather less significant but still of some interest.

The election brought a number of changes to the office staff of the NLF. R.J. Deachman was not an elected member; his place was filled by Walter Herbert, who had supervised party publicity in the West during the election from the Liberal offices in Winnipeg. Herbert was given Lambert's old position as secretary of the federation, but he was not involved in organizational work as Lambert had been. Instead, he looked after the production and distribution of publicity, as his background in advertising would indicate. This task he seems to have performed very well. Lambert was certainly far better pleased with Herbert's efforts than he had been with those of Deachman, whose departure was scarcely a cause for dismay. Journalist Bruce Hutchison described Herbert as 'brilliant,' and his talents were apparent enough to earn him a leading position in the wartime information bureau, and, briefly, a spot on the prime minister's own personal office staff where, according to Hutchison, he 'could endure for a time a party leader who telephoned at midnight to complain that the proposed menu of a public banquet was unsatisfactory, that peas must be substituted for beans and the whole program reprinted. In the end, he, like so many others, quit in disgust.'[26]

Some of the regular publicity activities of the NLF office under Herbert's direction in the late 1930s included the publication of the *Canadian Liberal Monthly*, which finally began to live up to its name by appearing on a monthly basis in February 1936. An average of 10,000 copies were distributed per month to elected Liberal members both federal and provincial, local organizational officials, and a 'selected list of Party supporters throughout the country.' Special review issues were given wider circulation for electoral publicity purposes. Some 200,000 copies of speeches by the prime minister and some of the more prominent cabinet ministers had also been circulated. A regular effort at planting material in the press resulted in Liberal publicity being 'used generously in both daily and weekly papers in all the provinces,' according to Herbert. In gearing up for the election expected in 1939 the national office set to work on a wide variety of special publicity projects including preparation of the *Speakers' Handbook* which provided quick information for the use of candidates; the production of leaflets and folders and the development of a 'uniform poster and banner campaign ... arranged for national appeal' – this to be worked out in co-operation with the Cockfield, Brown advertising agency; the arranging of national radio broadcasts by leading party luminaries; and the gathering together of a number of bright young journalists and academics to prepare memoranda on public policy issues for the use of candidates, officials, speakers, and campaign workers.[27]

An attempt was made in this period to generate some local Liberal activity around 'study groups' across the country, an idea advanced by Senator Cairine Wilson, and apparently premised on the notion that they would in no way attempt to replace electoral organizations but would rather focus on policy matters alone.[28] Although federation funds were requested for these groups, no concrete facts or figures seem to have been provided as to their actual size or extent of activity. Since they appear to have quietly faded away by the end of decade, it seems reasonable to conclude that they were never of much significance. Nor is it apparent how they could have been; given the tight control exercised by the party in power over policy formulation, it is not clear why rank-and-file supporters should have spent their time 'studying' policy.

The only concrete result of the study groups was an idea advanced through them by W. Ross MacDonald and Senator W.A. Buchanan that King and his cabinet ministers ought to give a series of radio broadcasts in 1938 to communicate to the Canadian public the nature of the work being done in the various departments. Lambert found the funds for this project, not without difficulty, and once the prime minister was persuaded that a request for a fifteen-minute national speech was not an unjustifiable importunity on the part of the party organizers, the series was launched under the overall direction of Lambert and the NLF office.[29]

Just as in the case of organizational work, publicity required the co-operation of the cabinet and members. As Lambert informed one of King's assistants, 'any attempt to have N.L.F. distribute large quantities of leaflets & pamphlets now without ministerial sponsorship in the form of an address beforehand was just waste of time.' Nor did cabinet ministers always make use of the NLF's efforts, especially in Quebec where the national party organization was generally kept at arm's length. The prime minister was himself a chronic complainer about the quality of the party publicity; his extreme fussiness about the most minute details, down to the grade of paper and the colour of the ink, was enough to drive most people to distraction, if they were not already inured to his peculiarities. Every small mistake made by the office only served to reinforce his believe that 'one has to follow literally every detail oneself.'[30]

Yet however exasperating King's behaviour could sometimes be, it was also manifestly the case that his meticulous attention to small detail was a major asset for the Liberal party, particularly as regards his voluminous correspondence with a wide variety of Canadians from all parts of the country and all ranks of society. King's dogged determination to read and reply personally to the staggering volume of letters he received constituted a sort of one-man publicity effort for the party. Not only did the party leader keep in close touch with the political situation in the various nooks and crannies far from Ottawa, but his carefully worded and diplomatic replies were a significant form of party publicity among the local notables of the smaller centres of the country, and, on occasion, among the higher notables of the larger and more powerful centres as well. He once lectured his personal secretary about the 'value of such correspondence that, from a strictly official view, appears to be not only unnecessary, but a waste of time. It is, I am sure, the little things that count for most in politics as in all else.'[31] When the volume of official business became too great for the prime minister to devote as much time to his personal correspondence, he made sure that intelligent and shrewd assistants like Jack Pickersgill would sift through the material and bring to his attention any letters which seemed to be of any political significance. No discussion of the Liberal party's public image in this area could thus be complete without due credit being given to King's Herculean efforts at personal public relations and personal information gathering. The clumsy attempts at 'regional desks' and other such devices by more recent incumbents of the office indicate the necessity to find some institutional substitute for a function which only the most austere and dedicated individual could perform on a sustained personal basis. In this sense at least, the Liberals under King's leadership enjoyed the luxury of a highly personalized national publicity office which the NLF could support and supplement but never really replace.

One particular problem faced by the NLF as a publicity organization in the late 1930s was the question of a French-speaking section. That function fell vacant when Adjuter Savard, the former assistant, departed for a position in the Press Gallery following the election of 1935. For the next three years the NLF operated without a French secretary, despite its efforts to provide publicity services in French as well as English. The problem was, as Lambert diplomatically explained, that the relations between the NLF and the Quebec Liberals 'had been, and still are, unique.' Liberals from that province, he went on, 'have not in the past shown any warmth for the idea of participation in the National Liberal Federation.'[32] This relationship will be explored in greater depth in Chapter 7; for now it may be noted that it was not until 1938 that a French secretary was secured for the office. He was Philéas Côté, a journalist and publicist who had studied at Laval and Harvard, who was later to pursue a career as a civil servant in wartime and as a Liberal MP following the war. Côté's appointment was approved by Lapointe and Power, and accepted by Lambert. The French-speaking side of NLF activities was not one of the office's strengths in this period, but Côté did something to alleviate that problem.

NATIONAL MEETINGS OF THE NLF

A meeting of the advisory council of the NLF was held in Ottawa in 1936, at which very little of any note took place, other than the confirmation of Lambert as president. Since the prime minister and most of his colleagues in the cabinet did not attend, citing the abdication crisis as their excuse, the meeting, which included about 160 participants, was characterized by a sense of irrelevance – Lambert later referred to the 'disappointing nature' of the affair.[33] The only flurry of excitement was generated by Lambert's uncharacteristically irascible reaction to an attempt by the Liberal women to gain a somewhat greater voice in the executive. Their main complaint centred around the failure of the NLF to ever hold executive committee meetings, despite a constitutional provision that a meeting be called at least once a year. Since the Liberal women, as well as the Twentieth Century club members, had been given recognition in the form of positions on the executive committee, they not unreasonably felt that they had thus been sidetracked into a merely symbolic or honorary presence. That, of course, was exactly where the party brass wanted them to be. But faced with a 'hectic morning' with an organized group of women 'on the attack,' Lambert's usual cool judgment seemed to evaporate. Despite his somewhat heavy-handed intervention stressing that geographical representation was a Liberal principle of more weight than the representation of women ('women or other cliques' as he put it privately), a resolution was put through calling for four annual meetings of the executive committee, four of whose eight members were women. Thus the small and compatible finance committee which had since 1932 been acting as the effective executive of the NLF would be paralleled by an acting executive committee with a strong women's representation.[34]

This small surge of internal party democracy upset Lambert to the point that he brought this 'very important change' to the attention of the party leader, explaining that it appeared to be 'part of a plan orginated in Ont. to get control of national organizn.' Lambert's reasoning was so tortuous, and the evidence so scant, that King simply threw up his hands in bewilderment: 'I could not make head or tail,' he noted in his diary, 'of what he was telling me of control women were getting of the Federation, and which, he thinks, is engineered as a part of a intrigue which, he believes, exists in Toronto on Hepburn's part in reference to the Federal Government.'[35] Lambert was imputing motives too devious by half. Two observations of note, however, emerge from this curious little affair. The first is that any attempt by the rank and file to exercise a greater say in the affairs of the NLF, especially the female rank and file, generally would be met by an hysterical reaction on the part of the leadership. Lambert's political judgment was usually very sound; any move toward greater internal democracy was enough to quite unsettle his normal equanimity. The second point is that Lambert would make very sure that the parliamentary luminaries would be present at any future meetings, on the assumption that any challenges to the NLF leadership would be intimidated by the presence of the prime minister and his cabinet.

There was no advisory council meeting the following year, but there was one scheduled for the spring of 1938. This time King and his ministers were in attendance, but the prime minister was not particularly impressed by the occasion: 'to tell the truth, I was disappointed at the size of the gathering, the limited numbers present from other parts of Canada and the unrepresentative rather than the representative nature of the gathering apart from the members of both Houses of Parliament which composed the majority of those present.' The only matter of any note to emerge from this convention was the passage of a number of resolutions vaguely critical of the Hepburn government which was by this time in a state of open war with the national party, including one motion which deplored 'Communism, Fascism, Nazism, Separatism, Sectionalism and Provincialism, and all other "isms" inconsistent with Liberal principles.'[36] That no doubt offered some small strength to King in his struggle with the 'provincialist' at Queen's Park. Nothing else of any significance took place, confirming the impression that the advisory councils were honorary affairs.

There were no more such meetings until 1943. In the last year before the war began, a national gathering of the Twentieth Century and Young Liberal clubs was held in Ottawa under the auspices and with the financial support of the NLF; the executive committee – which did operate after 1936 as a functioning body, but without the dire results predicted by Lambert – decided that the right of way should be given to that event as the 'outstanding' Liberal affair of that year. Then in August 1938 the NLF sponsored and organized an anniversary banquet for Mackenzie King in honour of his twentieth year of party leadership. This affair, with attendant publicity whipped up by Cockfield, Brown advertising men, was described by Lambert as 'very successful,' but was in King's own eyes a veritable personal disaster. His own speech, which was broadcast live across the nation, was, he believed, a 'complete failure.' Later, feeling 'weary and depressed' and convinced that he had 'let down the party completely,' and was 'humiliated in my own eyes beyond expression,' King did two very uncharacteristic things: he went out and had a drink and briefly speculated about quitting the party leadership, 'if there was anyone available' to replace him. The defeatist mood passed, of course, but King's experience of that night might have had something to do with the fact that he never thanked the NLF or Lambert for their work in preparing the event, an omission which Lambert duly noted among all the other snubs and grievances he collected over the years, which finally helped precipitate his departure from organizational work.[37]

THE 'BUSINESS' SIDE OF PARTY ORGANIZATION

As Lambert never tired of telling people, much more of his time was spent on the 'business' side of party affairs than on the publicity aspect. After the party returned to office in 1935,

Friends of the Liberal Party from all parts of Canada approached Ottawa to deal with different parts of the government, and the offices of the National Liberal Federation became a useful point of contact for the deserving petitioner – and also the end of the road for many of those who were not so deserving ... [A] great deal of time is spent each day in meeting a never-ending stream of people who come with the impression that if we do not hold the keys of the public treasury, we at least have a pass key; and we are in a position to deliver any kind of a post or contract. Most of our visitors from out of town, however, come for information about some departmental business, for a word of introduction to members of the Government, or for discussions of problems affecting party organization in their sections of the country.

For reasons already made clear, the linkage between these 'deserving petitioners' and 'friends' of the party on the one hand and the government departments on the other was by no means as firm as Lambert would have liked. Indeed, his discontent on this score was great enough to spur him to deliver a mild public rebuke to the cabinet at the 1938 advisory council meeting. 'Now with all due deference to the Government in power today,' he complained, 'I believe it can give us – the people who are trying to keep the machinery of organization intact – a little more co-operation than we have been getting during the past two years and half.'[38]

Mackenzie King's ground rules against toll-gating contractors had already been laid down in advance of the election at a meeting of the Toronto finance committee, as discussed in the previous chapter. Moreover, he reiterated this point and expanded upon it to his new cabinet. As Chubby Power was later to recall:

... one of the first things that Mr. King did at the time I was called to enter the Cabinet in 1935 was to say to us that whatever we thought might be our obligations to anyone these things were to be absolutely put aside. We were to judge policies and matters which came before the government irrespective of any feeling that we might have of obligations to anyone. Now he laid this down with great seriousness ... Let's say that that was the general policy. He was quite insistent on that. That is about the only thing he did say in the way of a preliminary speech. Quite insistent on that policy that he didn't think we should be influenced by anything that had gone before.[39]

In a sense, the ghost of Beauharnois continued to haunt King's fourth administration. There were more than a few occasions when men of some prominence within the party in various parts of the country discovered that the NLF was certainly not an automatic 'pass key' to the public treasury. One gentleman, who was president of the Toronto and District Liberal Association and a past national president of the Twentieth Century clubs, was turned down flat as a lobbyist for a cosmetics firm seeking to reverse an unfavourable tax ruling by Ilsley's Revenue Department, despite Lambert's plea for King's intercession, and was left to lament that after all his years of party work he was 'utterly bewildered' by his treatment. King himself did not want to be bothered with petty patronage and problems of government contracts; one night he threw out of his office a British Columbia MP and some west coast businessmen seeking a shipbuilding subsidy, while declaring himself to be 'irritated beyond words.'[40]

This still left a wide area for Lambert to operate in as a kind of 'fixer' or middleman between the party supporters and the government. There was first of all the matter of government business let without tender. Some of this, although on a strictly patronage basis, did not go through Lambert at all, but directly through the sitting member or defeated candidate to the department in question. The legal patronage lists, kept in the Department of Justice, of Liberal lawyers eligible for government work, were never touched by Lambert; these came strictly on the recommendation of MPs or candidates. In other areas where the national office had been the recipient of services donated in the campaign, Lambert would undertake to arrange the expected *quid pro quo*. Advertising was a prime example, but here ministerial prerogatives were often exercised with blithe disregard for Lambert's guidelines. Where the matter involved less important amounts of money, Lambert might make the arrangements with permanent civil servants rather than the ministers. One example of this concerned office equipment supplies. Certain stationery and office equipment suppliers had established long-term relationships with the party, demonstrated by small cash donations and the provision of cheap supplies or free loans of equipment at election time. To ensure that these friends of the party received their just reward after the Liberal victory, Lambert spoke to Watson Sellar, comptroller of the treasury, 'who agreed to cooperate on office machinery.'[41]

The available evidence would indicate that toll-gating was not normally practised where contracts were bid on tender. Lambert's importance in these cases was more after the fact than before. When a contract had been let, Lambert would approach the successful bidder and suggest, in effect, that they might demonstrate a suitable degree of gratefulness to the government which had made possible their good fortune. The suitable degree of gratitude usually ran somewhere between 1½ to 2½ per cent of the contract. The higher the contract, the higher the percentage would run.[42] While there is nothing in this practice which stands outside the letter of the law, neither is it without some doubtful aspects. For one thing there is Lambert's role as middleman to consider in so far as inside information helpful to bidders might be communicated to friendly firms. Secondly, one could usefully consider the possibility that all tenders might not be equitably arranged; while no direct evidence could be found of rigged bids, there are some hints here and there that all was not what it might appear to be on the surface. Finally, there would seem to be an implied threat involved in the 'levy' on contractors, that if they did not show the requisite degree of gratitude some unspecified difficulties might attend future efforts at gaining government business. All this is necessarily vague. What one might reasonably conclude is that the post-tender levy system appears to have been legitimate within the definition of the laws of the land, but that an inevitable ambiguity surrounds the process.

It was a common saying among politicians that manufacturers as a rule supported the Conservatives and contractors as a rule supported the Liberals.[43] Like most such conventional wisdom, this maxim was a bit of a simplification with a kernel of truth. Certainly Lambert spent much of his time in the late 1930s dealing with contractors, keeping them informed of prospects, getting in touch with ministers (mainly C.D. Howe whose transport portfolio included much business of interest to road, bridge, and harbour contractors), and calling on them after the awarding of contracts for the party's cut. Most of the firms with which Lambert dealt seemed to operate in Ontario and the Maritimes. Quebec was largely out of bounds; certainly Cardin's Public Works Department figures very little in Lambert's activities in these years, despite its obvious importance for contractors. Presumably that was the preserve of Cardin's Montreal machine and the local members in the various constituencies. When Chubby Power suggested that Cardin be named acting minister of transport after Howe was shifted to munitions and supply at the outset of the war, Lambert protested vociferously to King, who agreed that it would not be a wise choice. There seems to have been a serious problem which involved dredging contracts, Cardin's old bailiwick until 1930 which King had kept out of his hands in choosing his 1935 cabinet, because of suspicions concerning his connections to the Simards. Lambert, who had been involved in acting on behalf of an Ontario dredging company since 1934, was incensed when Howe apparently teamed up with Cardin and Simard and did not give a promised $1 million per year contract at Sorel to this company. Lambert referred to this as a breach of faith, but there was little he could do but complain.[44]

Despite the difficulties attendant upon the role of agent in a situation he could influence erratically but never control, Lambert did eventually manage to put the party's financial status on an improved footing by his activities with contractors. Perhaps he came closest to the exact description of his role when he told one interested party that 'he could not use my name in approaching people, but he was free to come to me as a Parliamentary agent and ask me to help get business for his clients.'[45] If contractors and other businessmen were willing to pay for these services – reasonably enough, *after* satisfaction had been obtained – the point was that the profit would go to the Liberal party and not into Lambert's own pockets as was the case with the more usual type of lobbyist. The result was that the Liberals by the time of the 1940 election actually had a solid national campaign fund; in fact, considerably more than their opponents. The businesslike basis upon which Lambert put the process of fund-raising, with the contract levy as the core, was largely responsible for this success. There is certainly ample evidence of the systematic nature of the levy system, such as the preparation of detailed lists of government contracts which were used in fund-raising drives.[46] The Lambert diaries are filled with information about donations extracted from bridge, road, and dock contractors throughout the late 1930s. Sometimes the amounts involved could be substantial: one post office building in Toronto apparently netted the party $50,000.[47]

The politics of roads, bridges, docks, and post offices were 'old hat,' as much a part of Laurier's era as of the age of depression and world war. There was a growing amount of public business that involved much more extensive amounts of money and hence much more scope for the Government party to gain access to sources of funding. C.D. Howe was at the centre of these developments, first as minister of transport with jurisdiction over land, sea, and air communication, and then as minister of munitions and supply with command over the military-industrial complex involved in a modern total war. One of the primary areas of heavy industry contracts was in the supply of railway cars to the publicly owned CNR. Lambert used his good offices to arrange the meeting of various producers with Howe. Satisfactory arrangements had been concluded with National Steel Car, Canada Car, and Eastern Car in 1937-8, when R.B. Bennett made a speech in the House of Commons charging the Liberals with toll-gating CNR contractors. Lambert had in fact only done his collections after the contracts, in line with his usual practice, but it appeared that the problem lay with Montreal Liberal MPs who had been doing their own levying on CNR suppliers, apparently with fewer scruples than Lambert, to the point where some suppliers had written letters of complaint to the leader of the opposition. This problem having been smoothed over, Lambert put the CNR railway car business on a fairly regularized basis by 1939 when he was able to tell a supplier that they 'would deal with me direct on car orders.' Lambert got full co-operation from Howe.[48] Some good friends of the Liberal party were involved in this, particularly Victor Drury of Canada Car, who contributed to the Liberal campaign fund. Another lucrative area for the party in supply to the CNR was in steel items, such as couplers, rails, and steel frames. Two firms which featured prominently here were Dofasco in Hamilton, whose president, Frank Sherman, was such a good friend of the party that he not only gave money but helped collect it in Hamilton as well, and Dosco in Nova Scotia, which Lambert's financial collector in that province believed good for $50,000 to $60,000 per year.[49]

Defence spending was another profitable area, and one which presented itself to Lambert with increasing frequency as the shadows of war lengthened in Europe and Canada turned to the necessity of bolstering her impoverished defence forces. The one major scandal which afflicted the Liberal government from 1935 to the outbreak of war revolved around defence spending. The Bren gun affair, which was serious enough to call for an official inquiry, also involved another side which never became public. On 18 March 1938 Lambert entered the following in his diary: 'Saw Hugh Plaxton who said contract for Inglis & Co. had gone through; it represented

5,000 British + 7,000 Can. Bren guns = $5,000,000. That 100th. shd. come to Lib. funds by 1940; or earlier – that an advance of 25th on that wd. be available in 6 mos. from now & then balance in 4 monthly periods.' Plaxton was a Liberal MP who was involved in the scandal through accepting expenses from the Inglis Company on a trip to England to help gain the contract for the company. Lambert began to note that there were suspicious aspects to the contract as early as May 1938, before George Drew had aired his charges which led to the inquiry. He called Plaxton to his office and stated that 'any transaction relating to political funds was out of the question.' It is not clear whether this meant that no Inglis money went to the party, although it should be noted that Lambert was strenuous in his efforts to ensure that no reference was made to political contributions in the terms for the commission which investigated the affair;[50] thus no indications of such contributions came out in the inquiry. In any event, there were many other defence contracts involving shells, aircraft engines, and other such material, upon which the party was able to quietly extract its regular levies.[51] King was at first worried by the Bren gun affair, descrying in it the dreaded potential for another Beauharnois.[52] But it was not another Beauharnois in so far as party funds were concerned, and Lambert's system was not challenged by this affair.

Another area of Howe's jurisdiction in the transport portfolio which aroused much interest on the part of Lambert and the 'friends' of the party in the late 1930s was air transport. This new and highly important form of transportation was just beginning to come into its own, both technologically and commercially, in the late 1930s.[53] Various interests were involved in efforts to carve out as large a share of this emergent market as they could. Since the entire business was under government regulation and would obviously be dominated by the actions of government, Howe and Lambert became focal points for the attention of such concerns as James Richardson's Canadian Airways, which represented a merger of both Winnipeg and eastern Canadian interests, including the CPR, whose president, Sir Edward Beatty, was a vice-president of Canadian Airways. The problem was given even greater urgency in the first few years of the King government after a series of meetings with the United Kingdom, Ireland, and Newfoundland resulted in an agreement for transatlantic air service, an agreement which in 1936 was extended to include the United States as well. The question of who would receive the plum of getting the carrier contract on this route excited much interest. At first Lambert believed that he had Howe's agreement to co-operate with the Richardson group. Richardson was a party supporter of some stature, and Lambert was more than pleased to press his case. Then, in late 1936, 'without explanation' in Lambert's words, Howe changed his attitude of friendliness to Richardson to one of violent opposition. This about-face was counted by Lambert as one of Howe's 'breaches of faith.' Howe's none too discreet criticism of Richardson and of the alleged impossibility of working with him forced Lambert to communicate to the prime minister the 'injurious political implications.'[54]

In 1937 the government passed legislation establishing Trans-Canada Airlines as a Crown corporation. In one sense this meant that no private interest triumphed to the extent of gaining a monopoly. On the other hand, private carriers were not eliminated, with the eventual extension of the CPR into the air lanes. Moreover, there was still the question of aircraft production to supply TCA; here, reports kept filtering in to Lambert about contracts without tender and 'corruption' in the air service.[55] In any event Lambert could only speculate, since his support of Richardson seemed to have shut him out of the business from the point at which Howe had turned against the Winnipeg financier.

Lambert's job did not end with the linking of government contracts to campaign contributions, however important that might be. Many 'friends' of the party were not, in the nature of their business, particularly interested in gaining government contracts. Many were much more interested in government *policy*, especially as it affected their operations or the general 'climate' of business in the country. Here Lambert's job was either to put the party supporters in touch with a relevant cabinet minister or to pass on the message himself. In other words, if party financial donors were seeking to purchase access to the party leadership, Lambert could be the conduit, either direct or indirect, for the message which they wished to impart. Given that most contributors were businessmen, the policy area of most concern was usually taxation, tariffs, or some aspect of government regulation of the private sector. Two typical examples from Lambert's diary of this type of relationship follow:

Called on Mr. Burton [Simpson's] who promised 2500 in April. He also talked about onus of taxation & hoped to see budgets ease sales tax & excise as well as cut tariffs on textiles...

...collected 1th. from Lesueur [Imperial Oil] who complained about income tax & asked me to speak to J.G[ardiner].[56]

To the extent that contact was thus maintained between the cabinet and the financial contributors through the national organizer, the party in office could maintain the necessary distance from its contributors while maintaining the necessary connection at the same time. But once again it is very difficult to sustain such generalizations in the face of the *ad hoc* nature of the arrangements in a federal cabinet. Lambert's relationship with some ministers was either so remote or so strained that he could not always act out such a role. On the other hand, some ministers had their own direct contacts with certain financial supporters and had little need for a middleman like Lambert either to raise financial support or to bring the concerns of the supporters to their attention. That Lambert did play this role is clear; to what extent others bypassed him to make more direct contact could only be determined by a knowledge of the actions of others at least as comprehensive as the knowledge we can gain of Lambert from the evidence he left behind. Since such detailed information is not available we can only speculate about the overall importance of Lambert's activities in relationship to the operations of the party and the government as a whole. No doubt he was less important than some of the 'friends' of the party hoped he was; yet he may well have been a little more important than the prime minister appeared to believe.

One relationship which can be traced out with some exactitude is that with J.S. McLean of Canada Packers. McLean, it will be recalled, had not only contributed money to the 1935 campaign but had taken collections from certain key companies personally in hand. McLean was thus more than an average 'friend' of the party: he was virtually a member of the party organization. He maintained a close connection with Lambert following the election and the latter immediately set to work to arrange little matters such as getting Canada Packers onto the suppliers' lists in military camps. By February of 1936 the company expressed itself 'satisfied with treatment now being received' and two days later Lambert received a donation of $2000 in gratitude.[57]

As McLean soon learned, however, even so cosy a relationship as this could founder when matters moved onto a higher plane of politics than simple patronage. In 1936 a report made privately to the Department of Trade and Commerce concerning Canada Packers and Swifts meat packing houses in Winnipeg raised certain charges and led to an investigation. Charles Dunning, minister of finance, told McLean the nature of some of the charges made in the report; McLean was enraged at what he believed to be unfounded accusations and felt that it was his right, 'as a matter of fairness, not as a matter of favor,' that he be allowed to see the report. Lambert was unable to get a copy for him, as was Howe, since it was considered a confidential internal document of the government. At this point McLean

decided to come down heavily on Lambert who went to see him in Toronto:

Saw J.S. McL. about the private report. He demands it on his rights, & not as a favor; but at same time stated that I was under obligation to get it for him because he
contributed to the election campaign. I pointed out that he had helped me in the
election
(1) because V.M[assey] asked him to.
(2) because he wanted to see [H.H.] Stevens crushed.
(3) That I agreed with his feeling of resentment vs. the private report; but that I was
not responsible for it at all & he shd. not mix up his arguments on it.

Lambert did undertake to arrange an appointment for McLean with the
prime minister. When this proved impossible, Lambert agreed to state
McLean's case to King, which he did formally in a letter. Lambert also carried the case to the trade and commerce minister, W.D. Euler, who recognized that Lambert's 'nose was out of joint' on this matter, but promised
little.[58]

It is not clear who gave the authorizations but McLean was eventually
allowed to see the report. When he did, he felt even more angry at King,
who apparently had not responded to his request. McLean felt that the
prime minister had not insisted upon 'fair play' in this matter, and his resentment carried over into the following year when he informed Lambert
that 'he would not contribute further except on his own terms.' These terms
included the removal of the offending report from the files of the Trade and
Commerce Department. Lambert advised him to take this demand to Euler,
which McLean agreed to do, and the latter said he would 'go to King if
necessary' as well. It seems either that McLean's terms must have been met
or that he found new reasons to actively support the Liberal cause, for by
1940 he was once more offering to collect funds from the retail chains, meat
packers, and banks, and would put himself down for a $25,000 donation.[59]
Thus it appears, in the long run, that a supporter of the weight of J.S.
McLean could have some influence, as a matter of 'fairness' rather than
'favor.' But even here the result was not automatic, by any means.

Another sort of deal with which Lambert would sometimes get involved
concerned the willingness of certain individuals to purchase senatorships or
lieutenant-governorships. Kirk Cameron, an elderly Montreal businessman
and regular party contributor, was willing to pay $20,000 for a Senate seat,
which he never did receive. Another deal involving the payment of $25,000
for a Senate appointment failed to come to fruition. On the other hand,

Lambert did successfully arrange the appointment of W.G. Clark, New Brunswick merchant and Liberal MP for York-Sunbury, as lieutenant-governor of his province. Protracted negotiations involving Lambert's collector in New Brunswick, financier and industrialist Neil McLean (later a senator himself), resulted in the closing of a deal involving $30,000 on 20 January 1940. Exactly two months later, Clark became the new lieutenant-governor of New Brunswick. Moreover, it seems clear that Albert Matthews, Bay Street collector for the party, who had expressed his desire for the vice-regal position in Ontario, must have contributed sufficiently to receive the appointment in 1938. Yet on other occasions Lambert made it plain that he would not undertake such cases, as with one applicant who offered $25,000 for a Senate appointment only to be told by Lambert that he 'hadn't a chance for a million.'[60] While it was certainly true that those who received major appointments were expected to pay for them in one way or another, whether by past contributions, cash on the barrel, or by future considerations, it is also apparent that Lambert was no Maundy Gregory selling peerages on commission as in the days of Lloyd George. The point is that the collective prerogative of the cabinet in these matters – and in the case of lieutenant-governorships the advice of the provincial party as well – generally superseded the ability of an extra-parliamentary figure like Lambert to build up a system in gaining dollars for appointments on a regular basis, despite the fact that the money was obviously there for the taking. The extra-parliamentary organization simply could not deliver on its promises with the regularity requisite for such a process to operate.

PARTY FINANCE: THE NLF

If Lambert faced considerable difficulties in getting a systematic fund-raising system in use in co-operation with the government departments and the cabinet, he faced further difficulties with regard to the disposition of what funds were collected. Lambert was fully responsible for the provision of money for the NLF office and its activities, but he was also deeply involved in more general campaign fund collections as well. This obviously entailed some important decisions on Lambert's part concerning which monies were to go where.

The NLF office was itself an important source of expenditure: Table 3.1 shows receipts and expenditures for the first three years following the return to office. By the late 1930s NLF expenses were running at about the same level as they had been in 1934 (compare Table 2.1), but instead of falling back on chronic bank overdrafts receipts now covered what were, after all,

Table 3.1
Finances of the National Liberal Federation, 1936-8

	Receipts	Expenditures	Balance
1936	$ 33,828.90	$ 31,737.76	$2091.14
1937	27,414.61	28,000.79	−586.18
1938	30,504.78	28,954.41	1550.37
Outside activities	58,100.00	58,100.00	
Total	149,848.29	146,792.96	3055.33

Source: WLMK, v. 252, "National Liberal Federation, December 1, 1935 to November 30, 1938" (215200)

very modest expenditures indeed. Even if Lambert's entry into the Senate early in 1938 could free some funds to pay the salary of a French-speaking secretary for publicity in that language, a budget of a little over $2000 per month for a national office of the party in power was not very formidable, when one considers that the amount had to cover everything from salaries to rent and telephone bills. The situation was stable enough by the end of 1938 that Lambert could inform the prime minister he held all the requirements for the ensuing year in trust. But he went on to point out that with reference to the nearly $150,000 he had collected in the previous three years:

Practically all of this financing I have done alone; and I mention this fact only because it represents a weakness in the organization of the Party at the present time. As President of the National Federation, I feel responsible for providing necessary finances to maintain the work of the National office here; but I have never at any time assumed responsibility for financing the Party's entire federal organization throughout Canada. Not only is it personally distasteful to have circumstances gradually resolving one into that impossible position, but it is against all the decent instincts of the Liberal Party to have that kind of a situation develop.[61]

Protest as he might, Lambert was drawn deeper and deeper into becoming the national campaign fund-raiser. His struggle to develop stronger provincial finance committees to take this 'impossible' burden from his shoulders was thus a major organizational concern in this period.

Lambert of course knew that the real centres of major campaign funding were Montreal and Toronto, and that the organization of those cities for financial purposes had to be the primary thrust of his efforts. But he did not stop here. Believing as he did that the Liberal party should be as decentralized and provincially autonomous an organization as possible, he also felt strongly that the various regions ought to pay their own way as much as financially feasible. Although there was a specific reason for emphasis on regional financial autonomy in the form of the challenge to the federal party mounted in Toronto in this period by the Hepburn provincial machine and its control over financial resources in that city, Lambert nevertheless was a sincere believer in the idea of a decentralized party and in making the constituent parts of the organization fiscally responsible. To this end, he successfully pressed in 1937 for an unusual degree of co-operation between his office and the cabinet in selecting provincial finance chairmen with the advice and approval of the regional ministers. Chairmen were named in each of the provinces, as well as for each of the two districts in Quebec; Ontario, however, remained a special case because of federal-provincial conflicts. Two years later Lambert was able to report to the prime minister on the eve of a possible federal election that 'in all of these provinces, with the exception of Ontario, I know collections have been made systematically, and I have no doubt that the Ministers in charge of the different Provincial areas have been co-operating fully in each case and know what has been done.'[62] Events were to show that this autonomy was not consistent across the country, and in a national election some regions could not be expected to bear all their costs themselves. But Lambert's initiative in this matter was an important one for the party; there can be no doubt at all that the degree of financial decentralization which was achieved was a significant step in the development of a more systematic financial basis for party organization.

Montreal demanded a good deal of special attention, particularly after the defeat of the Taschereau provincial government in 1936 led to increasing internal strains within the Quebec Liberal organizations. This will be discussed at greater length later in Chapter 7, but for now we might usefully focus on Lambert's role in reconstituting the Montreal finance committee and the Montreal district organization along lines more responsible to national co-operation than had previously been the case.

Quebec had been a problem for the NLF from its very beginnings, and the Montreal financial apparatus had been no more co-operative with the national organization than the Montreal and Quebec district organizers. Following the election victory in 1935, Lambert found that he was no more able than before the election to gain the financial support of Montreal for the operations of the NLF office. Donat Raymond informed the national organizer that he would be 'pleased to help at any time in making necessary contacts, but wd. not be responsible for any monthly help' – although it was precisely that kind of continuous support that Lambert was seeking in order to maintain a national office between elections. Even when he promised to deliver funds to Lambert, Raymond would often fail to live up to these promises. In one case his failure to provide $1000 to the national office apparently left him sufficiently embarrassed that he asked Lambert not to tell Frank O'Connor that he had failed. This Lambert flatly refused to do, and went on to lecture Raymond: '[I] said further that if our office was to do favors for Montreal we had to have support.' Lambert was particularly annoyed at the failure of Montreal to provide the necessary funds to pay the salary of a French secretary and the costs of producing and distributing a French-language version of the *Liberal Monthly*. He could see little reason why the largest metropolis could not pay for service in the French language from the national office, and was certainly not willing to see Toronto subsidize this sort of enterprise which could only be for the benefit of Quebec Liberals. Raymond for his part wished to shift the blame onto the shoulders of the Quebec ministers, or so he tried to do for Mackenzie King's benefit.[63] Some hints that the Simards would be willing to make regular donations never materialized. Raymond did provide some funds, although nothing like what was expected.

Lambert did have one man in Montreal who was more co-operative. Gordon Scott, an English-speaking businessman, worked closely with the national organizer, who was in fact a personal friend, in raising money on a more enthusiastic basis than Raymond. Lambert was sufficiently pleased with Scott's efforts that he made an unusual, and vain, attempt to gain recognition for his collector from the government in the form of a Senate appointment. Scott, Lambert told King, had 'rendered more valuable assistance to me and the national organization during the past two years than anyone else in Montreal.'[64] Lambert's plea went unheeded, reflecting his lack of influence with the prime minister and with the Quebec ministers, whose advice King needed in making Quebec appointments, thus affording one more example of how difficult it was for Lambert to build up the kind of organization he wanted and needed to do the job he had been assigned.

Two events conspired to strengthen Lambert's hand in Montreal in the late 1930s. The first was the defeat of the Taschereau government in 1936 which greatly weakened the independent provincial autonomy of the Quebec Liberals. The second event, which may have been in some degree related to the first, was a fresh outbreak of antagonism between Raymond and P.-J.-A. Cardin. Raymond had gone to King and denounced Cardin as 'belonging to a dangerous ring'; King had then related this to Cardin. Cardin then told the prime minister that he was willing to let Lambert take charge of Montreal finances, in order to get rid of Raymond.[65] King, and Lambert as well, recognized that it was necessary to have a local man established in that city, rather than to have an outsider like Lambert attempt to collect, but the dispute did offer the national party the opportunity to gain greater co-operation under new arrangements. Ernest Lapointe, who was the minister in overall charge of affairs in Quebec, seemed reconciled to giving Cardin clear command of Montreal district; Raymond had been angling for an appointment for his brother Maxime as minister to Paris, a plum which King was quite unready to provide.[66] Thus the decision was inevitable that Cardin should take charge of Montreal, and the prime minister gave his imprimatur to an arrangement whereby Cardin would be the chief organizer and Elie Beauregard, a lawyer with extensive connections in Montreal finance capital and industry, would take charge of financial collections, with the help of Scott. Some greater, although vaguely specified, degree of co-operation with Lambert would be involved. For his part, Lambert told King that he was 'willing to work with Cardin, but strictly on same basis as with other prov'ces & C[ardin] must be responsible for the man who would collect in Mtl. The P.M. agreed that my attitude towards collecting funds in Mtl. was sound.' Raymond, who was if nothing else tenacious, still held out for some part in this new arrangement, and eventually it was agreed that he could help, but only in co-operation with Lambert. Beauregard also suggested Aimé Geoffrion, a very prominent Liberal financier and corporation lawyer, and one other man to form a finance committee. This committee would, in Beauregard's words, 'do what they could to follow up information' received from Lambert, that is, to make appropriate levies on government contractors. In exchange for this new spirit of co-operation, Lambert arranged to open a special Montreal bank account and to give Beauregard power to make withdrawals or deposits at any time. Raymond handed over the crucial lists of contributors to Beauregard. Lambert then further arranged that Scott would handle funds for 'national business,' which would be kept separate from Beauregard's collections which were for Quebec and the Maritimes campaign chests.[67]

These complicated arrangements thus appeared to have culminated in a favourable resolution from the point of view of the national party organization, but Quebec was not that easily mastered by Ottawa. The following year Lambert and Scott were commiserating with one another about the lack of co-operation evidenced by Beauregard and his organization.[68] To some degree it was always a case of 'plus ça change, plus c'est la même chose,' but perhaps not quite. With the provincial Liberals out of the patronage trough, Montreal could not manage the same degree of autonomy as it had in the fat years of the Taschereau administration. Since the return of the Liberals to office in 1939 was effected with the massive intervention of the national party, both organizationally and financially (including some of Lambert's own national funds), even that event did not fundamentally change the new balance of power.

Toronto in the days of Hepburn's all-out war on the federal Liberals represented, if anything, a more serious problem than Montreal. In fact, the situation became so serious that Lambert had to start all over from scratch to reconstitute a financial apparatus in that city. Frank O'Connor withdrew from collecting as did one other member of the 1935 finance committee. Then E.G. Long, the most important figure from Lambert's perspective, died in 1938. The Toronto situation was in a shambles at the same time as Hepburn was doing his best to drive all possible support away from the federal party – his most crude and direct threat being that any contractor giving to the federal party would get no further provincial business.[69] Under such circumstances, Lambert found it 'almost impossible to get anybody' to replace Long. Since the Ontario Liberal MPs were 'wholly devoid of any suggestions,' Lambert had to intervene directly to build a new political as well as financial organization. A federal Liberal office was set up in Toronto without any connection to Hepburn's Ontario Liberal Association, but Lambert had to finance it from national funds. In order to put the city back on a self-sufficient financial basis, Lambert called a dinner meeting of younger Liberal businessmen, not attached to the Hepburn machine, and arranged for two new men, Peter Campbell and C.P. Fell, as joint treasurers. Lambert was hopeful of the prospects, although as Norman McLarty cautioned Mackenzie King, by the summer of 1939, the dollars of Bay Street were still '*in future* rather than *in esse.*' In any event, Lambert as a provincial autonomist was not pleased with 'this sort of arbitrary set-up' which left 'much to be desired in so far as Liberal interests in Ontario are concerned.'[70] Since Lambert saw his job in terms of securing the active co-operation of self-sufficient provincial units toward national purposes, Toronto represented one of the worst failures of Liberal organization in the

King government of the late 1930s. Certainly Toronto was the weak link in the generally strong financial organization which Lambert had helped put into operation across the country in preparation for the next election. Lambert and his national office could not be blamed for this result, which was rather the result of circumstances and the malevolent hand of Mitch Hepburn; indeed, Lambert's intervention, distasteful though it might be to him, was the one factor which saved the day for the national Liberal party. Less money was raised in Toronto in 1940 than had been raised in that city in the previous campaign, but it proved to be sufficient. Before Lambert's 'arbitrary' intervention even that possibility had seemed unlikely.

ELECTION ORGANIZATION

In the summer of 1939, with the shadows of war lengthening across Europe, Mackenzie King canvassed his ministers on the state of the organizational and financial readiness of the party in their regions in the event of a general election. As the prime minister put it, the NLF was supposed to be responsible for such information, but the national office was in a 'position to effect but little without the co-operation of the ministers.' It was important, he went on, that the NLF and the cabinet should 'know to what extent each may rely upon the other, as respects all matters pertaining to a campaign.'[71] In this, King was responding to some gentle but insistent prodding from Lambert whose complaints about lack of co-operation from the cabinet had become habitual, as well as reasonable.

The responses to King's inquiry were highly encouraging. The consensus among the ministers was that an immediate election would be highly successful from a Liberal standpoint; there was general support for an early dissolution of Parliament. The Maritimes and the Prairies both reported a satisfactory situation in their regions. Even in Ontario there was general confidence that an appeal to the voters would reveal strong public support for the King Liberals against the combined efforts of the Tories and the Hepburn machine, an opinion with which King himself was in full agreement. Only Quebec seemed to be doubtful, but here the real problem was not so much the standing of the party with the voters but the usual difficulties of sorting out responsibility among the various factions claiming control over campaign organization.[72]

The picture was also very encouraging from a financial perspective, a situation which was in itself a tribute to Lambert's effectiveness over the previous four years – although King characteristically gave no particular recognition for this achievement. As Lambert told the prime minister:

I can guarantee sufficient funds to meet the national expenses of a campaign if it comes this year. Those expenses would represent national advertising by newspaper and bill board; campaign literature ... cost of national speaking tours of the leaders of the party who would be subject to arrangements made by a national speakers' bureau attached to headquarters here; and the cost of greatly expanded office equipment at headquarters.

Local constituency requirements financially, cannot be met from National Headquarters. These expenditures must be provided for within the local constituency itself, or from the headquarters of each Provincial organization.

C.D. Howe, who along with Lambert was most responsible for the affluent state of the national party finances, referred to the NLF fund as 'substantial.' Since campaign contributions usually came in a rush at the time of the election itself, this situation seemed to indicate to Howe that the Liberals were in a 'vaster [sic] better' position than the other parties, especially the Tories who had fallen on hard times since the departure of R.B. Bennett and his Eddy match fortune. Even in Ontario, Howe was very hopeful that Lambert's young finance committee would prove itself in action.[73]

The only weak points outside of Ontario in a financial sense were Saskatchewan and Alberta. Saskatchewan was politically sound, and the Liberal machine was organizationally capable of delivering the votes on call. The problem was that it was an extremely expensive machine to maintain – $6000 per month to be exact – and Jimmy Gardiner did not believe for one moment in Lambert's concept of financial self-sufficiency as a rule for provincial units. As Gardiner insouciantly informed King, at least one-third of the election campaign budget in that province 'will have to be provided by the central office, or in other words by Senator Lambert.' Alberta was politically, organizationally, and financially feeble. J.A. MacKinnon, the Alberta Liberal whom King had finally placed in the cabinet, without portfolio, after the province had gone unrepresented for more than three years, reported that he might be able to raise sufficient money to pay for the contest in his own seat, but almost all the rest of the campaign funds would have to come from outside the province. Alberta's inability to finance itself had, according to MacKinnon, deeper roots than Liberal unpopularity and the effects of the Depression. As he stated simply, 'what little work has been done in Alberta federally has been largely done by outside contractors.'[74]

The situation in Europe becoming more and more menacing, King decided early in August against an immediate election, although he noted that the cabinet members 'were pretty generally disappointed' at the decision. King's instincts proved sound in light of the coming of war less than a month after the decision was made. In any event, he had the assurance of a generally satisfactory campaign organization ready to go into action whenever the call came. Since the prime minister was resolute against any sort of 'national government' coalition along the lines of the previous war, this assurance was a matter of some comfort. Once again, in the second month of the war, King returned to Lambert to ask that campaign literature be prepared for a possible campaign, and Lambert was again able to assure his party leader that there were sufficient funds held in a trust account to meet the expenses of a national publicity campaign.[75]

The moment for an election arrived on 18 January 1940 when Hepburn joined with the provincial Conservative leader George Drew to pass a resolution through the Ontario legislature condemning the federal Liberal government's prosecution of the war effort. King instinctively understood that with this act Hepburn had sealed his own fate and offered a golden opportunity to the federal party, just as he had quickly grasped that Maurice Duplessis had destroyed his Union Nationale government when he had called the snap provincial election in opposition to the federal government a few months earlier. 'Hepburn's action,' he wrote in his diary, 'has given to me and my colleagues and to the party here just what is needed to place beyond question the wisdom of an immediate election and the assurance of victory for the Government.' According to Bruce Hutchison, Lambert, vacationing in Virginia, read the news in a brief newspaper dispatch, remarked to his companion, "There's your election," and hurried to Ottawa.' King, in a rare show of confidence in his organizer, actually told Lambert, two days before the cabinet was informed, of his now famous manœuvre of calling for an immediate dissolution of Parliament in this speech from the throne at the beginning of the new session.[76]

As a link between the cabinet and the national office for the campaign, King chose Chubby Power. Lambert, already fed up with the entire business, offered to turn over the campaign completely to Power, but King wished to have the Quebec minister as the cabinet man in overall charge rather than responsible for the detailed work of the election. In fact, King had had Power in mind for this responsibility since June of the previous year when he had overridden Power's desire for an appointment to the Senate or the Tariff Commission with the promise of important duties in the coming campaign and an unspecified reward later.[77] As J.L. Granatstein comments: 'Power drank too much, and there were periods when he was completely incapable of carrying on the work of his portfolio. But when he was sober he was one of the best of ministers, and in addition he was one of the very few members of the Cabinet with an interest in and talent for party organization and the mechanics of electioneering. "What we could do without Power when it comes to matters of this kind," King noted, "I really do not know." '[78] Indeed, although King made it known to his errant minister that 'you have given me a great deal of anxiety, as doubtless you have given yourself,' he was loud in his praises of Power to other ministers such as Ernest Lapointe.[79]

Lambert told Power that 'each province wd. stand on its own feet financially, & I would look after national headquarters expenses for publicity etc.'[80] In a memorandum on the election campaign organization prepared at the beginning of February, Lambert was more explicit yet on his decentralization strategy:

The campaign will be fought by the Liberal Party as a federation of operating units.
Each Provincial Liberal Association will be primarily responsible for the conduct of the campaign in its own province. The National Liberal Federation, with its Women's and Young Liberal affiliates, will serve as a clearing-house and service station, to aid and inspire and advise the provincial units.
Thus, in every province there will be in effect two parallel, but not conflicting processes going on ...
From the standpoint of the National Liberal Federation's campaign, the Province of Quebec will be treated as a separate self-contained unit although there will be continuous and eager co-operation between Ottawa and Montreal in connection with such matters as advertising and literature and speakers.[81]

Radio and other media publicity were to be used extensively, since there was a war to be watched over in Ottawa by the cabinet and, more cynically, because King knew that the opposition parties lacked the funds which the government party could expend on media advertising.[82] A series of radio broadcasts by the prime minister and some of his more saleable colleagues was produced during the month of February, before King ventured forth on tour. As usual, a billboard and leaflet campaign was conducted in conjunction with the party's advertising agency – Cockfield, Brown – as was a newspaper campaign in dailies, weeklies, farm papers, and the ethnic press, particularly the Jewish press now that Canada had at last gone to war against fascism. Special concentration was given to the *Toronto Star Weekly* with its massive 400,000 circulation and its strong Liberal loyalties which led it to orchestrate Liberal publicity in its news columns as much as in its advertising. All in all, the campaign, in Lambert's words, was planned to bear the 'underlying basis of dignity and calmness suited to the primary fact that the whole nation is seriously engaged in the grim business of war.'[83] That theme seemed effective enough, and the opposition was sufficiently weak and confused to ensure a massive Liberal sweep – in fact a victory of such proportions as to actually yield a majority in the popular vote, which no single party had been able to accomplish since the election of 1911.

There can be no doubt that Norman Lambert had done a most creditable job in the five years in which the Liberal party had enjoyed office. To be sure, the Mackenzie King Liberals were a highly marketable commodity in 1940, just as the Manion Conservatives were non-starters. But if the job of a national organizer was simply to maintain the constituent units of the party in working order and to co-ordinate their efforts when the call came to organize the campaign on behalf of a record and programme which had been produced by the parliamentary party, then Lambert can only be judged a success. Only in Ontario had there been significant internal party disorders; King lamented in his diary in the last week of the campaign about the 'lack of organization ... in Ontario. I am afraid it is going to cost us seats.'[84] Yet even King placed the entire blame on Hepburn, and despite his fears about the 'completely new organization' which had had to be set up 'by inexperienced men,' the Liberals increased their popular vote in that province by more than 7 per cent over 1935 to reach an absolute majority, and improved their seat standing by one over the earlier election as well. In the heartland of Tory conscriptionist sentiment, the Conservative party failed to improve their electoral standing over their low point of five years earlier, and their new found ally, the Liberal premier of Ontario, suffered a blow from which he was never to recover. Thus Lambert's direct intervention in the organization of the largest province proved quite successful. However much one would wish to credit circumstances and the record of the King government, Lambert's efforts had obviously resulted in an organizational base commensurate with the general popularity of the party. In the rest of the country the picture had been even clearer. For once the exercise of office had not resulted in an atrophy of organization. After five years of power the party machinery had come back even stronger than before.

Yet the prime minister, whose 'slurs on the National Liberal Federation and its organizational efforts were habitual and almost always unfair,' to quote Granatstein,[85] was uninterested in giving Lambert any thanks for his contribution. On election night King 'took full credit for the results' on national radio and failed to even call the NLF office. A disgusted Lambert told Chubby Power that a previous statement to King that he wished this election to be his last would be reiterated to the prime minister as quickly as possible. When Power told King about Lambert's feelings, the prime minister protested to his organizer that he had been 'so busy phoning members & Ministers & preparing his radio speech that he didn't have time,' and rather lamely invited Lambert to lunch with him in a few days. In his own diary King expressed his irritation at the 'unreasonableness' of Lambert's attitude: 'After all, it was their place to ring me up and congratulate me. It was scarcely mine, as Prime Minister, to be the first to congratulate them though, naturally, they were in my thoughts for a word of very sincere thanks.' Apropos of this exchange, Granatstein justly remarks that 'if Mackenzie King was unloved by his subordinates, he had only himself to blame.'[86] One might add that Liberal party organization had decidedly improved in the decade since the defeat of 1930; the party leader's attitude toward the organization and the organizers had not changed.

CAMPAIGN FINANCE 1940

It is unfortunately impossible to reconstruct as comprehensive a picture of overall finances for the 1940 election as was possible for the previous campaign. It was well understood at the time that not only had Lambert been able to build up an adequate reserve to pay for the national campaign long before it began, but that more than sufficient funds flowed in during the campaign itself to pay for the expenses of the provincial finance committees as well. Of course, there is never 'enough' money to please some people in any campaign; the point is that what the Liberals collected was more than adequate for the task of piling up a massive majority over the hapless Manion Conservatives, who were in a desperate plight, being frozen out by almost all their traditional big business donors such as the CPR, the Bank of Montreal, and J.W. McConnell of the Montreal Star. In all, Granatstein estimates that the Tories were able to spend only about $500,000 at most on a national basis, and ended in debt.[87] Certainly the CCF with its miniscule national budget financed by one dollar annual memberships presented no comparison to Liberal finances.[88]

There is a complete picture of the amounts raised by the Toronto finance committee during the campaign. Lambert's fledgling collectors, Peter

Campbell and Percy Fell, ably assisted by J.S. McLean whose differences with the party leadership appear to have abated by this time, were able to collect $451,391 in a little over two months. While that total is less than the amount collected in 1935 in the same city, three factors should be noted: first, Lambert had, by means already described, put funding on a more regularized basis which meant that many contractors had already been 'taxed' on their government business before the campaign; second, what was done in Toronto was done not only with new collectors but against the active opposition of the provincial Liberal government and the provincial Liberal machine; third, other amounts were collected for other purposes – Gardiner drew funds directly to Saskatchewan and Lambert collected at least $25,000 separately for eastern Ontario.

In any event, the amount was more than adequate. Ten days before the vote Lambert met with his finance committee and came to the happy conclusion that 'after raising the candidates to a higher level all around' there would be $50,000 still left over.[89] Table 3.2 shows the distribution of donations by size, and Table 3.3 indicates the distribution of donations by major economic activity of the donors. Two interesting contrasts become apparent when these tables are compared to the similar tables compiled for the 1935 election (Tables 2.4 and 2.5). First of all, there is a noticeable concentration of contributions in the second election. Not only were there fewer donors in 1940 but there were also fewer small donors. In 1935 donations of over $10,000 accounted for 40 per cent of the total collected in Toronto; by 1940 contributions of $10,000 or more made up 60 per cent of the total. Second, there was a change in the composition of contributors, particularly a shift toward construction contractors as the largest single identifiable group of party supporters. The importance of this group more than doubled in relative importance from the previous election. On the other hand, the largest group in 1935, brewers and distillers, almost disappeared in 1940. The rise of construction contractors has already been explained; the fall of the liquor interests is not, to my knowledge, explicable, unless they were being warned off by the provincial Liberals, an explanation for which there is no documentary evidence available.

Mining retained an important share of party support, although it was down a bit from before. Despite Hepburn's single-minded advocacy of the cause of the northern Ontario mining entrepreneurs, they had not abandoned the federal field altogether. They could not, in truth, afford to do so, since the federal government maintained a sufficient presence in the provi-

Table 3.2
Contributions to Toronto Liberal finance committee, 1940, by size of
donation

	Number of donors	Percentage of total collected
$20,000 and over	7	38.7
$10,000 to $19,999	9	21.3
$5000 to $9999	18	23.3
$1000 to $4999	33	13.2
$100 to $999	48	3.5
Less than $100	9	
Total	124	100.0

Source: NPL, Diary, 1940

Table 3.3
Percentage breakdown of contributions to
the Toronto finance committee, 1940, by
major economic activity of donors

Construction contractors	18.5
Mining	12.5
Retail merchandising	12.4
Food products and processing	10.8
Iron and steel	9.8
Oil and chemical	7.8
Financial and insurance	6.8
Manufacturing	6.7
Entertainment and media	4.5
Textiles	1.4
Pulp and paper	1.4
Office equipment	0.9
Utilities	0.4
Transport	0.4
Breweries	0.2
Other and unidentified	5.4

Source: compiled from NPL, Diary, 1940;
Financial Post, Directory of Directors,
1940, *Survey of Industrials,* and *Survey of
Mines* to establish economic activity of
donors

sion of capital infrastructure (exploration, roads, etc.) and in the setting of tax conditions that the mining barons could not turn their eyes to the provincial party alone. Moreover, King's ministers of mines and resources, T.A. Crerar, had been an indefatigable champion of the mining companies' point of view in the King cabinet; the party felt sufficiently proud of its record in supporting the mine owners that it published a pamphlet extolling its aid to that sector of the economy alone.[90] The party expected some support in return, and it got it.

Another point to be noted is the importance of J.S. McLean, whose work for the party with the retail merchandisers, food processors, and financial institutions accounted for something between one-quarter and one-third of the money collected in Toronto. Finally, it should be pointed out that some sectors appear to be smaller than they were in reality because they relied on donations in kind more than in cash. Such is the case with the office equipment suppliers, who generally loaned machinery or donated paper or other supplies as their major contribution. The 'entertainment and media' sector also hides considerable contributions in kind, such as *Toronto Star* free advertising in the form of 'news' items, or the provision of advertising services directly for the party. One example of this is N.L. Nathanson of Famous Players who provided a billboard campaign at his own expense.[91]

A list of the contributors of amounts of $10,000 or more, which accounted for 60 per cent of the total follows:

Eaton's	$30,000
Dominion Foundries and Steel	$25,000
Imperial Oil	$25,000
International Nickel	$25,000
Hamilton Bridge	$25,000
Canada Packers	$25,000
Simpson's	$20,000
Tomlinson (contractor)	$15,000
Famous Players Theatres	$11,500
National Trust (four directors)	$10,000
Francheshini (contractor)	$10,000
Canada Locomotive	$10,000
Canada and Dominion Sugar	$10,000
Canadian Bank of Commerce	$10,000
British American Oil	$10,000
Algoma Steel	$10,000
Total	$271,500

It can readily be seen from this that most of the biggest contributors to the Toronto committee in 1940 were to be numbered among the giants of Canadian capitalism. Yet the mere donation of a large sum of money to the party was not sufficient to buy favourable government treatment for just anyone. Francheshini, a contractor who had done business with the Liberal government and played the party's rules for gratefulness, did not receive an equivalent display of thanks from the Liberal government: instead he was arrested under the War Measures Act and interned as an enemy alien for the duration of the war. The only comparable display of ingratitude came five years later when the Liberals rewarded their 1945 election allies, the Communist party, with mass arrests under the same War Measures Act following the Gouzenko spy revelations. But apart from Italian contractors and Communists, there is certainly no evidence that the party treated any of its more respectable supporters with such lack of consideration.

There is no information available on the total amount raised in Montreal in this election, although there is evidence that it must have been considerable. Certain big interests which had deserted the Tories over R.J. Manion's alleged 'radicalism' on the railway unification issue – the CPR, the Bank of Montreal, and the McConnell–*Montreal Star* interests – appear to have positively supported the Liberal cause this time out, although in what amounts one can only speculate. Moreover, Lambert's contract levy system was ready to reap benefits for the Montreal organization. Early in February Lambert went to Montreal, authorized the indestructible Donat Raymond to handle everything in Montreal, and gave him the names of three railway car companies which had not been canvassed on $16 million of government business. Since Raymond and Gordon Scott expected to collect at least 2½ per cent on such large amounts, these three companies would alone account for about $400,000. Whether they gave in such amounts is not known; the potential was certainly impressive. The other point of note about the Montreal finance operation in this election is that Lambert felt able to direct Raymond on the transfer of funds to the Maritimes, which he could not do in the earlier election. He asked the senator to send $50,000 to Nova Scotia and $20,000 to Prince Edward Island. New Brunswick did not require funds. Asking was not, however, receiving. A month later Lambert was still trying to get Raymond to put $25,000 into Nova Scotia, to which he had apparently committed himself, but without following through. It was not until the following year that Lambert learned that from Montreal 'additional amounts were given to private candidates' both in Nova Scotia and the

West. Lambert's informant would not under any circumstances 'name any names, for the latter had talked to Chubby Power,' who 'said Libs didn't like squealers & will be in power long time.'[92] Old ways died hard in Montreal.

Manitoba was a model of Lambert's conception of financial self-sufficiency. A total of $59,155 was collected under the direction of T.A. Crerar, who unlike some cabinet ministers took a very direct hand in collections, and J.C. Davis, the party treasurer who had replaced J.B. Coyne a few years earler. Only $56,338 was spent, leaving a prudent surplus of almost $3000: $15,000 was spent on the operations of the provincial headquarters; the remainder was distributed among the various constituencies, the average grant in this low-spending province being just over $2400 per riding. British Columbia did not come as cheap as this: $170,000 was spent by the Liberals in that province, and $30,000 was put into Vancouver Centre along by S.S. McKeen, the provincial treasurer.[93] In the latter seat, British Columbia cabinet minister, Ian Mackenzie, was able with that amount of money and the help of the Vancouver Liberal machine to narrowly squeeze past his CCF challenger. Since he had been widely expected to lose, at times by himself, Mackenzie's expensive victory was important to the party in the Pacific province. But national money had to go into British Columbia. It had not been self-sustaining as Lambert had hoped.

Saskatchewan, under the singular and highly personal direction of Jimmy Gardiner, presented financial problems to Lambert of quite a different, and more irritating, order. It was not merely that Gardiner blandly expected to be subsidized from national funds. Worse was his habit of competing directly for the same sources with the national party. Since Gardiner seemed to be the only regional leader outside of central Canada with access to eastern big business contributions, this was a problem unique to his provincial machine. The election campaign was only a few days old when Gardiner had already sent his own bagman into Bay Street, calling forth a protest from Lambert to the effect that Gardiner should co-operate with Campbell and the Toronto committee and not 'go off on his own.' Gardiner's man, after admitting that the Saskatchewan machine was too expensive, went on to state bluntly that he would quit if Lambert would assure him of $50,000. Lambert agreed to this and also allowed him to complete a transaction with British American Oil which he had already begun. Yet by the end of the campaign Gardiner was involved in obtaining a contribution from Acadia Sugar in Nova Scotia, of which he was magnanimously willing to allow the national party a small cut.[94]

On the whole, the 1940 financial operation worked very well indeed. Although it is not possible to estimate with any degree of accuracy just how much was spent on a national and provincial basis, it is more than apparent that funds were adequate, that the Liberals had considerably more money than their opponents, and that the structures set up for fund-raising and distribution worked with a reasonable degree of smoothness – given certain federal-provincial strains which were probably inevitable and, in any event, certainly not serious enough to disrupt the process which Lambert had set in motion.

THE NLF AND THE WAR

The declaration of war against the German Reich on 9 September 1939 fundamentally changed the nature of partisan politics at the national level in Canada. Although a general election was fought in 1940, events were set in motion at the very beginning of the war which put the matter of party organization and party structure on the back burner, so to speak. At least that was where the Liberals left the matter – with consequences for their political standing by the late years of the war.

On 7 September Lambert communicated to King his belief that with the coming of war the NLF office should be closed, since he could not 'see any good purpose in keeping it operating as a party office at this time' – to which King expressed 'general agreement.' King's agreement was indeed general, while Lambert's idea was specific. As Jack Pickersgill recalls, there was a certain failure of communication between the two men on this point: Lambert wanted the NLF closed; King, Pickersgill believes, wanted it 'toned down' but not closed.[95] It was not the first failure of communication between these two, but it proved to be the last, since it effectively led to Lambert's formal departure from political organizing.

On 14 September King spoke to his cabinet about his ideas on the partisan conduct of the war. King hated and feared the idea of a 'national government' coalition more than almost any other eventuality. But if the Liberals were to attempt to run the war effort without the cabinet level participation of other parties, the question of the relationship between the government and the party as a partisan organization had to be delineated at the start. As King put it to his cabinet colleagues:

... [W]e could so manage affairs as to get all the benefits of a national government without its inherent weaknesses and defects. That meant it was to co-operate with the other political parties in a fair way – not to be partisan in appointments, contracts, or anything else, but to view all obligations as a great trust ...

I then spoke of appointments and patronage. Said I loathed the partisan side of politics and was not prepared to countenance it. I did not mean the government should not make appointments of people in whom they had confidence, but I had tried to make plain in Parliament that, so far as business in war time corresponded with business in peace time, we would proceed as we ordinarily would, – contracts being subject to tender, and appointments made of those in whom we had special confidence, but ... we would have to deal with men and women of all parties. I said that if we did that, and brought in outstanding men of different parties, entrusting them with work, we would find that, at the time the elections came on, these men would come to be as part and parcel of ourselves ... I pointed out that, on the other hand, if we were partisan and wasteful, we would be criticized, and the opposition would come from all those seeking national government, with all the discontents on their side ...

I feel that if men play their part along the lines indicated, I have no doubt I am right and that the Liberal Party will continue to hold office at the end of the war and at the time of reconstruction. I feel that, in the interests of the country and freedom, this is most desirable. I stressed that point in talking with the Ministers – it was even more important we should continue in office, to prevent the whole nature of our institutions being changed through the national government or any other party gaining power meanwhile. [96]

What this meant in specific terms for the NLF was that Lambert was to keep the office ready for another election, but to maintain what a later generation of politicians would call a 'low profile.' Lambert had suggested that the staffs of the various party offices might be absorbed into the Wartime Information Board. King did not want non-partisanship taken *that* far.[97] It also meant that King, perhaps paradoxically, was unwilling to appoint Lambert to a position of any importance in the war effort because of Lambert's partisan association with the party organization.[98] Lambert, who seems to have genuinely wished to serve his country in some non-partisan position, was thus caught on the horns of an impossible dilemma: the NLF would be maintained for partisan purposes, but Lambert would not be given a position because he was considered too partisan. It was not always possible for lesser mortals to sort out the tangled complexity and subtlety of Mackenzie King's political genius. Some, like Lambert, eventually gave up trying.

The executive committee of the NLF met and tried to cope as best it could with the new situation by stopping publication of party literature and other visible activities, but at the same time sought to find the ways and means of maintaining a 'small office to preserve contacts with Liberal organizations throughout the country – having in mind a general election next year.' Lambert also told the committee that he 'couldn't see my way clear to attempt collections at this time.' At the beginning of November Lambert could no longer understand just what King wanted from the NLF and wrote to the prime minister announcing that he had 'now reached the point where I should appreciate your judgment and advice as to what course would be pursued by me, or for that matter by anyone else, in connection with the status of the Party's Organization, and particularly that part of it known as National Headquarters.'[99] Two weeks later, Lambert finally got to see the prime minister privately and immediately informed him that he 'felt at the end of my tether': '... that finances, and desire to do something useful, as well as to observe non-partisan standard, made it advisable to close, and wait until election was announced to set up an office. I offered to turn over everything to anyone else, but didn't want to leave P.M. or party in the lurch or be of embarrassment. I said we had funds in reserve for headquarters expenses in an election, but couldn't see feasible way of collecting usual subscription for Federation office.'[100] After complaining once more about the lack of co-operation with his office on the part of the cabinet throughout his tenure as NLF president ('I said that nobody had offered to help those who had helped us'), Lambert agreed that he would remain on for one more election. King then brought Lambert's representations to the attention of the cabinet, particularly the point about lack of co-operation, and formally requested Lambert to continue on until an election would bring out the full partisan activity of the party organization once again. Perhaps sensing just how deeply Lambert's feelings of hurt at the lack of recognition of his activities ran, King tried to mollify his sensitivity with a statement of appreciation for all that he had done for the Liberal cause, and added that he had tried to give his colleagues 'an appreciation of your services to the Party in these particulars. I realize, however, that, at best, only a part of what you accomplished can be made known.' Lambert agreed with King's plans, although he wanted to close the office down immediately, since he was being 'exposed to all sorts of needless demands from those in search of war business.' His final condition was the important one: 'With the conclusion of the next general election campaign, I should like to have it understood that I be relieved of my present responsibility for the maintenance of the National Liberal Federation, and the work of party organization. Apart from a personal desire to have an opportunity of applying qualifications and experience to other things, I think the cause of organized Liberalism in Canada stands to benefit through a change to a new and younger president.'

Following the election, when King's failure to thank Lambert rather gave the lie to his earlier expressions of appreciation, the prime minister confirmed the previous understanding that Lambert would be relieved of responsibility in the NLF. But even retirement from the partisan side of politics could not get Lambert the position he wanted in the wartime government. King thought it better to defer any such appointment 'for a time.' Instead, Lambert wrote in his diary, King 'wanted me to be a political godfather to the party, etc.'[101] There was a wealth of feeling in that 'etc.' from Lambert's pen. So ended the decade-long relationship between the Liberal party and the most talented and effective national organizer it had ever had, or was likely to get. And with Lambert's departure it is no exaggeration to say that an era ended in the party as a political organization. It is perhaps not without a certain poetic justice that this final interview between the prime minister and his organizer took place on April Fools' Day.

4

Crisis and reorganization of the Government party, 1940–5

Commenting on the 1949 Canadian general election, American political scientist William R.Willoughby recalled that 'a few years ago, certain Americans with Canadian investments became alarmed at the possibility of a Socialist government's coming to power in Canada and expropriating all foreign-owned factories, forests and mines. The American investors can now set their minds to rest. The Dominion – at least for the predictable future – is not going Socialist.'[1] Willoughby was right, although he might have made the same comment more appropriately after the general election of 1945. The war brought with it many changes in public attitudes towards politics and political values, not the least important of which was a striking shift to the left in public opinion. At the same time the Liberal government faced an organizational crisis brought about by its freezing of partisan activity at the same time as it remained a single-party war administration. This organizational crisis was thus compounded by a broader ideological crisis. Things had reached such a dismal state by 1943 that as intelligent an observer as Brooke Claxton could later recall that 'the Liberal Party was at its all-time low ebb.'[2] Yet from this low estate the Liberal party was able to fashion a major electoral revival which laid the groundwork for over another decade of national office. The resolution of the double crisis of the war years was a triumph of Liberal skill and a reaffirmation of that will to power to which so many observers have pointed as a characteristic of the party in this century. Moreover, the compounded crisis of the war affords a rare example of the fusion of party organization and party policy. Although it was only a brief encounter it was of considerable importance for the future of Liberal fortunes.

THE NON-PARTISAN PERIOD 1940-3

As indicated in the previous chapter, there had been a certain failure of understanding between Mackenzie King and Norman Lambert concerning the closing down of the party's national office at the beginning of the war. Now that the election of 1940 had been directed to its more satisfactory conclusion, and Lambert had finally taken his leave of the National Liberal Federation presidency, the question once more was reopened of the future of the office, and thus of national party organization.

King clearly did not want the office to be closed down entirely, and consequently new quarters were found for whatever minimal activities might be arranged. Lambert himself did not completely disappear from the picture. Since his contacts with the financial supporters of the party, particularly in Ontario, were crucially important, he was persuaded to stay on as part of the financial apparatus of the organization. He and his two men in Toronto, Peter Campbell and Percy Fell, formed a trust to administer funds on behalf of the NLF. Eventually, Campbell's services were secured as the main treasurer. As Lambert noted cynically in his diary, if Campbell were 'willing to give an unconditional acceptance afterward; he will be disillusioned later; but I'll give him whatever help he wants.' [3]

Norman McLarty, King's minister of labour until the end of 1941 and secretary of state from that point until the end of the war, was by now the Ontario minister charged with special responsibility for party organization, and along with Ian Mackenzie, Jimmy Gardiner, and Chubby Power exercised whatever loose supervision was necessary. Senator Adrian Norton Knatchbull Hugessen, the English-born son of British nobility and a director of Canadian Marconi Company, from whom King had extracted a promise of aid to the party when he had been called to the upper chamber in 1937, was being kept in line for the presidency of the now moribund NLF. Lambert and Campbell were able to arrange financing for a 'skeleton setup,' but a meeting of the interested parties early in 1941 agreed that 'without some definite line of action & policy an office here was a waste of time & money, that whole matter would have to be thoroughly discussed in Cabinet with P.M. present. Hugessen called the P.M. afterward, & said he was going to tell him that his comtee. was not agreed on what office should do.' [4]

At another meeting in the spring it was agreed that a formal announcement should be made that Hugessen had taken over from Lambert as acting president of the NLF, that the federation ought to be 'identified exclusively as an educational and promotional office,' and that 'matters pertaining to party organization involving patronage and party finances and the direction of elections should be directly under the control of a subcommittee of Cabinet.'⁵ By the late fall of the same year Lambert's finance committee agreed that there was 'no basis on which money could be raised or expended at this time' for an expanded political office. Hugessen was already proving a disappointment to King, who obviously wanted some level of partisan activity which the senator was unwilling to provide. Consequently, the postmaster-general, William Mulock, was brought into the picture to try to solicit some help to gear up the activities of the office. When Mulock attempted to get the former secretary of the NLF, Walter Herbert, to return to his old position, Herbert candidly replied that 'he wouldn't have anything to do with Liberal organization so long as King was leader.'⁶

The year 1942 was the turning point for the party's fortunes. Events which appeared to be favourable actually indicated growing weakness, beginning with three crucial by-elections held early in that year. In the historic Liberal constituency of Quebec East, corporation lawyer Louis St Laurent was attempting to replace the late member Ernest Lapointe as King's Quebec lieutenant. St Laurent was elected, but not before the entire Quebec East Liberal organization had walked out to protest his refusal to reject conscription in advance. In fact, he was elected with the aid of an *ad hoc* organization with strong support from Chubby Power's Quebec South machine.⁷ Success at this poll masked the dangerous issue of conscription in French Canada with all its debilitating potential for a party which rested on Quebec support.

Another crucial by-election was the famous affair of York South where Arthur Meighen, groomed for a comeback as Tory leader, went down to a startling defeat at the hands of the CCF.⁸ Although the Liberals did not officially contest this election, falling back on the tradition of not opposing by-election contests involving leaders of the opposition, and while it was generally believed that there was a tacit saw-off arrangement with the Tories involving the Welland by-election bid by King's nominee for the labour ministry, Humphrey Mitchell, in fact the Liberals actively supported the CCF against Meighen. Arthur Roebuck, who had been fired from Hepburn's cabinet in the late 1930s for his support of the union in the Oshawa strike, decided to hit back at the Hepburn people who were fully in support of Meighen, and took to the air waves on behalf of the CCF candidate. He also persuaded Mackenzie King that his old and hated Tory antagonist from the 1920s could be beaten.⁹ Brooke Claxton asked Norman Lambert to raise $1000 for the CCF, and Lambert, dealing with David Lewis and Andrew Brewin, complied.¹⁰ Peter Campbell was also brought into the fund-raising picture, and Claxton himself approached some possible sources. Although

J.L.Granatstein concludes that the $1000 was the extent of direct financial assistance, Claxton informed a close friend of his a week before the election date that he was in 'pretty close touch' with the CCF, and spoke in familiar terms of $2200 spent already and of the possibility of more for election day.[11] Whether this was Liberal money alone or Liberal plus CCF is not clear, but the fact of Liberal financial assistance is not in doubt.

The defeat of Arthur Meighen of course overjoyed Mackenzie King – and very seriously weakened the Tories. Yet there were two disquieting factors underlying this seeming triumph. First, there was the notable defection from the Liberal party of some highly important Liberal capitalists in Toronto in support of the conscriptionist Conservatives. Early in the campaign a Committee for Total War, popularly known as the 'Toronto 200,' was organized to finance and support a massive propaganda campaign in favour of Meighen and for conscription. This group, with distressing echoes of the Toronto Eighteen who had done so much to defeat Laurier in 1911, included at its head J.Y. Murdoch of Noranda Mines, who had actually collected money for the Liberals in 1935, and C.L. Burton of Simpson's, who was not only one of the party's biggest Toronto supporters in both 1935 and 1940 but was also a personal friend of Mackenzie King. The committee, which evidenced the fine hand of C. George McCullagh and his *Globe and Mail* as well as the old axis of the Hepburn machine and the mining interests, set about whipping up a jingoistic hysteria through the media. When King, on the night of Meighen's defeat, asserted that the Tory leader had been 'supported by financial interests and the press – everything in the way of organization and campaign power that could be assembled for any man...' there was considerable truth in the statement. Despite Meighen's loss, the question of the relationship to the Liberal party of big business had once more been opened up; it was, indeed, a hint of real difficulties ahead. But if the party had reason to be worried about its right flank, there was much more reason to be worried about the meaning of York South for the left wing of the political spectrum. The Liberals had helped the CCF defeat Meighen, but it slowly began to dawn on the brighter party members that in so doing they had helped bring a monster to birth which could end by devouring its erstwhile sponsor. The York South upset was the signal for a dramatic rise of the CCF in national popularity. When Meighen later blamed his defeat on a combination of the CCF, the Liberals, and the Communists, he was not entirely without foundation: Granatstein attributes his loss to a strong working class switch from the Tories to the CCF.[12] But this leftward shift of the electorate could just as well leave the Liberals beached while the CCF swept to national office.

The Welland by-election, in which King's choice for the labour portfolio, Humphrey Mitchell, was elected over the opposition of an independent candidate as well as a CCFer, presented problems of a different order. The local Welland organization demanded twelve to fourteen thousand dollars from national headquarters, citing alleged donations to the CCF from the CIO unions. Norman Lambert refused to have anything to do with the business, expressing his 'vehement contempt for the 12-14 thousand estimate of the Welland Liberals, as being a definite hold-up, & subversive of all decency in Gov't.' Peter Campbell could not apparently control the situation, and following the election Lambert wrote that 'nobody knows evidently where and how' over $20,000 had been spent.[13] The point was that a strong hand was needed to grasp the overall reins of national organization, and for the moment such a hand seemed to be missing.

The conscription plebiscite of 27 April 1942 – clever political stroke though it was – also served to reveal the organizational weakness of the government party. Norman McLarty was supposed to take charge of a publicity campaign to encourage a 'yes' vote, but instead, according to Granatstein, he created a 'shambles.' Another minister, William Mulock, proved no more competent; the campaign was left to run itself, financed by what Granatstein calls 'patriotic brewers, distillers, and manufacturing firms' whose contributions were declared tax-exempt by the minister of national revenue.[14] In Quebec, where the real problem lay, it proved almost impossible to get a single French-speaking Liberal of any note to support the 'yes' vote. Meanwhile, the *Ligue pour la défense du Canada*, the germ from which the *Bloc populaire* was later to grow as an electoral opponent of the Liberals, was carrying on a highly successful anti-conscription campaign under the direction of André Laurendeau of *L'Action nationale*, Georges Pelletier of *Le Devoir*, and Maxime Raymond, brother of Donat Raymond, now an independent member for a Montreal constituency in the House of Commons.[15] As Brooke Claxton wrote to a friend before the vote: 'It will not surprise you to learn that up to three days ago, literally nothing was done in the province of Quebec at all. In organizing the campaign in my own division, I have run into people of all races, who are sick and discouraged at the failure of the Government to come out and fight before the battle was lost. As you can imagine, I have had this out with Mr. King and his crowd a good many times.'[16] One of the chief difficulties, Claxton argued, was that the nominal head of Liberal organization in Montreal, P.-J.-A. Cardin, was 'crazy,' and had prevented anything resembling a real organization being set up. Although the results were gratifying to the government in so far as English-speaking Canada was concerned, the picture was very different in Quebec, where almost three-quarters of the electorate – and virtually all of the French-speaking voters – voted 'no.' There could be no doubt that the position of the Liberal party in Quebec was perilous, especially if the worst came to pass and conscription had to be imposed.

THE CHALLENGE FROM THE LEFT

Throughout the rest of 1942 and into the fall of 1943, as the war dragged on inconclusively, it seemed more and more that the Liberal government was heading into a political abyss and various forces seemed ready to engulf a party which had swept the country in a landslide victory only a few years earlier. In the late summer of 1943 the Liberal government of Ontario, now under the leadership of the only pro-King cabinet minister who had remained with Hepburn, Harry Nixon, went down to a staggering defeat, falling to a distant third place in the legislature. What was most ominous from a Liberal viewpoint was the sudden and powerful rise of the CCF who fell just four seats short of the Tories. If a new party of the left could displace the Liberals in Canada's largest province and heartland, then the possibilities for the rest of the country were darkening. King's worst fears were confirmed only five days later when Liberal candidates were defeated in four by-elections – by the *Bloc populaire* in a French-speaking Quebec riding, by CCFers in two western seats, and by a Communist in Montreal's Cartier constituency. Then in late September came perhaps the greatest shock of all to the Liberal party. A national Gallup poll showed the CCF leading both the Liberals and the Conservatives across the country. In Ontario they were running ahead of the Liberals; in the West the CCF had almost double the support which either of the two old parties could muster.[17]

The rise of the CCF as a credible challenger for national power has been extensively documented by others.[18] Yet it was not merely that a party which had seemed on the very brink of extinction four years earlier could by 1943 head the Gallup poll. Worse, much worse, from the Liberal's point of view, was that the high tide of CCF popularity was only a symptom of a massive shift of public opinion toward the left – a shift which was, on a much smaller scale, even sweeping a few Communists to electoral success in some of the larger cities. But the context was broader than Canada alone. Throughout the Western world, with the apparent exception of the United States, a radical political trend was emerging out of the war – a trend which was later to result in the defeat of Churchill by the Labour party in Britain at the war's end and was to establish the French and Italian Communist parties as mass parties of national electoral importance. Although Canada may have been a North American nation, she did not initially react with the exceptionalism of the United States to this trend. In the late years of the war it seemed for a time that, on the contrary, Canadian politics might change significantly.

Just how sharply public opinion was changing – and how much more radical it was then than today – can be glimpsed in a single poll out of many that might be referred to. Early in 1944 the Gallup organization asked Americans and Canadians the following question: 'Most people believe the government should not be controlled by any one group. However, if you had to choose, which would you prefer to have control of the government – big business or labour unions?' American and Canadian answers showed a startling divergence:[19]

	United States	Canada
Big business	63 per cent	35 per cent
Labour unions	37 per cent	65 per cent

Similarly, growing support was indicated for public ownership over private, as well as increasingly positive feelings toward Communist Russia.

To a Liberal like Mackenzie King, whose lifelong conception of the historical role of Liberalism was the co-optation and absorption of the political left, this transformation of public opinion constituted at the same time a stinging reproach and an invigorating challenge. Just as the First World War had force-fed the growth of the farmers' revolt, the outburst of labour militance in 1919, and the efflorescence of the social gospel and middle class radicalism – all of which had set the stage for King's *Industry and Humanity*, his textbook for corporatist co-optation of radicalism, and his accession to the Liberal leadership on a reformist platform – so too the changes of the second war presented him with an opportunity to 'redeem the time,' as he confided to his diary. Somehow the working people were rejecting his protective Liberal wing: that was his rebuke. Yet the changes in opinion were preparing the ground for a new wave of reform: that was his opportunity. The lost years, the two decades of conservatism and depression, seemed to fall away. He remembered the man he had been in the early days of reform, 'the singleness and earnestness of purpose... My life should have been more expressive of those forces within myself and its real purpose. I have felt a certain return of health and with it a willingness to try one more political campaign.' But as he went back to the hustings one last time, there was to be a difference: 'In my heart, I am not sorry to see the mass of the people coming a little more into their own, but I do regret that it is not a Liberal party that is winning the position for them ... My whole sympathies are with labour and I even feel I would rather be defeated as a Government, and have labour come into fuller rights, than to win and have labour deprived of greater freedom, if these were the necessary alternatives. I do not believe they are. I think, in the end, Labour can win the most by returning a Liberal Government, but I know much work will have to be done to effect that end.'[20] It was to that work that King was turning the Liberal party's attention.

The National Liberal Federation was scarcely functioning and would have to be rebuilt from scratch. Moreover the NLF could not command the kind of expertise in opinion manipulation which seemed necessary to confront a transformed public mind. In Ontario 42 per cent of working class voters told the Gallup poll that the CCF would best look after their interests; only 17 per cent trusted the Liberals.[21] To recast the image of the 'progressive' centre party in the face of this kind of statistic called for much more than the recycling of the old party stalwarts for another run of old-fashioned political speeches before traditional crowds of hereditary Liberal supporters. Either public opinion had to be changed or the Liberal party had to change its policies and its public face – and perhaps if the party was skilful enough, a little of both might be accomplished.

One set of forces already working on the problem of public opinion were the freelance anti-socialist crusaders: 'Bugsy' Sanderson, the pest exterminator; William Ewart Gladstone Murray, the disgraced former general manager of the CBC metamorphosed into the head of 'Responsible Enterprise'; Burdrick A. Trestrail, the untrammeled enterprise evangelist from Missouri. With some exaggeration, Gerald Caplan describes their combined 'red scare' campaign as the 'most massive propaganda drive in Canadian political history.'[22] Moreover, the pillars of corporate capitalism, especially finance capital, began shifting their own emphasis in advertising from identifying themselves with the war effort to drawing attention to the red menace.

Such excrescences were no doubt frightening to some, but the freelance crusaders were little more than ideological terrorists whose crudities might well be more useful to a resurgent Conservative party than to the Liberals who had always thought of themselves as posing a progressive centrist appeal to the working class.[23] One leading Liberal in Ottawa confided to a friendly editor that an intelligent reading of public opinion yielded quite different results than the right seemed to perceive: 'People,' Brooke Claxton wrote, 'are in a state of confusion because of the pace of the revolution.

Certainly they are ready for change, are not frightened of new ideas, are frightened of almost everything else. Uppermost is the fear of another depression. Associated with that are the two old parties. The CCF cleverly has succeeded in identifying itself with all forward-looking thoughts.' The 'record,' he concluded, is not worth a damn: 'the future is all.'[24] This came to the nub of the problem. The Depression had weakened faith in free enterprise; war and collectivist controls had restored prosperity and a sense of common purpose. People now had something to *lose*. The left could now be seen as a curiously conservative force, ready and able to protect the gains of the war in peacetime; the right was a force which might lose it all in a return to the prewar 'normalcy' of depression and despair.

Other friends of the Liberal party across the country were setting their minds to work on the problem and its solution as well. As journalist Leslie Roberts suggested to his friend Chubby Power, it was time for the Liberal government to outflank its rivals by 'courageously grabbing the post-war nettle':

John Bracken and [M.J.] Coldwell can only tell us what they will do, as, if, and when. The Government, on the other hand, can do something about it. Frankly, if it doesn't, then it is my conviction that the Liberal party will be swamped at the polls.

What do the Canadian people and what do the men in the service want? I think you could sum that up by saying that they want economic security ... full-time employment at wages commensurate with dignity in living, security of tenure of that employment. I do not think they'll settle for anything short of this. What is more I believe we can give it to them. I believe that if we are not ready for this responsibility on the day the shooting stops that we are in for a bushel of trouble ...

...[I]f capital doesn't come pretty soon to the idea of cooperation with Government and People in bringing about change, instead of resisting every forward-looking movement ... if entrenched wealth doesn't acquire a willingness to give part of itself away to the people, then the people will turn on it and rend it ... and defeat any government which clings to the economic ideas of, say, 1939. They just won't go down anymore. Maybe the successors of this Government won't succeed in bringing about Utopia, but they'd certainly snatch a bagful of votes on the promise thereof ...

This country can give leadership, to its allies and to all mankind, in the realm of forward-looking legislation. Are we ever going to stop playing follow-the-leader and act like the young and virile nation we actually are?[25]

Roberts had not only captured the essential lines of public opinion, as the polls now available make clear, but he also touched on all the essential points in the eventual Liberal response: that governmental reconstruction policies could offer a *concrete* response to the theoretical schemes of the socialists; that the concept of an alliance between the government, capital, organized labour, and the consumer was the central ideological thrust of a Liberal centrist appeal; and that a welfarist postwar policy could be made the basis of a nationalist programme to capture the patriotism of the collective war effort for the political benefit of the Liberal party after the European victory. There were the dim outlines here of a new national policy, for which the Liberal party was uniquely fitted to be the political champion and beneficiary. At this early stage the mechanics of the actual policies were still problematic, but the senior levels of the civil service could be tapped for the specifics. The Liberals, as a political party, could play their by now familiar role as the defender of the people against the big interests and the defender of the big interests against the people. And who better to play this role than the party of Mackenzie King, author of *Industry and Humanity*, conservative and reformer, who somehow managed to remain suspicious of the very interests which made his own political career possible while at the same time expressing his true devotion to the radical politics he was always working to co-opt and thus undermine?

But would big business recognize the manifest correctness of the Liberal position? There indeed was a problem, alluded to time and again by the references in this period by leading Liberals to the 'stupidity' and 'selfishness' of the big interests. As Charles Dunning had once confided to Mackenzie King when he had temporarily left politics for the world of high finance, he had been surprised 'at the very little the so-called financiers know – without their money many of them would amount to nothing.'[26] This was especially true when the times called for a rethinking of the hoary rhetoric under whose comforting homilies capitalists lived and thought. The Liberal party would have to undertake a major education course for business in the new economics. Even though Liberals knew that their historical task was to save Canadian capitalism from its own excesses and its own weaknesses, there was no guarantee that the objects of these attentions would recognize who their friends were. Yet while big business was ultimately crucial for the continued financial viability of a national party, and of course crucial to the effective functioning of any national economic policies of a government party, nevertheless, in a liberal democracy it was possible for a political party to turn to the voters and to draw on the weight of public opinion as a counterforce to the withdrawal of business support. This task was made easier by the fact that the Conservative party, responding to the same popular pressures, itself turned leftward after the Port Hope conference of 1942; big business thus had no 'safe' party of its own. If the Liberals could only co-opt the support of those who were turning leftward by seeming to offer a moderate, responsible, and, above all, a concrete and specific variant of what the CCF was preaching to growing congregations, then the tide of opinion could be harnessed for Liberal power. Presumably, at this point, big business would perforce recognize its real friends.

To be sure, Canadian capitalism was not bereft of new ideas and creative responses to a changed situation, even if the rhetoric of the divine laws of the free market continued apace with the growing, and profitable, partnership with government in the war production effort. It was particularly from the advertising agencies, which, by the nature of their work, had to be highly sensitive to the changing winds of public opinion and popular fashion, that perceptive responses were forthcoming. This can be seen in a document prepared in 1943 by Walsh Advertising of Toronto: a survey of the trend to the left in public opinion carried out on behalf of a large private corporation, but passed on to the Liberal party for its consideration. Walsh was by this time a major agency associated with the Liberal party in Ontario. Walsh noted that a nation-wide poll had 'seemed to indicate' that public opinion in favour of the nationalization of private enterprise 'was now close to a majority; that it had taken an enormous spurt in the last one to two months.' Significantly, the agency added: 'This was a staggering and startling piece of news for Ottawa and *prompt action was taken to prevent publication of the report*, for the present at least.'[27] Suppression of the bad news, however, could only delay the reckoning. Walsh had positive ideas as well. A national survey of attitudes was undertaken to determine why Canadian opinion was accelerating to the left while American opinion was moving to the right. The answer centred around the Canadian political culture, and especially its economic framework and the influence of European ideas and models. The CCF, Walsh argued, was not only a moderate bulwark against 'the more extreme left-wing party which ... might spring up and sweep into power – given such a situation, for instance, as heavy postwar unemployment,' but it was also a welcome antidote to rightward pressures in the Liberal party itself. And there was much in the CCF support which lent itself to Liberal co-optation.

Walsh interviewed labour leaders ('the men who are likely to settle the thinking of their followers') and discovered that, apart from a visceral mistrust of management, '*so far* – and they underline this, – they have committed themselves to no new economic system as the method of securing their desires ...' Labour distrusted the two old parties and saw the need for some form of independent political action. But a regulated capitalism might well be sold to them as a substitute for public ownership. Interestingly enough, they found that the 'staunch supporters among labour groups for private ownership are most vocal among the ranks of employees in public-owned corporations ...' The response of the 'tried and true politicos seek[ing] to toss tempting morsels to the wolves,' such as the Ontario cabinet minister who hastily called a press conference to offer a free refrigerator to every farmer, was irrelevant and absurd. Instead, only a competently managed and regulated capitalism could confront the discontent of the working people. Prophetically, the Walsh memorandum concluded with a reference to a speech by W.C. Clark, the deputy minister of finance and the architect of the postwar Keynesian fiscal and monetary policies. As Walsh interpreted Clark's views on taxation policy for the future: 'in the face of steady employment and the ability to spend as well as earn, the interest in isms, reconstructed systems and radical change would fade. It varies directly with the public uncertainty over employment.'

THE POLITICAL WATERSHED 1943

The story of how the Liberal government was able to piece together a programme for postwar reconstruction which was not only saleable to the electorate but was also effective in maintaining full employment throughout the transition from a wartime to a peacetime economy is perhaps more interesting from the point of view of the high degree of competence and intelligence in the civil service – people like W.C. Clark and his 'boys' in the department of finance – than it is from the perspective of the party as a political organization.[28] Yet in another sense this decisive turning-point both in the fortunes of the Liberals and of the Canadian nation does indeed relate to the Liberal party as an organization. First of all, the Liberal party was by now the Government party, and as such its ability to draw on the expertise and new ideas of the civil service and to put them into effect in an electorally successful manner was an integral aspect of its functioning as a political organization. The civil service was a resource unmatched by anything which the opposition parties could command in the way of ideas. The point was that the Liberals proved capable of using this resource with a considerable degree of success.

Three political figures, other than the prime minister himself, particularly stand out in this process of adapting bureaucratic inputs into party policy. Ian Mackenzie, whose dogged determination that effective reconstruction policies be implemented gives him a place in history which his personal shortcomings as an administrator would otherwise have precluded, was important in keeping the issue constantly before the attention of the cabinet and the prime minister.[29] Brooke Claxton, first as a parliamentary secretary, then as minister of national health and welfare from late 1944, was a source of political intelligence and encouragement to the government to proceed along the lines which were eventually followed. Finally, there was the backroom figure of Jack Pickersgill, only a few years earlier a thoughtful academic critic of the conservative trend in Canadian Liberalism during the Depression, and now a lively assistant in King's own office – and the only assistant King ever had who seemed capable of talking back to his boss. In the summer of 1943 Pickersgill submitted a memorandum to King which brilliantly summed up the outlines of the Liberal programme: a floor on farm prices; family allowances to head off the wage demands of labour; improved health assistance; and a massive housing programme and other government spending to keep the economy booming.[30] Later it was Pickersgill who finally persuaded a reluctant and suspicious Mackenzie King of the morality of family allowances.[31]

There were two other senses in which this adaptation of bureaucratic inputs into party policy were functions of party organization as well as the party in Parliament. First, the extra-parliamentary structures were reactivated in 1943, not merely to get electoral machinery geared up once again but also to bring together the grass-roots demands for change with the new ideas on how reform could be accomplished. This served the double purpose of linking the supporters of the party with the new policies being generated in the deputy ministers' offices in Ottawa, and of thrusting a useful weapon into the hands of the reform wing of the party in Parliament to do battle with the conservative and backward-looking elements which still exercised considerable power in the cabinet and caucus, the type of politicians of whom King once remarked that they seemed to think they still lived in the sort of country where a person could 'go out and shoot a deer or bison for breakfast.'[32] For once the extra-parliamentary party played an important, if intermediary, role in policy-making. The second reason why party organization became an important factor in this process is that the Liberal party was in a dreadful organizational crisis, one which was almost universally attested to by those who interested themselves in the party's political fortunes, and which was almost always traced to the non-partisan administration of the wartime government and its consequent downplaying of party patronage, the lifeblood of political organization. If the Liberal party were to become a viable vehicle for the implementation of reform policies, the party apparatus would have to work its way out of the hole into which it had been sunk by the relatively effective freeze on partisanship in government appointments. The desire for a renewal of patronage and the desire for reform policies might seem to be somewhat inconsistent partners, but in fact they went hand in hand.

Taking the question of patronage first, there can be no doubt that the claims of the Liberal government to have been reasonably non-partisan in the conduct of appointments to the various new agencies, boards, and commissions which proliferated during the war must be taken quite seriously. One need only turn to the chorus of howls and whimpers which issued from all parts of the country from local Liberal partisans about the placement of known Tories in various positions. As early as October 1939 Norman Rogers, then newly installed as minister of national defence, was writing to his cabinet colleagues drawing their attention to the public statement by the prime minister that no favouritism would be shown in appointments on a party basis, and spelling out to them that this definitely meant the exercise of 'no partisan or personal preferences' and no special favours in contracts.[33] Indeed, every effort was made to attract well-known Conservatives – unsuccessfully in the case of Senator A.D. McRae, the national organizer of Bennett's campaigns in the 1930s; successfully in the case of the Conservative leader in the 1940 election, R.J. Manion, who was appointed director of air raid precautions[34] – and the government was justifiably proud of the cleanliness of its record in this regard. Yet however grand this might sound in a speech to the Canadian people on sacrifice for the war effort, it sounded much less impressive to those Canadians who counted themselves as Liberal party activists and partisans in the constituencies. As one Liberal assistant to a minister put it succinctly: the 'abdication of patronage has deprived the Ministers and Members of the opportunity to make friends ... Each member is conscious of the falling away of supporters due to the fact that he can no longer dispense little favours, however trivial.'[35] Senator Wishart Robertson, named as party president in 1943, put the matter in a wider context:

Generally speaking, in the past, Liberal Governments could depend on the active and enthusiastic support of the Party organization. There is much evidence to bear out the fact that at the moment, the present Government does not enjoy this support in anything like the measure it has in the past ... [T]his Government, acting as a Party Government, deemed it necessary to dispense with the Liberal Party Organization as such, in the administering of its war policies, for the past four years. The position of Liberals as such in their respective communities, has become increasingly difficult, and unhappy. Quick to sense the situation, many governmental employees, both Liberal and Tory, have gone out of their way to ignore elected Liberal members, and individuals prominent in party organization ... Gradually the rank and file of the party resigned themselves to these conditions as being inevitable, and have become increasingly indifferent. They would probably agree that the Government's record was a good one, but their general attitude would be that it was not incumbent upon them to exert themselves to perpetuate the existing state of affairs ... I am quite sure in my own mind that there is a considerable number of Liberals who not only believe that defeat at the next election is inevitable, but who are quite convinced that it is by no means an unmixed evil.[36]

In other words, the traditional prerogatives of the ministers and the sitting members had been cancelled – for *raisons d'état* – and the rank and file of party activists, the men and women the party desperately needed at election time to suddenly spring into life in the form of myriad constituency organizations, had decided that without the glue of patronage there was little to interest them in adherence to party activity. To be sure, this diminution of party support was not tested in an actual election, at least until 1945 when the situation had significantly changed. But the regularity with which reports such as the above were received does lend credence to the observation. If so, the mid-war years offer striking evidence to support the hypothesis that patronage was a crucial element in party organization.

The watershed separating the period of partisan drift from the strong political recovery of the late war years was the reactivation of the National Liberal Federation through an advisory council meeting held in Ottawa in late September 1943. This meeting, easily the most important and interesting ever held by that body, was immediately preceded by a special parliamentary caucus called to mobilize parliamentary support for the new political initiatives. At the caucus, Mackenzie King launched into his favourite theme of the lack of organization: this time it was obviously true, even if it had been rather unfair on occasion in the past. The members met all day, into the evening, and on to the next day. King was blunt about responsibility:

I here and now say to my colleagues that I feel it is their duty, and it is the duty of Ministers of every province to be responsible first and foremost for the organization of their own province, and for all the federal organization collectively. That I did not end the responsibility there. That M.P.'s could help. I saw a number of Senators present. I would say there is not a Senator who did not owe his position for life as a Senator to the Liberal party. That I thought they owed it to the party to help in the work of organization.

King left the marathon caucus feeling that the 'two days have been the most profitable in the history of the party.'[37] Norman Lambert also attended the caucus, which he described as King 'raising particular hell,' and put his finger on a major weakness in King's logic: 'The result of the recent [provincial] elections he blamed on lack of organization, altho. later he declared that the Gov't couldn't be concerned with party matters & run the war effectively.'[38] As usual, however, King wanted to call in the organizers when they were needed, but he himself did not want to be bothered with the details, or more particularly, the responsibility. Not of course that he could be expected to undertake such duties while government leader in wartime. The point was that the old question of the relationship between the extra-parliamentary party and the party leader and cabinet was scarcely clarified by King's remarks.

Brooke Claxton took charge of preparing a series of policy resolutions to be presented to the NLF advisory council meeting which followed on the heels of the caucus. The resolutions, which were steered through the sessions, not without frank debate but without serious amendment, reflected the strategy of welfarism whose outlines had become fairly settled in the minds of the brighter and more forward-looking Liberals. Among the crucial planks in the platform were a strong emphasis on the role of goverment spending in creating full employment (in partnership with private enterprise, of course); a national housing programme; a greatly expanded social security plan which would include 'social insurance and assistance against the consequences of economic and social hazards' among which were numbered 'unemployment, accident, ill-health, old age and blindness'; specific improvements to the existing old age pensions; and the 'consideration of children's allowances.' And in what had by now become a customary curtsy to labour drawn straight from the pages of *Industry and Humanity,* the NLF affirmed that 'Labour is not a commodity but a partner in industry and a principal mainstay of national life. The Liberal Federation will support vigorous measures to make this partnership effective through labour-management councils and the participation, wherever appropriate, of representatives of Labour on wartime boards and other agencies of government.'[39] Almost all the resolutions were in fact implemented to some degree or other, including the very tentative support for family allowances. It was a welfare programme which not only stole just enough of the socialists' thunder to make it a credible reform platform, but was eminently practical and within the capacity of government to implement without seriously disturbing the balance of power between government and business. Even the most rockribbed reactionaries of Bay Street would eventually come around to the realization that healthy workers were better for business than sick ones. As the *Canadian Forum* remarked about the Marsh Report on social security, itself a report by a known CCFer authorized by the Liberal government: it was 'the price Liberalism is willing to pay in order to prevent socialism.'[40] That could just as appropriately be said about the 1943 advisory council resolutions.

The one major exception to the high degree of governmental acceptance of the NLF proposals was the section on labour quoted above. Rhetoric about labour not being a commodity but a partner was easy enough, but it does not seem that the Liberal government achieved a very high degree of concrete representation of labour on wartime boards, and nothing was ever done about 'labour-management councils.' Organized labour was by no means unconciliatory toward government – even the Communists prominent in the CIO unions were scrupulously following a 'popular front' win-the-war strategy following the Nazi invasion of the Soviet Union – but little was done to extend a corporatist hand from government to integrate the unions into the government-business complex which was waging the war. It is in many ways a curious failure, particularly in light of Mackenzie King's professed views on the subject. Some of the reasons for the failure can be traced to the hard-nosed reaction of business to the prospect of any participation by the unions. The businessmen who went to Ottawa to direct war production and administration were suspicious of precedents being set in the public sector which might be carried over into the private sector at the end of the war. The president of Ford Canada, for example, had flatly threatened to resign if any labour representative were named to the War Supply Board which he headed.[41] J.L. Cohen, labour lawyer of rather pronounced left-wing views, was fired from the National War Labour Board at the demand of the chairman, C.P. McTague, who was himself reincarnated as the national chairman of the Progressive Conservative party a year later.[42] The Liberal government was either unable or unwilling to run seriously against the grain of these attitudes, and the corporatist labour philosophy was left largely in the realm of rhetoric, where Mackenzie King had always lived most comfortably with it for over a generation. The one important initiative taken by the Liberals toward labour was the order-in-council of 17 February 1944 which guaranteed the right to collective bargaining and the right to strike. This order was of very great significance for labour, and its passage was certainly a strong act of support on the part of government for the labour movement.[43] What it involved was essentially an affirmation of the adversary system of industrial relations, which was no doubt realistic and sensible in the circumstances, but was not along the corporatist lines which *Industry and Humanity* and its offspring, the 1943 NLF labour resolution, followed.[44]

In the light of the somewhat ambivalent Liberal attitude toward labour, it is interesting to note that a real debate raged at the advisory council meeting on labour policy, a debate which even extended to such un-Liberal behaviour as personal attacks on the minister of labour, and such plain speaking as a statement by a prominent Liberal MP that the Labour Department was 'the main blight upon our escutcheon.'[45] The point of this ambiguity in Liberal policy is that while social welfare legislation was readily assimilable within a liberal centre-left ideological framework, and ultimately quite compatible with a modernized capitalist economy, the question of the relations between capital and labour and between labour and the state perhaps touched deeper and more sensitive roots of the dominant values and arrangements of a liberal-democratic political economy. In any event, organized labour was slowly moving toward more open ties with socialist or social democratic political parties. Despite King's long-standing concern that the Liberal party in this country escape the fate of the Liberals in England who had been outflanked on the left by a Labour party, the Liberals' leftward shift in the late years of the war was not sufficient to head off the historical development of a labour-socialist party – although of course this left party was never able to seriously challenge the Liberals for national power, an accomplishment for which the welfarist turn of the Liberal party in these years must be given at least some credit.

Dire warnings of the advance of socialism and worse were rife at the NLF meetings. Labour minister Humphrey Mitchell expressed his conviction that the 'whole continent of Europe will go Communist, whether we like it or not.' Another delegate offered this moderated version of Marx: 'The workers of the world ... comprise the majority of the people who live on this earth and there may come a time, sooner perhaps than we anticipate, when the workers of the world may decide that there is no satisfaction in a form of industry which gives them only wages.' And there appeared to be very widespread agreement with the answer to this trend as succinctly expressed by a British Columbia Liberal twice defeated by the CCF: 'Make no mistake about it, the best counter-irritant to the CCF is to go as far as you possibly can with social security out of the dividends of private enterprise.' That was the Liberal response in a nutshell. Whatever the business community might think of what was going on inside the two major parties, both the Liberals and the Conservatives were turning reformist in order to save capitalism. In this the two parties were in a sort of tacit alliance, one which redounded first to the advantage of the Liberals but kept the door open in the longer run for the Conservatives to return as the major alternative to the government party. As one British Columbia delegate asserted defensively to the advisory council: 'believe me, I feel that there is not a man or woman in this room who would not ally himself or herself with the Conservatives rather than see the CCF get into power in their province.' Cockfield, Brown advertising man, H.E. Kidd, later to become the national secretary of the NLF, in an internal agency memorandum early in 1943, suggested clearly that the attention of the voters was being focused on selecting one of two futures, a CCF future or a Liberal-Conservative future.[46] The new NLF president put the proposition even more forcefully in a party memorandum shortly after the NLF meetings: 'We can appeal to the moderate Conservative on the grounds that at this crisis someone has got to make the system of free enterprise work, and we are the logical ones to do it. While that principle is being established, the Conservative party can keep their organization intact, ready to take over when the country decides on a change.'[47]

Although Mackenzie King told Chubby Power that he would never form a coalition with the Conservatives, that indeed he would prefer to do so with the CCF,[48] there can be little doubt that the main thrust of the new Liberal reformism was to head off the CCF by co-opting its support, and that this involved a tacit alliance with the Conservatives in the sense of maintaining the 'two-party system' and the predominantly private enterprise economy which nurtured the two old parties. In other words, the policy initiatives of 1943 were ultimately conservative and highly supportive of the existing political economy, although they were also creative and adaptive in the sense of re-establishing the system's equilibrium in the face of what was widely perceived on all sides as a challenge of very serious proportions. All of which accrued to the Liberals' benefit.

If the extra-parliamentary party played an important role in this policy reformulation, it was not without qualms and anxiety on the part of the parliamentary leadership. In placing the resolutions passed by the resolutions committee before the general meeting of the council, Brooke Claxton cautioned the delegates to restrain any incipient enthusiasm for party policy-making:

...it should be recognized that we are meeting as a political party at a time when a Liberal administration is in power. That is quite a different situation to that facing a political party which is in opposition and which wants to get into power. Anything that we say here should be done by the Liberal government or by the parliament of Canada will at once put the government on the spot. If it does it, then it does it in accordance with the resolution put forward by the Federation; if it does not do it, it of course will be charged immediately with having had the opportunity of putting into effect Liberal principles and not having done so. So that it is probably unwise from a political point of view to put forward things which the government will not do or cannot do because of its responsibilities to the people of Canada ...

Further, this programme is not the platform on which the party would go before the people at an election. Before an election I would imagine that the government itself would draw up its own platform and that would be the platform on which they would fight ... This is intended to be more in the nature of a general statement and it must not be thought of as a platform.

Claxton also asked the indulgence of the meeting in a final request, that once the resolutions had been passed they not be issued immediately to the public and the press, but instead be entrusted to the NLF executive for the task of putting them 'into the best possible form and to remove all inconsistencies and possible errors.'[49] As if this were not enough, Mackenzie King was quick to instruct Claxton that 'care be taken not to issue it as a programme settled by the Liberal party, but merely as some suggestions from the Advisory Council to the Government.'[50]

All things considered, however, the 1943 meetings were closer to rank-and-file participation in policy than any other party gatherings held in the King–St Laurent era of the party. As Chubby Power confided happily to a friend following the sessions:

The Show went over far better than we could have anticipated. The two day caucus was a real one with minds spoken freely and ideas expressed forcibly. The Federation meeting also went off well. Plain speaking was the order of the day and there was sufficient of radicalism even to please you. I am convinced that whatever may befall, the rank and file of the Liberal Party are not turning Right.

...[E]veryone is thinking in terms of Post War and the bright New World which they wish to promise. The ball is now definitely passed to the Administration, and it is up to us to translate into legislation something that will appeal to our people. Meanwhile there will be a sincere attempt to strengthen the organization throughout the Country. The job is a terribly uphill one since there is no doubt but that the tide was running strongly against us.[51]

Organizationally, the NLF meetings were less spectacular in result than were the policy resolutions. An organization committee chaired by Arthur Roebuck, and including provincial representatives as well as Jimmy Gardiner and Chubby Power, called for a reopening of an active national office in Ottawa, devoting itself to the production of literature and assisting 'autonomous provincial organizations devoted to advocacy of Federal Liberal policies' wherever necessary – which was little more than a reaffirmation of the basic definition of the NLF office from the beginning. The committee was unanimous in agreeing that if the Liberals were to go to the polls within the year, they would face certain defeat. They also agreed that the 'major complaint is that the elected representatives of the people and their supporters have been deliberately ignored in favour of their opponents, and are not allowed to help in any way with the war effort and the machinery of the Government.'[52] This was not put in the form of a resolution for the general meeting. In fact, the committee had almost passed a resolution which would have suggested that the authority of the MP and of the party organization should 'replace government policy.' The idea was dropped, however, due to fear that it might be 'misinterpreted,' but it was privately communicated to the government that 'something of the members [sic] old time authority' should be restored, that, in other words, patronage be reinstated, except in matters directly related to the war effort where it was recognized that public opinion might be hostile to party favouritism.[53] The specifically partisan concerns over patronage were obviously less politically saleable items than were the sparkling new policy initiatives in social welfare. Yet from the point of view of the party's political fortunes, these concerns were of no less importance, even if they were treated with more circumspection in public.

Senator Wishart Robertson of Nova Scotia was appointed party president. Robertson had been a third-generation holder of a hereditary family seat in a provincial constituency, and had built up a certain local reputation as a businessman, mainly in forest products and automobile sales, which had been sufficient to land him the job of federal treasurer for the Liberal party in Nova Scotia in the late 1930s. Norman Lambert appears to have been reasonably well pleased with the choice of Robertson,[54] but others in the party were less impressed with his performance once in office. Jack Pickersgill recalls Robertson as having been 'dredged up from somewhere,' and a certain lack of confidence was clearly demonstrated when the party later chose another man to supersede Robertson as chairman of the 1945 election campaign.[55] The most important backstage development was not the choice of Robertson but the pledge by Lambert and Peter Campbell to underwrite the national office for $25,000 per year, with $15,000 of that total to be raised from cabinet ministers, senators, and MPs.[56] The NLF was back in business once again.

THE POLITICAL COUNTERATTACK 1943-5

The autumn of 1943 was particularly warm and lovely, with the trees in the Gatineau Hills north of Ottawa more brilliantly coloured than for years past; even the normally laconic entries in the Lambert diary became lyrical at the spectacle. And far off in the Soviet Union the Red Army was beginning its vast counterattack which was to break the back of the Nazi war machine. Yet despite the reorganization and rethinking that the Liberal party had gone through in September, rank-and-file Liberals across the nation were still convinced that the party's long political retreat was about to turn, not into a counterattack, but into a dismal and prolonged rout. Grant Dexter of the *Winnipeg Free Press*, a journalist with close connections to the Liberal party, was convinced that the 'very encouraging flurry of optimism' had drained away immediately after the meetings, that the cabinet ministers were burnt-out cases, that the party was 'back where they were and I can see no disposition to stand up to the C.C.F., to contest the field ...'[57] In December Lambert went on a tour of the West, and found that everyone he spoke to held out little hope for the government. The spring of 1944 brought yet worse news: the CCF swept to a mighty victory in Saskatchewan, taking 47 of 52 seats, and almost annihilating the vaunted Saskatchewan Liberal machine. If even Jimmy Gardiner's boys could not hold the line in the face of the socialist tide, what hope could there be for the much more disorganized Liberals in the rest of the country? Equally appalling from the Liberal perspective was the news that the CCF had carried about two-thirds of the votes of the servicemen overseas. Then the reopening of the conscription crisis a few days after the Saskatchewan election by the Tories could only presage more difficulties for the Liberals from the Scylla of Ontario and the Charybdis of Quebec. Perhaps C.D. Howe's despairing suggestion to Lambert of the previous summer, that the best the Liberals could do was to win the war and then 'fade out,'[58] was indeed the only honourable course left open.

The counsels of despair were not the only voices listened to by the Liberals. J. Gordon Fogo, a partner in J.L. Ralston's corporate law firm, and a prominent figure in wartime Ottawa on various boards, particularly in regard to labour relations, was appointed by the cabinet as party chairman, over the head of his fellow Nova Scotian, Senator Robertson, indicating a lack of confidence in Robertson and the NLF as an organization. Fogo was to be paid a salary of $15,000 per year, no mean sum in those days, and neither Lambert nor Peter Campbell in Toronto were pleased with this development. Campbell in fact told Lambert that he would do no more than serve out his remaining year as party treasurer.[59] Yet there were two points which seem to have escaped both Lambert and Campbell. First of all, Fogo's appointment demonstrated a renewed confidence in the party's ability to raise money – at a salary of $15,000 they would have to – and in addition Fogo was a very able figure; it is now generally recognized that Fogo was the closest thing the party ever got to Lambert himself. On the former point about the finances of the party, C.D. Howe was already gathering in funds from war contractors; although the party never did collect what it believed to be its due, it was once again acting like a party which was concerned with its political, as well as its governmental functions.

Fogo was himself very far from the mood of gloom and despondency which was immobilizing so many Liberals. In a memorandum prepared after the Saskatchewan election, for example, he pointed out that not only had the provincial Liberals helped to defeat themselves by an undue reliance on old-fashioned machine methods, but that it was by no means certain that the federal Liberals could not successfully appeal to many of the voters who had turned to the CCF provincially. Fogo cited the 'respectability' of the CCF candidates and the manifest ideological moderation of much of their support, and concluded that it was perhaps closer to the truth to say that the agrarian CCF was *progressive*, rather than socialist. This left an obvious opening for an ideologically revitalized and welfarist-oriented Liberal party on the federal scene, if that party were to play its cards correctly.[60]

With Fogo installed as general national organizer preparing for the coming election, and Jimmy Gardiner named as the cabinet minister responsible for the matter of organization,[61] the structures were falling into place. Cockfield, Brown advertising of Montreal was retained as the party's national advertising agency responsible for submission of detailed plans for publicity, as well as the preparation of other services such as polls and testing of slogans, etc.[62] The question of just what the NLF was supposed to be doing with these other centres of authority and responsibility taking over much of its former role is by no means clear. Two MPs, Gray Turgeon of British Columbia and J.-A. Blanchette from Quebec, were briefly attached to the NLF office, the former to oversee publicity and arrange speakers tours and the latter to take charge of organization and publicity in Quebec.[63] The female vice-president of the NLF was supposed to take a full-time position in the office but was instead seconded to the separate election organization under Gardiner and Fogo. Allen G. McLean, later to be the national secretary of the NLF following the 1945 election, was also appointed by Gardiner to take direct charge of the electoral organization. The NLF office, as such, seems in fact to have been somehow telescoped into the separate electoral organization. No further meetings of the advisory council were held since the September 1943 affair until after the 1945 election. At that time Senator Robertson apologized to the delegates for the fact that the NLF had not followed its constitutional provision to provide 'study and research groups' to look into 'social, economic, financial, and political matters.' The NLF, he went on, had 'no authority to do otherwise – such as engage in pre-election activities or organization – and indeed its personnel under the Constitution makes no provision for activities along anything in that line.' Such a constitutional constraint had never of course limited Norman Lambert from playing the role of national organizer, fund-raiser, and party president at one and the same time, but no matter. Wishart Robertson was not another Norman Lambert, and the cabinet in its wisdom had decided to simply circumvent the NLF altogether in order to set up an *ad hoc* election-oriented extra-parliamentary organization under more able direction. The NLF as such was unable to get out a single issue of the *Canadian Liberal Monthly* and the English and French secretaries who had been hired soon found employment elsewhere and were not replaced. The NLF office thus simply withered away, with some its staff simply being absorbed by the Gardiner-Fogo organization. Some of the activities of this latter group were carried on under the name of the NLF, and some under the name of the 'National Liberal Committee.' 'The net result of this,' Robertson admitted to the advisory council meeting held following the 1945 election, 'has been that in the interval between September 1943 and the present all of our activities have been carried on by the election organization, with which the members of your Executive have been closely associated.'[64] Just what all this organizational charade signified, other than an attempt to shuffle Robertson off the stage without officially removing him from office, is somewhat difficult to say. On the assumption of 'a rose by any other name, etc.' we may simply assume that whatever it was called the organization chaired by Fogo was the effective extra-parliamentary organization for the Liberals at this time, and leave it at that.

Under its new identity, the extra-parliamentary party began to carry on a considerable number of activities. A national meeting was held of provincial representatives, Young Liberals, and the womens' groups in Ottawa in early 1944 to initiate organizational and publicity work in the various provinces.[65] As always, the Liberal party could depend upon the continuing organizational strength of the party in the provinces – except in Ontario, which was still reeling from the combined effects of the Hepburn war against Ottawa and the catastrophic defeat of 1943.[66] Strong efforts were made toward a renewal of activity among the Liberal women and the

Young Liberal groups. The latter held a national convention in Winnipeg in the spring of 1944, which was then backed up by the establishment of a national office and the employment of a full-time secretary. Because of the apparent appeal of the CCF to young English Canadians and of the *Bloc populaire* to young Québécois, the party gave very special attention to the organization of the party's youth wing;[67] the Winnipeg convention garnered the party a gratifying amount of the very sort of publicity which they most needed. Other publicity ventures included the production of a weekly news commentary issued to the weekly press, eighty-five of which agreed to run it as a regular feature; the rebuilding of a national mailing list which eventually reached 148,000 names, of which 34,000 were French-speaking; the distribution of well over one million English pamphlets and a quarter of a million French-language pamphlets, up to the election period proper; the provision of assistance to the parliamentary caucus in terms of research and the distribution of mimeographed speeches, etc.; and the general handling of inquiries from the public.[68] Finally, there were the friendly members of the press, most notably the *Toronto Star*, who often acted as publicity adjuncts to the Liberal party.[69] In addition to these publicity activities there was also the matter of direct political organization, for which King called special meetings of the cabinet and caucus in the fall of 1944, with detailed reports on constituency standings.[70]

RECONSTITUTING PARTY FINANCE 1943-5

With the greatly expanded party activity under the direction of Gardiner and Fogo, the inevitable question of the funds to pay for the renewed burst of activity came once more to the fore. The figure of $50,000 per year was suggested at the 1943 advisory council meeting of the NLF finance committee as a working figure for a yearly budget, and Jimmy Gardiner was talking about the same figure early the following year. Lambert suggested that $2000 be raised in Montreal and $2000 in Toronto each month. Montreal was, as usual, the main problem. One prominent collector, Gordon Scott, had become an early war casualty. The indefatigable Donat Raymond was still holding on to some vestige of his former prominence as fund-raiser in that city, although he was now being slowly superseded by Senator Armand Daigle, a finance capitalist in Montreal with directorships in a number of industrial corporations. Raymond gave his promise to help Daigle and Aimé Geoffrion, who was also doing some collections. Yet Montreal did not come through as promised, as was that city's habit. Gardiner was pledged $25,000 by Daigle, but by the end of January 1944 he was reportedly 'sore' over the fact that only $5,000 had been delivered, and 'intended to have a showdown on the subject.' The resolution of this showdown is not known, but by 1945 Fogo informed McLean in the organizational office that Senator Daigle paid for the activities of the French section.[71]

The main centre of national activity in regard to finances was Toronto. Early in 1944 there was a reorganization of the finance committee in that city with strengthened links to the cabinet in the person of C.D. Howe. Peter Campbell went to Ottawa to meet Lambert, Howe, Power, and Gardiner to straighten out the situation. The assembled men were constituted as a general finance committee for the national party. Daigle would look after Montreal – where he had already collected $25,000 from the CPR, with another $50,000 to come – but was not a member of the national committee.[72] Lists were reactivated, and Lambert cautioned Campbell to make sure that Howe and Gardiner 'did their jobs in Toronto, & clear the ground before proceeding to actual collections.' Howe, as minister of munitions and supply, was the obvious figure to exact levies on war contractors. Howe, in turn, wanted Lambert to take up his old position as the collector of these levies. As Lambert noted in his diary: 'C.D.H. spoke to me at lunch about taking hold of finances of organization. I told him that Peter [Campbell] & I had talked about the subject after their last meeting, and I would help him organize the thing, after certain lists were supplied from M[unitions] & S[upply], but that I was not going to go to Toronto or any other place to collect funds.' The next day Lambert prepared a list of thirty-one names of 'people who served Gov't during last 4 years mainly through M & S who should be asked by C.D.H. to help now.' A month later Lambert told Howe that he was ready to go to Toronto to help Campbell 'at the proper time, but if I went into it, I didn't want any pressure or interference from any minister or any one else.'[73]

The usefulness of the munitions and supply lists for gaining party financing seems to have had some initial success. Or so one might surmise from the vastly expanded amounts expended on national organization, as compared to the 1930s. From the end of November 1943 to the end of November 1944 no less than $88,000 was raised under the general supervision of Campbell – which was about equal to the total expended by the NLF for the three years from 1936 to 1938 (see Table 3.1). Another financial statement at the end of 1944 estimated expenditures for the first four months of 1945 at almost $22,000.[74] Much more pre-election work was being done, especially that involving the party's national advertising agency. The point is that funds were available for this sort of extended expenditure pattern, which had certainly not been true in the past. It was thus all the more curious when difficulties presented themselves in financial collections during the election campaign itself.

As the attention of the prime minister turned to the election of 1945 his first thought concerning the supervision of the campaign was to turn to the man who had worked so well at that job in the past, Norman Lambert. After the politically damaging defeat of General A.G.L. McNaughton in Grey North by the Tories early in the year, King grew even more concerned that a firm and experienced hand be placed at the helm. On the eve of the by-election King mused that 'there is no one man that can be entrusted or who has political knowledge and skill to take charge of the organization. Lambert who could do very much is really unfriendly, for what reason except that he would like to have been in the government, I don't know. So there it is.'[75] King for once had hit the nail on the head so far as Lambert was concerned. The former NLF president felt very acutely that he had never been given any place in the wartime government. On one occasion he had almost been appointed chairman of the National War Labour Board, but at the last moment doubts about such a 'partisan' appointment assailed the prime minister and he instead appointed Humphrey Mitchell, later King's labour minister. Lambert drafted a letter to King expressing his feelings of hurt, but decided not to send it – although he noted in his diary that he had not changed his mind about 'the kind of courtesy extended in return for services rendered in previous years.' He had still not changed his mind by 1945, as became apparent when King called him to his office in March of that year. As recorded in Lambert's diary, King came to the point quickly: 'He said that "some of our friends" had spoken to him about asking me to take charge of election campaign organization, especially Ontario; to decide matters of publicity, etc., but not to raise money. I told him that I already had been helping by advising Campbell, Roebuck, Fogo & others who asked my advice; & would be glad to continue doing so, but I would not accept the nominal headship of the party organization.'[76]

King referred to his failure to call Lambert on the night of the 1940 victory, but Lambert wished to make the party leader understand that there was a wider issue involved than his personal feelings:

...it was rather because I felt that the Presidency or Chief Organizership of the party was an important post in the eyes of people in the country & in the party, and carried with it a responsibility on the part of the occupant of these posts to the membership of the party; because of this, recognition and full co-operation should be given to it by the P.M. & the Gov't. I had felt & still felt that one's identity with pol. organizn. was regarded as a stigma & a barrier by the P.M. & his colleagues, to any form of public service outside. As for example during the war years, I had wanted to do certain things as he knew, and was denied them because of too close an association with pol. organizn. If that could be regarded as a personal reason then it would have to stand ... He finally said that ... if he had hurt my feelings at any time he would like to make amends. I said that I appreciated his speaking to me in this way; and that I had entertained no personal feeling of any kind toward him, but just a strong objection & antipathy to being subject to invidious treatment as President of the N.L.F.; & because of that, bringing the post into an unfavourable light.

Lambert was expressing an old complaint of party organizers, one which was perhaps inevitable to some extent, although doubtless exaggerated in the case of Mackenzie King's leadership. King, however, could never quite understand what Lambert was getting on about; the prime minister's diary account of this meeting notes blandly that he had 'cleared up the whole situation pretty well' with Lambert, which was certainly not true. But he at least recognized that while Lambert might offer his services as adviser he could not be secured as the man to take charge.[77]

The alternative to Lambert was Gordon Fogo, who had come highly recommended to King by C.D. Howe.[78] Under Fogo's direction the usual preparations were made for publicity, this time with Cockfield, Brown advertising men in intimate communication on all matters of national publicity. This side of the national campaign will be discussed in greater detail in Chapter 6. In keeping with the leftward image the party had been cultivating since 1943, the national advertising campaign showed little concern with the past achievements of the government in winning the war, but instead emphasized its concrete plans for postwar reconstruction, and the avoidance of a return to the 1930s through a new role for the state in economic life. The welfare plans, such as family allowances, which were already on the books, offered the best advertisement possible of Liberal good intentions to protect the poorer and weaker, precisely those voters to whom the CCF had the greatest appeal. Propaganda appeals went out to specific sectors of the population, to farmers, to union workers, to returned soldiers, to small businessmen, and to housewives – with a dual emphasis in each case on the actual achievements of the government with regard to the special interests of the recipient, and on the plans the government had for future action. All this was summed up in the audacious, if not incongruous, slogan 'Vote Liberal for a New Social Order.'

Since the Tories had been so unfortunate as to have some purist party members oppose family allowances, it was easy for the Liberals to pin the 'reactionary' tag on them, in an election when that name seemed to be a guarantee of ill effect. On the other hand, the CCF had already waned from their peak of popularity of a year or two earlier. How much of that decline can be accounted for by the alert Liberal co-optation of their reform appeal, can of course only be the subject of speculation now. Certainly many in the CCF itself blamed their decline on the Liberals. The failure of the new party to sink roots in the electorate east of the Ottawa River was also highly damaging to their ability to mount a national campaign. In addition, there was evident disunity in the labour movement on the question of electoral support. The strong Communist party group in many of the industrial unions were following a line of alliance with the Liberals, both to defeat their rival on the left, the CCF, and to support the Moscow line of popular frontism, which actually succeeded briefly in placing a few communists in office in European governments of 'national unity,' such as in France. The Communists greatly weakened the pro-CCF actions of the Canadian Congress of Labour's Political Action Committee, and pro-Liberal groups in the Trades and Labor Congress actually obtained a TLC endorsation of the government. Pro-CCF labour elements were thus forced to the periphery – and in some working class constituencies, such as Paul Martin's Windsor riding, they found themselves facing an effective Liberal-Communist alliance.[79] This curious alliance gained the Communists little, but it did serve to disorganize the left and give the Liberals the thin end of the wedge, which they certainly used to maximum effect. Shortly after, they demonstrated their gratitude by arresting a batch of leading Communists under the War Measures Act following the Gouzenko spy disclosures. The only sitting Communist member, Fred Rose, was convicted of espionage. On the other hand, the alliance helped deny the CCF any extensive base in organized labour, which cut severely into their ability to mount a real campaign as a national social democratic party. It was a real clean-up by the Liberals. Thus ended the historic high point of the left in Canada.

What better way was there for Mackenzie King to go out as Liberal leader in his last national campaign? He had guided the party to adopt a welfarist platform, in keeping with his views in *Industry and Humanity*, which he had brought to the leadership of the party in 1919. He had headed off the possibility of a left-wing challenge to the Liberal party by co-optation rather than reaction, and had managed once again to place the Conservatives in the public mind on the right of the spectrum. Once again the Liberals were the triumphant centre. And this was clearly King's triumph as well. As Granatstein justly remarks: 'The victory belonged to King too, for it was the Prime Minister who pressed on in the face of the many difficulties, the Prime Minister who had pushed through the great social-reform program that more than anything else secured the Liberals their majority.'[80]

There was one other element which was crucial to the Liberal victory, and this too could be associated with King's leadership. Quebec had faced two conscription crises and the resignation of leading Quebec ministers in the national government. Yet despite the appearance of an anti-conscriptionist third party, the trauma of conscription had astonishingly little effect on the Liberal party's standing in that province. The Quebec situation is detailed later in Chapter 7. The point for now is that once again the old wisdom of Liberal politics, that so long as Quebec stays solid the party is virtually unbeatable, remained true in 1945. The CCF ran strongly in the West, and in Ontario the Tories were of equal strength to the Liberals. But in Quebec the Conservatives could muster only 8 per cent of the popular vote and the CCF only 2 per cent. With that kind of opposition, the Liberal party had little to worry about in its electoral heartland. But the threat from the *Bloc populaire* had been more serious – the spectre of a nationalist breakaway party sweeping Quebec was one to offer a real *frisson* to the federal Liberals. Yet the *Bloc* had come to very little in the end. The power of patronage and the fear of being outside the councils of the national government was apparently enough to give pause to the vast majority of French Canadians before voting for a third party; yet King's tortuously cautious handling of the conscription issue must be given credit for this result as well. By the time conscription had eventually been introduced, it was so late and so little that much of the opposition had drained away. Finally, the strong hold of the Liberal party on the Quebec media must be noted as another factor. Except for *Le Devoir*, with its tiny intellectual audience, the press was almost unanimously hostile to the *Bloc populaire* and favourable to the government. When this bias extended to simply blanking out the activities and public statements of the *Bloc*, it is little wonder that the party found great difficulty in getting its message across to the voters. In any event, the result was the same: a solid base from which the Liberals could pick up a majority in the rest of the country with no more than a respectable showing in the other provinces.

ELECTION CAMPAIGN 1945: FINANCE

If the organization put together under the direction of Gordon Fogo had proved adequate to the electoral appeal of the Liberal party nationally, it had not always been so clear that the party would find the money to pay for the election activities. This is doubly curious since the Liberal standing in the public opinion polls by the time of the election demonstrated that they were the stronger of the two alternatives to the CCF, and because, as already indicated, the party had been able to gather in a considerable sum in the period between the 1943 reorganization and the election. The financial problem ought not to be overemphasized; the party was hardly without adequate means with which to fight an election. Indeed, the most serious difficulty which arose during the campaign, a demand by the advertising agency, Cockfield, Brown, for immediate payment, was a difficulty brought about more by the agency's failure to understand the fact that contributions normally come in over the last few weeks of a campaign than by the party's inability to raise the required amount. Yet there were difficulties associated with fund-raising in this election which rather tend to indicate that the Liberal party was not yet *the* party of big business. The Conservatives were financially much better off than in 1940, while the Liberals were probably not quite as well off as they had been in that year.[81] Perhaps war contractors expecting a quick return to prewar 'normalcy' in government-business relations were unwilling to pay the Liberal levy on their war business – although as it turned out, of course, the Cold War rearmament was to offer more permanent inducements to retain the gratitude of government and the Government party. Perhaps as well the threat of a leftist party coming to office was no longer strong enough, or the business community was sufficiently isolated from, or indifferent towards, trends in public opinion that it was simply not spurred to offer lavish financing to the two mainstream parties. Or perhaps there was even some element of disgruntlement with the reformist trend which had been displayed by both old parties, and particularly by the Liberals.

There is some evidence that certain elements of big business wished to use the CCF scare to force the two old parties into some form of coalition or co-operation. Since Mackenzie King had adamantly held out against 'national government' throughout the war, this attempt was bound to be quixotic, but it did give the Liberals some trouble. Frank Sherman of the Dofasco steel works in Hamilton, and an old party supporter, informed Norman Lambert in January of 1945 that he and other manufacturers in Hamilton, including Stelco, were 'determined to insist on co-operation between Cons. & Libs as a condition of their support.' Lambert strongly suggested that such discussions might go on at the local level in Hamilton between the constituency associations, but that 'any effort to discuss it amongst others outside would be most harmful.'[82] Not too much seems to have come from this initiative by Hamilton capital. By April Stelco was giving a large amount of money to a Liberal party which had refused all attempts at co-operation, with donations going both to Toronto and to Montreal.[83] Moreover, Sherman himself once again played the role of party collector in Hamilton. C.D. Howe visited that city in the middle of May and asked for 'someone to follow up fast on his footsteps.' Sherman and a local contractor did the necessary fingering of contributions after Howe had established the necessity for gratefulness, and Lambert and Campbell then received the proceeds in Toronto.[84]

One of the problems troubling the Liberals in this election may have had more to do with their own disorganization than with any refusal on the part of business to support them. Lambert was disturbed by the profligacy of party spending in the late years of the war, and was worried that Peter Campbell was unable to effectively control the disposition of funds. This was a problem which stemmed directly from Lambert's own departure from the party apparatus. When he had occupied the position of chief organizer he had not only taken charge of fund-raising but had also exercised considerable control over the disposition of funds. Now there was an apparent bifurcation of these functions. In the late 1930s Lambert had providently squirreled a substantial sum away in readiness for the coming election. Campbell was unable to do this, partly because in the late war years the party was in a much worse political position and thus had more immediate needs than in the late 1930s, but also because everyone was holding out their hand for the most they could grab from the party finance committee. The Grey North by-election had been a sinkhole of funds, and one which had not even returned General McNaughton. Lambert was further shocked when he discovered that $35,000 had already been paid out to Ontario members in advance of the election; he told Campbell forthrightly that he was 'sunk' if he continued to be a party to such spending practices.[85]

About three weeks from the election day, Campbell told Lambert that over $700,000 had passed through his hands since October 1943 (that is to say, in a year and a half). At this stage he had $63,000 in hand and needed an additional $100,000 to 'get by on.' One week from the election Ontario alone was still short of requirements by $50,000.[86] The various provincial organizations were making no pretensions about financial self-sufficiency as in Lambert's days. For example, Manitoba, which had usually been one of the more reasonably autonomous units in a financial sense, 'raised hell' with Fogo over their share of the national budget and demanded $100,000 from Toronto. Campbell had by the end of May sent them $40,000 and Montreal had kicked in another $10,000.

There is no doubt that the fund-raising drive of 1945 did not come up to expectations, although how much this can be traced to the indifference of big business and how much to the disorganization of the Liberal campaign structures is not clear. Unfortunately there is no information available on the exact amounts raised and spent in this election comparable in detail to the information available on the 1935 and 1940 elections. Conservative R.B.Hanson may have thought that his opponents had a 'slush fund' of $5 million,[87] but that seems to be mere Tory fantasizing. It is not possible to say just how much the Liberals raised in Toronto and Montreal, but it is a pretty safe bet that it was much smaller than that rather garish figure. As seems so often to have been the case with party finance, there was perhaps less than met the eye in the mysterious doings of the bagmen in the backrooms of big business.

One way or another the threat of the CCF had been counteracted, the two-party, free enterprise system had been preserved, and the Liberals under Mackenzie King were once more comfortably installed in the seats of power to which they had become so accustomed, not to say fitted. Canadian capitalism had been saved, if not from communism, then at least from Fabian social democracy. That Canadian capitalists seemed curiously ungrateful to their political benefactors may, in the final analysis, only be a reflection of the fact that they had never, throughout the course of Canadian history, suffered the direct challenge of a mass socialist movement as many of their colleagues in Europe had suffered, nor even the challenge of a radical liberal reform movement as their colleagues in the United States had faced – or at least believed they faced – in the Roosevelt New Deal. Thus secure in their own minds, perhaps they never saw the leftward trend in opinion during the war as anything to get all that excited about; perhaps, considering how readily the Liberals were able to co-opt this sentiment, they were correct in their perception, If, on the other hand, the trend really had been significant, then the Liberals saved capitalism with only moderate support from the capitalists themselves. But that had been the essential message of King's *Industry and Humanity*, published a generation earlier: capitalism was too important to be entrusted to the capitalists alone. The Liberal party, through its ups and downs, its organizations and reorganizations, had in the end proved to be a structure capable of embodying that vision.

5

The Government party fulfilled, 1945-58

In the fifteen years since the fall of Mackenzie King's ministry at the beginning of the Great Depression, Canada had gone through 'ten lost years' (to borrow Barry Broadfoot's apt phrase) of economic disaster, followed by five and one half years of a total war effort. The Liberal party had gone through its own changes as well. Following the confusion of defeat and the 'valley of humiliation' of Beauharnois, there had been the rapid and vigorous extra-parliamentary recovery culminating in the electoral victory of 1935. Once in power the party had not quite followed the old tradition of letting the extra-parliamentary party atrophy while organizational responsibility devolved solely on the cabinet – although there had been strong tendencies in that direction, the able hand of Norman Lambert had prevented this development from going unchallenged. The well-organized and well-financed election victory of 1940 was in part at least a result of that continued organizational strength, combining traditional centres of influence and patronage in the cabinet with the active organizational and financial role of Lambert in co-ordinating government-business relations (to the extent to which he was allowed) and co-ordinating the activities of the provincial units of the national Liberal party organization. The war brought with it a partisan ceasefire at the national level, and a virtual scrapping of the national office and the position of national organizer. The precipitous decline of the Liberal party and the growing restiveness of the rank-and-file party activists brought home to the highest levels of the party the necessity of partisan organization to the functioning of what had perforce become the Government party. The fact that the ministers of the government were deeply engaged in administering the war effort and could not, for the most part, afford the luxury of partisan activity, meant that the extra-parliamentary party had to be called back into existence at the national level to direct the renewal of the party as an electoral, as well as an administrative, force.

In this task the extra-parliamentary organization was largely successful – although how much of the success followed from its efforts, and how much from extraneous factors, must remain a matter of speculation. Nevertheless, the fact was that the parliamentary party had felt the need to call upon the extra-parliamentary party in its hour of political need. Once the hour passed, however, and the parliamentary party was again safely installed in the offices of government, the extra-parliamentary party was quickly banished to the further reaches of political influence. This time the emergence of the cabinet ministers as the centres of whatever passed for organizational responsibility in the Liberal party in the postwar era, was much more complete and thorough than in the late 1930s. In a sense there was almost a reversion at the end of the war to the administrative and bureaucratic concentrations of the war period itself. Perhaps the Liberal party had finally found its true reflection in the managerial style of the war years. Not only did the Liberal government extend wartime controls much further into the peacetime period than had been contemplated at the end of the first war; not only did they willingly undertake a responsibility for maintaining full employment and a stable economy which would have been unthinkable before the war; not only did they carry over for another decade a level of centralization in the operations of Canadian federalism which would have been out of the question even in the depths of the Great Depression; but, more than all this, they carried over into peacetime a political identity which is best captured in the phrase, 'the Government party.'

Others have written more extensively of the Liberals' managerial style, of the virtual fusion of party and state, which became more and more apparent as the years of comfortable power wore on into the complacent and quiescent 1950s.[1] For the purposes of this account, we need no more than note some of the factors which bore an obvious relevance to the question of party organization, such as the almost total reliance on the senior civil service for policy ideas and initiatives to the virtual exclusion of any input from the party rank and file;[2] the highly centralized system of political organization focused around a federal cabinet which was increasingly 'nationalized' in its concerns and increasingly remote from the regional perspectives which the cabinet ministers had once represented; the successful cultivation of an electoral image more generalized, more diffuse, and more dependent upon the personality of the party leader than that of any of the opposition parties;[3] and, finally, a sense of confidence – buoyed by successive electoral triumphs, steady prosperity, and an apparently endless vista of economic growth fed by massive foreign investment – which grew imperceptibly into what the opposition was quick to call 'arrogance,' but which at the very least led to a palpable neglect of the political underpinnings of the power of the Government party and to a sense that 'the business of Canada was business' and that sound management would somehow take care of politics as well as the economy and public administration.

It is difficult, in surveying the last dozen years of the long Liberal ascendancy, to avoid the conclusion that the Liberal party had indeed become the Government party to the extent that the question of whether, for example, the bureaucrats were Liberals or whether, conversely, the Liberals had themselves become bureaucrats, is rather problematic. The Liberal party had become the representative of the two most powerful forces in Canadian life – the vastly expanded national state apparatus and the corporate capitalist interests not only of Montreal and Toronto but now of New York and Chicago as well – to the Canadian people; and the party in turn acted as the representative of the Canadian people to these forces. Since capitalism, supported by unprecedented state intervention and a huge rearmament programme, and protected by the ideological hegemony of the Cold War crusade against communism, appeared to be producing the goods, while the state's venture into social security programmes was sufficient to take the hard edge off the impact of economic dislocations, the representation of the bureaucrats and the capitalists to the Canadian people was a saleable electoral platform. Similarly, the role of the party as some vaguely mediating element between the citizens and these powerful forces seemed to suffice for the party as a political enterprise. What Donald Creighton has caustically termed the 'Mackenzie King millennium' had arrived. And when King himself retired from office in 1948 it seemed that nothing had changed. Like the deist universe of the eighteenth-century French *philosophes*, once set in motion the Mackenzie King millennium appeared to be self-regulating and self-generating. In fact, it was under Louis St Laurent that the system reached its culmination, and its highest stage of perfection.

What all this comes down to, in specific terms addressed to the question of party organization, is that in the last dozen years of Liberal rule the party had become the government, and this fused operation simply ran itself with very little intervention from specialized extra-parliamentary structures. The motor had been wound up and the machine ran on, so long as the underlying conditions of economic prosperity and political apathy pervaded the various sectors and regions of the country. Once one has said this, one has probably summed up the entire political history of these twelve fat but grey years of Liberal party activity. The rest of this chapter is merely an extended elaboration of this single theme.

The last years in office of Mackenzie King were not particularly eventful ones for the Liberal party, as the cabinet went on about its business, while marking time in so far as important political initiatives were concerned. The aging prime minister, particularly after the immediate postwar peace settlements and the initial transition to a peacetime economy, settled into a pattern best described by J.W. Pickersgill and D.F. Forster: '... the Prime Minister seemed to have lost his sense of purpose and to be concerned mainly with his place in history, his successor and, above all, his failing health and strength.' As they go on to point out, while King had no new ideas to promote 'he did not relax his grip on policy and was increasingly jealous of his prerogatives as Prime Minister and as leader of the Liberal party.'[4] Ironically enough, many of his complaints of his last days, that his colleagues and the senior bureaucrats were putting Canada under the control of the United States under the guise of 'internationalism,' or that the Finance Department was centralizing the operations of federalism too much, have come to take on a certain undeniable credence to more recent eyes. At the time, however, it was more apparent that the prime minister was out of touch with the directions and currents of thought among the cabinet ministers and the senior bureaucrats who were increasingly close to the ministers. The growing economic conservatism and growing reliance on American capital and American foreign policy initiatives which were to be so characteristic of the Liberals in the St Laurent–Howe era, were already manifest tendencies scarcely blunted by the prime minister's erratic and sometimes crotchety interventions.

One of King's greatest concerns in his last few years was what he believed to be the declining political fortunes of the Liberal party and the failure of the party to maintain proper organization following the 1945 election victory. Whether King's views in this matter were prescient projections of the eventual fate of the party, or were simply tiresome reiterations of his age-old complaints about 'lack of organization' with little regard to the actual truth of the allegations, may be left to the inclinations of the reader. As early as the fall of 1946, Liberal by-election losses in three constituencies led the prime minister to gloomy thoughts on the political future of the party and the possibility of another party, 'further to the left,' coming to office in the near future. As always, the problem was not Liberal policies, which were above reproach, but rather the lack of organization. 'Having no organization,' he wrote his diary, 'excepting what was arranged in the constituencies at the last moment, was of course a major factor. I do not see how the latter is to be overcome because none of the young Liberals are prepared to put time or money into an organization or to seek to find the latter. The older Liberals have lost or are losing their interest in the future of the party.'[5] King's worries were intensified by the fragile majority which the government held in the House of Commons, a majority threatened by defections and by resignations leading to critical by-election contests.

No doubt King had valid complaints about the tendency of the government party to let the organizational side of politics fall into disuse following an election, although as Norman Lambert's long-standing quarrel with the prime minister indicates, King himself had not, as party leader in office, either given sufficient recognition to the extra-parliamentary party or been willing or able to enforce the necesary political directives upon the regional cabinet ministers to make a parliamentary political organization entirely satisfactory. Certainly King's constant harping on the lack of organization seems to have arisen as much out of a desire to set up an easy scapegoat for mistakes made elsewhere as from a genuine concern over the party structure. These by now familiar and well-worn complaints fell on increasingly deaf ears along the government benches. Men like C.D. Howe and Jimmy Gardiner had heard it all before, many times, and they had also seen the Liberal party returned in election after election. Since they, along with their younger colleagues, would live to see the party returned again in the future, perhaps they were justified in their judgment that the old man was protesting too much.

Evidence that King's judgment was beginning to slip can indeed be seen in the doubts he harboured about Brooke Claxton's organizational abilities. Claxton, who was the cabinet minister directly responsible for liaison with the national party office and charged with general supervisory duties over electoral strategy, was almost wholly blamed by the party leader for the defeats in the three by-elections. This was not merely unfair in the specific case,[6] it also demonstrated a serious failure to recognize the man who was, above all, the organizational genius of the Liberal party in the immediate postwar period. No cabinet minister in fact showed any greater sense of responsibility for the organizational side of politics and none showed more consistently intelligent political judgment than Claxton. Claxton's retirement from both office and Parliament in 1954 left a grave gap in the Liberal party's political face, one which was acknowledged by the persistent recourse to his advice even from retirement.

At the beginning of 1947 the prime minister informed the first cabinet meeting that the most important matter on the agenda for the coming year was 'proper political organization,' which he also related to the antagonism which had been created between the federal government and the provinces, many of them led by Liberal governments, by the 'rigidity' of the federal Finance Department in federal-provincial tax arrangements. Remembering the political devastation wrought within the Ontario Liberal party by the Hepburn-King feud, the prime minister was clearly wary of upsetting federal-provincial unity within the party by centralist national policies. It was thus with particular enthusiasm and gratification that King greeted the Liberal victory in a by-election in Halifax in the summer of the same year, since it was the Nova Scotia government of former federal cabinet minister Angus L. Macdonald which had been a major provincial Liberal antagonist of the government's federal-provincial policies. Taken in conjunction with two earlier by-election wins in Quebec, Halifax seemed to indicate that the national party was back on the proper course. Characteristically, King did not give any particular credit to the party organization for these successes, although organization would have been quickly blamed for failure. King's interpretation was quite different: 'Today's victory in Halifax places an additional obligation to stay in public life for a while longer ...' When the prime minister finally decided to withdraw from public life, he made the announcement of his retirement at a meeting of the National Liberal Federation in January 1948, and he took the occasion to once again reiterate that the party needed more effective organization. As he later recorded in his diary:

If the party loses the next election, it will be due more to the inadequacy, insufficiency, etc., of the organization than to anything else. Indeed had I really first class assistance in party organization and felt the strength of it, I might well have felt that I, myself, could carry on through another campaign. It has been the worry of this each election that has made the task so heavy. Men with the right vision might well have seen that there is a power and joy in organizing a political party for victory which is equal to that of headquarters staff in fighting a battle. We have never had a headquarters staff worthy of the name, as long as I can remember. Excepting one campaign where Massey and Lambert threw their energies into the situation, has the Party ever had what it should have had in the way of a first class organization.

I am recording all these feelings as I have experienced them so that the story some day, if I am spared, can be told in its true light.[7]

Whatever else one may say of him, Mackenzie King was consistent on this point until the very end of his political career. It is also a small historical footnote that Lambert finally got at least partial recognition from his party leader for his efforts, even if it was only in the leader's private diary.

THE NATIONAL CONVENTION OF 1948

King's retirement from office precipitated the calling together of a form of extra-parliamentary structure which King himself had never allowed during his twenty-nine years of party leadership: a national party convention. Although the Liberals had been the pioneers in the use of party conventions in the nineteenth century, and had even under Laurier had occasion to call such meetings while the party leader was still in office,[8] King had adamantly opposed any national meetings taking place from the adjournment of the convention in 1919 which had chosen him as leader until the time his own retirement called for the choice of a successor. As events were to prove, he was also quite unwilling to allow the 1948 convention to interfere in any way with his own ideas on either leadership or policy. Certainly, throughout his long career as party leader King never gave the slightest indication that he harboured any belief in intra-party democracy, especially when the definition of party was extended beyond the cabinet and parliamentary caucus.

Immediately following the prime minister's retirement statement, a subcommittee of the NLF executive was appointed to work out arrangements for a convention in consultation with a committee of the parliamentary caucus. This joint committee issued a 'call for a national convention of the Liberal party' which stated the purposes of the convention to be threefold: to establish a party platform; to 'consider the question of Party organization'; and to select a new leader. Delegates were to be chosen from the following categories: Liberal MPs and senators along with defeated Liberal candidates from the previous election or new nominees; the nine provincial leaders; and the presidents of the NLF, the National Federation of Liberal Women, and the Young Liberal Federation, along with their counterparts from the various provincial associations, plus three officers from each of the university Liberal clubs; three delegates from each constituency to be chosen by local conventions called for that purpose. As well, the Liberal members of the provincial legislatures along with the defeated candidates or new nominees in ridings not represented by sitting members were to select from among their own number a body of delegates 'equal to one-fourth of the total number of representatives in each provincial assembly.'[9] The NLF executive was reconstituted as the committee in charge of the convention organization, along with some outside help, such as H.E. Kidd of Cockfield, Brown advertising who subsequently took over Allan McLean's job as national secretary of the NLF following the convention. The office staff of the NLF was put to work full time on the convention as well.

A number of problems arose in the course of delegate selection. There were no less than five provincial elections called in the interim between the 'call' and the convening of the convention. Then there was a problem of responsibility for overseeing the local conventions. Was the national party office to take direct charge of insuring that such meetings took place or was it the responsibility of the provincial Liberal associations? The national party was in fact more than happy to accede to demands for provincial control, since it had neither the time nor the machinery to properly undertake the task. The NLF secretary informed one provincial secretary that the 'provincial unit' was the 'basis on which the convention will run.' Special rooms were in fact set aside at the convention hall for provincial offices and it was expected that provincial caucuses would meet regularly.[10] Another thrust toward provincial autonomy came from Norman Lambert, now fighting a lone rearguard action against the growing centralism of the federal Liberal government in the postwar world. Lambert suggested that the chairman of the national convention should not be Senator Fogo, president of the NLF, but should instead be chosen by the Liberal premiers; Angus L. Macdonald of Nova Scotia was Lambert's own choice. Fogo reportedly 'felt it a body blow when Lambert had suggested this.' It was also a blow aimed at Mackenzie King, since Macdonald was the most autonomist and obstreperous of Liberal premiers in this period. King would have none of it. Provincial autonomy would not be taken to that length.[11]

The composition of the convention membership, as may be seen in Table 5.1, was largely drawn from the constituencies. Almost one-quarter of the delegates were members of the federal parliamentary caucus or were designated federal candidates. Almost 11 per cent were drawn from the provincial legislative caucuses, and fewer than 10 per cent from the national and provincial extra-parliamentary organizations, of whom almost half were from the university Liberal clubs. Regionally speaking, the domination of central Canada was rather less than one might otherwise expect considering that the convention was held in Ottawa. The hinterland areas of the country were well represented (see Table 5.2). Only two or three constituencies failed to send a full complement of three delegates each.[12]

Yet whatever the mathematics, whatever the paper figures may seem to indicate, the inescapable fact is that parliamentary domination was the rule at this convention. As Peter Regenstreif has pointed out, there were at this time very few constituencies in Canada which boasted representative associations; most were controlled by small cliques of local notables or the MP, with the provincial cabinet minister always hovering in the near background. Indeed, there is every likelihood that many of the so-called constituency delegates were not genuinely such, but rather hand-picked appointees

Table 5.1
Delegate composition, national convention 1948

	Number of delegates	Percentage of total
Federal caucus	**307**	23.6
MPs, candidates	245	
Senators	62	
Provincial legislators	**140**	10.7
Extra-parliamentary	**120**	9.2
National and provincial associations	12	
Liberal women	27	
Young Liberals	27	
University Liberals	54	
Constituency delegates	**735**	56.5
Total	1302	100.0

Source: NLF, *Report of the Proceedings of the National Liberal Convention, 1948* (Ottawa, n.d.), p. 25

of whoever was in local charge. Regenstreif goes on to press the point further:

If parliamentary domination was more than likely in the make-up of the convention, it was everywhere evident in the arrangements and proceedings ... [T]he composition of the two important sub-committees, on Resolutions and Political Organization, was heavily weighed [*sic*] in favor of the parliamentary party: the seventeen-member Resolutions Sub-Committee, through which all the resolutions emanating from the constituencies and provincial associations had to pass, had eleven of its members from the parliamentary party – five senators, three M.P.s and three cabinet ministers. Of the remaining six, four were from the hand-picked Federation Executive and the other two were the permanent General-Secretaries. The Political Organization Sub-Committee was almost entirely composed of members of the House. Of the twenty members, eighteen were M.P.s, one was Senator Lambert and the other was Ottawa Lawyer John J. Connolly, formerly executive-assistant to Angus L. Macdonald and within five years a Senator himself.

Table 5.2
Provincial representation, national convention 1948

	Number of delegates	Percentage of total	Provincial population as percentage of Canadian population 1941
Prince Edward Island	35	2.8	0.8
Nova Scotia	79	6.0	5.0
New Brunswick	72	5.5	4.0
Quebec	324	24.9	29.0
Ontario	391	30.0	32.9
Manitoba	97	7.5	6.3
Saskatchewan	110	8.5	7.8
Alberta	97	7.5	6.9
British Columbia	93	7.2	7.1
Yukon	4	0.1	0.1
Total	1302	100.0	100.0

Source: *Proceedings*, p. 25; 1941 Census data

As if this packing of the key committees were not enough, the parliamentary party went to extraordinary lengths to quell a somewhat obsessive anxiety that someone, somewhere, might express an unofficial idea. King wished to see the draft resolutions after they emerged from the resolutions subcommittee, but before they went to the convention floor so that the cabinet might prepare its own interpretation. Regenstreif reports an anonymous source to the effect that Norman Lambert successfully opposed this by asserting that if the cabinet wished to present its own programme, they should do so openly.[13] This appears somewhat puzzling since there is direct evidence in the King diary that the prime minister went over the resolutions with Brooke Claxton and Paul Martin two weeks in advance of the convention's opening, and made a number of changes, particularly along the lines of not being 'too specific, like setting out concrete measures, but to make general statements which can be well defended.' King's concern over the slightest hint of disharmony in Liberal ranks reached the point of outright paranoia, at least in his private diary, when he contemplated the awful possibility that Jimmy Gardiner, the only serious challenger to his designated successor, Louis St Laurent, should have the temerity to express his own policy platform to the convention as part of his leadership campaign. The submission of a personal policy, the prime minister asserted, was 'unconstitutional' for a minister of the Crown sworn to cabinet solidarity: 'He has no right in expressing a platform. He should leave the Government first if he intends to criticize.'[14] He was only restrained from 'strong action' by his knowledge that St Laurent was a certain winner in any event and his disinclination to 'create a scene.'

King summed up his views on the consideration of party policy by a national convention in slightly more calm terms while addressing the delegates:

A Prime Minister is not responsible to a party organization or to a political party; he is responsible to Parliament, and through Parliament to the people of the country as a whole. Unless we are to abandon the basis on which constitutional government rests, and substitute the decisions of a single political party for the authority of Parliament, and for the respect owing to the Crown, we cannot guard too closely against any course which, even to appearances, might tend in so disastrous a direction. The substitution, by force or otherwise, of the dictates of a single political party for the authority of a freely elected Parliament is something which, in far too many countries, has already taken place. It is along that path that many nations have lost their freedom. That is what happened in fascist countries. A single party dictatorship is, likewise, the very essence of Communist strategy.[15]

It was a virtuoso performance, vintage 1926. If Eugene Forsey did not comment on it, he should have.

Mackenzie King was letting matters get a bit out of proportion. There was not a chance of a resolution even mildly critical of the government being passed through this meeting, which was not a convention but a celebration. Others in the cabinet did not take the affair as seriously as the aging prime minister. In the recollection of Young Liberal delegate Dalton Camp, the intervention of Finance Minister Douglas Abbott in a committee considering taxation policy was rather more typical of the proceedings:

Finally, the Finance Minister appeared before us, sitting with legs crossed at the knee, an arm casually draped over the back of his chair, relaxed and smiling, a boardroom portrait of bland and effortless efficiency.

'Well, Mr. Chairman,' Doug Abbott said, his light voice buoyant with confidence and genial candour, 'let me just say this to you. It doesn't matter what resolutions you pass here. Pass any resolutions you like. But I am the Minister of Finance and so long as I am, I will do what I think is right.'

Saying that, he smiled – a handsome, radiant, ear-to-ear smile.[16]

Louis St Laurent summed up the entire situation with regard to the convention's policy-making role most simply and succinctly following his coronation as the new leader. 'I will do whatever it may be within my power to do,' he told the cheering delegates, 'to uphold the principles and advance the policies affirmed at this national Convention, as circumstances may permit them to be implemented.'[17]

Chubby Power, whose alienation from the directions being taken by the federal Liberals – following his own resignation from the ministry over conscription during the war – had grown apace with the increasing centralization and use of administrative discretion in the postwar period, felt that the only way he could possibly present the convention with his view on returning to 'true Liberalism' was to run as a candidate and thus have an opportunity to address the delegates for a few minutes. Other than Power, a lonely and isolated figure within the party by this time, the only glimmerings of dissent came from the Young Liberals, who were put down by their elders at every turn.[18] The ultimate indignity came when four of their number were patronized by being asked to address the convention for three minutes each. Some meek suggestions that the party should have greater participation in policy-making, that the cabinet alone was not the party, flashed momentarily across the proceedings of the convention, and were then forgotten. One of the young protesters, Dalton Camp, has described his feelings in being thus called before the meeting: 'I had the feeling of being on the end of a string looped around someone's fingers, helplessly manipulated, obliged to respond without thought or calculation to the urgencies of unknown or unseen forces. What, I asked myself, looking out over the crowd, did they want from me? Where was the revolt our presence was calculated to quell? Why was I being tokenized? ... [W]hatever I said came from a distracted mind, annoyed by the patronizing introduction, puzzled by my selection, and ignorant of any purpose.'[19] Camp did suggest to the crowd that if this party was unwilling to listen to the voice of the young people, some other party might. There was to be a time in the future when some Liberals might well have wished that they had done more than patronized young Dalton Camp. But at the time, nobody seemed to give a damn.

If the convention's ostensible purpose to consider policy was pretty much a failure, and if the parliamentary wing of the party, and especially the cabinet, effectively dominated the convention's proceedings in this area, the question of leadership selection was even more blatantly manipulated, this time in the most direct and personal manner by Mackenzie King himself. King had long before annointed Louis St Laurent, and everybody in the party knew it. The only other possible contender was Jimmy Gardiner who was something of a loner in the King government from the beginning, with his own independent organizational base in the Saskatchewan Liberal machine, strong regional support in the Prairies, and a blithe disregard for the proprieties of Liberal social manners which Mackenzie King held so dear. Gardiner was, in the view of the prime minister, an outsider, a man from the hinterlands in a party which to this day has never had a leader from outside central Canada; he was a rough, uncultured machine politician; he had been mysteriously connected with Mitch Hepburn when the King-Hepburn feud had been at its height; he had been a staunch opponent of those Liberals who had been associated with the Progressives and United Farmers movements in the 1920s. King was enraged almost beyond words that Gardiner should contest the leadership. He quickly decided to take matters into his own hands by developing a strategy of having a number of leading cabinet ministers enter the contest, and then withdraw while making known their support for St Laurent. C.D. Howe was the first minister contacted by King, and was followed by Abbott and Claxton. All agreed to the scheme with alacrity. Paul Martin was a more difficult case, since he clearly harboured his own leadership ambitions. Jack Pickersgill was put to work on the task of persuading the recalcitrant minister, which he accomplished without much difficulty.[20] Eventually, the convention was treated to the faintly ludicrous spectacle of six leading Liberals – Howe, Claxton, Abbott, Martin, Lionel Chevrier, and Stuart Garson – all going through the formal motions of withdrawing candidacies just before the balloting.

There had been some thought among the Maritimes delegates to nominating Angus L. Macdonald. Macdonald too would withdraw, but the move would be designed to serve ends other than those of Mackenzie King. Macdonald's nomination, by the premier of New Brunswick and the former NLF president, Senator Wishart Robertson, would give the Nova Scotia leader the opportunity to place before the convention the specific regional grievances of the Maritime provinces. When Robert Winters, soon to be the Nova Scotia minister in the next cabinet, caught wind of this scheme, his comment, reported by Dalton Camp, was to the point: 'in a pig's ass,' he muttered, hurrying off to snuff out the plot. Immediately the scheme collapsed, as premiers and smaller fry scurried to get out of the annoyed glance of the powerful of the party.[21] Chubby Power was past caring about the sanctions of the party hierarchy, and he stayed to the end, although he found himself a pariah at the convention, as numerous old friends in the party tried to avoid any public contact with him.[22] Power gathered 56 votes, not much of a tribute for one of the few leading Liberals who dared to speak his mind openly.

Jimmy Gardiner was a serious candidate, who in the end gathered 323 votes, not enough to challenge the commanding 848 votes which gave St Laurent his first-ballot victory, but enough to demonstrate that the Liberal party fell just short of total unanimity. Gardiner, who was described by Bruce Hutchison as a 'kind of sovereign power in loose diplomatic relations with the Canadian Government,'[23] had once again demonstrated that he was too tough a figure to be manipulated like the other ministers – although equally, his region was neither populous nor powerful enough to allow him to seriously challenge the entrenched might of central Canada. King's indignation at hearing Gardiner's appeal to the delegates was such that he decided to break his own rule of 'neutrality' (!) and voted on the first ballot in full view of the press.[24]

The charade ended on the first ballot. Yet even the forlorn candidacies of Gardiner and Power contributed to the legitimation of the new leader's authority. As John C. Courtney has concluded:

Gardiner's candidacy and, to a lesser extent, Power's, nonetheless provided a vital service to the Liberal party in 1948; they made at least a token competition out of what would otherwise have been, for all intents and purposes, a coronation. St. Laurent was clearly marked as Mackenzie King's successor and the party was anxious to have him as its leader. But whereas an unopposed candidate in a caucus selection system would be quite acceptable under certain circumstances, the same could scarcely apply in a convention system. To generate intra-party enthusiasm and to attract public attention, conventions need some genuine competition, even if only for one ballot. It is difficult to conceive of a situation in which it would not be in the party's interests to ensure that some respectable competition to the obvious winner was provided.[25]

Thus everything worked out for the best, and even the ragged spots in the control by the party hierarchy turned out to be enhancements of the party's image. We may leave the last word on this rather curious gathering to Dalton Camp: 'What one had come to marvel at most in Canadian Liberalism was its efficiency, its splendid imperturbability, the infallibility of both its fortune and its genius. The convention had been summoned to decide everything – and to decide nothing (or as little as possible) and to demonstrate that there are ways to maintain fealty other than through commitment to a cause.'[26]

THE ST LAURENT CABINET AND THE PARTY

One of the responsibilities charged to the national convention in 1948 had been to make recommendations concerning political organization. The convention was presented with a resolution calling for the hiring of a national organizer, two assistant organizers, a public relations officer, a press liaison officer, and a recommendation that national conventions be held at least once every four years.[27] The resolution was duly passed without a single dissenting – or even commenting – voice. Like most of the proceedings of the convention it then disappeared from history. Although H.E. Kidd of Cockfield, Brown advertising was appointed general secretary of the NLF in a move which might be seen as meeting the demand for a public relations officer, that appointment was already predetermined. No other moves were made throughout the rest of the St Laurent years which even approximated any of the other recommendations.

There was little interest in building up the extra-parliamentary apparatus in this era because under St Laurent's leadership the party reverted to near total control by the cabinet. The St Laurent years were not merely years of extreme centralization in Canadian federalism; this centralism was also mirrored in the centralism of the Liberal party itself. The old federal-provincial feuds of the Hepburn and Pattullo era were now only memories. One by one the provincial Liberal parties had either fallen under the increasing political and financial sway of the national party or they sat in helpless frustration in opposition while their federal colleagues struck bargains with provincial governments of allegedly opposite political stripe.[28] In Ottawa, the heavy one-party dominance of the House of Commons and Senate, not to speak of the Government party's intricate interconnections with the senior civil service, meant that opposition was at best peripheral and erratic. In this atmosphere the necessity for extra-parliamentary organization scarcely seemed very pressing, and to many it appeared to be merely quixotic. St Laurent inherited a cabinet which contained some of the more powerful figures in Canadian political life, and there was no shortage of bright younger talent to fill the breaches made by retirements. Here were the power brokers of postwar politics. That they should also be given clear responsibility for the political health of the Government party, as well as for its administration and policies, seemed only natural.

The personal style and interests of the new prime minister also had much to do with the reversion to complete cabinet control. Louis St Laurent was not merely replacing a former prime minister; he was replacing a man of whom one cabinet minister later recalled that 'his mere presence resulted in his dominating any situation whether in the House of Commons, in the drawing room, or at the cabinet table.'[29] There are two points of particular contrast between the two men which are germane to this discussion. First is the contrast which Gordon Robertson – who worked for both leaders – has drawn between King who ruled his staff by fear and St Laurent who ruled by love.[30] Robertson, and Machiavelli,[31] both conclude that it is better for the Prince to be feared than loved, if he must choose between the two, but that question aside it would seem that this contrast also holds for the relationship of the two prime ministers to their cabinet colleagues. King was not loved by his ministers; many, indeed, cordially detested him. But they viewed their leader with a mixture of awe and dread. Perhaps one of the few exceptions to this was J.L. Ralston, and his savage dismissal is one of the most dramatic incidents in the history of the Canadian cabinet. None of his colleagues disliked St Laurent, whose gentle manners, personal kindnesses, and unfailing courtesy made him appear the very soul of decency – especially in contrast to the unpredictable and sometimes vengeful old thunder god who had preceded him. But the obverse of this new style was a much looser rein.

The second point of contrast lies in the differing attitudes toward matters political and organizational. King, for all his personal pettiness and his disinclination to give recognition to party organizers, none the less showed a persistent interest in the matter and, to an extent at least, kept the legitimacy of the extra-parliamentary party before the attention of the cabinet. Since the tendency in the regionalized Canadian cabinet was to pull away from a national party structure toward regional groupings, it took such a commitment from the prime minister to maintain whatever extra-parliamentary structures did survive. King's commitment was partial, and erratic, but it existed. In the case of St Laurent no such commitment was ever entered into, let alone maintained. He showed neither interest nor aptitude for the details of partisan politics. Chubby Power's first impression of St Laurent as prime minister was that he treated everything about political organization as 'a bore and not important,' that he had no interest in the general political situation, and that 'Howe is the Boss of all political affairs.'[32] The combination of this lack of interest in political organization and the looser rein given to cabinet ministers meant inevitably that under St Laurent powerful cabinet ministers would draw into their orbit almost all partisan activity. As a direct consequence, the NLF was reduced to near extinction as a viable force in the life of the national Liberal party.

C.D. Howe, the 'minister of everything' as some were beginning to call him in the 1950s, was involved with partisan politics as much as with the serious business of mobilizing American capital for Canadian economic development. If St Laurent needed an English-Canadian lieutenant, Howe filled the bill. In Ontario Howe not only took direct organizational responsibility for the constituencies of northern Ontario but he was the pre-eminent minister for the party in all of Ontario. For example, in the 1953 general election H.E. Kidd at the national office explained to an executive of Cockfield, Brown advertising how responsibilities were divided for the largest province. The campaign manager reported to Howe, and 'any authority he exercises, he does so by virtue of Mr. Howe's consent.' Other Ontario ministers did have some regional importance, Kidd added, 'but of course Mr. Howe is *the authority*.'[33] The only other Ontario ministers of any importance were Paul Martin in the Windsor area, who had a certain reputation within the party for being a loner and somewhat self-serving, especially in regard to the consumption of campaign funds,[34] and Walter Harris, who showed a genuine aptitude for this kind of responsibility and gradually took charge of Toronto and Hamilton as well as his own area of western Ontario.[35] Harris' importance was growing during the years leading up to the defeat of 1957, but he was the only other Ontario minister who rivalled Howe in any sense. Other ministers from the province were either entirely local in their importance, such as Lionel Chevrier and George McIlraith in eastern Ontario or J.J. McCann in the Ottawa Valley, or of no organizational significance at all, such as Lester Pearson who was officially in charge of central Ontario but was only a front man for Senator W.A. Fraser who was not in the cabinet.[36]

Howe was not simply the boss of Ontario, important as that post might be. He was also the crucial cabinet minister for questions bearing on top-level patronage and financial backing for the national party. Until his retirement from politics in 1954, Brooke Claxton was the other minister with equivalent national organizational responsibilities, but in Claxton's case these had to do with advertising and publicity and liaison with the national office. Howe, as Claxton put it somewhat delicately, had to do with the 'other side of political organization.' The two men worked in tandem: 'I had to satisfy him,' Claxton recalled, 'that what I proposed was financially possible because it was politically desirable.' After Claxton's departure his place was taken by Jack Pickersgill, elevated from the civil service to the cabinet in 1953 and installed in the safe seat of Bonavista-Twillingate by Joey Smallwood.

Other than Howe, Claxton, and Pickersgill, no ministers seemed to possess any more than regional importance, although this could often be quite important in itself. In Saskatchewan Jimmy Gardiner continued on as the local party boss and the most important prairie politician in the cabinet.

Both Claxton and Pickersgill later expressed considerable scepticism about Gardiner's alleged political capacity as an organizer.[37] Stuart Garson was less than adequate as the Manitoba man in the cabinet. Alberta, always the weakest link in the Liberal chain, was represented by the weakest link in the cabinet, George Prudham, minister of mines and technical surveys from 1950 to 1957. Prudham not only drew well-justified criticism from the opposition for refusing to divest himself of his personal interest in a company which managed to do business with the federal government without tender,[38] but also proved highly unpopular with the Alberta Liberal party, such as it was.[39] In any event, any government with as wide national support as the Liberals had in this era could afford one weak link.

British Columbia threatened early in the St Laurent government to become another soft spot. The Liberal hold on the Pacific province had always been rather tenuous in the face of a very strong CCF movement. Coalition government in Victoria between Liberals and Conservatives to keep the socialists out of office had proved to be a considerable embarrassment to the federal party, but when the breakup of the coalition was followed by the victory of Social Credit, apprehension turned to outright panic in Ottawa. The British Columbia minister, Ralph Mayhew, was not considered to be very effective in a job which even Ian Mackenzie had been unable to carry out with conspicuous success, and pressures immediately mounted to replace Mayhew with younger and more able ministers. Ralph Campney, parliamentary secretary to Brooke Claxton, was willing to wait, but Jimmy Sinclair, parliamentary secretary to the finance minister, Douglas Abbott, was ready to try to force the prime minister's hand, by threatening to resign. He was dissuaded from this precipitous action by St Laurent who agreed with his views on Mayhew but pleaded that 'I cannot treat colleagues who have been completely loyal to me as though they were worn out machines.'[40] Nevertheless, within three months Mayhew was appointed ambassador to Japan, and both Campney and Sinclair were made members of the ministry, Campney in the national defence portfolio, and Sinclair in fisheries.

Quebec was, as usual, weak on paper, but a powerhouse when it came to counting the votes on election day. No very strong French-speaking cabinet minister emerged during St Laurent's years of leadership, and a succession of ministers undertook organizational responsibility in the two main districts, Montreal and Quebec, without any emerging as particularly important. But with a French-Canadian prime minister leading the Liberal government – and with at least a partial deal struck with Duplessis' unparalleled provincial machine[41] – the lack of strong cabinet representation was scarcely cause for anyone to lose much sleep.

The Maritimes were well taken care of within the cabinet. Milton Gregg in New Brunswick and Robert Winters in Nova Scotia were solid pillars of the party. And in Newfoundland after 1953 the combination of Jack Pickersgill and the protective wing of Premier Joey Smallwood was as potent and electorally profitable a political operation as could be found anywhere in the country.

There was a general recognition throughout the party of the decisive significance of the ministers for political organization, that in Paul Martin's words, all 'political activities would filter through the Ministers. It was the Ministers who would take charge of the various regions, select candidates and handle patronage.'[42] Any break in the continuity of ministerial responsibility for a region could be highly damaging. For example, a few months elapsed between J.L. Ilsley's retirement and the appointment of a new Nova Scotian to replace him in 1948. Although St Laurent was at this time only acting prime minister, Ilsley wrote to him to warn him of the patronage problems being created in the absence of a responsible minister and the 'political difficulties we shall be storing up for ourselves' the longer the province remained without an 'energetic and aggressive Federal minister.' Robert Winters was designated as the acting minister in a circular letter sent from St Laurent to all the Nova Scotia members. In other words, Winters' political appointment predated by a couple of months his official appointment.[43]

There was also widespread recognition of the ministerialist form of organization in the lower ranks of the party. When the problem of finding suitable political talent among the French-speaking Quebec ministers led St Laurent to throw out the idea of appointing an 'organisateur en chef' from outside the cabinet, Solicitor-General Joseph Jean was quick to label the idea as a grave error, since the major complaint from the party rank and file in the province was 'précisément le manque de contact avec le Cabinet et le Chef du parti et le manque de direction de la part de ces derniers.'[44]

The centralization of administrative and political functions in the cabinet placed a crushing burden of work and responsibility upon those ministers willing to play out their full roles. Some, of course, neglected one side of the job, and in the highly administrative and bureaucratic atmosphere of the St Laurent government of the 1950s this usually meant a neglect of the political side. Others found that their private lives were simply snuffed out. Brooke Claxton was the closest the government had to the perfect political man; 'only Mackenzie king,' James Eayrs writes, 'possessed more sensitive antennae: Claxton's were constantly attuned to the faintest murmurings of public opinion.'[45] As minister of the country's biggest spending department, in charge of the 'limited war' effort in Korea, as well as the minister with national responsibilities for Liberal party publicity and image-making, Claxton found that he was regularly spending much of his life on the road. His office calculated that in 1950 he travelled 51,315 miles, delivered 211 speeches, attended 131 meetings, held 307 appointments, was involved in 203 social functions, and spent 110 nights away from home. And of course every day away from the office only increased the administrative load accumulating in the department. Claxton concluded sorrowfully that Canadians, in the form of voters, parliamentarians, and media, were 'exceedingly demanding' of their ministers.[46] Finally, despite his enormous appetite for hard work and intelligent administration, Claxton decided he had given enough of himself and of his talents to the Canadian government and to the Liberal party, and in 1954 retired to the presidency of Metropolitan Life, where he knew that the remuneration was superior, the work easier, and the pressures far less.

C.D. Howe stuck with it until he was forcibly retired by the voters in 1957. Yet despite his long experience and his apparently inexhaustible energy, Howe showed the strains of office in other, and more politically damaging, ways. The increasing intolerance of criticism; the growing political insensitivity indicated by such infamous one-liners as 'what's a million?' 'who could stop us?' or 'nuts!'; the atrocious political misjudgment of the pipeline fiasco in 1956 – all these were perhaps signs not merely of a naturally abrasive and indiscreet personality, but of the increasing wear and tear of the relentless political grind as well. Even St Laurent himself, despite his apolitical manner, was a victim of the pressures of office in his last years. Old, tired, and – in the opinion of many – bored with the job, he went through the motions like a run-down automaton.

Ministerialist political organization worked well enough while the party was popular with the voters, and as long as the fusion between party and state remained more or less unchallenged. The difficulty lies in the question of whether it was ministerialist organization which accounted for political success or whether success allowed the ministerialist form of organization to flourish. No very satisfactory answer can be given, since data on which such an answer could be based scarcely exists. One might give greater weight to the second alternative, however, if for no better reason than the conventional wisdom of the politicians themselves that good political organization is an added luxury when the voters approve, and of no use when the voters turn strongly away; only when elections are close, the belief runs, is sound organization of decisive importance.[47] Employing this rough rule of thumb, one might argue that ministerialism was a luxury in 1949 and 1953, a failure in 1957, and of no significance in 1958. In fact, the defeat of 1957 meant the total breakdown of ministerialism, as the surviving ex-ministers, shorn of their departmental armour, and scrambling desperately for retention of their own seats in 1958, abandoned the field of party organization altogether. Ministerialist organization proved a profound liability for the party after defeat, particularly since the rapidity with which a second election followed allowed no time for the old pattern of extra-parliamentary resurgence while in opposition to develop. The 1958 election was thus fought by the Liberals with a near vacuum at the centre of their electoral organization. The habits of power, developed over two decades of authority, not only ill-suited the Liberals for the task of parliamentary opposition but also ill-prepared them for the problem of organizing out of office. Like self-confidence based on beauty, ministerialism was appropriate in youth, but grotesque in old age. Senator John Connolly, drafted by the party to direct the hopeless campaign of 1958, responded sharply to criticism from a British Columbia Liberal of the NLF's role in the 1957 defeat: 'As a matter of fact, the real responsibility for organization up to June 1957, was vested in the Ministers, in each Province. The Federation did not have the responsibility for organization and did not try to exercise it.' 'Perhaps,' he added wistfully, 'it should have.'[48]

THE NLF AND THE NATIONAL OFFICE

A section on the NLF and the national office of the party may, in the light of what has just been said, seem like an undertaking of dubious value. The NLF was certainly not a national institution in any accepted sense of that term, nor was it any longer a genuine federation. It was a small office doing rather unimportant work, barely noticed by the parliamentary party, by the provincial parties, or by the media. Under its auspices boring and irrelevant meetings were held infrequently at the Chateau Laurier and party propaganda was mailed out to a small number of convinced partisans who needed no persuasion. It is difficult to escape the conclusion that the NLF and its office were more in the way of a symbolic legitimation of cabinet rule within the Liberal party than active forces in their own right, that they were mere façades intended to maintain the fiction that there was a Liberal party 'out there' in the population, when in fact there was only the parliamentary party and its ministerialist leadership, together with a few financial collectors in the major cities and local notables in the constituencies ready to work at elections for reasons of patronage and favour from Ottawa. There is really little need to waste very much time on this paper creature, and hence every effort will be made to describe the main activities of the NLF in this era as briefly as possible.

Late in 1946 Ian Mackenzie reported to Mackenzie King that the NLF office was 'suffering from pernicious anemia,' without leadership or direction. The best he could say of the permanent secretary was that he was 'plodding and loyal, but should have help.'[49] Gordon Fogo succeeded Wishart Robertson as NLF president, and seems to have played a certain role as organizer and party trouble-shooter. He also took a direct hand in the operations of the national office, overseeing the activities of the secretary, Allan McLean, a Gardiner man from Saskatchewan, and keeping minute watch over the expenditure of money. Fogo's health was not good, however, and his death in 1952 left the leadership fo the NLF to Ottawa lawyer Duncan MacTavish who had married into the Southam newspaper family and was connected to a large number of local businesses in the Ottawa area. He was also a lobbyist for some large companies, among them the Boundary Pipeline Corporation seeking a licence for a gas pipeline from Alberta to the United States which was talked out by the opposition in 1952 in a debate which was something of a rehearsal for the 1956 fiasco.[50] The point is mentioned because it was not the only connection established between the Liberal party and the pipeline interests.

McLean was followed as secretary in 1949 by H.E. 'Bob' Kidd who came to the party via Cockfield, Brown advertising, which agency had not only loaned his services for the 1945 election and for the staging of the 1948 leadership convention but continued to pay his salary while he was secretary of the NLF for over a decade.[51] Kidd's appointment signalled the growth of advertising and public relations in politics to the point where those skilled in the techniques of mass selling were gradually becoming more important than old-fashioned politicians or organizers. But Kidd's years at the NLF represented a transition from the older era to the newer. Kidd never took charge in any sense of the Liberal party's policies; indeed, he was scrupulous in keeping in his place, which was very modest. Two incidents typify Kidd's attitude toward his job and the place of the NLF in an era of ministerialist party organization. The first concerned a story which appeared in the press directly quoting Kidd. Kidd immediately called the reporter on the telephone to protest being named in public as speaking for the Liberal party: 'It is a little embarrassing,' he explained. 'If anyone is to speak for the party it should be the President.' The reporter apologized, but added that 'we think you're the man who is there all the time and know the score better than MacTavish does, but I can see your point.'[52] Another involves a conversation between Kidd and his namesake, 'Cappy' Kidd, who was at the same time national director of the Progressive Conservative party. A reporter wished to write personality pieces on the two Kidds. The Liberal Kidd told the Tory Kidd that he had sent the reporter away, explaining that the national officers 'like to live anonymously and the personalities aren't such really as to attract any attention.' The Tory Kidd agreed. 'Well, we don't want publicity,' said the former; 'God, no! I don't want the damn stuff. It's very awkard,' agreed the latter.[53]

There was never the slightest question about where the power lay. When a Liberal newsletter once made a mildly humourous reference to the Senate, the ire of Liberal senators was drawn to the office and McLean's knuckles were rapped over this breach of loyalty. The NLF office once suggested the idea of co-ordinating publicity for a budget presentation. When the finance minister demurred, the plan was quickly abandoned.[54] The control of the selection of officers was entirely in the hands of the cabinet inner circle, despite the *pro forma* votes in advisory council meetings, or the decisions of the executive committee of the NLF. For example, when Fogo died in 1952 Jack Pickersgill from his (supposedly non-political) office as clerk of the Privy Council wrote to the prime minister that 'it is obviously important to have a certain number of members of the Executive Committee told in advance that Mr. Duncan MacTavish would be prepared to accept the presidency and that you feel this would be a desirable arrangement.'[55]

An institutionalization of cabinet supervision of the NLF was achieved in the St Laurent years which had never taken clear form in the King period. Claxton had been the very personalized link established before the 1945 election, and this arrangement continued after the change in leadership. Claxton's close personal friendship with Kidd greatly facilitated an easy rapport and co-operation on publicity matters. But by the early 1950s it had become apparent that the pressures of Claxton's position as defence minister while a war was being waged in Asia meant that he could give no more than 'spasmodic attention' to the activities of the national office. Hence Pickersgill suggested the formation of a small group of ministers to 'discuss useful lines of publicity and to give greater continuity to work of the Federation.' This committee, which was to be broadly representative on a regional basis, was instituted by the prime minister in 1952 and included, along with Claxton and Pickersgill, Stuart Garson, Robert Winters, Hugues Lapointe, Walter Harris, Paul Martin, and Alcide Côté. After Claxton's retirement, Pickersgill was placed in overall charge of the liaison committee, as it was known. On the other side sat the NLF president, Kidd, the French-language secretary of the NLF, Paul Lafond, and on occasion representatives of the party's advertising agency.[56] Regenstreif has aptly summed up the operations of this committee:

The Committee met every month at various places in Ottawa – in the House, at the Chateau Laurier, at the Rideau Club and at the Federation offices – sometimes with a full complement and sometimes with the attendance down as low as four. With J.W. Pickersgill usually in the chair, the meetings would last anywhere from 1¼ to 2½ hours and it was this body that took charge of all matters of organization at the national level for the party during this period. Among its activities, it reviewed each issue of the *Canadian Liberal* before publication, discussed the content CBC free broadcasts should have ... decided upon new candidates in a federal constituency to replace those who had died and approved the programme for the 1955 Advisory Council meeting, at the same time confirming the names to be submitted as the new Executive of the Federation to the Council.

The executive committee was the main body outside of the cabinet which had a voice in the supervision of the national office. The committee was not directly elected but was made up of appointees from the various constituent bodies of the Liberal party, plus the executive of the NLF elected by the advisory council. The provincial associations and representatives of the Liberal Women and the Young Liberals thus shared a place with the NLF president, vice-president, treasurer, as well as the two secretaries. The committee was also empowered to add more members, which it did, to the extent that it numbered up to thirty by the mid-1950s. Its meetings were private, with the press barred, so that rather more important matters might be discussed than were aired in the public advisory council meetings. Geographical factors ensured that only those members who lived in central Canada, and especially in Ottawa, were able to give any sustained attention to the workings of the committee. Nevertheless, it did have some utility to the party, again in Regenstreif's words, 'partially as a mechanism of liaison among the provinces and between the provinces and Ottawa, and as a helpful device for the transmission of the Leader's wishes to the party in the country.'[57]

Advisory councils were another matter. Frank Scott once termed the NLF 'that amorphous body of self-appointed notables occasionally summoned to give the appearance of democracy to the Liberal party machine';[58] the description was apt enough for the periodic meetings of the advisory council. There were odd occasions in the late 1940s when delegates to the advisory council meetings actually stepped ever so slightly out of the well-indicated paths laid down for them by the party leadership. In 1949 Brooke Claxton – who saw his role as that of a 'kind of messenger boy' between St Laurent and his cabinet and the council[59] – had to intervene twice against proposed resolutions, once successfully and once unsuccessfully. The successful intervention came on the more serious matter, having to do with the highly sensitive question of federal aid to higher education which happened to be Maurice Duplessis' current *bête noire*. Claxton suggested that 'if this resolution were passed it would embarass us and we would not be able to carry on our objectives. On that account I would suggest that the Resolutions Committee be asked to reconsider this matter. I suppose I have not a vote, but I raise the difficulty that I see, because I cannot see the wisdom of a Council such as this adopting things it cannot do, and just setting up a target for the attack of our opponents, if we do or do not do them.'[60] The committee took the hint and, in reconsidering the matter, withdrew the offending resolution.

In the 1950s advisory council meetings were called less frequently than before, and those that were held caused nary a ripple of controversy or criticism. At an executive committee meeting in 1954 MacTavish explained why no council meeting was called for that year: 'It was not appropriate, he thought, to ask people to come a long way to a Council meeting unless there was a satisfactory agenda and important business to transact. At the present time there did not seem to be any real need for a meeting.' At the advisory council meeting of 1955, the last before the Liberal defeat, held as all council meetings were in the Chateau Laurier in Ottawa, there were 324 officially in attendance, of whom 164 were voting delegates and the remaining 160 were 'observers' or 'guests.' In other words, it was as much a social occasion as a political gathering. Regenstreif may again be quoted on the significance of the advisory council: 'The conclusion is inescapable that any possibility of the Council asserting its independence, if it were so disposed, or even of carrying on free discussion was hampered by ministerial control and supervision. The fact that the press has access to the meetings, and that guests may attend its deliberations may be the most apt indications of the effectiveness and significance of the Council. The conclusion must be reached that it served more as an enthusiasm-generating body than one from which ideas or policy could originate.'[61]

To turn now to the national office of the NLF, the activities which were carried on a regular basis were of a generally mundane nature. The office staff could be as few as eight persons, as it was following the 1949 election, but generally fluctuated around fourteen to twenty, and sometimes reached fifty at election time. A national mailing list of Liberal supporters was maintained which sometimes reached as high as 50,000 English and 20,000 French names, but was always incomplete due to the slowness of MPs in supplying names to the office. After the 1945 election, MPs and defeated candidates were asked to submit lists of party workers in their constituencies: only nine bothered even to reply![62] Eight years later, sixty-three constituencies still had supplied no names to the mailing list, despite the 'frequent appeals' of the NLF.[63] Other activities included the reprinting of speeches, a clipping service, and occasional, although very minor, research assignments. Even here there was little co-operation from the parliamentary party members. A reprint of a speech by the prime minister in 1952 was ordered by only 76 MPs, and another by the defence minister in the same year was ordered by only 72 MPs for their ridings. A booklet on political organization prepared by the NLF office roused the interest of only 52 MPs and candidates.[64]

There had been sporadic attempts following the end of the war to revive the idea of the *Liberal Monthly* which had briefly come into existence in the late 1930s. Senator Fogo had to report to the 1947 advisory council that the idea of the *Monthly* had been once more deferred, mainly due to the lack of financing, since the party brass knew well that such a venture would never be self-funding.[65] A small newsletter, in English and French editions, was produced on a fairly regular basis in the postwar period, although the size of the readership would appear to have been small. Finally, a quarterly publication called the *Canadian Liberal* was produced, which attempted to combine party propaganda with more serious pieces by well-known journalists and academics. The magazine never attained a readership of much more than 5,000 subscribers, and the parliamentary party members were among the most delinquent of all. Kidd reported in 1953 that of the 184 Liberal MPs in the House, only 60 subscribed to the quarterly, and of 73 Liberal senators only 14 bothered to pick up the party magazine. Kidd went on to say that 'if the members don't think the material from the Federation is worth using, then we would be interested in having some suggestions but, so far, we have received none whatsoever.' When a special election issue of the magazine was offered free to the members, only 77 even asked for it![66]

The lack of interest in a party press was compounded by the problem of the two languages in Canada. It was difficult enought to get out an English-language magazine which could attract much attention, but there could be no question even of translating an English paper into French. Quebec Liberals were always insistent on the point that party publicity must be different in more than language, that there were, in effect, two political cultures in Canada, and the Liberal party would be running afoul of its strongest bastion of support if it neglected to treat French-language Liberals as a separate and distinctive category. As a Quebec MP told the advisory council meeting in 1947:

The same principles should be from Halifax to Vancouver, but you cannot speak the same language as an approach or put across the same message in Quebec as you possibly can do very efficiently in Ontario or British Columbia or the maritimes ... The thing that damages national unity in this country is to try to conceive in Quebec what can be conceived elsewhere. It is because you cannot change Quebec; you cannot change human nature. We are here. We are French peasoups, proud of it, and you cannot make us anything different.[67]

The NLF always tried to take account of this French fact. A French secretary assisted Kidd in the day-to-day operations of the office. Paul Lafond was by all accounts a very able and useful member of the office, and was really the second in command with regard to all its operations, not merely the French-language activities. A smaller French edition of the *Canadian Liberal*, called *Le Libéral,* was issued under Lafond's direction, but its financial status was even more tenuous than the English publication. Finally, as Kidd himself was quick to point out, despite the good intentions, the NLF office was 'not as bilingual as it should be.'[68]

It hardly seems that the NLF was fulfilling a very important role in the provision of party publicity. The point is not to criticize the office but simply to note that the market for inter-election partisan publicity was not sufficient to justify very much effort. One Liberal MP made a telling point while disparaging the small newsletter which the NLF produced at the time. Such publications, he suggested, are of 'very doubtful value' since 'most people follow such information in the daily press if they are at all interested.'[69] Despite partisan suspicions on the part of Liberal leaders themselves, the major media in Canada – the CBC, the Canadian Press, and the newspapers – were generally either sufficiently neutral or sufficiently pro-government in orientation that Liberal supporters needed no more partisan sources of information on a regular basis. Certainly they showed no noticeable demand for such.

A second, and equally important, point to be made about the NLF as a publicity office was that in terms of the one period when Canadians were accustomed to partisan political communcation as a legitimate intrusion on their consciousness – that is, election campaigns – the NLF was not directly involved in the creation of party publicity. This was instead the prerogative of that other national office of the party, Cockfield, Brown Limited in Montreal. In fact, the role of the advertising agencies in the party's affairs is sufficiently important to warrant a separate chapter (see Chapter 6). The point for now is that in terms of election advertising, Cockfield, Brown clearly superseded the NLF. The fact that Kidd while secretary of the NLF remained an employee of Cockfield, Brown clearly established the order of precedence. The NLF was in this sense a branch office of the advertising agency in Ottawa. This relationship became even more obvious at election time, when the agency turned its full attention to its Ottawa account.

One attempt to circumvent the general disinterest in partisan publicity was the idea of setting up a front organization called the 'National Editorial Bureau' which would produce a column for weekly newspapers, as well as short 'news' bulletins for radio stations. Two journalists were retained early in 1953 for this purpose. Great pains were taken to conceal the partisan intent of the venture. 'Our first objective,' one NLF memorandum rather melodramatically explained, 'is to gain the confidence of the news editors of the radio stations. The contents will gradually change, and material on topics closer to government policy will be included.' Employees of the NLF office were admonished not to leave copies of bulletins lying about the office for fear that visitors might make the connection. The cloak-and-dagger precautions were in vain. A check done on the distribution of the material found that only five weeklies across the country had picked up anything from the service, and very little had found its way onto any radio stations.[70]

One enterprise of some significance for which the NLF did take responsibility in this era was the production of the *Speaker's Handbook,* a compendium of handy facts about government achievements for the use of Liberal candidates in preparing speeches and local campaign material. This venture was, in Kidd's words, 'the most complicated and demanding task' facing the NLF, and was also the 'largest co-operative project undertaken by this Federation.'[71] The latter was a reference to the co-operation required of the ministers to provide the necessary information on departmental achievements, and particularly the breakdown of these achievements by electoral district in exact dollars and cents. The preparation of the *Handbook* usually took about a year from beginning to end, and close co-operation was normally enjoyed with the ministers' executive assistants.

Another area where the NLF did provide useful service to the party was in co-ordinating the itineraries of the ministers in their travels about the country. As early as the 1949 advisory council there were suggestions made that the NLF should attempt to schedule these travels for maximum political effect. But action was taken only when strong complaints began to filter into the highest levels of the party in the mid 1950s about ministers failing to co-ordinate their visits with local Liberal organizations, sometimes to the point of rousing vocal resentment among the local Liberals.[72] Reacting to these criticisms, St Laurent directed his ministers to list all their planned trips with the NLF office, which was given the responsibility of co-ordinating them for the general political benefit.[73]

In electoral matters the NLF had almost no role, beyond sending out a

letter at the prime minister's request to all the constituencies to request political intelligence pending a general election. Yet one such inquiry in 1952,
even with a covering letter from the prime minister, elicited only sixty-seven
replies.[74] Sometimes the office would offer assistance in sorting out the complicated question of appointments of returning officers in elections, but
even here it was normally under the direct supervision of the regional
ministers.[75] When the local organizations in by-elections sometimes sought
help from the national office, they were usually rebuffed or referred to the
appropriate minister.[76] One exception was Ontario riding in Oshawa, where
the NLF secretary took direct charge of a by-election in 1948. It is not quite
clear why this unusual arrangement was arrived at, but Liberal advertising
agents in the constituency requested that McLean, then the NLF secretary,
come down to Oshawa and take over. A total $18,489 was spent in a cam-
paign replete with all the modern publicity techniques, but the riding, which
had been Liberal, was lost to the CCF.[77] It was not an auspicious start for the
NLF as an electoral organization. Somewhat surprisingly, one finds that in
1952, in another by-election occasioned by the death of yet another Liberal
in the same constituency, the NLF was again imported to choose the candidate, the organizer, and to revamp the organization as a whole. This time
they lost the seat to Tory Michael Starr.[78]

The NLF office was in fact in such poor touch with local conditions in
most constituencies in Canada that when they were occasionally asked to
provide patronage lists in local areas or even to provide the names of constituency executives they were often unable to do so.[79] This raises the question
of the role of the NLF in patronage. In the days of Norman Lambert the national office, as was indicated earlier, had been a conduit of some significance for patronage matters. The presidents in this later period, Fogo and
MacTavish, may have played some role in this area, but it is doubtful that it
was on a very important scale. Again, the crucial significance of the ministers is the key point. Patronage was their prerogative, and was unlikely to be
surrendered to an extra-parliamentary organization of peripheral relevance
to the workings of the government. The national office did play some minor
role, sometimes redirecting patronage requests when there was a temporary
hiatus in ministerial representation in a province. The national secretary
might act as a kind of traffic controller for requests coming in from local
Liberals with grievances about patronage who did know who to contact in
Ottawa – although this was usually very 'small potatoes' in the patronage
scale – or for departments who did not know who to contact for nominees
in a local area. McLean while secretary devoted a certain amount of time to
patronage matters of a local nature, although these mainly concerned

Yorkton, Saskatchewan, McLean's own home constituency, unfortunately represented by the CCF.[80] Since McLean was a Gardiner man, he had a fairly close, if minor, relationship to the Saskatchewan Liberal machine. Following Gardiner's defeat at the 1948 convention, McLean was replaced by Kidd, who had no practical political background and rarely got involved in any patronage matters, except for those which touched on his own area of advertising. Here he sometimes represented not only Cockfield, Brown to the party (as well as the reverse) but also attempted to keep other Liberal agencies happy as well, by putting in the odd word here or there. In addition there was the task of making known to the appropriate departments the contributions made by the paper and office equipment companies during election campaigns through their free services and low-cost loans of machinery, as well as making known to Cockfield, Brown the names of approved suppliers for Liberal ad campaigns.[81]

None of these enumerated activities on the part of the national office add up to very much, in the last analysis. The conclusion stands that the extra-parliamentary office of the party was largely a symbolic legitimation of the real power centre in the cabinet. If it could provide the odd concrete contribution along the way, who was to complain?

AFFILIATED ORGANIZATIONS: THE LIBERAL WOMEN AND THE YOUNG LIBERALS

No attempt will be made to deal here in any detail with the two major auxiliary organizations to the NLF, the Liberal Women and the Young Liberals, for both were less important in themselves than in what they represented in potential to the national and provincial parties – although in very different senses. The Young Liberals were a recruitment channel to the party organization and to the parliamentary party, a legitimate route for upward mobility where young Liberals could gain a sense of importance and responsibility within a 'playpen' atmosphere, while at the same time gaining the kind of experience and contacts which could open doors to future participation in the big time. In an era when the gap between university graduation and responsibility and prestige was perhaps somewhat more difficult to bridge than it may be today, the Young Liberal organization was an important link, giving the party brass the opportunity to test the abilities and potential of the young in a safe subsidiary organization, while at the same time helping to harness their energy and enthusiasm to the party cause by the promise of immediate office and responsibility, albeit at a secondary level.[82] University Liberal clubs were also affiliated to the NLF, and acted as channels into the Young Liberals.

If the Young Liberals were an organizational expedient for recruitment and upward mobility, the Liberal Women's Federation was quite simply an organizational ghetto, a reservation where an important section of the electorate and of the party could be effectively contained and managed while any real participation in the party's leadership was prevented. The place of women in the party was demonstrated time and again whenever female Liberals tried to do anything more than to type letters or stand about pouring tea while modelling large floral hats. When one Liberal woman tried to take the initiative in organizing a Liberal association in a Newfoundland constituency in 1953, Kidd drafted a letter for the signature of the president of the National Federation of Liberal Women ordering her to desist from such activities.[83] Money for Women's Federation activities was another means of control, since the NLF president and treasurer held the purse strings. Control was most effective when particular projects were approved and underwritten, rather than when bloc grants were given on an annual basis. In the 1950s the former practice was generally followed, despite protests by the women.[84] It would be both tedious and superfluous to document this relationship at great length, since the ghetto model has since been officially recognized and rejected, first by the Liberal Women and then by the party as a whole. But in the 1940s and 1950s it occasioned only sporadic protests. In a rare burst of dissent, some western women delegates disrupted the smooth proceedings of the 1947 advisory council to move to reverse a constitutional change whereby female representation on the executive of the NLF had been reduced. The Young Liberals immediately took this as an attempt to diminish group influence, but one of the women stated flatly that women 'are really being deprived much more than the Young Liberals.' She went on to point out that, thirty years after being given the vote, women were no closer to effective participation in the inner councils of the party. She then suggested that this was not entirely their fault: 'I have worked in elections for twenty-seven years, and I meet the women all the way through. I find many women are not interested, because there is nothing to shoot for. If you are playing a game, it does not make any difference; if there is a fifty cent trophy, you work for it. What do we work for? Nothing but the domestics of the election.'[85] The women were ruled out of order, and everything returned to normal.

But the delegate had put her finger on the precise reason why women were organized by the party. The 'domestics of the election' – typing letters, licking stamps, knocking on doors, and holding teas – were an invaluable service to the party. To gain the use of this necessary labour force, the Liberal Women's clubs were a device to offer as symbolic and immaterial a return as possible while mobilizing enthusiasm. The abilities of women as workers – even sometimes as speakers – were highly prized and heavily utilized, but they were always kept pretty strictly in line. In this division of labour the maintenance of a *separate* but *subordinate* women's organization was decisive, both in the sense of mobilizing women and in keeping them out of the top levels of the party.

'It is perhaps fair to say,' one Liberal women wrote in 1952, 'that most of the women I have talked to look to the day when we will be working as equal partners in political parties, and that there will be no longer any point in having a political organization or federation for women any more than there would be to have one for red-headed or blue-eyed people.'[86] But this 'looking to the day' did not involve any important initiatives to bring the day about. That had to await the social changes of the late 1960s and the resurgence of feminism as a movement. In the 1950s that day still seemed a long way off. For this era, the contrast between the two affiliated groups is what stands out. If the 'playpen' atmosphere of the Young Liberals was at least a temporary transitional device for political socialization and recruitment, the 'kitchen' atmosphere of the Liberal Women's Federation was a permanent condition, symbolizing the structural subordination of women to men in the affairs of politics. One could grow out of the Young Liberals; one could not grow out of the Liberal Women's Federation. Young men became older men; women always remained women.

PARTY FINANCE

There are two introductory points to be made about party finance in the postwar era. First, it is obvious that the Liberal party was much better financed than before; it seems fair to say on the basis of the available evidence that the Liberals had largely solved the problem of funding in this period. The second point is that while the overall outlines of the picture are reasonably clear, there is much less detailed and specific information available for this era than for previous years. Sad to say, there was no diary-writing Norman Lambert collecting funds in the postwar era; or, if there were, the records have not been made generously available to the interested researcher. It is a matter of some irony that the closer the Liberals came to financial affluence, the less one can say about the matter with confidence. The two points, of course, may not be entirely unconnected.

We may begin at the top. It has often been remarked that the Liberal governments in this century have shown a marked preference for co-optation of leadership from outside the ranks of the professional politicians.[87] Perhaps the choice of Mackenzie King – then of the Rockefeller empire – over parliamentary veterans Fielding, Graham, and McKenzie; the choice of co-opted corporation lawyer Louis St Laurent over the machine politician Jimmy Gardiner; the selection of co-opted bureaucrat Lester Pearson over the professional politician Paul Martin; and finally the choice of Pierre Trudeau, with only three years of political experience behind him at the time of his accession to office – all tend to demonstrate a preference for the political amateur over the professional, a preference which also extends to the selection of cabinet ministers as well. While this tendency has been widely noted, the financial inducements to attract men from outside politics to give up their private careers has been less remarked upon. In fact, there has been a long-standing tradition within the Liberal party of stepping outside the limits of public remuneration for national office by mobilizing private funding to supplement the rewards of the public treasury.

Mackenzie King, as noted in an earlier chapter, benefited enormously from the assistance offered by P.C. Larkin of Salada Tea and other Toronto businessmen in the form of almost a quarter of a million dollars, along with the renovation and refurbishing of his personal residence – which had been willed him by Laurier's widow. Just how much this had to do with Larkin's appointment as high commissioner in London is a matter of speculation, but there was no shortage of wealthy businessmen who felt it worthwhile, for whatever reason, to become financial benefactors of leading Liberals. Indeed, King himself, even in his last years as prime minister, was still the object of these attentions. In 1946 J.W. McConnell of the St Lawrence Sugar and *Montreal Star* empires, who was an ex-Conservative kingmaker apparently converted to Liberalism by the war years, offered landscaping and gardening work to the Kingsmere estate. King gratefully declined the offer.[88]

When Lester Pearson was debating in 1948 the question of giving up his successful career as a diplomat to enter politics, the spectre of financial insecurity weighed heavily in his mind against the decision. At this stage, Walter Gordon, then in private business in Toronto, stepped into the picture to help his friend by raising the funds for a 'modest annuity which would temper this source of hesitations.'[89] Douglas Fisher has since written of this fund that 'the largest single donation came from the McConnell sugar interests [St Lawrence Sugar Refineries Limited] in Montreal.'[90] The editors of Pearson's memoirs have claimed that he knew nothing of the identities of those who had subscribed to the fund; the point has been questioned, particulary in relation to the somewhat curious immunity of the sugar interests from prosecution under anti-combines legislation throughout both the St Laurent and Pearson administrations. Again, there can only be speculation on the matter – and rather ill-informed speculation at that – but the doubtful aspects of the position of any leading politician who places himself in this situation need little comment.[91]

When King was attempting to persuade St Laurent to remain in public life to inherit the office of prime minister, St Laurent expressed grave misgivings. Among them was the financial question. In the account of St Laurent's biographer, the justice minister explained that he could not 'afford to remain in public life': 'friends had offered to help him financially if he remained in politics, but he was very reluctant to accept such assistance, because it might appear to imply some sort of obligation toward the donors. Once again, Mackenzie King had a ready reply: if *he* had not been helped by friends, he would not have been able to remain in public life either, and he had never felt any embarrassment on that score; in fact, nearly every political leader received financial aid to compensate for the loss of revenue resulting from his public service.'[92] St Laurent's mind was made up for him when a group of 'wealthy admirers' went ahead, 'without consulting him' according to Dale Thomson, and underwrote his financial situation. After satisfying himself that he was not thereby putting himself under any obligation to his benefactors, St Laurent accepted the assistance and went on to the highest office.[93] Chubby Power was twice offered financial assistance by Sir James Dunn of Algoma Steel to contest the party leadership.[94]

There were two main financial structures in the Liberal party below the level of private funding for the leaders. These were the regular election fund-raising committees situated in Montreal and Toronto, with smaller subsidiary committees in such centres as Winnipeg, Vancouver, Hamilton, and Ottawa. Peter Campbell and Bruce Matthews (son of former fund-raiser Albert Matthews) were important figures in this era from Toronto, and Senators Armand Daigle and Louis Gélinas in Montreal were successors to Donat Raymond, who seems at long last to have disappeared from the fund-raising scene. There was no diminution of the close connections between the fund-raisers and the donors already evident in the 1930s; the 'Masonic interest' of which Mackenzie King had earlier spoken continued apparently unabated. As a study done for the Committee on Election Expenses in 1966 concluded:

New collectors are recruited informally by already active collectors. A known Liberal who is also a rising young businessman will be approached very informally about collecting some money for the Party. Participation in fund raising is sometimes a family tradition. Since its personnel is renewed from within itself, the fund-raising structure usually continues even when the leadership of the Party changes. Thus the fact that established business contacts are the key to success in this aspect of Party activity leads toward the apparent autonomy of the fund-raising structure.[95]

There was no repetition in the St Laurent years of the Hepburn feud in Toronto, or of the Beauharnois affair in Montreal. Continuity and autonomy were the characteristics of the period in so far as the raising of funds was concerned. And at the centre of the operation there was C.D. Howe, the 'minister of everything' in Ottawa, carefully keeping watch over who did what government business and reminding them of the usefulness of tangible signs of gratitude to the Government party which made so much possible for them.

There is no reason to believe that the contract levy system initiated by Norman Lambert in the late 1930s was abandoned as the Government party grew older in the comfortable exercise of power. Indeed there is, on the contrary, every reason to believe that it was extended and made more comprehensive and efficient. One of the ironic consequences of the vast extension of state activity and intervention which followed the Liberal turn to the left in the late war years and the prolongation of an armament economy well into the Cold War years, was that the scope for party finance on the basis of government business was much increased. As the public sector of the economy expanded, so did the fund-raising potential of the Government party. If one looks at the spending of the Department of National Defence, for instance, it quickly becomes apparent that the Cold War and the Korean War were highly profitable undertakings for the Liberal party. Brooke Claxton, the minister of this crucial department, kept his own up-to-date lists of defence contractors with offices in his own Montreal constituency for fund-raising purposes in his own campaigns. The amount of government business was quite impressive. For example, one list used to solicit funds for the 1949 campaign listed defence suppliers for the last six months of 1948. For this period alone, Canadair was listed for $2.5 million, the CPR for $1.5 million, and Canadian Car and Foundry for close to $2 million. Altogether no fewer than twenty-six companies in Claxton's riding had done business with his department in this period.[96] Nor was Claxton the only one who kept such lists. On the contrary, they were a staple item for party perusal. Examples abound, but one which may be taken as indicative was an inquiry by Kidd at the NLF office on behalf of the NLF treasurer, Alan

Woodrow, into all construction suppliers to the Defence Department with more than $5000 business. The list grew quite detailed as Kidd searched out suppliers of 'pallets and small wooden boxes' and other minor items.[97] It is unlikely that these efforts were undertaken out of a pure thirst for knowledge.

Increasing government intervention in the economy also yielded significant gains for party fund-raisers. Corporation presidents might continue to ritually excoriate 'creeping socialism' and 'government dictatorship' to awed Rotarians and Jaycees, but they were of course reaping immense benefits from the old Canadian tradition of corporate welfare, now become bigger and better than ever. At the same time, the party which had initiated these dangerous experiments in collectivism was reaping its own benefits from the generosity of grateful corporate benefactors. The mining interests, who had played such an ambiguous role in the era of the King-Hepburn quarrel, offer a good example of this mutual accommodation between government, party, and business. Difficult world market conditions for gold led to greater and greater government assistance to the gold producers in the 1940s. But the mining companies, like Sam Gompers, always wanted more. In May of 1949 the finance minister, Doug Abbott, wrote to the Canadian Metal Mining Association and the Ontario Mining Association to accede to their request for extending the very generous tax write-offs already granted gold mines to all mining operations. The executive director of the CMMA assured Abbott that his actions had put the mining industry in his debt, and thanked him for giving them such 'prompt notification.' The promptness of the finance minister might have had something to do with the fact that a federal election was scheduled for 27 June, just a month away! To drive the point home, the Liberals placed an advertisement in the *Northern Miner* just before the election pointing out that the Liberal government had already provided no less than $9.5 million in assistance to eighty-eight gold mines, which worked out to an average rate of assistance of $4.23 per ounce in 1949.[98] There is no documentary evidence of mining company donations in this election, but if the Liberals' point was lost on the mining entrepreneurs, it was certainly not for want of trying.

The names of only a few of the large donors to the party in this era can be established for certain. Duncan MacTavish is on record as speaking of the CPR as 'pretty substantial contributors';[99] International Nickel was a contributor, both to the national fund and to local candidates in northern Ontario;[100] IBM also gave money to national headquarters and to local constituencies, such as in Ottawa;[101] some old stalwarts of Liberal campaign chests, such as Canada Packers, Swifts Premium, and Eaton's, continued their regular support into the postwar period.[102] But the fragmentary evidence on specific identities of donors need in no way deter the observer from the conclusion that the Liberals had by now gained a widespread financial base in most sectors of Canadian business. The well-known sixty-forty split in donations between government and opposition had by now become common, and many sections of the corporate world, such as the banks and financial institutions, apparently gave to both parties as a routine matter of good public relations.[103] When one adds the growing number of businesses with direct government business to those with such general motives as maintaining 'fire insurance,' purchasing potential access to the party leadership, or simply maintaining the two party system,[104] and when one remembers that the Liberals were the dominant and unchallenged party in federal politics, with little apparent chance of losing office, it is readily apparent that the party was rich with potential sources of financing.

There is also abundant evidence that the actual return was almost as rich as the potential. Just prior to the dissolution of the Twentieth Parliament in 1949, the chief financial collector in Montreal, Senator Armand Daigle, sent a short but eloquent piece of advice to the new prime minster. 'Mon cher M. Saint-Laurent,' he wrote, 'vous n'avez qu'à lui donner vos instructions et le tout devra se faire tel que vous le désirez.'[105] Chubby Power estimated that the party spent $3 million nationally and another $3 million in assistance to candidates in that election.[106] Senator Lambert maintained that in the 1953 campaign national support for local candidates was at least $3000 per constituency[107] – thus being far in excess of anything conceivable in the 1930s. The relative affluence of the Liberals reached its apogee in the 1957 campaign when the most careful analyst of that election has estimated that the government party spent two to three times as much as its main rival, which would put it in the range of between $6 to $7 million at all levels.[108]

These are all estimates, it must be emphasized, and may be more or less 'ball park' figures. It might also be noted that neither Power nor Lambert were significantly involved in the campaigns which they described, although they were no doubt well-informed observers. In the absence of detailed and accurate information, such estimates will have to be accepted, *faute de mieux*. Two points may be made, however. There was never as much money available as the advertising agencies wanted to spend on behalf of the party.[109] Second, the Liberals stood so high in the estimate of the voters and the opposition was generally so weak that the party did not need to spend vast amounts. In 1953, for instance, Claxton called in the campaign managers three weeks before the vote for the purpose of announcing that since the election was 'in the bag,' costs should be radically cut.[110] Yet in 1957, when the tide of opinion turned, the widely acknowledged fact of the Liberals' greater spending capacity could not save them. Finally, it might be pointed out that during and after the Diefenbaker landslide of 1958 the party found itself in straitened financial circumstances. In 1958 C.D. Howe, now a defeated minister helping out with finances, reported to one of the party collectors that 'everyone will have to do with less this year.'[111] In 1959 Daniel Lang, treasurer of the Ontario Liberal Association, reported to the NLF advisory council that 'I was somewhat relieved to find that most of the other treasurers of our Party throughout the country are in the same position in which I find myself, namely not in the position of being the custodian of the purse but more in the position of being the custodian of an overdraft.'[112] *Sic transit gloria.*

One area of expenditure about which information is available is the amount spent on national advertising through Cockfield, Brown. This is discussed in the following chapter. Anther area about which fairly precise information is available is expenditure by the NLF national office. Table 5.3 gives the total expenditures for 1946 to 1958. It is immediately evident that, by comparison to national office budgets in the 1930s (see Table 3.1), the NLF had gained considerably in financial stature. This can no doubt be taken as a reflection of the generally healthy state of party finance in this period. In election years the figures were swollen by campaign expenditures channeled through the NLF office, but even in off-election years it is obvious that the party, especially by the latter part of the St Laurent years, had been able to achieve a certain degree of continuous funding. Considering the traditional inability of Canadian parties,including the Liberals, to raise funds except in short, frenetic bursts just before elections, this level of financial continuity was an important development. It enabled the NLF to carry out the fairly modest tasks assigned it, and even allowed the declaration of annual surpluses,[113] a state of affairs which Norman Lambert had only been able to dream about twenty years earlier.

At the 1945 advisory council, the finance committee estimated that the annual budget of the NLF should be $60,000, to be raised by the constituent provincial associations on a quota basis.[114] This objective was not being met in the early postwar years. It soon became apparent that the NLF executive, including the treasurer and the president, would have to involve itself personally in fund-raising, since the provincial associations were not sufficiently reliable. This raises the question of parallel structures in Liberal fund-raising, and the somewhat shadowy relationship between the campaign finance committee in Toronto and Montreal on the one hand, and the NLF executive itself. K.Z. Paltiel has concluded that the NLF fund-raising structure was only 'formal,' while the informal structures carried out the

Table 5.3
Expenditures of the National Liberal Federation national office, 1946-58

1946	$ 27,025
1947	46,189[b]
1948	57,657
1949[a]	130,482[b]
1950	63,402[c]
1951	51,472[b]
1952	70,839
1953[a]	170,976
1954	82,251[d]
1955	83,344[b]
1956	116,956
1957[a]	223,520
1958[a]	174,762

[a]Election year
[b]Includes special expenditure on advisory council meeting
[c]Includes preparation of 1948 convention report
[d]Includes expenses of prime minister's tour, and expenses of Young Liberal convention
Source: NLF, v. 798, financial ledger; v. 800, 'Statements of receipts and disbursements'; v. 862, 1949 advisory council

'essential' fund-raising tasks.[115] Regenstreif has also pointed out that 'In the 1950's the Presidents of the Federation, Fogo, Woodrow, MacTavish and Matthews also engaged in collecting funds for the party (not for the Federation which has a regular contribution schedule worked out by the Honorary Treasurer). However, this is not normally the function of the President. Fund raising happened to be the *forte* of these Presidents, especially the latter two, and it would have imposed some hardship on the party had these men terminated this activity upon assuming their new position.'[116] Such fine distinctions appear rather doubtful. In the absence of any examples to the contrary, it would seem altogether more appropriate to conclude that the NLF presidents were regularly assumed to be fund-raisers, and that the presidency was considered a convenience for the task, conferring public honour and legitimacy on the collector.[117] This in turn facilitated the ability of the NLF itself to gather in the revenues necessary for day-to-day operations through a close interconnection with the regular campaign fund-raising structures.

The provincial quota system got onto somewhat firmer ground in the 1950s. Early in 1952 Gordon Fogo, before his sudden death, called together the provincial treasurers for a dinner at the Seignory Club and worked out a new set of quotas. Alan Woodrow and the new president, Duncan MacTavish, kept up the pressure for the rest of the year on the provinces to fulfil their pledges. Despite some of the usual foot-dragging, most of the cheques came in one by one, and the federation's revenues rose. Particularly noteworthy, by way of contrast with past performances, was a fairly reliable level of financial support from Montreal, where Senator Louis Gélinas was able to fulfil that province's large quota. At the end of the year it was decided at a luncheon held by C.D. Howe that in light of the probability of an election the following year, alternatives with regard to the future of party financing should be developed to supplement the provincial quota system.[118] While the evidence is very sketchy, there does seem to be some reason to believe that after 1952 the distinction between the NLF budget and the regular campaign fund became even hazier than before, that in some fashion the two fund-raising structures became more finely meshed. Certainly the revenues available to the NLF grew considerably in the latter years of the St Laurent government, as a glance at Table 5.3 will confirm. There are also rather puzzling discrepancies in the records available for NLF finances for this period, which might be explained by the possibility that some funds raised were going into reserve campaign chests to await elections. In any event, the relative affluence of the party is not in doubt in this period, and even if some provinces, notably Saskatchewan and British Columbia, failed to fulfil their quotas, the Montreal and Toronto finance committees did not appear to experience many difficulties in taking up the slack.[119]

A final point regarding party finance in this period is the very considerable contributions in kind rather than in cash which had become available to the Government party. There were first of all the advertising agencies, whose contributions were highly important. But at a lower level of importance were a number of other firms eager to contribute free services or loan equipment on the understanding of a mutually profitable deal with the party which also held the keys to the public treasury and government business following elections. Office equipment suppliers, printers, engravers, and stationers were among the more prominent businesses engaged in this practice. There were in fact traditional Liberal firms which held a monopoly in dealings with the party in their particular line of interest. As with the advertising agencies, there were often grey areas in these deals, with delicate negotiations on the exact amount of the discounts offered being worked out between the NLF president or treasurer and the company in question – and with further delicate negotiations involving government departments after the election. Gestetner gave a reproduction machine free to the NLF in 1957, but Addressograph-Multigraph offered used equipment free with the purchase of other equipment.[120] Two engraving companies, Bomac Electrotype and Rapid Grip and Batten, donated services in election campaigns which were valued in the thousands of dollars.[121] T.B. Little Company regularly supplied the party with stationery at discount prices, through the advertising agency.[122]

The media sometimes provided services to the party as well. The *Toronto Star* was the most faithful of Liberal newspapers, and its assistance always went beyond favourable coverage. In the 1949 campaign the *Star* set up three special offices in Quebec, and hired a stable of Francophone reporters to follow the Conservative campaign around the province. The purpose was to discredit the Tories in Ontario by publicizing campaign statements which might be construed as too nationalistic for English-Canadian ears. The entire operation cost the *Star* at least $5000 and the results were forwarded directly to the Ontario Liberal campaign committee, as well as being used in the *Star* itself. The *Star*'s campaign to link Conservative leader George Drew with Maurice Duplessis and the wartime internee Camilien Houde reached an appalling climax of yellow journalism and bad taste on the Saturday before the election, when a particularly revolting picture of Houde was featured on the front page topped by a triple banner headline: 'KEEP CANADA BRITISH, DESTROY DREW'S HOUDE, GOD SAVE THE KING.' The third line in this trinity was later changed to a more direct, 'VOTE ST. LAURENT.'[123] The *Star* was only the most spectacular example of the Liberal media. When entrepreneur Jack Kent Cooke took over *Saturday Night* magazine, he offered the journalistic services of his 'stable,' which also included *Liberty* magazine, to the Liberal party. Articles were arranged in conferences between reporters and the NLF. One article which boosted the government appeared in *Saturday Night* just in time for the 1953 election, and prompted effusive thanks from Duncan MacTavish for the use of such a 'respected and objective [*sic*] source as *Saturday Night*' which would 'undoubtedly have a great impact on public opinion.'[124] Electronic media were also involved: radio stations sometimes gave discounts to Liberal speakers, while charging full rates for the opposition parties.[125]

Another important source of media support was N.L. Nathanson, whose Famous Players Corporation had an obvious stake in maintaining good public relations with the Canadian government, considering that it represented American domination of an important communciations industry, the cinema. Nathanson was a traditional Liberal supporter, whose services on behalf of Liberal campaigns went back to the 1930s. Famous Players and

Associated Screen News provided considerable help in film publicity for the 1948 national convention and even produced and donated a documentary on the life of Mackenzie King which was used for propaganda purposes by the party. In 1948-9 Nathanson, this time in conjunction with Universal-International in New York, produced a film on the new Liberal leader, in both English and French versions, the distribution of which was further facilitated by co-operating cinema chains. Yet another film portraying 'Uncle Louis' was produced for the 1953 election by the same combination of Famous Players and Universal-International. In the pre-television era, these heavily subsidized film efforts obviously constituted a very considerable contribution to Liberal election publicity.[126]

In summary, the available documentary evidence offers only a fragmentary picture of party finance in this era. What is certain is that the party had considerably enhanced financial resources. It would appear that the Liberals had more, but that we know less about it. But it also seems safe to conclude, on the basis of what is known, that the pattern of fund-raising established in the 1930s under the direction of Norman Lambert continued into the 1950s. Fund-raising in the Liberal party during the period covered in this study evolved in a linear pattern. The financial structure of the party in the 1950s was like that of the past, only more so.

CAMPAIGN ORGANIZATION

There is little which need be said at this stage concerning campaign organization, for two reasons. First, the matter has already been discussed in earlier sections of this chapter. Second, there is already in existence a very comprehensive discussion of Liberal party national campaign organization in this era, in John Meisel's *The Canadian General Election of 1957*.[127] Meisel's analysis of Liberal organization in this campaign may be taken as a model for other, earlier postwar campaigns – with the significant proviso that the Liberals of course lost in 1957, while winning easily in the two previous elections. Defeat in 1957 did not represent a change in campaign style, or even a failure to live up to the standards of organization in the past. In 1957 the Liberals more or less faithfully copied their successful formula from the past. It was the audience that had changed.

In 1949 and 1953 Brooke Claxton acted as co-ordinator of the overall campaign effort from the Windsor Hotel in Montreal in 1949 and from Ottawa in the following campaign. Claxton's job was to watch especially over the national office and the advertising agencies in the central direction of publicity.[128] The cabinet ministers would be expected to oversee the highly autonomous regional campaigns organized through the provincial associations and the constituencies. Money would flow out from the centre, along with campaign literature and prominent speakers. So long as the ministers' campaign trips were co-ordinated – Jack Pickersgill as well as the national office took a hand in this – the general rule was that what went on within the provinces was essentially a provincial responsibility. Yet paradoxically, perhaps, it might also be said that the Liberals in the St Laurent era ran highly national campaigns, in the sense of the issues and the direction of publicity. 'Uncle Louis,' the grand old man of Canadian politics, the kindly national patriarch, was the central theme of all the Liberal propaganda.[129] The paradox is more apparent than real. The popular appeal was made as broad and as unspecific as possible, and the personality of the national leader was an appropriate focus for this kind of appeal. Yet however national the image to be sold, the mechanics of the sales campaign were generally farmed out to the constituent units of the party. An increasingly centralist party continued to draw electoral strength from a campaign organization which was surprisingly decentralized, although the content of the message was strongly national in scope. Perhaps the combination of these elements was both inevitable and inevitably unstable. The elections of 1957 and 1958 certainly demonstrated that the previously successful formula could become unstuck.

Brooke Claxton was gone from the campaign high command in 1957, but his place was adequately filled in by Jack Pickersgill. There was no shortage of money, as previously indicated, and the same personality-centred campaign was carried on at the level of publicity. The ministers carried out their traditional role of overseeing the local campaigns in their provinces, with the usual differences in interest and competence among their number. Defeat in that election rapidly destroyed the basis of Liberal campaign organization. The cabinet ministers were now ex-ministers, and the survivors were more worried about their own seats in 1958 than in looking after regional campaigns. Demoralization was rife throughout the Liberal rank and file as defeat seemed certain in the face of Diefenbaker's appeal for majority government. Across the country defections from the ranks, or at least a distinct lack of spirit and enthusiasm, severely weakened the provincial campaign committees. The 1958 campaign, *ipso facto*, was run on a much more centralized basis than before; Senator John Connolly and Chubby Power and the small staff of the NLF national office, took 'control' of the overall campaign, to the extent that one could speak of control. Duncan MacTavish raised money.[130] C.D. Howe at first offered to help the campaign, but was 'so shocked by the direction of the campaign that I decided to take no part in it, other than to help with the financing.' The example of this type of campaign organization was not encouraging, to say the least, but then it had never been seen by the party as anything but making the best of a disastrous collapse. As Senator Connolly later told Kidd, 'looking back I think the Party never had a chance for this election ... Perhaps it was as well that the future was hidden from us, because the amount of work which was done was tremendous.'[131]

There seems to be no reason to conclude that campaign organization had failed the Liberals in 1957, although it could with justice be said of 1958. The point is that the organization of the campaign weakened as a result of defeat, rather than the other way around. The downfall of the twenty-two-year Liberal régime – the 'twilight of the Grits' passing into night, in Eayrs' memorable phrase[132] – must be explained otherwise than by poor campaigning.

'THE TWILIGHT OF THE GRITS'

Ex post facto explanations of historical events are notoriously easy. Nothing is so simple, or so facile, as the quick search for the 'causes' of great events. Enough is now known about the complexity of voter perceptions of parties and leaders to render suspect any easy identifications of electoral defeat with this or that issue – an 'issue' which may very well have been such to politicians, journalists, and political scientists, but not in any significant way to the voters. There will be no attempt here to suggest any comprehensive rationale for the sudden demise of what had been the longest continuous rule by a single party in Canadian history. There have of course been many explanations offered, from the allegedly irresistible charismatic power of John Diefenbaker, to Jack Pickersgill's considered view that Canada was simply bored with too much good government.[133] Yet Regenstreif is quite right to deride this 'grasping at straws.' As he points out: 'In 1957, there were no tangible indications that the Liberals would be beaten or, even in the opposition's darkest moments of reflection, could be. All the hindsight and *post hoc* gazing at entrails cannot change that objective fact.'[134]

If the question of grand causation is set aside, some points relevant to the focus of this study may be noted. In the aftermath of the defeat some figures in the party began asking what had happened, and why. Some of their reflections touched directly on problems of party organization, and particularly on the effects of long one-party domination on the organization of the Government party.

First was the question of the age of the leadership, and its growing inability to remain in touch with changes in the real world. The spectacle of the pipeline débâcle, in which a C.D. Howe apparently gone out of control destroyed support for the party left and right while a bored and listless prime minister sat slumped in his Commons seat, was not the stuff out of which strong electoral images were made. But the aging of the leadership was a symptom of an aging of the party as a whole, and particularly a growing closed-mindedness, an ossification of the political imagination. Howe later told a friend that both he and St Laurent had been to blame, but that their failure reflected a larger failure: 'At the time of the 1953 election, I had an understanding with our leader that we would both retire after a year or two in office and give the new leader time to get organized. Unfortunately, our leader changed his mind about retiring, which was a mistake,both for him and for the party. The plain fact is that the Liberal dynasty had run out of ideas.'[135]

The only link between this septuagenarian leadership and any new ideas was the senior bureaucracy, which obviously had its own problems of ossification after twenty-two years of symbiotic relations with these same Liberals. In 1955 J.E. Hodgetts prophetically noted that the line between politics and administration having become virtually invisible, cabinet ministers and civil servants had become a single 'solid corps of senior officials' which 'looks complacently into a common mirror and receives an acceptable answer to the collective question "Who is now the fairest in the land?" '[136] Indeed, it is one of the interesting aspects of examining the St Laurent papers in the Public Archives to find that there were, in the late stages of the St Laurent government, two levels of public opinion; the first was the official version, passed on by the cabinet itself, the bureaucracy, the universities, the major newspapers, and all the other élite opinion leaders; the second can be glimpsed in the letters which came to St Laurent and to his ministers from humble Canadians without the position or eloquence to make their voices felt in any public way. These letters reached deluge proportions by the time of the pipeline fiasco, but even before that event one can catch sight of a Canada which existed outside the élite centres, a Canada which, for one thing, was very much more nationalistic than its rulers thought either sensible or desirable. As early as 1951 Jimmy Gardiner was bringing some letters to the attention of the prime minister indicating growing resentment of American domination of Canadian life. St Laurent's response was incredulity: 'It is rather hard to believe,' he informed his agriculture minister, 'that there can be any general feeling throughout the country that we are giving control of the country to the United States.' In the typical reflex of the self-satisfied politician, he then went on to suggest that 'if such a view is at all generally prevalent, there is something pretty seriously wrong with our government publicity, and we should lose no time in correcting it.'[137] Gardiner worried about what the opposition might do with this feeling. The answer came six years later. But the Liberal party in its metamorphosis into the Government party had lost touch with opinion not sponsored by the élites with which it was in daily and intimate contact.

Another aspect of the same problem was the growing centralization of the government and its increasing isolation from regional grievances, a development which again cost it dearly at the hands of Diefenbaker. The voices of regional protest had become stilled, or at best were so quiet and self-conscious as to scarcely make a dent in the overall complacency. Yet the signs were there, if anyone had cared to read them. At an NLF executive committee meeting in 1954, Walter Tucker, Liberal leader in Saskatchewan, gently suggested that the Liberal tendency to govern Canada as a unitary state 'was hurting the party in the long run in the West.' Tucker suggested that more latitude for the expression of independent regional opinion for the MPs should be allowed by the party, since the alternative, if the Liberals became too rigid in their policies, was that the western electorates would turn to the opposition parties. The president of the Saskatchewan Liberal Association cited a growing feeling among the voters in his province that the Liberal party represented the domination of the West by the central provinces through the mechanism of party discipline over the local MP. The voters were asking themselves, he suggested, why they should vote for Liberal MPs who were unable to speak for the interests of their constituents.[138] It was an old complaint, but the Liberals should have had enough historical sense to have taken it seriously. A string of Liberal defeats in provincial elections leading up to the 1957 election may have been more than a contributing cause of the latter defeat, through the prior loss of provincial organizational strength – it may well have indicated a regional revulsion against Liberal policies. In any event, by the time of the 1957 vote there were only three Liberal governments left in the ten provinces, and one of these, in Manitoba, was a Liberal-Progessive government which was not on good terms with the Ottawa party and did nothing to help it. Only Newfoundland, a throwback to the ministerialist days of the western provinces in the late nineteenth century when politics equalled government appropriations, boasted a finely meshed federal and provincial Liberal machine which was able to deliver the votes. Everywhere else the picture had become much bleaker for the Liberals.

It is difficult to avoid the conclusion that the party, in becoming the Government party, had willfully cut itself off from important sources of information which were vital to its continued viability as an electoral, as well as an administrative, enterprise. The slow but sure strangulation of any vestige of an extra-parliamentary party, and the corresponding transformation of the NLF into a mere symbolic legitimation of ministerialist government, meant that one possible channel of rank-and-file opinion had been stilled. As Norman Lambert sarcastically commented: 'the East Block had become the "mirror and sounding board" – not the Federation.'[139] While the experiments with intra-party democracy in policy-making in the 1960s may give one pause as the the representativeness of party conventions, it is surely the case that a greater use of the party membership might have at least given the leadership a wider awareness of trends in opinion.

Lambert had a wider point as well. His concept of the NLF had always stressed the *federal* aspect; in an exchange with Lester Pearson in 1964 Lambert decried some centralizing tendencies he saw in the Liberal government of that period. Pearson viewed the period after 1957 as a 'revolutionary period in thinking of people in relation to political parties.' Lambert countered that on the contrary there had been a 'reaction to excessive centralized direction and power':

The provincial units which had been responsible in restoring and maintaining Liberal strength, during the thirties, were rendered inoperative during the next fifteen years, by a centralized domination of administration from Ottawa. My old friend C.D. Howe became the main-spring of the party organization, not on the strength of any lines of legislative policy, so much as upon his command of the ways and means of running the election [*sic*] of '49, '53 and '57. The disastrous result of 1958 was not so much a Conservative Party victory as a rebuke to 20 years of increasing centralized power.[140]

None of these problems of centralization and isolation at the top were inevitable – if the party had been able to develop as flexible and self-renewing a leadership structure as, say, the Ontario provincial Conservative party has enjoyed over the past thirty years. Yet there were also some structural reasons why the decline of the party as an organization *was* in some senses inevitable, by contrast to a private corporation or a public bureaucracy. The key to this structural fault lay in the reward system of political parties: patronage. This is indeed the decisive difference between a party as an organization and corporate or bureaucratic organizations. The latter rely on reward systems which turn on cash remuneration and promotion. A political party, at least in the Canadian context, lacks the financial resources to make direct cash remuneration a crucial reward for service, except at the very lowest level of payment for scrutineers, drivers, etc., in individual polls. Above this level, cash rewards are rarely commensurate with services rendered. While the CCF-NDP might well operate on the analogy to a charity drive, drawing voluntary help in fairly large numbers, the Liberal party could rely only very incompletely on voluntary services. Indeed, the 'psychic' pay-offs of participatory policy-centred politics which rose to the surface in the 1960s as a new form of reward system to draw support for the electoral organization, were never developed in the 1940s and 1950s to any significant extent; certainly the 1948 national convention had made no attempt to even give the appearance of participation by the party rank and file. Except for a brief flurry of activism centred around the 1943 advisory council resolutions moving the party in the direction of reform in the face of the CCF threat, there is little or no evidence of Duverger's 'contagion from the left' affecting the cadre structure of the Liberal party in this era. On the contrary, continued electoral success for the party offered the strongest of inducements to retain a cadre-ministerialist structure, since the Government party continued to exercise control over a wide range of rewards appropriate to such a structure, in the form of political patronage. But the use of patronage proved curiously self-limiting as a reward system.

The difficulty centred around the role of the party as an intermediary institution between the private sector and the state bureaucratic apparatus. If the major function of parties in liberal-democracies is, as many have suggested, recruitment to political office, the party also plays some role in staffing those offices within the state system which remain subject to political nomination. In Canada the Civil Service Act has resulted in a dual level of patronage appointment: at the bottom of the state structure, in some of the least remunerative positions, and at the highest levels, in the range of offices from lieutenant-governor, senator, through the diplomatic service, to the judiciary, to deputy ministers, to positions on the numerous boards, commissions, and Crown corporations which proliferated during and after the war. The crucial problem with most of these latter rewards, however, was that once a party supporter was awarded an appointment he was generally thereby recruited into the state system and lost to the party as an active worker. The Senate was a major exception, since continued partisan activity was considered quite legitimate in this body. The Senate, however, presented two drawbacks. The regional constraints on appointment limited its patronage value and there was no way in which the party could enforce partisan activity as a senator, once he was appointed – many a time a senator fell back on what amounted to lifetime tenure, and simply removed himself from party activity. Many of the other staple rewards had the effect of removing the recipient, *ipso facto,* from the political sphere altogether. Judicial appointments, for example, so important a reward for a political system still dominated by the legal profession, could not legitimately be combined with any public partisan commitment. And, to be sure, there is abundant evidence that the Liberals respected the fairly rigorous separation of the state and political systems. Yet however appropriate this division was to the tenets of liberal-democracy, and however much it may have facilitated smooth intermeshing of the various state élites during the long years of Liberal rule, it nevertheless presented the Liberal party with a cumulative organizational problem: the steady dispersal of necessary talent and enthusiasm out of the party and into the state system.

A document in the Brooke Claxton papers entitled 'The Reason Why' dealt at length with some of the underlying reasons for Liberal decline. Among them, patronage as a problem featured prominently. The government, the report suggested, had

suffered a steady process of attrition through the promotion of the most able of the younger Liberals to positions of responsibility outside of politics and government. Over 22 years it was inevitable that a good portion of the brighter members in the ranks of the younger lawyers should be Liberals. It was not only in accordance with the practice, it was inevitable that a good many of the vacancies in the judiciary should be appointed from their ranks ... Usually they were people of above average ability, frequently of cabinet timbre. Each Liberal appointment meant a loss in the fighting forces of the party, and 22 years brought a lot of them. Unfortunately, not much was done to fill up the gaps in the ranks. For an able and ambitious young man there was not much future in becoming another Liberal supporter when there were already so many of them. More and more the Liberal ranks, both in Parliament and outside, were filled by the residue of those left behind by promotion of one kind or another.[141]

Among those who stayed in Parliament, the notorious frustration of promising backbenchers condemned to years of 'unrewarded impotence,' was a discouragement to new candidates of quality presenting themselves in the constituencies, particularly in light of the Liberal propensity for direct cooptation of leadership from outside the political system altogether. The result was a tendency for the party organization to die more from 'self-satisfaction' than from the attacks of the opposition: 'With the passage of time any organization tends to contain more and more of the people who have not had the ability or independence to move out, if they haven't moved up. [M]ediocracy [*sic*] begins to take over and people of ability are attracted less and less. Meanwhile the mediocre follow the only path they can; they break into divisive groups competing for every place, asserting with fatal truth that each of them is at least as good as the other fellow.' The party had thus become 'fettered to a conglomeration of ageing organizers whose greed increased as their energy declined.' If there is truth in this, then our earlier description of the campaign organization in 1957 being essentially the same as in the earlier, successful campaigns might now be slightly amended. The structure was the same, the same motions were rehearsed once more, but perhaps the material out of which the structure was built had declined in quality and substance. The 1958 election, then, simply completed the demolition of an organization suffering from internal decay.

And laid the groundwork for organizational rebirth, for the startling fact is that within five years the Liberal party had returned from its worst rout in the twentieth century to its accustomed seats of power, where it has remained, not always comfortably it is true, but with that same tenacious persistence which characterized its will to power throughout the King–St Laurent period. Now that more than a decade of renewed Liberal mandate is once again stretching into an indefinite future, one begins to see the acute precision of Regenstreif's characterization of 1957 to 1963 as the 'Diefenbaker interlude.' More than this, one can also begin to glimpse the overall continuity of the Government party, extending back in time to Mackenzie King's masterful opportunism in building a majority centre party out of the political and economic chaos of the Great Depression. Driven out of office in 1957-8, the Liberal party showed remarkable regenerative powers and an undiminished ability to exploit the difficulties of the Conservatives to their own considerable political advantage. The story of this phoenix-like rebirth is not within the scope of this study, and has been analysed elsewhere.[142] From our perspective, the point is twofold: the concept of the Government party is not specific to a particular historical period and a particular government, but seems to have a more persistent identification with the process of national government in the Canadian federal system – perhaps the much discussed system of 'executive federalism' is in part a reflection of the fusion of party and state at the national level. The point cannot be elaborated here, but the importance of the continuity of a government party at the national level cannot be dismissed. The final point is that, in defeat, the Liberal label was still an attractive enough franchise to draw the talents and energies of precisely those young elements which had been either blocked in their progress or drawn out of the party through appointment to the state system while the party had remained in office. The manpower turnover within the party from 1957 to 1963 was tremendous. A brief period of defeat thus offered the party a relatively painless method of renovation and renewal. For the Government party, even the occasional defeat proved both functional and salutary. Just how different the Liberals are from the Conservatives can be seen in the fact that defeat has certainly never done anything for the Tories, other than confirm them in their apparent role as the permanent Opposition party.

6

The Liberal party and
its advertising agencies

... we stripped away all the mysticism of political campaigns and "sold" Liberalism as we would sell any other product or service – by modern merchandising methods ... Walsh has always approached its political assignments with the same techniques that it employs successfully to sell automobiles, fountain pens, hosiery, etc. for other clients ... Given a free hand, Walsh proceeded to formulate a plan that would sell a Government to a people, just as we would sell any other product or service to people ... [I]nferior products can annihilate superior ones, if shrewdly, consistently and heavily impressed upon the public.

Walsh Advertising Agency,
A Formula for Liberal Victory (1948)

Jello isn't very solid either, but they sell a hell of a lot of it.

American political public relations man

The rise of the advertising and public relations industries in the twentieth-century capitalist economy has been one of its more noteworthy structural changes. The saturation of existing markets, the shift of emphasis from production to consumption, the concentration of ownership in huge monopolistic multinational corporations, and the intensive development of the mass media, have all contributed to an increasingly important role for what has been termed 'marginal product differentiation' – a type of economic activity which contributes neither to higher product quality nor to lower prices (which perhaps is more likely to contribute to higher prices and lower product quality) but which serves to allocate an increasing proportion of resources to non-productive use: at best, the creation of a cultural milieu of images, sounds, and phrases appropriate to a corporate capitalist civilization. Nor have the socialist nations been remiss in attention to the media of mass persuasion; any lag exhibited in this regard is more likely the result of technical inferiority than of principle.

Obviously these developments have not bypassed the political sphere in Western liberal democracies. The historical context within which the ad man and the PR man have replaced the traditional political boss is indeed very suggestive of the relationship between politics and the wider world of economic activity. Although product *advertising* was a more or less internal development of industry, *public relations* – the creation of a favourable image of a company or organization in public opinion – has a more interesting history from a political point of view. It is important first to note that the public relations industry was in itself created as part of a political, although not a partisan, response to a challenge to corporate power in American society. The attitude of capitalist enterprise in its more uninhibited formative period was best summed up in the famous statement of Cornelius Vanderbilt in 1882: 'the public be damned.' By the 1920s, pioneer technicians of opinion manipulation like Edward Bernays and Ivy Lee were selling their skills to big business under the name of the 'engineering of consent.' The world of difference in this forty-year transformation was spurred by the spectacular success of the left-wing reformers in early-twentieth-century American politics in utilizing the mass media to persuade public opinion. The 'muck-raking' journalists like Lincoln Steffens and Upton Sinclair threw such a salutary scare into American capitalists that the latter set about appropriating the use of mass media techniques for their own purposes: the creation of a public opinion favourable to the giant corporations and thus to American capitalism in general. Their success in this endeavour has been such that since the 1920s the impressive array of modern methods of opinion-moulding have been largely developed in the service of private economic power rather than against it.[1]

In this context it is not surprising that PR and ad skills should have been put to the service of the 'two-party system,' that euphemism which in North American parlance means making democracy safe for 'free enterprise.' It is not only that the 'safe' parties can naturally command more financial resources with which to purchase these skills; it is also largely the case that the PR and ad men are drawn toward those parties which seem to express the political and economic perspective of their own profession. When one adds to this the powerful motive of political patronage in government advertising contracts in Canada (about which much more later), one has the formula for an impressive dovetailing of interests between the major parties and the advertising world, especially in the case of the Liberal party which

for the period studied here was the dominant or 'Government' party in federal politics.

It must also be said, however, that the historical context of political PR
suggests another side to the question which the opponents of 'political
hucksterism' have rarely taken into account. It would seem that the rise of
mass advertising techniques in politics tended to coincide with the decline
of traditional, localized, patronage-oriented, machine politics. As patron-
client politics has been slowly transformed into the more universalist categories of bureaucratic politics, techniques of communication with the *mass*
of voters has obviously become a more pressing concern. This does seem to
involve, in a curious way, a greater emphasis on issues.[2] Although ad men
are commonly denounced for debasing politics with personalized images,
they are in another sense technicians advising their political clients in the
best way to present their electoral promises and programmes to the widest
possible mass audience. Just how far one can blame the ad men themselves
for a state of affairs which may be more a symptom than a cause of the
lowest-common-denominator standard of mass society, is a matter of some
considerable conjecture, which I could not hope to answer here. Nor will I
attempt to answer the question of the empirical effect of advertising on partisan voting behaviour.[3] Instead, in keeping with the overall focus of this
study, I will examine the *organizational* aspects of political advertising: the
links between the ad agencies and the party, and the effects of advertising
on the party organization. And here, it must be said at the outset, the effect
of the ad men was indeed to focus the attention of the party on its ideas and
programmes. However much the packaging and selling of these programmes might displease the high-minded and the fastidious, the ad agencies were in another sense clearly in the balance against the older, localized
patronage politics. As agents of mass socialization for the newer bureaucratic politics, their influence ought not to be underestimated.

The merger of professional public relations and political parties has gone
much further in the United States than in Canada, perhaps because of the
more open American system of government, with its lack of party discipline, its much wider number of elective offices, and its greater use of referenda. There are simply more individual politicians in America who require
the personal services of PR and ad men – and more interest groups who feel
that an investment in public opinion manipulation will pay off in
influencing the votes of individual representatives. It may also be that Canadians are less devoted than Americans to 'selling' as a way of life. In 1966
Canadians spent on an average less than half of what Americans spent on
advertising.[4] American public relations has developed an entire industry de-

voted to 'campaign management': firms whose primary purpose is to direct political campaigns, whether individual candidacies, referenda issues, or pressure campaigns on particular issues before Congress or the state legislatures. As early as the 1930s the bellwether of American modernity, California, had already given birth to the pioneer campaign management agency, Whitaker-Baxter's Campaigns, Inc. By the 1960s one writer was able to list no less than forty-seven such firms in full-time operation.[5] Typically, campaign management firms take overall charge of all aspects of a campaign, including not only publicity but such details as finance as well (a single bill will be presented following the campaign, thus relieving the candidate of one of the major campaign problems – paying for services as they are provided). The campaign management firms have excited much comment in the United States, much of it critical and indeed anxious. Some firms, such as one in California, go so far as to stipulate that their candidates, at least to those minor posts which proliferate on American ballots, should be neither seen nor heard in person – the reality might interfere with the carefully managed image. To anyone with even a residual attachment to traditional liberal democratic values, there is something distinctly scary in these developments. The selling of Richard Nixon to the American voter might even suggest the need for a Misleading Advertising Act to cover political promotion as well as commercial.[6]

There have been similar developments in Canada, especially in the larger provinces. The campaigns of the Davis Conservatives in Ontario in 1971 and the Bourassa Liberals in Quebec in 1973 bore many of the earmarks of carefully controlled American image management. There are also differences in Canada as well. The more centralized and disciplined nature of parties in the parliamentary system, the much smaller number of elective offices, the more circumscribed use of the media, may all in part indicate why campaign management *firms* have not made an appearance in Canada. Instead, regular commercial advertising agencies have been the institutional vehicle normally commanded by parties in this country. The difference is presumably in the degree of specialization: political advertising does not seem to be big enough business in itself to call forth agencies specializing in political campaigns alone. Another critical institutional difference in Canada is the patronage nature of official government advertising, which does not seem to be matched in the United States. In Canada, government and political advertising are inextricably linked; the specific techniques of political advertising are therefore developed within the same agencies whose multifaceted commercial techniques are required for general governmental advertising as well.

ADVERTISING AGENCIES AND POLITICS IN CANADA

It is thus to the advertising agency that one must turn in Canada to study the link between politics and the techniques of modern mass persuasion. K.Z. Paltiel has noted the decline in the influence within parties of the press barons of earlier eras, like the Siftons, the Atkinsons, and the Lord Atholstans, and their replacement by the ad men – in conjunction with the rise of radio and television: 'The advertising agency and the public relations consultant have taken the editor's place in the counsels of the parties. The rise to party prominence of such advertising men as Senator Keith Davey, the former national Liberal organizer, Senator Allister Grosart who performed a similar function for the Conservatives during Mr. Diefenbaker's rise to power, and Mr. Dalton Camp who precipitated the latter's undoing, bear witness to this process.'[7] And it was the Liberal party which from the 1930s through the 1950s led the way into the new era of political advertising – whether as a cause or an effect of its superior political and financial status among federal parties at this time being difficult to determine. In any event, analysis of the relationship of the party to the advertising agencies in this formative period does seem a particularly worthwhile endeavour, both from the point of view of the party and from that of political advertising. With regard to the former, Peter Regenstreif reported that there 'are many within the party' who claimed that the Liberals' major agency, Cockfield, Brown and Company, 'was the central office of the party, particularly around election time.'[8] Unfortunately, Regenstreif was either unable or disinclined to follow up this suggestion in any detail. There is now sufficient documentation available that a detailed examination of the role of the agency – as well as that of other subsidiary agencies – is both possible and necessary.

An advertising agency, as described by Dalton Camp – who ought to know – is a place where 'one finds grown men, swathed in soft grey flannel suits, wearing foulard ties and pocket handkerchiefs, agonizing over the right phrase to describe the delectable flavour of Wrigley's Chewing Gum.'[9] Advertising agencies arose to serve two major purposes: to provide technical expertise in preparing the promotions of clients (concepts, copy-writing, artwork, and so on); and to represent clients with the media in buying space and time.[10] The two functions are not necessarily related directly, but they have evolved historically as Siamese twins. Indeed the method of remuneration developed in Canada is a direct result of this fusion. The client pays the costs incurred by the agency in the preparation of the advertisements and the cost of the media space and/or time. The media rebate 15 per cent of the latter charge to the agency. This 15 per cent along with an additional 2 per cent rebate from the print media, if the charges are paid within a specified period (a banking function for an agency awaiting payment from the client), constitutes the basic return to the agency. A second major consideration to be kept in mind is that the relationship between an ad agency and a company contracting for their services is essentially that of an agency-client type, which is merely to say that the agency is hired to advise, but that ultimate decisions remain in the hands of the client. Of course, the specific nature of the relationship will vary from case to case, but the basic role of the agency is that of servant rather than master.[11]

The First World War gave a major impetus to the development of advertising and most particularly to the involvement of advertising agencies in the preparation of government propaganda appeals to citizens on such issues as voluntary enlistment and the sale of government bonds. The many businessmen who took up leading positions in the government war effort naturally turned to the publicity methods with which they were already familiar, and to the agencies with which they were familiar. Following the introduction of conscription, advertising agencies found their way into politics as well. H.E. Stephenson and C. McNaught note that 'the same advertising agency which had explained the terms of the Military Service Act to the public was allotted the task of preparing the publicity campaign for the Union Government' in the election of 1917.[12]

There is only scattered evidence on the extent to which advertising agencies were utilized by parties in political campaigns of the 1920s and 1930s. Paltiel has stated that it was in the 1940s that 'both the Liberals and the Conservatives began to employ advertising agencies to help plan their campaign activities.'[13] Although the use of agencies and their services did become more pronounced in the 1940s, and while it does seem to be true that more formal bargains were struck between the party and its agencies in this decade, the relationship in fact appears to have more venerable roots, reaching into the 1930s at least. In the 1935 federal campaign, for example, slightly over $50,000 was spent nationally on radio publicity through the agency of Cockfield, Brown and a further $17,000 was spent on billboards and weekly newspaper advertisements through the agency of R.C. Smith. The publicity end of a special dinner commemorating the twentieth anniversary of Mackenzie King's leadership of the party held in Toronto in 1939 was handled by Harry Cockfield, a principal partner in Cockfield, Brown.[14] Moreover, as will be shown later, the distribution of advertising dollars from the government among the various friends of the Liberal party in the advertising world was already a major patronage problem for Norman Lambert in the late 1930s.

The Second World War gave an even greater impetus to the advertising industry than its predecessor. By 1944 almost $37 million was being spent nationally on advertising through agencies (about half the total amount spent on advertising) and the agencies were earning almost $6 million in fees. Significantly, two-thirds of the total billings were going to eleven agencies each making more than $1 million per year in gross revenue.[15] Giants were already emerging within the industry.

The federal government was leading the way in the use of advertising, particularly through its gigantic Victory Bond campaigns, the greatest promotion campaigns ever to take place in Canada up until that time. Throughout the war the federal government spent at least $30,444,537 on advertising, of which more than two-thirds went through ad agencies.[16] In fact, by war's end, the federal government headed the list of the largest advertisers in the land.[17] This meant that there was a very substantial 'pork barrel' for advertising patronage in the making; it also meant that the attention of politicians would inevitably be drawn to the potential of ad agencies for political as well as governmental work. Everything was in the cards for a happy and lasting *ménage à trois* between the government, the party, and the ad agency.

To the Liberals a more specific spur came with the realization of the sagging popularity of the wartime government and the sudden perception of a strong electoral threat from the left. The now famous Gallup poll of 1943 which showed the CCF leading both the Liberals and the Conservatives in national popularity was a salutary shock to a party which had carried the country in a landslide vote only three years earlier. The awareness that not only did the government need to better its image but that public opinion on a wide spectrum of issues had shifted clearly to the left, presented the Liberals with a decisive challenge which called for the services of experts, not amateurs or old-fashioned machine politicians. Besides, Mackenzie King himself had long been a strong believer in the management of public opinion as a leading factor in the management of public affairs. His actions as a labour expert, in the employ of the Canadian government and of the Rockefeller empire, had revolved rather more importantly around the manipulation of public opinion than around the solution of the substantive issues of labour disputes.[18] The general reorganization of the Liberal party in the face of the new challenge from the left has already been outlined in Chapter 4, but one facet of the strategy devised to renew the party's electoral hold on the country was to turn to the services of the advertising agencies which were at that moment shaping Canadian public opinion on behalf of the war effort. If experts could package and sell a war, presumably they could package and sell the Liberal party.

Not that the Liberals were lacking in ideas for substantive approaches, although the ideas came largely from the senior levels of the civil service. The new Keynesian economics being channelled into Canada by W.C. Clark and his bright young men in the Department of Finance did offer a strategy which could not only avoid a return to depression at war's end (which was the chief fear of the public) but could do it through the wide extension of public welfare and social security programmes: a winning combination of policies with which to face a strong social democratic challenge. The advertising agencies were to have a viable product to market, but the Liberal party clearly realized that a good product alone would not necessarily be accepted on its own merits. Hence the need to develop an appropriate sales pitch. The civil service and the cabinet would produce the product and the ad men would undertake the job of selling it. Just what this meant in specific terms may be seen in an almost embarrassingly frank presentation made in the form of a large, glossy brochure by Walsh Advertising to the National Liberal Federation detailing Walsh's contributions to the New Brunswick provincial Liberal victory in 1948 (Walsh was the official Liberal agency in both the 1944 and 1948 McNair campaigns).[19] Although Walsh was not chosen as the Liberals' national agency, it did represent the party in Ontario and New Brunswick; its thinking as exemplified in this brochure does perhaps represent an insight into how ad agencies saw their role in political assignments in the 1940s. Certainly Walsh seems to have thought so highly of it that they specially deposited a copy in the Public Archives of Canada, presumably for the edification of future generations.

Whether edifying or not, the gist of the Walsh 'formula for Liberal victory' was as follows. After being retained by Premier McNair as 'advertising and public relations counsel' to the New Brunswick Liberal Association, Walsh was given the full co-operation of the civil service and free access to all government records; thus saturated with information, Walsh ad men were able to put together a *Speaker's Handbook*, the 'foundation' of the campaign. Then the actual campaign work was begun: province-wide newspaper advertisements on every theme, and with a local 'dealer tie-in' – the name of the local candidate included; radio bulletins so short that by the time the low attention span of the listener led him to turn the dial, the message was already over; and so on.

Rather more interesting than Walsh's specific techniques, however, was their philosophical rationale, a vision of political man as standing somewhere between a Hobbesian consumer and a Benthamite behaviourist:

Walsh has always approached its political assignments with the same techniques that it employs successfully to sell automobiles, fountain pens, hosiery, etc. for other clients. Perhaps that is the secret of the agency's success in the political field. After all, voters are human beings. And all human beings are motivated, in all their actions, by a comparatively few well-known and measurable impulses. These may be broadly defined as Fear, Hunger, Sex, and Rage. To reach and incite these impulses, there are five portals of entry – sight, sound, touch, taste, and smell – with the first two being of paramount importance.

Given a free hand, Walsh proceeded to formulate a plan that would sell a Government to a people, just as we would sell any other product or service to people ...

Walsh researchers, having probed deeply into the 'subconscious or inner feelings of the people,' had concluded that Canadians were, 'in their secret hearts,' *satisfied* with what they had, but were equally *afraid* of losing it. Liberalism was the political product which could best answer this consumer dilemma, by a positive exploitation of this fear: if the idea of *progress* could be distinguished in the voters' perceptions from that of *change*, and the former identified in the public mind with the familiar and habitual act of voting Liberal, then the future of Liberalism would be assured: '... Liberalism was presented not as a political party, nor as a vague, ideological theory, but as a *mass* expression of each individual's inherent human desire for progress and security. The objective was to make each individual discover within himself the exciting realization that Liberalism and his own personal hopes and aspirations are synonymous ... In other words, we gave people the opportunity to gratify the inherent desire for change and to mitigate an equally inherent fear of the unknown in a single action – voting Liberal.' Walsh was also at pains to point out that while the Liberal party was doubtless a worthwhile product, there was no guarantee that a good product can sell itself. Indeed, inferior products can annihilate superior ones, 'if shrewdly, consistently, and heavily impressed upon the public.' In case the Liberals missed the significance of this point, Walsh was careful to add that 'only professional advertising people of long experience can do this ... We at Walsh are not politicians. But we are professional students of human behaviour and human reaction to stimuli.'

It would be easy to dismiss this kind of sales pitch as little more than repellent self-puffery, of the kind which has made 'Madison Avenue' an epithet among civilized people. And indeed Walsh Advertising seems to stand out even among its colleagues of the day for brashness and self-assertion. Not everyone was impressed with Walsh's mastery of propaganda. Dalton Camp, whose own copy bested Walsh in New Brunswick in 1952, recalled:

The press burbled with self-indulgent Liberal advertisements, each from the same mould, cast-iron in its dullness, as though any sound would make a symphony, any statement win a vote ... their advertising seemed possessed by an awesome, compulsive arrogance; a propaganda machine which, once started, could not be stopped from its volcanic regurgitations, soiling every page, intruding into every radio program, in every paper, on every station ... I concluded sorrowfully that I might be the only one who would ever read them except the Walsh copywriter, his copy chief, the account executive, and the Premier of New Brunswick.[20]

Yet the comments of the opposition aside (and marginal product differentiation is nowhere more intense than among rival ad agencies), it should be said that the Walsh brochure does offer an insight into the thinking of ad men in politics, and most particularly into the kind of sales appeal used for the Liberals in the 1940s.

COCKFIELD, BROWN AND THE NATIONAL PARTY

The agency the Liberals chose to advertise their wares nationally was not the fast-talking Walsh group, but an agency that, being Number One, did not have to try harder: Cockfield, Brown and Company, of Montreal, Toronto, Vancouver, Winnipeg, and anywhere else where there was money to be made from salesmanship. Cockfield, Brown was not only the biggest advertising concern in the country; its president claimed in the late 1950s that *per capita* it was the largest agency in the world. Beginning with a merger of a Toronto and a Montreal firm in 1928, Cockfield, Brown began its existence with over $2 million in billings and never looked back. One of Cockfield, Brown's special assets was its research department, apparently the first such department in a Canadian agency; its research capacity was certainly one of its attractions to clients such as the Liberal party.[21] But Cockfield, Brown was politically attractive to the Liberals as well. In the 1935 federal election, the Toronto office contributed $2,000 to the Liberal bagman on Bay Street.[22] In the 1940 election, the Montreal office of Cockfield, Brown was the chief Liberal agency, assisted by Walsh and Canadian Advertising of Montreal. And Cockfield, Brown was already gaining a lion's share of the lucrative government advertising pot. It was only natural when the government decided in 1940 to set up a special group of large agencies to push the War Savings Campaign, that one of the agency's two principal partners, Harry Cockfield, should have been chosen as chairman of the campaign.[23] The most successful ad agency in the country and the most successful political party seemed to be made for each other.

Two key figures in speeding this marriage were Brooke Claxton for the party and H.E. 'Bob' Kidd for the agency. Claxton has been described by Donald Creighton as a 'large, shambling, inept man, with a high-pitched grating voice.'[24] The grating quality of his voice may or may not have been observed by those more friendly to Claxton's politics than Professor Creighton, but to describe him as 'inept' seems to constitute a particularly inapposite piece of partisan blindness. Brooke Claxton was the organizational genius of the national Liberal party in the 1940s and early 1950s. Along with Jack Pickersgill, he probably had more to do with the organization of national campaigns than any other cabinet minister. That this involvement coincided with the period of some of the Liberals' greatest electoral triumphs is unlikely to have been entirely accidental. A man with an academic background, Claxton was much more than an old-fashioned organizer. Although he had a quick eye, not to speak of a strong stomach, for some distinctly traditional patronage practices – such as collecting campaign contributions from a carefully tended list of corporations receiving contracts from his own mammoth Defence Department 'pork barrel,'[25] he was still something of the intellectual in politics who always kept watch on issues as well as on organization. And part of his concern with issues was an interest in their efficient packaging and selling. Claxton seems to have been one of the first federal politicians to take real advantage of the services of the ad agencies to advance his own career as well as the fortunes of his party.[26]

Kidd was an ad man who had 'worked with and in the Liberal organizations since 1925,' first in Vancouver where he arrived after immigrating to Canada after the First World War, and later in Montreal where he moved within the Cockfield, Brown organization.[27] Kidd seems to have had a predilection for putting his advertising and PR skills into the service of Liberal politics, and by 1949 was to become the secretary of the National Liberal Federation. Unlike some of his more recent professional colleagues in similar positions, his self-effacing manner prevented him from rising above a service capacity in the party; indeed, there is no evidence that he ever harboured ambitions to do any more than that. As a servant of the party, however, his role was not at all unimportant, even if less glamorous than that of the Keith Daveys of a later era.

In Claxton's first entry into politics, his successful capture in 1940 of the Montreal seat of St Lawrence–St George from the Conservatives to whom it had been entrusted since 1925, he personally retained the services of Cockfield, Brown. Following the election, a small debit balance in Claxton's account with the agency was written off, and his agent thanked Cockfield, Brown for a 'further contribution to his cause.' Kidd, who was a close personal friend of Claxton, undertook to advance the latter's political career with some PR work between elections. A year after Claxton's first appearance in Ottawa as an MP, Kidd was working on some press publicity for him. 'In my opinion,' he suggested to Claxton, 'it would do no harm to begin and to maintain a carefully directed publicity drive, the purpose of which would be, primarily, to acquaint the Canadian people with your career and to make people who don't know you as enthusiastic and devoted as those who have had the good fortune to work with you during the last campaign.' Claxton, professing himself to be 'just a little embarrassed,' nevertheless admitted that he 'like[d] this very much.'[28] Kidd then began a systematic effort to send out copies of Claxton speeches and personal information to editors around the country. As he explained: 'A tremendous effort is necessary to sustain ... the increasing rate of public attention which an individual like yourself is gradually attracting. It is easier to start it than to sustain it, but I would say that in sustaining it alone, can you look for reasons for ultimate success and power, and once you are firmly established as a national figure (it may well happen this year or next) I believe you will agree that you have acquired political capital of considerable value.'[29]

Kidd was right: within two months Claxton was appointed parliamentary secretary to the prime minister, was given major responsibility for steering the revived National Liberal Federation along the desired lines, and within a year and a half was appointed minister of national health and welfare. His political capital proved to be of considerable value indeed. In this rise to prominence Claxton's own abilities can hardly be discounted. Yet he himself put considerable value on the publicity skills of Kidd and Cockfield, Brown. Sometimes, however, the frothy effusiveness of the PR practitioner made even its beneficiary wince. When Kidd described a Claxton speech on foreign policy as 'masterly ... a document of historic significance,' Claxton was somewhat taken aback. 'I must say,' he replied with disarming candour, 'that when I delivered it I thought it a very poor speech and just another set of platitudes ... "governor generalities." '[30] At least it can be said for Claxton that he was too intelligent to believe his own publicity.

The other side of the agency-party relationship even at the local level is demonstrated by an inquiry from Kidd in late 1942 concerning an advertising account with the Montreal Tourist and Convention Bureau which Cockfield, Brown wanted. Claxton, who seems to have had some influence with the bureau, promised to push for making money available for such an account.[31] But compared to the advertising dollar of the city of Montreal, Ottawa was the big time; here, Claxton would no doubt be a friend in court. Such a friend was worth cultivating.

In the spring of 1944 Cockfield, Brown's research department conducted an opinion poll in St Lawrence–St George on Claxton's behalf – in itself a somewhat innovative practice at that time – and from March of that year to the beginning of the 1945 election campaign the agency did $2585 worth of paid work for Claxton in his constituency. In the 1945 campaign itself, Claxton spent $5109 on advertising (almost 40 per cent of his total budget) of which $2750 went to Cockfield, Brown. By this point, numerous other ad agencies were clamouring to get on the bandwagon as well; trying to find a place for them all in the campaign was something of a problem. That these services were by no means all over-the-table agency-client contracts can be seen by notations in Claxton's campaign records of 'donations, etc.' from the agencies or their personnel. And a massive, ninety-page, typewritten analysis of the campaign in detail, with recommendations for improved efficiency in the future emanated from the Cockfield, Brown offices after the election. Claxton wrote a warm letter of appreciation to the agency for their assistance that 'took so many forms that it is hard to single any out, but perhaps the most gratifying was the way in which your executive were always willing to help me personally.' None of his political attachments, Claxton averred, were more valuable than those with the Cockfield, Brown people, 'as friendly as they are able.' '*Everyone*,' he concluded, 'thinks my own publicity in St Lawrence–St George was the best any candidate had in any election.' Years later, in reply to the receipt of a Christmas present from Cockfield, Brown, Claxton gracefully stated that 'my connection with Cockfield, Brown and Co. has been one of the happiest results of my being in public service. Nothing has contributed more, both to such success as I have had, and to the enjoyment (such as it is) of this life.'[32]

Such a mutually beneficial arrangement could not be confined to a single Montreal constitutency, or to a single Liberal member, however important. In 1943, the watershed year for the organizational revival of the Liberal party nationally, a formal arrangement was made between the National Liberal Federation and Cockfield, Brown. The latter would become the party's single national agency on a continuing basis. Other agencies might work on the provincial campaigns, responsible to provincial committees, but only Cockfield, Brown would have responsibility for the national advertising. What the precise terms of the agreement were is unfortunately not clear from the documentary evidence now available. Nor is this altogether surprising, considering the circumstances: as the author of an internal Cockfield, Brown memorandum two years later rather delicately put it, 'the agreement we entered into with the party was a confidential one. I hope that neither its terms or conditions are known to anyone outside our office.'[33]

The reasons for this reticence are obvious: the relationship was to be a patronage one, party work in return for government contracts. This has indeed been the classic arrangement with ad agencies in Canadian politics, one now so well known as to have been officially noticed in a public government report in 1969.[34] The use of political advertising as a 'loss leader' by agencies is thus no longer a very startling piece of news. What is still murky, however, is the exact nature of the bargain struck. At one pole one might imagine the entire range of advertising services offered at cost, with the agency's commissions from the media being rebated to the party. And, to be sure, at one point the president of the NLF, Gordon Fogo, did inform the secretary of the NLF that the arrangement with Cockfield, Brown was 'not intended to show them any ultimate profit.'[35] A few years later the same secretary, in dealing with another ad agency involved in a by-election, suggested that 'in all the advertising we have done the 15% commission has been paid by the newspapers to the advertising agency. In most cases the advertising agencies have rebated this to us.'[36] If such were in fact the practice in all cases, the donation to the party would be very considerable indeed. But this appears to be highly overstated.

One problem with the model of political advertising at cost in exchange for government advertising for profit is the sheer diseconomy of such a bargain from the agencies' perspective. Not only is there uncertainty over the outcome of an election and thus of the ultimate pay-off, but the volume of government business necessary to recoup the loss involved in the political advertising would seem to be quite enormous. As one expert in the advertising field told the Task Force on Government Information in 1969:

If an agency spends, in time, talent and out-of-pocket, $15,000 on a political campaign (and this is not a large amount, if one considers men assigned to travel with a candidate plus the back-up staff), then taking into account the 15 per cent commission agencies get from the media on billings, it will take $100,000 in government billings to replace this amount. And on the basis of current agency net profit, it may take a million dollars before the agency breaks even. That is one of the reasons that some very good agencies will not touch government business. They cannot afford to get embroiled.[37]

Granted that the net profit of the industry may have been different in earlier decades, the point remains: the *quid pro quo* cannot, in the nature of things, be a simple equation. As the task force concluded, ad agencies 'do indeed get paid for much of the work they perform during elections. They get a 15 per cent commission from the media on billings; that is their normal commission on any kind of advertising assignment. What they do not normally get paid for are such extras as special television effects, art work, and men assigned to travel with candidates.' As O.J. Firestone suggests, agency earnings on political accounts may, in a narrow sense, be greater than on commercial accounts, since 'as a rule, advertising agencies do little media, product or consumer research, and a minimum of artwork, in political advertising.' However, the *net* position of the agencies may normally be worse on political accounts, because they are also required to provide other services 'such as public relations services for a minister or other help for individual politicians trying to get elected.' The final result is well summarized by Firestone: 'Agencies continue to mix commissionable advertising efforts with unpaid political work. Then they rely on getting government advertising to make up for any losses or non-earnings they have had during an election campaign.'[38] The specifics of any particular agency-party relationship will thus have to be discovered, not inferred.

It is difficult to establish the precise dollars and cents bargain struck between the Liberals and Cockfield, Brown. One problem is the rather loose terminology that often went back and forth in communication between agency and party. Echoing Fogo's statement quoted earlier, Kidd informed Fogo's successor, Duncan MacTavish, that 'I believe Cockfield, Brown has taken the position that they do not wish to consider service to the National Liberal Federation from a profit standpoint. They are more than pleased to be able to make the resources of the organization available to the Party whenever they are required ...' This self-sacrificing statement was, however, to back up an agency invoice including a $650 commission. If the party were to 'raise our eyebrows at this charge,' Kidd went on, the agency would withdraw it. In the event, the commission and similar charges were paid.[39] Indeed, it is clear from the documents that the Liberals did normally pay the commission on their regular media advertising.[40]

If commissions were normally charged, which is hardly suprising, the question remains as to what Cockfield, Brown's actual contribution to the Liberal cause constituted, apart from the services they could offer any commercial client. Claxton informed Mackenzie King after the 1945 election of the status of Cockfield, Brown's contribution: 'It is often thought that the commissions earned through handling political advertising would leave a firm doing political business with money in pocket. This was not the case with Cockfield, Brown. In direct expenditures and contributions of money, Cockfield, Brown and Company spent $9,000.00 more than they received from all sources, and, in addition, made contributions in the services of the experienced senior executives for which no charge was made.'[41] A straight financial contribution to Liberal campaigns might be part of this bargain. This could take the form of a write-off of a portion of the agency's fees. In 1953 this write-off totalled $5000. Contributions might also be given on special occasions, such as the 1948 national convention, when $3650 was billed without commission.[42]

Above and beyond this type of clear-cut contribution there were other services provided free as well. For example, certain cabinet ministers were given special consideration. In the 1949 and 1953 elections, 'as a gesture of good will,' Cockfield, Brown provided free posters for Robert Winters' campaign in his own constituency. In a by-election organized under the general supervision of Walter Harris, a Cockfield, Brown man was loaned free, expenses included, for the direction of the advertising campaign. Paul Martin had a special relationship to Cockfield, Brown (as did Martin's ministry) which even superseded the normal devolution of advertising at the Ontario constituency level to the Walsh agency. C.D. Howe was also the beneficiary of some Cockfield, Brown largesse on occasion. Often such matters seem to have been played by ear: if the agency thought it could collect, it would; if unsure, it might write off an outstanding amount.[43] The situation was not always obvious, to either side.

It was obvious that such *ad hoc* arrangements could lead to misunderstandings. In 1953 the party arranged to have an agency man, W.A. Munro, set up in the Chateau Laurier to direct the Ottawa end of the prime minister's advertising campaign for the election of that year. There was a catch, however. As Duncan MacTavish put it somewhat delicately at a joint strategy meeting of the party and the agency: 'it would be very helpful to us if Bill [Munro] would consider himself as part of the team now and when he is in Ottawa for his favourite client, to consider ways and means of doing a little work for us at the same time.'[44] The 'favourite client' referred to was none other than the Trans-Canada Pipe Line Company, then seeking government favour in Ottawa. The minister facing the company's pressure, Howe, was furious and fired off a blistering letter to MacTavish: 'This seems to me very dangerous business. Bill Munro is now representing a pipeline company in Ottawa, and appears to be very active in that regard. In the Chateau Laurier he would be most conspicuous, particularly as I understand his rooms would be used to entertain the press.' Munro, moreover, belonged to Cockfield, Brown 'which firm gets the bulk of the government business. It seems to me absurd that they would charge one hundred dollars a day to the Liberal party ... for the part-time services of one of their men. If Bill Munro is not anxious to work for the Liberal party at a price the party can afford to pay I would like to know it.'[45]

The situation was not in fact quite what Howe believed it to be. The propriety of the ad agency man representing both the party and a private company dealing with the government was dubious at best. But while the party was paying for the hotel suite and expenses, the time of Mr Munro and his secretary came compliments of Cockfield, Brown and Co.[46] There was thus a *quid* for the *quo*. But the incident illustrates an inherent problem in the agency-party relationship: the *ad hoc* nature of the arrangements left them open to misinterpretation, even from within the party. And the question of conflict of interest between party and commercial clients was very much an open one. During the bitter pipeline debate three years later a Tory MP informed the House of Commons that 'the public relations director of Trans-Canada Pipe Lines is ensconced in Suite 514 of the Chateau Laurier Hotel, and he is the same man who was the public relations director of the prime minister in his last election campaign. I understand he is turning out some speeches ... they may have been some of the speeches we have heard in this House.' As Dalton Camp was later to put it, Cockfield, Brown was 'so powerful and influential a firm as to represent the Government of Canada, the Liberal Party, and Trans-Canada Pipe Lines all at the same time.'[47]

In the 1940s such considerations did not intrude. But the loose and somewhat indeterminate nature of the party-agency bargain did intrude, very early, and very rudely, in the history of the relationship. And the trouble that resulted was so great as to endanger the marriage at its outset.

After the initial arrangement was made, the Liberals, mindful of the spectre of the CCF hovering menacingly on their left, wished to begin a public relations campaign well in advance of an election which could by law come no later than 1945. Cockfield, Brown prepared a pre-election plan in December 1943 which was submitted to Senator Wishart Robertson, president of the NLF, in January. In the same month H.E. Kidd of the agency appeared before Jimmy Gardiner, Chubby Power, and Ian Mackenzie for the job of directing the campaign from the Ottawa end. His services were to be 'loaned' from the agency for the duration.[48] Kidd arrived in Ottawa to work with Claxton and Jack Pickersgill from the prime minister's office, and later with Gordon Fogo as party chairman, on plans for the coming campaign. An extensive survey of a sample of forty-three ridings was undertaken to test the party's standing as well as to try out some possible election slogans for consumer reaction.[49] But problems arose almost at once. The party decided against immediate commencement of the campaign. A second pre-election campaign plan, with an estimated budget of $150,000 for all media was approved by the cabinet's publicity committee in April, with special reference to the coming Saskatchewan provincial election, which was seen as the major test of the CCF. Although the programme was authorized by Jimmy Gardiner, and the first ads set in type, 'financial arrangements were not completed' and the campaign largely remained in the Cockfield, Brown files. In any event, the Liberals spent two and a half times as much on election advertising in Saskatchewan in 1944 as they had in the previous provincial election, but only about one-fifth of the total, a mere $5505, was channeled through Cockfield, Brown as the national agency.[50] The nub of the problem was the puzzling difficulty the Liberals were experiencing in raising money nationally. Traditionally, inter-election periods have been the most difficult time for Canadian parties to collect money, but as the election period in 1945 was to demonstrate, the Liberals were, for reasons which remain quite unclear, in some trouble concerning fund-raising in the late stages of the war years.[51]

It is not possible to reconstruct a coherent picture of just how much money was being spent by the Liberals on advertising in the first year of their arrangement with Cockfield, Brown. The secretary of the NLF reported that $14,537 had been paid to the agency from March 1944 to January 1945, but invoices totalling some $23,000 were sent from the agency during the same period. How much was paid for, how much written off, and how much represents duplication of other charges is impossible to sort out. The point is clear, however, that whatever funds were forthcoming fell far short of the first hopeful estimates of the agency. For example, one item alone in the original December 1943 plan had included a series of twenty-six quarter-hour radio broadcasts for which production and time charges would have totalled $73,000. The Liberal party simply did not command the financial resources to pay for the publicity campaigns familiar in the world of private enterprise.[52]

Nor could the party count on the kind of continuous and steady financing that private corporations relied on. And Cockfield, Brown was evidently unprepared for dealing with such a client. The Liberals were in a difficult situation: they knew that a massive advertising campaign would be required to ensure the defeat of the CCF, but they were not at all sure how to pay for it. Early in 1945 Kidd and Fogo worked out a tentative campaign estimate that 'would come to a pretty substantial figure' – around $200,000. Since the total cost of the national advertising campaign to the NLF in 1940 had been only $68,222.30 (Quebec included), this would indeed indicate a major increase. But as *Marketing*, the advertising journal, correctly prophesized at the beginning of the election campaign: 'The power of advertising will be a strong factor in the forthcoming federal and Ontario provincial elections but there will not be nearly as much advertising as the various parties and candidates wish to employ.' After the election was called, a scaled-down budget was agreed upon for $143,000. Ultimately, all that and possibly a little more was in fact expended.[53] But the process was painful, to say the least.

Trouble began almost as soon as the campaign got underway. Cockfield, Brown demanded payments in advance of expenditures. The party could not find the dollars: Fogo, 'at the end of his tether,' told the prime minister that $35,000 was desperately needed for publicity expenditures. With Norman Lambert's quick intervention, the money was advanced by Senator Armand Daigle, one of the party's Montreal bagmen, but the agency was indignant.[54] Kidd, already beginning to see things somewhat more from the party's point of view, tried to mollify his employers by pointing out that the Liberals were now (after the advance) $8,000 ahead:

I would like to take this opportunity to point out that Mr. Fogo has at no time protested against payments in advance of expenditures – these payments are an indication of his integrity and intention to abide by our agreement. What he did hope to receive was a few days breathing space when his maximum outgo hit at a time when funds were just coming in.

It would be extremely unfortunate, and I think bad faith on our part, if we broadcast the impression that the Liberal party were hard up for funds. This is not so – and we have no reason for saying so.

In a memo a few days earlier Kidd pronounced his intention to comment on the behaviour of the agency 'at some future date when there is time to view these events in their proper perspective.'[55]

The money did come through; *Marketing* complimented Cockfield, Brown on the quality of its Liberal advertisements,[56] and 'Unity-Security-Freedom ... Vote for a New Social Order' proved to be a more compelling selling point than the CCF programme of nationalization. The marriage between the Liberal party and Cockfield, Brown had proved itself, but not before some rough ground had been passed over.

One significant result of the 1945 campaign was the Liberals' realization of the invaluable service of H.E. Kidd as the institutionalized link between the party and the agency. Kidd had worked 'day and night for the Federation for eighteen months,' Brooke Claxton testified to his cabinet colleagues. And to Mackenzie King, Claxton confided that Kidd's work had 'extended far beyond the preparation of advertising material ... he was in Ottawa assisting in the whole work of organization ... '[57] In effect the Liberals had gained the services of a full-time national organizer for the duration, as well as a direct link to their ad agency. Properly grateful, the party helped secure him a vacation in the West Indies, when the pace of his activities in the party's service led to health problems after the election.

Following the election Kidd returned to Cockfield, Brown's Montreal office. But his heart does not seem to have been in it. Complaining to his friend Claxton about the boring detail of normal commercial work, he sounded a plaintive note: 'Please remember me to Jack Pickersgill and other friends. Needless to say, I find it difficult to adjust myself to commercial activities. I miss keenly the broader horizon and the more interesting tasks which occupy the minds of the men at Ottawa (in my opinion!).'[58] It seems that this sense of 'broader horizons' drew Kidd strongly toward party work; perhaps there is a hint here of the pyschological considerations that can on occasion attract men from the private sphere to the insecurities of politics. After directing the advertising for the 1949 election, Kidd tried to convey to the surviving principal of the agency, G. Warren Brown, the peculiar flavour of an election campaign:

It has been very interesting to get a glimpse of a political party in battle. You hear strange voices on the telephone from all parts of the country ... Men and women never heard of before – all confident, demanding and determined. I hardly realized the large number of people who are engaged in a political campaign. In our case it is absolutely true to say that the strength of the Liberal Party's power lies not in the Cabinet so much as in the roots of the organization which extend deep into the electorates of every province.[59]

Kidd was to provide perhaps the most significant contribution the agency was to make to the Liberal party. After taking charge of the publicity side of the national Liberal convention to choose King's successor in 1948, Kidd was appointed secretary of the National Liberal Federation, a post he was to hold for over a decade. Regenstreif reported that upon assuming this new office, Kidd 'severed his formal connections with his old firm.'[60] This was not in fact the case. Kidd continued to be a member of Cockfield, Brown and was even, in 1956, promoted to the office of vice-president 'in charge of the Ottawa office of Cockfield, Brown.'[61] In fact, there was no real Ottawa office, other than the NLF offices, but Kidd did double duty as both party secretary and agency representative, using two separate letterheads for his correspondence. While working for the Liberals he continued to do agency business, such as handling the account of the Canadian Bankers' Association. This was not necessarily to the detriment of the party; the latter association carried on anti-socialist propaganda in elections which the Liberals felt to be to their benefit.[62] But the point is that the NLF for over a decade was under the permanent direction of a member of the party's ad agency. The most striking evidence of all of the intimacy of the agency-party relationship is that Cockfield, Brown paid Kidd's salary throughout the period of his work with the NLF.[63] Considering Kidd's position in the agency this must have constituted a very considerable contribution to the party, and must certainly figure as a major part of the *quid pro quo* of the patronage relationship. Even if the party had paid for his services, the fact yet remains that the permanent call on the services of someone of Kidd's talents, not to speak of contacts in the media throughout the country, would have just as surely been of invaluable assistance. Some of the implications of this cosy arrangement were not lost on the opposition in Ottawa. In 1951 the CCF leader, M.J. Coldwell, frustrated by rather devious attempts of the government to cover up the extent of Cockfield, Brown's government advertising business, cast some less than oblique references in Kidd's direction: 'It seems to me that Cockfield, Brown and Company are receiving very large advertising fees from this government, very large commissions therefore for the magazines and periodicals. And when we know who is the representative of Cockfield, Brown in this city – the national secretary, I believe, of the Liberal association – it seems to me that they are getting a very large amount of advertising, and that the commission is very considerable.'[64]

The relationship was not without its critics from within the party as well, although they did not normally dwell on questions of patronage. Many of the complaints came from the more old-fashioned politicians and organizers who had an instinctive mistrust of the slick new operators from the world of Madison Avenue. Norman Lambert was suspicious of the agencies, believing that the increasing tendency to turn over campaigns to their direction 'was one reason for the great increase in the amount of money spent by the parties because the advertising company finds ways of spending money.' Chubby Power felt that the ad men were one of the biggest problems in political campaigning, due to their lack of political principles, and that in any event they were not worth their cost.[65] After the liberal defeats of 1957-8 C.D. Howe suggested privately that 'in my opinion, Cockfield, Brown have not done much for us over the year, except advocate spending money uselessly.'[66] One Liberal MP, in answer to a request from the NLF for ideas on improving party organization, was more direct yet: 'I may be old fashioned,' he admitted, '[but] I would steer clear of the average professional advertising agency, the only thing they can convince *me* of – is a desire to be sick.'[67] Nor was such criticism only confined to outsiders. As one highly successful Tory ad man admitted publicly, 'I had come to the conclusion that advertising agencies in politics were wasteful, their judgement often atrocious, and that many of their decisions were likely to be based on their interest in a profitable campaign, rather than on an effective one.'[68]

But Dalton Camp was talking mainly about Tory agencies, which, in the days of Liberal dominance in the 1940s and 1950s, were notoriously inefficient in selling their product. Cockfield, Brown had a more saleable product and thus the agency itself took on an added lustre. This was especially true when Louis St Laurent took over the party leadership. Here was the ad man's dream, the perfect human material for the image merchants. The prosperous, dull, conservative 1950s found their personalization in the paternal, authoritative, kindly figure of 'Uncle Louis.' Cockfield, Brown lent their best efforts to the careful cultivation of this image; in a real sense, the elections of 1949 and 1953 were the first Canadian elections dominated by a consciously manipulated media image of the party leader.[69] The ad agency was subtly changing the nature of campaigning, and the Conservatives scarcely understood what was happening to them. As Camp recalls:

The Liberal Party seized the new instruments of communication and used them confidently, deliberately, and effectively ... [St Laurent's] image was vague, somewhat fuzzy, seen through filters of sentiment, layers of gauze woven by exuberant flacks and romantic commentators. But the evidence, as presented in assiduously retouched, richly-coloured photographs, was testimony enough to convince Canadians that, after a long period of spinster rule by a man essentially drab and determinedly colourless, they were now led by another who could have been the head of the house of 'One Man's Family.'

On reflection I am struck by the fact that, while this was happening in the campaign of 1953, none of us at Tory headquarters seemed aware of it. While the advisors and strategists pored over every published word uttered by the Prime Minister and his cabinet, no one looked up to see that the Liberal leader had changed his clothes.[70]

On occasion, Conservatives even let it be known that if Cockfield, Brown were ever interested, the Tory party would be glad to take the Liberal propagandists to their very own bosom. One day in 1953 Kidd chanced upon Grattan O'Leary and was told: 'You know, you people do an exceedingly fine job for your clients. I wish you were doing our work. You seem to have acquired a certain political flair for what you are doing, and something which we can't seem to find with our people.' Then, Kidd recalled, 'he sort of smiled and shrugged his shoulders.' Wistfully might the Tories envy the Liberals their image-makers; in the glory days of C.D. Howe's 'who can stop us?' there was little enough chance that the country's biggest and most successful ad agency would be lured away to support the sagging ranks of George Drew's opposition. As Kidd commented on one Tory overture, 'if our work is noted by the Opposition, I hope it must also be satisfactory to our principals.'[71]

Cockfield, Brown and the Liberal party were in one sense very much alike. Dalton Camp, a judicious observer of agency techniques, writes that a Cockfield, Brown campaign 'would be efficiently conducted, the material would bear the mark of professional skills, but it would also be bloodless, even somewhat alien ... [Cockfield, Brown ads] were, for the period, slick and patronizing, which is to say they bore the unmistakable imprint of the agency's competence, as well as its opinion that they were being prepared for the eyes and ears of yokels.'[72] Efficiency, competence, bloodlessness, and condescension: an epitaph many would give to the St Laurent Liberal party as well as to their ad agency.

Of course there were many tasks to which an advertising agency could be put, other than the planning and execution of a national advertising campaign during elections. One was the continual cultivation of the media for the enhancement of the Liberal image day to day. Kidd was tireless in the NLF offices in monitoring the press, planting stories, admonishing hostile reporters, and generally watching for opportunities to put the best Liberal face forward. In these endeavours the Montreal office of his agency was always willing to help. The Cockfield, Brown research department, a pride of the agency, was sometimes called upon to supplement the inputs into the party's fact files from the civil service, helping to provide favourable data for party speakers.[73] Opinion surveys in the constituencies were another item, although in this era it seems that primary reliance was placed on the Gallup polls. The agency handled the distribution and advertising of the CBC 'Nation's Business' broadcasts by cabinet ministers. And special occasions, such as the rather infrequent national conventions, national summer conferences, or special testimonial dinners for prime ministers, which required press liaison and public relations services, invariably found Cockfield, Brown men in charge of such arrangements.[74] In other words, in an era of growing media emphasis, ad men were beginning to displace the old style political organizers who had traditionally looked after these matters.

There were other purposes to which the agency could also be put which were rather less obvious – and less legitimate as well. There is definite evidence that in the 1945 campaign at least $15,948 was collected in campaign funds from four companies, Massey-Harris, Dominion Woollens and Worsteds, Firestone Tire and Rubber, and G.H. Wood and Company, in the form of cheques made out to Cockfield, Brown and not to the Liberal party.[75] The attraction of this arrangement from the contributors' point of view was that the donations could be written off for tax purposes as advertising expenditures. There was a certain hesitation on the part of the agency concerning the problem of receipting these donations, as well there might be, since the procedure was quite certainly illegal. But illegal or not, it did continue, and while no documentary proof of the practice could be found beyond the 1945 election, there is evidence that contributions to parties through advertising agencies have been a continuing feature of the political scene in Canada.[76]

As the years went by, the agency-party relationship became closer and closer. After the 1953 election a cabinet subcommittee on publicity began fairly regular meetings as an institutionalized link between the cabinet and the NLF. In 1956-7, with another election on the horizon, the committee was expanded to include Cockfield, Brown staff, to plan the outlines of the campaign.[77] The combination of the regional power brokers of the cabinet, a representative of the prime minister, the NLF, and Cockfield, Brown was a summation of all the important organizational forces in a national campaign. The intimacy of the party-agency relationship meant advance knowledge of election dates was entrusted to the agency – with concomitant problems of security when the agency was eager to get started. Only the Cockfield, Brown officials were allowed to see the advance plans for the 1953 election, as the NLF reminded the agency of the party's 'dependence on you to protect its position ...'[78] In other words the ad agency was privy to the kind of arcana normally reserved to the inner circle of the cabinet.

FEDERAL-PROVINCIAL ORGANIZATION OF ADVERTISING

The generally decentralized nature of Liberal campaign organization was paralleled by decentralization of campaign publicity. The 1945 campaign proved that an arrangement with a national agency need not preclude the use of other agencies at lower levels. As one party document noted: 'In the 1945 election publicity was decentralized. Each provincial committee and in many instances the constituency committees, had their own publicity people. The duties of publicity people in the provincial and constituency levels being to insure the greatest possible presentation in newspapers of the activities of their candidates.' The practice continued in later elections. There was certainly no shortage of agencies ready and willing to offer their services to a party which gave every indication of continuing its control over the Ottawa government advertising dollar into the indefinite future. As Kidd reported in 1953, one ad man met with Liberal officials, offering on behalf of his agency 'to accept any assignment we care to give him, in the hope that he may get some reward after the Liberal Government has been given a new mandate.'[79]

Walsh Advertising, the Ontario provincial Liberal party agency, regularly took charge of that province's publicity in campaigns. Walsh's president, W. George Akins, chaired a provincial standing committee on publicity, which also included individuals from other agencies with special tasks: for example, G.A. Phare of R.C. Smith and Son, a pioneer in radio advertising, took charge of Ontario radio spot ads in 1949.[80] One agency which was assiduous in cultivating the Liberal party was MacLaren's of Toronto, one of the largest and fastest growing agencies in the country. Already involved in 1949, MacLaren's was making cash contributions to the Liberal cause in the early 1950s. In 1953 MacLaren's offered various forms of help to the campaign.[81] MacLaren's was later to be the agency that picked up the pieces after the Liberal disaster of 1958.

Putting all these agencies into harness simultaneously was not always an easy task. In 1945 the NLF treasurer recommended that Vickers and Benson of Montreal be given a 'substantial' amount of Liberal advertising. The secretary of the NLF wondered if his impression was correct that the arrangement with Cockfield, Brown included the understanding that 'they were going to divide some advertising among certain Liberal companies.' Gordon Fogo was clear in his mind: 'As I understand our arrangement ... it will not readily lend itself to distribution of the advertising amongst several concerns.'[82]

Fogo was speaking of the national campaign, of course, but what he seemed to have forgotten was that in Liberal campaigns there were always two 'national' organizations – one in English Canada and another in Quebec. The publicity organization was parallel in this regard as well. Although it was the Montreal office of Cockfield, Brown which was involved in national party work, Quebec always remained a special case, out of reach of the agency's control. Vickers and Benson did gain a portion of the business in that province, which was not altogether surprising in light of the fact that a Liberal MP from Montreal was an executive of the firm.[83]

A persistent problem was that of French-language ads. Outside Quebec, these sometimes rested with the NLF and Cockfield, Brown.[84] But the 'special situation' of Quebec was recognized in the original agreement between the party and Cockfield, Brown. The agency agreed to work with the

Quebec organization and to 'bring in as our associates for the French advertising the Canadian Advertising Agency.'[85] By 1949 Vickers and Benson was involved in some of the French advertising as well. In the same year Claxton concluded an understanding with the Quebec party organization that English and French ads would be handled separately, without regard to province.[86] In this election, a committee of six Quebec ministers and senators with organizational responsibility made final decisions on copy and distribution. Nor was this seen as mechanical translation of English into French; instead 'des changements radicaux' were necessary. 'Il s'agit,' as one committee member put it, 'non pas de traduire, mais d'adapter les idées de base des brochures à notre milieu particulier le Canada-français.' And the NLF's French secretary agreed wholeheartedly. A key figure in linking this Quebec committee and its publicity to the national campaign in 1949 and 1953 was Brooke Claxton; the maintenance of continuity and co-operation was 'very largely on a personal basis.'[87]

There was a delicate problem involved in all this, one which had as much to do with the advertising business as it did with political organization, and which was to come to the fore in the 1960s as the impact of the Quiet Revolution came to bear on the cultural and linguistic dimension of advertising in Quebec. Briefly, it was this: the powerful socializing effects of modern advertising were increasingly perceived in Quebec as yet another imperialistic arm of English-speaking assimilation. The crude translation of English copy (and hence of English cultural assumptions) into literal French sometimes led to ludicrous and even insulting results. Among those French Canadians who accepted the basic framework of North American capitalism, the question of establishing a French presence in the advertising world – either through separate agencies or autonomous French-language sections in English agencies – was becoming an important issue.[88] Although this problem was only in its infancy in the 1950s, it was not without its implications for anyone, including political parties, planning large-scale advertising campaigns in French Quebec. And to the Liberal party, with its own roots sunk deep in the province in the form of an organization with a prickly sense of 'special status,' the implications were evident enough.

Cockfield, Brown had a relatively large French-speaking section in Montreal, and even liked to style themselves the 'largest French speaking agency in the world';[89] on the eve of the 1957 election, they began a real push to take over the French-language advertising. In late 1956 the agency began to campaign to persuade leading Liberals of their ability to handle the task. 'It is essential,' they recognized, 'that we put our best foot forward insofar as our French speaking people are concerned.' To this end an organizational chart was devised for an all-French effort: '... this is the first time in Cockfield, Brown history,' an agency memorandum stated, 'that we have mounted a 100% French-speaking team from start to finish opposite any single project. This is a most interesting development and a great challenge to all concerned.' Leading Liberals were impressed. Louis Gélinas, prominent Montreal financial collector, allowed that if the agency were all it had been 'cracked up to be,' he would back their offer. Organizer Roch Pinard met Duncan MacTavish in New York and raised the possibility of a changeover to Cockfield, Brown.

Technical competence was not the only consideration. Brooke Claxton's advice was sought from retirement: he emphatically asserted that Cockfield, Brown's obvious superiority was quite beside the point, and argued on the contrary that the 'controversy which would build up around Cockfield, Brown would be unpleasant and difficult.' Co-operation with those agencies already involved, he concluded, would be much preferable. Kidd, despite his affiliation, agreed: 'our purpose is to serve the Party to the best advantage of the Party and we certainly don't want to introduce controversy in a situation which is so sensitive and which has a fairly complicated history of internal dissension.' Neither did he feel that Cockfield, Brown's 'French-speaking element' should be entirely excluded from the French-language advertising.[90] A compromise was eventually reached, which also continued into the campaign of 1958 when Gélinas again pressed Cockfield, Brown's claims against the strong advice of Chubby Power who championed Canadian Advertising. A neutral party emissary finally arranged a mutually satisfactory saw-off.[91]

Quebec advertising may have been a special case, but even the distribution of responsibility to other agencies at the provincial level was not without its inter-agency rivalries and complexities. In effect, the strains which often accompanied federal-provincial relations within the party organization were reflected in strains between federal and provincial ad agencies. This point should not be overemphasized: in general the decentralized publicity organization worked as well for the Liberals in these years as did their decentralized campaign organization. Efficiency and co-operation stand out far more than division and conflict. But this success was not without at least some attendant strains. Ontario was one example, and its problems were directly related to the failures and disasters of the provincial Liberals. Ottawa Liberals won elections with tireless regularity; Toronto Liberals lost with equal reliability. Ad agencies associated with the Toronto Liberals found correspondingly greater difficulties in successfully practising their trade. Hence, at federal election time the serene functioning of the

Cockfield, Brown – NLF machine would sometimes sputter and cough at the provincial intakes. One Ontario agency prominent in the mid-1940s – R.C. Smith Advertising – was eased out the picture altogether by the end of the decade.[92]

Walsh Advertising was the pre-eminent provincial agency in Ontario in the 1940s and 1950s, and was always attempting to move in on the national account as well, with little response from national party figures who tended to be deeply suspicious about both the competence and the expensiveness of Walsh's services. William Mulock, the wartime postmaster-general, was the spokesman for Walsh in the federal cabinet, who had vainly tried to head off the arrangement with Cockfield, Brown, but there was little if any support for the brash Toronto agency outside of Mulock. Indeed, Norman Lambert complained about the massive bills Walsh had piled up in directing publicity for the disastrous Grey North by-election defeat of General McNaughton; defeat did not stop Walsh, however, as Lambert commented ironically about the president of the agency early in 1945: 'Fresh from North Grey with Mulock's backing Aikin [sic] on behalf of his firm is out to buck up the Liberals, rally them from recent defeat, with large sized doses of his particular brand of public relations work.'[93] Walsh was always ready to formulate self-assertive and sometimes eccentrically grandiose plans. The standing committee on publicity of the Ontario Liberal Association, chaired by Walsh's president and staffed with other Walsh men, issued a report in late 1952 suggesting a vast scheme of provincial, regional, and constituency meetings of publicity officers under the 'expert guidance' of 'advertising specialists,' and the creation of a regular party press as a 'ready medium of official party communication.'[94] Since the NLF had been providing such a press to a generally unappreciative and uninterested party audience for years, since an Ontario Liberal paper had gone under for lack of sales, and since there was no possibility of raising the funds necessary for the Walsh vision, Kidd in Ottawa might have been grinding his teeth in frustration. The air of unreality in Toronto was heightened when set against four successive election routs, in two of which the Liberals had been reduced to a third party in the legislature. Such foolishness scarcely enhanced the confidence of the federal party in either its Ontario party or its Ontario ad agency.[95]

It was no doubt considerations of this sort that led to certain manœuvrings in both Ottawa and Toronto prior to elections. Early in 1953 Kidd reported to his agency that the man in charge of the Ontario part of the coming campaign, Harry Hamilton, was setting up a committee. 'Naturally,' George Akins of Walsh 'will want to dominate Mr. Hamilton's thinking on publicity matters and on everything else if he can.' Kidd allowed that 'the Liberal Party must welcome all offers of energy and assistance.' But he went on to point out that the Ontario Liberal Association, dominated by Walsh, 'is not in any way connected with or responsible to Mr. Hamilton's federal campaign committee,' and added that Cockfield, Brown 'should protect its "flank" in Ontario,' guarding against Akins promoting too many Walsh people into key positions. 'I have always thought so,' Kidd explained, 'but I understand why it has been difficult to ask anyone in the Toronto organization of the company to take an interest in Liberal politics.' (Without the attraction of government patronage in Toronto it is easy to see why.) Kidd did suggest to MacTavish that a Toronto Cockfield, Brown man be added for 'federal-provincial liaison,' which argument MacTavish accepted. In the end the NLF treasurer, Alan Woodrow, and two Cockfield, Brown men were added to the Ontario committee, but the latter appointments were made 'very discreetly' – 'for obvious reasons,' as Kidd put it.[96] By 1957 the Toronto office of Cockfield, Brown was much more integrated into the national advertising campaign. It may be that Walsh was being discreetly elbowed out of the picture, although the documentary evidence available does not permit firm conclusions.

Another province where the publicity situation presented a face of some complexity was 'that great and uncertain political country' of British Columbia.[97] Of course the political situation in British Columbia was confused enough from the federal perspective during the days of the coalition government. But following the Social Credit victory in 1952, political advertising was even more confused, owing to Premier W.A.C. Bennett's blithe disregard of national partisan allegiances in dispensing advertising contracts. Whether Bennett actually believed in non-partisan allocation of the government ad dollar, or whether, as may be more likely, he preferred to make his own alliances without reference to what was done east of the Rockies, the result was the same: a situation unique to that province. For example, James Lovick and Company was the agency for the Alberta Liberal party and also ran government tourist campaigns in British Columbia, campaigns so partisan as to rouse BC Liberal leader Arthur Laing to denounce 'purely political propaganda to advertise Premier Bennett.'[98] British Columbia was, as so many easterners before and since have discovered, a world of its own. This could cut both ways. In 1957-8 Cockfield, Brown was able to pick up the lucrative contract from the BC Travel Bureau to advertise centennial celebrations; it was quite unthinkable that such a contract would have come their way from, say, Tory Ontario.

In 1945 the Stewart, Bowman, and Macpherson agency ran the provincial side of the federal campaign, with promises to Cockfield, Brown of 'all kinds of co-operation.' 'I need hardly tell you,' Kidd reminded his agency's Vancouver office with barely repressed bitterness, 'that this proved an illusion in as much as he [Stewart] persuaded the newspapers to give him the space he required, and squeezed out national advertising on the party's important subjects such as family allowances, full employment, etc.'[99] Relations with the BC Liberals had reached such a low level by 1949 that the secretary of the NLF could not even get a reply from the secretary of the BC Liberal Association even after a stream of letters to Vancouver. Understandably, in such circumstances the federal party decided to try to put its own people in charge of federal publicity. A tour by St Laurent in April of 1949 was publicized by the Vancouver office of Cockfield, Brown, which reported to Kidd that they had 'arranged publicity, news reels, window displays, radio broadcasts, eclipse of the moon, and earthquake.' Modestly, they added: 'Hope our efforts will reflect the glory of Cockfield, Brown and H.E. Kidd.' After the provincial electoral disaster of 1952, in which the coalition's account was handled ineptly by Stewart, Bowman, Macpherson, the time had come for a clean break with the past. Cockfield, Brown was asked to handle publicity in British Columbia for the federal election the next year. Yet such was the peculiar nature of the province that not even this could put Ottawa's fears to rest. Kidd put his foot down firmly on the idea that the agency's Vancouver office should handle not only the provincial campaign but the placing of national ads as well, and admonished Montreal not to give Vancouver authority to do anything 'on our account.' 'Not that I don't trust them,' he hastened to add, 'but the people of BC are known to be enthusiastic. Sometimes their enthusiasm takes them the wrong way, but we have hopes that the faithful will respond ... to the clarion call of the Great White Father.' The Great White Father's call seems to have had disappointing results. Or at least one might infer this from the fact that the next election in 1957 saw BC publicity handled by McCann-Erickson, a Canadian subsidiary of one of the largest American agencies.[100] Somehow neither the Liberals nor Cockfield, Brown ever quite solved the problem of acclimatization to the west coast.

ADVERTISING EXPENDITURES

Throughout the period 1944 to 1958 it is not possible to reconstruct the total amount of money spent by the Liberals through ad agencies at all levels. It *is* possible to estimate how much was spent on national advertising through Cockfield, Brown in general elections. Table 6.1 gives the overall

Table 6.1
Estimated amounts spent on national advertising for the
Liberal party through Cockfield, Brown in general elections 1945-58

1945	$161,361
1949	188,890
1953	178,867
1957	164,119
1958	146,620

Sources: invoices, statements, etc., NLF, v. 602, 809, 815, 836, and 843

picture. Although these figures are only estimates, they are probably reasonably accurate. One of the striking features is the steady decline in total expenditures from 1949 to 1958. There seems to be a combination of factors at work. Neither in 1953 nor (mistakenly) in 1957 was there much fear of losing, and expenditures were held down. Then in 1958 the situation was so hopeless that money was scarce anyway. Another observation must be one of surprise at the generally low level of national expenditure, compared to amounts at least doubled in the late 1960s and early 1970s.[101] The big difference, aside from inflation, is that television had not yet come into its own in this era. Moreover, then as now, considerable amounts were spent at the provincial level. For example, in 1953 it was estimated by one source that $82,000 was spent separately in Ontario: about 46 per cent of the national total.[102] Finally, as already explained, French-language advertising was also excluded from the national totals.

Naturally enough, Cockfield, Brown wished to encourage greater spending. Their first hopeful estimate in 1957 was for a budget of $548,666. By the end of that disheartening campaign they had to settle for little more than one-quarter of that figure. In 1953, after a final, reduced estimate had been accepted, Claxton called a meeting of NLF and Cockfield, Brown representatives in his office three weeks before the polls and announced a 'radical scaling down' of advertising spending. As one participant in the meeting later recalled, 'Mr. Claxton announced that the election was in the bag and the purpose of the meeting was to save every possible expenditure.' The change was fundamental: in 1949 advertising had been a 'major vehicle' for the party campaign. Now it was felt that the Liberal image could live off its own fat; 'getting out the vote' would be the major thrust. The howls from Cockfield, Brown and from some provincial quarters were loud, but Claxton was, as usual, right.[103] All of which seems to indicate that the Liberal party was selling itself as much as it was being sold by its ad men.

Table 6.2
Breakdown of space and time charges for Liberal advertising, by media and by province, general election 1953

	$	%		$	%
Print media:					
Dailies	19,562	20.0	Ontario	43,100	44.1
Weeklies	30,960	31.7	Quebec	16,850	17.2
Weekend	19,168	19.6	British Columbia	9188	9.4
Farm	7861	8.0	Manitoba	8511	8.7
Financial	831	0.9	Saskatchewan	7932	8.1
Labour	1628	1.7	Alberta	6128	6.3
Foreign-language	3948	4.0	Nova Scotia	2425	2.5
Veterans	315	0.3	New Brunswick	1888	1.9
			Newfoundland	1213	1.2
Radio	13,518	13.8	Prince Edward Island	431	0.4
			Yukon and		
			Northwest Territories	126	0.1
Total	97,791	100.0		97,792	100.0

Source: NLF, v. 815, Cockfield, Brown account, 28 Oct. 1953, media breakdown, Nov. 1953

How the money was spent can be seen in Table 6.2 based on the 1953 campaign. Most of the Liberal radio time was under the direction of the provincial committees, although Cockfield, Brown did provide a man to coordinate the distribution of transcribed radio speeches throughout the country.[104] Production costs, especially for 'spot' bulletins on private stations, normally rested with the provinces and their agencies. Similarly, the special status of Quebec in advertising, as outlined above, accounts for the relatively low figure for that province in the table.

One factor inflating these rather modest figures was the practice of charging 'political rates' by the media. Even hiring such a prestigious agency as Cockfield, Brown to purchase space did not prevent newspapers, especially weeklies, from taking the opportunity to gouge the political parties for a little extra. This practice – now illegal under the Election Expenses Act of 1974[105] – was a major problem in the 1940s and 1950s. The worst of it was that neither the party nor its agency could budget accurately for this factor, since the papers in question often quoted a commercial rate and then invoiced the agency at a higher, 'political' rate. Despite a general feeling that the practice was 'scandalous' and 'virtually dishonest,' there was little the party could do in the face of a threatened publicity shut-out in rural areas served by weekly papers.[106] And the drain on the publicity budget could be considerable. In 1949, 218 out of 656 weeklies upped their rates *after* accepting lineage, representing a 41 per cent increase in charges over the original quotations. Some Saskatchewan papers went from two to ten cents a line. An advertisement in 1953 was placed in eighty papers – twenty-nine of which had 'known' political rates, others of whom might charge such rates without quoting them. Even some major dailies, such as *Le Devoir*, charged political rates.[107] And this despite the fact that many papers, particularly small weeklies, were dependent to a considerable degree on the placing of federal government advertisements for much of their operating revenue. This ingratitude was irritating to the Ottawa Liberals, to put it mildly.

Cockfield, Brown's activities for the party were not confined to election campaigns. A regular year-to-year advertising and publicity arrangement was also in force, which might vary in extent according to the political circumstances and the party's financial position. In 1954, $5879 in publicity expenditure was billed through Cockfield, Brown by the NLF; this dropped to a mere $644 the following year, but rose to $7281 in the pre-election year of 1956.[108] These figures, it might be noted, represent actual amounts paid out by the NLF to the agency; in the nature of the *ad hoc* party-agency relationship, this may be an underestimate of the actual volume of business.

THE TELEVISION MEDIUM AND LIBERAL ADVERTISING

The role of the advertising agency in national Liberal campaigns in this era may seem, when all is said, to have been modest and conservative by present-day standards. Certainly there is little or no evidence of the ad men controlling or directing the party's policies. The 'boys in the back room' were obviously *advisers* in certain technical aspects of media use; ultimate power lay squarely in the cabinet and the office of the prime minister. Not a single instance can be found in the available records of the ad men persuading the party to adopt a particular issue, or not adopt another. Kidd tried to serve both his masters, the party and the agency, with equal fidelity – and with equal sense of his own subordinate position. If anything, when relations became strained, Kidd tended to take the party's interests as primary, and to plead its case with the agency. So far as the nature of the product being sold, the relations between the Liberal party and Cockfield, Brown were along the classic lines of the agency-client type. Cockfield, Brown packaged and sold what the party produced. The ad men may have worn grey flannel suits, but *éminences grises* they were not. Others have suggested that in the

1960s and 1970s the ad men have taken on a more direct policy-making role in the party councils.[109] But it was not so in this earlier era.

Cockfield, Brown's political advertising was not as aggressive or as ostentatious as the kind of political puffery already evident in the United States in this era. Indeed, in striking contrast to the tinsel and plastic garishness of American presidential campaigns, the national campaigns orchestrated for the Liberals seemed restrained, dignified, deferential – perhaps even a bit dull, a trifle *bureaucratic*. The quiet, competent style had the same solid stamp as that of an official government poster: authority without overstatement. Indeed, those schooled in the Cockfield, Brown style could be quite put off by signs of 'Americanization' of Canadian politics. One agency man accompanying the prime minister on a 1953 election tour of Windsor reported with evident distate to Duncan MacTavish that Paul Martin's local organization had been influenced by the techniques of American ad men from across the river – a master of ceremonies telling the rally crowd how to respond, the use of cue cards, etc. 'The worst aspect of the Windsor show resulted from a resort to American electioneering methods which shook me almost through the cement floor of the arena ... It must be remembered that Windsor is at all times influenced by methods employed across the line and, while the above tactics shocked us, they probably went quite unnoticed by the Windsorites.' But reporters from the Parliamentary Press Gallery, he added, 'were not impressed.'[110]

The decisive watershed separating this older era of publicity from that of today was, of course, television. Television was just making a first appearance in Canada in 1953 and was of no significance in the national election of that year. But 1957 and 1958 witnessed the first extensive use of television in a general election. That this coincided with the end of the twenty-two year Liberal era may be merely accidental, but it is much more likely that there is some connection between the two events. The entire publicity programme built up by the Liberals and their ad agency, and the resulting image of the party in the minds of voters, was in many respects a pre-television, print-media phenomenon. The restrictive rules established by the CBC against 'dramatization' meant that *any* use of television in this era would be limited and primitive, but even at this level the Liberals were quite lost in the new medium. While some solid empirical evidence would be needed to show that Diefenbaker rose to power on the strength of his television image – evidence that is simply not available – it *is* certain that television was an unmitigated disaster for the Liberals, a disaster so frightful that the party leadership itself was appalled and shaken. It is worth looking at this story, for in retrospect one can almost mark the end of an entire era in Canadian political campaigns.

Some preliminary investigation of the use of television in the United States was undertaken by Cockfield, Brown in 1953 with the NLF footing the bill, but little or no use was made of the medium in that election, except for some CBC free time, with the latter providing technical assistance. Considerable preparatory work was undertaken prior to the 1957 election, with Kidd suggesting to Cockfield, Brown that an 'all out effort on television for the party' should be mounted. Television, he predicted with considerable accuracy, will be 'the biggest headache of all,' and suggested the need for a lot of expert help. A man from CBC Montreal was installed in a special studio in Ottawa to prepare Liberals for the new medium. Later a Quebec broadcaster by the name of René Lévesque was added for French-language work. Closed circuit lectures and demonstrations were provided, but despite having 'at our disposal the best of equipment, knowledge, and enthusiasm to have done a first class job ... it was never given a full rein of appreciation.' This latter statement was merely diplomatic. In fact, 'the principals in the contest' – the cabinet ministers – took no notice of the services being provided them. Only one minister, Ralph Campney, bothered attending a single session. The trouble was, as Kidd confided to his agency, that 'the attitude of most politicians ... is one of caution and fear.' Some had appeared in free time shows in 1956 with consequences 'disastrous for the personalities involved ...' St Laurent refused to appear on such programmes: 'He recognizes that ultimately he will make his appearance on television, but he prefers to see what his colleagues will do on the television screen.' The example was not encouraging, and by late 1956 signs of panic were beginning to appear in the party.[111]

Early in the 1957 campaign the extent of the disaster became apparent when the long-awaited appearance of the prime minister on the television screen called forth an anguished plea from the arch-Liberal *Winnipeg Free Press*. Under the heading 'LIBERALS, BE HUMAN' the *Free Press* noted sorrowfully that St Laurent, reading from a manuscript on his desk, 'refused to make any concessions to the television camera.' Liberals, the editor concluded, were 'just not at home in [this] merciless medium': 'If you cannot loosen up and act like ordinary people,' he advised earnestly, 'it would be decidedly to the advantage of the Liberal party to give up the television time that has been allotted to you.'[112] This Hobson's choice was indeed all that was left to the party by this stage. From $30,000 to $35,000 had been spent on production. Close to $15,000 more had been invested in buying time for 'spots' and ten-minute programmes in Ontario. But the party had 'convincing evidence that our TV programmes were doing us more harm than good ...' All further television was cancelled in mid-May, despite the fact that cancellations would in many cases be billed anyway by the stations. This painful, and costly, decision was necessary, Kidd told MacTavish, not because of the technical backing, which was 'marvellous,' but 'because our masters have not seen fit to make use of the facilities we established for them here ... '[113]

To make matters worse yet, the Liberals were also the victims of what appears to be either a misunderstanding or worse with regard to television production. A Toronto film and television producer, S.W. 'Spence' Caldwell, offered his services for the 1957 Liberal television effort. The NLF understood that he would charge only costs and out-of-pocket expenses, for as Caldwell told Kidd 'several times,' he did 'very substantial business in Ottawa and there were other reasons why he was most anxious to do everything he could to facilitate the presentation of the Liberal case on TV.' Or, more succinctly, he was quoted as saying: 'we want to earn as many gold stars as we can.' Kidd became suspicious of Caldwell, however, sensing 'that he had set a trap for us,' a sort of 'Trojan Horse operation.' When the election results were known, MacTavish recalled, Caldwell 'changed [his] tune' and began charging large amounts. Some money, $10,000 at least, was paid, but Caldwell billed the party for an additional $43,852.72 in 1958, and continued to try to collect this amount, along with threats of legal action, into the 1960s. The Liberals successfully stood fast against this claim, but well might Kidd conclude, from all points of view, that the party needed some basic discussions on television and its use, for 'future ways of handling this difficult and cruel medium.'[114] C.D. Howe summed up the situation most admirably with reference to his own defeat in Port Arthur by Douglas Fisher of the CCF: 'My opponent,' he informed another defeated Liberal MP, 'was a polished television artist, and his gains all took place within the area covered by television. I may tell you that television is no good for us 'old boys.'[115]

ELECTORAL DEFEAT AND THE AGENCY-PARTY
RELATIONSHIP

The 1957 electoral disaster marked the end of an era in more ways than one, for it also signalled the beginning of the breakup of the relationship between the Liberals and Cockfield, Brown. Despite the fulsome praise traditionally lavished by both partners to the agreement on each other, there was one key consideration which kept the marriage happy: the electoral success of the breadwinner, the Liberal party. When the party was no longer in a position to follow through on its contribution – the government advertising pot – the romance turned sour. Cracks began to appear immediately after the election with a somewhat cool exchange of letters between Kidd in Ottawa and Cockfield, Brown in Montreal on the agency's billing. An executive committee meeting of the agency made an accounting of its overall contribution. 'It was the feeling of the meeting that the amount of our work and efforts should be made known in the right places, and in this connection Duncan MacTavish was parctiularly mentioned.' But 'recognition' was not enough. Some $17,000 was assigned to such items as travel, staff time (195 man days), and research, and the agency wished to explore the possibility of collecting as much as possible of this amount from the party. Kidd, clearly angry, stated that research was a service the agency would normally render a client, that there was no prior agreement on such a billing, that the party was being charged for the time it took the agency to answer inquiries, that in sum 'this is a new development in the relation between Cockfield, Brown and the Federation.' So far as staff time went, Kidd asserted that 'this is an attempt to assess the value of the company's services to the Party and probably should be placed opposite the total revenue secured [for] the company, not only in the various election campaign expenditures, but on other matters as well.'[116]

It was the last part of Kidd's argument which was the weakest, in light of the fact that the Liberals no longer held the government's purse strings. Hence the agency was changing its perspective on the whole matter. The first victim of this change was Kidd himself. He was given a choice of staying with the party or returning to the agency. Kidd's heart by now seemed to be much more with the party than with the agency and he formally resigned his position with the latter about the end of 1957 and accepted a full-time appointment as secretary of the NLF, a post he had in fact held for the past nine years. His old friend Brooke Claxton was troubled by this development, justly warning him that his future in the NLF might not be secure inasmuch as Duncan MacTavish would not be around forever as president. It was 'quite possible and even probable, that the incoming President and Executive may have quite different ideas about the Federation's work and the manner of carrying it out ...' After the 1958 Conservative landslide, the Liberal party began to look to revamping its party organization, and the 'old guard' – of which Kidd was seen, rightly or wrongly, as a representative – was under fire. By the close of 1959 it had been decided to replace Kidd as secretary. In vain Claxton appealed to A.B. Matthews, Bay Street bagman and now NLF president, to remember Kidd's contributions to Liberal election publicity since 1945: 'With all the emphasis I can use I say that Bob had more to do with this than any other single person, that it was superbly well done and that no one could have worked more effectively over longer hours or with greater success. Beyond question he has sacrificed his business career and his health in the interest of the Liberal cause.' Jack Pickersgill still recalls with some bitterness the 'rather brutal' firing of Kidd.[117] Sentiment, however, has little place in either politics or business, when losing numbers start appearing on the board.

Early in 1958 a changeover also occurred in the top ranks of Cockfield, Brown, but the agency decided to stick with the Liberals in the election of that year. Yet the writing was on the wall. And other agencies were more than willing to move in and pick up the pieces, foremost among them MacLaren's of Toronto which 'contributed' the services of Richard O'Hagan full time to the NLF during the 1958 campaign, services described by Senator J.J. Connolly, the campaign co-ordinator in Ottawa, as 'invaluable.' Walsh also tried to move in on the national scene, as did the Ronalds agency. But MacLaren's was by 1958 the largest agency in Canada, topping Cockfield, Brown for the first time in total billings. A cynic might suggest that only the best would do for the Liberal party, and in early 1959 the Ontario party dropped Walsh and appointed MacLaren's, presaging a changeover on the national level in the same direction. As if in confirmation of MacLaren's growing partisan role, the Diefenbaker government dropped its last official government account with the agency, the Fisheries Department, and hired a Tory firm.[118]

Thus MacLaren's took over where Cockfield, Brown left off, and the agency that in the days of the pipeline debate had represented the Liberal party, the government of Canada, and Trans-Canada Pipe Lines, all at the same time, relapsed into a position of political neutrality, to which they have steadfastly adhered ever since.

The experience of 1943 to 1958 did not seem, in the end, to have commended itself to the agency as an example for a reinvestment in the Liberal party for the future. Either the agency was not as alert as MacLaren's to Liberal resilience (or Conservative weakness) or they decided that, win or lose, the game was not worth the candle. The point of this history is not, however, Cockfield, Brown's reaction to changing fortunes, but rather that, with a change in names and personnel, the party-agency relationship quickly resumed, apparently under essentially the same ground rules. It would seem that the structural or organizational basis of the relationship remained as compelling as always. And perhaps in an age of television, even more compelling.

GOVERNMENT ADVERTISING PATRONAGE

Having examined the agency-party relationship from the electoral view-point, it remains to examine the reverse side of the coin: the partisan nature of government advertising distribution among the agencies.

After helping elect the Conservatives in New Brunswick in 1952 while on leave from his ad agency, Locke, Johnson & Company, Dalton Camp recalls that he had never considered gaining government advertising accounts. The readers of Mr Camp's memoirs may permit themselves a slight incredulity on this point, while taking more seriously his memory of what transpired in a meeting between himself and the new premier, Hugh John Flemming. The latter showed Camp a letter from the president of Walsh Advertising, suggesting a renewal of Walsh's account with the New Brunswick Tourist Bureau:

'Seems like a nice fellow,' Flemming said, placing yet another call.

'Two months ago they were down here telling people you weren't good enough to be Premier of New Brunswick,' I said, somewhat more heatedly than intended.

Flemming looked puzzled. 'What's that?' he asked.

'They're the Liberal agency,' I said, my irritability barely contained.

He put down the phone, the light of revelation in his eyes, a smile playing on the corners of his mouth.

'Well,' he said, softly, reflectively, almost to himself, 'We can't have that, can we?'

And so it came to pass that Locke, Johnson & Company Ltd. became the agency for the New Brunswick Travel Bureau ...[119]

Camp adds that the return of this trophy to his agency gained him a promotion and, more importantly, experience in the travel industry. The mixture of politics and travel advertising has turned out well for Mr Camp. Today, the firm of Camp Associates rests its business almost entirely upon two pillars: the accounts of the Ontario and the New Brunswick governments, especially their tourism budgets.[120]

Camp Associates are by no means the only agency to have relied heavily on political connections for their clientele. One of the few wholly French-language agencies in Quebec history was Huot Advertising, which at its peak grossed $2 million in billings. Huot was, however, fatally dependent on the patronage of the Union Nationale party, and when the Quebec Liberals won in 1960 the agency 'began a downfall from which it never recovered.' In 1963 it was merged into a new agency.[121]

The federal Liberals have always been shrewd enough to avoid too heavy involvement with agencies whose overall dependency on the party might prove unhealthy. Certainly neither Cockfield, Brown in the 1940s and 1950s nor MacLaren's in the 1960s and 1970s could be considered *dependent* on the party's fortunes, given the wide range of lucrative commercial accounts both agencies boasted. Nevertheless, the electoral success of the party could bring a very welcome and profitable dollop of government business on top of their commercial accounts: the icing, as it were, on the largest advertising cake in the country.

Given the patronage nature of the party-agency relationship, and given the number of agencies which offered their services at election time, it was inevitable that conflict and jealousies should arise over the distribution of the government advertising dollar. Norman Lambert's role as the patronage 'fixer' behind the scenes from 1935 to 1940 was nowhere more evident than in the settling of the various claims from the advertising agencies which had helped the party in the 1935 election. One of the chief problems was that C.D. Howe did not particularly like Cockfield, Brown and preferred to give his business to MacLaren's. Lambert continued to argue Cockfield, Brown's case until Howe finally agreed that he would leave the advertising contracts to Lambert, with his own advice to be taken into consideration. Other ministers were not always so co-operative, and were apt to give contracts to their own favourites despite the impact on the overall distribution, and ministerial perogatives were such that Lambert sometimes had to throw up his hands in resignation. One such incident occurred in 1939 when P.-J.-A. Cardin, minister of public works, switched his ministry's advertising from MacLaren's to a Quebec agency; Lambert simply told MacLaren's that he could give them introductions, but could not look after their business for them. It appears that in this era at least, part of the bargain struck between the agency and the party included a straight kick-back on the contracts awarded. For example, when the Agriculture Department was considering Cockfield, Brown, Lambert told the agency that a 5 per cent return to the party was expected; the agency representative seemed to be in agreement with this arrangement. When the Department of Trade and Commerce gave their advertising to MacLaren's in 1938, Lambert spoke to an agency representative who confirmed that $2000 would go each year to the NLF in gratitude. Other variations on the *quid pro quo* can also be found in the Lambert diaries. For example, in 1941 Harry Cockfield informed Lambert that Howe was supporting his agency for the tourist publicity budget; in return for this support, Cockfield, Brown was putting on a 'big publicity campaign' in Howe's Department of Munitions and Supply 'at cost.'[122] There were many possible forms which the patronage relationship might take; generalizations appear difficult. One theme common to the twenty-two years of Liberal rule after 1935, however, was that Cockfield, Brown got too much business in relation to the party's other agencies. This cry, originating from the competition and sometimes picked up by certain cabinet ministers, was no doubt an inevitable result of Cockfield, Brown's pride of place as the national agency for the party.

Following the 1945 election Kidd's first assignment upon his return to Cockfield, Brown was to 'provide immediately a breakdown of advertising expenditures made by the Government since 1940 through the various advertising agencies.' Claxton invited Kidd to come to Ottawa and offered the assistance of an official to go through the departmental records.[123] The problem was the age-old political problem of successful parties – the just distribution of patronage. All the agencies which had done their bit during the election had to be rewarded, but Cockfield, Brown kept a watchful and proprietorial eye over the proceedings to ensure that its senior position in the agency hierarchy was respected. When Kidd moved over to the NLF as secretary he sometimes had to placate rival agencies with data showing their share of the pie.[124] Indeed, there even seem to have been conscious efforts to downplay the amount of billings received by Cockfield, Brown, for the benefit of the opposition, and even perhaps for that of the other agencies. This becomes more obvious in the light of Tables 6.3 and 6.4, which summarize what little information was made public about government advertising accounts in this period.[125]

A number of aspects of these figures require explanations. First of all, there is no breakdown available by specific agency for the 'Advertising Agencies of Canada,' the non-partisan group set up to promote the war effort, even though three-quarters of the total advertising spending during the war went through this group. Harry Cockfield of Cockfield, Brown was the chairman of the consortium and it is not unreasonable to suppose that this agency received a good proportion of the total business; on the other hand, known Tory agencies were also cut in on this deal as well.[126] 'Associated Advertising Agencies,' which appeared briefly around the war's end, was a consortium of Liberal agencies only, but the specific breakdown of account allocation among agencies is unknown. By the 1950s the picture becomes clearer, with Cockfield, Brown; MacLaren's; Walsh; and Ronalds each taking between one-fifth and one-quarter of the total business on the average. Canadian retained a smaller share. R.C. Smith, once closely connected to the party,[127] seems to have fallen into disfavour and to have dropped altogether from the picture by the last couple of years of the St Laurent government. The 'other' category includes a shifting miscellany of agencies

Table 6.3
Federal government advertising contracts by agency, 1940-56
(Crown corporations excluded), in dollars

	1940-6	1945-7	1949-50	1952	1953	1954	1955	1956
Cockfield, Brown	1,121,212	861,020	933,469	852,912	880,890	927,468	913,677	1,008,775
MacLaren's	444,421	301,906	803,329	1,043,291	773,825	1,109,460	949,105	1,155,781
Walsh	689,197	688,388	510,327	1,015,678	884,230	1,090,054	731,910	789,196
Ronalds	12,654	96,418	380,058	804,827	794,324	775,595	687,907	845,949
Canadian	478,770	195,133	121,253	97,157	63,572	104,459	83,072	86,427
R.C. Smith	1,613,402	955,450	110,128	10	6237	11,720	7798	
'Advertising Agencies of Canada'[a]	17,748,464	5,350,578						
'Associated Advertising Agencies'[b]	568,592	837,510						
Others	1,295,589	635,932	96,308	64,735	83,557	55,165	56,327	55,731
Total	23,972,301	9,922,335	2,954,872	3,878,610	3,486,635	4,073,921	3,429,796	3,941,859

[a] A special non-partisan grouping of ad agencies during the war, chaired by Cockfield, Brown, but including Conservative agencies as well.
Marketing, 8 Sept. 1945
[b] A consortium of Liberal agencies
Source: see note 125

Table 6.4
Federal government advertising contracts by agency, 1940-56
(Crown corporations excluded), in percentages

	1940-6	1945-7	1949-50	1952	1953	1954	1955	1956
Cockfield, Brown	4.7	8.7	31.6	22.0	25.3	22.8	26.6	25.6
MacLaren's	1.9	3.0	27.2	26.9	22.2	27.2	27.7	29.3
Walsh	2.9	6.9	17.3	26.2	25.4	26.8	21.3	20.0
Ronalds	0.1	0.1	12.9	20.8	22.8	19.0	20.1	21.5
Canadian	2.0	2.0	4.1	2.5	1.8	2.6	2.4	2.2
R.C. Smith	6.7	9.6	3.7		0.2	0.3	0.2	
'Advertising Agencies of Canada'	74.0	53.9						
'Associated Advertising Agencies'	2.4	8.4						
Others	5.3	6.4	3.2	1.7	2.4	1.3	1.6	1.4
Total	100.0	100.0	100.0	100.0	100.0	100.0	100.0	100.0

Note: percentages may not total exactly due to rounding
Source: see note 125

Table 6.5
Total publicity billings by Canadian Government
Travel Bureau through Cockfield, Brown, fiscal years
1942-58

1942-3	$ 15,670
1943-4	
1944-5	27,362
1945-6	
1946-7	604,785
1947-8	500,726
1948-9	737,750
1949-50	910,568
1950-1	608,377
1951-2	857,733
1952-3	930,568
1953-4	896,184
1954-5	952,825
1955-6	948,025
1956-7	929,353
1957-8[a]	730,897
Total	9,650,823

[a]In 1957-8 the bureau also spent $521,654 through three
new Conservative agencies: Locke, Johnson ($455,982),
Hayhurst ($53,363), and Harold F. Stanfield ($12,309)
Source: *Public Accounts,* 1942-58

with very small bits of business with different departments, including small
amounts going to foreign agencies for promotions abroad. Here and there,
Conservative agencies (McKim; McConnell, Eastman; J.J. Gibbons, etc.)
do appear with small contracts but never as major advertisers.

Long-term agency-client relationships were built up with particular government departments: MacLaren's was largely centred on finance, defence,
and the RCMP. Walsh specialized in defence, labour, post office, trade and
commerce, and veterans' affairs; Ronalds in defence and finance. Cockfield,
Brown's departmental specialization was even more concentrated, being
centred almost exclusively on the single biggest advertising account in Ottawa, the Canadian Government Travel Bureau. Table 6.5 shows the total
billings by the Travel Bureau through Cockfield, Brown from 1942-3 to
1957-8. In the twelve-year period from the end of the war to the defeat of
the Liberals in 1957-8, Cockfield, Brown did $9,607,791 worth of business
with the bureau.

Yet even with this steady source of earnings, Cockfield, Brown does not *seem* to have been 'top dog' among the agencies, with either Walsh or MacLaren's or both apparently out-billing them in any given year; in fact, this appearance is quite misleading, but it was one which both the government and the agency were at pains to cultivate, even to the extent of deliberately covering their trail in replies to parliamentary questions. On more than one occasion, written returns to questions evaded stating the amount spent by the Travel Bureau on the entirely disingenuous pretext that the media, not the bureau, paid the agency commission. But the greater problem was that the bulk of Cockfield, Brown business lay with Crown corporations which did not report the disposition of its advertising dollars: TCA, CNR, and the Canadian Steamship Lines (accounts which dovetailed neatly with the Travel Bureau account). The total advertising budgets of TCA and CNR are only available from 1950 and after (see Table 6.6). Unfortunately we cannot be sure what proportion of these figures was billed through agencies, and how much of that through Cockfield, Brown. In the case of CNR, however, Donald Gordon testified before a parliamentary committee in 1956 that Cockfield, Brown and Canadian Advertising had together done $454,408 worth of business in Canada for CNR (in what proportion was not clear), and that Cockfield, Brown had indirectly handled an additional $500,404 in billings in the United States through an American 'correspondent' agency, presumably taking a small cut in the process.[128] A similar agreement was in force for TCA's American advertising, but on the Canadian side Cockfield, Brown was the sole agency. Whatever the exact amounts earned by these accounts, it is obvious that they were quite sufficient to establish Cockfield, Brown's pre-eminence in the government feeding trough. That it was impossible to precisely quantify this pre-eminence no doubt well suited both the agency and the party.

Crown corporations did have a certain autonomy from political influence, and Cockfield, Brown began to suffer from the restiveness of both the CNR and TCA in the late years of the St Laurent government. In 1956 the CNR decided to rationalize the somewhat curious arrangements for its American advertising, by eliminating the middle man and dealing directly with an American agency – in this case the giant McCann-Erickson agency, just then moving into Canada. TCA moved in the same direction with its American accounts. Worse for Cockfield, Brown was CNR's decision to phase the agency out of its Canadian account as well, and to shift over fully to Canadian Advertising. When TCA put out for bids from other agencies as well, questions were inevitably raised about Cockfield, Brown's reputation, questions which seemed to embarrass Donald Gordon. In the end, TCA

Table 6.6
Total advertising and publicity expenditures, TCA and CNR,
1950-8

	TCA	CNR
1950-1	1,182,938	1,247,466
1951-2	1,137,532	1,317,215
1952-3	1,183,906	1,416,590
1953-4	1,513,726	1,426,754
1954-5	1,830,414	1,608,785
1955-6	2,186,660	1,613,470
1956-7	2,010,898	1,737,000
1957-8[a]		1,975,586

[a]For this year, TCA lumped 'sales and promotion' together
Source: *Public Accounts,* 1950-7

stuck with the agency which had served them since their inception,[129] but the loss of the CNR must have been a major blow.

If all were not well with Cockfield, Brown's government business by the mid-1950s, the election defeats of 1957 and 1958 gave the *coup de grâce* to the agency's presence in Ottawa – and to that of the other Liberal agencies as well. Within a month or two of Diefenbaker's accession to office in 1957, *Marketing* was reporting wholesale shifts in departmental advertising from Liberal to Conservative agencies, such as McKim's (the agency of Tory president Allister Grosart); Foster; Locke, Johnson (Dalton Camp); and newcomers such as O'Brien of Vancouver (headed by a personal friend of John Diefenbaker). Walsh, Ronalds, and Canadian were quickly pulled out of a massive campaign for the Bank of Canada already underway, and Walsh, always the brashest of agencies, decided to contest the matter in court, filing suit in Exchequer Court for $160,580 and costs. The suit was counterpetitioned by the government, and the matter seems to have disappeared from further view. Considering Walsh's own *modus operandi* in the nether world of party advertising and government patronage during the Liberal years, it is not altogether obvious what legal or moral claim it had in mind – in any event the partisan changeover in 1957 only confirmed (as the Liberal return in 1963 reconfirmed) the patronage nature of government advertising. Ironically enough, the only bit of government business retained by Cockfield, Brown during the Diefenbaker years came from the same source which had given the agency trouble in the Liberal era because of its relative political independence, TCA. In 1960 the public airline undertook once again a prolonged search for a new advertiser, interviewing no less than twenty-seven agencies, but decided to divide its business between Cockfield, Brown and the Conservative agency of Stanfield, Johnston and Hill.[130] By this point, of course, Cockfield, Brown was already easing its way out of partisan identification.

In conclusion one is led to the observation that from the point of view of the agency, the patronage business was ambiguous. When it was good – as it was during the 1940s and 1950s – it was very good. It would certainly appear, in the absence of contrary evidence, that for Cockfield, Brown, MacLaren's, Walsh, Ronalds, and perhaps Canadian, the many fat years of government earnings must have very handsomely compensated them for whatever sacrifices they made to the benefit of the Liberal party. Certainly Cockfield, Brown must have been averaging somewhere between $1.5 and $2 million worth of billings per year in the 1950s, which would seem to indicate an adequate return on their rather modest political investment. But when things went wrong, they went very, very wrong – as they did from 1957 to 1963. It is obviously a chancy business, and for any agency it must be something of a calculated gamble.

From the party's point of view, the risks would seem to be less. After all, the rewards will come not from the party's own resources but from the public treasury – with the added bonus that official government advertising can often be employed to enhance the political image of the party in power. Indeed, with the tremendous growth of government advertising in recent decades, the thin line between 'state' publicity and publicity for the *party* in office, especially near election time, becomes more and more difficult to distinguish. It is scarcely possible to say, for instance, if an official advertisement announcing the extension of a welfare programme, replete with highly visible references to the minister and the prime minister, is more of a governmental or political advertisement; the connection is obviously so close that there is little point in even attempting to make distinctions. It is simply the media-era version of the local wharf construction announcement. The major difference from the past is the key intervening role of the advertising agency between the party and the electorate. There seems every reason to believe that this role is becoming more, rather than less, important.

One example of the deepening relationship between the agencies and the political process is the recent extension of advertising services to party leadership campaigns and even to constituency nominations – a paradoxical result of the so-called 'democratization' of the Liberal and Conservative parties in the 1960s. Another factor supporting the party-agency relationship is the massive growth of provincial budgets in the 1960s and 1970s. The concomitant rise in provincial expenditures on advertising has apparently lessened the risks incurred by political agencies, who may now fall back on friendly provincial treasuries when the wrong party is in office federally. Camp Associates, for instance, can presumably wait out the eventual return of the Tories to Ottawa in relative affluence so long as Ontario and a Maritime province or two retain Conservative administrations. Another example of the same phenomenon is the career of the NDP agency, Dunsky Advertising of Montreal, which offers publicity assistance to a federal party with little or no hope of achieving office in the foreseeable future. That something more than faith in the social democratic cause may be involved in this otherwise charitable activity can be seen in the fact that Dunsky not only holds the accounts of the major trade unions affiliated with the party, but became the chief agency for the provincial NDP governments of Manitoba, Saskatchewan, and British Columbia. The latter account included the billings of the largest automobile insurance agency in North America, the nationalized Insurance Corporation of British Columbia, but was entirely lost to Dunsky with the defeat of the Barrett government in 1975.

With these types of intricate interconnections established between advertising agencies and all three major political parties in the country, it is unlikely that the agency-party relationship will change drastically in the near future. If anything, with rising levels of expenditures on both party and government advertising, the agency-party relationship is undoubtedly even stronger today than at any time in the past. Thus the examination of the relationship between the Liberal party and its advertising agencies from the 1930s to the 1950s is of much more than antiquarian interest; it is an examination of a present situation in embryo and early development.

PART II

Federal-provincial relations
within the Liberal party, 1930-58

Part I has dealt with the evolution of the Liberal party from a national perspective. Given the profoundly regional character of the Canadian political system, it would be a grave distortion to simply treat the Liberal party as a national entity, without an attempt to inquire into its regional and provincial roots and into the difficult and complex question of federal-provincial intra-party relations. Indeed the Liberal party generally prided itself on its decentralized structures and on the autonomy of its provincial units. Some of this pride was based more on rhetoric than reality, yet there was much substance to the claim that the party's organizational strength lay in local bases in widely divergent areas of the community.

The problem with local autonomy, however, lies in the immense divergences between different regions with regard to economic and political power and significance. In the Canadian case the fundamental imbalance between the central heartland of Ontario and Quebec and the hinterland or peripheries of the western and Atlantic provinces has been of crucial importance to national development, federalism, and the very evolution of national identity. The Liberals have in recent years become pre-eminently a party of the centre, while the Conservatives and New Democrats are more and more parties of the periphery. In the King–St Laurent period the lines were less clearly drawn, with the Liberals drawing political strength from a wider regional basis. Yet even then there was no question that the Ontario-Quebec heartland dominated the Government party, just as it dominated the nation.

This domination is easily accounted for. Until the 1950s the Ontario and Quebec constituencies in the House of Commons accounted for 60 per cent of the total seats, and even with redistribution in the 1950s the proportion fell to just below 57 per cent. Moreover, almost all the money raised by the national party came from either Montreal or Toronto. Politically and financially there was never any question of where the power lay.

This central domination presents one with a major problem in examining federal-provincial relations within the party. There is, not surprisingly, a wealth of information on Ontario and Quebec since it was these provinces which preoccupied the attention of the national party. Consequently, the chapters on the central provinces are detailed and, within certain limits, exhaustive. On the other hand, for the very reason that less attention was paid to the peripheral provincial parties, there is less detailed information available, and the chapters devoted to the West and especially to the Atlantic region are much less detailed and make no claim to be exhaustive in any sense. There is, moreover, an additional problem of space with regard to the West. The amount of material available, on the Prairie provinces in particular, actually exceeded what could be incorporated within the reasonable boundaries of the present study. Since each of the western provinces is politically unique, with its own special historical pattern of development, a comprehensive examination of the Liberal party in the West would demand a number of distinct studies, more than could be attempted here. In the case of the Atlantic provinces, the general neglect of this region within Canada is mirrored by a lack of documentation at the national level. A more specific local investigation would be required to yield better results, a project which unfortunately lays outside the scope of this study.

The reader is thus advised that the focus of Part ii is more closely directed to Quebec and Ontario than to the other provinces. I would like to emphasize that this bias was to a certain extent inevitable, given the unacceptable alternative of either writing another book to do justice to the peripheral provinces or ignoring them altogether, which would be yet more of an injustice.

7

Quebec

In any study of federal-provincial relations within the Liberal party, just as in any study of federalism in Canada, an initial acknowledgment must be made that Quebec is a province 'pas comme les autres.' The point may seem somewhat trivial in the light of the heightened awareness of the cultural, ethnic, and linguistic uniqueness of Quebec which has emerged from the national traumas of the 1960s and 1970s, but it may be rescued from triteness within the historical context of this study. The emergence of bilingualism and biculturalism in the last decade and a half as standard fare for political discussion ought not to blind observers to the relative novelty of the terms of reference of the Quebec-Canada debate, post-1960. Reading the urgencies of the present back into the past is, of course, not an unusual use, or misuse, of history. However much it may make the past serve the present, it does little for the past itself. In the face of some very convincing strictures against this kind of historical rewriting,[1] one hesitates to make too much out of the special status of Quebec in an historical study of federal-provincial relations, even within a political party. Yet the fact remains that a close examination of the Liberal party – the party which dominated, to the near exclusion of any other, in this period in Quebec – indicates that the Quebec wing of the party, whether federal or provincial, did exercise a degree of special autonomy unparalleled, as a general rule, in the English-speaking regions.

Quebec *was* different. Since the national Liberal party's success was founded on the solid electoral support of Quebec, a support which never faltered until the Liberals themselves went out of office in 1957-8, to the party it was usually a case of *vive la différence.* To the Conservatives, who for one reason or another could never fathom the special conditions and complexities of Quebec, that difference remained a vexing mystery.[2] But if the Liberals in Quebec represented a success story at the federal level throughout most of this period, the same could not be said for the provincial party; indeed, by the 1950s it had become apparent that the federal party's success had been built in part upon a limitation of the provincial party's potential. Thus a study of the relations between the national party and the Quebec wings, both federal and provincial, as well as the relations between the two Quebec wings themselves, offers a double interest: the specific political working-out of the federal bargain between English and French Canada within the confines of the dominant national political party in this era, and the relationship between a federal party and its provincial counterpart during a period of success at one level and general failure at the other. Some interesting and suggestive commentaries on both these problems emerge from this examination.

TRADITIONAL STRUCTURE OF PARTY ORGANIZATION

Until very recently the structure of Liberal party organization has been basically the same for both the federal and provincial parties, and is best described in the phrase used by Georges-Emile Lapalme: 'un parti d'organisateurs.'[3] By this phrase is meant essentially a 'cadre' party in Duverger's terms, but the key role of the *organisateur* in Quebec parties is a variant of the practice found in English Canada. Not until after the Second World War were there any constituency *associations* along the lines of those found in English Canada. Instead, the party 'skeleton,' as it were, was composed essentially of organizers, from two *organisateurs en chef* for the province as a whole to local organizers for each constituency, to the *chefs de poll* at the smallest electoral unit. Along with the organizers were the *trésoriers*, or fund-raisers – who were no doubt often the same persons. Of course, both elected and defeated candidates were the key figures in the local constituency; but their relationship to the local organizers could vary greatly from constituency to constituency – and, in any event, the defeated candidate might himself be the organizer. Data on this is unfortunately very incomplete, and, while we later look at one constituency as a case study, the relevant point for now is that there was never, either federally or provincially, until the 1950s, any 'party' with a constitution, membership cards, and structures in which the ordinary voter could participate. Although the existence of such formal organizations in English Canada could often be very misleading to anyone seeking the real centres of party authority in the constituencies, in Quebec there were no formal structures either to lead or to mislead the student of party organization.[4]

We can speak with greater confidence about the higher levels of party organization, the main outlines of which are reasonably clear. First of all, and interestingly enough for those who tend to think of Quebec as a political monolith, there was never a single Quebec organization, but two – one centred on Quebec City, the other on Montreal. While the provincial Liberal leader and the leading Quebec cabinet minister in Ottawa federally were considered in overall charge of their respective parties, the Montreal and Quebec districts were always effectively two separate organizations, with their own offices and their own *organisateurs en chef*. Moreover, as we shall see later, this organizational division has often accompanied very real conflicts between the two districts on policy, rooted in differing economic interests.

The Montreal federal district organization involved some thirty-seven constituencies (forty-seven after the redistribution of 1953) west of Trois-Rivières, administered from a Montreal office. A further division, on ethnic lines, was accomplished by detaching the six English-speaking districts of western Montreal. The French organization was directed by P.-J.-A. Cardin from the early 1920s until 1942. Ernest Bertrand and Alphonse Fournier took over following Cardin's resignation from the cabinet, and were in turn succeeded by Alcide Côté and Roch Pinard. After 1940 the English district was under the supervision of Brooke Claxton until his retirement from politics in 1954, when he was followed by George Marler.[5] These men were not only regional representatives in the cabinet, but their particular cabinet posts were those well suited to the kind of patronage politics on which political organization in Quebec rested. Cardin was minister of public works from 1935 to 1942, and Fournier was his successor in this office to 1953. Bertrand was postmaster-general from 1942 to 1949; Côté was also in charge of the Post Office in the early 1950s. These two departments were among the most important patronage departments in the government, and neither bore a heavy administrative load, thus freeing the ministers for political work. Secretary of state – the office held by Pinard – was more or less honorific. In the 1920s Cardin had been minister of marine and fisheries, a post of rather specific importance in the light of Cardin's close association with the Simard shipbuilding interests in his constituency, who were prominent financial contributors to the Liberal party.[6]

The Montreal office was under the day-to-day direction of Senator Elie Beauregard, an associate of Cardin with very extensive connections to Montreal industry and finance. In the 1950s Jacques Vadeboncoeur, who held no elective office, took over from Beauregard. The exact relationship betwen the cabinet ministers and the district *organisateur en chef*, such as Senator Beauregard, would of course vary with the individuals involved.

The Quebec district, constituting twenty-eight constituencies to the east of Trois-Rivières, was under the supervision of Senator Philippe Paradis until 1931. Following him was Chubby Power. Working with Power were such persons as J.-A. Lesage, Quebec City businessman, and later Senator Fernand Fafard. Ernest Lapointe, and later Louis St Laurent, were higher authorities than Power, but neither, and especially St Laurent, shared Power's evident talent and enthusiasm for organizational work. Both Lapointe and St Laurent held the key portfolio of justice – which not only was of some policy importance to Quebec but which also involved considerable patronage of a more 'elevated' nature – judicial appointments, government legal work, etc. – befitting the dignity of Mackenzie King's Quebec lieutenant. When St Laurent became prime minister, Power relinquished his role and Hugues Lapointe – the son of Ernest – and Maurice Bourget took over. Lapointe had been minister of veterans affairs, but after 1955 became postmaster-general. Bourget was not in the cabinet, but was parliamentary secretary to the minister of public works. The Quebec City office was for many years under the day-to-day supervision of Wilfrid Hamel, mayor of Quebec City, followed later by Bourget.[7]

The two districts were drawn from divergent economic bases. Before the Second World War Montreal Liberals were closely associated with the great industrial, financial, and commercial interests of that city. Although St James Street had no profound attachment to the Liberals, as such, and while some elements (such as Lord Atholstan of the *Star* and the CPR owners) might be more inclined to the Conservatives, the almost total identification of the French-speaking population with the Liberal party after conscription in 1917, meant that the Liberals were the sure winners. Moreover, almost all the prominent French-speaking Liberal members from Montreal and its immediate surroundings were themselves closely associated with the large capitalist interests. Of course, not all the capitalists of Montreal had identical interests: most were high-tariff supporters, but low tariffs were in the economic interests of some. Each faction had its political representatives.

By contrast, the Quebec district was based on a less industrialized economy. Quebec district Liberals were drawn more from the traditional agricultural and professional traditions of French Canada.[8] Some, such as Lapointe, appear to have had no connections with large capital whatsoever. Resource extracting industries were involved: both Power and Edouard Lacroix were personally associated with the lumber industry, and St Laurent made his fortune as a corporation lawyer representing American pulp and paper companies.[9] But the resource industries had very different interests from the industrial and financial capitalists of Montreal. Quebec Liberals had more moderate views on the tariff, were better disposed toward the farmers of Ontario and the West, and were generally less concerned with policies to bolster Canadian industrial growth.

The differing economic bases of the two districts had important implications for policy, and also for party finance. Most of the potential party funds were in Montreal, although smaller amounts were drawn from Quebec. Several prominent Montreal Liberals were both leading contributors themselves and important channels for corporate donations as well: senators such as Donat Raymond, Marcellin Wilson, W.L. McDougald, Jacob Nicol, and later Armand Daigle, P.-H. Bouffard, and Louis Gélinas, were familiar in the boardrooms of many of the most powerful corporations in Canada. The dependence of the Liberal organization on these kind of men for funds was a difficult problem for a party which nationally wished to move in policy directions not always approved by Montreal capital – a point which will be examined later. The Beauharnois scandal of the early 1930s illustrates another problem of the Montreal financial apparatus, namely, the problematic nature of national control and the ever-present danger of politically damaging scandals coming to the surface.[10]

One Montreal organization which stands somewhat apart from the structures just outlined was the Reform Club. This appears to have been a combination of a social club, with the usual amenities characterisitic of such organizations, and a forum where the wealthy and powerful of the party in Montreal (*les grands,* as they were known) could gather under agreeable circumstances to discuss the proper course which the party should take. The Reform Club, which dated back to the days of Laurier, had 850 members by 1947, of whom 670 were French-speaking and 180 English-speaking, many of the names being those of prominent businessmen and professionals. The influence of this group on the party excited much comment and resentment from the lower ranks, although it is rather more likely that individuals associated with the club exercised such influence, rather than the club as an organization. There can, however, be little doubt that it facilitated fund-raising.[11]

A highly relevant question from the point of view of this study is how the federal and provincial wings of the party were related to the organizational structure here outlined. Of course, the elected *chefs* of the federal and provincial parties were different persons, but beneath this level the question becomes more complex. Peter Regenstreif asserts that 'since the days of Laurier, federal and provincial organizations were kept scrupulously apart in the province.'[12] Such a claim appears to have very little basis in fact. Indeed, one of the major sources of tension between the federal and provincial parties since the First World War has been precisely the lack of clear organizational differentiation. At various times the second organizational level, that of the *organisateurs en chef* of the two districts, has been simultaneously both federal and provincial; at other times separate groups have existed. At the local, or constituency, level, while firm data is not generally available, the overwhelming impression is that the constituency organizers and *chefs de poll* were generally the same persons federally and provincially. The case of campaign funds is more shrouded in mystery: fund-raisers (as well as contributors) were usually the same persons. Norman Lambert reported from his long experience that relations between the federal and provincial wings in financial matters were 'more complicated than negotiations over Federal-Provincial tax agreements.'[13] An important factor in setting the terms of these negotiations was the relative strength of the two wings, whether one was in power, or both, or neither, as well as the acceptability of their policies to the financial supporters.

There was never, before the 1960s, any *formal* organizational division between the federal and provincial wings, below the level of elected officials. Informal arrangements were the rule, and, while harmony and cooperation were sometimes characteristic of federal-provincial relations, in the longer historical perspective the tendency was toward tension and conflict.

CONSTITUENCY ORGANIZATION

There is very little data available on constituency organization, but a case study can be made of one federal constituency from the 1920s to the 1940s. Quebec East, the 'showpiece' seat of Sir Wilfrid Laurier, Ernest Lapointe, and Louis St Laurent, hardly constitutes a typical Quebec constituency: in all probability it was much better organized than seats with less prestigious members; but a close look at Quebec East may nevertheless disclose some idea of constituency organization.

Electoral organization was extensive and strong. Lists were maintained of voters with their affiliations. On election day itself the organization would number in the many hundreds, many of them paid – at an average cost of about $100 per poll for all the workers in that unit. There would also be a generous amount of support from local businessmen and professionals who would donate money, lend premises or automobiles, or give their services direct, all of whom would normally be thanked personally by the candidate after the vote. All these election day activities would be supervised by the permanent organizers and poll chiefs who would act as advisers or informants on patronage matters between elections.[14]

As a cabinet minister Lapointe could hire an executive assistant, who could act as the minister's agent in constituency affairs. For example, L.-P. Picard, until becoming an MP himself in 1940, acted as the organizer for the riding from his office in Ottawa. Another man, a Quebec City lawyer, was Lapointe's deputy in the constituency itself. Under them there were, in the late 1930s, forty-four *chefs de district,* organizers at the local district, or poll, level. While there was no 'official' Liberal constituency organization, there were in this same period no less than seven self-styled Liberal 'clubs,' or 'associations,' with such names as the Club Mercier, Fédération Laurier, etc.[15] These clubs, each with their own permanent premises and their own officers, appear to have been focal points for various factions within the constituency, each jostling one another for favour from Lapointe. The main purpose of the clubs would appear quite simply to have been the control of patronage.

Although the civil service reforms of 1918 had reduced the number of patronage positions open to federal politicians, it had by no means eliminated them. We have already noted that such departments as the Post Office and Public Works, at one level, and Justice, at another level, were still important patronage dispensers. While they could not compete with the provincial government on this level, there were still many federal government jobs exempted from civil service regulations, and it was around these that constituency politics were organized.

Following the return of the Liberals to power in 1935, Lapointe divided his constituency into four districts for patronage purposes, and asked the various clubs to name representatives to dispense patronage, ten in total, while cautioning them to make choices which would represent 'autant que possible les diverses nuances d'opinion libérale dans le quartier.'[16] The latter warning was necessary because the federal Liberals in 1936 were badly divided, down to the lowest level, by the question of the status of the *Action libérale nationale* group in provincial politics. The ALN people had broken with the party provincially but many remained Liberals federally. Those who saw themselves as 'rouge à Ottawa, rouge à Québec' wanted the rebels ousted from patronage privileges, if not from the party as a whole. Lapointe was, however, not unsympathetic to the ALN supporters, and the picture was further complicated by the fact that Oscar Drouin, the provincial member for the same area, had flirted briefly with Maurice Duplessis' new Union Nationale government, before returning to the Liberal fold. But the Drouin and Lapointe organizations were largely the same, and Lapointe was concerned to retain the support of Drouin and his people. Drouin's brother, Paul, a leading ALN spokesman, was one of the representatives chosen for patronage purposes, along with other ALN supporters. New clubs were formed as angry 'loyalists' protested to Lapointe, and struggles for patronage between the two groups were a constant problem. A curious mixture of 'bread and butter' politics and ideology characterized these struggles. The ALN group wanted to retain the support of reformers and nationalists for the federal Liberals, the loyalists wanted strict federal-provincial purity; the means in both cases was the distribution of patronage.

The Quebec Harbour Commission was a prime area for patronage, shared among the various Liberal members in Quebec. When the Liberals returned to power in 1921 many employees of the commission who had worked in Conservative campaigns were replaced by Liberals. 'For instance,' Chubby Power recalled, 'short work was made of men who had been poll leaders in the Lower Town and had actively tried to intimidate most of our reputable workers.'[17] In 1930 the victorious Conservatives reversed the situation. When the Bennett government was beaten in 1935, Lapointe faced not only the usual demands for removing the *bleus* but a particularly desperate intensity of feeling because of the Depression. The Depression, however, also severely limited the number of patronage positions. The Harbour Commission, which in the heyday of the prosperous 1920s had employed at least temporarily as many as three thousand persons per year[18] – a very considerable patronage plum – was reduced to one-tenth that size by the exigencies of the Depression, and the trend was downward. The man in overall charge of patronage for Lapointe was keenly aware of the problems this was causing the party: ' ... nos amis libéraux critiquent l'attitude du Commission du Hâvre car l'économie qui s'opère à cet endroit est vraiment désastreuse au point de vue politique.'[19] Picard, Lapointe's assistant, asked the commission to provide full statistics on all their employees from 1921 to 1936. Following the 1935 election, of some 360 harbour employees, 146 were new, 105 were reinstalled after being fired by the Conservatives five years earlier, and only 109 were holdovers from the pre-election period.[20] Since the total number of employees had dropped from over 450 in 1934 to 360 in 1935, it would appear that less than one-quarter of those employed before the election were able to hold their jobs. Moreover, not only were 250 appointed by the Liberals but this was done in strict accordance with a pre-arranged formula for distribution between the various Quebec constituencies. Complaints that Chubby Power was cutting in on other members' patronage called for an inquiry. The Harbour Commission, which kept printed forms to list the electoral constituencies of its employees, readily provided the figures: 30 per cent were from Quebec East; 28 per cent from Quebec South (Power's riding); 23 per cent from Quebec West;

and the remaining 19 per cent was divided among local rural ridings. The commission's employment agent expressed his honest disgust at 'l'insinuation de certains députés à l'effet que préférence serait donnée aux employés de Québec-Sud.'[21]

The kind of local struggles which could take place between members of the same party over patronage are illustrated by what happened when the federal arsenal was moved across the river to Valcartier, in Montmorency constituency. The local member, Wilfrid Lacroix, was delighted at the possibility of new patronage, 'des travaux de peu d'importance, mais qui me permettront d'aider grandement mes électeurs.' Lapointe, however, was not about to let any patronage slip out of the hands of his constituency. He asked Ian Mackenzie, the minister of national defence, to ensure that the arsenal was staffed in the same proportions as held in the Harbour Commission, with only 20 per cent for rural constituencies, including Lacroix' seat, and added that his agent would supply Mackenzie's officers with the names of eligible candidates from Quebec East. Lacroix wanted at least 60 per cent, since Valcartier was in his constituency, but his weight could scarcely match that of Lapointe and Power. Furious at what he believed to be a 'boycottage systématique,' Lacroix tried to appeal over Lapointe's head to Mackenzie King, denouncing, with a fine sense of distinction, 'le patronage politique éhonté et dégoûtant!'[22]

Although patronage was an essential part of the political system at the local level, the twin blows of civil service reform and the Depression had severely restricted the number of positions open. But as patronage diminished, the intensity of conflict over patronage within Liberal ranks increased. Supposedly a means of building party support, patronage seemed to be more a disuniting factor. Powerful and unchallenged electorally, the Liberal 'machine' of Quebec East was not, underneath, a machine at all, but a collection of small oligarchies bitterly competing for a few scraps of patronage, a situation best described in the title of a book on party politics in the 1960s, 'le panier de crabes.'[23] Assailed on the one side by partisans hungry for blood, and on the other by respectable citizens and clergy disgusted by the dismissals of poor workers in a Depression winter,[24] Lapointe at times wondered how useful the system was and so expressed himself on occasion to his leader in Ottawa.[25]

By the late 1930s an attempt was made to contain the internal dissension in the constituency by moving against the proliferation of 'clubs,' of which Lapointe himself disapproved. In 1938 four Liberal clubs fused, with Lapointe's blessing, into one group, the idea being 'former une association libérale pour le comté du genre des associations existant dans la province d'Ontario.' Using a charter copied from an Ottawa area Liberal association, this was brought about by the end of 1938.[26] This was no democratization of the constituency organization, but it did presage a move away from the old system which was to come about more generally in Quebec in the 1950s and 1960s.

The independence of the local organization was demonstrated in 1941 when Louis St Laurent was drafted to fill Lapointe's place after the latter's death. When St Laurent refused to speak against conscription, the entire organization walked out, leaving the political novice all alone to face a by-election. However, various other elements, including Power's Quebec South organization, stepped in to fill the breach. St Laurent's high position in the government brought its own rewards to the local organizers, including those who had walked out, and the dissension was soon stilled.[27]

This sketch of a single constituency has admittedly been inadequate. But some conclusions can be drawn. Constituency politics were essentially the politics of patronage – in all its various forms. The electoral machine of Quebec East ran on patronage. Second, as the scope for patronage narrowed internal party cohesion tended to weaken. Third, and somewhat paradoxically, with narrower powers of patronage at the disposal of the member, the organization was better able to assert its independence when united. Fourth, there were no clear distinctions between federal and provincial organizations, the personnel of which appear to have been more or less interchangeable. Finally, because of this interchangeable organizational structure, internal problems at one level were immediately translated into the other level, complicating the operation of the federal wing (in this case) with the divisions of the provincial wing.

THE THIRTIES

The Liberal party in Quebec which emerged from the 1920s was a classic political machine appropriate to a highly patronage-oriented political culture. It was also a machine heavily dominated by the provincial party. Throughout the 1920s the party had been virtually unchallenged either at the federal or the provincial levels. In organizational terms, it was a case of 'rouge à Ottawa, rouge à Québec': a single, unified organization delivered the votes in both kinds of elections. The interests of the two wings could be easily meshed, since the federal Liberals were enjoying an extravagant level of popularity resulting from their opposition to conscription during the war, and the provincial government of Premier L.-A. Taschereau found it very useful to run provincially against Arthur Meighen and the spectre of 'Tory imperialism.' At the same time the provincial party had more resources at its command, since the federal party was now constrained in its exercise of patronage by the passage of the new civil service legislation of 1918 while the provincial party benefited from the old practice in Quebec whereby parties in government became self-financing through a kick-back system of letting contracts and natural resource concessions.[28] It was even widely believed that Taschereau directly subsidized the federal party from the provincial war chest, especially when the federal party was out of office.[29]

In the Quebec district, Senator Paradis, a commercial traveller who had established a small business, was given various government jobs and preferences in contracts, thus freeing him for political work. Paradis' business brought him in contact with middle and small businessmen and merchants around the province. Leading Montreal Liberals, such as Aimé Geoffrion and Senator Raymond, provided the necessary links to big business. The party organization had direct, personal contact with the premier through the medium of weekly poker parties and periodic weekends at fishing camps. Young Chubby Power was carefully groomed as Paradis' successor, while being given legal work from the Lands and Forests Department, which enhanced his standing with his main legal clients, the lumber and paper interests. When he took over from an ailing Paradis for the 1931 provincial election, he was taken into the cabinet room, introduced to the members by Taschereau, and given express authority on electoral matters. The public image of the *organisateur en chef* was, as Power suggests, a curious mixture of distaste and respect. Politics was a rough and often corrupt affair in Quebec, and the *organisateur en chef* was the chief Machiavelli of a devious system. On the other hand, he was also viewed by the wealthier and more respectable elements of society as a focal point for access to the premier and the patronage and favours he controlled. Power stated as a condition of accepting the post in 1931 that Taschereau make clear that patronage should rest solely in the hands of the cabinet and the elected members and also appoint a committee of prominent businessmen, such as Jules Brillant (later one of the most powerful businessmen in Quebec) and Edouard Lacroix (a lumber merchant), in order to spread more widely the responsibility: as a federal MP Power did not wish to become deeply involved in provincial patronage.[30]

The precise role of an *organisateur en chef* was, as Power recalled, dependent upon the state of organization at the constituency level, and the relationship of the organizer with the premier, or the cabinet minister responsible for the area. It does not appear to have been a job with fixed responsibilities. Instead, the nature of the work could vary greatly from time to time. Candidate selection was one important role, especially where the local organizers had made what was taken to be a poor choice, were themselves divided, or unable to provide a candidate at all. Co-ordination of publicity, the mobilization of speakers, arrangements for tours of the party leaders, the organization of gangs to protect meetings and break up opponents' meetings, and other such matters were important at election time. The organizer was usually expected to furnish advice to the leadership on local sentiment, or in contemporary terms to act as a ready Gallup poll. The most important responsibility of the *organisateur en chef* was, however, the dispensing of campaign funds to candidates.[31] The treasurer, from Montreal, collected the money and the Quebec organization allocated it, to the office or to the constituencies. How this money was to be spent at the constituency level was a matter of tactics. Certainly much of it went into small-scale patronage for the voters in the form of alcohol, money, food, stockings, etc., characteristic of the electoral mores of Quebec.

Candidate selection was a relatively simple matter: any Liberal incumbent was assured of the party nomination except in the most extraordinary circumstances; since Liberals were relatively unchallenged either federally or provincially, most members could return from election to election if they wished.[32] The lack of internal party democracy was matched by an overall party system which could in no sense be termed democratic. Provincially, maldistribution of seats in favour of the rural areas was the rule. In 1926 over 53 per cent of the seats in the legislative assembly were held by constituencies which were over 70 per cent rural. Put another way, 29 per cent of the total electorate, mostly rural, controlled the majority of seats, while 46 per cent of the electorate, mostly urban, who resided in the twenty-one largest constituencies, were represented by only 25 per cent of the assembly seats.[33] The rural areas, it might be added, were those most concerned with patronage as an end in itself. Consequently, rural areas controlled but did not lead. Paradoxically, the Liberals used this solid rural support to carry out a policy of industrialization and resource extraction. Even when this directly conflicted with rural interests, no significant opposition was raised, such grand policy matters apparently going over the heads of those preoccupied with the more immediate patronage benefits to be derived from supporting the party in power. When Duplessis later came to power in 1936 the rural areas supported him just as solidly: one is reminded of Goldwin Smith inquiring of a British Columbian what his province's politics were and being told 'Government appropriations.'[34] The use of nationalist appeals by Arthur Sauvé's Conservatives in the 1920s was confronted, and blocked, not by ideological counter appeals but by the efficient use of a new form of patronage. Centralized provincial control over a new network of highways necessitated by the automobile was widely extended. The results were devastating. In one seat an incumbent Conservative retired in favour of a Liberal so that the area would get a new highway.[35] The beauty of the system lay in its perfection. Those who put up the funds got what they wanted – tax concessions, licences, leases, etc., for resource exploitation and industrial development; the party was able to indefinitely perpetuate itself in power; and those who ultimately benefited the least were precisely those who kept the system going through their votes.

As a consequence of all these factors, the provincial party was organizationally more powerful than the federal party, so long as it stayed in office. This power was enhanced by the relative political weakness of the federal party in the 1920s during minority governments, and by the attempts by King to draw support from the western Progressives, which were highly unpopular with the party's Montreal financial supporters. King, as party leader, had been following a precarious balancing act between the two conflicting pressures of protectionist Montreal capitalism and liberal western agrarianism. Montreal was represented within the federal cabinet in the early 1920s by Sir Lomer Gouin, the former premier of Quebec. King found an ally, however, in the person of Ernest Lapointe, and a base of support in the Quebec district Liberals, who, lacking direct ties to Montreal capital, were more flexible and moderate on economic questions, and more sympathetic to negotiations with the Progressives. The victory of the Quebec district over the combination of Montreal and the provincial party was finally signalled in 1924 with the resignation of Gouin, the emergence of Lapointe as King's chief Quebec lieutenant, and the appointment of P.-J.-A. Cardin, a Montreal member bitterly opposed by the Gouin-Taschereau group, as the minister charged with chief organizational responsibility in the Montreal district. Cardin's testing under fire in the 1925 election, when the old Montreal organization boycotted the campaign, proved a success, and by the latter half of the 1920s Lapointe and Cardin had emerged as the undisputed leaders of the federal party. Consequently, there was a certain reversion of unreconstructed Montreal conservatism to the provincial party alone, and a few lines of conflict began to appear between the federal and provincial parties, most notably concerning the issue of old age pensions. Yet Chubby Power's appointment as Quebec district organizer for the 1931 provincial election clearly demonstrated that the cleavage was less important than co-operation within the party: at the organizational level the party was still pretty much of a seamless fusion of the two wings.[36]

The defeat of the federal Liberals in 1930 and the reversion from minis-

terialist organization to the development of an extra-parliamentary structure (see Chapters 1 and 2 above), revealed some significant facts about the
relationship of this Quebec organization to the federal parliamentary leadership. Even before the 1930 election Quebec organizers had refused to co-
operate with the national Liberal office, and had adamantly opposed the
setting up of constituency associations, or even the institution of Twentieth
Century (Young Liberal) clubs in the province. As Power told King: 'I cannot go so far as to say that the machine which has been evolved is a perfect
one – but I firmly believe that it is the best which can be created in this
constituency and I very much resent the unwarranted interference of
outsiders.'[37]

The creation of the National Liberal Federation presented a direct challenge to this autonomist stance. Since Mackenzie King had no desire to
tackle Quebec feelings directly, and since the party was still electorally
strong in the province – although the Conservatives did make substantial
inroads into Quebec in the 1930 election – the response to Quebec's opposition to a new extra-parliamentary structure was to grant that province a
'special status.' Quebec was the only provincial unit of a new federation, except for Prince Edward Island, which did not possess a provincial Liberal
association. Thus the lack of constituency associations was matched by an
absence of any formal province-wide body. Quebec delegates to NLF meetings were either the federal and provincial parliamentary leaders or their
appointees. Of course, this was in fact little different than in the English-
speaking provinces, where extra-parliamentary structures masked effective
parliamentary domination. The difference was that in Quebec neither political culture nor electoral defeat gave any impetus to the creation of extra-
parliamentary forms. As Escott Reid succinctly commented after one interview with a Quebec politician, 'no homage is paid to democratic theory.'[38]

Where there was a *real*, as opposed to a rhetorical, difference between
Quebec and the rest of the party with regard to national organization, was
in the terms of reference which Norman Lambert was given when he took
over the job of national organizer. As Lambert himself later recalled, he was
told by King and the other party leaders when he accepted his appointment
in 1932 that while the NLF was a 'federal chain of representative provincial
associations,' Quebec was in a separate category: 'it was understood definitely ... that Quebec did not want any interference in its local counties
from a federal Bureau.' His instructions on this point were simple: King
told him to 'leave the Province of Quebec alone.'[39] Moreover, as already indicated in earlier chapters, Montreal was not a very regular financial supporter of the NLF over the years, and sometimes was altogether remiss in

this regard. Finally, in terms of the distribution of election funds during campaigns, the Maritime provinces were largely left to the mercies of the Montreal finance committee; Norman Lambert's sporadic attempts to ensure what he considered an equitable and effective distribution to that region usually ended in failure. Both organizationally and financially there can be little doubt that Quebec possessed a 'special status,' quite different in nature from the English-speaking provinces. Linguistic and cultural distinctions no doubt had something to do with this status, but it was also true that these basic differences were reinforced and compounded by significant differences in the structure of political organization and the nature of the electoral culture in the province.

Relations between federal and provincial wings of a political party are obviously dependent on their relative political strength, among other things. In the mid 1930s there was a significant shift in the fortunes of the two wings which was to have a very high degree of salience for their future relations. In 1935 the federal Liberals returned to power in Ottawa with the largest majority of seats ever achieved until that time. In Quebec, Liberal representation jumped from forty seats in 1930 to sixty. The same year the Taschereau administration, badly split down the middle, barely survived an election against the new coalition of Conservatives and anti-Taschereau Liberals put together under the supervision of Maurice Duplessis, and was soon plunged into the humiliation of a legislative session in which charges of corruption and nepotism were publicly proved. The political fortunes of the 1920s and early 1930s had been reversed; the federal Liberals were now politically the more powerful of the two wings of the party.

When King chose his new cabinet in 1935, Lapointe was certainly the most important Quebec member. Cardin had fallen out of favour, since King suspected him of corrupt dealings with the Simards over dredging contracts under his old portfolio of marine and fisheries. But by his toughness in negotiations Cardin forced King to take him back, this time in public works.[40] Cardin was to remain in control of the Montreal organization until he left the cabinet during the war.

The provincial party was at the same time in its death throes. A group of left-wing Liberals led, ironically enough, by Paul Gouin, the son of Sir Lomer Gouin, set up L'Action libérale nationale to reform the provincial Liberal party from within. Harold Angell suggests that the leadership of 'administrative' parties like the Taschereau Liberals can be broken only by a split in the tight inner circle. This is what happened in the early 1930s.[41] Even when the ALN group broke with the provincial Liberal party completely, and allied themselves with Duplessis' Conservatives, the dominant

Quebec district group of federal Liberals retained much sympathy for the rebels.[42] This, Power recalled, 'brought about a dangerous coolness between the federal and provincial wings of the Liberal party,' although Taschereau, perhaps recognizing his own unpopularity, wanted to maintain at least the semblance of party unity. An 'armed truce' was arrived at, by which both provincial old guard and ALN people took part in the 1935 election on behalf of the Liberals. When Taschereau was finally driven from office, federal Liberals took part in the choice of successor, and gave some support to the new leader, Adélard Godbout, in the 1936 election which brought Duplessis to power. For his part, Mackenzie King confessed 'complete indifference,' both because he had been quite shocked at the revelations of a Taschereau 'family compact,' and because he believed it 'easier to govern at Ottawa with the provinces *contra*. Also it will help us in dealing with other provinces, and in meeting constitutional questions, etc.'[43]

When an 'administrative' party goes out of power, the leadership is no longer self-financing. The fund-raisers and local organizers with independent means can form centres of opposition: Angell points to the attrition rate of leaders of opposition parties in Quebec to prove this point.[44] Certainly the contrast between the tightly controlled hierarchy which characterized the provincial party in the Taschereau period and the disorganized factionalism which followed lends credence to Angell's view. The vestiges of the Taschereau group, still ensconced in important positions in the party organizations, were more eager to revenge themselves on Liberals of other views than to build an effective opposition to the Union Nationale. More moderate elements were above all concerned to bring dissident ALN supporters back into the Liberal fold. A provincial convention was called in 1938 but the federal party was warned that the convention was being organized 'by the same handful of Montreal politicians, who are mainly responsible for the party's loss of prestige in recent years,' and that it would serve more to disunite than to unite the party. A correspondent of Mackenzie King noted that this group 'would rather see the party in opposition than give up their grip on its control.' The federal Liberals appear to have heeded such warnings. Lapointe, Cardin, and Elie Beauregard, Cardin's federal *organisateur en chef* for Montreal, took an active part at the convention both publicly and behind the scenes, to assure that the dissident group, led by Edouard Lacroix and representing Paul Gouin, were not read out of the party as the Taschereau group wanted. Godbout, re-elected as party leader, wrote a profuse letter of thanks to Lapointe about the convention 'dont vous avez contribué dans une si large mesure à assurer le succès.' Following the convention factionalism continued, with various leading personalities in the party involved. Nor was the federal party immune as provincial factionalism inevitably spilled over into the senior level, through the largely synonymous organizational structure.[45]

Byzantine internal politics were of course doing the Liberals no good. As a party, the provincial Liberals were utterly disorganized, and made no progress toward restoring their former efficiency. The federal Liberals had every reason to deplore this state of affairs. The lucrative party war chest and extensive patronage which came with provincial office would be more than welcome to the federal party organization. In fact, the federal party was besieged by Liberals turned out of their jobs by Duplessis and looking for federal help. Moreover, the federal party was fearful of the impact that the Union Nationale might have on the Liberals' chances in the next federal election. As Wilfrid Lacroix put it succinctly to Lapointe: 'Notre politique est magnifique, mais vous savez comme moi l'importance des travaux de Voirie dans une élection.'[46]

At the national level, the weakness and disarray of the Quebec Liberals presented the federal party with the opportunity to establish a more effective framework for the integration of the Quebec federal wing into the national party operations. This took a number of forms, beginning with King's firm and persuasive insistence that Ernest Lapointe, who was tired, sick, and discouraged, remain as the chief Quebec lieutenant through another election; Chubby Power, who had 'burned the candle at both ends,' was kept on, with some reason to be grateful to the prime minister; and, in Montreal, generally fruitless attempts were made to displace the mistrusted Cardin as leading minister.[47] Financially, the definite break between King and Donat Raymond over the refusal of the prime minister to appoint Raymond's brother as minister to Paris, opened the way toward a restructuring of the Montreal finance committee, which eventually yielded a more co-operative fund-raising set-up in that city. This restructuring was made all the more urgent by the evident attempt by Mitch Hepburn's Ontario machine to make a deal with the Montreal fund-raisers to blockade the federal party.[48] The Hepburn ploy failed miserably, and federal influence over Montreal in fact continued to grow. Finally there was the appointment of a French-language secretary for the NLF national office and the projection of national publicity efforts into Quebec, as well as the English-speaking provinces. King's original prohibition of NLF activities in Quebec had been rendered somewhat obsolete by the changing political circumstances. As Lambert told an NLF executive committee meeting in 1937, he felt that the 'time is ripe to do some organizational work' in Quebec, 'provided the French Canadian Cabinet Ministers are heartily behind the project.'[49] On a number of fronts, then, it was clear in the late 1930s that the federal party was the ascendant star in Quebec Liberalism.

Yet this ascendancy within the Liberal party did not mean federal domination in Quebec-Canada relations. There were already signs that the Union Nationale was capable of establishing a hold on Quebec which could force the federal Liberal party to make deals and accommodations with the provincial government. Some scattered evidence of Liberal-Union Nationale electoral collaboration at the constituency level was available to Ottawa in the form of rumour. More troublesome than this was the political incapacity of the federal government to confront provincial policies considered repugnant to the national interest. The best example is Duplessis' notorious 'Padlock Law,' which King personally abhorred but felt helpless against. The greater power of the central provinces as against the hinterland regions is vividly illustrated in federal disallowance of Alberta's Social Credit legislation as compared to its laissez-faire response to the Padlock Law. Mackenzie King was of course able to rationalize this double standard, but in the privacy of his own diary he confessed that 'it is not a decision which does credit to Liberal thought, at a time when Liberalism is being crushed in other parts of the world.' Still, Duplessis could effectively divide Quebec from Canada on this issue, and, again in King's own words, 'in the last resort, the unity of Canada was the test by which we would meet all these things.'[50]

THE SECOND WORLD WAR

The lengthening shadows in Europe in 1938-9 fell across the relationship between the federal government and Quebec, with the revival of all the old divisive issues of the imperial connection, war and peace, and – lurking in the wings – the awful spectre of conscription. Here the importance of Lapointe to the Liberal party became more and more crucial. Early in 1939 both King and Lapointe made matching speeches on the Canadian position vis-à-vis a war in which Britain would be involved. The two speeches were carefully tailored to strengthen the delicate position of a government poised between its anti-conscriptionist base in Quebec and its imperialist English-speaking support in Ontario, as King's comments in his diary brilliantly demonstrated:

If I had made the speech Lapointe made, the party might have held its own with the Jingos in Ontario, but would have lost the support of Quebec more or less entirely. If he had made the speech I did, he might have held Quebec, but the party would have lost heavily in Ontario and perhaps some other parts on the score that Quebec was neutral in its loyalty. Together, our speeches constituted a sort of trestle sustaining the structure which would serve to unite divergent parts of Canada, thereby making for a united country.[51]

Duplessis' effective exploitation of Quebec nationalism might seem to have presented an impasse to a federal government thus committed to maintain this difficult balance. The way out of the impasse was unexpectedly offered by Duplessis himself, when he called a snap provincial election at the outset of the war. By making opposition to the federal government the major issue of the election, Duplessis managed to be too clever by half.

The federal ministers from Quebec were not slow to grasp the opportunity which had been handed to them by Duplessis. Power told Norman Lambert that the federal ministers had been directly challenged and would have to respond to the premier's 'foolish act.' The ministers told King that they were in the 'best of spirits' and optimistic about success, if they could impress upon the voters that a federal Liberal government with adequate Quebec representation was the best guarantee of keeping conscription off the agenda. King, always cautious, worried lest they irrevocably commit themselves in public to resignation were conscription ever to be introduced, but he could see the force of their argument to the Quebec population.[52] The pledge by Lapointe, Cardin, and Power to act as the rampart against conscription within the federal cabinet if the provincial Liberals were elected was stunningly successful. To those who argued that federal politicians should keep their noses out of provincial contests, Lapointe had a straightforward answer: 'Les ministres et les députés fédéraux de cette province sont des citoyens qui, comme des autres, ont intérèt à la bonne administration des affaires provinciales ... Chaque député fédéral est libre de ses actions dans le domaine provincial et c'est une impertinence que de vouloir leur contester ce privilège.'[53]

Not only did the federal party provide the provincial party with the decisive issue but they also threw out the feuding and ineffective provincial organization, and took direct charge of the campaign in its entirety. Power ran the Quebec district and Cardin and Beauregard took charge of Montreal. Candidates considered too nationalistic or unreliable in their federal party loyalty were either forced to withdraw or given no financial support.[54]

Most importantly of all, the federal party took direct charge of mobilizing the financial resources of English-Canadian capitalism to defeat Duplessis. J.W. McConnell, of St Lawrence Sugar and the *Montreal Star*, a long-time Tory, suddenly discovered the patriotic importance of supporting the Liberals, and offered his money, as well as withdrawing editorial support from Duplessis. McConnell wished to make his new loyalties known at the top, and so called on Mackenzie King to announce his support and to offer to bring the financial support of other Montreal Conservative business interests as well.[55] McConnell himself gave at least $10,000. While McConnell put in a good word with his St James Street colleagues, Jimmy Gardiner's Saskatchewan Liberal machine put up $25,000 as a loan to the Quebec party, while Gardiner himself went to canvass Toronto, where he contacted one man with extensive contacts in the mining industry as well as such old standbys of Liberal fund drives as J.S. McLean of Canada Packers and C.L. Burton of Simpson's. Gardiner returned to Ottawa with large sums of 'patriotic money' as well as the editorial support of C. George McCullagh's *Globe and Mail*.[56] Finally, Norman Lambert's national fund was drawn into the election as well, despite Lambert's reluctance. As soon as the election had been called, Power, Cardin, and Gordon Scott, Montreal federal fund-raiser, had approached Lambert to lend them money from the extensive campaign chest built up by the national organizer over the past four years. Lambert could not finally hold out against the combined intervention of the Quebec ministers, Gardiner, and even the prime minister himself, and agreed to the transfer of at least $60,000 to Montreal and Quebec from the national funds – most, or all, of it to be paid back when circumstances permitted.[57]

The results of this marshalling of resources on behalf of the provincial Liberals were gratifying to the patriots of English Canada. For the provincial Liberals, the case was rather more complex. When the new Godbout government took over after the election, the provincial Liberal party was, in appearance, restored to its former position of power, but the appearances were quite deceiving. The provincials had taken office by the grace of the federal party alone. The Godbout government was a client government, and the King-Lapointe government was its patron. Godbout knew out of whose hand he fed, and not once during his term of office did he try to bite that hand. The landslide victory of 1939 ironically marked another stage in the prolonged decline of the provincial Liberals. The fact that success had come to them as a direct gift from their 'grands frères' at Ottawa locked them into a vicious circle out of which they would not be able to break for over twenty years. The patronage accruing to a party in office in Quebec was not sufficient in itself to build up the provincial party. The context within which the party had achieved office proved to be a more salient factor in the long run.

The most surprising aspect of the famous conscription crisis of 1944, from the point of view of the federal Liberal party in Quebec, is that it did such little damage to the party, either in terms of organization or of electoral success. Whether or not this remarkable result was a function of Mackenzie King's skill in the politics of compromise or had more general causes, is a subject of historical conjecture which need not concern us at this point.[58] But when the decision was finally introduced to send conscripted soldiers overseas, the expected revulsion in Quebec against the Liberal party did not take place. To be sure, the Godbout government had been turned out of office, but that had taken place over three months before the conscription decision and at a time when there was relatively little public discussion of the issue. Moreover, Godbout's party had actually received a slightly higher popular vote than Duplessis, although this is partially explained by the overwhelming English-speaking Liberal vote.[59] In any event, the main issue against the provincial Liberals was the all too evident fact of their total dependence on the federal Liberals – an issue that in itself did not depend upon conscription. To Power, Godbout was being made the scapegoat for federal sins.[60]

Perhaps the major share of the credit for preserving federal Liberal hegemony in Quebec should go to the Conservatives, upon whom King could always depend in emergencies. By their fanatical devotion to conscription as an end in itself, and to the greater glory of the British empire, the Conservatives ensured that they could never be a successor to the Liberals in Quebec. The Union Nationale had solved the problem of the unpopularity of Conservatism among French Canadians by forming a new, autonomist party with no formal ties to the federal Conservatives. But this was a solution for the *bleus* of Quebec, not for the federal Tories.

Although Cardin had quit the cabinet at the time of the first conscription crisis in 1942, and despite the fact that Power quit at the time of the actual imposition of conscription in 1944, there was no party revolt of major proportions, other than a few members walking out of the Liberal caucus, all of them later returning to the party. The main storm centre of dissidence was around the figure of Cardin, who did attempt to field a 'front nationale' slate of candidates drawn from the *Bloc populaire,* Union Nationale, independent Conservatives, and nationalist Liberals; but this motley crew of disparate tendencies never got off the ground. Cardin, as enigmatic and secretive as always, may have been trying to put together a Cardinist group of clients with political and financial dependency on him personally. The possibility of an alliance with Power in the Quebec district, which would have been essential to such an operation, was apparently turned down by Cardin for reasons which remain mysterious, but might have to do with Power's independence from Cardin's influence – or so Power himself suspected. Senator Beauregard was involved in this intrigue, and it appears that C.D. Howe, of all people, was the national Liberal in whom this group was placing its trust. Whether Howe was to be a lever on King, or whether they wished to replace King with Howe, remains a murky aspect of a Byzantine affair – in either event the alleged Quebec nationalism of a group tying itself to someone like Howe lends a comic, even farcical, air to the strange and sometimes inexplicable manoeuvres.

There is little point in attempting to follow the twists and turns of these inept schemers since all their efforts came to nothing in the end.[61] Eventually, as a kind of consolation prize, Cardin was allowed to run once again in his own constituency as an 'Independent Liberal,' unopposed by an official party candidate. The *Bloc populaire*, which did seriously put up a slate of candidates to challenge the federal government, was unable to make much of a dent in the Liberal armour. Without the organizational services of either Power or Cardin, and with the direction of the campaign dumped in the hands of the inexperienced solicitor-general, Joseph Jean, by King's new Quebec lieutenant, Louis St Laurent (who had himself departed the country for the United Nations conference at San Francisco),[62] the Liberals nevertheless managed to roll up a commanding victory in Quebec in the 1945 election: fifty-four Liberals and two Independent Liberals made a total of only five less than in 1940. In the rest of the country the Liberals did much worse than in 1940; once more Quebec had saved the party. And, out of the war, another era of 'rouge à Ottawa, bleu à Québec' had emerged, which was to prove to be a very durable combination of political opposites.

ROUGE A OTTAWA, BLEU A QUEBEC 1945-58

With Duplessis consolidating his power in Quebec in the postwar period, while the federal Liberals were reigning supreme in Canada as a whole, the provincial Liberal party was finding itself in a most peculiar position. Godbout, who has specifically requested the federal liberals to stay out of the 1944 election, was now reduced to calling on their aid in 1948. It was Godbout's misfortune as a provincial politician in Quebec to retain a strong sense of loyalty to the federal Liberals. A more opportunistic, or realistic, leader might have deliberately chosen to pick a quarrel with 'les grands frères' at Ottawa, but Godbout would not engage in such tactics. At Godbout's 'urgent request,' St Laurent agreed to intervene, as a 'citizen of Quebec' rather than as a member of the government.[63] Power was also persuaded to lend his organizational talents to the campaign as chairman of a provincial Liberal committee on organization. But as Power suggests, St Laurent's participation was a 'dismal failure,' a 'washout,' and a 'flop,' the electoral organization was incompetent and ineffective, and, most significantly of all: '... we found that our federal Liberal allies were not very helpful. Some almost openly proclaimed their neutrality, some engaged on the hustlings, but in constituencies other than their own, in order not to arouse the animosity of their local Union Nationale member.'[64] On election day the Union Nationale took eighty-two seats, and the Liberals were reduced to a remnant of eight, the lowest number ever to represent the party in the legislature since 1867. The following year Godbout was appointed to the Senate, the least the federal Liberals could have done in gratitude for over a dozen years of consistent loyalty. But if Godbout did receive some token of gratitude, the provincial party had received only the dubious assistance of Louis St Laurent, and the collaboration of their 'friends' with their enemies. The latter point, that of collaboration, was soon to assume greater proportions, but it is significant that as early as 1948 federal-provincial party unity was beginning to break down, not on the official or formal level, but on the practical level of constituency politics.[65]

With Godbout gone to the Senate, it was necessary to find a new provincial leader. The provincial party did not, however, have the primary say in this decision. The old Cardin organization in Montreal, led by Senator Beauregard and the Simards, decided on Georges-Emile Lapalme, a young and able federal member from the Montreal district, who since his first election in 1945 had shown a distinct flair for organization. A close friend of Edouard Simard, Lapalme was built up as a candidate by having a collection of his speeches and writings published. The Simards offered to give Lapalme personal financial backing if he would undertake to lead the provincial party, but Lapalme, fearing scandal, said he would look after his own financial affairs. The Montreal district federal Liberals, under the direction of René Beaudoin, did give Lapalme all the political backing he needed to easily crush his opponents at the 1950 provincial leadership convention.[66]

Duplessis called the Liberal convention a 'convention fédérale-provinciale' and Lapalme himself readily admitted that not only had he been established in his new position by the federal organization, but that he found himself in control of a party which lacked its own organization and secretariat, and its own financial means. The provincial party treasury was in debt by some $6000. Lapalme recalled that 'En 1950, je ne sais plus qui en défrayait le coût, mais je crois bien que les années de vaches maigres du parti provincial ne lui permettaient plus de solder sa part des dépenses communes.' Whatever motives of the old Cardin-Simard forces in placing

Lapalme at the head of the party might have been, they soon learned that he was his own man, and no one else's mouthpiece. To Beauregard's evident dismay, Lapalme told the convention that 'malgré notre insolvabilité, je crus nécessaire de créer une organisation absolument indépendante ayant pignon sur rue.' The theme that was to dominate the efforts of the provincial Liberals for the next decade, the creation of an independent organization with independent financial foundations, was thus struck at the very moment when a federal MP was installed by the federal party as provincial leader. The dismal fate of Adélard Godbout's 'petit frère' party had been taken by Lapalme as a warning beacon, indicating a course for sure disaster.

But a new, independent course was by no means easy, and concealed its own dangers. Unseen by the media and the public, a schism quickly developed within the party between Lapalme and his small group of reformers, and a pro-federal group opposed to an independent provincial organization. Lapalme was scornful of the latter, referring tothem as 'la foule des amis du pouvoir' and 'les courtisans et les éternels gagnants de la politique.' When the provincial party was stronger than the federal, as in Taschereau's days, Lapalme knew that these 'parasites' had attached themselves to the provincial wing.[67] But the federal wing was all powerful and the 'amis du pouvoir' did control the financial means. Lapalme, the 'federal' candidate, was henceforth *persona non grata* with Ottawa, and the provincial Liberal party was forced to wage war on two fronts throughout the 1950s, the one front public against the Union Nationale, and the other, more covertly, against the Ottawa Liberals.

In organizational terms the task facing the provincial party was staggering. Lapalme later recalled that when he took over in 1950 there was 'pas une seule organisation vivante dans le province,' and only one provincial deputy between Montreal and Gaspé. 'Et quand nous avons entrepris la tournée des comtés, nous avons été obligés de chercher avec une loupe les organisations Libérales que la défaite de 1948 avait balayées un peu partout.'

A vague resolution passed at the 1950 congress called for new structures, and a group of young reformers, such as Jean-Marie Nadeau, Jean-Louis Gagnon, J.-P. Grégoire, and Maurice Lamontagne, argued for a democratized party organization with membership participation in policy-making and 'une vie permanente de l'organisation ... au niveau de "poll." '[68] But the reality with which Lapalme had to work was not of the kind to lend optimism to reformers:

En réalité, le parti, c'était le chef et n'éprouvait autant que lui la solitude dans laquelle il oeuvrait presque toujours. La politique, dans le fond, malgré l'effort sporadique de quelques réunions faussement appelées congrès, c'était lui qui la faisait d'année en année. Pour sortir de son isolement, il ne pouvait en appeler à des organismes tout faits et préparés, avec des cadres; il convoquait nommément des individus qui avaient sa confiance ...

Dans l'esprit du public et des militants, le parti s'incarnait dans les deux bureaux de Montréal et de Québec. Ce qui ne représentait que la permanence de l'organisation se transformait selon eux en une figuration vivante du parti. Dans les comtés, on trouvait des associations *bona fide*, sans liste de leurs membres et, quand ceux-ci voulaient s'adresser au parti, ils s'acheminaient tout simplement vers l'organisation centrale.

La politique, après cent ans, n'avait engendré chez nous que des partis d'organisateurs, incapables de prouver d'ailleurs qu'ils appartenaient à un parti. L'affirmer suffisait.[69]

Not only was the party an empty shell, so to speak, but the shell itself was made in Ottawa. The two small provincial party offices in Montreal and Quebec were separate, but this was mainly show. René Beaudoin at first ran the Montreal district for both wings, as did Wilfrid Hamel in Quebec City. In the latter district, Senator P.-H. Bouffard doubled as treasurer at both levels – and went on a European trip accompanied by an influential fund-raiser for the Union Nationale,[70] an act which scarcely inspired confidence. At one point the tiny provincial offices almost had to be closed down, for want of money. And *Le Canada*, a newspaper which Lapalme and Beaudoin were planning to use as a vehicle of Liberal ideas, was closed down by Senator Daigle, federal fund-raiser, because of its deficits.[71] At times it seemed to Lapalme as if the federal party was planning his destruction. For example, André Montpetit, whom Lapalme had chosen as Montreal *organisateur en chef* as a provincial replacement for Beaudoin, was appointed to the Supreme Court at the same time as Senator Ferland, Lapalme's law partner – just months before the 1952 provincial elections. 'Le ciel,' Lapalme recalled, 's'obscurcissait tout d'un coup. D'un côté, c'était la mort de notre bureau d'avocats, de l'autre c'était le vide à l'organisation ... J'en avais mal au coeur.' Jean-Marie Nadeau was chosen as Montpetit's successor.

Lapalme's social progamme was considered too radical for most of the party's traditional financial backers. A speech advocating labour and welfare legislation considered 'advanced' in Duplessis' Quebec, brought grimaces from *les grands* of the party who were present. 'Ce n'est pas avec des discours comme celui-là,' a powerful Liberal told Lapalme, 'que vous trou-verez de l'argent.'[72] The prophecy was sound: the Liberals' treasury was nearly bare and remained so. It was in this financial state that the party faced in the 1952 election an adversary possessing apparently unlimited financial means.[73] And the following year the federal Liberals, drawing on many of the same sources, were estimated to spend $2 million in Quebec alone.[74] Of course, some money was available for the provincial party; as Lapalme put it, there were always those willing to take out 'fire-insurance policies.' But between the quasi-taxing power of the Union Nationale, and the demands of the 'safe' and business-oriented St Laurent-Howe Liberals, there was little left over for the provincial Liberals. There might have been more, of course, if Lapalme had not acted so 'dangerously.'[75] But that was the whole point: how could an independent policy be followed without some independent and assured financial base.

Despite the financial miseries of the party, despite its internal federal-provincial struggles, and despite the widespread electoral fraud and corrup-tion practised by its adversaries, the Liberals under their new leader im-proved their standing substantially in 1952, tripling their representation to twenty-three seats, and increasing their share of the popular vote by 10 per cent. But they were still far from overtaking the formidable machine of Maurice Duplessis. And in the task of building an opposition which could dislodge this machine, Lapalme became increasingly aware that one of his main adversaries was the federal wing of the Quebec Liberals. Not only was money withheld, not only did the federal party put obstacles in the way of provincial organization, but the federals were also engaged in positive col-laboration with the Union Nationale, both on the constituency level in elec-toral terms and on the highest level in terms of policy.

Lapalme claims that he knew nothing of collaboration between the fed-eral Liberals and the Union Nationale when he took over as leader.[76] Yet as has been suggested earlier, clear evidence of 'non-aggression' pacts between federal Liberal MPs and provincial UN deputies was already obvious as early as the 1948 provincial election. Such collaboration was in fact widespread, especially in rural areas, by the 1950s. In the 1949 federal election and in by-elections following, the UN machine demonstrated its power by support-ing various 'independent' Liberals against official Liberal candidates. Three were elected in the general election and four in by-elections. All were wel-comed into the Liberal caucus after a brief interval, and Quebec Liberal MPs took due notice of Duplessis' warning.[77] In the 1952 provincial election federal non-intervention became the rule, from St Laurent who 'remained discreetly quiet' during the contest except to denounce as 'absolutely false' a Union Natione advertisement asserting that taxes had been imposed by the federal government to pay for Lapalme's campaign, to a substantial number of federal MPs whose electoral organizations were withheld from provincial use.[78] In the federal election the following year, Frédéric Dorion, the Conservatives' Quebec organizer, tried to pretend that Duplessis was supporting his party. But in fact Duplessis kept aloof publicly, while 'the word was spread quietly to vote "bleu à Québec, rouge à Ottawa." '[79] A deal had emerged. The Union Nationale had control of enormous patronage and graft, and also had control over much of the Quebec press. These were valuable commodities to be exchanged for non-intervention agreements by federal Liberals.[80] As Regenstreif has described the system:

By 1955, approximately 30 federal Liberal Members, sitting for mainly rural constituencies, had entered into these agreements, which consisted of little more than a reciprocal undertaking between federal MP's and Union Nationale Members not to participate in the election campaigns of their counterparts. The federal Liberals involved found these agreements especially enticing. There was little patronage available for them in federal politics, where civil-service rules are relatively stringent and where there is less opportunity for outright corrupt behaviour. On the other hand, provincial politics in the province has traditionally been characterized by just the opposite. So for the previous few years, the province had witnessed the spectacle of Liberal candidates campaigning vigorously in federal elections, not so much for the privilege of representing their constituencies in Ottawa, but in order to be in on the graft pouring in from Quebec City, which would automatically be theirs as a result of the pacts.[81]

If four out of ten federal members were collaborating in this manner, the impact provincially would be even greater, since the rural areas, strongly Union Nationale, were considerably more overrepresented on the provincial electoral map than on the federal.

It has often been asserted that the kind of agreements just described were not undertaken with the approval of St Laurent. There is no definite evidence to the contrary, but St Laurent's actions scarcely gave the impression of a leader who wished to do battle with Duplessis, and did often lend some credence to the image often put forward in nationalist circles of 'un seul grand parti, dont le chef national est M. Saint-Laurent et le chef provincial, M. Duplessis.'[82]

Shortly after St Laurent became prime minister, an Ottawa-Quebec rapprochement seemed to be coming about. At the 1950 Dominion-Provincial Conference, Duplessis seemed conciliatory, and St Laurent, in the words of his biographer, 'grasped eagerly' at the outstretched hand.[83] In 1951 it was widely noted that Duplessis was not engaging in his usual attacks on Ottawa, while at the same time one of St Laurent's sons was appointed by Duplessis as aide-de-camp to the lieutenant-governor. Federal-provincial agreement was reached on universal old age pensions, and a provisional one-year agreement was made for federal aid to universities. All this may have been innocent enough, and even constructive. But the case of iron ore exploitation was, from the point of view of the provincial Liberals, both embarrassing and disturbing.

Under both Godbout and Lapalme the provincial Liberal party had strongly opposed the granting of iron ore concessions in Ungava to American companies for what most observers felt were absurdly low prices. For example, shortly after the war, an American steel corporation was granted a $200 million concession for a royalty of one cent on every ton of iron ore extracted – while at the same time the Newfoundland government was collecting thirty-three cents per ton on similar mines in Labrador.[84] Of course, the company was undoubtedly paying somewhere between one and thirty-three cents, the difference going directly into the Union Nationale treasury – and the provincial Liberals were attempting to make these corrupt deals into a political issue. Then, in 1951, St Laurent spoke out in the House of Commons in favour of Duplessis' natural resource policies. George Marler, the assembly leader, told Lapalme: 'C'est horrible … nous étions atterrés.' The reaction among provincial party rank and file was violent; numerous organizers walked out in disgust. Lapalme believed it was a signal which allowed 'nombreux libéraux fédéraux de libérer ce qu'ils appelaient assez drôlement leur conscience en votant pour Duplessis.' Lapalme issued a strong public statement expressing his party's anger at St Laurent's speech, preceded by a coldly worded letter to St Laurent stressing that the public statement was 'une absolue nécessité' for the provincial party.[85] To the press and public it seemed as if the 'non-aggression' pacts between federal Liberals and Union Nationale members had been matched by a 'non-aggression' pact between the party leaders as well.

In 1954 there were signs of a rift between St Laurent and Duplessis. Stories about the corruption and brutality of the Duplessis régime had even reached the *haute bourgeoisie* of Grande-Allée, and the St Laurent family was upset.[86] St Laurent hired Maurice Lamontagne as a special advisor just after his pro-federalist book[87] had been published: Duplessis was furious. In September St Laurent spoke in Quebec and, in an apparent provocation said that Quebec was only 'une province comme les autres.' In the ensuing controversy, great verbal violence was generated on both sides. But it was only sound and fury. As his biographer somewhat delicately put it, 'St. Laurent began to realize the dangers to Canada on an all-out test of strength, and his instinct for moderation and compromise gradually took over.'[88] When compromise did come, it was, predictably, at the expense of the provincial Liberals.

The Quebec government had for years been talking about a provincial personal income tax, but the federal government had been strongly opposed. The provincial Liberals, asserting that any provincial entry into the personal income tax field would thus involve 'double taxation,' opposed Duplessis in the assembly. Suspicious of the federal Liberals' intentions, George Marler spoke directly to Douglas Abbott, the finance minister, pointing out that if the federal government was planning to give a tax abatement to match the provincial imposition the provincial Liberals would support Duplessis. Abbott categorically replied that there was no chance of this 'whatsoever.' Jean Lesage said as much in the House of Commons. But as Lapalme later wrote bitterly, federal resistance was 'dure comme du roc. Comme du roc qui s'effrite au souffle de vent.'[89] In early October St Laurent met with Duplessis in Montreal's Windsor Hotel and resolved their differences in Duplessis' favour: the provincial tax would stand, and the federal government would grant a 10 per cent abatement to eliminate 'double taxation.' Blair Fraser reported that J.-P. St Laurent, the prime minister's son, had said: 'My father is fed up with Lapalme and would rather deal with Duplessis.'[90] As it was, the provincial Liberals were left in the worst of all possible worlds. They had opposed a popular autonomist move, leading to charges of tutelage to Ottawa, and even to the loss of members; they then had the rug pulled out from under them by Ottawa itself. When St Laurent met Duplessis at the Dominion-Provincial Conference in 1955, Dale Thomson reports that the latter was 'surprisingly affable.'[91] If St Laurent were genuinely surprised at Duplessis' attitude, he must have been the most naïve man in Canada.

The Windsor Hotel incident was probably the low point in relations between the federal and provincial Liberals in the 1950s. But the real importance of the incident is that it constituted, in effect, the last straw. In retrospect, Laplame saw this as the turning-point in freeing the provincial Liberals from what one editor was later to term its 'mauvais génie,' the federal party.[92] Since the federal party was a positive detriment to the provincial wing, the provincials could only gain by striking out on their own path. From this point on, the provincial Liberals were to enter seriously into the painful task of building a viable party which would eventually be able to stand independently of any federal support.

In 1955 the first congress of the *Fédération libérale provinciale* (FLP) was held. This was the project first suggested by Lapalme in 1950, and was almost exclusively the work of the provincial party. With the founding of the FLP, the provincial party took a major step toward building the basis for an independent party. This was not altogether clear at the time: St Laurent attended the congress, and despite the misgivings of some, the public impression was that the bad old traditions of Godbout's dependence on Ottawa were being maintained. Gérard Bergeron comments that 'les éléments autonomistes du Québec, trouvèrent insolite la présence du premier ministre, mais l'admiration vouée quasi unanimement à la personnalité de M. St. Laurent noyait à l'avance toute velléité de protestation.'[93] Pierre Laporte warned prophetically of defeat in the 1956 elections.[94] Moreover, the relationship of the FLP to the party organization and to the elected members was shrouded in ambiguity.

But beneath the surface it is clear that decisive changes were in the making. First of all, there were elements in the party, such as Nadeau, Gagnon, and Lapalme himself, who were geuninely concerned to democratize the party structure and to turn the old cadre party into something like a European mass party; there was brewing in the Quebec of the 1950s a new wave of democratic reform that was to come to the surface in 1960, and the Liberal party was a focus for at least some of that feeling. But there were more pressing, and more practical, reasons for party reform. The old cadre party had, quite simply, broken down. It could not finance itself from traditional sources, and it had not demonstrated any ability to deliver the votes. To move from under the shadow of the federal Liberals and to defeat Duplessis it was necessary to broaden the party's narrow base. As Paul-André Comeau has asked, cannot 'democratization' be seen 'purement et simplement une partie de la stratégie électorale? Ce serait un excellent moyen de rallier les partisans désorganisés par une série de défaites consécutives et de raviver leur enthousiasme.'[95] A mass party also offers the possibility of an alternative to traditional sources of funds – which in the Liberal case had virtually dried up in any event. Lapalme's memoirs suggest quite strongly that finding new sources for party finance was one of the major reasons for breaking away from the old 'parti des organisateurs.' Of course, the idea of financing the party through membership dues was not easily accomplished. Lapalme recalls that 'la cotisation, chez des gens habitués à recevoir et non à donner, suscitait les commentaires le plus primitifs: "Quoi! Il faut payer maintenant pour être libéral!" '[96]

In retrospect it has now become clear that the old party structure never did wholly give way. At both the constituency level and at the top the old power centres have merely adapted themselves to the new structures without losing their grip. Similarly, the party treasury later grew when the party came to power, and not from $2 memberships. But all this has only become evident since the mid-1960s. In the 1950s it appeared as if the FLP 'prenait figure d'innovation à la fois au sein du parti libéral et aussi dans le contexte culturel québécois.'[97]

In 1956 the liberals sustained another major electoral defeat, and the FLP emerged from its second congress in a stronger position vis-à-vis the increasingly discredited party organization. Despite Lapalme's enthusiasm ('La Fédération, c'est le parti'), there were critics who spoke darkly of the Liberals' 'congrès de la dernière chance.'[98] But, significantly, a report was unanimously accepted which affirmed 'l'indépendance du parti libéral provincial vis-à-vis du parti libéral fédéral. Ces deux partis, dans le respect de leur autonomie, assureront dans leur domaine respectif la réalisation de l'idéal libéral.'[99]

The new weight of the provincial party made itself felt on the issue of 'collaboration.' The new party journal, *La Réforme*, began to publicly denounce the 'non-aggression' pacts which had so poisoned federal-provincial party relations. Then, before the 1956 election, Lapalme confronted the federal Liberals on the issue. The latter publicly confessed their sins and promised to act more responsibly in the future. Perhaps it was the signs of rejuvenation among the provincial Liberals which brought about this apparent change of heart. A somewhat astonished Pierre Laporte wrote in *Le Devoir*: 'Il [Lapalme] a peut-être réussi à apeurer les fédéraux. Car en collaboration comme en bien autres choses ... la peur est souvent le commencement de la sagesse.'[100] In the elections, the federal wing did participate, to no great effect so far as the Liberal fortunes went, but to very great effect so far as the attitude of Duplessis went.

Angered by what he considered a betrayal of a sensible agreement , Duplessis set out to teach the federal Liberals a lesson in the federal election of the following year, by knocking selected Liberal MPs out of office. John Meisel reports that the Union Nationale organization was placed at the disposal of the Conservatives in at least sixteen constituencies, including Trois-Rivières, Duplessis' own provincial seat. In other seats, no Conservative was nominated to allow a UN-backed Independent to challenge a Liberal incumbent. In some areas old 'non-aggression' pacts between the Liberals and the Union Nationale remained in force. But where the Union Nationale did oppose the Liberals, Meisel reports, 'it did so lavishly and in a manner which has made notorious the electioneering techniques employed by M. Duplessis' party.'[101] Nine Conservatives, two Independents, and one

Independent Liberal were elected: a modest dent in the Liberal monolith, but a fatal one. The nine Quebec Tories were enough to give the party a narrow margin over the Liberals nationally, and Louis St Laurent was out of power. For the first time since 1896 neither Ottawa nor Quebec had a Liberal government. And if the federal Liberals were looking to their Quebec wing for sympathy and support, they must have been taken aback by Lapalme's cool response: 'Quant à l'effet que peut avoir ce résultat sur l'avenir de notre parti provincial, on nous dit de partout dans la province que ce résultat ne nous nuira pas. On pense probablement au fait que le parti libérale provincial ne pourra plus être la cible dont on se servait pour atteindre le parti libéral fédéral.'[102]

END OF AN ERA 1957-8

At first the provincial Liberals did not seem prepared to take a more autonomist route, despite the federal defeat. The 1957 congress of the FLP saw the affiliation of the organization to the National Liberal Federation.[103] An official report put forward the proposition that the NLF should 'représente les croyances et aspirations de toutes les provinces et de tous les groupes ethniques pour le plus grand bien de notre province et de notre pays.'[104] Moreover, Lionel Chevrier, the new federal Quebec lieutenant, was the guest of honour at the closing banquet. Lapalme, for various reasons, no longer seemed to be in control of his party, and opposition groups were manœuvring for control. In the struggle for power, it was a federal MP, Jean Lesage, who had always maintained a strong federalist front, who easily won out over two autonomist figures from the provincial party, Paul Gérin-Lajoie and René Hamel – drawing the jibe from Duplessis that the provincial party was 'l'appendice, la succursale du parti fédéral.'[105] Duplessis, as it turned out, was wrong. Appearances were deceiving, just as they had been when Senator Beauregard, René Beaudoin, and the Simards had installed Laplame as provincial leader eight years earlier.

The 1958 election saw not only the decimation of the Liberals nationally, but the election of an astonishing bloc of fifty Conservatives in Quebec, with the help of the Union Nationale machine.[106] At the convention which had chosen Lester Pearson as national leader the Quebec Liberals were still unsure enough of themselves that a very tough Quebec resolution which would have drawn public attention to the notorious federal collaboration with the Union Nationale was not pressed on the resolutions committee. After the electoral disaster of 1958, the provincial Liberals had no more reason to feel inferior: their federal counterparts had shrunk remarkably in size, prestige, and self-confidence. The restructuring of the provincial party was apparently paying off in a widening membership, and it was the turn of the federals to look to Quebec for an example. A representative of the FLP, participating in a meeting of the consultative council of the NLF in late 1958, reported that 'on peut dire sans pécher par vanité, que la Fédération Libérale du Québec, avec sa structure libérale au Québec, avec sa structure et ses réalisations, a fait l'envie de nos amis des autres provinces. Le chef libéral de la Nouvelle Ecosse a même fait un discours, non prévu à l'ordre du jour, pour proposer que la Fédération du Québec serve d'exemple à tous les libéraux du Canada.'[107] When a year and a half later, the Liberals under Lesage swept to power in Quebec, the once-powerful federal wing was even more envious. And envy soon turned to chagrin as the Lesage Liberals struck out along autonomist paths which were to shake Canadian federalism to its roots.

The federal party in Quebec had appeared to be a powerful electoral machine. Yet it is not merely hindsight to recognize that its unblemished record of success until 1957 hid severe, and growing, weaknesses. There was a sense in which the Liberals by the 1950s were running on a crude and deceptive platform in Quebec: vote for a French-Canadian prime minister. This essentially racial appeal masked the intense centralization of federalism carried out under the aegis of St Laurent, but it also masked the growing void in principle and policy at the core of the federal Liberal party in this era. The party was in fact little more than an electoral machine, decorated with a stuffed figurehead of a leader, who was in reality losing both his interest and his grip. Underneath this façade the organization itself was riddled with decay, indicated both by the failure during the St Laurent years to generate a second echelon of party leaders for the federal wing and by the fatal dependence upon the co-operation of the Union Nationale. St Laurent so overshadowed all other Quebec Liberals, the personality cult was developed with such assiduous and lavish attention, that no successors appeared in the wings, and no lieutenants were given the necessary prestige to carry on the tasks of organization and politics required to maintain the party in a state of renewal. The dependence on the Union Nationale was not only organizationally dangerous, as the 1957 election demonstrated only too well, but it also paralysed the party in a policy sense, constricting its ability to strike an ideological stance in tune with changing times in Quebec. It was only the provincial Liberals, led by one former federal Liberal who had turned away from the federal party, and based on new and more democratic party structures, who seemed capable of adapting to the new conditions. The very depth and extent of the federal defeat in 1957-8 illustrates the void in the Liberal party which the St Laurent personality cult and its racial overtones had previously hidden. With the departure of St Laurent there was not much left save an electoral machine in a very poor state of repair.[108] The devastating shocks suffered by federal governments at the hands of the provincial Liberals in the 1960s could be attributed, in part at least, to the legacy of the St Laurent years in the Liberal party, and the atrophy of the federal wing of the party under the illusory façade of easy electoral success. It was to take a decade of flux and confusion within the ranks of the Quebec Liberal party before the adhesion of Pierre Trudeau, Jean Marchand, and Gérard Pelletier to the federal wing would pay off in renewed federal authority and prestige in Quebec.

FEDERAL-PROVINCIAL CAREER PATTERNS

A crucial point of relevance to federal-provincial party relations identified by E.R. Black is that while policy objectives and organizational requirements are often quite different in the federal and provincial arenas, 'both sets of leaders must rely in large measure on the relatively small group of people and on the same resources in their field work.'[109] This was certainly true for the Quebec Liberals previous to the 1960s. Although no systematic study has been done of federal-provincial membership participation patterns, the fragmentary evidence available points to a persistence of the traditional system.[110] A study of the nature of Liberal allegiance among party members and workers – how many are oriented primarily toward the federal sphere, how many toward the provincial sphere, and how many toward both equally, and how these patterns have developed over time – would be invaluable. Lacking such an analysis, it is necessary to turn to other evidence.

One indication of relationships over time can be gathered from the career patterns of elected officials. Although adequate data on Liberal members of the Quebec national assembly was not available for the period considered here, a full study of the political careers of the members of the House of Commons and Senate from Quebec was possible.[111] A total of 286 persons elected from Quebec sat in the House from 1921 to 1967 under the Liberal label. If this group is broken down by the decade in which the federal political careers of the members began, it is then possible to analyse the interrelationship of federal and provincial career patterns (see Table 7.1). Thus, over a half-century period, eight out of ten federal Liberal MPs from Quebec have remained wholly within the federal sphere. Only a meagre 12.6

Table 7.1
Elected career patterns of federal Liberal MPs from Quebec, 1921-67, by decade in which federal career began

Decade elected	Federal career only		Federal and provincial careers		Defeated provincially		Total
	N	%	N	%	N	%	
Before 1920	40	78.4	8	15.7	3	5.9	51
1920s	35	81.4	8	18.6			43
1930s	28	77.7	6	16.6	2	5.7	36
1940s	46	73.0	12	19.0	5	8.0	63
1950s	30	88.2	2	5.9	2	5.9	34
1960s	54	91.5			5	8.5	59
Total	233	81.5	36	12.6	17	5.9	286

Source: information compiled from J.K. Johnson, ed., *The Canadian Directory of Parliament, 1867-1967* (Ottawa, 1968)

per cent have pursued provincial careers as well, and this has trailed off in recent years.

Of course it may be objected that those who began their federal careers in the 1950s and 1960s have not had time to show a full career pattern. However, when the trends among those with both federal and provincial experience is examined, we find that the tendency has been for MPs to have come into Parliament with *previous* provincial experience (see Table 7.2). What is indicated here is either an increasing specialization of MPs in federal politics alone or a shift from a provincial to federal pattern to a federal-to-provincial pattern. The relatively high number among those who began their political careers in the 1940s in the House of Commons and later moved into provincial politics might point to the latter conclusion. More significantly, when the cabinet experience of those MPs who have pursued both federal and provincial careers is examined, we find a strong predominance of those with *provincial* cabinet experience (see Table 7.3). Of the 36 federal MPs with provincial experience, 16 (or 44 per cent) achieved cabinet rank in Quebec governments. Since only 37 of the 250 Liberal MPs with federal careers (or 15 per cent) achieved federal cabinet rank, it would seem that movement between the two levels of government has been mainly a movement of those seeking higher office, or at least heightened prospects of such promotion. Only three men have reached cabinet rank in both governments, and two of these, Sir Lomer Gouin and Jean Lesage, were provincial

Table 7.2
Elected career patterns of Liberal MPs from Quebec with both federal and provincial experience, 1921-67

	From provincial to federal	From federal to provincial	Both	Total
Before 1920	6	2		8
1920s	5	3		8
1930s	4	1	1	6
1940s	5	7		12
1950s	1		1	2
1960s				
Total	21	13	2	36

Source: *Canadian Directory of Parliament*

Table 7.3
Cabinet experience of federal Liberal MPs from Quebec with both federal and provincial careers, 1921-67

	Federal cabinet	Provincial cabinet	Both	Total
Before 1920	2	1		3
1920s		3	1	4
1930s		3		3
1940s		6	1	7
1950s	1		1	2
1960s				
Total	3	13	3	19

Source: *Canadian Directory of Parliament*

premiers. Most significant is the group who began their federal careers in the 1940s and later moved into provincial politics, no less than seven achieving cabinet rank in the later period, in Lesage's so-called *'équipe de tonnere.'* The revival of the provincial Liberal party in the 1950s seems to have acted as a pole of attraction drawing away some of the federal party's human resources.

Except for the case of the 1940s generation and small movements of élites, the federal sphere would appear to be fairly well insulated; this insu-

Table 7.4
Quebec federal Liberal MPs with previous experience as elected
municipal officials, 1921-67

| | Previous municipal experience | | Total |
	N	%	
Before 1920	15	27.8	51
1920s	12	25.6	43
1930s	13	36.0	36
1940s	12	19.0	63
1950s	7	20.6	34
1960s	13	22.2	59
Total	72	25.2	286

Source: *Canadian Directory of Parliament*

lation has not changed drastically over the twentieth century. Indeed, previous experience as an elected *municipal* official has been a far more common career pattern for federal Liberals than provincial experience (see Table 7.4).

Finally, we may look briefly at Liberal senators from Quebec. Forty-seven Quebec senators sitting in this period listed their party affiliation as 'Liberal.' Table 7.5 shows their career patterns. Except for a brief period in the 1940s following the defeat of the Godbout government, when four provincial ministers (including Godbout himself) were given appointments, the Senate has not been used to reward those with only provincial careers. Of course, Quebec was unique among the provinces in possessing its own appointed legislative council, which no doubt relieved provincial pressure on the Senate. It might also be noted in passing that of the seventeen senators without careers as elected officials, at lease eleven can be readily identified as either fund-raisers or organizers, many of them for both the federal and provincial parties – the two parties at the extra-parliamentary level.

In terms of elected members, then, the federal Liberal party in Quebec has had a distinct identity of its own vis-à-vis its provincial wing, and there is some evidence that this insularity of the personnel of the two spheres of legislative activity is increasing. It should also be noted, however, that the relative ease with which federal Liberal candidates have normally been elected in Quebec, together with the greater uncertainty of provincial party fortunes, has no doubt reinforced the tendency of federal MPs to stay in the same legislative body. It is thus not altogether clear that this federal career

Table 7.5
Elected career patterns of Liberal senators from Quebec, 1920-67

Decade appointed	Federal only	Federal-provincial	Provincial only	No elected career	Total
Before 1920	7	2		4	13
1920s	7	1		2	10
1930s	3			1	4
1940s	3		4	7	14
1950s	2			1	3
1960s	1			2	3
Total	23	3	4	17	47

Source: *Canadian Directory of Parliament*

pattern necessarily reveals any fundamental divergence within the party organization (or among the party supporters) and indeed the historical evidence we have drawn on in this study would rather tend to indicate the over-lapping of organization, personnel, and resources between the two wings, at least until very recently.

8

Ontario

Ontario, the largest province in terms of population and incomparably the most politically influential in English Canada, has been a cause of much ambiguity in the minds of Liberals throughout the twentieth century. In federal politics it has never been as reliable a source of Liberal support as Quebec, but the Liberal party has usually had reasonable success at the polls. In provincial politics, on the other hand, the story is quite different; throughout most of this century Ontario has been a Tory province. Since 1905 there have been only two exceptions to the Conservative hegemony: the short-lived United Farmers government from 1919 to 1923, and the nine chaotic and turbulent years of Liberal rule under Mitch Hepburn and his successors from 1934 to 1943. Ironically, for the federal Liberals this solitary example of Liberal provincial success also marked what must be called the worst federal-provincial struggle which the Liberal party ever had to wage within its own ranks. The only comparable intra-party war was the three-year period from 1963 to 1966 when Jean Lesage's provincial Liberals in Quebec were in the midst of their Quiet Revolution and a weak minority Liberal government in Ottawa vacillated before the provincial challenge. Whatever the respective socio-cultural and economic significance of these two very different federal-provincial struggles, there can be little doubt that for sheer personal rancour and partisan violence the Hepburn-King feud of the 1930s and the early war years has no match in the record of the Liberal part in this century. The electoral disaster of 1943, which the provincial party has never been able to reverse, did very little, if any, damage to the federal party which in the years since has consistently done much better at the polls than its provincial counterpart, and has moreover found little difficulty for the most part in reaching mutually satisfactory accommodations with the Conservative rulers of the largest province. As in the case of

Quebec, the Liberals of Ontario illustrate the fact that a government party in Ottawa can get along well without successful partisan support in the major provinces – that, indeed, they may very well get along better without it.

THE PROVINCIAL LIBERALS BEFORE HEPBURN

One of the underlying weaknesses of the provincial Liberal party in Ontario in failing to translate the old nineteenth-century Mowat coalition of the rural southwest, town manufacturers, and Roman Catholics into effective twentieth-century terms was their apparent inability to understand the qualitative changes which the new century was bringing in the Ontario political economy.[1] As early as the census of 1911 over half the population of Ontario was classified as urban, and this demographic landmark only reflected the fact that the economy had shifted decisively from agriculture to industry. As Charles W. Humphries has written:

The Conservatives observed the change and acted; the Liberals, with few exceptions, failed to appreciate the altered circumstances and, consequently, were unmoved by them. At the century's turn, the Conservatives increasingly represented the new interests of the growing cities and towns and they were rewarded for their perception; the Liberals remained tied to a declining rural population – in some instances the decline was real and, in others, relative – and they were penalized for their insensitivity.[2]

The most recent, and the most comprehensive, analysis of the Ontario Liberal party in the 1970s echoes this judgment on the party of seventy years ago in terms almost unchanged. 'The future of the Liberal party in Ontario must surely be bleak,' write John Wilson and David Hoffman. 'In a developed industrial society they cannot expect to recreate the old Mowat coalition.'[3]

The Liberal party of Ontario before the accession of Mitch Hepburn as leader was in a sorry state of disorganization and demoralization. There was a continuing rural base for the party which gave no particular promise of extension into the urban areas of south-central Ontario. The party was, moreover, saddled with the dour face of prohibition, the legacy of Newton Rowell. And the Ontario Liberal Association, the main organizational force for the party in the province, was clearly a federal, not a provincial, institution. Even provincial riding associations were 'dead,' in the words of the provincial leader.[4] In Toronto the party was in desperate condition, a weakness which also was reflected in the federal party's inability to elect members in the nation's second largest metropolis. To the rest of the party outside Ontario, the contempt for what J.W. Dafoe called 'those time-serving pussyfooters, the Liberals of Toronto,' was high indeed.[5]

The double electoral defeat of 1929-30 obviously called for serious rethinking on the part of the Ontario Liberals; even the provincial leader, W.E.N. Sinclair, favoured the calling of a provincial convention at which the party leadership would be decided by the delegates. Into this situation stepped the ebullient young federal member for Elgin West, Mitch Hepburn. Bored with life as a backbencher in Ottawa, and resentful of the federal party which had neither helped him in his own upset victories in 1926 and 1930 nor offered much encouragement to him as a sitting member, Hepburn was ready for a new and exacting challenge in other fields. Ontario certainly offered such a challenge.

There were powerful forces gathered in opposition to the brash newcomer. J.E. Atkinson of the *Toronto Star*, as influential a Liberal press baron as there was in Canada at this time, was distinctly hostile. More importantly, Mackenzie King was plotting with some leading figures in the organizational and financial branches of the provincial party to keep Hepburn out of Queen's Park. King's opposition, covert but pointed, revolved around two main objections: he feared opening up a by-election in a riding which could well go Conservative and he did not particularly like Mitch Hepburn's personality and way of life. 'Drinking and getting mixed up with women' were scarcely King's ideal of the public image of Liberalism; to the sober and high-minded national leader, Mitch Hepburn had all the distasteful characteristics of the boy from the wrong side of the tracks.[6] The personality factor in the distance between the two men must be emphasized from the start. King might have detested Vincent Massey, but the latter's social position and wealth ensured King's grudging respect. Hepburn had none of the qualities which could rouse either admiration or deference in King. For his part, Hepburn was never much impressed with King's stuffy Victorian probity. These personal divergences might not in themselves have accounted for the schism which was later to open between the federal and provincial parties in Ontario. But when superimposed over more underlying economic and political factors, they did much to exacerbate the division.

The Ontario Liberals were so badly disorganized, however, that the national leader was unable to effectively oppose Hepburn, despite the efforts of party organizers. In December of 1930 Hepburn was elected party leader by a provincial convention. The former leader, W.E.N. Sinclair, dashed off a bitter letter to Mackenzie King: 'His friends are not my friends. Whatever faults I may have, I know he is of a much inferior type of mind to my own.

His personal habits do not appeal to me. We have nothing in common. I am prominent in my profession and he has no training. His chief qualification consists in making rabid speeches, one sentence of which at any time may be his undoing. If he does not make a rabid speech, he makes no speech at all.'[7] If King could no more respect Hepburn's personality than could Sinclair, he at least respected the ability to achieve political success. Once Hepburn had won the leadership, King tried to put the best face on the situation by disingenuously informing the new leader that he had always favoured his candidacy, and moreover pointed to the opportunity for a new era of friendly co-operation between the federal and provincial wings of the party in Ontario. King was also busy trying to mollify other Liberals equally suspicious of the young man with the dubious personal reputation. 'After all,' he assured one anxious correspondent, 'the Tory Party has not had as leaders men of such exceptional character and ability that that party should be permitted to profit by any limitations on the part of those entrusted with responsibility by our friends.'[8]

THE HEPBURN PARTY 1930-4

Hepburn retained his seat in Ottawa until the next provincial election was called, four years later; thus freed from day-to-day responsibilities in the legislative assembly, he set about energetically reorganizing the Liberal party across the province. The first step was to take the control of the remnants of the party machinery away from the federal party. The Ontario Liberal Association, with its headquarters in Toronto under the day-to-day charge of Harry Johnson, was turned into an instrument of the provincial leader. This operation was not as difficult as it might have been at other times, since the defeat of 1930 had left the federal party weak and leaderless in Ontario. It did involve a jurisdictional quarrel with some federal figures who were attempting a party reorganization in the federal ridings at the same time. The hiring of a federal field organizer caused some considerable conflict in the early 1930s which finally had to be resolved by the capitulation of the federal party, and the recognition of the final authority being vested with Hepburn's people. The deal which emerged by the time of the five Ontario federal by-elections in 1934 was, essentially, that there would be a single organizational apparatus under the control of the provincial leadership but at the service of the federal party.[9] This agreement, which was to cost the federal party very dearly in the years ahead, was made possible not only because of federal disorganization in the province but also, and perhaps much more importantly, by the growing ability of Mitch Hepburn as leader to cope with another necessary prerequisite of political success, fund-raising. While there were considerable difficulties encountered in raising money in the period immediately following Hepburn's accession to the leadership, these difficulties were gradually resolved. A popular subscription fund achieved some modest success, but far more significant was Hepburn's growing closeness to a certain group of powerful and wealthy capitalists, particularly the mining entrepreneurs of the northern Ontario mining frontier, as well as some other leading industrialists.[10]

There were two distinct dimensions to Hepburn's involvement with these capitalists. In personality terms, Hepburn was readily susceptible to the attentions of the wealthy, a characteristic to which many witnesses bear testimony. Fast living, fast drinking, and fast women were Mitch Hepburn's style of life, and those who could provide them in abundance were sure to be met with warm gratitude. Since Hepburn lacked Mackenzie King's post-Beauharnois scruples about political obligations, the tying of financial support to party policy was a far easier matter at the provincial level. That there can be no doubt about this is readily apparent from the policies pursued by the Hepburn government after the victory of 1934, as will be subsequently demonstrated. Yet Hepburn's personal vulnerability to the seduction, as it were, of the wealthy, is only part of the picture. Of much wider significance, both for the Liberal party and for the Canadian political economy, is the fact that Hepburn, the individual, stepped into an historical situation 'made' for someone of his style. As many observers have noted, the underlying economic basis of Confederation was shifting away from the old centralization of the National Policy era towards a regional decentralization based on new forms of economic activity. As Harold Innis wrote in 1941:

The political and economic structure of the federation of Canada with its emphasis on coal and iron, rigid debts, and protectionism has tended to conflict with the political and economic structure of the provinces with their emphasis on the new industrialism of hydro-electric power, oil, and minerals. The results have been evident in the financial and labour problems of the iron and steel, coal mining, and railroad industries, of federal debts, and of interprovincial and international constitutional stalemates. The disequilibrium which marked the extensive intervention of the federal government in the construction of transcontinental railways ... enormously stimulated the production of minerals and hydro-electric power and the use of oil. It strengthened the position of provinces with mineral resources in a progressively industrial civilization and weakened the position of provinces in which wheat production had been stimulated.[11]

When one adds to this the specific factor that in the world depression of the 1930s general currency devaluations had raised the price of gold, thus giving a strong boost to the exploration and development of the northern Ontario gold reserves, at the very moment when the rest of the Canadian economy was in a profound decline, then one has all the ingredients for a significant transfer of power and influence toward the regional economy of Ontario. Mitch Hepburn was more than willing to strike bargains with the mining capitalists and their allies in the Ontario economy in order to shift power within the Liberal party from Ottawa to Queen's Park. The structure of the Liberal party in Ontario in the 1930s was thus placed under very severe strain by this combination of economic change and a leader willing to make the most of his new resources.

To take advantage of the situation, Hepburn had first to win office in the province. That proved to be much less difficult than anyone in 1930, including Hepburn himself, could have imagined. The Depression helped discredit Toryism and Hepburn was able to carry out a remarkably successful personal campaign in 1934, a campaign that made the most out of the electoral potential, in conditions of economic chaos and political despair, of populist rabble-rousing, demagoguery, and messianic enthusiasm. The Conservative débâcle was awesome in its proportions, as their share of seats in the legislature fell from ninety-two to seventeen. The Liberal percentage of the popular vote rose from less than one-third in 1929 to half in 1934. Ontario politics had been drastically realigned for the first time since the end of the Mowat era more than a generation earlier. This extraordinary feat cannot be attributed to the Liberal party as a party, but to Mitch Hepburn as a charismatic leader.[12]

In the face of this brilliant personal triumph by a man whom Mackenzie King and other influential Ontario Liberals had tried to keep out of the party leadership only four years earlier, the national leader of the party reacted in a manner so bizarre as to strain the credulity even of a hardened student of King's personal peculiarities. When the news of the Liberal sweep reached Ottawa on election night, King was hurled into the depths of an extreme spiritual crisis, precipitated by the fact that Sir Wilfred Laurier had appeared to him in a vision a few days earlier and predicted a Conservative victory. 'Sick at heart,' King spent much of the night in agony over this 'betrayal' by his friends in the beyond.[13] This singular example of King's private mental universe is mentioned here only as an indication of the deep-seated antipathy which King harboured toward Hepburn, an antipathy so deep that it found expression in his dreams. Publicly, as always, King was the perfect party leader, hearty in his congratulations and collegial in his advice to the new premier. The private turbulence of mind was, however, a much more accurate indicator of the road ahead than the public propriety.

Having won an immense personal victory, Hepburn set out to consolidate his own control over the party in Ontario even further. No meetings of the Ontario Liberal Association were called while Hepburn remained leader. This rejection of the extra-parliamentary party was facilitated by Hepburn's appointment of T.B. McQuesten, the president of the association, to the cabinet.[14] The small group of organizers around Harry Johnson at the party's Toronto headquarters were henceforth little more than the adjuncts of the premier's office. If it had been a Hepburn victory more than a Liberal victory, it was also to be a Hepburn government more than a Liberal government, and a Hepburn party more than a Liberal party.

None of these developments were, of course, welcomed by Mackenzie King. Yet if Hepburn had confined his activities to the provincial field alone, matters might not have gotten out of hand. Indeed, King tried very resolutely to draw the line between the two spheres of the party as soon as Hepburn had been elected. Hepburn asked for one of King's federal members for his cabinet, a request which King was more than happy to grant, since he was glad to be rid of the member in question, Peter Heenan. Beyond releasing this doubtful asset, King made it clear that he wished to give no advice to Hepburn on appointments. The clear implication was, of course, that King expected that Hepburn would not offer patronage advice following a federal victory by King. Moreover, in answer to the many entreaties which flooded his office to put in 'a word with Mitch,' King scrupulously refused to pass on any names whatsoever – even when they came from as prominent a figure as former premier E.C. Drury.[15] One case in which King was misrepresented by a job-seeker as having given his endorsation raised a strong protest from Hepburn. King quickly moved to allay the premier's fears:

As I said to you in our first conversation, after the election, I felt your colleagues would resent any attempt on my part to go over their heads in matters which were likely to be of concern to them or to their departments; also, that I was sure you yourself would feel embarrassed were I to be making suggestions, with which you might not agree. I pointed out to you, as you will recollect, that as leader of the federal party I felt it was most desirable that I should be able to tell those who applied to me to use my influence with you on their behalf that I could not do anything of the kind, as it was all-important that I should not be held, either by them or by you or by anyone, directly or indirectly responsible for any actions of the provincial government. You may recall my mentioning that I had followed this course with the Premiers of all the provinces ever since the time I was chosen leader of the federal party. Events, over and over again, have proven to me how wise this course has been. I am sure you will find it the same yourself in your relations ... with myself in federal matters, should I again have the duty of participating in the government at Ottawa.[16]

Hepburn's views on federal-provincial party relations, however, appear to have differed significantly from those of the federal leader. While resenting any suggestion of federal interference in his new administration, he was also setting about the business of making the federal wing of the party dependent on him and his provincial party. His financial and organizational support for the five by-elections in Ontario in the fall of 1934 (see Chapter 2), and his personal and financial support for the federal campaign of 1935, fell into a consistent pattern of provincial control over party machinery and provincial aid to the federal party in electoral contests. Since Hepburn himself had never received any financial or organizational assistance from the federal party, he felt that he owed no favours in return. On the other hand, because of his assistance to the federal wing, he felt that favours were in fact owing to him. This asymmetrical relationship was obviously neither understood nor appreciated in Ottawa.

THE KING – HEPBURN FEUD: CAUSES

The inevitable break between the two parties began in earnest over this very matter of appointments to the federal cabinet. Frank O'Connor of Laura Secord Candy Shops, the principal provincial fund-raiser, was rewarded for his support of the federal campaign with a Senate appointment, but no other notable recognition to the Hepburn people was granted by Mackenzie King, despite the very substantial and valuable assistance they had rendered the federal party throughout the campaign. Hepburn expected a cabinet post for one of his supporters, and directly asked King to appoint Arthur Slaght, newly elected member for Parry Sound and a Hepburn man.[17] Norman Rogers, an academic about to be directly co-opted into the King cabinet, and a man considered by Hepburn as an outsider, warned his prime minister to be wary of the 'Hepburn ring' and of Slaght as a 'danger' to the federal party. Joseph Atkinson of the *Star*, also a Hepburn-hater, advised King not to take Slaght into his cabinet since he was 'in with the mining crowd.' King concluded that doubts about Slaght's loyalty precluded his inclusion. To Hepburn he addressed what Neil McKenty terms a 'patronizing lecture' on constitutional division between the two levels of government.[18] King was at pains to point out his own previous refusal to advise Hepburn on his selection of ministers, and went on to add that, however appreciative he might otherwise be of the Ontario premier's friendly advice, the constitutional responsibilities of a prime minister ruled out a too close relationship with party colleagues in the provinces:

What I have said as to the maintenance of a strict independence between us as individual leaders, has become increasingly imperative with the knowledge that a Dominion-Provincial Conference will be held in the immediate future, at which all-important questions of finance, jurisdiction, and the like, will come up for consideration, and, I hope, satisfactory adjustment. I have felt that I should be in a position, when the Conference assembles, to assure all the governments represented that my action in the formation of the federal government had in no way been influenced by any consideration other than that of the public interest as I was free to disclose it to all; also that I had, for the reasons mentioned, purposely avoided conferring with any of the provincial Premiers or members of provincial governments ... in the formation of the federal administration. They would, therefore, know in meeting the federal government, that neither fear nor favour towards any of the provincial governments had played any part in the formation of the federal ministry ... Obviously, I could not ask the counsel of any one of the eight Liberal Premiers without being equally prepared to seek the counsel of the other seven, and that, even if it were advisable, would be quite impossible.[19]

The response to Hepburn was stiff, but correct. Hepburn had no effective answer, yet the Slaght affair was a festering sore to which the Ontario leader would return again and again. And there was no shortage of minor patronage irritants to keep up the friction between the two governments, one example being T.B. McQuesten's provincial Highways Department, which never got along with Ottawa on highway construction and road contracts.[20]

As early as the spring of 1936 Hepburn was already attempting to use his financial whiphand over the federal party to force it into line with his wishes. A public organizational break was formalized in the fall of that year when a friendly 'dear Mitch' letter from Norman Lambert requesting the premier's attendance at the annual meeting of the National Liberal Federation in Ottawa was met with the following reply from Queen's Park:

We will not be represented at your annual meeting. I am also asking Mr. [Harry] Johnson to keep his organization separate and distinct from yours ... I am constantly being pressed from all sides to make representations to the Federal Ministers and in accordance with the intimation given to me by Mr. King shortly after the federal election I have carefully refrained from doing anything of such a nature which I know would ultimately be embarrassing not only to Mr. King, but to myself as well. In future it will be our intention, and may I make this very clear, to keep our organization separate and apart from yours.[21]

In the spring of the following year Hepburn made his famous public statement that while he remained a Liberal he was 'not a Mackenzie King Liberal any longer.'[22]

An analysis of the causes of this split reveals a complexity of factors, many of which are difficult to disentangle. The participants themselves, especially Hepburn, are poor witnesses to the origins of the quarrel, inconsistent, evasive, and sometimes dishonest, even to themselves. One gathers the bewildering impression of politicians nurturing deep personal enmities being swept up by forces which they barely understood, but which impelled them along paths of behaviour which were damaging to their party, but which also satisfied their personal feelings of hostility and aggression. Perhaps the best that can be done now is to attempt to isolate as many of the threads as possible.

Of the two main figures in the drama, Mackenzie King is perhaps the more easily understood, at least in terms of his public positions. It is Hepburn who presents the chief puzzle; it is Hepburn's apparently aberrant behaviour which must be explained in relation to the patterns which generally prevail in relations between federal and provincial wings of Canadian parties; it is Hepburn's record in office which seems more eccentric. Observers of the Hepburn government have divided on this question into those who fall back on the irrational in politics as the final answer, and those who see a deeper, impersonal rationality at work beneath the surface. Richard Alway puts the irrationalist explanation best: 'For those who believe that in the political sphere decisions are made as the result of a process of rational and deliberate analysis, a study of the Liberal party in the Province of Ontario during this period must, in many ways, prove a singularly disillusioning experience.'[23] Arguing from the other direction, from economics towards politics, Viv Nelles offers a strikingly different perspective:

Ontario politics in the thirties moved with a rhythm imparted by the Ontario Hydro-Electric Power Commission ... To some observers the convolutions and reversals of government policy during this period have a certain arbitrariness about them that is most easily explained in terms of the intemperate personality of the Premier ... If the fact that the Ontario government was in the power business is borne in mind, then the erratic course followed by the politicians makes sense.[24]

While Nelles' rather too exclusive preoccupation with hydro as an economic explanation can be quarrelled with, there is much apparent irrationality which may indeed be explained on grounds of economic, if not political, logic. There was some method in Hepburn's madness, although the methods were more often than not those of businessmen who were using the politicians.

The list of Mitch Hepburn's 'friends' during his years in office is instructive. Besides Frank O'Connor, who has already been mentioned, they include Sir James Dunn of Algoma Steel; James Gundy of Wood Gundy, and holder of no fewer than thirty-two directorates, including the control of British Columbia Electric and Canada Cement; J.P. Bickell, president of McIntyre-Porcupine mines; 'Sell 'Em Ben' Smith, New York mining stock promoter; Larry McGuinness, the Toronto distiller. These men and others met with Hepburn on numerous occasions, and were members of the Centurian Club which had been organized by C. George McCullagh, the young mining millionaire and publisher of the *Globe and Mail*. Mackenzie King might have had his Rockefeller and his Larkin, but Hepburn's relationships with his friends from Bay Street and Wall Street were far less circumspect, less discreet, and, it must be concluded, much less innocent.

To begin to sketch in the connections between Hepburn's policies and the interests of his high-powered friends, we may begin with Sir James Dunn. Dunn bought 20 per cent equity in Algoma Steel in the 1930s, and then used his influence with Hepburn to get a promise of a provincial subsidy on iron ore: this promise was used by Dunn to gain majority control of the company. When the promised provincial subsidy was in fact brought in, it was Dunn, rather than the premier, who made the official announcement. This subsidy was of considerable importance in putting the twice-bankrupted corporation back on its feet financially. As Alway suggests, these two stages of assistance meant that Dunn 'had been refinanced through the efforts of the Hepburn administration.'[25] Dunn was grateful for this personal attention, as shown by his support for the provincial Liberals and a long, shadowy war which he appears to have waged against the federal party leadership, especially King and C.D. Howe. Dunn acted as an emissary between Hepburn and Maurice Duplessis when the two premiers were cementing their anti-federal alliance in the late years of the decade. Dunn let it be known to King that Hepburn had after all given him a $2 million subsidy on the Algoma steel works, while the federal party had declined any assistance to him in his hour of need.[26]

The gold mining interests offer, if anything, an even more striking example of the subservience of the Hepburn government to the dictates of private profit. As has previously been indicated, the price of gold had risen substantially in the conditions of world depression, and the gold entrepreneurs represented the one clear success story of Ontario capitalism in this decade. The men who were opening up the mines, and making fortunes in the process, were distinct throwbacks to an earlier era of capitalism, the era of self-made millionaires, cowboy entrepreneurs, and robber barons – a type which stood out in singular contrast both to the grey finance capitalists of the corporations, as well as to the general misery and suffering of the mass of the population caught up in the unemployment and destitution of the Depression. They had little sense of social grace, no sense of political finesse, and a hard-edged determination to get what they wanted at any cost. Mitch Hepburn was right at home with them.

The clouds on the gold mining horizon were two in number, and both related to the peculiar position of gold on the world market. Government taxation and labour union militancy could cut into the huge profits since the price of gold was outside the control of the producers and increased costs could not be passed on to the buyers. The attitude of the mining interests to government and unions was hence more extreme than that which characterized most forms of capitalist activity. It might even be described as paranoiac. Thus when the gold mining crowd channelled financial support to the federal Liberal campaign through Hepburn and O'Connor in 1935, they expected to be paid off in government policy reversing the hated bullion tax which the Bennett régime had imposed. Hepburn acted as the spokesman of these interests at the 1935 Dominion-Provincial Conference, and when King refused to repeal the tax Hepburn argued on grand constitutional principle that the federal government ought to vacate the entire field of natural resource taxation in the spirit of the British North America Act. On the other hand, he also let it be known that if he did indeed have sole control of taxation on mining, the level would be much lower – even though Ontario mining companies already enjoyed one of the lowest taxation levels in the world. Nelles sarcastically comments: 'All taxpayers should have such friends.'[27] The irony is that for all their laissez-faire rhetoric, the gold entrepreneurs were inextricably tied to the state and closely linked to political parties. As Harold Innis wrote in typically cryptic, but pregnant, terms: 'Governmental intervention is a result of unpredictable resources and in itself becomes a disturbing factor. The enormous stakes have a dangerous influence on political life. No adequate objective tests have been devised, with the result that political issues tend to become determining factors. Exploitation of virgin resources in mining, as in lumbering, tends to involve political manipulation.'[28]

The remarkable figure of C. George McCullagh serves to illustrate some of the political ramifications of gold. McCullagh, a handsome and even dashing figure, was a self-made millionaire by the age of thirty in the midst of the Depression. With a fortune built on gold stocks, and with the assistance of William Wright of Lake Shore and Wright-Hargreaves gold mines, McCullagh merged the old Liberal *Globe* and the Tory *Mail and Empire* into the *Globe and Mail,* an organ which he viewed as representing the British Empire and the Ontario mining industry. Although McCullagh was later to turn against Hepburn and the Liberal party, in the mid-1930s he was intimately connected to its operations, as well as to the personal fortunes of the premier, through gold mining stocks which he purchased for Hepburn without the latter's name being mentioned as owner.[29] McCullagh's influence over his political protégé reached a climax in the events surrounding the strike at the General Motors plant in Oshawa in 1937. This incident in fact was crucial to the developing split between Toronto and Ottawa; the role which McCullagh and the gold interests played in the affair is thus of considerable interest.

The Oshawa strike was, in Irving Abella's considered words, 'a turning point in the history of the Canadian labour movement. It marked the birth of industrial unionism in Canada.' It may also, in the longer view of history, have helped mark what Abella again has called the 'strange death of Liberal Ontario'[30] – although, paradoxically, it rather seemed at first to have been a major popular triumph for the provincial Liberal party. Yet while the provincial response to the strike, and to the CIO unions which were then organizing in the province, seemed to have consolidated the electoral position of the party with the Ontario voters in the election which followed the strike, as well as consolidating the position of the party with the big business interests, the strike policy of the government not only widened the gap between the provincial and federal parties, and caused a rupture in the provincial cabinet, with the dismissal of two progressive ministers, but also in the long run appears to have sealed the fate of the Liberal party with the unionized working class electorate, and offered an electoral opening to the CCF. The net result of Hepburn's violent anti-union policy was to bring to reality the nightmare that had haunted Mackenzie King: the outflanking of the Liberal party on the left by a social-democratic labour party, and the reduction of the Liberals to a paler and less effective version of the Tory party. Hepburn's swing to the right over the Oshawa strike was a textbook confirmation of King's wisdom in persistently maintaining a centre-left position and a co-optive rather than repressive stance toward labour.

Hepburn's direct intervention in the Oshawa situation against the very recognition of the United Auto Workers union as a bargaining agent for the workers led inexorably to the demand for federal intervention in the form of the RCMP. Although there were elements in King's cabinet, and influential figures in the federal Liberal party, who were more than ready to take this step, to Mackenzie King the idea of the federal state intervening with its armed might on behalf of General Motors was sheer insanity. 'In the years that I have been Leader of the Liberal Party,' he wrote in his diary, 'I have not known a situation as injurious to Liberalism or as serious to the Country as that with which it is now faced as a consequence of Hepburn's rash and unwarranted action.' King derided as 'ridiculous' the argument that American unions should be kept out of Canada, since that battle had already been decided forty years earlier with the coming of the AFL to this country. To those who were opposed to union organization of an entire industry, King countered with labour's 'right to sell its services in a way likely to be most beneficial to itself.' 'No Liberal government,' he asserted flatly, 'could take any other position.'[31]

Hepburn's Liberal government was, however, taking the directly opposite position – although the removal from the provincial cabinet of David Croll and Arthur Roebuck (the latter leaving with the memorable phrase that he would rather 'march with the workers than ride with General Motors') indicated that the decision was not universally applauded in the party ranks. How could Hepburn's behaviour be explained? That Hepburn the onion farmer from Yarmouth Township understood little about the world of the industrial working class was obvious. But the rather typical rural insensitivity of Ontario Liberals to the cities could offer only a very partial explanation of such a vehement stand. Hepburn had staked his own position and that of his party on this issue. The stakes were apparently very high, but what exactly were they? Mackenzie King, as well as many other observers then and later, thought they knew perfectly well what interests Hepburn was protecting. As King wrote in his diary the night that Hepburn wired for RCMP reinforcements, Hepburn had tried to identify his actions with anti-communism:

In this he has gone out of his way to raise a great issue in this Country, the frightful possibilities of which no one can foresee. The truth of the matter is that he is in the hands of McCullagh of the Globe, and the Globe and McCullagh, in the hands of financial mining interests that want to crush the C.I.O. and their organization in Canada. The situation as he has brought it into being has all the elements that are to be found in the present appalling situation in Spain. Hepburn has become a Fascist leader and has sought to have labour in its struggle against organized capital, put into the position of being under Communist direction and control. Action of this kind is little short of criminal.[32]

To King, then, the possibilities were not merely that Hepburn would destroy the Liberals as a centrist party, but that he would push the workers into the arms of the communists who were at this time active in the ranks of the CIO.[33] Such dedicated efforts to intensify class conflict were directed by reactionary capitalist interests, centred around the gold mining promoters who wanted effective unions kept out of their mines at all costs. King had put his finger squarely on the real source of the Ontario government's stand in Oshawa.

The peculiar vulnerability of gold mine profits to wage increases has already been mentioned. Not that the companies were about to go bankrupt if unions forced wages up – far from it, in 1936 northern Ontario mine profits had reached as high as 50 per cent on total production! But the mine owners were ready to protect every penny of their enormous profits against the incursion of unions, and Mitch Hepburn was willing to throw his entire ministry into support of that struggle. Reports which had reached him from police agents and mine owners in the north had convinced him that the CIO was about to organize the mine workers. His stand in Oshawa was a test case to smash the CIO before it could strike at his good friends in the north. To say this is not to impute motives; Hepburn himself is the best witness. In a public statement he told the province that he was 'more concerned with the CIO threat in the mine fields than in the automobile industry ... for Oshawa is only an attempt by the CIO to pave the way for its real drive against the fundamental wealth of this province – its mine fields ... Let me tell Lewis [American president of the United Mine Workers] here and now that he and his gang will never get their greedy paws on the mines of northern Ontario as long as I am prime minister.' Privately, he was even more adamant. As if to underline the real basis of the situation, there was a major gold-stock collapse on the Toronto Stock Exchange on 19 April, a collapse attributed mainly to rumours of CIO activities in the gold mines.[34]

The influence of C. George McCullagh and the *Globe and Mail* in all this was widely noted at the time. The rival *Toronto Star* traced much of the CIO policy to Hepburn's 'large fund of inexperience' and to his 'intimacy' with McCullagh, 'who knows nothing of trade unionism, but who is deeply concerned with gold mining.'[35] Mackenzie King's private insistence on Hepburn's 'fascism' – a judgment echoed by many around him[36] – was by no means the product of an overheated imagination. McCullagh later went on to found the Leadership League, backed by his own demagogic radio speeches, which, with an emphasis on cleaning out 'politics,' restoring the 'discipline' and 'moral fibre' of the nation, and the necessity for strong leadership, did indeed bear many fascist overtones.[37] That such movements found little mass support in Canada does not detract from the significance of such a tendency among certain sectors of Ontario capitalism close to Hepburn.

Just how extreme Hepburn's views on the union issue were is indicated by the astonishing fact that at the very height of his ephemeral popularity over Oshawa, the premier actually tried to sink the Liberal party into a coalition with the Conservatives, for the purpose of cementing a non-partisan front against 'communist' labour agitation in the province. This dream of big business – a suspension of party politics on behalf of emergency protection of business profits – might even include, Hepburn told a startled Tory leader, Earl Rowe, his own retirement from the premiership, the elevation of the leader of a mere seventeen Tory members of the legislature to the highest office, and the right to name half the cabinet. That Hepburn was not acting on his own in this was clearly indicated when he told Rowe that upon his acceptance Rowe's debts would be covered and he would be provided with an 'honorarium' of 'several hundred thousand dollars.' The coalition was explicitly linked by Hepburn to the concept that only a strong government could 'beat the CIO and stop them from getting into the mines.' Hepburn also had one other major enemy: 'I will never be satisfied until King's political heels go through the wringer,' he told Rowe.[38] Rowe refused to be drawn into this dark and perplexing scheme, but his chief lieutenant in the Conservative ranks, Colonel George Drew, resigned in protest over Rowe's reluctance to end the two-party system in order to combat what Drew liked to call 'communism.'

Hepburn's attempt at a rapprochement with the Tories in his own province had failed – although perhaps only because of the premature disclosure of the plan by the *Star* which wished to sabotage it – but Hepburn went on from the aftermath of the Oshawa affair to denounce and repudiate his own national leader, to declare war on the federal Liberal party, and to seek an interprovincial alliance with the Union Nationale administration of Maurice Duplessis in Quebec for the purpose of attacking and defeating the Liberals of Ottawa. To say that the gold mines of northern Ontario had had an effect on the course of Canadian politics in the 1930s would be an understatement. To say that Mitch Hepburn was a creature of these interests would be no exaggeration.

If Hepburn seemed to have been acting as a mouthpiece for other people's interests over gold mining and the Oshawa strike, there was another major economic issue of the 1930s in which the Ontario government was itself a direct, rather than indirect, participant. Ever since the nationalization of the private power interests under a Conservative government earlier in the century, the provincial government had been in the hydro-electric power business. Ontario Hydro was, as Viv Nelles has brilliantly demonstrated in *The Politics of Development*, much, much more than just another Crown corporation. Although the crusading advocate of public power, Sir Adam Beck, had passed from the scene, the activities of Ontario Hydro continued to play a major role in Ontario politics. Indeed, it was a scandal in Hydro, skilfully, even ruthlessly, exploited by Hepburn and Arthur Roebuck, which helped bring down the Conservative government in 1934. Many of the leading preoccupations of politics in the Hepburn years revolved around power questions, and many of Hepburn's many shifts and oscillations in relation to the federal government can be explained in terms of the inner logic of the power business.

When Hepburn came to office he found himself presiding over what seemed to be a power surplus. After purging the leadership of Hydro, Hepburn went on to take the dramatic move of repudiating contracts made by the previous administration for the import of power from three Quebec power companies, including Beauharnois. The courts subsequently ruled out the legality of repudiation. Hepburn then faced the embarrassing task of restoring the contracts and finding an outlet for the power. The obvious answer was the traditional one of exporting surpluses to the United States. This involved the approval of the federal government, as well as the American government. The latter announced that it was unwilling to accept Hydro's terms, just at the moment when Hepburn had been mounting a massive lobby in Ottawa to gain support for Arthur Slaght's private bill for an export licence. The provincial government was caught between an American and Canadian government, both of which Hepburn believed were conspiring to force Ontario into supporting the St Lawrence Seaway project, to which Hydro was now opposed. Instead, Ontario wanted to carry out a Long Lac diversion, which would not fit in with the Seaway project at all. There the matter rested, at dead stalemate. Federal-provincial relationships, and the relations between the federal and provincial Liberal parties, were severely strained by this stalemate, which was exacerbated when Duplessis weighed in on the side of the Ontario premier. As Nelles sums up: 'Ontario Hydro provided the substance of dominion-provincial disagreement; Mitchell Hepburn supplied the rhetoric.'[39]

In keeping with his normal style, Mackenzie King contributed little in the way of public rhetoric to this dispute; he instead maintained what a later generation would call a 'low profile.' But in private, King was scathing. In his diary he wrote that

This is a clear case of seeking to pay part of his [Hepburn's] election debts through an obligation entered into with the big power interests of Quebec on the one hand, who have been the allies of the big moneyed mining interests on the other. We have right in Ontario today what they have in Italy and Germany in the leading political organs being controlled by moneyed power; the head of the Government completely indifferent to Parliament playing a demagogic role for the sake of power, but really hand and glove with financial interests using the State to serve their own ends.[40]

There were many in the federal party who believed that Hepburn's actions on hydro power represented a little more than the public interests of a Crown corporation. Arthur Roebuck told King that his dismissal from the provincial cabinet had been only ostensibly due to the CIO strike in Oshawa, that the 'true explanation' lay in Hydro, 'and in the fact that I have apparently stood in the way of future private profits from that public enterprise.'[41] King had other circumstantial evidence that Hepburn had received campaign funds from Quebec power interests, particularly Beauharnois, now under the control of Sir Herbert Holt's Montreal Light, Heat, and Power, and that Hepburn's motive in opposing the Seaway project was to allow the Quebec private power companies to export their own surpluses. There was much talk in Ottawa about the 'power ring' which allegedly controlled Hepburn and Duplessis.[42] Information on this count is much sketchier than in the case of the gold mining interests and the CIO. Final judgment as to the facts must be reserved. But there is no doubt that the idea had wide credence among the Ottawa Liberals. As such, it formed part of a pattern which placed Hepburn and the provincial Liberal party behind an entire series of private interests having to do with natural resource development, all in opposition to the federal government, and dedicated to advancing their own interests through the advance of provincial power within Canadian federalism.

One final incident in the long list of disputes between the two wings of the party may be touched on briefly at this point. The patronage question of the lieutenant-governorship of the province in 1937 was scarcely of equal consequence with the large issues of labour unions and power exports, yet it serves to indicate that the depth of the division was such that it would be manifested in trivial and formal matters as well as important ones. Hepburn had decided after his second victory at the polls in 1937 that he wished to close down Chorley Park, the residence of the lieutenant-governor, presumably as a sort of populist gesture against extravagance in government. When King balked at Hepburn's advice to replace the incumbent, Dr. Herbert Bruce, with Duncan Marshall, Hepburn's defeated agriculture minister (the latter had an 'uncouth manner,' King noted), Hepburn went ahead and advanced the date for the closure of Chorley Park as an act of defiance. A last-minute compromise was reached when King agreed to appoint the unwanted Marshall to the Senate, and replace Dr Bruce with Albert Matthews, former Toronto financial collector for the party. Chorley Park was closed, never to reopen. The entire affair had, in King's own words, the aura of 'opéra bouffe.'[43] There was almost no matter which could escape the relentless enmity between King and Hepburn in this period.

These disputes, great or small as the case may be, were constantly deepened and reinforced by the personalities of the two men. Hepburn was convinced that King had always been 'out against him,' that he was being patronized in his dealings with the crusty old gentleman in Ottawa, in short, that he was a victim of a certain degree of snobbery. Hepburn was always reporting his feelings of 'hurt' over remarks made about, or allegedly made about, him in Ottawa.[44] King was not personally wounded by the things Hepburn said about him, because he felt himself superior to the Ontario upstart to start with: he no more minded Hepburn's attacks, he told George McCullagh, than he would a 'dog barking at the front door.' Instead of injured pride, King manifested an icy and sometimes brutal contempt. Hepburn was an 'ass,' an 'alcoholic,' a 'gangster,' a 'dumb ... greedy dog,' a 'fascist.'[45]

That Hepburn's personal life was somewhat more garish than that usually associated with Ontario politicians was a fact widely noted at the time. A British journalist recounted the following visit to the office of the premier in 1936:

From the room behind him came the sounds of radio dance music and ice tinkling in glasses and girls' voices ... Mitchell Hepburn led me into the room where the radio was playing, and introduced me to his friends. They were his doctor and a member of his Government and two attractive girls who sprawled on a sofa and called the Prime Minister 'Chief' ... A big broad-shouldered fellow with the supple movements of a trained athlete mixed drinks ... It was evident that he acted as a sort of bodyguard-cum-gentleman's servant to the Prime Minister. The latter called him 'Eddie,' but the girls just called him 'Bruiser.'[46]

Another contemporary account of Hepburn's life as a politician comes from Escott Reid, who spent a hectic day or two with him in 1932:

The evening he had been in Toronto, Harry Johnson, the Lib organizer for Ontario, had taken him on a party with some newspaper men ... He had had a good deal to drink and had a bad head the next morning. The next evening in Peterboro after the banquet we gathered with a gang of stalwarts in a room in a hotel and drank more whisky. One man talked to Hepburn about a war disability he should have but apart from that little business was done. It was all socialbility [sic]. After that there was a talk at Judge Huyck's and at about two in the morning he started off to Pt. Hope to catch the Toronto sleeper in order to be in the city for a meeting the next day. Only a tremendously strong man could stand the strain of that week in and week out. He apparently never reads anything but the newspapers and memoranda furnished him by others, cranks or friends or party organizers, but even if he had the capacity and desire to read he would find little time for it.[47]

Rumours which circulated about Hepburn's racy life were not exaggerations. As Harry Johnson once told Norman Lambert: 'if you hear anything break regarding Hepburn & women, you'll know it's probably true.'[48]

It goes without saying that such behaviour was not such as to endear the provincial leader to Mackenzie King. And, indeed, King most often personalized the dispute between the two governments to a 'lack of character' on the part of Hepburn and his associates, men whom he felt 'belong to a different class of persons, a class to whom business of government should never have been entrusted,' 'unprincipled men, fond of drinking, good fellowship, and really uncomfortable in the presence of men of perspective, culture, and integrity.' In an inspired phrase, King once referred to the Hepburn people in his diary as 'beggars on horseback.'[49] Beyond the self-serving rationalizations and simple snobbery which characterized much of King's attitude towards Hepburn, this phrase quite brilliantly captured the essence of the social forces which Hepburn represented. The rising young demagogues of the provinces and the capitalist interests which they advocated, represented the *nouveaux riches*, with all the rough-edged aggressiveness and lack of manners usually associated with such forces attempting to push their way on stage against the opposition of the older, better entrenched, and more mellowed forces of the established order. Mackenzie King and Mitch Hepburn may have personalized their conflict since it was an easier and more manageable way of dealing with what was after all a rather complex set of changing circumstances and contradictory interests. Yet the extent to which these two men appropriately personified in their own lives the conflicting forces at work is itself an interesting, even remarkable, historical observation.

One other factor having to do with personality ought to be mentioned as salient to the outcome of the conflict. Hepburn's particular personality and style of life did not prepare him very well for the kind of struggle he had to wage with King. His mercurial and erratic temperament, his predilection for the bar room brawl as a means of settling differences, as well as the generally debilitating effects of his somewhat dissolute habits, made him in the end an easy mark for the patient, sober, and cunning old politician in Ottawa. As Hepburn's sympathetic biographer puts it, 'Mitch Hepburn's "loose living," excessive drinking, philandering, and partying impaired his physical well-being, blurred his judgment, shortened his political career, and complicated his family life.'[50] Hepburn the man burned his candle at both ends, and ended up extinguished. His antagonist, as always, survived.

THE KING – HEPBURN FEUD: STRATEGY AND TACTICS

Until this stage we have tried to indicate some of the underlying factors which went into the making of the dispute. It remains to examine the strategy and tactics of the two sides as they fought the issues out. It is clear from the historical record that the protagonists had more or less well-defined goals, had developed broad strategic plans to achieve these goals, and particular styles of behaviour with regard to tactical situations. The Hepburn strategy will be examined first, since Hepburn was the initiator of the conflict, and then the federal reaction to Hepburn's challenge. One external factor intervened which fundamentally altered the balance of power between the two forces: this was Canada's entry into the Second World War, which will be discussed separately in the next section.

The most immediate weapon which Hepburn could utilize was the control of the provincial leader over the party organization in the province, and the exclusion of the federal party from direct access to the party machinery. Since the Liberal party had never developed separate federal and provincial organizations to any extent, a strong provincial leader could squeeze the federal leaders out of the picture by the simple expedient of dominating the existing party machinery. Three factors facilitated this strategy in Hepburn's case. First, he achieved power in Ontario while the federal party was out of office, and did so largely through his own efforts. Thus freed of obligations, he could set about systematically taking charge of the party apparatus, with a virtual monopoly of patronage powers. Second, the Ontario leadership of the federal party was particularly enfeebled at this time and offered little effective resistance to Hepburn's takeover. Later, new men such as C.D. Howe and Norman Rogers were to achieve stronger leadership positions, but they required time to develop. Third, and most importantly of all, the provincial party had access to funding from which the federal party could be excluded. This financial whiphand was the most crucial factor of all; it was, in one sense, the instrument to achieve all of Hepburn's goals with regard to the party.

Hepburn's moves in the period between his provincial victory in 1934 and the federal victory the following year have already been indicated. Subsequent to the installation of the new King government in Ottawa, and the open falling-out of the two parties over such matters as Hepburn's advice on cabinet selection and the Dominion-Provincial Conference of 1935, Hepburn's formal break with the NLF was matched by an explicit exclusion of the federal party from the Ontario machine. Early in 1938 Hepburn told three Ontario MPs that he 'had instructed the provincial organization not to take any part in federal affairs and that he had forbidden the use of the federal party of the Liberal office in the King Edward Hotel,' and that provincial ministers would be forbidden to support the federal party in a federal election campaign. Given Hepburn's complete domination of the Ontario party organization and his refusal to allow any representative gatherings of the Ontario Liberal Association to take place under his tenure of office, his personal fiat in such matters was more or less unquestioned. Moreover, when the premier could back his moves with the threat of such patronage clubs as raising hydro rates and stopping all road work in the event of King calling a federal election, it may be seen that he had very real resources at hand.[51]

Another level at which the organizational weapon was employed was in the constituencies. A number of areas of the province, notably Hamilton, Ottawa, and the Lakehead, were the scenes of federal-provincial factionalism as the Hepburn forces tried either to take over the federal riding associations or to freeze the federal members out of the picture. Such devices as 'independent Liberal' candidates with provincial support or even the threat of Hepburn backing for Tory candidates could be used to some effect in certain local situations. Hamilton, where the president of the Ontario Liberal Association and provincial minister of the patronage-rich Highways Department, T.B. McQuesten, was the provincial member, was one example of the success of this strategy, where federal riding associations eventually had to be rebuilt from scratch. As one Liberal associated with the federal party in Woodstock informed King in 1938, 'life is very difficult these days for a sincere Liberal,' either in the local riding association, where Hepburn influence had extended itself, or in the Twentieth Century club, which 'seems to be dying out in Ontario very quickly and what little of it there is left is used as a cheer leading section for Hepburn.'[52]

An .extension of Hepburn's divisive strategy was to carry the battle into the federal Liberal caucus at Ottawa itself. Certain Ontario MPs were known to be Hepburn men. Among them were Arthur Slaght, the crux of the patronage dispute over the 1935 cabinet selection; W.H. Moore, who was a bitter opponent of King's ever since the Beauharnois affair had brought the leader's wrath down upon his head; and W.A. Fraser and Ross Grey, who in Norman Lambert's view were drawn into the Hepburn orbit through 'bridge contracts.' When Hepburn was turned down by the federal cabinet on hydro exports in 1937, he made open threats to the cabinet about the loyalty of the Ontario MPs.[53] The government back benches are, however, notorious seedbeds of discontent in majority government situations. Much more alarming to King was the possibility that Hepburn's reach may have extended into the cabinet itself. There is no substantive information indicating anything in the nature of an actual conspiracy against King's leadership on the part of his ministers, although there were three of the prime minister's colleagues sometimes rumoured to be close to Hepburn. Jimmy Gardiner, who was always the most independent of ministers, had frequent meetings with Hepburn in which the dispute between the two parties was discussed in considerable detail, and some courses of action to resolve the situation debated. There was, of course, a thin line between acting as a representative of one side in discussions with the other, and acting as a kind of double agent for both sides with the possibility of personal advantage to be gained thereby. Norman Rogers, for one, was convinced that Gardiner was disloyal, and told King so. Gardiner himself relayed the message to his prime minister after one session with the Ontario premier that Hepburn wished to replace King with himself, Gardiner, as national party leader. This confidence tends to indicate that Gardiner was not in fact acting with Hepburn, and King confided to his diary that he thought his agriculture minister was simply playing both sides, while remaining basically loyal. He was less sure about Ian Mackenzie, another minister close to Hepburn personally. King also suspected Chubby Power, although the evidence for Power's role is doubtful at best: perhaps it was no more than King's suspicion of 'Irish Catholic drinking men.'[54] In any event, the very existence of such suspicions, not only among the cabinet ministers themselves but even in the back benches and to some extent in the press, was itself a weapon in Hepburn's hands. The appearance of disunity at the heart of the federal Liberal government itself could only strengthen Hepburn's hand in the ruthless game being played out between the two men.

The takeover of the party organization, the exclusion of the federal party, attacks on the federal constituency organizations, the spreading of disunity into the federal caucus, and perhaps even into the cabinet itself, all these were made possible by one decisive resource held by Hepburn: the power of the purse. Hepburn's superior command over financial resources was his ultimate trump card. It was one which he played again and again, with devastating effect.

Late in 1937 King visited Hepburn personally in his Queen's Park office in a vain attempt to resolve the situation with some summit diplomacy. As the prime minister noted in his diary, Hepburn:

spoke of how during the campaign of 1935, he had, as he described it, placed the entire organization of his party at the disposal of the Dominion Government [sic]. He seems to have the idea that every man who contributes funds in Ontario is contributing to an Ontario organization. With equal truth, one might say that the Dominion had placed its entire Ontario forces at the disposal of his Government in the Ontario campaign. He spoke of what O'Connor and one or two others had done. Where he is entirely wrong is in assuming that contributions made to either campaign belonged to an organization which was distinctly provincial or federal. Such has never been the case in Ontario. [55]

However comforting such constitutional arguments based on prescriptive rights might be to the national leader, they were entirely beside the point. Hepburn had simply changed the basis on which business had previously been done in the Ontario Liberal party.

Some of the factors which went into Hepburn's financial control – his access to the natural resource extracting industries; his ability to attract such efficient collectors as Frank O'Connor; and his lack of scruples in attaching donations to promises of government policy – have been discussed above, as well as in Chapters 2 and 3. Hepburn was also willing to use his patronage powers to cut the federal party off from their own sources. The provincial Liberal party treasurer, Bethune Smith, informed one of Norman Lambert's federal collectors that 'any money spent in Ontario on roads or anything else by Ottawa must accrue to Ontario.' If that threat did not carry sufficient weight, the federal party already had evidence of one contractor being cut out of two provincial jobs by McQuesten's Highways Department as a 'penalty' for having contributed to the federal party, and of another construction company being warned to stay away from the Ottawa party if it wanted any further provincial business.[56] It is interesting to note that Bethune Smith, who was a brother-in-law and legal guardian of future Conservative MP George Hees, was close to the federal Conservative party even in this period. In the 1940 general election he contributed at least

$10,000 to the Conservative national campaign fund.[57] In other words, Hepburn's men were willing not only to cut federal collectors off from their sources, but to offer support to the federal party's opponents as well. Norman Lambert summed up the entire situation with precision early in 1938 when he entered the following equation in his diary:

Elections account = looks bad,
Political expenditures = rotten.
Effect of swinging influence to provinces.[58]

Hepburn had one further tactic to be employed in his struggle with King. This was to strike alliances with political forces hostile to the federal party. When George Drew became provincial Conservative leader in Ontario, Hepburn more or less revived the scheme which he had proferred to Drew's predecessor, Earl Rowe. This time, however, no formal coalition was entered into; rather a tacit alliance was established. Drew saw no reason to deter Hepburn from warring against the federal Tories' greatest enemy in Ottawa. Hepburn at the same time hoped to protect his own position internally in order to devote more time and energy to the external foe.

Much more significant than this alliance, however, was Hepburn's well-publicized foray into interprovincial alliances with the Union Nationale government in Quebec. Not only did the Ontario premier make common cause with Maurice Duplessis on the federal-provincial issues of the day, such as their united front against the Rowell-Sirois Commission, but it is important to understand that Hepburn tried to extend his *intra-party* struggle into Quebec as well. With Duplessis in Hepburn's 'hip-pocket,' in Harry Johnson's phrase, Hepburn decided in 1938 to deal what might have been a death-blow to the federal party's finances by extending his blockade to the other major Liberal fund-raising centre, Montreal. Johnson was delegated to contact Montreal collectors Donat Raymond and Gordon Scott to sound out the possibility of a working arrangement to force the federal Liberals either to drop King in favour of Gardiner as prime minister or to come to terms with Hepburn's demands, including the right to name at least one cabinet minister from Ontario. Hepburn also dropped hints to some Ontario MPs that if Lapointe and Rinfret were removed from the federal cabinet Duplessis might 'either quietly support the federal Liberals in Quebec or at least mind his own business.' Thus the bare outlines of a deal between the Ontario Liberals, the Union Nationale, and the federal Liberals in Quebec can be glimpsed, a deal in which the provincial régimes would emerge with at least partial control over the federal cabinet.

The moment for Hepburn's move into Montreal Liberal circles was opportune in one sense: Raymond was at the point of an open break with King over the latter's refusal to appoint his brother as minister to Paris. Gordon Scott, however, was not disposed to add his participation to the conspiracy. Instead, Scott immediately informed Norman Lambert, who told King. Scott then visited the prime minister in Ottawa and recounted the details of the Johnson mission to Montreal.[59] Raymond was eased out of financial collections in the city and the Ontario scheme failed to get off the ground. This attempt to extend the federal-provincial battle onto the national stage by outflanking the federal party leadership with regard to party funding even outside his own province represented perhaps the most ambitious of all Hepburn's tactics. That it failed was crucial to the defence of the federal party against the Ontario challenge. That it was even attempted demonstrates just how serious matters had become in the Liberal party with regard to Lambert's 'swinging influence to provinces.'

Such were the main outlines of the Hepburn strategy. On the other side of the battle lines, the strategy of Mackenzie King was rather different in style, as might be expected. The prime minister was inclined to wait the affair out patiently, while maintaining a calm, above-the-battle stance becoming to the dignity of the high office he held and the authority and prestige of the government which he led. Despite the constant, sometimes maddening, provocations, King consistently refused to fight on Hepburn's terms, which were those of the bar room brawl. He was guided in this not only by his own sense of dignity, but by a shrewd understanding of the instability of his opponent: 'As he [Hepburn] gets more irritable through alcoholic strain,' King mused in his diary in the thick of the fight in 1938, 'other breaks will come and he will go to pieces. That is my reason for holding back and saying nothing for the present.' In short, King thought it wisest to 'give him enough rope ...' King's conciliatory and patient attitude won support from both the press and the public. Alway suggests that Hepburn simply 'could not understand' these tactics; the premier *wanted* personal attacks in return, in order to put the fight on a basis with which he was familiar and comfortable. 'It was,' Alway concludes, 'very much the case of the reckless swashbuckler pitted against a wily and experienced fencing master.'[60]

The old fencing master was not content merely to evade the lunges of his opponent. By 1938 King was quietly preparing the ground for a counterattack. When a Saskatchewan provincial minister reported that Hepburn had said that he was willing to destroy the Liberal party in order to destroy Mackenzie King, the latter knew that the rope was long enough.[61] Following the abortive attempt to enlist the Montreal finance committee on Hepburn's side, King called a cabinet meeting at which he disclosed what had happened and then asked Jimmy Gardiner to tell his colleagues what Hepburn had suggested to him at their secret meetings. This Gardiner did, fully and frankly, in King's view. King then went on to state that the time had come to confront Queen's Park since King now had definite evidence that Hepburn had not only tried to sell out his own party in Ontario by entering a coalition with the Conservatives before the 1937 election, but, worse yet, Hepburn had come to an understanding with R.J. Manion and the federal Tories for the next national election. He went on to detail some of the patronage and financial clubs which Hepburn was using on MPs and on backers of the federal party in Ontario. In other words, King put it squarely to his ministers that Hepburn was a 'traitor' to his party and must be stopped. When questioned as to the strategy of counterattack, King suggested that it would be preferable for the ministers themselves to make public statements against Hepburn; this would of course bring Hepburn out in reply, and at this point 'I could then follow the matter up, and would not be put in the position of seeming to defend myself; that it was the Government that was at stake.'

Privately, King remained doubtful about the loyalty of some of his colleagues, but he also was sure, if he forced the issue at this point, 'that they all knew that I am the only one who can hold the Party together and carry it through the next campaign.' What the rest of the ministers did not know was that Howe and Rogers were already preparing to take the fight to Hepburn directly. These two crucial Ontario ministers had been in consultation with the prime minister over the situation in Port Arthur, where the Hepburn forces had been attempting to unseat Howe at a nominating convention. Rogers accompanied Howe to the meeting and both men issued strong statements of denunciation of the Hepburn-Duplessis 'conspiracy.' The opposition to Howe melted away at the appearance of this onslaught, and he was renominated unanimously. Without having to commit himself publicly, King had forced the issue through the intermediary of his two most important Ontario ministers. Thus King had been able to line up his cabinet behind him, and to place Hepburn on the defensive. When Hepburn reacted predictably by telling newsmen that he was going to vote for Manion in the next election, King was elated. Hepburn was beginning to tie the rope around his own neck.[62] At this point, King himself stepped publicly into the dispute with a statement supporting Rogers.

With the cabinet behind him, King's next move was to line up the Ontario federal caucus – as well as to flush out any jokers in the deck. A special meeting was called of Ontario MPs, defeated candidates, and senators at which their loyalty was 'unreservedly' pledged to Mackenzie King. Recalcitrant members not present were pressed to sign the resolution, with the prime minister's own office managing the affair behind the scenes. Frank O'Connor did not sign, but he was ill. Two other noteworthy absences were Arthur Slaght and W.H. Moore. But, on the whole, it was a major triumph for the prime minister's leadership, even if many of the members, in Alway's words, 'probably felt squeamish about a meeting which obviously put them very much on the spot.' That, of course, was the whole point. As a gesture toward reconciliation, a small subcommittee was struck to explore the possibility of Hepburn returning to the fold, but nothing came of this initiative. The next stage in this process of consolidation was to take the case to the entire Liberal caucus, which was done early in the new year.[63]

The subsequent step in King's plan was to attempt to draw some of Hepburn's men back into the federal orbit. The patronage powers of the federal government could in some cases be used to this effect. Once Frank O'Connor had been appointed to the Senate, his independence from Hepburn's influence grew to the point where as early as 1936 he was defying Hepburn's financial blockade of the federal party and continuing to raise some money for the national party.[64] By early 1939 King was actually ready to appoint Arthur Slaght to the cabinet – the very point which Hepburn had been so insistent upon three years earlier – apparently on the assumption that the appointment might offer 'the link through which proper relations can be established anew with the Ontario Government.' The difference would now be that Slaght would be in the cabinet by grace of King and not Hepburn. Slaght, however, declined this somewhat surprising offer. Arthur Hardy, the wealthy and powerful party backroom figure, who had been close to Hepburn in the early days of his provincial leadership and who had privately supported him on his anti-CIO stand in 1937, grew worried about the 'astonishing personality' of the Ontario leader and his potential for becoming the 'laughing stock of the country.' Hardy told King that he had since 1919 contributed about $200,000 to the Liberal party, of which $25,000 had gone to Hepburn. Since he had believed that this would benefit the federal party in Ontario, he had now changed his mind: he would not 'say anything against the present regime but will not contribute a word or a dollar.'[65]

Another level of struggle was entrusted to Norman Lambert, who was asked to rebuild a viable financial structure in Toronto to compete against Hepburn's blockade. Old friends of the federal party in that city, such as J.S. McLean of Canada Packers (who said he had 'no use' for Hepburn) and C.L. Burton of Simpson's, were enlisted to co-operate with federal collection efforts. The new Toronto finance committee set up by Lambert has already been discussed (see Chapters 3 and 4), but the point here is that the federal party was by no means without resources in the financial front.[66] Lambert's contract levy system was bound to yield some returns to the federal party, however much Hepburn tried to scare away contractors. While the provincial party might have more patronage at its disposal and fewer legal barriers to directing government business to friends of the party, it was also true that the federal government was a large, and growing, operation with which many businesses would wish to come to terms. As the shadows of world war lengthened over the little political stage of Canada in the late 1930s, the rise of defence spending as a major component of federal spending opened up whole new avenues for federal party funding. Hepburn had used the natural resource companies to great effect, but they were, after all, only one section of Canadian capitalism; the federal party was quite capable of enlisting the support of other sectors on their behalf. The large electoral fund amassed by Lambert for the 1940 election campaign clearly indicates that in the end Hepburn's blockade, however irritating it had been at earlier stages, failed in the long run.

The final stage of King's strategy was to take the issue to the Ontario constituencies and the voters. First, the federal party decided to demand that the Ontario Liberal Association hold a convention at which the dispute could be openly debated. When this initiative was rebuffed it was decided that 'direct action' should be taken by federal MPs to set up a new provincial association. By the summer of 1939 a new 'National Liberal Committee for Ontario' headed by 'Bart' Sullivan of Hamilton had been set up – appropriately enough in the *Toronto Star* building. The new organization was financed out of Lambert's national fund, and indeed was largely a result of Lambert's own careful behind-the-scenes management, despite his personal dislike of 'this sort of an arbitrary set-up.' At the same time, efforts were being redoubled in the constituencies where the provincial machine had made inroads into federal strength in recent years, especially in Hamilton and Toronto, to build independent, federally oriented associations in preparation for the next election.[67]

Underlying all these moves was the growing confidence in Ottawa that Hepburn was only a 'paper tiger.' Following his dismissal from the provincial cabinet over the CIO issue, David Croll was elected mayor of Windsor by a large majority, despite Hepburn's 'vigorous personal intervention' against him. Moreover, there was consensus among the party leaders in Ottawa that in the event of an open electoral confrontation between Hepburn and the federal party, the federal party would win. The combination of Hepburn's provincialism and his methods of political confrontation were widely believed to be working in favour of the federal party with the large mass of the electorate. Evidence of this, and of the continued fidelity of local party activists to the federal, as well as provincial, party, was not slow in coming to Ottawa's attention.

Hepburn's real problem, as Alway has pointed out, was at the constituency level, where the integration of federal and provincial organizations was generally so close, and the personal obligations of mutual support entered into by federal and provincial members so well established, that Hepburn was quite simply unable to break the traditional web of interdependence. Not a single federal nominating convention in an Ontario constituency in 1939 failed to attract the attendance of the local Liberal MLA. When the NLF held a twentieth anniversary dinner for Mackenzie King in Toronto, as a clear act of defiance of Hepburn, fourteen provincial members braved the wrath of their leader by attending. While King had managed to whip his own dissidents more or less into line by his clever tactics, Hepburn's caucus was increasingly divided. Harry Nixon, who was perhaps the second most prominent member of the provincial cabinet, was quite openly at odds with the premier on the question of relations with the federal party. Even Harry Johnson, Hepburn's organizer, did his best to maintain links with the federal organization.[68] The problem with Hepburn's flamboyant attack on Ottawa was that the local party activists did not see themselves as provincial Liberals first, and federal Liberals second. Much less did they see themselves as pawns to be suddenly shuffled across the board to work for the traditional enemies, the Tories. In the local committee rooms they were becoming increasingly puzzled, resentful, and worried about what Hepburn was doing to their party. Hepburn's charisma had taken him just so far; provincialism which jumped traditional party lines took him no further. In the end, it was Mackenzie King who demonstrated sounder political instincts, despite Hepburn's frequent aspersions on the prime minister's advanced age and allegedly anachronistic ideas.

THE SECOND WORLD WAR AND THE FALL OF HEPBURN

It would appear that the logic of events was impelling the provincial Liberals toward defeat. In terms of political resources and personality factors, King held the stronger hand. But the intervention of an external event, the coming of war in late 1939, fundamentally transformed the situation and altered the balance of forces in a way which sealed Hepburn's fate.

The first effect of the war on the federal-provincial dispute was to turn public opinion against narrow provincialism in politics. This nationalizing effect on opinion can hardly be overestimated in its ultimate significance for federal-provincial relations. Populist provincial leaders like Hepburn suddenly found that the old standby of provincial rights and kicking Ottawa no longer generated much response among the voters, whose attention had shifted to the national cause of winning the war. When the Rowell-Sirois Commission held hearings in British Columbia, for example, Premier T.D. Pattullo once more reiterated his familiar attacks on the federal government; this time he suddenly found himself alone, as brief after brief sought ways to support the federal government in the war effort. Not only did opinion shift toward the federal government, but under the powerful authority of the War Measures Act, Canada's 'other constitution' in D.V. Smiley's phrase,[69] the actual powers of the provincial governments were severely curtailed.

The war had been only a few months old when Hepburn lost his erstwhile provincial ally with the sudden defeat of the Union Nationale in Quebec. As his defences crumbled around him, Hepburn desperately sought alternatives. One was to strike a firm alliance with George Drew and the provincial Conservatives as a united front against Ottawa around a win-the-war strategy. If provincialism no longer had resonance in the population, then perhaps super-patriotism could mobilize the masses against Ottawa. Accordingly, a delegation of Hepburn, Drew, and the lieutenant-governor, Albert Matthews, visited Ottawa in October to discuss 'ways and means by which Ontario can best serve Canada in this great crisis.' This 'bizarre delegation,' in Jack Pickersgill's phrase, gave Ottawa the impression of renewed co-operation. The Ontario premier, however, gave quite a different version to a reporter from the *Toronto Star*. Despite Hepburn's reversal of his opposition to the St Lawrence Seaway project – which was couched in the language of sacrifice, but which actually reflected a new set of interests surrounding Ontario Hydro's planning – his suggestions about how Ottawa should be running the war effort were not greeted with immediate enthusiasm by the federal government. Hepburn, hurt and angry as usual, began, in his biographer's words, to crusade for 'what he almost considered his own war effort.'[70]

Matching Hepburn's provincial common front with Drew was the attempt at the federal level to force the installation of a 'national government' of the two major parties. Nothing could of course be better calculated to rouse the violent antagonism of Mackenzie King than this coalition scheme, haunted as he was by the memory of what Union government had done to the Liberal party in the previous war. The fact that support for 'national government' within the federal caucus came from the same people who had been closest to Hepburn previous to the war, was for King the last straw. Arthur Slaght led the move from within the Liberal party. Rumours were rife of plots to remove King and form a coalition government, with provincial backing. King's imagination ran rampant: 'the whole business is part of a conspiracy in which the cloven hoof of the gang is only too apparent.' A vast conspiracy took shape in the prime minister's mind which included an astonishing panoply of Canadians, including Hepburn, Drew, C. George McCullagh, John Bassett of the *Montreal Gazette*, the mining companies, the private power interests, Sam McLaughlin (owner of General Motors), the CPR, Arthur Slaght, W.H. Moore, Social Credit (a 'Communist Nazi organization'), W.D. Herridge, and even the CCF![71] It was not clear from this who was left in the country to defend King's government. In fact, his situation was very strong, whatever his personal paranoia.

Early in 1940 the long-awaited 'break' came in Queen's Park, when Hepburn introduced his resolution condemning the federal war effort in the Ontario legislature. At long last King knew that Hepburn had finally hanged himself, on the very rope which King had generously extended him over the years. King wrote the next day in his diary that Hepburn had fallen into the same trap that had swallowed up Duplessis a few months earlier: he had done 'just what is needed to place beyond question the wisdom of an immediate election and the assurance of a victory for the government.' Not only did Hepburn's action give the federal Liberals the issue on which they were to receive an overwhelming mandate from the electorate, but it also split the provincial party. Twenty to twenty-five Liberals hid in the corridors when the resolution was put to the vote, and ten openly opposed it. Of those who did join in the vote along with the Tories, another twenty-five later supported the federal party in the election campaign. At least five members of Hepburn's cabinet itself actively supported the federal campaign, including Harry Nixon who appeared on a public platform beside King, after a well-publicized controversy with his premier. After the rout of the Tory opposition, Manion wrote to thank Hepburn for his efforts against the 'fat little jelly fish out at Kingsmere' who 'somehow' always 'seems to come out on top.'[72]

Following the federal victory, it was clear to most observers that Hepburn's days were numbered. The federal party felt secure enough in Ontario to close down the special organization previously set up in competition with Hepburn's machine, and give the director of the office a job in the government at Ottawa. At the same time cries were heard within Ontario for the calling of an Ontario Liberal Association convention. Hepburn hung on to the remnants of power, and made one last effort to strike out at King by supporting Arthur Meighen in the York South by-election of 1942. His reverse in that endeavour was the seal on his coffin. Strange, eccentric, and perplexing actions followed, as the premier made gestures towards Social Credit in Alberta, towards the Communists (the menace of which he had tried to rid the province only a few years earlier, now become patriotic allies of the Liberal party), towards some vaguely defined 'All-Canada' movement. His actions were, in his biographer's words, 'confused, incoherent, almost irrational.' Many suspected that the man had simply gone over the edge. Finally, in late 1942, Hepburn resigned the office of premier. His reasons were bizarre, 'the product of an imagination diseased and warped by hatred for King.'[73]

Even in taking his leave, Hepburn stirred up divisions within his already shattered party. Once the autocratic hand which had tightly controlled the party machinery for twelve years was lifted, the party began, not surprisingly, to fly off in all directions. Yet Hepburn had appointed his own successor, Gordon Conant, without consulting even his cabinet or caucus, let alone any more representative body of the Ontario party. Since Conant was not viewed as a good choice, resentments were rife. At this point, Mackenzie King decided to intervene directly by asking his Ontario ministers to instruct their riding associations to call for a provincial convention. As the calls for a convention began flowing in, Hepburn continued his erratic course, entering the Conant cabinet as finance minister only to be fired shortly after. But the federal party was now ascendant. Eight federal cabinet ministers attended the convention, determined to put an acceptable man into the position. Harry Nixon, who had been the leading pro-King minister in the Hepburn cabinet, won easily over Arthur Roebuck and two other candidates. Along with the routing of the old Hepburn forces, the aroused delegates to the convention took their revenge on the people who had turned the Ontario Liberal Association into a dead letter during the Hepburn years. The constitution of the OLA was drastically revised to bar cabinet ministers, elected parliamentary members, or civil servants from holding the office of OLA president. This was a direct rebuff to T.B. McQuesten who as highways minister and OLA president from 1930 to 1943 had refused to call a single meeting.[74] There could be no doubt about the significance of the convention for the long dispute between the two wings of the party. As King wrote with great self-satisfaction in his diary:

it was a King-Hepburn battle so far as the province generally was concerned, with a complete routing of all the Hepburn forces, and he and his right and left bowers wounded and bleeding on the field – no one prepared to lend them succour of any kind ... it is a great triumph – a wonderful expression of loyalty. It reveals the extent to which, despite 'everything,' I have been able to keep the party together, in provincial as well as federal politics and this by 'non-resistance,' by refusing to enter a quarrel and through allowing my enemies to confound and destroy themselves. Again I say it is the evidence of a moral order that controls in the end.[75]

Questions of the moral order aside, it is evident that Mackenzie King's superior strategy as well as the superior political resources of the federal party, and the external intervention of the war, had defeated Mitch Hepburn's ambitious but ill-considered attack on the national Liberal party. What King's victory over his rival could not do, however, was to restore the provincial Liberal party in the eyes of the voters. Seldom has a government leader in this country acted in a manner so calculated to discredit his own party; in his last days Hepburn could just as well have been acting under the orders of the rival Conservative party for all the destructive irrationality of his behaviour. When Nixon led the shattered party to the polls for the first time in six years, it was to a defeat which was more thorough and more devastating than that which Hepburn had dealt the Tory party in 1934. The Liberals fell from 51 per cent to 31 per cent of the popular vote, and lost fifty seats, leaving them a distant third in the legislature behind the victorious Conservatives and the rising CCF. King noted with satisfaction that the only ministers to survive the débâcle in their own seats were three King loyalists, and went on to confess that 'in my inner nature I feel a sense of relief that a Cabinet that has been so unprincipled and devoid of character has been cleaned out of Queen's Park, and that a new Administration, be it what it may, will have to take over affairs for a time. Instead of injuring the federal party, excepting temporarily, it may help to save us in the end. It will show our men, above all, the need for unity and for organization.'[76] King was right that this defeat would not hurt the federal party, but the provincial party has never recovered. Thus the interesting result of the King-Hepburn dispute was a lasting asymmetry in the partisan structure of Ontario politics at the two levels.

THE ONTARIO LIBERALS SINCE HEPBURN

The story of the Liberal party in Ontario politics since the fall of Hepburn is a story of sustained failure, with a monotonous cyclical recurrence of defeat, reorganization, change in leadership, further defeat, and so on. It would be tedious to recount these developments in detail. Money was one problem: there was never enough of it after Hepburn's brief period of affluence. The 1945 provincial election was so badly financed that the party had to give up radio time to the Tories which they had earlier reserved. By 1946-7 the OLA office was struggling along on an annual budget of about $12,000. One party worker complained that the 1948 election was run on a 'shoe string.' In 1955 the entire provincial advertising campaign was only $63,000 – about half what Hepburn had been able to spend almost twenty years earlier.[77] There is even some fragmentary evidence that the federal party barred the provincial party from some of their sources on occasion.[78]

Leadership was another problem endemic to the provincial Liberals. From Hepburn's resignation in 1942 through 1958 the party underwent no fewer than seven changes in leadership, including a last desolate attempt at a comeback by Hepburn himself in the 1945 campaign. Farquhar Oliver was leader twice, having been recycled in 1952 after Walter Thompson had to retire in the face of concerted opposition at an annual meeting.[79]

Money and leadership were problems within a larger context; the chief difficulty of the provincial Liberals was their unpopularity. On 4 June 1945 the provincial party collected a mere 30 per cent of the popular vote; a week later, the federal Liberals captured 42 per cent of the vote in a federal general election. That pattern has since continued. The provincial party has in the postwar period only exceeded one-third of the popular vote on two occasions. The federal party has, on the other hand, been the dominant party in seven out of eleven general elections. The widespread recognition in the aftermath of the Tory victories of 1943-5 that a political watershed had been passed, that in the words of one federally oriented faction in the Toronto district riding associations in 1946, 'we are dead provincially speaking for the next twenty years,'[80] was bound to have a debilitating effect on the very potential for political renewal. The same problem which plagued the provincial Liberal party in Quebec in this same period – the draining away of the party's human resources to the national party – was obvious to all in Ontario. A consequence of these factors was a pathetic desire of the provincial party to hang onto the coat-tails of the federal party for dear life. Provincial constituency associations merged with federal associations, thereby hoping to share in the bounty of popularity and good organization; by the mid-1950s, three-quarters of the riding associations in Ontario were joint federal-provincial affairs. At the behest of provincial leaders, joint committees of federal and provincial members of the legislatures were sporadically established to 'co-ordinate federal-provincial matters.' None of these devices sufficed to restore provincial fortunes. All that remained was a residual sense of property rights over the ruined mansion of provincial Liberalism, which the mortgage holders in Ottawa were more than happy to indulge. 'We of the National Liberal Federation,' Duncan MacTavish wrote patronizingly in 1953, 'have to be careful to avoid any appearance of attempting to dominate provincial organizations and this sort of thing has to be carefully handled.'[81]

It has sometimes been suggested that the federal Liberals had arrived at a mutual non-aggression bargain with the provincial Conservatives. There is little or no substantive evidence for this hypothesis, but even if no explicit arrangements were ever made it remains obvious that neither Ottawa nor Queen's Park showed much inclination to throw all their resources and prestige into battle on behalf of their unhappy counterparts at the other level of government. It is difficult to escape the feeling that somehow or other a *modus vivendi* had been reached. There can certainly be no doubt that, from the federal point of view, dealings with Drew, and particularly with Leslie Frost, were far less difficult than they had been at the best of times with Mitch Hepburn. That observation alone must have given the federal party pause when considering assistance to their provincial wing.

Yet if the federal party offered little positive help to the floundering provincials, it must also be pointed out that the strength of the federal party was indirectly responsible in one sense for the very continuation of the provincial party. As John Wilson and David Hoffman have ably summarized the situation:

...[I]t may well be asked why the Liberals have not long since ceased to be an important element in Ontario politics. For it is not simply the case that they are unable to attract sufficient support to match the performance of the federal party; they are often victims of the very success they enjoy nationally. Their most promising men have generally preferred to move to Ottawa, where opportunities to participate in government were more likely to occur. Coupled with this has been the continued inability of the national party to foster the growth of a permanently strong provincial organization. Moreover, since the period of Hepburn's leadership such help as has been made available has been more in the nature of interference than assistance.

But, paradoxically, the success of the national party may also be the principal reason for the Ontario party's ability to hold its own in the provincial system. The mere existence of a viable Liberal party at the federal level legitimizes the continued, if unsuccessful, competition of its provincial counterpart, and the need to maintain even a nominal federal electoral organization in the province encourages political activity on behalf of the Ontario party.[82]

FEDERAL-PROVINCIAL CAREER PATTERNS

One further exploration may be made of the relationship between the two wings of the party in this period. An examination of the elected career patterns of federal MPs from Ontario for the period of this study indicates a striking insulation of the two spheres of political activity. Table 8.1 shows that almost nine out of ten Liberal MPs from Ontario in this era had careers which were federal only. Of the fifteen MPs with dual federal-provincial careers, twelve had had provincial experience previous to entering a federal career; two went from the federal to the provincial sphere; one went from provincial to federal back to provincial again. Three MPs had been provincial cabinet ministers before entering a federal career; three others went from federal politics to provincial cabinet posts. The latter category accounts for all those who went from the federal to the provincial sphere; it might thus appear that only the promise of cabinet rank was sufficient to attract Liberals from national to provincial politics. Conversely, only one federal cabinet minister in this period had an Ontario provincial career – in this case, both before and after his federal career. Only ten of the 136 Ontario MPs had unsuccessfully contested provincial office at some point in their careers, but even if this number is added to those elected to provincial office the total comes to only 18 per cent. In other words, there is no doubt that the vast majority of federal Liberals had no demonstrated interest in provincial careers. On the other hand, 40 per cent of the MPs had had previous experience in elective *municipal* office before entering federal politics.

The career patterns of twenty-eight Ontario senators appointed by Liberal governments during this period can also be examined. Half of them had previous careers in federal politics, but less than one-fifth had provincial experience. There was only a single case of a former provincial member without federal experience being appointed to the Senate, but Duncan Marshall's appointment had been a highly unusual instance of bargaining between the federal and provincial parties. It might also be remarked that two of the three former provincial cabinet ministers (Croll and Roebuck) appointed to the Senate had left provincial politics in open opposition to the party's provincial leadership. Finally, ten of the senators could readily be identified as having some association with the extra-parliamentary organization or financial apparatus of the party previous to their appointment. Moreover, eight out of fourteen (57 per cent) of senators without elected experience could be thus associated with party organization. The senate, it can be safely concluded, was used as a reward-system for former federal

Table 8.1
Elected career patterns of federal Liberal MPs from Ontario, 1930-58, by decade in which federal career began

Decade elected	Federal career only		Federal and provincial careers		Total
	N	%	N	%	
Before 1930	17	81.0	4	19.0	21
1930s	43	91.5	4	8.5	47
1940s	46	90.2	5	9.8	51ᵃ
1950s	15	88.2	2	11.8	17
Total	121	89.0	15	11.0	136ᵃ

ᵃTotal excludes the Hon. A.L. Macdonald, former Nova Scotia premier who was elected to an Ontario seat during the Second World War and returned to Nova Scotia politics.
Source: information compiled from J.K. Johnson, ed., *The Canadian Directory of Parliament, 1867-1967* (Ottawa, 1968)

members from Ontario or for those who had served the federal party without holding elective office. It was not used to reward those who had assisted the provincial party alone.

In the case of both MPs and senators it is obvious that there was a very high degree of insulation between the two spheres of Liberal party activity. Yet, as with the case of Quebec analysed in the previous chapter, there is little evidence that this separation at the élite level was matched by separation of the local constituency organizations and local activists into distinct groups oriented toward one or the other sphere. While empirical data on this latter point is very incomplete, the available evidence seems to suggest the contrary. Some more recent quantitative data for three Ontario constituencies in fact suggests that the pool of Liberal activists at the local level tends to be either federal-provincial in orientation or federal alone.[83] In other words, the long-term legacy of Hepburn's assault on the federal party has been to diminish the pool of human resources available to the provincial party, while failing to attract any such resources away from the federal party.

This was a poor legacy indeed which Hepburn left his provincial party. The consequences of challenging the elder brother in Ottawa were awesome. The case of Ontario, as well as that of Quebec, indicates that there were very strict limits to the degree of provincial party autonomy possible in federal-provincial party relations, at least in an era when the federal party was dominant in its own sphere of activity.

9

The West

As the seedbed of radical and third-party politics in Canada, the West always presented certain problems to the national Liberal party. Mackenzie King's first few years as Liberal leader were plagued by the rise of farmer and progressive movements, mainly, although not entirely, rooted in the western environment. While his strategy of undermining the Progressives through the symbolic co-optation of their policies was successful in the short run in swallowing up the new party in the House of Commons during the 1920s, it also contributed to the diffusion of partisanship on the Prairies. The defeat of free trade in the 1911 election – when the Liberals had finally, after a decade and a half of office, come down on the side of reciprocity so popular with the farm population – along with the experience of Union government during the war, had already prepared the ground for third-party politics. The signal success of the Progressives in exercising leverage on the minority King government while losing their identity at the same time was a paradoxical lesson in the utility of stepping outside the framework of traditional but decreasingly relevant partisan loyalties. Even when the Progressives had virtually disappeared as a federal force, the catastrophe of the Great Depression on the Prairies quickly demonstrated that two-party politics had no continuing hold over the majority of western voters when the old parties no longer seemed to be producing results. A significant number of westerners were quite prepared to use third parties as vehicles of protest – whether in the hope of eventually replacing the old parties or with the more modest aim of forcing them to recognize western grievances.

After 1935 the Liberals never regained the level of electoral support which they had enjoyed before the war. They were generally weaker in the West than in any other part of the country. Yet in the period of Liberal domination of national politics from 1935 to 1957 the party did manage to

Table 9.1
Popular vote percentages polled by Liberal candidates in the western provinces in federal general elections, 1930-58, by province

	Manitoba	Saskatchewan	Alberta	British Columbia
1930	37.2	46.5[a]	30.0	40.9
1935	40.5[a]	40.8[a]	21.2	31.8
1940	47.8[a]	43.0[a]	37.9[a]	37.4[a]
1945	34.7[a]	32.7	21.8	27.5
1949	47.9[a]	43.4[a]	34.5	36.7[a]
1953	40.2[a]	37.7	35.0	30.9[a]
1957	26.1	30.3	27.9	20.5
1958	21.6	19.6	13.7	15.1

[a]In these instances the Liberals received more votes than any other party
Source: information compiled from H. Scarrow, *Canada Votes* (New Orleans, 1962)

maintain a presence in the West which was by no means inconsiderable. After the Diefenbaker landslide of 1957-8 the Liberals have of course gone into a much more profound decline in the West than at any time in the past. But in the period examined in this study the Liberals continued to be a major participant in western politics. Provincially, the party continued its traditional strength in Saskatchewan, even after it went out of office in 1944, and in British Columbia it continued, alone or in coalition, until the early 1950s to participate in provincial office. In Manitoba a long period of blurring partisan lines eventuated in the re-emergence of a Liberal party as the dominant provincial force. Only in Alberta did the Liberals collapse as a coherent and viable provincial alternative as early as the 1930s. In federal politics, the Liberals from 1935 through to the 1953 general election led the polls in the western provinces more often than they trailed – although they never gained over 50 per cent of the popular vote in any western province. Again it was Alberta which was the weakest spot for the Liberals, yet even here they usually came in second. Table 9.1 indicates the level of popular vote support for the Liberal party in federal elections in the four western provinces. Only by the time of the Diefenbaker sweep in 1957-8 had the Liberals declined to virtual third-party status in this region.

However much westerners tend to think of a western regional identity within Canada, and however much one may generalize about western politics, it is not the West as a monolithic unit which appears to yield the most useful insights into political phenomena in that area. Each of the western provinces has its own distinctive history and its own unique blend of political institutions and values. Even when, as at certain periods in the past, the economic structures and conditions have been closely parallel from one province to another, as in the cases of Alberta and Saskatchewan in the 1920s and 1930s, the political response has been markedly different – thus the paradox of Social Credit in Alberta and the CCF in Saskatchewan which neither the sophisticated Marxist analysis of C.B. Macpherson nor the sophisticated political sociology of S.M. Lipset has been able to resolve. In the case of the Liberal party, each of the western provinces presents a different set of circumstances and a different set of responses. Each is interesting in itself, and thus each province will be treated separately. Generalizations about the region as a whole will be left to the end.

MANITOBA

Manitoba is the oldest of the Prairie provinces, with class and ethnic politics already taking shape as early as the 1880s.[1] By the First World War Winnipeg was clearly established as the gateway to the West, a kind of mini-metropole in the western hinterland with emerging industry, a large immigrant, working class slum, and a degree of class polarization which exploded in the Winnipeg General Strike of 1919, the most significant single labour action in Canadian history. North Winnipeg was from that time forward a seedbed of social democracy and radical politics, while to the south in the same city a nascent western bourgeoisie with its own strident class consciousness had emerged victorious from its epochal confrontation with the working class. At the same time the rest of the province remained rural and agricultural, qualities which alternately gave rise to militant protest politics in the form of the United Farmers and the Progressives at one moment and an implacable conservatism at the next. The gradual development of the mining frontier and the transformation of ethnic into class politics outside of Winnipeg has finally resulted in the victory of a social democratic government under Ed Schreyer in 1969. Throughout the period with which we are more directly concerned, Manitoba politics presents a confused face ranging from class politics to non-partisan 'business' government. The economic and class divisions of the province, combined with cross-cutting ethnic cleavages, made for such a volatile mixture that everything from third-party politics to non-party politics flourished at one time or another. The Liberals usually managed to weather the storms and survive the shifts. On the whole, the story of the Liberals in Manitoba is another chapter in their history of adaptation and survival in peculiar local conditions, until the 1950s when their disintegration in Manitoba accompanied their decline in the country.

In the early part of the twentieth century the Manitoba Liberal party emerged as the reform party in the province representing strands of radical thought from feminism to temperance to the social gospel to the single-tax movement.[2] Around the period of the First World War the party was able to attract such stalwarts of the reform movement as Nellie McClung, the pioneer feminist. When the farmers exploded into national politics at the end of the war, it was notorious that the Manitoba Progressives were extremely close to the Liberal party. Such figures as T.A. Crerar, the national Progressive leader, and Norman Lambert, the provincial party secretary, would shortly return to leading positions within the party of Mackenzie King. Yet by the 1950s and still more recently, the Liberals have become the distinctively conservative party in the province, standing to the right of the Progressive Conservatives. At the same time – although this may be merely coincidental – they have also declined to the point of imminent extinction as a political force.[3] The complexities of this historical process are intriguing.

In Manitoba, unlike the experience of the other two Prairie provinces, rural progressivism not only came up against the hostility of the central Canadian metropoles but also against the existence of another, distinctive, non-agrarian class force: the urban working class politics of North Winnipeg as manifested in the Winnipeg General Strike. The ambiguous radical-conservative face which the Canadian farmers' ideology has presented in successive historical periods was put to the test of strong labour participation in protest against the economic system very quickly in Manitoba. Just as in Ontario where the farmer-labour alliance failed to weather the distrust of the independent commodity producer for the wage labourer, so too in Manitoba the hint of revolutionary syndicalism in the General Strike was enough to thrust the conservative face of the farmer ideology to the fore. When the United Farmers of Manitoba formed the third provincial farmer government in Canada in 1922, following Ontario and Alberta, they brought with them the anti-party sentiment and the rural Protestant anti-permissive moralism which characterized the farmers elsewhere, but scarcely a trace of the social radicalism which was the other prominent feature of the movement. The result was an emphasis on non-partisan 'business' government, which tended to avoid legislative innovations and sought to blur both partisan and ideological cleavages under the banner of sound economical administration. A dull greyness descended over Manitoba public life which was to last for well over a generation, a period in which the triviality and parochialism of small town municipal politics enveloped the provincial stage as a whole, and in which political conflict and debate was played out on the margins or under cover, if at all. It was a situation for which the Liberal party was eminently well suited, although its adaptation was not without strains.

The major question before the party in the 1920s was how to win back the Progressives to the Liberal fold. Some believed that those who had defected should be punished by exclusion, as a warning to others. Jimmy Gardiner, to whose leading role as Liberal purist on the Prairies we shall return, both in regard to his native Saskatchewan and to neighbouring Alberta, had a brief but disastrous moment of influence in Manitoba as well. Gardiner was allowed to unleash his Saskatchewan Liberal machine in Manitoba in the 1927 provincial election in support of a straight Liberal ticket in every constituency. The electoral result was more to the advantage of the Tories than to the Liberals, but the permanent organizational result within the Liberal party was a split between the so-called 'die-hards' who wished to maintain Liberal purity at all costs and the co-operators who wished to build an electorally promising alliance with the farmers. By 1929 Mackenzie King, whose instincts were always to co-operate with the progressive elements, had decided with J.W. Dafoe of the *Free Press* that an understanding between the groups should be actively pursued. By 1932 the Liberals formally merged with the Progressives to form the Liberal-Progressive party, thus making the discrediting of the Gardiner 'die-hard' position official.[4]

While this meant the return of Liberals to participation in the provincial administration, it obviously left unanswered the problem of federal alignments, which was a constant source of irritation for the federal party organizers leading up to the 1935 election. The federal party was at this juncture extremely fortunate to have Norman Lambert, ex-Manitoban, as its national secretary. Lambert had an intimate knowledge of the intricacies of that province and valuable contacts with both the Liberal and Progressive groups. His chief goal was to bring the federal party into open support of the provincial merger and to head off the 'die-hards.' Lambert involved himself directly in provincial fund-raising and in the appointment of provincial as well as federal organizers. The cross-currents were heavy, however, and provincial divisions were inevitably manifested at the federal level. By early 1933 Lambert was admitting in his diary that the federal party could make no headway 'just now,' and in the national arena the moves toward establishment of the National Liberal Federation and its provincial funding received no support from Manitoba whatsoever.[5] The picture fell into somewhat greater resolution with a Liberal-Progressive meeting at Brandon in the spring of 1933 which endorsed the new party. The meeting had 'the earmarks of spontaneity,' Crerar reported to Mackenzie King. He added, significantly, that 'Lambert deserves a great deal of the credit for the success that attended it.' A convention at Portage la Prairie later the same year saw what one observer termed the 'usual fight' with the 'usual results': the 'die-hards' mustered less than a quarter of the delegates and were soundly defeated. A hard core of 'die-hards,' centred in Winnipeg, continued to harass the mainstream of the party by setting up competing youth groups, packing selected party meetings, and attempting to take over particular constituency nominations. But all was in vain, for the concept of fusion was not only accepted by the majority of Manitoba Liberals themselves but was being sponsored by the national party as well. The issue eventually faded away, but not before Lambert had to intervene much more extensively in the local affairs of the party than he himself would have preferred.[6]

In the 1935 election the Liberal party did well out of its new arrangements. Ten out of eleven sitting Conservatives were defeated and the Liberals swept fourteen out of a total of seventeen seats in the province. The new CCF party took two seats but these were both in the north end of Winnipeg. Outside of that social democratic ghetto, the Liberals had established a strong federal presence. Five years later in the wartime election of 1940 they did even better, coming close to an absolute majority of the popular vote. Provincially, the urge to non-partisanship went further yet in the late 1930s as the Conservatives were brought into the provincial government, leaving the CCF and the Communists as the only extant opposition elements. In line with this disposition to unity, the Liberal-Progressives suggested that provincial cabinet ministers should stay out of federal elections altogether. Conservatives were doubtful about going that far. Then, before the 1940 election, the CCF and Social Credit were asked to join the government as a co-operative war measure. Sitting MPs were given acclamations. When Premier John Bracken resigned in 1942 to become leader of the renamed Progressive Conservative party of Canada, the CCF abandoned its support of the provincial government. Significantly enough the Liberals showed no signs of following, despite the fact that the former premier was opposing their federal counterparts. Indeed, the Liberal-Progressive-Conservative government continued intact through the 1940s. The provincial elections of 1945 and 1949 were 'formalities' in which half the seats in the legislature were filled by acclamation. The Social Credit party had been swallowed without trace, the Communists routed. Only the CCF remained in opposition. Debate in the legislature had virtually ceased and the cabinet had become a kind of super regulatory board.[7]

These developments had serious consequences for the nature of liberal democracy in Manitoba. Not surprisingly, almost all legislative innovation came to a halt, and even public discussion of politics reached desperately low proportions. But it also had pernicious consequences for the Liberal party, consequences which the provincial Liberals never fully comprehended but which set them firmly on the road to political extinction. By the end of the 1940s business elements in south Winnipeg were growing restive with the stagnant, rural-oriented administration of Douglas Campbell, Bracken's successor. Duff Roblin, grandson of former Manitoba premier Sir Rodmond Roblin, won election to the legislature in 1949 as an Independent Conservative and together with anti-coalition business elements managed to remove the Tories from the government in 1950. The Liberals, bred by a generation of co-operation with everything else that moved politically in the province, did not react to this new challenge. There is some evidence that Premier Campbell continued to try to placate the Conservatives by distributing patronage to them – including, according to one observer, federal patronage which Louis St Laurent was willing to dispense on Campbell's advice.[8] Meanwhile the political initiative was passing into the hands of Roblin's revitalized Tories. The provincial government myopically believed that it could save itself by attacking the federal Liberal government in Ottawa. In the 1957 federal election the Liberals suffered a crippling defeat in Manitoba, dropping seven out of eight seats, and sinking from 40 to 26 per cent of the popular vote. Premier Campbell shrugged off the disaster with the following words: 'I never did run as a Liberal – I helped turn out the Liberals in this province.'[9] The following year he was himself turned out by the provincial electorate. Neither the federal nor the provincial Liberals have ever come back.

The pattern of provincial politics has resolved itself into a social democratic dominance with the Conservative party as the main opposition element, with the Liberals retaining just enough marginal existence to keep the NDP in office. Paradoxically, the Manitoba legacy of non-partisan government has prevented the establishment of an anti-socialist coalition which was successful in British Columbia in 1975 in defeating an NDP government. The choice before the Liberal party eventually became that of losing their identity within a coalition with the now much stronger Conservative party, or facing eventual extinction as an independent political force. They have chosen the latter. Nor has the federal party done any better in the province since the Diefenbaker realignment of western voting.

SASKATCHEWAN

'The continuity of Saskatchewan politics since 1905,' writes David Smith, 'has been found in the Liberal party.'[10] It is doubly remarkable that a

Liberal party should maintain itself successfully for so long a period in a prairie environment where Liberals have experienced more difficulty than in any other region of the country. It is not merely the Saskatchewan Liberal party which is unique; Saskatchewan itself differs markedly and significantly from all the other western provinces in terms of its political development. The high degree of party competitiveness and the obdurately two-party nature of that competition mark Saskatchewan off from its western neighbours with their histories teeming with non-partisanship, anti-party parties, shifting coalitions, and quasi-party systems.[11] Moreover, any generalizations about the third-party tendencies of the West are contradicted by the example of the Saskatchewan Liberal party. Not only was this party tenacious in its adhesion to its traditional party label but it also demonstrated an unparalleled solidarity with its federal wing in Ottawa. Organizationally the closest thing to a continuously functioning political machine to be found anywhere outside of Quebec, it displayed a style of partisan, patronage politics which appears to confound many generalizations made about the issue-oriented nature of the western political culture. Finally, in the person of Jimmy Gardiner, one-time premier of the province who went on to Ottawa in 1935 to become minister of agriculture for a twenty-two-year period, Saskatchewan provided the single most dominant figure in western politics in the period of this study, a man so powerful that his influence could be felt within the Liberal parties in Alberta and Manitoba as well as over both the provincial and federal wings of the Liberal party in his own province.

The Saskatchewan Liberal party always held firmly and unswervingly to the principle that it must remain undefiled by any form of fusion, coalition, co-operation, or any other unnatural arrangement with any other party, group, organization, or force with political ambitions. The party itself would welcome identifiable groups within its own structures, so long as they become loyal and partisan Liberals. Politically active elements of the farm community were absorbed by the Liberal party after the First World War far more successfully than in either of the other two Prairie provinces; as a direct consequence, the Liberals were able to retain both power and identity in the face of the Progressive onslaught which virtually destroyed the Liberal party in Alberta, and forced it to undergo a major transformation in Manitoba. This Liberal attitude also insured, paradoxically, that when farm and labour discontent once again reared its head in the 1930s and 1940s it took the clear and decisive form of a highly organized political party able to confront and defeat the Liberals on their own terrain of partisan political warfare. When the CCF took office in 1944 there were few vestiges of that debilitating anti-party tradition which had so crippled the earlier farmers' movements. The CCF was as well, or better, organized than its Liberal rivals, well financed – albeit in a different manner than the Liberals – and resolute on the question of maintaining the partisan identity of its government, which it was to do successfully for twenty years. Yet if the Liberal insistence on partisan politics helped strengthen its socialist rival's ability to hold onto office, it also helped maintain the identity of the Liberal party even in the years of opposition. In contrast to Manitoba, where the urge to co-operate with everybody from Progressives to Conservatives finally denatured the Liberal party of its very identity, the Liberal party in Saskatchewan survived even a generation of opposition to return to office in the 1960s as the sole example of a provincial Liberal administration in the West since the 1950s, and the only 'pure' or straight Liberal administration in the West since the early 1940s. In the 1970s it remains as the sole example of a western Liberal party which is even able to maintain a position as an official opposition.

The Saskatchewan Liberal machine before 1929 has been ably analysed in a pioneering article by Escott Reid written over forty years ago.[12] Because this case has been studied so closely and so well there is little reason here to repeat Reid's findings, which may be summarized as follows: the Saskatchewan Liberal party exemplified machine politics in perhaps the fullest sense ever seen in the West; patronage was what held the machine together, a function performed neither by ideology nor issues; and the machine continued to perform continuously between elections as well as at election time – a characteristic which sharply distinguishes it from so many other patronage-oriented but more ephemeral political organizations. This machine, moreover, was equally adaptable to either federal or provincial politics, without discrimination. When the party resumed provincial office under Jimmy Gardiner in 1934, there was an immediate return to old machine practices, including the abolition of a provincial Civil Service Commission created by the previous government.[13]

There was never any question that Gardiner was as interested in federal as in provincial politics. He played a crucial role in organization and finance during the period of Liberal reconstruction in the Bennett period, although not always to the benefit of those who were in charge of federal organization. Gardiner had a unique ability to raise funds from major eastern corporations which no other western Liberal possessed, and he repeatedly used his entrée into the boardrooms to gain control over funds whose allocation he alone supervised. Gardiner's special relationship with the CPR and the problems posed to Norman Lambert by Gardiner and his agents raising money separately from the same sources which the regular federal collectors were soliciting have already been discussed in an earlier chapter.[14] It was not merely that Gardiner acted independently. Worse was the fact that the famous Liberal machine was expensive to operate, far too expensive in the eyes of many, so that Saskatchewan tended to suck more than its share of scarce party funds into its orbit. As one leading provincial Liberal explained to Mackenzie King, everyone who worked for the Liberals expected something in return. 'You have to pay to get them to the polls, you have to pay your canvassers, you have to pay your scrutineers, it is pay, pay, pay. So long as there are plenty of funds this condition will continue and become increasingly aggravated.'[15] The problem was that with the Depression and with the Liberals out of office nationally, there were no longer 'plenty of funds.' But given no discernable diminution of demand, the aggravation only increased. Even with Gardiner's freelance fund-raising the Saskatchewan Liberals overspent their resources in the 1935 federal election by $12,000, even after no less than $30,000 had been drawn out of the 'provincial treasury.'[16] There were many in Ottawa who were of the firm opinion that Gardiner's machine was not merely profligate with money but was not as effective as it was reputed to be by its own champions.

Immediately following the return of the Liberals to office in Ottawa, Gardiner set about preparing for his own removal from the provincial scene and his elevation to federal cabinet rank. It is an indication not merely of the close meshing of the federal and provincial wings of the party at this time, but even more of the higher prestige attaching to the senior governmental level that a provincial premier should readily give up his leading position to become one minister among many in the nation's capital. Yet, in this, Gardiner was merely following a long tradition in the province: four out of the ten premiers of Saskatchewan have had previous careers as federal MPs, while three pursued subsequent federal careers in Ottawa.[17] Indeed, Gardiner's immediate Liberal predecessor as premier, Charles Dunning, had gone to Ottawa as a minister in the King government in the late 1920s. In moving to Ottawa, Gardiner left behind him a new premier, W.J. Patterson, who was no threat to his own power and prestige in the Prairies. At the same time he had to face down the possible rivalry of Dunning who, though not a candidate in 1935, was being sought by King to resume his old finance portfolio. Gardiner negotiated with King from a position of some strength, attaching conditions to his acceptance of the agriculture portfolio having to do with responsibility for the Wheat Board.[18] More than this he successfully headed off any possibility that Dunning would be viewed as a Saskatchewan minister. When King asked Gardiner if he had the 'confidence' of eastern big business, the latter asserted that he did 'even more than Dunning.' King sensed in the premier a 'desire to get closer contact with the big interests, realizing a sort of power in that connection.' Despite his misgivings that the 'little beggar' was 'running the danger of getting out of his depth,' King not only gave him the Agriculture Department, with some Wheat Board responsibilities, but also promised the Saskatchewan machine control over federal patronage in the province, and gave further assurances that Dunning would come in only as an eastern minister, leaving Gardiner as 'the most important Western minister' and 'master of an empire there.' Dunning, in the event, ran in a by-election in far-away Prince Edward Island. King had secured the services of the boss of the Saskatchewan machine. It is just as clear from the prime minister's diaries that he viewed Gardiner as merely a regional figure, best kept as much as possible in his own bailiwick.[19]

King's distrust of Gardiner continued and to an extent even deepened in the years in which they were cabinet colleagues. Although Gardiner's personal morality was, unlike that of Mitch Hepburn, above reproach, his political morality was not. Indeed, King often privately linked him with the hated Ontario premier. There was some circumstantial evidence pointing to some association between the two and even to some co-operation between the Hepburn and Gardiner political organizations.[20] More to the point perhaps was King's distaste for the patronage politics which both men pursued too openly and unashamedly. Gardiner was always trying to chip away at the civil service merit system to open up more patronage positions for his machine, or to find various clever devices to hand out jobs and money to supporters. After one such attempt in 1939, King angrily wrote in his diary that 'it is perfectly damnable to have one's own colleagues betraying the very principles of Liberalism which all of us are trying to uphold in public life. I really feel about Gardiner that he is more and more of a machine politician, and that Dunning was perhaps right in his estimate of his tendencies in that direction. My opinion of him is not what it was some time ago.'[21]

That Gardiner was a 'machine politician' there can be little doubt. He was not above excoriating public works officials for their letting of contracts on public buildings in Saskatchewan on the basis that they 'seem to have a weakness for wishing to get someone who has engineering or some other technical knowledge even if they have to go outside the town where the building is being constructed.'[22] Revulsion at this kind of administration went beyond King himself. When the provincial Liberals were swept from office in 1944 by the CCF, there were many in the national Liberal party who were quick to lay much of the blame on the sordid politics of Saskatchewan

Liberalism. For example, a document in the files of the NLF, probably penned by Gordon Fogo, was blunt:

Saskatchewan citizens had become heartily fed up with the rule of the so-called Grit machine, and with some justification. After all, the province had never known anything but a Liberal government for 34 out of its 39 years, and patronage had flourished. The fact that many appointees did an efficient job was outweighed by the numbers of local bosses and hangers on, many of whom became pretty arrogant. And the name of J.G. Gardiner was associated with that machine more than that of any other man. There's nothing sinister in the idea of seeing your friends get the plums; but the feeling was widespread that this business was carried much too far, that too many of the rewarded didn't earn their keep.[23]

There were other reasons for Gardiner's sometimes questionable standing among his colleagues in Ottawa. One of the more important was his rigid insistence on Liberal purity and his aversion to any form of co-operation with any of the various western protest groups which sprang up over the years. As previously suggested, this was the dominant Saskatchewan 'line' within the party, and was not without some historical justification. Yet Gardiner was placing himself against the record of Mackenzie King himself who in the 1920s had skilfully played the game of co-optation of the Progressives and encouraged similar behaviour on the part of other western Liberals. Moreover, by the 1930s King was disposed to attempt the co-optation of labour and radical elements here and there. Thus Gardiner's straight and distinctly unoecumenical Liberalism was not at all congenial to his prime minister. Gardiner also had the irritating habit of extending this doctrine to the neighbouring Prairie provinces as well, where his unchallenged dominance over the Liberal party in the region allowed him to intervene on more than one occasion, sometimes to the active resentment of local Liberals of a more co-operative frame of mind.

It is ironic that the one important figure in the Prairies who remained fully loyal to both federal and provincial Liberalism and who could, moreover, usually deliver on the promise of support, should have remained to the end of his twenty-two-year tenure as agriculture minister an outsider to the inner circle of the Liberal party, but that does indeed seem to be the case. Nowhere is his outsider status more obvious than in his forlorn bid for the party leadership at the time of King's retirement in 1948. The savagery with which the old leader moved to ensure not merely the defeat but the humiliation of his longtime colleague is eloquent testimony to the arm's length nature of Gardiner's association with the national party.[24]

So long as the Liberals remained in office at both levels the uneasy relationship could be smoothed over. In a sense, whatever tensions did exist were the luxury of the successful, which Liberals in other, leaner areas of the West might well envy. With the accession of the socialist CCF party to provincial office in 1944, however, that situation changed. Gardiner himself never saw reason to alter his strict Liberal views. As late as 1952 he could reiterate: 'Our only organization is a Federation based on Provincial organizations. It seems to me that if the strength of such an organization is to be maintained we must have a strong Liberal organization prepared to know what Liberalism is and advocate it in or out of office and to do this the organization should be prepared to go to bat whenever a battle is being fought Provincially or Federally.'[25]

Others did not see it that way in all cases, especially as the provincial party languished for two decades in opposition, while their federal counterpart continued to hold sway for much of that time. The usual unpopularity of many federal policies handed ammunition to the CCF who were able to brand the provincial Liberals as the puppets of Ottawa. There was, in fact, some truth in this charge. Gardiner used his influence to direct the provincial party into paths acceptable to the federal wing. For example, in the 1948 provincial election the Liberal leader, Walter Tucker, himself a former federal MP, was 'totally dependent upon Ottawa for assistance.' Organizational and financial means lay within Gardiner's hands, and he would not allow the provincials to attack federal policies, however unpopular, and further used his influence to sabotage a plan of Tucker's to promote joint action with the Conservative party in the nomination of candidates.[26]

The lasting result of this dispute was a growing estrangement between Gardiner and Tucker, and a feeling among many provincial Liberals that the federal minister was undercutting the provincial leader. Poor financing, inadequate manpower, and a distinct federal orientation in both political organization and the distribution of patronage all tended to point to a provincial dilemma. The case for openly breaking with the federal party has been succinctly put by Smith: 'If the Saskatchewan Liberals broke free of federal domination, they could expect more and larger favours in terms of patronage and grants than they now received. In addition, a break would deprive the CCF of one of its favourite pastimes – imputing blame to provincial Liberals for federal government actions.'[27] On the other hand, Tucker was unwilling to initiate such an action, fearing that the division would only reinforce the certainty of future defeat and the decline of the party. This view prevailed, but after another electoral defeat, Tucker gave up and returned to federal politics.

When the provincial party chose a successor to the leadership in 1954, it broke openly for the first time with Gardiner. Indeed, the new leader, A.H. 'Hammy' McDonald, was a former Conservative who had won a seat as a coalition candidate in 1948 despite Gardiner's opposition. McDonald's victory ushered in the first full-scale, federal-provincial, intra-party dispute experienced in the province. The battle was waged over the filling of positions within the party organization, and the party was more or less paralysed by the division. The dispute reached the glare of full publicity when ten northern constituency associations met to offer their support of McDonald against Gardiner. While both sides drew back at this point, the Liberals lost a significant proportion of their popular vote while going down to their fourth successive defeat at the hands of the CCF in 1956, with Social Credit picking up support in areas where the Liberals were most divided. The national secretary of the NLF observed that much of McDonald's difficulties were 'because of differences he has encountered with Mr. Gardiner.'[28]

Nor were the federal Liberals doing as well as they had before the CCF victory. In the 1945 federal election only two Liberal members survived a CCF onslaught, with the prime minister himself losing his Prince Albert seat. The Liberals came back in the St Laurent landslide of 1949, but the CCF showed clear electoral superiority in both the 1953 and 1957 elections. The latter election, of course, saw the national defeat of the Liberal administration. With their grip over both federal as well as provincial patronage gone, the Saskatchewan Liberals were reduced to a sorry state which was only deepened by the fact that the new Conservative prime minister himself came from Saskatchewan, and was about to construct a lasting base of enthusiastic western farm support for the Conservative party. In the Diefenbaker victory of 1958 the Liberal vote in Saskatchewan declined to under 20 per cent, and not a single member survived. One of the victims was Jimmy Gardiner, whose long career thus came to an end. It was the end of the Liberal era in Saskatchewan as well. Although the party was able to return to provincial office in 1964, it was under the leadership of an ex-CCF convert, Ross Thatcher, whose fervent and dogmatic anti-socialist and free enterprise rhetoric gave a right-wing ideological cast to the provincial party which it had never before worn so openly, and embroiled it in disputes with the more progressive and welfarist federal Liberal party under Lester Pearson. Such intra-party ideological divisions were unheard of in Jimmy Gardiner's day.

The summation of this period of the Liberal party in Saskatchewan must be mixed. A greater degree of partisan purity and a greater degree of federal-provincial integration than were exhibited by the Liberals elsewhere in the West were both a source of strength and weakness for the party. On the whole, however, it must be the strength which remains as the last word. For the Saskatchewan Liberals did better than other western Liberals at the first and decisive test: they survived.

ALBERTA

To move from Saskatchewan to Alberta is to move from one political world to another, despite many similarities in the economy and society. Nowhere was the sharp transition more decisive or more painful than for the Liberal party. If Saskatchewan was a reasonable success for the Liberals in the period of this study, Alberta was a dismal, irretrievable failure – the very worst the Liberals have ever suffered in any province.

In the 1970s the Liberals have been reduced to a fringe third party in Alberta, unable to elect a single member federally or provincially. This condition has deep roots which extend back to the 1920s and 1930s. The remarkable unpopularity of the Liberal party in this province is a continuing phenomenon of successive decades of Canadian politics. The general disorganization and political ineptitude of the Liberals in Alberta is perhaps as much an effect of this unpopularity as it is a cause. But to examine the Alberta Liberals during the period of Liberal dominance in national politics is to cast a cruel and invidious light on one hopelessly ineffective section of a strong national party.

Like its sister province of Saskatchewan, Alberta began its political history under a Liberal provincial government. The influence of the federal Liberal government of Sir Wilfrid Laurier was not without significance in this early period: the first lieutenant-governor was a staunch Liberal and the distribution of federal patronage was used 'unblushingly' to build up the Liberals within the new province. Alberta departed from the Saskatchewan model abruptly, however, in 1921 when the United Farmers of Alberta swept to office, displacing a scandal-ridden Liberal régime. Premier Charles Stewart had vainly attempted to co-operate in some form with the rising forces of agrarian discontent, but the Alberta farmers were too well organized and too intent upon smashing the party system altogether to allow themselves to go the way of the Saskatchewan farmers who were at the same time being co-opted by the Liberals in that province.[29] The UFA was clearly the most left wing of the three farmer governments which took provincial office after the war, yet during the two subsequent elections the Liberals failed to polarize the opposition and saw their share of the popular vote decline further. The sinking popularity of the provincial Liberals and

their fading organizational strength inevitably was reflected in federal politics as well. As Mackenzie King philosophically put it on the eve of the 1930
federal election: 'It is quite true that the attitude of Liberals of the Province,
in Provincial politics, may have a bearing on the result in Federal politics
but that is something, whether for good or ill, which lies beyond the control
of those who are responsible for the administration of Federal affairs, or the
work of organization of the Party.'[30] In that election, the Liberals retained
only three members from Alberta in the federal House.

There were further embarrassments to come from the provincial Liberals. One of the most damaging, yet at the same time most puzzling, had to
do with the Liberals' alleged responsibility for the seduction suit against the
UFA premier, John Brownlee, which led to Brownlee's retirement from public life and contributed to the decay of the UFA's political popularity. This
case, which was widely viewed as a frameup, somehow redounded to the
disadvantage of the Liberals, who were active in pressing the scandal in the
media. To this day there are Albertans who allude to this muddy affair as a
root cause of the Liberals' low estate. As one recent observer of Alberta politics has written, the Social Credit party, which picked up the pieces from
the disintegrating UFA, did not exploit the scandal, nor did they have to:
'The Liberals, whose hunger for spoils was palpable, did the job only too
well – destroying in the process, not only Brownlee but themselves. It was
not lost on people that the Liberals were the main ones trying to make mileage out of the Brownlee affair, that they were behind much of the newspaper publicity and the whispering. Their own efforts boomeranged on the
provincial Liberals and gave them a stamp for cynicism.'[31]

More to the point was the manifest inability of the party to offer an alternative to the UFA in the desperate Depression conditions of Alberta in the
early 1930s. This province, which was one of the worst hit in the country by
the economic collapse, was obviously ripe for political radicalism, yet its
own increasingly discredited provincial administration was the left-wing
UFA. Social Credit, with its peculiar blend of monetary radicalism and old-
time religious conservatism, turned out to be the answer, an answer so ex-
plosive that Alberta politics was turned upside down in the charismatic triumph of William 'Bible Bill' Aberhart in 1935. In this cataclysm the Liberals proved to be quite simply irrelevant. Even before the Social Credit
sweep, the lengthening shadows of monetary reform had fallen across the
Alberta Liberals who tried their best to get on the monetary bandwagon before it was too late. As early as 1933 Alberta Liberals had recognized that
'this monetary question is the one uppermost in the minds of the people,'
and had submitted a brief to the MacMillan Commission on Banking and

Currency that same year which suggested a mild form of social credit–type reform.[32] In this same mood, the Alberta Liberals tried to organize a western Liberal conference to develop what they called a 'western policy with proper Western appeal.' Mackenzie King was aghast. 'There is nothing,' he wrote the Alberta leader, 'which can prevent victory to the Liberal cause between now and the time of a general election but possible cleavages and divisions in our own party. The possibility of anything of the kind, we must avoid at all costs.' King did not leave it at that, but moved to line up such prominent western Liberals as Jimmy Gardiner and BC premier, Duff Pattullo, to oppose any such a regional conference. In the end the Alberta Liberals had to confine themselves to a purely Alberta conference. Held at the end of 1934, the conference passed resolutions calling for government control of the credit system to replace that of the banks and even for three social credit 'experts' to submit a plan for social credit to the Alberta legislature.[33] When Aberhart took the province by storm the next year, it should hardly have been a surprise to anyone in Ottawa who had been closely watching the infection within the Liberal party. Nor should it have been much of a surprise to the provincial Liberals when they saw their own campaign workers either not show up on election day or actually turn out for Social Credit.[34]

With the victories of Social Credit provincially and the Liberals federally in the same year, the political pattern for the next generation was set. Yet even as the Liberals were returning to power in Ottawa, Alberta was not joining the bandwagon. Only one in five Alberta voters endorsed the Liberal candidates in the federal election, and only one of these was returned to Parliament: James MacKinnon from Charles Stewart's old seat in Edmonton West. Alberta, it seemed, was to be the poor cousin in the Liberal family. This unenviable status was exemplified in various ways. One was vicious infighting over whatever federal campaign funds were sent into the province. The federal financial collectors were dubious about any contributions to this province, given the poor return on the investment, but whatever money did make its way there tended to become the subject of competing attentions – between the federal and provincial parties and even between various figures claiming to be responsible party organizers. During the 1935 campaign Norman Lambert was constantly harassed by competing claims from a province that the national party had already written off in advance.[35] Another aspect was the predominance of urban lawyers in the Alberta party, a cause of much internal dissension which could be readily traced to the attractions of federal legal patronage and judicial appointments in a province ruled by a party opposed to that in Ottawa. It scarcely mattered, so it was alleged, whether these lawyer leaders and organizers actually succeeded in electing many Liberal members since their major aim was to monopolize the federal patronage.[36] Then there was the problem of the strong tendency within the provincial party to seek fusion with other groups or to otherwise avoid the stigma of the Liberal name – with obvious debilitating effects on the federal Liberal party. We shall return to this point presently.

One of the problems left by the feeble Liberal vote in the 1935 federal election was the gap in Alberta leadership in Ottawa. Charles Stewart, who had been something of a dubious asset to the federal organization in any event, was now lost through defeat. James MacKinnon, a successful Edmonton businessman and sole Liberal MP, showed promise but was inexperienced. He was put in charge of the north of the province. Senator W.A. Buchanan of Lethbridge was put forward by southern Liberals as their spokesman.[37] Irritated by the poor Liberal showing in the province, Mackenzie King decided to punish Albertans by excluding them from the cabinet. Once before, in 1921, King had given Alberta cabinet representation by putting Charles Stewart in a Quebec seat, but he vowed never to repeat such a manoeuvre. To calls that MacKinnon be named to the cabinet, King could reply with cold frankness as late as 1938: 'Do you really think that Alberta has given such support to the present administration as to warrant our showing our appreciation by giving the Province Cabinet representation at this time?'[38] In lieu of an Alberta minister King turned to Jimmy Gardiner, whose status was more that of a prairie regional leader than a purely Saskatchewan figure. Thus for almost five years Alberta Liberalism's main link with the national party was through a cabinet minister from a neighbouring province.

Gardiner was clear from the start that his job was not to control patronage, which he wished to channel through MacKinnon and Buchanan, but to offer advice and guidance on political conduct with regard both federal and provincial wings of the party. In this, MacKinnon regarded himself as Gardiner's 'lieutenant.' It was an unusual situation but Alberta was certainly an unusual case. According to Norman Ward's detailed analysis of this period, based on the Gardiner papers, it was relatively and perhaps surprisingly free of the antagonisms which one might assume would characterize the intervention of an outsider in internal provincial affairs. Perhaps the Liberals' very confusion and disorganization helped smooth the way for Gardiner; any help and guidance would be appreciated. Yet however closely Gardiner worked with MacKinnon on federal organization, with an end to eventually handing over responsibility to the Alberta member when the time was ripe, the relations with the provincial party were not always harmonious, as Ward himself has made clear. The problem here was the desire of one faction of the provincial party to break out of the Liberal framework toward some kind of 'unity' or fusion alternative to the Social Credit government which could include Conservatives, United Farmers, and any other elements willing to submerge their partisan identities in a common front. When this faction gained the apparent approval of the new provincial leader of the Liberal party, E.L. Gray, elected in June 1937, there were inevitable difficulties with Gardiner, whose firm belief in straight Liberalism was imported into Alberta from Saskatchewan where it had flourished so well. It is ironic that Gardiner and even Mackenzie King had been involved in the long and difficult process to find a man to take on the unenviable job of Alberta leader.[39]

Yet the new leader quickly demonstrated that he possessed a mind of his own and was unwilling to accept Gardiner's interpretations of political wisdom. There was some reason for this inasmuch as Alberta was very hostile ground at this time to traditional party politics; the Liberal name was by no means as compelling a rallying cry in Alberta as it was in Saskatchewan. Moreover, there was considerable sentiment among anti–Social Credit elements in the province to set aside the old, and many believed, outmoded partisan differences in the common cause of ridding the province of a new and dangerous heresy. Gray saw this possibility as a hopeful indicator of the road ahead and set about to attempt to work with such groups as the People's League and the Unity party. Gardiner told Norman Lambert that the People's League was nothing but a Tory plot and that he, Gardiner, 'would rather support Aberhart than a coalition with the Tories.' Lambert, who had bitterly protested the decision to make Gardiner responsible for the province and had decided to cut off any federal money while the arrangement continued, 'expressed apprehension at any attempt to divert Gray from the course he designated for himself ... and that every encouragement should be given to him in his attempt to unite all elements in the province against Aberhart.' Despite King's suspicions that Gardiner 'is apt to be rigidly Liberal,' he nevertheless concluded that 'he is right on the whole in this.'[40] The problem was that there were competing factions within the Alberta party, and both views could enlist support.

Matters came to head with the federal by-election in Edmonton East in 1938. Gardiner called in his Saskatchewan machine to help organize the contest for the Liberals. Gray was apparently kept out of the campaign for much of the time by the federal constituency organization. The Liberals were beaten by Social Credit. Mackenzie King took some comfort in a second place finish: 'I imagine,' he confided in his diary, 'having our campaign run by men from other provinces may have operated a little against us. On the other hand, I am sure that Gardiner's management of the campaign has been responsible for us getting the vote we did.' There were those in Alberta who agreed, but it seems that by this stage there were more who disagreed, with increasing vehemence. Correspondence received in the prime minister's office ran heavily against Gardiner. Criticism came from the highest levels of the Alberta party, federal as well as provincial. Senator Buchanan told King's private secretary that it had been a great mistake to leave Alberta to Gardiner, that 'the methods which succeed in Saskatchewan will not work in Alberta,' that provincial autonomy must be respected, and that the importation of the Saskatchewan Liberal machine had done no good to the Liberal image in a province already hostile in general to partyism. And, finally, James MacKinnon, who had once seen himself as Gardiner's 'lieutenant,' wrote a long letter complaining to King about 'Saskatchewan domination' and asking for a cabinet position for himself to allow for effective organization of the province.[41] In January 1939 King finally accepted the force of the argument and brought MacKinnon into the ministry without portfolio. Thus the period of Saskatchewan domination of the Alberta party came to an official end.

Even during Gardiner's interregnum the provincial party went its own way. At one point a curious incident developed around the office of lieutenant-governor which might have sunk the Alberta Liberals once and for all, if not for Gardiner and King's timely intervention. There had been no doubt that Alberta Liberals saw the vice-regal office as crucial not merely in a patronage sense but in a more openly political sense of a Liberal appointment presiding over a Social Credit government. Indeed, federal disallowance of Social Credit legislation in 1937 demonstrated that the power of the federal government expressed through its various manifestations under the British North America Act could indeed come into play in the political struggle over radical Social Credit legislation which impinged on the distribution of powers and, equally important, impinged on the property rights of eastern creditors.[42] That the federal Liberal government was willing to invoke the rarely used power of disallowance against Alberta's legislation, while at the same moment declining to use it against Ontario's hydro contract repudiation and Quebec's 'Padlock Law' which violated civil liberties, is an indication of the relative power of Ontario and Quebec as against Alberta, whatever the connotations of federal domination. When the position of lieutenant-governor was open in 1936, leading Alberta Liberals lobbied Ottawa on behalf of various candidates, stressing that, in Senator Buchanan's words, 'no weak-kneed, ill-informed individual should be considered,' given the 'greater responsibility that the position has assumed as a result of the political developments' since Aberhart's victory.[43]

The appointee, J.C. Bowen, proved to be definitely strong-kneed. Not only was there no problem in getting his agreement to reserve the controversial legislation, but he quickly became embroiled in a personal struggle against his premier which at one point came close to calling parliamentary government into question. As the situation worsened, Aberhart closed down the lieutenant-governor's residence – as Hepburn did in Ontario – and even cut off funds for such matters as personal transportation and stenography.[44] The blow to vice-regal dignity of having to beg someone to type his letters was too much. Bowen told MacKinnon not to be surprised if he were to see 'sensational headlines in the Press soon.' He went on, 'if I were to dismiss the outfit, Gray could form a Unity Government, go to the country in the fall and win.' The proposal was put to Gray who, astonishingly, thought it a good idea. When he revealed the scheme to Gardiner and King, however, all hell broke loose. King was beside himself with amazement and indignation. 'It is sheer madness,' he declared, a madness which could bring down the Liberal government in Saskatchewan where an election was being fought, and 'might bring on a sort of civil war in Alberta.' Gray was contacted immediately by both King and Gardiner, and MacKinnon was told to telephone the lieutenant-governor and order the abandonment of the entire scheme. King told Gray that the constitutional issue would be similar to that of the King-Byng incident in 1925, but with the Liberals now on the wrong side. Gray and Bowen bowed to the superior political wisdom of Ottawa and what might have been one of the most serious crises in the history of Canadian parliamentary government became instead only a curious footnote documenting the political unreality of Alberta Liberalism.[45]

Gray persisted in his more reasonable course of seeking a common political front against Aberhart for the next provincial election. It seems in retrospect that the anti-party feeling in the province at this point quite probably rendered a Gardiner-style straight Liberal ticket undesirable. Indeed, any suggestion that Gray was tending toward Liberal partisanship was linked in the public mind with alleged federal domination. When Gray saw his national leader for the first time in late 1938, he thanked King for having dissuaded him from going along with the dismissal of Aberhart, but went on to say that the Liberals might surprise King by the way in which they would contest the next provincial election, that party labels might count for little, and opposition to Social Credit might encompass many different tendencies. King replied that this was fine, even when it included agreements with Tories. He cautioned, however, that in federal politics the party 'should stick pretty much to a straight Liberal fight.'[46] When another provincial election was fought in 1940, there were only two official Liberal candidates in the field, one of whom was elected. There were no Conservatives running under that name. Instead there was a full slate of 'independents,' mainly Liberals with some Conservatives and United Farmers mixed in. This group of candidates came within a margin of 1335 votes of outpolling the Social Credit party in the popular vote, and elected nineteen members to Social Credit's thirty-six. The fledgling CCF picked up 11 per cent of the vote but no representation. Social Credit had in fact been reduced from a popular vote majority in 1935 to 43 per cent in 1940; the 'Independent' slate actually increased the combined Liberal-Conservative vote in 1935 by 50,000.[47] It was by no means a discreditable performance for Gray's approach, but having failed to dislodge Social Credit from office when at its most vulnerable – following a backbench revolt against Aberhart which had called his leadership into question – the great and crucial opportunity had been missed. The chance would not come again for over another generation, as Ernest Manning, Aberhart's successor, consolidated the party's position, and the discovery of oil put the government almost literally out of reach of opposition.

The wartime federal election in the same year also saw an artificial postponement of the Liberals' difficulties in Alberta. With attention shifting to the conduct of the war the Liberals were actually able to outpoll all their opposition, including Social Credit, and elect seven Liberals to Ottawa. It was gratifying to the national Liberal party but it was the last time they would ever finish first in a federal election in Alberta.

From this point until the defeat of the St Laurent government in 1957, Liberal politics in Alberta settled into a pattern. This pattern was dreary but predictable. Since the federal party was in office, even though Alberta voters did little to support it the Alberta Liberals were dominated by the federal wing. This domination took the form of clear financial dependency. In the late 1930s under Gardiner's wing the party had received national funds through Saskatchewan, despite Norman Lambert's displeasure. During the war years the new financial man in Toronto, Peter Campbell, became the source for all Alberta Liberals to see for money. Lambert continued to advise against large transfers on the basis that Alberta should learn to collect its own funds from its own sources. In fact, Alberta Liberals remained dependent on federal funding right through to the 1970s, despite the revolution which the discovery of oil made in the structure of the Alberta political economy.[48] The Alberta party was plagued by hangers-on seeking access to federal patronage for a minimum of political effort. There was also a problem of cabinet representation. After MacKinnon was called to the Senate in 1949 his position as provincial representative in the cabinet was taken over by George Prudham, an Edmonton building supply contractor. Prudham was not a success, either as minister or as Alberta representative. The subject of public criticism for continuing to do business with the federal government while holding office, Prudham was also remarkably insensitive to the needs and desires of the provincial Liberal party.

The provincial party, against all adversity, actually had begun to stage something of a political recovery. After a last fling with 'unity' in 1944, when the Alberta Liberals literally disappeared from the political landscape of the legislature, and after going without a provincial leader for seven years, the party got together once again in 1947 having learned, in Senator Buchanan's words, 'one of the most fateful lessons any party can learn, which is that you cannot philander with other parties and retain your objectivity.' The new leader, J. Harper Prowse stated that 'after banging our heads against the wall for ten years, the Liberal party has realized that there was no sense following along that line. Representation in opposition in the legislature was becoming smaller from year to year. And, not only that, but the disastrous part was that having admitted in the provincial field that there was not a useful difference between the two parties in the philosophies they pursued, we found the net result was that we had cut our own feet out from under ourselves in the federal field as well.'[49]

However much those sentiments may have warmed the heart of Jimmy Gardiner, Prowse was quickly to discover that federal-provincial relations within the party were much more ambiguous than he had believed. For one thing he discovered that as soon as he became a Liberal Albertans began looking on him 'as some kind of spy for the enemy down east.' Moreover, the federal party appeared reluctant to aid its provincial wing for fear of raising the resentment of the Social Credit administration with which it had learned to co-operate in Dominion-provincial relations.[50]

Surprisingly enough under the circumstances, the provincial party began to gather electoral momentum through three provincial elections, until by 1955 it accounted for almost one-third of the popular vote and was able to field a legislative contingent of fifteen MLAs, larger than any Liberal representation since the election of 1917. The party had clearly established itself as the major opposition to Social Credit, easily outstripping the Conservatives and the CCF. Along with this gathering strength, the party under Prowse also began to take a more aggressive and demanding stance toward the federal wing and its Ottawa representative, the unfortunate Mr

Prudham. Prowse even went to Louis St Laurent to request Prudham's replacement in the cabinet. The increasing provincial dynamism of the Alberta Liberals was reflected in the unified Liberal Association of Alberta which became more directed toward the provincial field at this time.[51] The decision of Prudham not to run again in the 1957 federal election may give further indication of this provincial assertiveness. As it turned out, Prudham removed himself just in time, for the Diefenbaker onslaught of 1957-8 wiped out all the hardwon gains of the previous decade and transformed provincial as well as federal politics in the province. The next Alberta election in 1959 saw the Liberals lose fourteen of their fifteen members; in the 1958 federal débâcle the Liberals polled less than 14 per cent of the vote in the province while the Conservatives took almost 60 per cent.

Alberta was the Liberals' chief embarrassment for the entire period of this study. The Alberta Liberals tried to find success through the submergence of their provincial identity, and when that failed they attempted to return to their partisan origins. The latter strategy ultimately failed as well. Neither approach did much for the federal wing which remained consistently weak throughout the period. When the provincial wing showed a brief capacity to gather some strength, strains were immediately cast upon a relationship of stagnant federal domination. In short, there were obvious difficulties in maintaining a party in local adversity during a period of national hegemony. The Liberals were lucky that Alberta was such a small province.

BRITISH COLUMBIA

Canada's Pacific coastal province is even more sharply differentiated from the other three western provinces than they are from each other. Economically very diverse and never dependent upon a single staple product as the Prairies were upon wheat, British Columbia also very early developed a degree of industrial class conflict and class consciousness which is perhaps unique in North America. Militant trade unionism and working class political action, which from the beginning took on socialist and sometimes even Marxist characteristics, were matched by a hard-nosed frontier capitalism capable of mobilizing the middle and lower middle classes to the defence of 'free enterprise' and the protection of business profits. More than anywhere else in North America, politics in British Columbia has been class politics. An economy based on resource extraction within what Martin Robin has called a 'corporate frontier' developed the political economy of a 'company province,' in which the characteristic class polarization of the company town has become something of a paradigm for the province as a whole.[52]

While *class* politics are a major feature of this province, *party* politics have not been. Party loyalty has always been weak on the west coast since the late nineteenth century when Goldwin Smith was told by a British Columbian that his politics were 'Government appropriations.' Party politics did not effectively exist in the BC legislature until the first decade of this century: until this time there had been a loose form of group government in operation. There was then a period of about forty years in which the Liberal and Conservative parties did dominate political divisions in the province, although centrifugal forces were usually pulling away at the kind of party solidarity familiar in more traditional areas of the country.[53] The rise of the CCF finally led to a breakdown of partisanship during the Second World War, when Liberals and Tories formed a coalition administration to block the socialists from office. This arrangement persisted until the early 1950s, with attendant strains upon federal partisanship for the duration. Then in 1952 an ex-Conservative, W.A.C. Bennett, welded a diverse group together under the banner of 'Social Credit,' a hybrid plant which flourished for twenty years with little or no connections to any external party identifications which existed elsewhere. More recently Social Credit expanded its base to gather in former Liberals and Conservatives and defeated the short-lived Barrett NDP government of 1972-5. British Columbia has been without a government reflecting the traditional lines of the two mainstream parties for well over thirty years: in this sense, it is further from national party traditions than any other province. It is the only province in which neither of the two major national parties plays any significant provincial role.

Like California to its south, British Columbia is notorious for the volatility of its voting patterns. The lack of firm partisan traditions allows for sudden and bewildering shifts in the electorate.[54] This presents obvious problems to party organizers; party structures have consequently been particularly weak here, even in relation to a country not notable for its well-organized parties. As if all this were not enough, national parties have also had to face the barrier of geographic distance in attempting to integrate their federal and provincial wings. With air travel and television the Rocky Mountains are no longer so important as they once were in separating British Columbia both physically and culturally from the rest of Canada. In the period of this study, however, the isolation of the province was a formidable fact in itself. The local Liberals made it clear to Mackenzie King that 'they are rarely, if ever, visited by important men and that this proves that they are really not considered in the Canadian scene.' The problem was particularly acute for British Columbia's regional representative in the federal cabinet. As Ian Mackenzie told the editor of the Vancouver *Sun*, 'it is not possible for a Cabinet Minister from British Columbia, who does justice to his own Department here and who is occupied, as I am, with other matters be yond his own Department ... to give that attention to local problems which is necessary ... I am able to visit the province only about three or four times a year and then the visit is of a very short duration ... On account of the vast distances from which I am removed from my constituents it is impossible for me to keep entirely in touch with local conditions and opinions.'[55]

Despite the barriers to partisanship, the Liberals enjoyed a recovery and period of considerable provincial strength in the 1930s. The Great Depression struck British Columbia, as a province dependent on primary production, with particular force, and helped destroy the credibility of the provincial Conservative administration, which was breaking up even before its defeat at the hands of the Liberals under T.D. 'Duff' Pattullo in 1933. In fact Pattullo had spurned an offer of coalition proffered by the Conservative premier just before the election. It was a wise rejection. Pattullo, whose origins as an Ontario 'Grit' gave him 'a respect for party tradition *per se* which none of his predecessors had shared and which, in actual fact, few British Columbians appreciated,'[56] had laid the basis for an effective party organization down to the local level, over which he kept personal control.[57] Pattullo's Liberal party was something of an anomaly in British Columbia but so long as Pattullo remained premier it showed considerable political strength. Elected on the slogan of 'work and wages,' Pattullo undertook an extensive and controversial programme of public works, a 'little New Deal,' to combat the Depression. His proto-Keynesianism proved popular and the Liberal party an effective enough vehicle for this type of centre-left politics.[58]

While Pattullo was riding high, the federal wing of the Liberal party was less successful. Although they had actually picked up support in British Columbia while losing the country in 1930, their proportion of the vote dropped in 1935 in the face of the CCF's sudden rise. More important than comparative electoral support, however, was Pattullo's authority and prestige among BC Liberals compared to that of federal Liberal leaders, and his tight control over Liberal organization. This inevitably led to federal-provincial intra-party strains which were exacerbated by growing tensions between Pattullo and King after the federal victory in 1935. Even before the federal return to power the task of reorganizing the party in preparation for the 1935 election proved very difficult. The first problem faced was that of a regional leader. Ian Mackenzie, a Scottish immigrant whose Highland brogue was so thick as to draw the jibe that he spoke neither of Canada's two official languages, had gone from provincial to federal politics in the 1930 election as

member for Vancouver Centre. Despite the misgivings of political colleagues that 'his principal handicap will probably be the fact that he had
not heretofore apparently taken himself or life very seriously,' Mackenzie
seemed the best choice around which to build a federal Liberal organization. This was not accomplished without difficulty, as Norman Lambert's
diaries for the early 1930s make clear. Mackenzie did well enough under the
circumstances in the role of patronage boss and regional organization chief.
He also managed to survive an attempt by the Vancouver *Sun* editor to
boost him as a leadership rival to Mackenzie King in the early 1930s. Despite Mackenzie's insistence that BC Liberals must formulate their own policy appropriate to that province even if it meant criticizing King and the national party, he in fact remained loyal to his leader who reciprocated by
backing him in local squabbles.[59]

One of the major problems which British Columbia introduced to Ottawa was named Gerry McGeer. McGeer was an ambitious, hot-tempered
Irish politician encumbered by some strange and unorthodox policy ideas.
He was in fact a monetary crank who wrote lengthy pamphlets on monetary
reform which were social credit in general inspiration although not in partisan identity.[60] When Pattullo achieved office in 1933 he excluded McGeer
from his cabinet and vowed that the latter would never get another Liberal
nomination.[61] McGeer was not so easily put down, however, and managed
to get himself elected mayor of Vancouver and federal member for that city
in 1935. At Ottawa he acted as a Liberal opponent of the Liberal premier of
his province. Despite Mackenzie King's evident dislike of Pattullo he was
never so foolish as to ally himself with McGeer, who seems to have been an
opponent of almost every other Liberal on the coast.[62] But if McGeer were
a nuisance, his fellow Vancouver Liberals were the centre of a continuing
storm within the BC Liberals. Premier Pattullo was a man who had built his
political strength in the interior of the province and was suspicious of the
metropolitan influence of Vancouver. The Liberal party in that city was the
closest thing to a political machine to be found in the province; Bruce Hutchison called it 'notorious.'[63] The Vancouver 'gang,' led by the Farris broth-
ers and Brent Brown, did not co-operate with the regular Liberal organization centred in Victoria. This caused great difficulties for the federal party,
with Lambert receiving desperate appeals from Liberal MPs outside of Vancouver during the 1935 election for funds direct from the east, since the
Vancouver machine which monopolized local sources had frozen them out,
while the Pattullo party was reserving its funds for provincial affairs.[64]
Then, immediately following the electoral triumph of that year, King was
chilled to receive a call that the 'Farris and Brent Brown gang' were

involved in a possible election scandal. Happily for King, nothing became public to mar his election victory.[65]

Internal Liberal intrigues were more than overshadowed in the latter part of the decade by the public conflict between the Liberal premier of British Columbia, Mr Pattullo, and the Liberal prime minister of Canada, Mr King. The King-Pattullo dispute may not have taken on the epic proportions, or the vicious personal characteristics, of the King-Hepburn affair, but it was deep and abrasive and it did the Liberals of British Columbia no particular good. Pattullo came from a similar background to King and indeed the two men had known one another in their youth. In this case familiarity bred, if not contempt, at least distaste – particularly on the part of Mackenzie King. King's cautious conservatism, especially in fiscal matters, appears to have been offended by Pattullo's free-spending 'work and wages' approach to the Depression. On meeting the premier early in 1936, King scribbled the following entry into his diary: 'Would spend millions – no sort of person to govern.' He later amplified his judgment with such epithets as 'entertains the most absurd notions,' 'very hard to take seriously, he is so vain and self-satisifed, and has such visionary ideas.' Throwing up his hands, the prime minister concluded: 'I really do not know what is going to happen to the country in the course of time with the kind of men who are gaining control of public affairs, and who use the public treasury as if it was something to be given away rather than guarded.' Pattullo, for his part, warned that 'we are fast approaching the situation where there will be an open difference of opinion' between the two governments, and appealed to King on the basis of party solidarity to heal the breach in order to 'save the Province and the Liberal Party from the political goblins.' The political goblins were the CCF, who had outpolled all other parties in the 1935 election.[66] Despite this tug at King's partisanship and despite his willingness to back the federal government against the combination of Hepburn's Ontario and Duplessis' Quebec which he saw as merely another form of 'eastern domination,'[67] Pattullo could not persuade King to go along with his spending plans; soon a host of conflicts sprang up between the governments. One of the major ones was the projected bridge over the Fraser River at New Westminster which Pattullo wished to build at considerable expense, some of which he asked Ottawa to underwrite.[68] A federal cabinet committee approved the spending of a million dollars of federal money on the project, but the prime minister, enraged, closed the matter 'summarily': 'Our ministers are far too prone to save themselves unpleasantness on the part of Provincial Governments, regardless of the costs. I took the position that I did not care how embarrassing this stand might be to myself, my business was to defend the Treasury, and I intended to do so.' Strengthened by his re-election as premier with an increased mandate in the spring of 1937, Pattullo took the opportunity to goad the prime minister to 'create and lead public opinion, rather than be driven by its variable moods.' This bit of advice was to encourage federal support for the Alaska Highway project, but it was scarcely attuned to King's philosophy of government.[69] The gap between the governments instead widened.

The King-Pattullo dispute inevitably translated itself into federal-provincial tensions within the BC Liberal party. The premier exercised firm control over the party machinery and was usually able to override opposition generated by the federal wing. Yet when the Vancouver machine opposed an attempt by Pattullo to split the party organization along federal-provincial lines in 1937, the Vancouver group won. The British Columbia Liberal Association remained a dual association until 1941, 'fairly well integrated' in the words of one observer.[70]

In the wartime election of 1940 the federal Liberals led the polls in British Columbia and took ten of sixteen seats. Yet Pattullo continued his opposition to federal domination, despite warning signs that in wartime a platform of provincial rights had quickly lost its appeal. Like Hepburn he failed to understand the 'nationalizing' effect of war mobilization, and like Hepburn he paid the price. In the provincial election of 1941, which he entered upon with great confidence, his party's standing dropped by a third. The CCF led the polls in the popular vote and reached the rank of official opposition in the legislature. Immediately the demand arose from within the party to form a coalition with the Conservatives to keep the CCF 'goblins' from the gates. Pattullo, with his deep traditional attachment to the Liberal party, could not co-operate with such a move; when within two months the party had endorsed coalition, Pattullo resigned and handed the government over to his finance minister, John Hart, who then formed a coalition government. Pattullo prophetically warned that the shift to non-party government had created a political vacuum into which a completely new party could move.[71] Ten years later Social Credit did exactly that.

A provincial Liberal-Conservative coalition existing alongside continued partisan rivalry in federal politics was a prescription for internal party strains. The coalition itself was an uneasy arrangement for the distribution of patronage between the two parties. Just as with the Union government at Ottawa during the First World War, such an arrangement proved inherently unstable and contradictory. The Liberals, it appears, did rather better than their Tory partners in the delicate game of one-upmanship in control of patronage and candidate nominations.[72] But to the federal Liberals there were very disquieting aspects to this deal. There was a tendency for Liberal organization to atrophy in ridings represented by Conservative members; there was a trend toward co-operation extending to more than the joint nomination of candidates; there was the debilitating effect on the voters' recognition of the party in federal election when it was losing its identity in provincial elections; and there was the reluctance of provincial Liberals to intervene in federal elections on behalf of their party colleagues.

Federal Liberals had remained strangely neutral when the coalition was struck in 1941. Rumours persisted that King had secretly supported the idea to get rid of Pattullo. Ian Mackenzie had said and done nothing one way or the other. At times the federal MPs might intervene on behalf of one faction in an internal conflict within the provincial party.[73] When Hart retired as premier in 1947, the rival candidates were Gordon Wismer, 'renowned boss of the Vancouver-Centre Liberal machine' who had used his position as attorney-general to build a province-wide patronage system around the distribution of liquor licences, and Bjorn 'Boss' Johnson, a man from the interior who mobilized anti-Vancouver machine sentiment in the party. Federal Liberals, particularly James Sinclair and Ralph Mayhew, stepped in to support Johnson, who won the party leadership. Wismer continued to control party organization and patronage under Johnson, but a growing restiveness against coalition and the hegemony of the Vancouver machine took form under the leadership of Arthur Laing, some federal Liberals, and the Young Liberals of the province. Laing was elected provincial party president as an anti-coalitionist. Thus an internal struggle within the provincial wing of the party was matched by increasing pressure from the federal wing. As BC Senator S.S. McKeen, a federal organizer, bluntly told the NLF advisory council in 1947, 'we have suffered from a coalition government, and though we did, through that means, put in a government there which would defeat the Socialist government [sic], at the same time it did much to hurt the cause of Liberalism in the province, for it had the effect of rather deadening some of our organizations.'[74]

Federal-provincial tensions rose in 1949. A provincial election closely coincided with a federal campaign; the stress became quickly evident. A BC Liberal informed Paul Martin in Ottawa that 'owing to the fact that our Provincial election is to be held on June 15th, the main Federal campaign will have to be compressed into the period June 16 to June 25th. It has been decided that there would be no objection by the Coalition interests in B.C. if we invited to B.C. yourself and Milton Gregg while the Provincial campaign is on.'[75] He immediately added that federal campaigns should remember that the CCF, *not* the Tories, should be the targets of partisan attacks. In fact, communications between the provincial and national party offices had literally broken down. When British Columbia's cabinet minister, Ralph Mayhew, inquired if an NLF pamphlet had been sent to the coast, the NLF secretary was forced to admit: 'As a matter of fact we have sent a great deal of material and I have written a number of letters to the Provincial office, but so far I do not appear to have had any reply. It makes it a little difficult at this end to know whether the services we are trying to establish with the Provincial associations are in line with their needs.' Mayhew's office had to intervene directly to gain any federal-provincial co-operation during the campaign, although in fact little was actually achieved.[76]

The coalition eventually came apart from internal contradictions much more than from external pressures. The strain of trying to handle patronage and to maintain the uneasy balance between two jealous and quarrelsome parties became too great by the early 1950s. Although the Liberals had been the main beneficiary of the 1949 provincial election, emerging with clear-cut superiority to the Conservatives in legislative representation, the opposition from anti-coalition Liberals reached a peak in 1951, coming mainly from Young Liberals, Liberal associations in Tory seats deprived of patronage, and from federally oriented Liberals. With direct intervention by federal members, the president of the BC Liberal Association denounced the premier and called a party meeting to consider the 'dangerous state of the party's affairs.' When the Tory finance minister began attacking the federal Liberal government on federal-provincial tax negotiations in 1952 without consulting the cabinet, Premier Johnson fired him. The other Conservatives left and the coalition had ceased to function.[77]

What followed the collapse of the coalition was W.A.C. Bennett's Social Credit party – an eventuality foreseen by Pattullo when the Liberals had first disregarded his advice by entering into a coalition in the first place. The strength of anti-socialism as a rallying point for the middle and lower middle class voters was proved once again by the rise of this exotic hybrid party, but this time the Liberal party was left by the wayside. The immediate effect within the party itself was to weaken the provincial wing considerably to the benefit of the federal wing. Arthur Laing, who had been an anti-coalition Liberal in the past, was elected provincial party leader in 1953 and entered upon an unhappy career in opposition to the rising star of 'Wacky' Bennett.

In the provincial election of 1953 the Liberals were suddenly cut off from funding as BC businessmen began loading their eggs in the Socred basket. Some indeed did contribute to the Liberal party but earmarked their donations for the federal Liberals only, for use in the federal campaign the same year.[78] Thus the provincial party was cast into a situation of financial dependency on the federal wing – a new and unpleasant situation for a party which until then had been more successful financially in provincial rather than in federal politics. It might be noted, however, that BC contributions to the federal BC Liberals did not necessarily help the national Liberal party in its attempts to finance the national party office. It was in fact a constant complaint in Ottawa that British Columbia never paid its share of national expenses and never attained the state of financial self-sufficiency which the postwar prosperity and industrialization in the province warranted. Yet despite this situation the financial domination of the provincial by the federal wing within the province was now an established fact.[79]

The federal wing was strengthening itself in other ways. The removal of Mayhew from his position as BC cabinet minister in 1952 and his replacement by two energetic and able younger men – Ralph Campney and James Sinclair, had given new life to federal Liberalism in the province.[80] Reorganization at the constituency and provincial level was underway and the necessity of federal-provincial co-operation was being emphasised. An executive assistant to Sinclair, schooled in electoral politics by Brooke Claxton, undertook to supervise the liaison with Ottawa during the 1953 campaign. National Liberal politicians, even from outside British Columbia, were suddenly in demand for speaking engagements. This spirit continued after the election and the NLF office in Ottawa began to feel that British Columbia was once more part of the national Liberal picture.[81] At the same time the crisis in the provincial party was becoming acute. Laing's opposition to Social Credit policies, such as the deals with the pulp and paper corporations for timber rights, was rejected by the federal Liberals from the province. As in Quebec at the same time, the federal Liberal party had decided to support the resource extraction policies of the provincial governments at whatever cost to Liberal opposition parties in these provinces. Federal pressure began to come down on Laing and general confusion grew within the party. When Laing was personally defeated in the 1956 provincial election which also saw Social Credit strengthen its grip over the province, Laing's position was precarious. As the secretary of the NLF remarked to Duncan MacTavish, 'the attitude of the people of British Columbia towards the St Laurent government is certainly quite different from their attitude toward the Provincial leadership ... I think Arthur Laing did a magnificent job within the limits of his personality and resources but apparently that was not good enough and probably will not be good enough in the future.'[82] The following year Laing was forced out as leader, with federal pressure one of the precipitating factors. Judith Ward sums up this period of intra-party tension: 'The sources of federal-provincial tension were contained within the situation wherein the federal leaders held unusual power in an organization which was designed to allow provincial autonomy and had operated in the past under provincial control.'[83]

The irony in all this is that the Diefenbaker cataclysm of 1957-8 wiped the federal Liberals off the electoral map of British Columbia as effectively as Social Credit had destroyed them provincially. In 1953 the Liberals had led the polls in British Columbia and elected eight members; the Conservatives had finished fourth and elected only three. In 1957 the respective positions of the two parties in the popular vote were reversed and the Liberals elected only two to the Conservatives' seven. The following year the Liberals were unable to elect a single member and their share of the vote fell to a dismal 16 per cent, the second worst showing which they made in any province, next to Alberta. The Conservatives took almost half the vote and elected eighteen out of twenty-two members. In fact, the Liberal vote in British Columbia had been declining steadily since 1949. In the end neither provincial coalition with the Tories nor federal partisanship made any difference: both strategies ended in the same desolation.

FEDERAL-PROVINCIAL CAREER PATTERNS

Assessing the federal-provincial career patterns of Liberal MPs from the West in the period of this study confirms some of the trends established in the similar analyses done for Quebec and Ontario. Table 9.2 shows that three-quarters of all Liberal MPs from western constituencies had federal careers only. Only about one in five had dual career patterns. When broken down by province, however, a striking difference appears. Saskatchewan shows a lower rate of federal careers only and almost 30 per cent with dual careers – a figure which rises to over one-third of the total if one includes those MPs who had sought provincial office unsuccessfully. The closer degree of federal-provincial party integration in Saskatchewan under Jimmy Gardiner which was noted in the section on Saskatchewan is thus confirmed by the career patterns of its MPs.

Table 9.3 breaks these figures down by decade in which the federal career was begun. The pattern appears to be fairly constant over time with the exception of the 1930s when a greater degree of career overlap did occur. It might also be pointed out that 33.7 per cent of the MPs had had previous municipal experience before entering on their federal careers, a figure which is higher than that for provincial careers. Taking the case of those with dual career patterns, it was found that nineteen of the twenty-one had moved

Table 9.2
Elected career patterns of federal Liberal MPs from the West, 1930-58, by province

	Federal career only		Federal and provincial careers		Defeated provincially		Total
	N	%	N	%	N	%	
Manitoba	22	84.6	3	11.5	1	3.9	26
Saskatchewan	24	64.9	11	29.7	2	5.4	37
Alberta	11	78.6	2	14.3	1	7.1	14
British Columbia	15	71.4	5	23.8	1	4.8	21
Total	72	73.5	21	21.4	5	5.1	98

Source: information compiled from J. K. Johnson, ed., *The Canadian Directory of Parliament, 1867-1967* (Ottawa, 1968)

from provincial to federal politics; the two other cases were federal-provincial-federal. In other words, federal dominance seems to obtain even among the dual career patterns. Another point is that transfers from one sphere to the other often involve élite politicians. Six former provincial cabinet ministers made the move to federal politics and five of these subsequently held federal ministerial office as well. Five were former provincial party leaders, and three provincial premiers. The two triple career pattern cases are accounted for by unsuccessful provincial party leaders who left federal politics to take up the provincial leadership and then returned to Ottawa after failing (Walter Tucker in Saskatchewan and Arthur Laing in British Columbia). There is thus strong reason to believe that movement from the provincial to the federal sphere is attractive to élite figures who have some assurance of transferring to the federal cabinet.

Table 9.4 examines the Senate appointments made from the western provinces by Liberal governments from 1935 to 1957. Over half the senators with previous elected careers had been involved in federal politics alone, while only one-quarter had been in provincial politics alone. It should also be pointed out that all five senators with provincial career patterns could be identified with federal party organization and/or finance. Thus even though as elected politicians they had limited themselves to the provincial sphere it is safe to assume that their federal organizational activity played an important role in gaining their Senate appointments. Three out of the five appointees without any elected careers could similarly be identified with the party organization at one time. It thus appears that there were no appoint-

Table 9.3
Elected career patterns of federal Liberal MPs from the West, 1930-58, by decade in which federal career began

Decade elected	Federal career only		Federal and provincial careers		Defeated provincially		Total
	N	%	N	%	N	%	
Before 1930	19	79.2	4	16.7	1	4.2	24
1930s	16	64.0	9	36.0			25
1940s	33	76.7	7	16.3	3	7.0	43
1950s	4	66.7	1	16.7	1	16.7	6
Total	72	73.5	21	21.4	5	5.1	98

Source: *Canadian Directory of Parliament*

ments to the Senate which could be seen as rewards for purely provincial Liberal politicians. Federal service of one kind or another, even if in conjunction with provincial careers, was the *sine qua non* of reward. It should finally be pointed out that the proportion of federal-provincial and provincial careers is almost entirely accounted for by one province, British Columbia. There is no ready explanation for this anomaly.

CONCLUSION

The comparison of the Liberal parties in the four western provinces in this period reveals a somewhat bewildering kaleidoscope of differences. In two provinces, Manitoba and British Columbia, the party undertook to shed its partisan identity for a coalition arrangement from which it believed it would benefit but which eventually ended in electoral disaster. In Saskatchewan a straight partisan purity was maintained which seems to have served the party in the long run better than coalition. In Alberta coalition was attempted but only in opposition and failed to achieve electoral success; eventually the Liberals virtually disappeared from provincial politics while attempting to maintain their partisan identity. Federal-provincial tensions within the party were inevitable when coalition arrangements were in effect, and were much less in evidence when the party maintained its provincial integrity as in Saskatchewan. Even here, long years of federal success alongside provincial defeat tended to exacerbate the latent conflicts between the two wings of the party.

Table 9.4
Elected career patterns of Liberal senators from the West, appointed 1935-57

	Federal only	Federal-provincial	Provincial only	No elected career	Total
Manitoba	3			2	5
Saskatchewan	2		1	1	4
Alberta	4			2	6
British Columbia	2	4	4		10
Total	11	4	5	5	25
Per cent	44	16	20	20	100

Note: all five Senators with provincial elected careers alone were identified with federal party organization or finance; three out of the five senators without elected careers were similarly identified.
Source: *Canadian Directory of Parliament*

In the end, nothing the Liberals tried in the West worked very successfully. The Diefenbaker transformation of the electoral map in 1957-8 had a much more deadly effect upon the Liberals in the West than in any other region of the country. The Liberals had always been weaker here than anywhere else since the rise of third-party politics at the end of the First World War. The precariousness of the Liberal position in this region was dramatically confirmed by the enormity of the Diefenbaker landslide and the long-term political realignment which it effected in the West. Whether it was the unpopularity of the Liberals which led to the thoroughness of the Conservative triumph, or whether the popularity of the Tories was simply reflected in the devastation of the Liberals, is a question which cannot be answered here. The result was the same in any event. No organizational device was sufficient to save the Liberals in the face of this fundamental fact.

There is another way of looking at this history. If we remove our focus from the Liberal party and replace it with a focus on the western provinces themselves, the conclusion may be very different. From a position of decisive subordination to central Canada during the period of the National Policy, a position of inferiority even under the provisions of the British North America Act applied to the new Prairie provinces with regard to control over natural resources, and from the depths of the economic catastrophe of the Great Depression which struck the West with particular force, the West's position within the Canadian federation did improve – never to the satisfaction of westerners, to be sure, but in certain measurable ways an improvement nevertheless. In this process of regional development the West's innovative and experimental approach to the party system must be counted a positive factor. Westerners made their discontent known through the instrumentality of the party system by disruption and self-assertion. That this made life difficult for the Government party is simply a sign of some modest success.

10

The Atlantic provinces

If Ontario and Quebec form the central heartland of Canada, the Atlantic provinces and the West form the periphery or hinterland. Yet there is a considerable disparity between these two hinterland regions. Where the West has been self-assertive and independent in its political choices, the eastern provinces have been timid, conservative, and deferential. The economic underdevelopment of the Maritimes has never been in doubt; there is growing evidence that this is not merely the result of benign neglect on the part of central Canada but the direct consequence of national economic policies: to borrow from the jargon of economic dependency literature, the Atlantic region may well suffer from the 'development of under development.'[1] Despite the superficial similarities with the West, the differences are much more pronounced. Economically, the Atlantic provinces did not produce a great staple product for world markets like prairie wheat. More relevant to our present concerns, they failed to develop third-party politics as a vehicle for regional protest, as the West had done so successfully. Having failed to develop alternative parties to the centrally dominated 'national' parties, the Atlantic provinces also failed to turn the provincial wings of the national parties into instruments of autonomous political expression against the hegemony of central Canada. The word 'failure' is used advisedly; the consequences of Atlantic loyalty to the national parties are all too apparent in contrast with the advances made by westerners who either went the third-party route or turned sections of the national parties into instruments of regional protest.

The Atlantic provinces are text-book models of the kind of smoothly integrated federal-provincial party organization which Sir John A. Macdonald had envisioned for his Tory party in the years following Confederation, or which W.H. Riker would take as evidence of an integrated federal system.[2] As is well known, Sir John's vision was highly centralist. The Maritimes demonstrate conclusively that his concept of federal-provincial party integration would indeed insure federal domination. To this day, Maritime voters have remained faithful to the parties of their forefathers. In the period of this study this fidelity redounded mainly to the benefit of the Liberals. From the early 1930s through the mid-1950s the three original Atlantic provinces returned Liberal provincial governments and generally returned Liberal pluralities in federal contests as well.[3] The McNair government in New Brunswick fell after seventeen years of Liberal domination in 1952. Robert Stanfield's Conservatives ended twenty-three years of Liberal government in Nova Scotia in 1956, and the Tories briefly came to office in Prince Edward Island in 1959, breaking a twenty-four-year Liberal reign in that tiny island. In Newfoundland, from the time of Confederation in 1949 until 1971, Liberal Joey Smallwood exercised an almost unprecedented one-man domination over a province which was readily translated into Liberal domination in the federal sphere as well. Just as good news is no news, the efficient functioning of the party machinery for federal as well as provincial purposes offered such minor difficulty to the national Liberal party over the years that little or no attention was paid to the region. If the old political wisdom that it is the squeaky wheel which gets the grease holds true – and a comparison of the Maritimes with the rest of the country appears to bear it out – then the Maritimes did little squeaking and received still less grease. And if the rewards for loyalty are few, the returns to scholarly research are fewer yet; there is a paucity of material on the Liberal party in the Maritimes – both have been taken for granted. Inevitably, if lamentably, this chapter must be short.

Some general remarks can be made on the Maritimes political culture and on the Liberal party within this context. There is a great deal in common in the Atlantic region which permits of cross-provincial generalization, but this will be followed by short sections detailing some specific features of federal-provincial party organization in each of the three Maritime provinces. The major exception to most generalizations about the Atlantic provinces is Newfoundland, which not only had a separate political and social history until 1949, but exhibited significantly divergent political patterns following Confederation. A special section is thus devoted to the newest province at the end of the chapter.

MARITIMES POLITICAL CULTURE

Two quotations sum up as well as any academic treatise the specific nature of the Maritimes political culture. The first is from a leading member of the

Maritimes political élite, Angus L. Macdonald, premier of Nova Scotia for sixteen years and a minister in the wartime government of Mackenzie King. In discussing with J.L. Ralston whether reformed Tories should be given positions within the Liberal party, Macdonald expressed his doubts in the following terms: 'I feel that we must always keep in mind that the Liberal party will endure long after we have gone, and that nothing should be done to impair its permanent force in the political life of this country.' The second is from an ordinary voter from King's County, Nova Scotia, who wrote Robert Winters, Nova Scotia minister in the St Laurent government, about the lack of road work for Liberals in his area: 'I am sorry, if things does not change, we will have to change our politics; it is not the Govement, that makes people change, it is the small fellows, road forman, like Douglas Lonegan; of Aylesford R.R. 4; King's Co., N.S. This man should be taken in hand imedemiately; and there is others on this road who does not get work.'[4]

Party politics in the Maritimes are traditional party politics, perhaps to a greater extent than anywhere else in the country. Gilbert and Sullivan would feel very much at home in a region where almost every boy and girl is born a little Liberal or Conservative – and, more often than not, die in the same state. Of course even partisan voters do switch from time to time; otherwise there would be few changes of government. But more than in most parts of Canada the Liberals could count on a reasonably stable base for their party organization in the Atlantic region. The second point is that party politics in this area have been patronage politics, including all the highly localized and particularistic features with which this type of politics is associated. Traditional party loyalties and patronage politics obviously go hand in hand hand and are mutually reinforcing. While the CCF-NDP has carved out a small but precarious base in the coal and steel area of Cape Breton, the rest of the Atlantic area has remained remarkably resistant to the incursions of third parties.[5] Since new third parties have no provincial patronage at their disposal, and no realistic chances of gaining federal power and patronage, a patronage-orientation among Maritime voters offers little incentive for altering the party system. The Committee on Election Expenses in 1966 noted that the Maritimes was an area of high election expenditure,[6] and all honest writing about the politics of the Maritimes must face up to the web of small-scale patronage and 'corrupt' practices which surround the electoral process in that region. There is nothing here to distinguish the Maritimes from the province of Quebec; the Ottawa River is the traditional dividing line for this aspect of political culture. But one fact does distinguish the Maritimes from Quebec, and here the difference is decisive. The Maritime provinces have always retained a high degree of party competitiveness. Although the Liberals were generally more successful than the Conservatives in the period we are examining in this study, there was always a viable party alternative in the form of the Conservative party. In Quebec, on the other hand, the quasi-one-party state of the Union Nationale at its zenith virtually precluded any reasonable measure of party competitiveness. Maurice Pinard's model of one-party dominance as the precondition of third-party growth certainly fits the Maritimes picture.[7] Indeed, by the late 1950s in anticipation of and in conformity with the national trend toward the Diefenbaker Conservatives, all three of the Maritime provinces had Conservative administrations. Here, as in many other instances, Newfoundland is the major exception; under Smallwoood the opposition was virtually eliminated by one-man rule.

The Atlantic provinces are thus characterized by a traditional, but competitive, two-party system operating within a highly patronage-oriented political culture. The effects of this structure on the attitudes of voters are paradoxical. The appearance of sophisticated analyses of survey data gathered in the late 1960s now allows for a more empirically sound set of generalizations about regional political cultures. Richard Simeon and David Elkins conclude that the Maritime voters, especially in the lower income strata, are likely to exhibit both a high degree of distrust of their elected politicans and political process and a low level of efficacy, or belief that they can do anything about their complaints. They are disaffected but at the same time uncritical. Moreover, they exhibit relatively high levels of political participation, especially at the more basic levels such as voting. In other words, the organization and leadership which can translate dissatisfaction into radical or protest politics has not appeared. In its absence, patronage politics encourages participation but fails to foster trust or efficacy.[8]

Politics in the Maritime provinces has thus tended to revolve less around issues and the bureaucratic outputs of the system than around small-scale patronage arising out of the electoral process itself. The parties as organizations have consequently been even less issue-oriented than their counterparts in Ontario and the West. To a very considerable extent party organization in the Atlantic region has been associated with the organization of patronage, its distribution, and its employment in the business of enlisting party workers as well as voters. The role of patronage as the medium of political exchange and its profound significance as the connecting link between voter, party worker, elected candidate, and government is well brought out in an interview which Escott Reid conducted with the president of the Nova Scotia Liberal Association in 1931. This gentleman informed Reid of a typical case of a position of janitor in a post office which had fallen vacant. The designated deserving Liberal fell afoul of Civil Service Commission regulations, and the Liberal organization in the constituency spent eighteen months working on this problem: 'it was the subject of many stormy meetings and he had no doubt it occupied at least one meeting of the cabinet at Ottawa.' Reid wondered if the energy expended had not been out of proportion to the results which the party could reasonably expect. The seasoned Maritime politician had no doubt of the importance of the matter; it would have caused dissatisfaction all over the constituency among Liberals if the man had not received the appointment:

The party workers would have said: 'What is the use of working for the Liberal party when it does nothing for its friends when it is in office?' It was not simply that the party workers wanted jobs for themselves to reward them but that they wanted the feeling of power which the ability to acquire jobs for supporters in their polling sub-division gave them. If a party worker from a small village could come to him and say 'I want to do something for so and so. He is dissatisfied with the party. Could you get him the job of boarding a horse for the express company?' and he got the job for him, the worker would feel that he had some part in the governing of the country. The motives which moved men to work for the party were mixed: it might be money, or prestige or power, or the emotional relief which came to a man who could say to himself when he was annoyed by some official: 'I will get at you, you bugger, when my party gets into power.'[9]

The federal Civil Service Act of 1918-19 and the establishment of the merit principle in wide areas of the Ottawa bureaucracy was a source of irritation and even bewilderment in the Atlantic region. Provincial governments in the area did not follow suit and thus after the First World War it was the provincial governments which became the major source of patronage for Maritime politics. Provincial patronage was so extensive that it even extended to jobs within companies doing business with the provincial governments.[10] Yet such was the strength of traditional party loyalties and so close the meshing of federal and provincial politics that this provincial command over the most valuable resources of politics was rarely used to establish provincial control over the federal wings of the party. It must of course be emphasized that the federal government continued to exercise many patronage prerogatives after the Civil Service Act came into being. Moreover, in a poor and economically underdeveloped region like the Maritimes, federal patronage would take on an importance perhaps not matched in wealthier and more self-sufficient regions. Nevertheless, it remains a striking testimony to the integration of federal and provincial politics within the Liberal party that provincial advantages were far more often used to assist the federal wing than to hinder it. For example, in the summer of 1935 the Liberal premier of Prince Edward Island wrote to the then leader of the opposition in Ottawa, Mackenzie King, to assure him that the provincial Liberal government would 'conduct itself diplomatically in the matter of appointments in the interval before the impending federal election.' Or as one Nova Scotia local organizer complained in the 1950s: 'Of course, many things enter into political organizations at various level [sic], but the key to the whole situation is "patronage" and "the hope of patronage." We, the Liberals of Annapolis-Kings, have neither and our own organization would be dead as a dodo if it were not for provincial patronage.'[11]

One area where the federal party had no difficulties in playing by the local rules was in election expenditure. The passing of money or gifts as inducements to vote was, and is, prevalent in the Maritimes. The Liberals collected most of the money destined for the Maritimes in Montreal. A federal election was a means whereby cash from St James Street could flow into the hands of party workers and voters in a chronically depressed region. This is a form of transfer payment which never shows up in discussions of federal-provincial financial arrangements but which is perhaps more real and tangible to ordinary Maritimers than the more rarefied levels of intergovernmental finance. The question of the prevalence of *quid pro quo* arrangements for voting is a sensitive one; even among Maritimers genuinely straightforward about patronage, the suggestion of bribery or corrupt practices at elections generates defensiveness. Yet there is no doubt that the practice has been widespread. J.B. McNair, a successful Liberal premier of New Brunswick, estimated that the proportion of 'bribable' voters in his province varied, but that in some constituencies it could be as high as half the electorate. To the poor voter this system perhaps offered a small bit of welfare. And, to be fair, there were standards of conduct associated with these electoral mores: party workers were adamant that, once bought, most voters would honestly stay bought.[12] In any event, the Liberal party encountered no difficulty in accommodating itself to these local customs, however much the national party might like to serenely ignore the sort of things done to send its supporting troops to Ottawa. Successful as the party was in the Maritimes, there was never even the hint of any suggestion that Maritime politics should be reformed. No doubt one of the secrets of Liberal success nationally was its ability to adapt itself with facility to local political cultures and local political practices.

If there was generally little tension between the federal and provincial wings of the party, there was one feature of patronage politics which did create persisting tensions of a different order within the party organization. Patron-client relationships tend to generate personal factionalism and petty cliques. Liberal organization in the Atlantic provinces was never altogether free from this nagging problem, but it was generally at such a localized level that it constituted a minor nuisance beneath the concern of Ottawa or even of the regional cabinet minister. Occasionally, when a member died or retired, the local organization would tend to disintegrate, since it had been little more than a personal following in the first place. At this point someone higher up might have to intervene to set the party in motion again behind a new candidate. Sometimes personal jealousies and factionalism might endanger the party in a particular election. Since much of the trouble would originally arise over patronage, government largesse could equally be employed to smooth over the difficulty. Here again the Liberal party benefited from the fact that success breeds success. In power provincially in most of the Atlantic provinces and in Ottawa for most of the period of this study, the Liberals commanded sufficient resources to handle such problems with relative ease.[13]

The Liberal party was, and is, part of the landscape of the Atlantic provinces, a traditional institution in a notably traditionalist area. The relative tranquillity of its political life in this region has been matched by its lack of dynamism in pursuing programmes of modernization. With the possible exception of a brief flurry of reform by the Louis Robichaud government in New Brunswick, there has been little inclination on the part of the Liberal party in the Atlantic provinces to undertake an interventionist or even progressive role. Smallwood's Newfoundland Liberals perhaps represent a more complex case, but that province is, as already noted, a rather special one, to be treated separately. Stable two-party politics have generally meant stagnant two-party politics: the legislative experiments and innovations which have marked the third-party politics of the West have never been in evidence in the East. What Lord Bryce said of the American parties in the late nineteenth century is wholly applicable to the Maritimes parties – they 'now continue to exist, because they have existed. The mill has been constructed and its machinery goes on turning, even when there is no grist to grind.'[14]

NEW BRUNSWICK

New Brunswick is the one Atlantic province with a large Francophone Roman Catholic population. The Acadians rest in somewhat uneasy equilibrium with an English-speaking population which takes its Protestantism and its Loyalist heritage very seriously. Voting patterns have followed this division with predictability. French and Irish Catholics strongly support the Liberals; Protestants of British origin heavily support the Conservatives. Since over a third of the New Brunswick population is of French extraction, and about half of the Catholic religion, the Liberal party has a fairly stable and persistent base.[15]

As Hugh Thorburn has written, the 'pervasive localism' of New Brunswick politics prevents many generalizations about party organization.[16] Although the nature of local party organization varies from rural to urban areas and from one section to another, there has never been any important friction between the federal and provincial wings of the Liberal party. It has always been considered the normal course of events for Liberals to contribute equally to both levels of political activity. Indeed, federal-provincial co-operation was so close that Ottawa Liberals sometimes failed to appreciate the situation, taking their cue as they did from central Canada. For example, Mackenzie King cautiously warned his postmaster-general, Peter Veniot, not to intervene too obviously in the 1930 provincial election, so that he might not alienate voters who were inclined to the Conservatives provincially, but undecided federally. Veniot thought the suggestion senseless: 'It is impossible for me to refrain from taking part as the provincial and federal organizations march hand in hand. If I do not help the provincial party they will not help me in federal elections.'[17] As one New Brunswick MP informed the NLF in 1948, local organizational structures – polls organized on a parish basis – functioned impartially at federal or provincial elections. In practically all instances over a twenty-five-year period of his own experience, he added, the arrangement 'has proven quite satisfactory.'[18]

When the McNair government went down to defeat in the provincial election of 1952, the Liberals took the opportunity to rejuvenate their somewhat complacent organization. A provincial office in Fredericton was financed by a constituency levy system – a first in the province – and attempts were made to publish a newsletter and to reactivate moribund constituency associations.[19] Results became apparent as early as the federal election the following year when somewhat greater particiation in the campaign became evident. By 1960 Louis Robichaud led the provincial Liberals back to office.

NOVA SCOTIA

Liberal politics in Nova Scotia from the 1930s through to the mid-1950s were dominated by one man – Angus L. Macdonald. A 'majestic father figure,' in J.M. Beck's phrase, Macdonald easily dominated the extra-parlia-mentary party organization in a province which has a long tradition of lead-ership domination. If anything, the party organization tended to atrophy somewhat in the latter years of the Macdonald era so that religious faction-alism following Macdonald's death quickly led to the victory of the Con-servatives under Robert Stanfield who was able to establish his own domi-nation of the province for over a decade. Yet even at the zenith of Macdonald's power and prestige, 'Liberal party workers attributed their al-most continuous success to superior organization on both the provincial and county levels, and, because the lower echelons of the party help to allo-cate the local patronage, the Liberals had no trouble in maintaining a co-herent organization at the polling district level.'[20]

Unlike New Brunswick, there was more obvious evidence in Nova Scotia of dissatisfaction with federal domination and even a willingness on the part of Macdonald as premier to criticize national Liberal policies. Particu-larly in the postwar period, the Nova Scotia leader gained a certain reputa-tion in the country as a 'provincial rights' man over issues such as federal-provincial fiscal arrangements. The autonomist rhetoric, however, did not carry over into intra-party conflict as happened elsewhere in the country. Macdonald himself left the premier's office during the war to take up a cabinet post in Ottawa, representing an Ontario constituency. He made very little impression on wartime Ottawa; apparently the charisma of the highland kilt did not pass the Nova Scotia border. And at the constituency level there is no evidence that consciouness of provincial grievances ever in-terfered with the smooth meshing of federal and provincial Liberal organi-zation. Since politicians respond above all to the visible power of votes, there is something futile in the spectacle of a provincial wing of a national party expressing rhetorical disagreement with their federal wing while at the same time refusing to back their position with organizational power. The ti-morous and half-hearted attempt to bring Maritime issues before the na-tional Liberal convention in 1948 mentioned in an earlier chapter seems to sum up the situation only too well. It was the Nova Scotia cabinet minister in Ottawa who snuffed out the attempt.[21] Beck suggests some of the implica-tions of the Nova Scotia record:

How much the provincial interest has suffered in the efforts to maintain harmony between the federal and provincial sections of the old parties is not calculable. It is pertinent to wonder, however, whether Nova Scotian MPs and MLAs have been too concerned with maintaining over-all party solidarity at the cost of safeguarding pro-vincial interests; whether their representatives at Ottawa have been content with little more than temporary sops; and whether it would have been to the advantage of Nova Scotia to have the followed the course of the Prairie provinces by returning third-party representation in strength to both the federal and provincial parliaments.[22]

The point is, of course, academic. Nova Scotians chose, and continue to choose, to reject the Prairie course. In the end, the federal Liberals could treat Nova Scotia in the same way as they treated New Brunswick. It was a faithful, if sometimes complaining, ally.

PRINCE EDWARD ISLAND

Canada's smallest province is politically unique. Nowhere else is there a provincial political unit based on the kind of face-to-face intimacy usually associated with small municipalities. In such an atmosphere there was little or no need for party organization for formal mobilization of the vote, and Island Liberals rarely worried about such exogenous concepts as provincial or even constituency associations. The four counties of the province were the basis of whatever party organization existed beyond the local or poll level. Although there was no evidence of 'serious inconvenience' to Liberal success – provincially the party remained in office from 1935 to 1959 with preponderant majorities in the legislature – the federal party was often irritated that Prince Edward Island should be the only province outside of Quebec with no provincial association to represent them in the NLF. Periodic attempts were made to prod the Islanders into emulating the rest of the country, but with mixed success. When a PEI Liberal Association was finally formed, it was, in the words of the official party historian in the province, 'largely a paper organization – it had no funds, no power, and little support from the rank-and-file.' Indeed, so unimportant was this organization that it took some years before Ottawa even noticed its existence.[23]

Prince Edward Island was so much taken for granted by Liberal governments in Ottawa that even the merely symbolic representation normally accorded provinces ignored on more substantive matters was sometimes allowed to lapse. During the King–St Laurent era this was virtually the only province allowed to go without cabinet representation on occasion. Alternatively, the Island might be designated as the seat of mainland party notables in search of a safe constituency, from Mackenzie King himself in 1919 to Charles Dunning in the late 1930s and J.L. Ralston during the Second World War. Yet such was the condition of economic dependency on Ottawa that very little autonomist sentiment appears to have manifested itself within the Liberal party in this era. Indeed, the large growth of federal spending in the late 1940s and 1950s under Liberal auspices was employed by provincial Liberals as an argument for maintaining a tight degree of political integration between the two levels of government. J. Walter Jones, premier from 1943 to 1953, used his federal Liberal connections as a major electoral selling point. The argument that it was necessary to maintain the same political colours provincially as were dominant in Ottawa in order to ensure the continued flow of federal dollars into the province met with consistent success at the polls. As a consequence, there was considerable confusion between federal and provincial issues. But as one observer has written: 'With nearly two-thirds of its budget coming from Ottawa, the province jealously guarded whatever advantages it could claim at the nation's capital.' In 1956, however, the federal goverment finally went too far in its neglect. In that year the Dominion Bureau of Statistics reported that a mistake had been made in calculating the province's population in the 1951 census. The federal minister of finance, Walter Harris, then announced that the Island had been the object of a $1.4 million overpayment in federal *per capita* grants calculated on the erroneous DBS figures. Harris demanded repayment, and a provincial delegation went to the capital to plead their case of fiscal incapacity. When Ottawa remained impassive, relations cooled considerably between the provincial and federal governments. In the 1957 federal election Liberal premier A.W. Matheson offered little help to federal Liberal candidates and all three Liberal MPs were defeated – a modest contribution to the national victory of John Diefenbaker's Tories.[24] With a Conservative government installed in Ottawa, the Island voters then defeated the Matheson government in 1959 and replaced it with a provincial Conservative counterpart.

NEWFOUNDLAND

Newfoundland is such an atypical case of federal-provincial relations within the Liberal party that any examples drawn from this province might seem to be of dubious relevance to the rest of the country. Not only was Newfoundland the only province without a long period of residence within Canadian political structures to temper and shape its own distinctive identity, but the circumstances of its entry into Confederation and of its early history as a province of the Dominion consolidated its uniqueness. Whatever else one may say about Newfoundland there is no doubt that it is a province quite unlike any other. More than one observer has compared Newfoundland's politics to those of an emergent Third World nation.[25] The closest one can come to a model for federal-provincial party relations in this country is the relation between Ottawa and the nascent parties in the West before the coming of provincial status. Yet even here the analogy is weak, for under Smallwood the Newfoundland Liberals exercised much more influence within their own sphere than the early western wings of the national parties ever did. Yet however unique the Newfoundland case, illumination is cast on the nature of the Liberal party in this era by examining its actions in bringing Newfoundland into Confederation and in maintaining, with great success, Liberal domination of both federal and provincial politics for a generation after Confederation. In the very extremity of conditions on the island, certain aspects of the Liberal party, obscured elsewhere by generations of tradition, may be seen in new light.

The distinctive features of the Newfoundland political culture have been the subject of a surprisingly large literature. There appears to be considerable agreement among writers on this subject; some may emphasize certain features more than others, but the outlines of a consensus are readily visible.[26] The severe level of economic underdevelopment, the marginal nature of the island's relationship to the centres of production and distribution of the North American capitalist economy, the dependence on precarious forms of primary production such as fishing and the peculiar structure of that latter industry, the outport pattern of settlement, the domination of the province by St John's and by the tiny clique of extravagantly wealthy Water Street merchants, the political chaos and financial insolvency of the years leading up to Confederation, and the unparalleled domination of the politics of a province by one man – all these factors, as well as many others, have tended to produce a politics which is perhaps less that of the classic patron-client model characteristic of the other Atlantic provinces and Quebec, than a blend of paternalism and personalist rule without the intervention of intermediary levels of brokers between the leader and the mass. Newfoundland exhibits machine politics without a political machine, and patronage politics without a web of clientist relationships from top to bottom. The analogy to newly independent Third World nations just emerging into self-government under the direction of a charismatic leader may be slightly exotic, but it perhaps gets the sense of the situation. In any event, the meshing of this peculiar blend of political culture at the provincial level with the national political system was accomplished with relative ease by means of the Liberal party. Thus the machinery of the modern bureaucratic state in Ottawa was enlisted on behalf of the Newfoundland leader's paternalist politics; in return, the federal Liberal party was virtually guaranteed a minimum of five seats in the federal Parliament. It was a minor, but suggestive, triumph for the adaptability of the Government party in manipulating the state for the benefit of party. Benefits may well have flowed in the other direction as well, but let there be no mistake that the Liberal party profited handsomely from this arrangement.

Smallwood's domination of the political life of the former colony was never in doubt after his successful championship of Confederation as the way out of the economic and political impasse which gripped Newfoundland following the war. Not only were there no formal structures set up within the Liberal party to accommodate membership participation in its operations, but there was always considerable doubt as to whether any party actually existed outside of Smallwood himself and the candidates whom he handpicked for election. In the fishing outports, 'Joey' was in an unchallenged position of direct influence over the scattered and socially isolated voters. The benefits from Confederation, especially the family allowance 'baby bonus,' were tangible payoffs for political support to which Smallwood seemed to personally control access. Unlike the patronage politics of the Maritime provinces and Quebec, in Newfoundland it was precisely the bureaucratic outputs of the federal government which were the staples of political obligation in the hands of the local party leader. The only persistent source of opposition came from St John's where the anti-Confederationists, metamorphosed into 'Conservatives' by the coming of Confederation, carried on a hopeless and disorganized sniping from the political fringes. Yet precisely because the St John's élite had so totally dominated the rest of the island before Confederation, Smallwood was able to exploit the political vacuum in the outports to establish a direct relationship with the voters without the intervention of local élites as brokers. He neither owed his political resources to anyone within Newfoundland nor did he have to come to terms with pre-existing élites. Given this clear field, Smallwood further chose not to establish new structures to support his rule, but rather to operate in a highly personal manner, embodying the functions of the party organization with his own office and person. Thus no political machine came into existence, nor anything remotely resembling a modern extra-parliamentary party structure. No convention of the Newfoundland Liberal party was called for over twenty years after a founding convention in 1949 unanimously selected Smallwood as the provincial leader. Joey ran a tight ship.

From the beginning, the national Liberal party came to recognize the potential value of absorbing Newfoundland as a province and Smallwood as a political resource. The ubiquitous figure of Jack Pickersgill was an important link between Smallwood and the Ottawa government.[27] The story of the constitutional arrangements for Confederation has been often told; the political arrangements have attracted less attention. The political arrangements with the Liberal party began where all real politics in this country begin – with money. Harold Horwood, a pro-Confederation journalist, and two financial men, Phil 'Ten-Percent' Forsey and Ray Petten, later a senator and financial collector for the party, set out to make contacts for waging a pro-Confederation campaign in the 1948 referendum which was to decide Newfoundland's fate. Although outsiders to Ottawa, these gentlemen were not without knowledge of who was who in that foreign capital. In Horwood's words, they 'went first, of course, to the fountainhead, C.D. Howe, who controlled the purse strings and everything else in the Liberal party.' Howe did not wish to be publicly associated with financing a political campaign in another country, so he sent them to Senator Gordon Fogo, the party treasurer. Fogo averred that he could not give them money from the regular party funds. But he could give them a list of donors who 'might be induced to contribute.' Horwood continues: 'most of these, it turned out, were brewers and distillers and vintners – people who were in a rather sensitive position, and who, if the word were dropped from the Liberal party that they should do a favour for somebody else, would be very apt to do the favour.' They collected a quarter of a million dollars.[28] Another valuable political resource which Confederation put into Smallwood's hands was the promise of senatorships, which he used to line up financial support even before the terms of union had been agreed to. Two Water Street millionaires were induced to break anti-Confederate ranks to support the Smallwood campaign: as Horwood remembers, 'it was a speculation which assumed there was a possibility that we would win, and if we did win there was a chance of getting a senatorship.' One of these donors succeeded in buying a senatorship; the other, unfortunately, was convicted of income tax evasion before his reward could be bestowed.[29] As it turned out, Smallwood's political skills were not matched by financial astuteness; since his main talent for money was in spending it, he put himself and the Newfoundland Liberals in constant difficulty. The contacts established with mainland financial sources were useful on more than one occasion in bailing Smallwood out of self-inflicted money problems.[30]

In the long run, the most important resource which Confederation placed in Smallwood's hands was access to the federal treasury. At the time of the original Confederation debates in 1865 one participant had sarcastically referred to the proposed Dominion authority as 'this one most magnificent government cow.' Understandably enough, it was this image which attracted the 'most calf-like appetite' of the impoverished Newfoundlanders.[31] From the point of view of Newfoundland politics, the most important aspect of this state of economic dependency was the boost which it gave to Smallwood's domination of the island. Smallwood was able to present himself not only as the man who carried Newfoundland into Confederation but also as the man who brought the expanded system of welfare and transfer payments to the outports, and who could, by extension, have them cut off again if the voters were unwise enough to send Tories back to Ottawa. However unsophisticated such credulity in the voters might appear to outsiders, the traditional paternalism and low level of social mobilization in the outports did little to prepare the people for dealing with a modern bureaucratic state. The charismatic leader then becomes a decisive intervening figure. It was a role which Smallwood exploited to the full. Indeed, be exploited it so well that he became a kind of local boss with unprecedented power and autonomy within the national Liberal party. It is difficult to recall any provincial Liberal leader who simultaneously managed to wield such influence within his own sphere and at the time time to retain the closest level of co-operation with the national party. Hepburn became the boss of Ontario, but this status was achieved at the expense of his position as a national Liberal, a situation which ultimately led to his provincial downfall. Smallwood managed to play both the federal and provincial sides with unparalleled success. The peculiar situation of Newfoundland obviously had much to do with this, but it was Smallwood's special genius to turn a condition of abject economic dependency into a position of political strength. And it was the genius of the national Liberal party to accommodate itself with such facility to Smallwood's conditions for federal-provincial party relations.

Even before Newfoundland's official entry into Canada, Smallwood had already been able to name Newfoundland's first federal cabinet minister. Following his sweep of the province in its first provincial election, Smallwood emerged as the campaign manager for the federal Liberals in the first federal election a month later. As Richard Gwyn writes, 'from then on, for the next generation, MP's went to Ottawa by his grace, and Senators by his favour.'[32] No separate federal party organization was set up; the same men and the same issues which dominated the provincial campaign also dominated the federal contest. 'What the 1949 federal campaign showed above all else,' Peter Neary suggests, 'was that federal politics in Newfoundland would be a mere adjunct of provincial politics and that the real political sovereign of the province would continue to reside in St. John's.'[33] When Louis St Laurent toured the province during the campaign it was under Smallwood's personal patronage; apart from his connection with Smallwood the Canadian prime minister had no independent following in the province. This situation has continued. S.J.R. Noel sums up the post-Confederation experience in these words: 'Federal politics have been, in practice, an extension of provincial politics – a further test of the premier's popularity ... the federal Liberal party has had no independent existence in Newfoundland ...'[34]

The great master stroke of Smallwood's political genius with regard to the Liberal party came with his enlistment of Jack Pickersgill as member for Bonavista-Twillingate. The story of how this prairie boy turned Ottawa mandarin and wire-puller was presented to the outports and accepted as Newfoundland's very own man in Ottawa is a classic study in the political audacity and imagination of the Liberal party; it is a tribute both to Pickersgill's abilities and Smallwood's power that this bizarre arrangement not only worked, but worked brilliantly. Pickersgill found himself a safe political base from which he could indulge his Liberal loyalties with greater seemliness than from the supposedly non-partisan position of clerk of the Privy Council; Newfoundland received the benefit of the indefatigable and talented efforts of a powerful and able man in Ottawa to single-mindedly draw the maximum amount of federal dollars into the province; Smallwood gained access to a Newfoundland spokesman who 'knew where all the bodies were buried in Ottawa,'[35] but who as a mainlander could not present a major alternative to Smallwood himself. In the end, Pickersgill adapted himself so well to his constituency that be became independently powerful in his own right, but he never used this to challenge Smallwood while the latter was premier.[36]

Admiration for the sheer cleverness of Smallwood and the Liberal party in Newfoundland ought not to obscure the darker judgments which many observers have made of the Smallwood era. Particularly by the 1960s – following the tragic events of the loggers' strike in 1959 – many began to see the Smallwood régime as a decaying and backward autocracy which had not only failed to produce economic development but had seriously obstructed the growth of political maturity in the island population. Inefficiency, stagnation, scandal, and the hints of one-man power grown inward, out of touch with reality and intolerant of dissent, within a general malaise and loss of direction and purpose; these too were the legacy of the clever dovetailing of interests between the federal Liberals and the ambitions of Joey Smallwood. The Liberal party drew the maximum political benefit to itself from the opportunity to integrate Newfoundland into the Canadian federal state; immediate material benefits flowed to Newfoundlanders from the arrangement, although real long-term economic development has eluded them. But in no sense did the Liberal party act as the instrument for the democratization of Newfoundland's seriously underdeveloped political life. We may conclude with Peter Neary's judgment on the Liberal party in this province:

Tragically, it all too often used the unquestioning trust which had been placed in it to exploit rather than to remedy the political immaturity of Newfoundlanders. Thus, despite the idealism of Mr. Smallwood's speeches in 1948 and 1949, the threat of punishment or the promise of reward has been much more characteristic of the Newfoundland Liberal on the hustings than has been rational argument ... Newfoundland now [1969] resembles the Quebec of Mr. Duplessis – a place of cheap, docile labour and an anachronistic freedom for private enterprise to exploit the public domain. In his own way Mr. Smallwood, too, has been cast in the role of *roi nègre* ... But just as many in Newfoundland who know better have been able to turn a blind eye to the abuse of power in the province, so has the federal Liberal party. It has left the organization of the federal constituencies in Newfoundland to the provincial Liberal party and it has accepted the support it has received in Newfoundland without questioning how that support has been obtained. In this way, it too, has fostered political immaturity in the island ... The federal party has put political expediency before principle and left its lieutenants in Newfoundland free to act in a way it would not care to be associated with elsewhere in Canada.[37]

FEDERAL-PROVINCIAL CAREER PATTERNS

This short excursus on Newfoundland serves to indicate the uniqueness of the newest province, yet it is an exception which in its own way demonstrates the truth of the earlier generalization made about the Atlantic provinces, that the Liberal party enjoyed closer federal-provincial co-operation here than anywhere else in the country. This degree of federal-provincial integration is further illustrated by an analysis of federal-provincial career patterns of Liberal MPs during the period of this study. Table 10.1 shows that the Atlantic provinces exhibit more intermingling of federal and provincial career patterns than any other area. The general trend toward insulation of the two spheres from one another is also apparent in the Maritimes. The pre-1930s figures of 83 per cent of Liberal MPs with either provincial careers or failed attempts at provincial office does decline quite drastically to the 1950s figure of only 10 per cent. Yet on the average over the entire time-span, more than 41 per cent exhibited dual careers – a figure substantially higher than anywhere else for the Liberal party or for national averages of all MPs for the same period.[38] Even when Newfoundland is

Table 10.1
Elected career patterns of federal Liberal MPs from the Atlantic provinces, 1930-58, by decade
in which federal career began

Decade elected	Federal career only	Federal and provincial careers	Defeated provincially	Total
Before 1930	1	3	2	6
1930s	11	9	5	25
1940s	14	5		19
Including Newfoundland	*17*	*7*		*24*
1950s	9	1		10
Including Newfoundland	*14*	*2*		*16*
Total	35	18	7	60
Including Newfoundland	*43*	*21*	*7*	*71*

Note: figures exclude Charles Dunning, an outsider sitting in Prince Edward Island, with provincial experience as premier of Saskatchewan.
Source: information compiled from J. K. Johnson, ed., *The Canadian Directory of Parliament,
1867-1967* (Ottawa, 1968)

Table 10.2
Elected career patterns of Liberal senators from the Atlantic provinces, appointed 1935-57

	Federal only	Federal-provincial	Provincial only	No elected career	Total
Maritimes	5	6	10	5[a]	26
Newfoundland		1	1	6	8

[a]Includes one senator who listed his party affiliation as 'independent'
Source: *Canadian Directory of Parliament*

included, the proportion only dips to 39.4 per cent, despite the fact that
Newfoundland had been without self-government for many years preceding
Confederation. This much closer integration of the two levels is further indicated by the type of appointments made to the Senate from the Maritimes
during the years of Liberal rule in Ottawa. Table 10.2 shows that 62 per

cent of Liberal Senate appointments have gone to provincial political figures or to those with dual career patterns. Of the ten appointments with provincial careers only, eight had been provincial cabinet ministers. Thus it seems that the Senate has been used as a reward system for provincial politics to a much greater extent in the Atlantic provinces than elsewhere. Since the provincial wings of the Liberal party always were willing to give support to the federal party whenever called upon, this seems only equitable.

The problem with which we began this chapter remains, even after the various pay-offs and arrangements associated with élite accommodation have been noted. Fidelity to the two-party system and close federal-provincial co-operation within the Liberal party in the Atlantic provinces certainly paid off for the federal Liberals, and produced tangible rewards for the local Liberal activists. Yet the long-term economic stagnation of the Atlantic region during this era may well suggest that, in the larger sense, federal-provincial party integration is a form of unrequired generosity on the part of a peripheral region within the Canadian federation. The West knew better.

Conclusion:
Party and state in the Liberal era

It is now possible to summarize the main conclusions of this study. There are two limitations immediately apparent on theoretical generalizations. First, the major thrust of this study has been descriptive rather than analytical, based on the sufficient grounds that so little has been known about Liberal party organization and financing in this period that the mere marshalling of the historical evidence from primary sources is of legitimate interest. Second, the limitation of this study to the period from 1930 to 1958 forbids facile generalizations linking the party structures of that era to those of today. It would be a tempting, but inevitably superficial, exercise to draw out lines of historical development from this earlier period to the present. It is to be hoped that studies like the present one will in fact make such broader analyses possible, but such a task lies outside the scope of this work. The conclusions are thus confined to what can be inferred directly from the evidence here presented.

ENVIRONMENTAL CONSTRAINTS

The environmental constraints on the Liberal party would appear to have been dominated by three factors. The Canadian political system is liberal-democratic, which, as C.B. Macpherson has ably argued,[1] is a system characterized by a fundamental, or structural, ambiguity: the coexistence of the democratic and egalitarian values of the political institutions based on universal adult suffrage and the inegalitarian nature of the liberal capitalist economic structures upon which the political structures arose historically. The Liberal party was operating in an environment in which two sometimes contradictory forces were at work in shaping the party's role. On the one hand, the party had to finance its operations as a party as well as to manage a capitalist economy as a government, both of which left it vulnerable to the demands of the corporate capitalist world. On the other hand, the party had to get votes, which left it vulnerable to the demands of public opinion. Contradictions were not always in evidence between these two forces, but when they were the party was in a state of crisis. Crisis can mean not only danger but opportunity. The Liberal party demonstrated superior skill at calling in one of these forces to redress the balance when the other became too dominating. In the King period this often meant calling in the force of the voters to compensate for the opposition of the private economic interests, but in the St Laurent period it more often meant calling in the force of corporate capitalism to restrain and manage public opinion. In either event, both the political power of the voters and the economic power of corporate capitalism were in effect resources with which the party, as an intermediary force, could bargain. The ambiguity of this role was heightened, and even cultivated, by the ambiguous ideological role of the party fashioned by Mackenzie King. That the party never rejected the support of the vested capitalist interests, while at the same time never entirely losing its credibility with the voters as a party of democratic reform, left it precisely the flexibility and freedom of action to 'wheel and deal' in the centre of the political spectrum and to make the kind of practical accommodations necessary to maintain its hold on power.

The third environmental factor, this somewhat more specific to Canada, was the regional diversity and political fragmentation inherent in a federal society as decentralized as Canada. This factor is at the same time so obvious as to be almost taken for granted, and yet so important that it can scarcely be overestimated. The relatively weak impact of the dominant *class* cleavages of modern industrial society on Canadian party politics in the face of economic regionalization and cultural divisions not only simplified the role of the Liberals as the centre party exploiting the ambiguities and contradictions of liberal-democracy – rather than becoming a victim of them, as in the case of the British Liberal party – but also gave a very particular cast to the structure of the party. It is no exaggeration to say that the structure of the Liberal party in this era can *only* be understood in the light of the impact of federalism on the inherited political structures of the British parliamentary system.

PARTY FINANCE

The relationship between the party and its financial supporters was a complex one, to a degree which rather forbids easy generalizations. The celebrated Beauharnois affair of 1930 was a highly misleading guide to the financial state of the party. The penury into which the party fell following the defeat of that year illustrates two points: first, whatever the motives of corporate donors to political parties, a party which sustained a major defeat was quickly abandoned. This was particularly crucial for the Liberal party whose traditional links had been more to government contractors than to significant sections of big business whose interests closely related to party policy or ideology. A party which depends heavily on government contractors is in obvious difficulties when faced with a period out of office. The second point to emerge from this period is that the party was clearly unwilling to compromise its policies in return for financial support. In the case of the banks and the mining companies, as well as the railway unification issue and the wheat marketing board, there is evidence that the party – and here the decisive role of the party leader must be emphasized – would not alter policy at the behest of businessmen armed with financial inducements. On the other hand, the party's own ideological bent, while it might distance itself from some capitalist interests, drew it close to certain sectors of the corporate world. Capitalism is not a monolithic set of interests, except in those comparatively rare moments when it is challenged by other classes from below or external enemies from without. There were always some sectors of the corporate world, even if not the greater part, which were willing to work with the Liberals, particularly where their interests coincided closely with Liberal policy. Even while still in opposition there were those who found such an identity of outlook – particularly the retail chain stores and the meat packing industry. Later, the Liberal party in office was able to greatly widen the scope of its friendly relations with the corporate world, as the identity of interests broadened and deepened with the years of power.

With the victory of 1935 a major structural problem in financing the party – its separation from office – was ended. Another problem soon manifested itself, however, in the form of Mitch Hepburn's financial blockade of the federal party. The capacity of a strategically well-situated provincial party to dominate certain crucial sectors of private financial support for the party, in this case the resource industries, and to use this financial power to attempt to force its own policy goals on the federal party, was a salutary lesson to the national party both as to the growing decentralization of the structure of Canadian federalism as a result of the growing peripheralization, or Balkanization, of the economy, as well as to the continuing vulnerability of the party, even in office, to the withdrawal of financial support for the campaign fund. Any government in a liberal-democracy is aware of the crucial significance of 'business confidence.' This general dependence of governments on the private sector was matched by the dependence of the Government party on the continued support of the same interests for the party treasury. In both cases, on the other hand, the party was not without resources of its own with which to bargain – although in neither case was it in a position to ignore these interests altogether. The party's principal resource was its continued hold on office. Hepburn's blockade could only work in the long run if he were able to dislodge the Liberals from power at Ottawa. Failing that, the Liberals would have to be dealt with as the Government party, and business could not afford to ignore the implications of this for its continued relations with government.

The contract levy system which Norman Lambert enforced in the late 1930s was predicated upon the desire of business to maintain good public relations with government as a major purchaser of goods and services from the private sector. This system not only was maintained after Lambert's departure from active party work, but was extended and deepened. Two developments made this consolidation possible. The enormous growth of government intervention in the private sector, arising out of the demands of the wartime economy and the commitment to interventionist Keynesian fiscal policies following the war, along with the maintenance of relatively high levels of defence expenditure in the Cold War period, had a specific meaning for the financing of the Government party. A greatly expanded state sector which involved government in continuous interaction with private corporations as sellers of goods and services to this sector, enhanced the scope for party finance – on a contract levy system where tenders were in force, or on a straight patronage basis where public bidding was not the practice. That this growth of state activity was expressed initially through the federal government, and that this centralization was closely associated with the policies of the Liberal party, also meant that the position of the federal party was reinforced in relation to its provincial counterparts. Of course, business generally wishes to retain good relations with government parties, especially when government intervention in the private sector becomes less predictable than in the past. There is also the motive of wishing to purchase access to decision-makers in case of difficulty. Thus, with or without the specific connection of government contracts, the federal Liberal party was able to increase its capacity for financing its activities as a partisan organization through the 1940s and into the 1950s. Another sign of this improved financial position was the growing regularization of funding over the inter-election period, reflected in the growing ability of the party in the 1950s to finance its day-to-day operations on a normal business basis – a condition which had certainly not existed in the 1930s.

Party finance was not an isolated factor; party organization was intimately, even inextricably, bound up with the problem of party finance. Adequate financing was the necessary, although not the sufficient, condition for the vitality of the party as an organization. The genesis of the National Liberal Federation in the early 1930s was as much, if not more, a matter of fund-raising as it was a matter of creating an extra-parliamentary organization for electoral purposes. Vincent Massey was selected by the party leader most of all because of his presumed access to sources of party funds, and his desire for post-election assignment to the London High Commission was used by Mackenzie King as a club to force Massey unwillingly to abandon a policy-making role to concentrate on fund-raising. Norman Lambert, as Massey's successor, was above all a finance chairman and 'fixer' for linking financial supporters with government business. Following the war the close connection between the NFL officials and fund-raising continued, from Gordon Fogo through Duncan MacTavish through Alan Woodrow to Bruce Matthews.

This concentration of the extra-parliamentary party on fund-raising may indicate an endemic condition of cadre parties, with their aversion to mass membership participation in policy-making or leadership selection, and their extreme vulnerability to a small number of corporate donors, but it also illustrates two specific factors of the Canadian political experience in this era. First, the Liberal party, especially under King's leadership, was haunted by the spectre of the Beauharnois affair, and found considerable political utility in a formal separation of the fund-raising apparatus from the parliamentary leadership of the party. Duverger's notion of 'contagion from the left' impelling cadre parties into extra-parliamentary organization proves to be of limited significance here. There is very little evidence of demands for participation by the rank-and-file membership in policy-making or even leadership selection in this era of the Liberal party's history. Nor is there much, if any, evidence of a perception of electoral threat from mass party techniques of campaigning. The move of the Liberal party toward extra-parliamentary organization had much more to do with the demands of party finance.

The second major factor forcing the national party's attention on party finance was the divergence between the concentration of economic power in the private sector – both in the corporate and in the regional sense – in a small handful of influential corporations in Toronto and Montreal and the decentralized nature of the formal political system. As a political organization, the Liberal party was based on the constitutional distribution of elective offices into more than two hundred local constituencies and nine provinces (ten after Newfoundland's entry into Confederation). However much the central regions might dominate the party as a whole, such centralization could in no way match the centralization of private economic power. Indeed, the autonomy of the local units of the party in a political and electoral sense was one of the characteristics of the Liberal party as an organization, and the very structure of the formal institutional arrangements of election under the parliamentary system of single-member constituency voting ensured that this would be so. Consequently, the scope of such political activities as electoral organization and policy-making on the part of an extra-parliamentary national office was necessarily limited; on the other hand, the importance of the small number of party donors in two concentrated geographical locations meant that local units of the party at the provincial and constituency level were generally incapable of generating the necessary contacts for fund-raising purposes – but for the crucial exception of the provincial units in these area. With this exception and its consequent problems aside, it is clear that party finance would necessarily be one area of party activity best left to an extra-parliamentary wing of the national party. Hence the high degree of concentration on this one activity most relevant to the extra-parliamentary national party.

PARTY ORGANIZATION

There is no doubt that the Liberal party was a cadre party in many of the senses that Duverger uses the term: parliamentary in origin, small in membership, deriving support from local notables, etc. Yet I have already suggested that there is little evidence of Duverger's 'contagion from the left' as a factor shaping the party's structure. The growth of an extra-parliamentary party alongside the parliamentary party did not come about as the emulation of a successful mass socialist party organization on the left – since such never did develop fully at the national level in Canada – but rather as the consequence of electoral defeat, in 1930, or the fear of defeat during the Second World War. Even when, as in the latter case, it was fear of a leftward trend in public opinion and the possible capitalization of the CCF on this trend which moved the party to change its approach, the specific *organizational* changes introduced in the party were not very significant; changes rather took place on the level of policy and party programme. There was no democratization of the party organization or any shift of influence from the parliamentary to the extra-parliamentary party; rather the parliamentary leadership skilfully manipulated the extra-parliamentary structure to help initiate desired policy changes. Once the next election was won, the organization reverted to its former state.

The point is that a cadre party operating in a federal system is particularly vulnerable in an organizational sense to the loss of office, not only because the fruits of power are useful resources for party organization but also because the party lacks a firm and loyal *class* basis of support in the electorate. Moreover, the fact that the party's provincial bases are not really bases at all, but rather problematic elements in the overall structure of the national party, with different electorates, different concerns, and even different sources of party funding, means that a national cadre party out of office cannot rely on the provincial parties as a second, fall-back position for the national party in its hour of organizational need. Conversely, if it does (as in the case of Ontario in the 1930s), it may be creating organizational and political problems for itself in the long run.

The alternative in this situation is for the defeated cadre party to create an extra-parliamentary structure to undertake some of the functions normally carried out by the cabinet ministers while in office. This in turn reflects the particular cast which federalism gives to cadre parties in office, which can be called a *ministerialist* system of party organization. This system places a premium on the regional representativeness of the executive, and encourages the emergence of regional power-brokers as key cabinet ministers, who thus play a double role as administrators and as political leaders of regions. When the administrative powers of patronage are severed from the political role of regional power-broking, ministerialist organization becomes a liability rather than an asset to the party. Hence the attempt to create an extra-parliamentary wing of the party as an electoral alternative, particularly when the party leader, as in the case of King from 1930 to 1935, is unwilling to personally assume the organizational burden.

On the other hand, when the party returns to power the extra-parliamentary party diminishes drastically in importance in the face of the return to ministerialism. In the case of the Liberal party after 1935, however, one can see a new factor entering into the parliamentary versus extra-parliamentary equation. In the absence of strong class bases to national politics, cadre-ministerialist party organization rests most comfortably on what can be loosely called a patron-client model. The regional discontinuities of the country lend themselves to a clientist type of politics in which one sees vertical integration of subcultures and horizontal accommodation among the élites generated by these subcultures. So long as politics revolves mainly around questions of patronage and regional bargaining, ministerialism fits in well with the needs of the party as an organization. Even out of office, as with the creation of the NFL in the early 1930s, the promise of future patronage considerations is a powerful weapon to line up political support. Yet to the extent that the forces of industrialism and urbanism and events such as depressions and world wars intrude on this somewhat petty little political stage (the provincialism and sordidness of which was noted by earlier outside observers such as Lord Bryce and André Siegfried),[2] the attention of governments is drawn inevitably toward wider problems, which demand universalist, bureaucratic solutions rather than the old-fashioned particularistic solutions of patronage political cultures. Under the pressure of these external forces, ministerialist government becomes administrative government, politics turns into bureaucracy, and the Liberal party becomes the Government party. Paradoxically, ministerialist organization thus becomes an impediment to the political health of the party as a patronage organization, as well as the source of the necessary instruments of that type of politics. In these conditions there is a continued need for some sort of extra-parliamentary wing of the party to maintain the necessary contacts between the party's external supporters and the largesse of the government, to co-ordinate the patronage side of the party's operations, and to remind it constantly of its role as an electoral as well as an administrative organization. Thus the NLF did not disappear entirely after the return to office in 1935, as had happened in 1921. The partisan ceasefire in the war years coupled with the intense and accelerated bureaucratization and centralization of the wartime government led to such a political crisis for the Liberal party that it found it necessary to call the extra-parliamentary party back into existence to help get the electoral machine functioning once again. Ministerialism thus generated its own limitations.

The electoral victory of 1945, in which the party's ability to respond to *class* politics as well as regional politics was tested, and the return of prosperity in the aftermath of war, laid the foundations for an apparent reversal of the relationships just indicated. After the war the extra-parliamentary party was relegated to the status of a mere paper 'democratic' legitimatization of ministerialist organization. Even party publicity was in effect 'farmed out' to a private advertising agency in return for government business, thus directly linking party publicity with state publicity. The Liberal party's transformation into the Government party had reached its logicial culmination, with the virtual fusion of party and state. The Liberals won two general elections under this arrangement, and convinced most observers that they could continue indefinitely. But they lost the third election, and then suffered a devastating collapse when faced with the necessity of running while out of office, suddenly bereft of ministerialist organization, yet lacking any real extra-parliamentary party organization.

Ministerialist organization thus appears as a curiously ambiguous factor in party organization. Partly as a result of this ambiguity, the role of the national leader in the Liberal party was of paramount importance. When the party was out of office in the early 1930s the leader was in a very real sense the sole representative of the national party. In the aftermath of defeat, it is no exaggeration to assert that Mackenzie King had become the sole personal embodiment of the party in any significant way. The parliamentary party remained, but without clear responsibilities, and often without either the inclination or the ability to function as a continuing party organization. Hence King's frantic efforts to set up an extra-parliamentary organization for purposes of election planning and especially fund-raising, since the responsibility for these activities was forcing an intolerable burden on his own shoulders. It should also be noted that when out of office the potential patronage powers of the leader of the opposition in a future government are almost the only inducements available to the party for organizational purposes. This places the leader squarely at the centre of the political stage, to a degree which would appear to almost match the domination of the party by an incumbent prime minister. There is no doubt that Mackenzie King returned to office in 1935 in a stronger and more commanding position over his parliamentary party and his ministers than that which he had enjoyed before defeat. The circumstances of that period of opposition may have been exceptional, and no attempt should be made to generalize on the role of the leader of a party on the strength of this example. What is clear, however, is that the crucial role of the leader in the party organization was enhanced by this experience, and that the creation of an extra-parliamentary party was not a detraction from the role of the leader but rather an instrument of the leader's continued influence over all aspects of the party's operations.

The well-known patronage powers of an incumbent prime minister, his direct relationship with the voters, his prerogative of dissolution, and his financial control over the fortunes of individual candidates, all demonstrate that the role of the party leader while in power is of enormous importance. Yet ministerialist organization, as well as the concentration of the prime minister on policy and administrative matters, tended to push the Liberal party in power toward a somewhat more diffuse distribution of responsibilities for party organization than had been the case while out of office. This tendency became quite striking when a new leader, Louis St Laurent, who showed not the slightest interest in matters of party organization, allowed a still greater degree of devolution of responsibility in these matters to his ministers. Paradoxically perhaps, the greater strength of ministerialism in the St Laurent years is itself an indication of the discretionary role of the leader in shaping the party organization; Liberal leaders had the capacity to leave their personal stamp on the party structure, even if, as in St Laurent's case, this stamp was delegation of authority to his cabinet colleagues. Under King's direction the party organization, as well as the cabinet, was under tighter control. Yet it must also be pointed out that this greater control was only a matter of degree. It is clear from the historical record that King's ability to dominate his colleagues was limited, the limits being well recognized by King himself. Ministerialism was more than a tactic of a certain kind of prime minister; it was a structural feature of cabinet government in a regionally divided society. The historical circumstances and the accident of personality might allow greater or lesser scope for ministerialism, but the *fact* of ministerialism was not subject to these vicissitudes. National party organization when the Liberal party was in office derived its basic structure from the interplay of the leadership of the prime minister and the ministerialist distribution of responsibilities.

The domination of the extra-parliamentary by the parliamentary leadership was an inevitable feature of a cadre-ministerialist party in a federal political system. This did not make the administrative task of the extra-parliamentary officials an easy one, in the sense of a division of responsibilities and recognition for their work. In the case of both Vincent Massey and Norman Lambert, the problems of status and position were acute. Massey was obviously over-qualified in the sense of social prestige and self-evaluation for the instrumental task which King had set him. The severe personal problems which beset the relationship between the NLF president and the party leader during Massey's short tenure indicated that in future less 'weighty' persons would have to be selected for the NLF . Norman Lambert was much less prestigious a figure than Massey – as well as being more appropriate for the position in terms of skills and interests – but Lambert's difficulties in dealing with the party leader arose from another, although related, source. In order to do the job of national organizer, fund-raiser, party 'fixer,' and director of the party publicity office, Lambert believed that as NLF president he must be given official recognition by the party leadership, in order that the requisite authority be vested in the position. The reluctance of the party leader to grant this recognition, and the consequent inability of Lambert to deal on a level of equal footing with the cabinet ministers, meant that his capacity to carry out his duties was constantly hemmed in by frustration and sometimes by direct opposition of elements of the parliamentary party.

In this situation there would appear to be more than the structural constraints of ministerialism and federalism at work: to King, party organization work was 'dirty work,' slightly tainted, not quite respectable, and above all to be kept at arm's length to avoid any possibility of his own office being infected with scandal. To St Laurent, party politics was rather boring and unworthy of much attention, best left to those with a taste for that sort of thing. In either event, the result was the same: the extra-parliamentary party lacked prestige and authority. Lambert, as well as some of his financial collectors, found this invidious position intolerable, and eventually parted ways with the Liberal parliamentary leadership. While direct historical evidence of dissatisfaction on the part of later incumbents in the NLF presidency is lacking, it is clear that none of Lambert's successors held positions of any greater prestige than Lambert. If they were satisfied with their role it could only be because their expectations were lower than Lambert's had been. Finally, when one reaches the level of the secretariat of the national office, there is no question of the strictly instrumental role expected of these officers. People like H.E. Kidd and Paul Lafond displayed the utmost modesty and self-effacement in their dealings with the parliamentary leadership, as well as in their relationship to the NFL president and executive. They were the closest thing in the Canadian context to party bureaucrats. It is a mark of the domination of the parliamentary leadership as well as the weak level of extra-parliamentary organization in this country that these party bureaucrats never became, as sometimes happened in th European context, 'apparatchiks,' men of indirect but powerful influence on the party. Since they were not holding the levels of power they could not manipulate them. More to the point, there is no evidence that they harboured such ambitions; if they had, they would not have assumed such positions.

The weakest aspects of the extra-parliamentary party in this era were the policy-making function and the question of leadership selection. Mackenzie King derived his ultimate legitimacy as party leader from the 1919 convention, but it was a legitimacy which he never allowed to be put to the test of renewal by the assembled party membership. Since there was no provision in the party constitution and no overwhelming party demand for national conventions during King's tenure, a generation passed without a single assembly embodying the membership base of the party in any significant sense. The advisory council meetings held infrequently over the years were the closest approximation to conventions but in terms of numbers and of authority they were far from substitutes. Advisory councils were effectively dominated by the parliamentary party and rarely fulfilled other than honorific and formal duties. The one apparent exception was the 1943 meeting which adopted the welfarist programme which the party carried into the 1945 election campaign. This was not the result of autonomous action, however, but of superbly executed manipulation by a parliamentary leadership which wished to legitimize new directions in policy which had been planned by the civil service and advisers to the prime minister.

Massey's attempts at policy-making in the early 1930s met the active hostility of the party leader and the indifference of the parliamentary caucus as a whole. That the party leadership expended considerable anxiety and energy at the various advisory council meetings over the question of preventing anything remotely critical of the parliamentary party's policies from being aired is a striking indication of how far parliamentary control over policy went: the extra-parliamentary membership was not only to be powerless in deciding policy, but it had to be *seen* to be powerless as well. The smallest hint of disagreement over policy among Liberals – which is to say, the hint of any dissension from the policies adopted by the parliamentary leadership – was to be avoided at all costs. Democratic legitimation of the internal processes of decision-making in the party was accepted, but only at the most rarefied and abstract level, that of the mandate of the party leader derived from the majority vote of a party convention at one point in time. The autonomy of the parliamentary party in policy-making was justified in rhetorical terms by the invocation of the constitutional supremacy of Parliament. Whatever the merits of that argument, it was rendered somewhat problematic by the increasing bureaucratic influence on the policies of the parliamentary leadership, to the extent that by the last years of the St Laurent period virtually all Liberal policy was formulated by the permanent civil service. Policy-making was delegated to an institution which was, in the formal sense at least, non-political as well as non-partisan. The exclusion of the extra-parliamentary party membership from policy-making may thus be viewed as a matter of practical expediency rather than as one of constitutional principle. The party membership was not judged competent to formulate policy.

The 1948 national convention which chose Louis St Laurent as King's successor best illustrates these relationships within the Liberal party. The extraordinary lengths to which the party leadership went, in this unique example of a national party meeting throughout the period of this study, to prevent any public manifestation of criticism or disagreement within the membership extended not only to policy questions but to the matter of leadership itself. The evidence clearly indicates that the convention format was manipulated throughout to ensure that King's chosen successor should receive as little opposition as possible. On the other hand, the necessary democratic legitimation seemed to demand that St Laurent receive some token opposition. Both imperatives were carried out in a remarkable example of stage-managed conflict, in which the two genuine opponents of St Laurent were effectively utilized for maximum public effect and minimum internal impact. Even in the case of the selection of the party leader, then, the 'democratic' mandate becomes highly questionable, and the domination of the party by the parliamentary leadership is seen to be decisive.

Conventions at the constituency level during this era would appear to have served equivalent legitimation purposes for the parliamentary élite. Nomination votes by the constituency association membership were often, although not always, called before elections. Rarely were these exercises more than empty formalities. Sitting members were virtually assured of renomination; defeated candidates from the previous election had the inside track; and if neither of these conditions obtained, the local cabinet minister and his organizers would normally anoint the man they wanted for the nomination. The association would then ratify the choice. It did not happen like this in every instance, but it was the general rule. Observers of contemporary Canadian political culture who have noted the 'quasi-participative' nature of Canadian democracy[3] might examine the role of the Liberal party, the dominant party in Canadian politics for well over a generation, in the political socialization of its members and supporters. The Liberal party was certainly no training ground for participatory democracy, however loosely that phrase might be defined. If anything, the dominant values which it propagated as a mediating institution between the state and the mass of the citizens were those of deference and unreflective loyalty.

Deference and loyalty are political values appropriate to the clientist web of relationships which formed the basic structure of the party. Clientist relationships, moreover, flourished in the era of one-party dominance, when the Liberals as the Government party monopolized the basic medium of exchange in patron-client politics: patronage. But the general condition referred to earlier, the transformation of politics into bureaucracy in the period of one-party dominance, had a double effect on the party as an organization. The use of the state as a reward system for party loyalty effectively drained away the human resources of the party as a partisan organization into levels of the bureaucracy and judiciary where they could no longer be of political use to the party. Second, as an inevitable consequence of the first problem, the party had to rely heavily on direct co-operation from the bureaucracy or the private sector to replenish its parliamentary leadership. Thus it merged more and more intimately with the senior civil service, both in terms of policies and personnel, and with the corporate élite outside the state system itself but in regular contact with government. For these organizational reasons, as well as for the more general ones mentioned earlier, the party became less and less distinct as an entity, its separation from the state system and the private sector more and more blurred. The Government party was becoming in a curious sense a non-partisan party, so long as its hold on office was not challenged. Some might prefer to argue that it was a case of the bureaucrats being made into Liberals. Yet however one approaches the question, it seems reasonable to conclude that the Liberal party, as a political party, was growing less distinct, that the party was more a vehicle for élite accommodation, involving not only the élites of the two linguistic and cultural groups in Canada but the bureaucratic and corporate élites as well, than a partisan organization. When partisanship got in the way of élite accommodation it was partisanship which was usually discarded. No better example of this can be found than in the examination of federal-provincial relations within the Liberal party in this era.

FEDERAL-PROVINCIAL PARTY RELATIONS

The relations between the federal and provincial wings of the Liberal party were examined in some depth. The conclusions of this examination may be most usefully divided into two parts: the central provinces of Ontario and Quebec and the hinterland or peripheral area of the West and the East.

Quebec, as the homeland of French Canada, held a special status within the national Liberal party, based on tradition and a mild form of consociational tolerance. Yet it was Ontario, with its strong and semi-autonomous economic base, which mounted the toughest challenge to the dominance of the national party in this era. In both cases the federal party ran into difficulties with its provincial counterpart, to a moderate degree in Quebec and to an extreme degree in Ontario. In Quebec, electoral defeat for the provincial party in the mid-1930s gave the federal party, which remained ascendant in its own electoral sphere, the opportunity to control the provincial party, even to the extent of guiding it back into office briefly. Eventually, the federal party settled into a pattern of constituency collaboration with its provincial party's enemy, and more or less accommodative intergovernmental relationships with the Union Nationale in terms of federal-provincial affairs, including accommodations which sometimes drastically undercut the political position of its provincial counterpart. In Ontario, a politically (and even financially) stronger provincial party in the mid-1930s waged open war on the federal party, even extending its campaign to Quebec, both on the intergovernmental and political fronts. This vigorous challenge was finally defeated by intelligent mobilization of the federal party's resources, and the intervention of an external event, the coming of the

Second World War. Following the provincial defeat, the federal Liberals managed very well in Ontario by allowing a much weakened and discredited provincial party to flounder unaided in the further reaches of opposition, while dealing with the Conservative provincial government in federal-provincial relations with little regard to partisan considerations. Thus, in both cases, the long-run result was the same: the federal party prospered in the two largest provinces without a strong provincial wing. Little was done to aid the provincial parties, and, in the Quebe case, much was done to damage the provincials. This distant relationship was matched by an emphasis on intergovernmental relations with the provincial administrations of the opposite political colour. In other words, executive federalism overrode federal-provincial party solidarity. The Government party at Ottawa preferred to deal with other governments.

Intra-party relationships with the hinterland regions of Canada were not normally troubled by financial competition between the federal and provincial wings. The financial superiority of the federal party was almost always evident. In the Atlantic provinces this financial strength in conjunction with competitive two-party systems and patronage political cultures resulted in highly integrated party organizations and low levels of intra-party strains. Newfoundland was a somewhat exceptional case, representing one-man provincial rule in close co-operation with the federal Liberal party and the federal state, but even here there was a close meshing of the two parties, albeit with rather more provincial direction than in the Maritime provinces. Basically the Atlantic provinces represent a case study of the Liberal party as an integrative device within Confederation drawing the provincial units into the federal sphere of influence and control, a political reflection of economic and administrative domination of poor and underdeveloped provinces by the federal government.

The West presents a striking contrast with the Atlantic region. Although very much in a state of economic inferiority to central Canada, the western provinces resisted a status of political inferiority to the Government party at Ottawa, first by giving relatively weak electoral support to the party in federal elections and second by tending to strike out on experimental routes with the party system in provincial politics. Thus the Liberal parties in Manitoba and British Columbia entered coalitions at the provincial level while maintaining their full partisan identities in federal politics. Even in Alberta unsuccessful moves were attempted in this direction. In all cases severe intra-party strains became apparent. Only in Saskatchewan was a consistently high level of federal-provincial party integration maintained, due to tradition, strong partisan leadership, and relative provincial political

strength. Yet even in Saskatchewan prolonged relegation to provincial opposition bred growing internal party disunity. The Liberal party at Ottawa
during its long period of domination grew further apart from its provincial
counterparts in the West which were either co-operating with its federal
party competitors or floundering in opposition. Eventually, a pattern of intergovernmental relations with provincial administrations ranging in partisan colouration from quasi-Liberal to social democratic to Social Credit began to predominate over the kind of intra-party integrations which the
Saskatchewan Liberal machine had once represented. The Liberal party's
experiences in the West were very different from those in central Canada.
Yet the same basic result was reached from different routes: executive federalism proved stronger than federal-provincial party solidarity.

The underlying reasons for the prevalence of executive federalism over
political federalism in Canada have been explored at length by other writers. Attention has also been given to the general question of federal-provincial intra-party relations.[4] This study in effect constitutes a documentation
of the growing 'confederalization' of the Liberal party over a period of almost thirty years. It should be emphasized that this process does not necessarily imply the attenuation of federal dominance over provincial wings of
the party. Indeed, in most cases examined, the federal party emerged as the
more successful. That this took place in the two central provinces, those
best situated in economic, political, and even cultural (in the case of Quebec) terms to mount effective challenges to federal domination of the Liberal party, is a striking indication of the ability of the senior level of the
party to maintain it superior position. But confederalization did mean the
separation of the two wings in terms of senior personnel, career patterns,
party finance, and even ideology. This means that by the 1950s the Government party in Ottawa was loosely linked with unsuccessful opposition parties in Quebec City, Toronto, and three western provinces – parties whose
weakness was more or less enforced by the very success of the federal party.
Nor was this distinctly asymmetrical relationship simply an accident; rather
it reflected a crucial problem in federal-provincial relations.

The problem revolves around the inevitable conflict in which two wings
of the same party in the same province must engage for the available human resources. An increasing separation and insulation of the two wings at
the level of parliamentary leadership was never matched by an equivalent
separation of the membership at the constituency level. The critical problem faced by all parties of the mobilization of the party rank and file at election time to perform the multiple organizational tasks necessary for successful electioneering, could become itself a cause of contention and

competition between two wings of the party in the same area. Only in the extreme – and in the Canadian context, unlikely – eventuality of complete jurisdictional accord between the province and the national government might political conflict at the governmental level not cause conflict at the party level. Another factor capable of overriding intra-party divisions might be a cross-provincial ideological cohesiveness within the party; in the case of a brokerage party like the Liberals, this was never true in practice, and doubtful in theory. Nor could pure patronage politics serve to override divisions. The instance of Quebec East cited in this study rather indicates that a preoccupation with patronage politics was itself a disturbing factor in federal-provincial intra-party relations.

E.R. Black has suggested that 'just as the virtual independence of a provincial government's policy-making depends to a considerable extent on its provincial resources, so the effective control of provincial organization by the local officers depends upon the local unit's political resources in comparison with those of the central party: such resources are considered to be size and commitment of membership, financial capabilities, quality and appeal of leadership, and, of course, electoral success.' Black then goes on to note that while the policy objectives and organizational requirements in the federal and provincial arenas are often quite different, nevertheless 'both sets of leaders must rely in large measure on the relatively small group of people and on the same resources in their field work.'[5]

In the case of Hepburn's challenge to federal domination, it was precisely this lack of organizational differentiation at the local level which proved to be his undoing. To blockade successfully the federal party Hepburn had to mobilize the local Liberal activists to withdraw their allegiance and support from the federal Liberals. This he attempted to do by discrediting the federal party in the eyes of Ontario voters and by forming alliances with federal Conservatives. Yet so long as the Liberals remained in office in Ottawa, this campaign achieved little success. Thus Hepburn was driven by the logic of his position to more and more extreme opposition to his own national party. Since he was ultimately unable to extend his efforts beyond his own province, the much wider base of the national party was not sufficiently undercut to give tangible evidence of success. Hence his struggle developed in a manner which seemed irrational and self-defeating to the local Liberal activists. The financial resources of the provincial party were not enough to counteract the political resources of the federal party, especially after the outbreak of the Second World War. In the end it was the provincial party which was driven into opposition; the provincial Liberals have never, since Hepburn's failure, attracted the kind of local organizational strength characteristic of the federal Liberals in that province.

In Quebec a superficially different, but essentially similar, pattern developed. Provincial disputes spilled over into federal constituency politics; the federal party reasserted stability by the subordination of the provincial wing, first by directly placing it in office, later by abandoning it to successive terms of opposition while collaborating with its opponent. The capacity of the federal wing to enforce a permanent opposition status on its provincial counterpart derived from its superior political and financial resources accruing from the national office, and its evident unwillingness – except in the very special circumstances of 1939 – to utilize these resources on behalf of the provincial party. Superior political and financial resources combined to ensure superiority in the attraction of human resources. Yet, in the long run, the provincial Liberals were able to rebuild their strength, not through prior solution of their financial problem but by generating new and separate organizational structures which could serve as alternative sources for the mobilization of human resources. In other words, political resources were developed independently of the federal party.

To a degree in Manitoba and much more so in British Columbia, coalition arrangements in provincial politics put severe strains on constituency organization and the loyalties of local party activists. There is definite evidence for British Columbia that the federal Liberals were in a much stronger position when the provincial party went into opposition in the 1950s than when it had been the dominant provincial coalition partner earlier. Saskatchewan, in the period of joint Liberal rule in both capitals from 1935 to 1944, appears to offer a contrast, inasmuch as party integration was smoother than it was later when the provincial party was out of office. In this case, Saskatchewan is closer to the example of the Atlantic provinces where intra-party unity was bought at the price of clear federal domination – exercised in the Saskatchewan case, however, with some autonomy at the level of the federal cabinet by Jimmy Gardiner as the regional prairie power-broker at Ottawa. In other words, federal Liberal domination within Saskatchewan did not preclude regional representation of some significance within the cabinet, a regional power which was backed precisely by the high level of intra-party integration and the bargaining leverage this placed in Gardiner's hands. Saskatchewan thus represented a model of party politics as a vehicle of regional representation quite different from those adopted elsewhere in the West. The Liberal parties of the Atlantic provinces, on the other hand, did not appear to utilize party integration as a bargaining lever within the federal cabinet to the same extent. Here party loyalty overrode regional discontent and the same local activists could be mobilized equally for either level of electoral politics with the same well-integrated set of rewards backed by the political financing of Montreal and the co-ordinated patronage inducements of the federal and provincial states. Only in Newfoundland is there real evidence of this Liberal loyalty being translated into any real provincial influence on the federal party, but here the small size of the province and its state of underdevelopment and poverty severely limited its power. The Maritimes aside, it is clear that in the case of Saskatchewan federal-provincial integration as a vehicle of provincial political representation is not without strain when one party loses office. In the late 1940s and 1950s it became apparent that a certain tension between the two wings at the leadership level was being reflected in problems at the local level.

There is a sense, then, in which federal and provincial wings of a party are often locked into a rather self-destructive relationship. If, as many observers have argued, political parties act mainly as recruitment agencies for the staffing of elective office – and the weakness of the Liberal party as a channel of demands on the political system through extra-parliamentary policy formation appears to give added weight to this emphasis – then federal and provincial wings of the same party are necessarily locked into competition for the same pool of human resources. Provincial weakness matched by federal strength guarantees the latter wing against too much competition. Dealing with governments of another political colour at the provincial level, on the other hand, avoids this problem. The claims of other governments can be treated as a matter of intergovernmental negotiation. The claims of party become a complicating factor, adding new levels of conflict which can be avoided when the problem is simply intergovernmental. The intra-party dimension of federal-provincial relations is thus a matter of *additional* complexity. It is difficult to generalize beyond this from the limited time period which has been examined, but it does seem safe to conclude that a Government party will prudently seek to avoid such complications. They may opt, as the federal Liberals did in Ontario and Quebec, for underwriting the position of their provincial wings as permanent opposition parties, thus keeping the party name before the provincial voters while at the same time minimizing their impact on the federal level. Thus the dominant strategy of the federal Liberals in confronting this organizational problem in Ontario and Quebec was to downplay partisanship between levels of government.

In a country as diverse and as decentralized as Canada, and especially in the case of provinces as crucially influential in relationship to the federal government as Ontario and Quebec, a party in power in Ottawa could not afford the intra-party strains involved in attempting to use the party as an integrative device in federal-provincial relations. Instead, the Liberal party reverted to intergovernmental, even interbureaucratic, relations as the major channels of accommodation. This not only helped account for the weak and underdeveloped nature of extra-parliamentary national party organization in this era, but also strongly reinforced the tendency already present in the Government party to transform politics into bureaucracy and party into state.

Perhaps this may be the final, paradoxical, conclusion to be drawn from this study. The curious lack of definition of Canadian parties, which has troubled so many observers of our politics, is only reinforced as the evidence concerning their structures is marshalled. The Liberal party was an organization seeking not so much to consolidate its distinct partisan identity as to embed itself within the institutional structures of government. Its fulfilment was not so much organizational survival as it was institutionalization as an aspect of government: control over recruitment channels to senior levels of office. The deadening of political controversy, the silence, the greyness which clothed political life at the national level in the 1950s, were reflections of a Liberal ideal of an apolitical public life. In place of politics there was bureaucracy and technology. This in no sense meant that Canada stood still. Profound changes were taking place in the nation's political economy. But these changes tended to take place outside the realm of traditional political debate. Instead, it was between the great bureaucracies, whether public (federal and provincial) or private (Canadian and American), that debate and policy refinement took place. The Liberal party had truly become the Government party – an instrument for the depoliticization and bureaucratization of Canadian public life. The vision of Mackenzie King in his almost forgotten *Industry and Humanity* had begun to take shape: 'whether political and industrial government will merge into one, or tend to remain separate and distinct' was King's question for the future in 1918. He concluded that 'the probabilities are that for years to come they will exist side by side, mostly distinguishable, but, in much, so merged that separateness will be possible in theory only.'[6]

The pipeline fiasco of 1956 and the Liberal defeat the following year were episodes in an apparent crisis of the Government party and its vision of the world. Whether this crisis was merely an ephemeral case of instability, or something more serious, is a question which cannot be answered here. It is enough to point out that many of the structural preconditions of Government party organization, as described in this study, remain in place today. On the other hand, the extent of political fragmentation, conflict, and instability in Canada since the Diefenbaker interlude of 1957-63 makes the continuation of the Liberal party as the permanent Government party much more doubtful than in the King–St Laurent era. To Liberals, at least, the world was simpler then.

Notes

Full bibliographical information on all secondary sources cited in the course of this book is given in the notes which follow. The core of the research was almost entirely found in primary sources, mainly collections of private papers of cabinet ministers, political figures, and party material gathered in the Public Archives of Canada or the Douglas Library, Queen's University. The most important collections are noted below, along with the short-form citations adopted in the notes for ease of identification. Various other collections of papers were consulted, many of which did not prove to contain pertinent information. Certain collections were of very marginal significance and are cited in full in the notes when the occasional reference is made to them.

A. PUBLIC ARCHIVES OF CANADA, OTTAWA

Brooke Claxton Papers (cited in notes as BC)
C.D. Howe Papers (CDH)
William Lyon Mackenzie King Papers (WLMK). Unless otherwise indicated, citations are from the First Series, General Correspondence. For diary entries from 1939 to 1945, references where possible are to the more readily accessible *The Mackenzie King Record*, ed. J.W. Pickersgill and D.F. Forster, 4 vols. (Toronto, 1960-70), cited here as MKR.
Ernest Lapointe Papers (EL)
National Liberal Federation of Canada Papers (NLF)
Ian Mackenzie Papers (IM)
James L. Ralston Papers (JLR)
Escott Reid Papers (ER)
Louis St Laurent Papers (LSTL)

B. DOUGLAS LIBRARY, QUEEN'S UNIVERSITY, KINGSTON

Charles A. Dunning Papers (CAD)
Norman P. Lambert Papers (NPL)
Charles G. Power Papers (CGP)

NOTE: Full references have been given to specific documents cited, that is, dates, authors, nature of document. Wherever possible, locational information has also been provided, such as volume number, file reference, or page number. In the case of well-indexed collections such as the King papers, such information is readily available and fully reliable. In some other collections, such as the Power papers, which were still largely unorganized when examined, locational data may not be of lasting usefulness, but is cited as fully as possible.

INTRODUCTION

1 'The Liberal Party,' *Canadian Forum* (Nov. 1955); reprinted in J.L. Granatstein and Peter Stevens, eds., *Forum: Canadian Life and Letters, 1920-70* (Toronto, 1972), pp. 302-5
2 'Political Science in Canada and the Americanization Issue,' *Canadian Journal of Political Science*, VIII, 2 (June 1975), p. 223
3 T.H.B. Symons, *To Know Ourselves: The Report of the Commission on Canadian Studies* (Ottawa, 1975), II, pp. 70 and fn. 46, 136
4 'The Liberal Party of Canada: A Political Analysis,' Cornell University, 1963
5 Cairns, 'Political Science in Canada,' p. 225
6 *The Theory of Social and Economic Organization* (New York, 1964), p. 408
7 James Bryce, *The American Commonwealth* (2nd ed., London, 1891); Ostrogorski, *Democracy and the Organization of Political Parties* (new ed., Chicago, 1964); Weber, *Theory of Social and Economic Organization*, pp. 407-12, and H. Gerth and C. Wright Mills, eds., *From Max Weber: Essays in Sociology* (New York, 1958), pp. 77-128, and other works by Weber; Michels, *Political Parties* (new ed., New York, 1962); Duverger, *Political Parties* (London, 1954)
8 R. MacGregor Dawson was one of the few Canadian political scientists of the older generation to deal seriously with party organization. *The Government of Canada*, revised by Norman Ward (5th ed., Toronto, 1970), pp. 413-500. Escott Reid was an early proponent of this type of analysis but was lost to the diplomatic service early in his career. See his classic study of the Saskatchewan Liberal machine in the 1920s, reprinted in H.G. Thorburn, ed., *Party Politics in Canada* (3rd ed., Scarborough, 1972), pp. 23-34. More recent examples of interest in such analysis may be found in J.L. Granatstein, *The Politics of Survival: The*

Conservative Party of Canada, 1939-1945 (Toronto, 1967), and Walter Young, *The Anatomy of a Party: The National CCF, 1932-1961* (Toronto, 1969). A recent introductory text on political parties also signifies renewed interest in party organization. C.Winn and J. McMenemy, *Political Parties in Canada* (Toronto, 1976), pp. 152-91.

9 Frank Sorauf, 'Political Parties and Political Analysis,' in W.N. Chambers and W.D. Burnham, eds., *The American Party Systems: Stages of Political Development* (New York, 1967), p. 36

10 Richard Rose and D.W. Urwin, 'Persistence and Change in Western Political Systems since 1945,' *Political Studies*, XVIII, 3 (Sept. 1970), p. 295

11 *Party Systems and Voter Alignments: Cross-National Perspectives* (New York, 1957), p. 50

12 'Electoral Mobilization, Party Competition, and National Integration,' in J. Lapolombara and Myron Weiner, eds., *Political Parties and Political Development* (Princeton, 1966), p. 258

13 *Nationalism and Social Communication* (Cambridge, Mass., 1953)

14 M.A. Schwartz, *Politics and Territory: The Sociology of Regional Persistence in Canada* (Montreal, 1974), examines regional impacts on the party system, but mainly in terms of voting support.

15 D.V. Smiley, *Canada in Question: Federalism in the Seventies* (2nd ed., Toronto, 1976), pp. 83-113

16 *Studies in Canadian Party Finance* (Ottawa, 1966), pp. 23-147 and 459-594. See also K.Z. Paltiel, 'Contrasts among the Several Canadian Political Finance Cultures,' in A. Heidenheimer, ed., *Comparative Party Finance* (Lexington, Mass., 1970), pp. 107-34

17 'Political Parties and the Community-Society Continuum,' in Chambers and Burnham, *The American Party Systems*, pp. 152-81

18 A good critical overview is R.R. Kaufman, 'The Patron-Client Concept and Macro-Politics: Prospects and Problems,' *Comparative Studies in Society and History*, XVI (1974), pp. 284-308.

19 Vincent Lemieux, *Parenté et politique* (Quebec, 1971); Lemieux and Raymond Hudon, *Patronage et politique au Québec: 1944-1972* (Sillery, 1975). For English Canada, see S.J.R. Noel, 'Leadership and Clientelism,' in D.J. Bellamy, J.H. Pammett, and D.C. Rowat, eds., *The Provincial Party Systems: Comparative Essays* (Toronto, 1976), pp. 197-213.

20 K.D. McRae, ed., *Consociational Democracy* (Toronto, 1974); Robert Presthus, *Elite Accommodation in Canadian Politics* (Toronto, 1973)

21 *Parenté et politique*, p. 234

22 *Cabinet Formation and Bicultural Relations: Seven Case Studies*, Study no. 6 of the Royal Commission on Bilingualism and Biculturalism (Ottawa, 1970), p. 172

23 NLF, v. 596, A.G. McLean, memorandum to J.G. Fogo, 15 April 1946

24 BC, v. 61, national executive committee meeting, 24 Feb. 1954

CHAPTER ONE
Background to the Liberal revival, 1930-2

1 Paul Stevens, 'Laurier, Aylesworth, and the Decline of the Liberal Party in Ontario,' Canadian Historical Association, *Historical Papers, 1968*, pp. 94-113; reprinted in Stevens, ed., *The 1911 General Election: A Study in Canadian Politics* (Toronto, 1970), pp. 211-19. See also Robert Cuff, 'The Conservative Party Machine and the Election of 1911 in Ontario,' *Ontario History*, LVII, 3 (Sept. 1965), pp. 149-56; reprinted in *ibid.*, pp. 205-10.
2 See Laurier LaPierre, 'Politics, Race and Religion in French Canada: Joseph Israel Tarte,' unpublished PH D thesis, University of Toronto, 1962; and H. Blair Neatby, *Laurier and a Liberal Quebec: A Study in Political Management* (Toronto, 1973), especially pp. 122-49.
3 Testimony of Commissioner Clarence Jameson to the 1923 House of Commons Special Committee on the Civil Service, quoted in J.E. Hodgetts *et al., The Biography of an Institution: The Civil Service Commission of Canada, 1908-1967* (Montreal, 1972), p. 48.
4 The 1921 federal election campaign in Ontario had to be run by national headquarters in Ottawa for, as Rodolphe Lemieux succinctly put it: 'In Ontario ... there are thousands of liberals but no liberal party'; quoted in Margaret Prang, 'Mackenzie King Woos Ontario, 1919-1921,' *Ontario History* (March 1966), p.17.
5 Peter Regenstreif, 'The Liberal Party of Canada: A Political Analysis,' unpublished PH D thesis, Cornell University, 1963, p. 130; see also John C. Courtney, *The Selection of National Pary Leaders in Canada* (Toronto, 1973), p. 72.
6 Regenstreif, *ibid.*, pp. 130-3; NLF, v. 865, 'Memorandum on Party Organization,' 1919
7 National Liberal Convention, *Official Report* (Ottawa, 1919), p.83
8 Regenstreif, 'The Liberal Party,' p. 135. This is the best source available on national organization in the 1920s, especially pp. 133-7.
9 Both of King's official biographers cite the warm confidence in which King held Haydon. R. MacGregor Dawson, *William Lyon Mackenzie King: A Political Biography, 1874-1923* (Toronto, 1958), I, p. 361; H. Blair Neatby, *William Lyon Mackenzie King: The Lonely Heights, 1924-1932* (Toronto, 1963), II, pp. 130-1.
10 Senate, Special Committee on the Beauharnois Power Project, *Proceedings and Evidence* (1932), p. 243
11 John C. Courtney, 'King and Political Leadership,' paper delivered at the Mackenzie King Centennial Colloquium, University of Waterloo, 16 Dec. 1974
12 Regenstreif, 'The Liberal Party,' pp. 261-70, 136

13 Neatby,*King*, ii, pp. 301-12. Two months after the election King could still make the following entry in his diary: 'The country was happy & contented, mffrs. [manufacturers] & labour alike but for the election propaganda.' wLMK, Diary, 22 Sept. 1930. The appointment of Charles Dunning as finance minister seemed to King a useful move in the direction of business co-operation with the Liberal party. The letters of congratulations to Dunning on his May 1930 budget read like a 'who's who' of Canadian finance and industry of the time, and Liberal informants in the Montreal and Toronto business communities believed the dominant business view of the budget to have been very favourable. CAD, v. 9, Gordon Scott to Dunning, 7 May, J.N. Godfrey to Dunning, 13 May 1930.

14 wLMK, v. 171, King to Buchanan, 19 Aug. 1930

15 *King*, ii, p. 399

16 wLMK, v. 188, Power to King, 27 Jan. 1931 (160112)

17 wLMK, Diary, 2 April, 2 May, 16 April 1930. Raymond saw his role as a 'trustee' for the party funds. Senate Committee on Beauharnois, p. 147

18 wLMK, v. 175, Haydon to King, 8 Jan. 1930 (148887-91)

19 wLMK, Diary, 29 July 1930

20 See below, Chapters 2 and 3. It must be noted that a large proportion of the Beauharnois money went to the Quebec provincial Liberals. See Canada, House of Commons, Special Committee on the Beauharnois Power Project, *Reports and Minutes of Proceedings and Evidence* (1931), pp. 824-5. King, who never trusted Donat Raymond, wrote in his diary on 28 July 1931 that $300,000 remained in the hands of the provincial Liberals. It is not clear if this statement represented actual knowledge of the facts, or merely conjecture on King's part.

21 wLMK, Diary, 29 July 1930. Worse yet was Toronto bagman Percy Parker whose demands for a Senate seat drove King to distraction, and who even made unpleasant appearances in King's dreams. wLMK, v. 179, Parker to King, 20 Jan.; Diary, 1 Jan. 1930. Concerning Quebec, see Neatby, *King*, ii, pp. 329, 340. Neatby doubts that this disaffection was decisive in the result.

22 wLMK, Diary, 4 and 29 June, 26 July 1930

23 McRae might have been helped by the fact that even previous to the election the Conservative office had, in McRae's own words 'a budget of from $25,000 to $30,000 a month, which I understand Bennett paid out of his own pocket.' Quoted in J.L. Granatstein, *The Politics of Survival: The Conservative Party of Canada, 1939-1945* (Toronto, 1967), p. 71

24 wLMK, Diary, 8 Aug., 20 Sept. 1930; 9 Feb., 31 March 1932. Moore, member for Ontario constituency, was a director of Massey-Harris and the author of a couple of books on politics including *The Clash*, a rather tolerant English-Canadian view of the conscription crisis of 1917.

25 CAD, v. 8, Dunning to J.A. Cross, 22 Aug. 1930; v. 10, Dunning to W.R. Howson, 7 Dec. 1931

26 WLMK, v. 181, King to Rundle, 6 Nov. (154089-93); Rundle to King, 12 Dec. (154095); King to Rundle, 15 Dec. 1930 (154097). As a consolation prize Rundle gave a personal donation of $500. Rundle to King, 15 Jan. 1931 (160583)

27 *Ibid.*, Diary, 13 Jan. 1931

28 Neatby, *King*, II, pp. 294-5; WLMK, v. 187, King to James Malcolm, 5 Nov. 1931 (159585-90); Diary, 16 Dec. 1931

29 WLMK, v. 174, King to W. Harvey-Jellie, 13 Nov. 1930 (148812)

30 *Ibid.*, v. 173, T.C. Davis to King, 31 July (147396-7); King to Davis, 6 Aug. 1930 (147398). One supplicant was a former premier of Ontario who was turned down flat: v. 186, E.C. Drury to King, 29 Jan. (15458-62); King to Drury, 30 Jan. 1931 (158463-5)

31 J.L. Ralston was saddled with responsibility for meeting 1930 debts from Nova Scotia, and as late as the fall of 1933 Norman Lambert was being turned away by Ralston who was still trying to settle the Nova Scotia accounts. JLR, v. 12, H.R.L. Bill to Ralston, 6 Dec. 1932; NPL, Diary, 17 and 18 Oct. 1933

32 WLMK, v. 172, P.-F. Casgrain to King, 27 Oct. 1930; v. 179, P. Paradis to King, 27 Oct. 1930

33 *Ibid.*, v. 197, Massey to King, 12 Oct. (167933-7), King to Massey, 13 Oct. 1933 (167937-8); v. 184, King to Cannon, 18 Feb. 1931 (157023); v. 188, W.R.P. Parker to King, 28 July 1931 (160008-9). The amount of the Beauharnois contribution was so niggardly as to call forth the comment by a Toronto Liberal MP at the House Beauharnois inquiry that 'men who get only $1,000 [*sic*] should be removed from office; it is absurd.' House Committee on Beauharnois, p. 826. WLMK, v. 187, B.K. McCreath to King, 10 Nov. 1931 (159116-20). King also mentioned a debt of $30,000 in his diary on 18 Aug. 1930.

34 WLMK, v. 206, A.C. Hardy to King, 31 Dec. 1935 (176999). The senator in question, Sydney Little, had earlier suggested to King that one way out would be 'selling his Senatorship.' Diary, 25 Aug. 1932. King did not approve of that course.

35 King seemed to feel that Cairine Wilson, the first female senator ever appointed, owed a special debt over and above the normal senatorial obligation. Invited to tea at the Wilson home, King professed disgust in his diary at the wealth 'which has been made so largely out of the country and the Party.' Mrs Wilson, he concluded in pre-emptory fashion, 'ought to turn over her sessional indemnity to the Party.' 31 Oct. 1930. King, it appears, was not above using a sexual double standard in making such judgments.

36 WLMK, v. 186, Hardy to King, 4 Dec. 1931 (158413-4). There is a voluminous correspondence in the King papers on the Spence-Hardy affair, mainly in v. 193, nos. 164612-22; v. 189, 160803-10. See also v. 191, Haydon to King, 5 Feb. 1932 (162909-10). Haydon's own problem is noted in v. 185, Haydon to King, 5 May

1931 (158473); v. 191, King to J.C. Elliot, 2 July 1932 (162476-7); Elliot to King, 15 July 1932 (162478-9). Hardy was still pushing his claims against Spence as late as 1937, and expressing his willingness to drive the latter out of the Senate as a bankrupt, if necessary: v. 235, Hardy to King, 20 Aug. 1937 (201903-5).

37 The case was McCoombe *v.* George and King. After the settlement King reflected that 'it is shocking though to think that no one seemed ready to lend a hand, not even ... men who were made senators by the party. The complete absence of any organization is a terrible thing to have to face.' Diary, 7 March 1931. Another threatened legal action involved the National Press Ltd. – which was connected in some murky fashion to the Beauharnois affair – in charges that the Liberals owed $26,544 for advertising from the 1930 campaign. This case seems to have been settled out of court, but the details are unavailable. WLMK, v. 192, A.H.A. Lasker to King, 13 June 1932 (163296-8)

38 *Ibid.,* v. 175, Haydon to J.G. Gardiner, 6 Nov. 1930 (149097)

39 *Ibid.,* Diary, 5 Nov. 1930, 21 Jan. 1931; v. 173, Raoul Dandurand to King, 5 Oct. 1930 (147305-6); v. 184, King to A.E. Ames, 21 Jan. 1931 (156666-70).

40 *Ibid.,* v. 184, King to F.-L. Béique, 7 March 1931 (156728-9); 'Statement of monies contributed to the national office since January 16, 1931' (158476-7). Another source also lists Frank O'Connor of Laura Secord Candies as donor: v. 188, O'Connor to H.R.L. Henry, 28 Nov. 1931 (159948)

41 *Ibid.,* Diary, 24 Jan. 1931. King's comment on Hardy was that 'he has been a good & true friend': v. 196, Hardy to King, 30 Jan. 1933 (166629). See also v. 200, King-Hardy correspondence (170907-28). The latter fund totalled $2850 for 1934 and included donations from nine individuals, including Hardy himself, whose names were all made known to King.

42 Dawson, *King,* pp. 398-9; WLMK, Diary, 24 Aug. 1930. King estimated his major expenses as $5000 to $7000 in taxes per year, and $4000 for servants in his two residences. For the 'tradition,' see Dale C. Thomson, *Louis St. Laurent: Canadian* (Toronto, 1967), pp 213, 216; Denis Smith, *Gentle Patriot: A Political Biography of Walter Gordon* (Edmonton, 1973), p. 28.

43 WLMK, Diary, 26 Nov. 1931; NPL, v. 2, Hardy to Lambert, 12 Aug. 1950

44 WLMK, v. 186, Gerald Larkin to King, 7 Dec. (158923); v. 187, Albert Matthews to King, 18 Dec. (159686-7); v. 186, King to Larkin, 9 Dec. 1931 (158924-6)

45 In the absence of any full-length study of the scandal, Neatby's chapter in his *King,* II, pp. 369-90 offers the best secondary treatment. The main primary sources are the two volumes of evidence heard by the House and Senate committees of investigation.

46 *King,* II, pp. 332, 381

47 Norman Lambert was one who believed King knew about Beauharnois all along, basing his belief on private statements by King's personal secretary, H.R.L.

Henry, and a former cabinet minister, James Malcolm. See NPL, Diary, 26 July 1933, 11 July 1941. Malcolm reportedly went so far as to assert that the whole affair was caused by King and Dunning diverting the plan from Shawinigan to Beauharnois because of campaign funds. In the absence of any collaborating evidence other than Lambert's diary, however, no conclusions can be drawn. More recently, press attention has been drawn to the disclosure that at least $25,000 was deposited by Senator McDougald in a Boston bank account of Mackenzie King in 1927 and 1928. W.L. McDougald papers, Public Archives of Canada, deposits to account of W.L.M. King, 29 Dec. 1927 and 1 Oct. 1928. Despite suggestions that this links King directly to the Beauharnois affair, the evidence is rather circumstantial. Since the same papers reveal that McDougald was involved in the P.C. Larkin Laurier House fund, there is at least as much reason to believe that these donations were connected to the latter as to Beauharnois. King in fact paid McDougald back $15,000 when he demanded his resignation from the Senate. Neatby, *King*, II, p. 383, claims that this McDougald money was indeed for the Larkin fund – although this of course still leaves the $10,000 in 1927 unaccounted for. It might also be pointed out that McDougald had agreed to take over King's personal liabilities in the latter's election in North York in 1925. McDougald papers, King to McDougald, 21 Dec. 1925. For some of the newspaper controversy regarding the significance of the McDougald papers, see J.L. Granatstein, 'Was King Really Bribed?' *Globe and Mail*, 18 Jan., letter to editor by Bernard Ostry, 22 Jan., and reply by Granatstein, 26 Jan. 1977. See also Geoffrey Stevens, 'Frustrating, Fascinating Reading,' *ibid.*, 12 Jan. 1977
48 WLMK, Diary, 26 June 1934
49 King instructed Charles Stewart that no further contributions to the party treasury should be accepted from McDougald, and then returned $15,000 which McDougald had donated years earlier to the Larkin fund for King. WLMK, v. 189, King to Stewart, 26 Aug. (163904-5); Diary, 23 Oct. 1931.
50 As King put it in his diary on 10 July 1931: '... a sort of grouping all of which has the appearance to an evil mind of design.'
51 Leslie Roberts, *So This Is Ottawa* (Toronto, 1933), pp. 196-7
52 WLMK, Diary, 18 July; v. 188, Rogers to King, 8 Aug.; Diary, 28 Oct. 1931
53 Senate Committee on Beauharnois, p. 189
54 WLMK, Diary, 12 Feb., 4 May, 26 Nov. 1932
55 *Ibid.*, Diary, 24 Feb. 1931; v. 184, King to Crerar, 7 Nov. 1931 (157568-73)
56 *Ibid.*, v. 187, MacDougall to King, 20 Nov. 1931 (159202-8). The personal impact of the financial problem on those unfortunate enough to be employed in political organizational work could often be catastrophic, as evidenced by the sisterly advice offered a secretary in the Saskatchewan Liberal office by Charles Dunning's secretary in Ottawa, recommending that she give up her party job and

come to work for the civil service: '... I think it much more likely to be remunerative than organization work.' She then recounted the story of one woman in the Ottawa Liberal office who was left 'to pay the rent and all the expenses of the organization until she had exhausted her own funds to the tune of some $2,000; then there was bitter discussion as to who would or would not pay the bill with the result that [she] does not now speak to a number of prominent politicians.' CAD, v. 8, Miss Craig to Miss Burton, 15 Aug. 1929.

57 Spender, *Sir Robert Hudson: A Memoir* (London, 1930); WLMK, Diary, 17 Oct. 1930, 15 Dec. 1931. It is an interesting observation that, despite the belief of many Conservative historians that King was pro-American and anti-British, whenever he wished for guidance on specifically political questions he seemed always to turn to British sources. The notion that it was the British parliamentary and party system which served as a model for Canada seemed to exclude American comparisons almost altogether.

58 Spender, *The Public Life* (London, 1925), II, pp. 86-92. See WLMK, v. 189, King to Spender, 4 Nov. 1931 (160812-6). It is a matter of rather pungent irony that the sale of offices for campaign funds was apparently much more flagrant in Britain than in Canada. See also H.R. James, *Memoirs of a Conservative: J.C.C. Davidson's Memoirs and Papers* (London, 1970). Colonial admiration for the motherland was characterized more by filial piety than by realism.

59 For a suitably stage-struck, society-page family biography, see Mollie Gillen, *The Masseys* (Toronto, 1965).

60 King to Massey, 18 Dec. 1931, quoted in Massey, *What's Past Is Prologue: The Memoirs of the Right Honourable Vincent Massey* (Toronto, 1963), p. 210

61 WLMK, Diary, 14 and 24 Aug. 1931; v. 186, Hardy to King, 31 Aug. 1931 (158368)

62 *Ibid.*, v. 186, 'Memo of Outstanding Accounts at National Liberal Office,' 28 Oct. 1931 (158481). $1500 had been paid off a month later: 'Memo of Present Standing Accounts, etc.,' 27 Nov. (158580-1); v. 187, King to Massey, 6 Nov. (159666-70); v. 185, King to Dandurand, 16 Dec. (157471-5); v. 187, 'Minutes of the First Meeting of the Executive Committee of the National Liberal Association,' 25 Nov. 1931 (159554-5)

63 *Ibid.*, Diary, 23 and 25 Nov. 1931

64 WLMK, v. 193, 'Report on National Organization Campaign,' 6 Jan. 1932 (164080-2). Some Liberals were rather less than delighted. One local correspondent of King's wrote scornfully of 'those high grade people' living a 'life of pretentious ease,' 'very ornamental but they don't win elections ...': v. 190, Alex Darrach to King, 16 June 1932 (162058-60). Another suggested Massey might be of help 'if he is not going around with a seven-piece orchestra and a uniformed chauffeur in a limousine': v. 200, G.N. Gordon to King, 29 Nov. 1934.

65 *King*, II, p. 388. Among these were Senators Lemieux and George Graham, J.E. Atkinson of the *Toronto Star*, Frank O'Connor, Gerald Larkin, and A.E. Ames.

66 WLMK, v. 193, Charles Stewart to King, 27 May (164686-90); v. 191, Hardy to King, 18 April (162869); Diary, 9 and 10 March, 29 May 1932

67 *Ibid.*, v. 179, Paradis to King, 29 April (152793); Paradis to Edith O'Malley, 24 April (152794-7); v. 180, Power to King, 24 April 1930 (153176-8); also in CGP, 1968, Box 1. When Norman Lambert took over as national organizer, King 'advised him to leave the province of Quebec alone.' WLMK, Memoranda and Notes, v. 192, memorandum, no author; 'Re: Meeting of Executive Committee of National Liberal Federation, March 16, 1937' (C135210-13). As late as 1941, Lambert noted that 'Mr. Cardin and Mr. Power are still identified with that view.' NPL, v. 8, file 9, Lambert, 'Memorandum regarding the National Liberal Federation,' May 1941

68 WLMK, v. 192, Massey to King, 5 Feb. (163830); King to Massey, 9 Feb. 1932 (163831)

CHAPTER TWO
Organizing for victory, 1932-5

1 WLMK, Diary, 7 Sept. 1932

2 CDH, v. 109, file 75(9), Fraser to Robert Winters, 8 Feb. 1960

3 WLMK, v. 88, nos. 160101 to 160162, contain correspondence between Power and King in 1931 on Power's plans. See also Norman Ward, ed., *A Party Politician: The Memoirs of Chubby Power* (Toronto, 1966), pp. 261-77, for Power's own account of the organization of the caucus.

4 WLMK, v. 201, King to R.A. MacDougall, 19 May 1934 (171850-3)

5 *Ibid.*, Diary, 26 Nov. 1932; 4 July 1935; 15 Feb. 1933

6 NLF, v. 861, 'Mr. Massey's Report to the National Liberal Advisory Committee,' 1 and 2 Dec. 1933

7 J.W. Pickersgill, 'Senator Norman Lambert – An Appreciation,' *Journal of Liberal Thought*, II, 2 (Spring 1966), pp. 140-1

8 Massey report, 1933. This is repeated by Peter Regenstreif, 'The Liberal Party of Canada: A Political Analysis,' unpublished PH D thesis, Cornell University, 1963, p. 168. Massey's own report ends with figures on NLF finances which contradict the existence of $50,000 in individual membership fees. From Nov. 1932 to Oct. 1933, the NLF received total revenues of only $23,766.30, of which all but $725.35 came from provincial associations. The following year, revenues amounted to $24,058, of which only the miniscule amount of $53.43 was identified as deriving from 'popular subscriptions.' NPL, v. 8, folder 9, Ryan and Gorman, CA, 'Financial Statement of National Liberal Federation of Canada.' It would seem that the 50,000 members may have more likely constituted a mere mailing list.

9 Regenstreif, 'The Liberal Party,' pp. 166-8

10 JLR, v. 12, 'Minutes of the Organizational Meeting of the National Liberal Federation of Canada,' 25 and 26 Nov. 1932; Massey report, 1933

11 WLMK, Diary, 26 Nov., 28 July 1932

12 To the long list of Lambert's virtues, the contemporary historian is tempted to add his fortunate habit of diary-keeping, which has resulted in the astonishingly comprehensive record of his, and the party's, activities now open to study in the Douglas Library at Queen's University.

13 NLF, v. 861, 1943 advisory council, *Minutes*, pp. 31-2

14 Massey report, 1933

15 NPL, Diary, 20 July 1933, 3 and 23 Jan. 1934

16 WLMK, v. 190, P.-F.-A. Casgrain to King, 15 Jan. 1932 (161818-21)

17 ER, v. 1, interview with Savard, 6 July 1932

18 NPL, Diary, 18 Jan. 1934, 26-7 Feb. 1935

19 Massey, *What's Past Is Prologue: The Memoirs of the Right Honourable Vincent Massey* (Toronto, 1963)

20 WLMK, Diary, 7 July 1933; 10 April 1934; v. 200, King to Rodolphe Lemieux, 16 Jan. 1934 (171566-7)

21 R. MacGregor Dawson, *William Lyon Mackenzie King: A Political Biography, 1874-1923* (Toronto, 1958), I, p. 303

22 On King's ideological response to the Depression, see W.J. McAndrew, 'Mackenzie King, Roosevelt and the New Deal,' paper presented at the Mackenzie King Centennial Colloquium, Waterloo, Ontario, 16 Dec. 1974, with commentary by F. Gibson; H. Blair Neatby, *The Politics of Chaos: Canada in the Thirties* (Toronto, 1972), and 'The Liberal Way,' in Victor Hoar, ed., *The Great Depression: Essays and Memoirs from Canada and the United States* (Toronto, 1969). Bruce Hutchison also offers some insights, although exaggerating King's 'radicalism': *The Incredible Canadian* (Toronto, 1952), pp. 148-201. Ramsay Cook has written that Massey was planning on writing a book about Canadian Liberalism and had approached J.W. Dafoe of the *Winnipeg Free Press* for ideas and suggested readings on the subject. *The Politics of John W. Dafoe and the Free Press* (Toronto, 1963), p. 206. This is the only reference I have found to such a proposed book, but it it easy to see why the idea would have been given up in the face of King's hostility to public revisions of Liberal doctrine. Blair Neatby, *William Lyon Mackenzie King: The Prism of Unity, 1932-1939* (Toronto, 1976) III, emphasizes the point that King was much more respectful of the views of the Liberal parliamentary caucus than of the party organization.

23 Massey report, 1933

24 JLR, v. 12, Ralston to Ralph P. Bell, 10 Feb. 1933

25 NPL, Diary, 6-15 Feb. 1933; WLMK, v. 197, Lambert to King, 4 Feb. 1933 (167137) and attached memorandum (167138-40)

26 Massey, *What's Past Is Prologue*, pp. 214, 216

27 See R.B. Bennett *et al.*, *Canadian Problems* (Toronto, 1933), for the published volume which emerged from the Conservative meetings. Michiel Horn, 'The League for Social Reconstruction, 1932-1936,' *Journal of Canadian Studies* (Nov. 1972), pp. 3-17

28 NPL, Diary, 27 March, 17 May, 8 July 1933; see also Neatby, *Politics of Chaos*, for details of King's reactions to the summer school idea.

29 WLMK, Diary, 3, 8-9 Sept. 1933

30 *The Liberal Way: A Record of Opinion on Canadian Problems as Expressed and Discussed at the First Liberal Summer Conference* (Toronto, 1933)

31 WLMK, v. 201, King to MacDougall, 19 May 1934 (171850-3); Diary, 10 April 1934. Massey described this encounter as 'stormy' and definitely cancelled his western trip. NPL, Diary, 10 April 1934

32 NPL, Diary, 6 April, 11 Sept. 1934

33 WLMK, Diary, 5 Aug. 1934

34 *What's Past Is Prologue*, pp. 221-3; see also Neatby, *King*, III, p. 121

35 NPL, Diary, 10 and 14 Oct. 1935

36 *What's Past Is Prologue*, p. 223

37 NPL, Diary, 7 July, 18-19 Oct. 1932

38 WLMK, v. 197, Massey to King, 10 July (167902-3); Diary, 20 July 1933

39 NPL, Diary, 21 Jan. 1934; WLMK, Diary, 10 April, 29 June 1934

40 NPL, Diary, 14 and 17 Oct. 1935; WLMK, Diary, 22 Oct. 1935. On the overall process of cabinet selection, see F.W. Gibson, 'The Cabinet of 1935,' in Gibson, ed., *Cabinet Formation and Bicultural Relations: Seven Case Studies*, Study no. 6 of the Royal Commission on Bilingualism and Biculturalism (Ottawa, 1970), pp. 105-42.

41 WLMK, v 188, John Newlands to King, 25 Feb. (159893); T.B. McQuesten to King, 3 July 1931 (159518-9)

42 *Ibid.*, Diary, 30 June; v. 188, King to McQuesten, 7 Aug. 1931 (159522-3)

43 It is an interesting commentary on the Liberals' co-optive strategy that the NDP, despite its strong financial and organizational backing by the Steelworkers union, is unable to mount a real challenge to the Liberals in this predominantly working class district of a steelmaking city. It is equally interesting that the present minister of labour in the Trudeau government is the member for Hamilton East, the Hon. John Munro.

44 WLMK, Diary, 11 Aug. 1931

45 *Ibid.*, v. 190, King to Deachman, 5 Oct. (162272-3); v. 192, King to Massey, 4 Oct. 1932 (163852-3)

46 'The Effect of the Depression on Canadian Politics, 1929-32,' *American Political Science Review*, XXVII (June 1933), p. 458

47 NPL, Diary, 18-21 April, 24-6 May, 9 June, 6, 8, and 13 July 1933; WLMK, Diary, 8 July 1933

48 NPL, Diary, 17-18 July, 3-18, 30 Aug., 18 Sept. 1933. WLMK, Diary, 19 July, 14 Sept.; v. 197, King to Lapointe, 24 Aug. 1933 (167188-90)

49 NPL, Diary, 31 July 1933

50 See Roger Graham, *Arthur Meighen: And Fortune Fled* (Toronto, 1963)

51 NPL, Diary, 8 Dec. 1932; 21, 29-30 Aug., 20 Sept., 21 Oct., 11 Nov. 1933

52 WLMK, Diary, 23 Oct. 1933

53 *Ibid.*, v. 197, King to Lemieux, 15 Nov. 1933 (167233-4); v. 196, draft letter to Peter Heenan (166688-95), W.A. Fraser to King, 8 Nov. 1933 (146305-7)

54 *Ibid.*, v. 201, Massey to King, 28 July 1934 (172351-5)

55 *Ibid.*, Diary, 28 July; v. 199, King to Elliott, 17 July 1934 (170506-8). NPL, v. 13, file 3, E.G. Long, financial records, 1934. The breakdown of spending was as follows: Kenora, $9000; Toronto East, $4800; Frontenac, $3500; North York, $2500; Elgin West, $2000.

56 *Ibid.*, v. 192, King to Massey, 31 May 1932 (163839-41). NPL, Diary, 7 Dec. 1932; 6 Jan., 26, 29 April, 1 and 5 June, 7 July, 26 Aug. 1933; 22 April, 9 July 1934

57 NPL, Diary, 10 July 1934; WLMK, v. 200, Lambert to Stewart, 11 Aug. 1934 (171477-8)

58 WLMK, v. 200, Lambert to Massey, 11 Aug. 1934 (171479-80). The decision to formally include the NLF within the responsibilities of the Toronto finance committee was taken at a meeting in Toronto in which Lambert, Massey, four Toronto collectors, and the secretary of the Ontario Liberal Association were present. NPL, Diary, 14 Aug. 1934

59 NPL, Diary, 7-8 Nov. 1934. On this occasion, the Bank of Commerce, at the urging of J.S. McLean of Canada Packers, came to the rescue with $2500, enough for another month.

60 Wallace Clement, *The Canadian Corporate Elite: An Analysis of Economic Power* (Toronto, 1975), p. 236

61 NPL, Diary, 14 Dec. 1933. WLMK, v. 198, Raymond to King, n.d. (168442), King to Raymond, 7 Dec. (168443), King to Massey, 7 Dec. 1933 (167966-7)

62 NPL, Diary, 21 April 1934. King also suspected – without any proof – that Cardin and other Quebec figures might have profited indirectly from Beauharnois. 'They have no conscience in some things ...' he wrote. WLMK, Diary, 28 July 1931

63 WLMK, Diary, 20 and 26 June 1934

64 NPL, Diary, 18 Dec. 1934, 20 Feb. 1935

65 *Ibid.*, 25 July; v. 2, file '1935,' Lambert to Raymond, 29 July 1935

66 *Ibid.*, 18 Dec. 1934, 20 Feb. 1935

67 T.W. Acheson's study of the 'Changing Social Origins of the Canadian Industrial Elite, 1880-1910,' *Business History Review*, XLVII, 2 (Summer 1973), shows that in 1910 the Toronto area was the only region in Canada where the majority (60 per cent) of the élite sample listed Liberal affiliation. Donald Creighton has written of

Laurier's 'new Liberal plutocracy' which turned against him in 1911. *Canada's First Century, 1867-1967* (Toronto, 1970), p. 124

68 WLMK, v. 193, W.R.P. Parker to King, 10 Dec. 1932 (104119); v. 195, J.W.A. Clark to King, 6 Jan. (165573) and 19 Jan. 1933 (165574-5)

69 NPL, Diary, 8 June 1933; WLMK, Diary, 2 Dec. 1933. King made no promises as a general rule; Hepburn had already made promises to Arthur Roebuck, Duncan Marshall, and Harry Nixon, in order 'to get platform speakers,' and did not wish to have his hands tied further.

70 WLMK, Diary, 26 Oct. 1933

71 This personal fund ran close to $2000 per year by 1934-5; contributors included Hardy himself, Gerald Larkin, Frank O'Connor, A.J. Freiman, Ottawa MP Thomas Ahearn, Reginald Scarfe, and Alf. Rogers. Hardy said that he did not want anyone to 'touch this fund who cannot do so with real ease as I don't want you to be under an obligation to anybody.' WLMK, v. 206, Hardy to King, 2 July 1935 (176968); see also *ibid.*, Hardy to King, 21 June 1935 (176962); NPL, Diary, 2, 17, and 29 Jan. 1934

72 WLMK, Diary, 26 June 1934

73 *Ibid.*, 3 Aug. 1934; NPL, Diary, 28 Aug. 1934

74 NPL, Diary, 11 Sept. 1934

75 See J.R.H. Wilbur, 'H.H. Stevens and the Reconstruction Party,' *Canadian Historical Review*, XLV, 1 (March 1964), pp. 1-28, and *The Bennett Administration, 1930-1935*, Canadian Historical Association, Historical Booklet no. 24 (Ottawa, 1969), for details of the Stevens inquiry background. C.L. Burton's biography, *A Sense of Urgency: Memoirs of a Canadian Merchant* (Toronto, 1961), gives his perspective on the affair.

76 Burton, *ibid.*, p. 339. 'I was not as greatly impressed by the suggestions as I might have been ten years later in my life [that is, 1936],' Burton writes.

77 WLMK, v. 199, Burton to King, 13 June (169856-60), King to Sam Factor, 23 July 1934 (170546-7); NPL, Diary, 22 Feb. 1934

78 WLMK, v. 201, Massey to King, 5 Oct. 1934 (172378-9); NPL, Diary, 11-12 Sept. 1934

79 WLMK, Diary, 1 Dec. 1934. Senator Hardy undertook to ask O'Connor to raise funds, since he knew 'of no one who can collect funds in Ontario as he can'; the senator also felt that King should not have to place himself under any 'obligation' by having to ask O'Connor personally. *Ibid.*, v. 206, Hardy to King, 10 Jan. 1935 (176947-8)

80 NPL, Diary, 30 March, 3 April 1934. It is not altogether clear who the contractor involved was, and Neil McKenty fails to identify him. *Mitch Hepburn* (Toronto, 1967), p.72. That it was Harry McLean of Dominion Construction is, however, almost certain from the evidence of the Lambert diary. There is no evidence

respecting the conditions of the contract in question, whether it was let by tender or not, etc., but the $200,000 kickback, amounting to 8 per cent of the total, was a sufficiently high percentage for those days to suggest somewhat unusual circumstances.

81 *Ibid.*, 10, 15-16 May 1935

82 *Mitch Hepburn*, p. 69

83 NPL, Diary, 11 Sept. 1935

84 *Mitch Hepburn*, pp. 68-70. Bickell was president of McIntyre-Porcupine Mines, a very big gold producer.

85 CAD, v. 10, Dunning to E.M. MacDonald, 21 Aug. 1935; NPL, Diary, 9 and 16 Aug., 9 and 20 Sept. 1935

86 NPL, Diary, 12 Sept., 4 Oct. 1935

87 The central place of financial capital in the Canadian political economy is best described by Clement, *The Canadian Corporate Elite*, pp. 44-122. See also R.T. Naylor, 'The Rise and Fall of the Third Commercial Empire of the St Lawrence,' in Gary Teeple, ed., *Capitalism and the National Question in Canada* (Toronto, 1972).

88 NPL, Diary, 27 and 28 Sept. 1935. The Bank of Montreal told Lambert (31 Oct. 1935) it preferred to give through its Montreal office.

89 See Neatby, 'The Liberal Way,' pp. 98-100. WLMK, v. 202, Rundle to King, 27 Jan. (173307-10), King to Rundle, 3 Feb. 1934 (173311-3), H.R.L. Henry to Rundle, 23 Feb. 1934 (173318)

90 NPL, Diary, 2, 3, 10, and 27 Sept. 1935; v. 13, 'E.G. Long' budget, 3 March 1936

91 For the general background, see V.C. Fowke, *The National Policy and the Wheat Economy* (Toronto, 1957), pp. 256-67. There had been a national wheat board established briefly at the end of the First World War, but it had lasted only two years.

92 NPL, Diary, 11 and 20 June, 4 July 1935; WLMK, Diary, 18 June 1935

93 NPL, Diary, 3 Aug. 1934; WLMK, Diary, 3 Aug. 1934

94 See, for example, Ralph Miliband's *The State in Capitalist Society* (London, 1969), for one of the most careful and subtle Marxist analyses of these relationships.

95 WLMK, Diary, 16 June 1932

96 See R.R. James, *Memoirs of a Conservative: J.C.C. Davidson's Memoirs and Papers* (London, 1970). The practice began under the virtuous Gladstone and reached its apogee under Lloyd George, who charged £100,000 for a peerage, £30,000 for a baronetcy, and £10,000 for a knighthood. Party brokers took a personal commission on these transactions.

97 NPL, Diary, 3 April 1935

98 *Ibid.*, 20 and 26 Sept. 1935

99 *Ibid.*, 2 and 25 July 1935, 6 and 14 July 1933; WLMK, v. 175, S.W. Jacobs to King, 15 Jan. 1930 (149558-9)

100 NPL, Diary, 24 Dec. 1934. WLMK, v. 205, J.C. Davis to Lambert, 27 April (175688), Lambert to Davis, 1 May 1935 (175689); v. 202, King to Rogers, 26 Sept. 1934 (173197-8)

101 NPL, Diary, 5 Nov. 1935, gives Donat Raymond's final figures on Montreal. The Lambert diaries contain a complete list of contributors in Toronto from 1934 through 1936, and then again for the 1940 election campaign. These handwritten entries are matched by typed lists in NPL, v. 13, folder 3, which are exactly similar in both names and amounts. A few years later, Lambert, in a letter to King, provided slightly different figures on overall amounts, indicating $550,000 in Toronto and $635,000 in Montreal. WLMK, v. 270, Lambert to King, 24 July 1939 (228966-9)

102 Depending on the importance of a local candidate in the eyes of corporate interests, the donations might be of significance. Frank O'Connor told Lambert in the midst of the campaign that W.H. Moore, whose seat was in Oshawa, was 'being well looked after by General Motors,' as was Thomas Vien, former member, now running in Montreal-Outremont. NPL, Diary, 1 Oct. 1935

103 *Ibid.*, 30 Sept., 5 Oct. 1935. $28,000 went direct to Vancouver machine politicians Wendell Farris and Brent Brown, and $22,000 to provincial ministers Gordon Sloan and John Hart. The 'gamble' in question is not specified in the Lambert entries, but it may have had something to do with Premier T.D. Pattullo's plans to build a $4 million New Westminster Bridge, presumably with the fiscal aid of a sympathetic new Liberal government installed in Ottawa. See Margaret Ormsby, *British Columbia: A History* (Toronto, 1958), p. 461; Martin Robin, *The Company Province: Pillars of Profit, 1934-1972* (Toronto, 1973), II, pp. 19, 43; see also Chapter 9, below

104 NPL, Diary, 5 Nov. 1935

105 NPL, v. 8, folder 9; interview with Hon. J.W. Pickersgill, 15 July 1974

106 WLMK, Memoranda and Notes, v. 162, f. 1474, 'Liberal Publicity Campaign' (C116251-76); v. 192, memorandum, 'Re: Meeting of Executive Committee,' 16 March 1937 (C135210-13)

107 The concept of main corporate affiliation is largely based on the *Financial Post's Directory of Directors*, which asks each respondent to indicate which of their corporate directorships constitutes their 'principal occupation.' This method is adopted by Clement, *The Canadian Corporate Elite*, pp. 202 (and n. 16), 223.

108 The mining interests had also contributed at least $23,000 to various individual candidates in Ontario. NPL, Diary, 4 Oct. 1935

109 McCarthy turned down a post-election offer of the ambassadorship to Washington. WLMK, v. 207, McCarthy to King, June (178333), 21 Oct. (178336-7), 10 Dec. (178338-40), King to McCarthy, 9 Jan. 1935 (178341)

110 *Ibid.*, v. 181, Rowell to H.R.L. Henry, 15 March 1930 (154042-3); CGP, series 4, transcript of interview with C.G. Power by John Meisel, 15 May 1960

111 H.V. Nelles, *The Politics of Development: Forests, Mines & Hydro-electric Power in Ontario, 1849-1941* (Toronto, 1974), pp. 435-6, 438

112 JLR, v. 12, Ralston to Angus L. MacDonald, 2 April 1932

113 *Ibid.*, Ralston to R.P. Bell, 29 Dec. 1930; *ibid.*, v. 27, Ralston to M.B. Archibald, 20 Jan., Ralston to H.A. Waterman, 30 March 1935

114 NLF, v. 863, 1958 advisory council, speech of R.A. MacDougall, pp. 650-2

115 NPL, Diary, 26 March 1935; see also WLMK, v. 200, King to J.J. Gillis, 16 July 1934 (170787-8)

116 WLMK, v. 200, S.H. Green to King, 2 June 1934 (170843); NPL, Diary, 22 July 1935

117 WLMK, v. 202, Power-King correspondence; JLR, v. 28, Power to Ralston, 22 July 1935

118 NPL, v. 13; WLMK, Memoranda and Notes, v. 162, 'Liberal Publicity Campaign'

119 JLR, M.B. Archibald to W.S. Thomson, 13 Aug., Archibald to Ralston, 13 Aug. 1935

120 Massey, *What's Past Is Prologue*, p. 222

121 WLMK, v. 210, W.R.P. Parker to King, 17 Oct. (180647-9), and Sept. 1935 (180652-62). Nathanson was a long-standing Liberal supporter whose out-of-pocket efforts on behalf of the party would continue into the 1950s. Nathanson's Liberal links appear not to have damaged the ability of Famous Players, the American cinema chain which Nathanson headed in this country, to maintain its domination despite challenges sometimes raised by those who wished to see the cinema medium in Canadian hands. Unlike radio and television, film was, for reasons we can only speculate about, never considered a 'national' concern to be protected from foreign control. When Louis St Laurent retired as prime minister in 1957, he was made a director of Famous Players. L. and F. Park, *Anatomy of Big Business* (Toronto, 1973), p. 58. Clearly there was a mutual regard between the Liberals and Nathanson's corporation.

122 WLMK, Memoranda and Notes, v. 192, report by Norman Lambert to NLF advisory council, fourth annual meeting, 10 Dec. 1936 (c135190-5)

123 *Ibid.*, v. 195, Atkinson to King, 14 Dec. 1933 (165145); v. 202, Bernard Rose to King, 22 Jan. (173205), King to Rose, 23 Jan. 1934 (173206-7)

124 *Ibid.*, v. 207, McClung to King, 12 Feb. (178342-3); v. 211, King to Norman Rogers, 6 March 1935 (181485-9)

125 See Mark Moher, 'The "Biography" in Politics: Mackenzie King in 1935,' *Canadian Historical Review* LV, 2 (June 1974), pp. 239-48; NPL, v. 13, Ontario budget

126 WLMK, Diary, 5 July 1935; NPL, Diary, 12 Oct. 1935. Statistics are from Scarrow,

Canada Votes (New Orleans, 1962), pp. 76, 90. On the election in general, see J.M. Beck, *Pendulum of Power: Canada's Federal Elections* (Scarborough, 1968), pp. 206-22; and Escott Reid, 'The Canadian Election of 1935 – And After,' *American Political Science Review*, xxx (Feb. 1936).

127 WLMK, v. 211, Norman Senior to King, n.d., 1935 (182161-4)
128 Apologies to Frank Scott
129 *Pendulum of Power*, p. 219

CHAPTER THREE
Building the Government party, 1935-40

1 WLMK, Memoranda and Notes, v. 162, file 1475, Dominion Securities Corporation, letter to shareholders, 19 Oct. 1935 (c116322)
2 Quoted in Pendleton Herring, *The Politics of Democracy* (New York, 1940), p. 350
3 NLF, v. 861, 1943 advisory council, transcript, p. 34
4 WLMK, Diary, 21 March 1936
5 See WLMK, Diary for Oct. 1935, *passim*. The best secondary source on the 1935 cabinet selection, with special reference to Quebec, is F.W. Gibson's fine article on 'The Cabinet of 1935,' in Gibson, ed., *Cabinet Formation and Bicultural Relations: Seven Case Studies*, Study no. 6 of the Royal Commission on Bilingualism and Biculturalism (Ottawa, 1970), pp. 105-42.
6 WLMK, Diary, 16 Dec. 1936
7 NPL, Diary, 11 Jan. 1944
8 WLMK, Diary, 14 April, 27 Jan. 1937
9 O.D. Skelton, *Life and Letters of Sir Wilfrid Laurier* (new ed., Toronto, 1965), II, p. 103
10 NPL, Diary, 20 Jan. 1934
11 WLMK, Diary, 22 and 23 Oct. 1935, 5 Aug. 1936; NPL, Diary, 23 Oct. 1935
12 NPL, 3 July, 21 Oct. 1935
13 NLF, v. 861, 1943 advisory council, transcript, pp 33-4
14 NPL, Diary, 28 Oct. 1935; v. 2, file '1935,' Lambert to King, 5 Nov., King to Lambert, 23 Nov. 1935; Diary, 25 Oct. 1936, 15 Dec. 1935
15 NPL, 13, 20, and 21 Dec. 1935; v. 2, file '1936,' King to Lambert, 11 Jan. 1936; WLMK, Diary, 20 Jan. 1938. When Lambert was finally appointed, along with former Ontario agriculture minister Duncan Marshall, King maintained that these appointments were 'the only two that I have ever made in my life, with respect to which I had given some prior undertaking.' The Marshall appointment arose out of a complicated affair involving the Hepburn government and the lieutenant-governorship of Ontario (see Chapter 8, below).

16 WLMK, v. 224, King to Matthews, 10 Dec. 1936 (192481-2)
17 NPL, Diary, 16 Dec. 1936
18 WLMK, Diary, 16 Dec. 1936
19 *Ibid.*, 10 Jan. 1936, 14 Oct. 1937, 9 Aug. 1938; v. 192, memorandum, E.A. Pickering for King, 21 April 1937 (135214)
20 *Ibid.*, v. 270, Lambert to King, 24 July 1939; Diary, 14 Nov. 1939, 31 Aug. 1937
21 NPL, Diary, 25 Oct. 1936
22 See Chapter 6, below
23 WLMK, Diary, 29 Jan. 1940. The most recent examination of the workings of cabinet government in the 1970s concludes that 'contemporary cabinet deliberations cannot be compared to a meeting between an all-powerful head of state and his courtiers. They bear closer resemblance to the relationship which might exist between a feudal baron and his independently powerful vassals.' Robert J. Jackson and Michael M. Atkinson, *The Canadian Legislative System* (Toronto, 1974), p. 57. This was at least as true in the 1930s and 1940s, if not more so.
24 NPL, Diary, 12 June, 21 Dec. 1936, 11 Nov. 1937
25 WLMK, v. 252, Lambert to King, 30 Dec. 1938 (215198-9), also in NPL, v. 2, file '1938'; NPL, Diary, 20 Jan. 1939, 1 Aug. 1940
26 *The Incredible Canadian* (Toronto, 1952), p. 233
27 WLMK, v. 270, memorandum, W.B. Herbert for Lambert, 17 July 1939 (228970-3). These outside people included Grant Dexter of the *Free Press*, Wilfred Eggleston, and Philip Vineberg, a young Liberal lawyer just completed post-graduate studies. *Ibid.*, Lambert to King, 24 July 1939 (228966-9)
28 *Ibid.*, report by Mrs Skinner to NLF advisory council meeting, 10 Dec. 1936 (135205-7)
29 *Ibid.*, v. 236, W.R. MacDonald to King, 11 April (203346-7), 21 July 1937 (203350-1); Memoranda and Notes, v. 193, file 1763; v. 252, Lambert to King, 29 Aug. 1938 (215181); Lambert 'Preliminary Draft of Proposal for Radio Publicity,' 26 Aug. 1938 (215183-94)
30 NPL, Diary, 20 July 1938; WLMK, Diary, 10 Sept. 1939
31 WLMK, v. 182, memorandum for H. Baldwin, 6 Feb. 1930 (155261). King was citing a letter of sympathy sent to H.S. Southam of the Southam Press on the passing of the latter's mother. The very grateful reply by Southam caused King to gleefully note that 'at one time we were not at all sure of having the Southam Press with us ...'
32 *Ibid.*, v. 192, memorandum, Lambert for King, 10 Dec. 1936 (135180-9)
33 WLMK, Memoranda and Notes, v. 193, memorandum, E.A. Pickering for King, 23 April 1938 (C135262). General material on the meeting is in *ibid.*, v. 192, nos. C135169-207

34 NPL, Diary, 10 and 12 Dec. 1936; WLMK, Memoranda and Notes, v. 192, memorandum, Lambert for King, n.d. (c135180-9)

35 NPL, Diary, 16 Dec. 1936. Two days earlier Lambert had written that the women's moves had been prearranged and were 'not unrelated' to Hepburn's efforts to 'upset whole N.L.F. picture.' WLMK, Diary, 16 Dec. 1936

36 WLMK, Diary, 18 May 1938; Memoranda and Notes, v. 192, minutes of advisory council meeting, 18 May 1938 (c135235-8)

37 NLF, v. 861, 1943 advisory council minutes, Lambert address, pp. 28-9; WLMK, Diary, 8 Aug. 1939. King did thank Norman McLarty for his part, but not Lambert. NPL, Diary, 20 April 1945

38 WLMK, Memoranda and Notes, v. 192, reports by Lambert to advisory council, 10 Dec. 1936 (c135190-5) and 18 May 1938 (c135227-8)

39 CGP, series 4, transcript of interview by John Meisel, 15 May 1960, p. 13

40 WLMK, v. 282, correspondence from nos. 238453-78; Diary, 20 May 1938. On rare occasions he might personally thank a financial donor, if requested to do so, and might even put forward a name for the consideration of the cabinet for an appointment. *Ibid.*, v. 207, King to Gordon Leiter, 16 May 1936 (178100); v. 206, A.I. Garson to King, 16 Dec. 1935 (176552-3); and memorandum, 10 Jan. 1936 (176554). But these instances were more the exception than the rule.

41 NPL, Diary, 22 April 1936

42 Two of Lambert's collectors in Toronto were seeking 1½ to 2 per cent in 1938. *Ibid.*, 18 Oct. 1938. On the other hand, another businessman was told by Lambert in 1940 that 'on a million dollar business,' the Montreal collectors Raymond and Scott would 'expect at least' $25,000 – or 2½ per cent. *Ibid.*, 6 Feb. 1940

43 CGP, Meisel interview, p. 14

44 NPL, Diary, 31 May 1940; 11-14, 23-24 Dec. 1934; 18 July 1938

45 *Ibid.*, 21 March 1938

46 See, for example, *ibid.*, v. 8, folder 7, 'Memorandum of firms in the Province of Ontario and business transacted with them,' 1935 to 1937-8. This document was 63 pages long, with additional supplement.

47 Typical of the sort of transactions involved is this entry for 5 June 1939 when Lambert called one of his contractors and informed him that 'his Moncton job was 159,000 as vs. 140,000 last year, therefore another payment in addition to Saturday's 2,500 would be expected later.' See also *ibid.*, 11 and 15 May, 20 Sept. 1939

48 *Ibid.*, 12 March 1938, 10 Jan. 1939. On 18 Feb. 1940 Lambert recorded in his diary that a detailed suggestion for giving three specific orders to a Nova Scotia firm was readily accepted by Howe.

49 Lambert noted complaints from a competitor about how much CNR business Dofasco received. *Ibid.*, 21 March 1939. On Dosco, see *ibid.*, 27 Nov. 1938

50 *Ibid.*, 17 May, 7 Sept. 1938. Drew's charges became public with the 1 Sept. 1938 issue of *Maclean's Magazine.*

51 See, for instance, NPL, Diary, 12 June 1938 for an arrangement with Vickers aircraft.

52 WLMK, Diary, 30 Sept. 1938. Characteristically, King also put the entire affair down to the 'question of men who drink,' as well as to Mitch Hepburn.

53 See G.P. de T. Glazebrook, *A History of Transportation in Canada* (Toronto, 1964), II, pp. 256-64, for an introduction to the position of air transport in this period.

54 NPL, Diary, 25 Oct. 1936, 24 Oct. 1946

55 *Ibid.*, 19 July 1936. According to Robert Chodos, *The CPR: A Century of Corporate Welfare* (Toronto, 1973), Howe had tried to arrange a semi-public airline, with private participation, but the CPR balked when it was not allowed half the directors.

56 NPL, Diary, 21 March 1936, 12 Dec. 1939

57 *Ibid.*, 14, 24, and 26 Feb. 1936

58 *Ibid.*, 26, 27, 28, and 29 Aug., 1, 2, and 3 Sept. 1936; WLMK, v. 219, Lambert to King, 2 Sept. 1936 (188500)

59 NPL, Diary, 23 and 24 Oct. 1936, 11 Feb. 1937, 24 Feb. 1940

60 *Ibid.*, 21 and 29 Dec. 1936, 8 Jan., 3 and 5 March 1937, 30 Jan. 1940

61 WLMK, v. 252, Lambert to King, 30 Dec. 1938 (215198-9), also in NPL, v. 2, file '1938'

62 WLMK, v. 270, Lambert to King, 24 July 1939 (228966-9)

63 NPL, Diary, 7 Jan., 1 April 1936; WLMK, Diary, 31 Aug. 1937

64 WLMK, v. 192, Lambert to King, 28 Nov. 1932 [*sic*] (163260-1). Lambert obviously misdated his letter, which would appear to have been written in 1938.

65 NPL, Diary, 8 and 12 March 1938. Late in 1937 King had visited Raymond at his Montreal mansion. 'He talked much,' King recorded, 'about not trusting Cardin & his grafting propensities. These millionaires are strange people.' WLMK, Diary, 1 Oct. 1937

66 NPL, Diary, 10 March 1938; WLMK, Diary, 5 Dec. 1938

67 NPL, Diary, 16, 22, 24, and 25 March 1938

68 *Ibid.*, 6 July 1939

69 *Ibid.*

70 WLMK, v. 270, Lambert to King, 24 July 1939 (228966-9); v. 273, McLarty to King, 15 July 1939 (230796-804)

71 CAD, v. 11, King to Charles Dunning, 10 July 1939. Similar letters were sent to all the cabinet ministers.

72 WLMK, v. 270, J.L. Ilsley to King, 22 July 1939 (228482-3); Diary, 20 July 1939

73 *Ibid.*, v. 269, Howe to King, 11 July 1939 (228207-11), with enclosures

74 *Ibid.*, v. 267, Gardiner to King, 15 July 1939 (227063-5); v. 272, Mackinnon to King, 18 July 1939 (230675-7)

75 *Ibid.*, Diary, 14 Nov. 1939

76 *Ibid.*, 18 Jan. 1940; Hutchison, *The Incredible Canadian*, p. 272; NPL, Diary, 23 Jan. 1940

77 *Ibid.*, 30 Jan. 1940; CGP, 'Political Jottings,' v. 2, 'Memorandum of conversation with Mr. King, June 26, 1939,' 27 June 1939

78 *Canada's War: The Politics of the Mackenzie King Government, 1939-45* (Toronto, 1975), p. 82

79 CAD, box 3, 2(b), file 'federal election 1940, Liberal campaign,' 'Private and Confidential, Memorandum re 1940 Election Campaign,' 1 Feb. 1940. WLMK, Diary, 23 June 1939

80 NPL, Diary, 23 Jan. 1940

81 CAD, 'Memorandum re 1940 Election Campaign.' No author is named, but it is characteristic of Lambert's style and approach. Granatstein, *Canada's War*, p. 83, identifies it as having been prepared 'probably by Norman Lambert.'

82 NPL, Diary, 30 Jan. 1940

83 CAD, 'Memorandum re 1940 Election Campaign'

84 WLMK, 19 March 1940

85 *Canada's War*, p. 75

86 NPL, Diary, 28 March 1940; WLMK, Diary, 29 March 1945; Granatstein, *Canada's War*, p. 92

87 *The Politics of Survival: The Conservative Party of Canada, 1939-1945* (Toronto, 1967), p. 50. See also Granatstein's article, 'Conservative Party Finances, 1939-1945,' in Committee on Election Expenses, *Studies in Canadian Party Finance* (Ottawa, 1966), pp. 273-81.

88 K.Z. Paltiel, H.P. Noble, and R.A. Whitaker, 'The Finances of the CCF and the NDP, 1933-1965,' in Committee on Election Expenses, *ibid.*, p. 324

89 NPL, Diary, 16 March 1940

90 CAD, box 3, 2(b); NLF, pamphlet no. 7, 'The Mining Industry and the Mackenzie King Government,' lists the many aspects of the Liberal government's 'fair deal' to the mining industry, including such bonanzas as a 'total tax exemption' for metalliferous mines, begun in 1936 and extended on to at least 1943 and $7 million government expenditure on mining roads. After noting that 86 new gold mines had opened since the return of the Liberals to office, the pamphlet quite properly concludes that this progress did not 'just happen,' that is was the 'result of energetic and determined federal government policy ...' One might also note that from the point of view of the party, mining road development was doubly advantageous, since they also collected 1½ to 2 per cent on the road contracts.

91 NPL, Diary, 8 March 1940

92 *Ibid.*, 6 Feb., 14 March 1940, 14 Feb. 1941

93 *Ibid.*, v. 8, file 9; Diary, 2-3 April 1940

94 *Ibid.*, 2-3 Feb., 20 March 1940

95 *Ibid.*, 7 Sept. 1939; interview with Hon. J.W. Pickersgill, 15 July 1974

96 WLMK, Diary, 14 Sept. 1939

97 NPL, Diary, 27-28 Sept. 1939

98 Even before the invasion of Poland, King had shown his desire to avoid placing any party organizers in important national defence positions. In July he had turned down the nomination of Jules Brillant to the Defence Purchasing Board 'as he had been a political organizer in Quebec.' He could, however, countenance his appointment as a director of the Mortgage Loan Board. WLMK, Diary, 5 July 1939

99 *Ibid.*, v. 269, memorandum, W.B. Herbert to King, 'Meeting of Executive Committee of NLF, 19 Sept. 1939' (228035-6); NPL, Diary, 19 Sept. 1939; WLMK, v. 270, Lambert to King, 1 Nov. 1939 (229009), also in NPL, v. 2, file '1939'

100 NPL, Diary, 14 Nov. 1939

101 WLMK, v. 270, King to Lambert, 18 Nov. 1939 (229020-1), also in NPL, v. 2, file '1939'; WLKM, v. 270, Lambert, 'Memorandum re Mr. King's personal and confidential letter of November 18th,' 20 Nov. 1939 (229023-4), also in NPL, v.2, file '1939'; WLMK, Diary, 1 April 1940

CHAPTER FOUR
Crisis and reorganization of the Government party, 1940-5

1 'Canadian Politics,' *Political Science Quarterly* (March 1951)

2 NLF, v. 863, NLF advisory council minutes, 27-28 Oct. 1952, p. 228

3 NPL, Diary, 25 Oct., 4 Dec. 1940, 20 Jan. 1941

4 *Ibid.*, 17 Jan., 13 Feb., 2-3, 30 April, 9 May 1941

5 *Ibid.*, 8-9 May 1941; v. 2, file '1941,' Lambert to Ian Mackenzie, 10 May 1941, with 'Memo of luncheon on Friday, May 9'

6 *Ibid.*, 25 Nov. 1941

7 Norman Ward, ed., *A Party Politician: The Memoirs of Chubby Power* (Toronto, 1966), pp. 133-4

8 On the York South by-election, see J.L. Granatstein, 'The York South By-Election of February 9, 1942: A Turning Point in Canadian Politics,' *Canadian Historical Review*, XLVIII, 2 (June 1967), and *The Politics of Survival: The Conservative Party of Canada, 1939-1945* (Toronto, 1967), pp. 100-12.

9 Granatstein, *Politics of Survival*, p. 108, n 101

10 NPL, 30-31 Jan., 1 Feb. 1942

11 BC, v. 31, Claxton to George V. Ferguson, 3 Feb. 1942

12 Granatstein, *Politics of Survival*, pp. 104-5, 110-11; MKR, I, p. 348

13 NPL, Diary, 18-19 Jan., 24 Feb. 1942

14 Granatstein, *Canada's War: The Politics of the Mackenzie King Government, 1939-1945* (Toronto, 1975), pp. 225-6. NPL, Diary, 27 April, 1942. Lambert was told by C.D. Howe that Sir James Dunn of Algoma Steel had offered $5000 but that Howe 'wouldn't touch it.'

15 It will be recalled from the previous chapter that Maxime Raymond had been rejected by King as a nominee as minister to Paris in the late 1930s. This not only embittered brother Donat's relationship to King but freed Raymond to become a major opponent of the Liberal party in Quebec. The results of not using the patronage weapon were, in this case, quite serious.

16 BC, v. 31, Claxton to Ferguson, 10 April 1942

17 Canadian Institute of Public Opinion, 30 Sept. 1943

18 See, *inter alia*, Walter Young, *The Anatomy of a Party: The National CCF, 1932-1961* (Toronto, 1969), and Gerald Caplan, *The Dilemma of Canadian Socialism: The CCF in Ontario* (Toronto, 1973). The smaller surge in support of the Communists is documented in Ivan Avakumovic, *The Communist Party in Canada: A History* (Toronto, 1975).

19 NLF, v. 694, NORC, *Opinion News*, II, 4 (22 Feb. 1944). The figures here are given as a percentage of those giving a definite response; 25 per cent of the Canadian and 29 per cent of the American sample were unable or unwilling to answer the question.

20 MKR, I, pp. 564, 571-2

21 Caplan, *The Dilemma of Canadian Socialism*, pp. 110-11

22 *Ibid.*, p. 126

23 Many Liberals were suspicious about the possible Tory taint of some of these operators. Later their partisan connections became fairly well known. See, for instance, NLF, v. 613, T.L. Anderson to H.E. Kidd, 25 Feb. 1949, on Trestrail's connections to the Conservatives. It was, however, generally believed that Murray was non-partisan. IM, v. 23, Ian Mackenzie to Gladstone Murray, 15 Feb. 1944

24 BC, v. 31, Claxton to Ferguson, 5 Oct. 1943

25 CGP, 'Political Jottings,' v. II, Roberts to Power, 23 Sept. 1943

26 WLMK, Diary, 2 April 1932. Dunning later proved his point by becoming one of the most powerful businessmen in Canada in the 1940s.

27 NLF, v. 603, W. George Aikins to Senator Wishart Robertson, 13 Dec. 1943 (emphasis added)

28 See John Porter's classic discussion of 'Dr. Clark's boys' in *The Vertical Mosaic: An Analysis of Social Class and Power in Canada* (Toronto, 1965), pp. 425-8. The most recent, and the most comprehensive, analysis of the development of postwar plans is Granatstein, *Canada's War*, pp. 249-94. It is not going too far to suggest that Granatstein's well-documented evidence of the importance of social welfare planning has altered the hitherto accepted version of wartime priorities.

29 Granatstein is the first historian to note Mackenzie's importance in this matter, *Canada's War*, pp. 249-94

30 J.W. Pickersgill, *The Liberal Party* (Toronto, 1962), pp. 32-6

31 Granatstein, *Canada's War*, p. 281

32 *Ibid.*, p. 283, citing Angus L. MacDonald's diary

33 IM, v. 7, Rogers to Mackenzie, 3 Oct. 1939

34 *Ibid.*, v. 52, Mackenzie to A.D. McRae, 5 June, McRae to Mackenzie, 6 June, Mackenzie to King, 29 Oct., 22 Dec. 1941

35 CGP, 'Political Jottings,' v. 2, Norman Senior, memorandum, 11 Sept. 1943

36 NLF, v. 620, Robertson, memorandum re NLF, 23 Oct. 1943

37 MKR, I, pp. 574-5, 578, 581. The decision to call these meetings was a very hasty one, involving less than a month between the decisions and the meetings.

38 NPL, Diary, 24 Sept. 1943

39 NLF, 'The Tasks of Liberalism: Resolutions approved by Advisory Council, NLF,' Ottawa, 27 and 28 Sept. 1943

40 See Granatstein, *Canada's War*, pp. 255-62; and *Forum*, XXII (1943), p. 292

41 WLMK, Diary, 15-16 Nov. 1939, 27 Jan. 1940

42 MKR, I, pp. 571-4; Granatstein, *Politics of Survival*, p. 177

43 Granatstein, *Canada's War*, p. 280

44 For a brief attempt to place *Industry and Humanity* within a liberal corporatist framework, see my review of the new reprint edition, *Canadian Journal of Political Science*, VII,1 (March 1974), pp. 166-7

45 NLF, v. 851, 1943 advisory council, p. 256

46 *Ibid.*, pp. 252, 267, 269, 97; BC, v. 44, memorandum, Kidd to C.L. Smart, 15 June 1943

47 NLF, v. 620, Robertson memorandum, 23 Oct. 1943

48 MKR, I, pp. 585-6

49 NLF, v. 861, 1943 advisory council, pp. 181-2. One delegate, Toronto municipal politician Lewis Duncan, who suggested a more widespread policy role for party members, later joined the CCF.

50 MKR, I, p. 585; WLMK, Memoranda and Notes, v. 302, Claxton to King, 7 Oct. 1943 (C209005-6)

51 CGP, 'Political Jottings,' v. 2, Power to Leslie Roberts, 4 Oct. 1943

52 CGP, v. 2(b), box 7, file 'NLF,' 'Notes of a meeting of the Organization Committee held 27th September 1943'

53 NLF, v. 620, Robertson memorandum, 23 Oct. 1943

54 NPL, Diary, 27-8 Sept. 1943

55 Interview with Hon. J.W. Pickersgill, 15 July 1974

56 NPL, Diary, 29 Sept. 1943. As late as August of the same year, C.D. Howe had made one last effort to entice Lambert back into the presidency of the NLF, but he

was turned down. 'Until the leaders in the Gov't,' Lambert told Howe, 'make up their minds to have a long term creative organization which they are not afraid to recognize at all times, nobody wants the job of Pres. of NLF.' *Ibid.*, 5 Aug. 1943

57 Quoted in Granatstein, *Canada's War*, pp. 271-2

58 NPL, Diary, 5 Aug. 1943

59 *Ibid.*, 3-4 May 1944

60 NLF, v. 596, Fogo memorandum, July 1944

61 NPL, Diary, 28 Dec. 1943

62 See Chapter 6, below, for a detailed account of the relationship between Cockfield, Brown and the Liberal party

63 CGP, v. 2(b), box 7, file 'NLF,' memorandum, 'Political Parties Today,' n.d., no author; Norman McLarty to C.G. Power, 4 Oct. 1943, with accompanying 'Memorandum re National Liberal Federation'

64 NLF, v. 861, 1945 advisory council, speech of Senator Robertson, pp. 5-6. WLMK, Memoranda and Notes, v. 301, Claxton to King, 28 June 1944 (C208540-6), v. 302, Claxton to King, 6 Jan. 1944 (C209035-6)

65 NLF, A.G. McLean speech, p. 45; MKR, I, p. 643; IM, v. 23, J.G. Gardiner to Mackenzie, 7 Feb. 1944

66 Lambert believed that Ontario was the only province which needed organization to 'complete the national picture.' NPL, Diary, 5 May 1943

67 The Winnipeg meeting involved some considerable expense. The Quebec delegation alone ran up a bill of $11,500 which was underwritten by the Quebec provincial Liberals and the federal Liberal organization in Montreal district. CGP, v. 2(b), box 7, file 'NLF,' Florian Fortin to J.-A. Blanchette, 20 Aug. 1944

68 NLF, v. 861, 1945 advisory council, pp. 35-7, 46-7; v. 596, A. McLean to Fogo, 3 July 1944; v. 597, memorandum, Fogo to King, 15 Sept. 1944. CGP, v. 2(b), box 7, file 'NLF,' Fortin to Blanchette, 20 Aug. 1944

69 Early in 1944, H.E. Kidd of Cockfield, Brown and Senator Robertson had an interview with Joseph Atkinson of the *Star* who pointed out that the Liberals should be able to reply instantly to attacks on the government, and 'offered to be the instrument for reply if factual material in answer to accusations were made available to his men on the same day the attack is news.' BC, v. 44, Kidd to Claxton, 27 April 1944

70 NLF, v. 597, King to McLean, 25 Aug. 1944; MKR, II, p. 95

71 NLF, v. 861, 1943 advisory council, p. 101. NPL, Diary, 26 Jan., 23 July 1943; 6 and 29 Jan. 1944. Gordon Scott had been appointed to Howe's department at the beginning of the war, but died when a Canadian boat on which both he and Howe were travelling to England in 1940 was torpedoed. See Leslie Roberts, *The Life and Times of C.D. Howe* (Toronto, 1957), pp. 83, 97-8. NLF, v. 596, Fogo to McLean, 10 March 1945

72 NPL, Diary, 7-8 March 1944. This reference to the CPR as contributor is particularly intriguing since it was at this very time that the cabinet was discussing the demand of the company that it be allowed to compete with TCA on international air transport routes. In fact, the decision reached, apparently at King's strong behest, was to have Howe issue the strongest statement ever put on record favouring government monopoly and the exclusion of the CPR altogether. Despite personal visits from the president of the corporation, D.C. Coleman, King refused to back down, and even charged Coleman with financing the Tories. MKR, I, pp. 645-9. It is not known if the promised $50,000 actually was paid, after this development. See also Robert Chodos, *The CPR: A Century of Corporate Welfare* (Toronto, 1973), pp. 91-3

73 NPL, Diary, 9, 15, and 16 March, 28 April 1944

74 *Ibid.*, 9 Jan. 1945; NLF, v. 596, financial statement, 31 Dec. 1944; WLMK, Memoranda and Notes, v. 302, 'NLF: Statement of receipts and disbursements, Nov. 1, 1943 to Oct. 31, 1944' (c209030-1)

75 King did not view this as a sign of Conservative resurgence, and felt that the CCF were still 'more to be feared than the Tories,' but that the Liberal defeat might induce anti-Conservative voters to desert the CCF for the Liberals. MKR, II, pp. 289, 291

76 NPL, Diary, 7, 10-11 Nov. 1941, 8 March 1945

77 MKR, II, p. 323. Lambert hoped to be named to the Canadian delegation to the UN conference at San Francisco. Walter Herbert, former NLF secretary, told Lambert that 'if King takes you to California, I'll forgive him for everything in the past.' NPL, Diary, 11 March 1945. King didn't, and Herbert didn't. And as late as 1949 Lambert was still nursing his grievances, according to Chubby Power, whom he often visited. 'Throws in the odd word of course,' Power complained, 'as to how badly I am being treated, I suppose to keep me interested, then continues on his own griefs.' CGP, 'Political Jottings,' v. 5, 5 April 1949

78 MKR, II, p. 296. NLF, v. 596, has considerable material on the national election organization.

79 The story of the Liberal-Communist alliance of 1945 is a rather murky affair indeed. See Gad Horowitz, *Canadian Labour in Politics* (Toronto, 1968), pp. 85-131; Young, *The Anatomy of a Party*, pp. 254-85; Irving Abella, *Nationalism, Communism, and Canadian Labour: The CIO, the Communist Party, and the Canadian Congress of Labour, 1935-1956* (Toronto, 1973), pp. 66-85; Avakumovic, *The Communist Party in Canada*, pp. 139-70. During the Gouzenko trials, the Liberals were embarrassed over public claims by leading Communists, such as Sam Carr, of direct contacts in 1945. NLF, v. 619, NLF press release, 18 April 1949. There is little doubt, however, that these claims were substantially true.

80 *Canada's War*, pp. 409-10

81 Granatstein, *Politics of Survival*, pp. 190-1. See Granatstein, 'Financing the Liberal Party, 1935-45,' in M.S. Cross and R. Bothwell, eds., *Policy by Other Means: Essays in Honour of C.P. Stacey* (Toronto, 1972), for the only detailed analysis of Liberal financing in this election.
82 NPL, Diary, 10 Jan. 1945
83 *Ibid.*, 26 and 30 April 1945. The total amount of Stelco's contribution is not known, but a 'further' $15,000 went to Senator Daigle in Montreal.
84 *Ibid.*, 16 and 17 May 1945
85 *Ibid.*, 28 Feb. 1945
86 *Ibid.*, 25 May, 2 June 1945
87 Granatstein, *Politics of Survival*, p. 189

CHAPTER FIVE
The Government party fulfilled, 1945-58

1 See, *inter alia*, Peter Regenstreif, *The Diefenbaker Interlude: Parties and Voting in Canada* (Toronto, 1965), pp. 10-26, and the same author's unpublished doctoral thesis, 'The Liberal Party of Canada: A Political Analysis,' Cornell University, 1963, pp. 91-8; Frank H. Underhill, 'The Revival of Conservatism in North America,' *Transactions of the Royal Society of Canada*, LII (June 1958); John Porter, *The Vertical Mosaic: An Analysis of Social Class and Power in Canada* (Toronto, 1965), pp. 405-15, 451-6
2 See J.E. Hodgetts, 'The Liberal and the Bureaucrat,' *Queen's Quarterly*, LXII (Summer 1955), pp. 176-83, and 'The Civil Service and Policy Formation,' *Canadian Journal of Economics and Political Science*, XXIII, 4 (Nov. 1957), pp. 467-79; John Meisel, 'The Formulation of Liberal and Conservative Programmes in the 1957 Canadian General Election,' *ibid.*, XXVI, 4 (Nov. 1960), pp. 565-74
3 Regenstreif, *Diefenbaker Interlude*, p. 14, has compiled CIPO data on the 1953 election which demonstrate the broad base of Liberal support.
4 MKR, IV, p. 5. See also Arnold Heeney, *The Things That Are Caesar's: Memoirs of a Canadian Public Servant* (Toronto, 1972), pp. 82-95, for a sympathetic but critical view of King's last years from one who knew him well; and Bruce Hutchison, *The Incredible Canadian* (Toronto, 1952), pp. 417-24. As might be expected, the most acerbic and caustic comment comes from James Eayrs, *In Defence of Canada: Peacemaking and Deterrence* (Toronto, 1972), III, who saw him as 'ill in body, ill at ease, sick at heart ...' Eayrs adds (pp. 5-6) that 'Prime ministers whose reflexes fail towards the close of their career may make life awkward for their colleagues; prime ministers who develop quirks and aberrations along with their faltering synapses threaten parliamentary

government itself. This threat was posed for Canada during Mackenzie King's last two years of power.'

5 MKR, III, p. 349

6 *Ibid.*, pp. 373-4. In fact, Howe had more responsibility for organizing these by-elections than Claxton. There is good evidence from King's diary that his growing dislike of Claxton was activated by jealous pique at Claxton's demonstrated ability at the Paris peace conference. See Eayrs, *In Defence of Canada*, III, pp. 20-1

7 MKR, IV, pp. 6, 75, 210-11

8 A Liberal convention had been held in 1893 for discussion of policy; the 1919 convention had originally been called by Laurier to examine policy and organization following the Union government split in the party, but Laurier's subsequent death turned it into a leadership contest. John C. Courtney, *The Selection of National Party Leaders in Canada* (Toronto, 1973), pp. 59-65

9 NLF, *Report of the Proceedings of the National Liberal Convention, 1948* (Ottawa, n.d.), pp. 14-15

10 NLF, v. 529, W. Hale to A.G. McLean, 12 April, McLean to Hale, 5 April 1948; v. 595, McLean to Arthur Laing, 5 April 1948

11 MKR, IV, pp. 280-1

12 NLF, *Report of the Proceedings*, p. 21

13 'The Liberal Party,' pp. 205-6, 207

14 MKR, IV, pp. 348-9

15 NLF, *Report of the Proceedings*, pp. 113-14

16 *Gentlemen, Players and Politicians* (Toronto, 1970), pp. 4-5

17 NLF, *Report of the Proceedings*, p. 231

18 CGP, 'Political Jottings,' v. 5, noted that 'any attempt by the Young Liberal groups to put forward any new ideas or express any criticism was promptly squelched.'

19 *Gentlemen, Players and Politicians*, pp. 2-3; NLF, *Report of the Proceedings*, pp. 167-72

20 MKR, IV, pp. 352-3, 354, 357

21 *Gentlemen, Players and Politicians*, pp. 5-6

22 Norman Ward, ed., *A Party Politician: The Memoirs of Chubby Power* (Toronto, 1966), pp. 395-8

23 *The Incredible Canadian*, p. 437

24 MKR, IV, pp. 362-3

25 *The Selection of National Party Leaders*, p. 199

26 *Gentlemen, Players and Politicians*, p. 7

27 NLF, *Report of the Proceedings*, p. 163

28 For a much fuller discussion of these developments, see Part II, below.

29 Brooke Claxton's words in BC, v. 224, 'Memoir Notes'

30 Remarks at the Mackenzie King Centennial Colloquium, Waterloo University, 16 Dec. 1974. See also W.A. Matheson, *The Prime Minister and the Cabinet* (Toronto, 1976), pp. 149-59, for a judicious comparison.

31 *The Prince* (New York, 1950), chap. 17. Machiavelli concludes that 'men love at their own free will, but fear at the will of the prince, and ... a wise prince must rely on what is in his power and not on what is in the power of others.'

32 CGP, 'Political Jottings,' v. 5, 15 Dec. 1948. Power later recalled that there was only one occasion on which St Laurent discussed organization with him. Before an election, Power and Maurice Bourget gave the prime minister a list of candidates in Quebec for his approval. St Laurent passed over the entire list without comment except for one man, whom Power wished removed for fear of losing the seat. St Laurent said: 'I think he'll pull through. Family influences and the family name will be enough to pull this one through.' The candidate lost. *Ibid.*, v. 36, transcripts file II, interview with John Meisel, 17 May 1960.

33 NLF, v. 827, Kidd to T.L. Anderson, 10 April 1953. In the same election, the NLF hired an organizer 'on orders from Mr. Howe.' *Ibid.*, v. 621, Kidd to Duncan MacTavish, 16 July 1953

34 Interview with Hon. J.W. Pickersgill, 15 July 1974. Other Windsor area Liberal MPs were sometimes heard to complain that Martin took a disproportionate amount of the national money allocated to the area.

35 LSTL, v. 138, file 0-20-5, Harris to St Laurent, 10 Nov. 1952; NLF, v. 617, Harris to Kidd, 1 Dec. 1952; v. 633, Kidd to Pickersgill, 13 Dec. 1954; v. 632, Harris to Kidd, 8 May 1956; Pickersgill interview

36 Pearson recalled the 'redoubtable' Fraser as 'a vigorous party orator and a gifted tub-thumper' – qualities which Pearson himself notoriously lacked. J.A. Munro and A.I. Inglis, eds., *Mike: The Memoirs of the Right Honourable Lester B. Pearson, 1948-1957* (Toronto, 1973), II, p. 9

37 BC, v. 224, 'Memoir Notes.' Claxton stated that 'it always struck me that he was a great political handicap.' Pickersgill, when interviewed for this study, was, if anything, more outspokenly contemptuous of Gardiner.

38 Dale C. Thomson, *Louis St. Laurent: Canadian* (Toronto, 1967), pp. 344-5

39 LSTL, v. 225, file 0-20-5-P, J. Harper Prowse to St Laurent, 20 Dec. 1956

40 *Ibid.*, v. 138, file 0-20-9, Sinclair to St Laurent, 10 July 1952; Pickersgill, memorandum for file, 18 July 1952, an interview St Laurent and Sinclair, draft letter, St Laurent to Sinclair. Rivalry between Sinclair and Campney is noted in Provincial Archives of Manitoba, Ralph Maybank papers, Diary, 28 Nov. 1949, and Campney to Maybank, 4 Nov. 1952.

41 See Chapter 7, below

42 Quoted in Tom Axworthy, 'Innovation and the Party System: An Examination of the Career of Walter L. Gordon and the Liberal Party,' unpublished MA thesis, Queen's University, 1970, p. 160

43 LSTL, v. 61, file C-20-2, Ilsley to St Laurent, 17 Sept. 1948; draft letter, St Laurent to Nova Scotia members, 24 Sept. 1948

44 *Ibid.*, v. 62, file O-20-4, Jean to St Laurent, 23 Sept. 1948

45 *In Defence of Canada*, III, p. 26

46 BC, v. 224, 'Memoir Notes'

47 Pickersgill interview

48 NLF, v. 847, J.J. Connolly to Herc Munroe, 22 March 1958

49 IM, v. 23, Mackenzie to King, 29 Oct. 1946

50 William Kilbourn, *PipeLine: Transcanada and the Great Debate* (Toronto, 1970), pp. 32-3

51 See Chapter 6, below

52 NLF, v. 629, record of conversation between Harold Greer and Kidd, 31 July 1953

53 *Ibid.*, v. 826, record of conversation between H.E. Kidd and 'Cappy' Kidd, n.d. (sometime during the 1953 election campaign)

54 *Ibid.*, v. 596, Fogo to McLean, Nov. , McLean to Fogo, 22 Nov. 1945; v. 616, Kidd to Douglas Abbott, 23 March, memorandum, MacTavish to Kidd, 10 Feb. 1953

55 LSTL, v. 137, file 0-20, memorandum, Pickersgill to St Laurent, 12 July 1952. C.D. Howe suggested an alternative, which was in fact followed. The party treasurer would take over as acting president for the interim, which public exposure might aid in his fund-raising activities. *Ibid.*, Pickersgill to Howe, 21 July 1952

56 *Ibid.*, v. 134, file N-14-P, Pickersgill to St Laurent, 29 Jan., 17 March, 27 May 1952; v. 223, file N-14-M, St Laurent to Pickersgill, 4 Nov. , Pickersgill to St Laurent, 15 Nov. 1954. NLF, v. 635, Kidd to MacTavish, 17 Aug., MacTavish to Kidd, 23 Aug. 1954

57 'The Liberal Party,' pp. 196, 178

58 F.R. Scott, 'Alignment of Parties,' *Canadian Forum* (March 1947); reprinted in J.L. Granatstein and Peter Stevens, eds., *Forum: Canadian Life and Letters, 1920-70* (Toronto, 1972), pp. 237-9

59 Quoted in Joseph Wearing, 'Mutations in a Political Party: The Liberal Party of Canada in the Fifties and Sixties,' paper presented to the Canadian Political Science Association annual meeting, Edmonton, June 1975, p. 6

60 NLF, v. 862, 1949 advisory council, p. 104

61 BC, v. 61, executive committee, NLF, 24 Feb. 1954; NLF, v. 863, 1955 advisory council; Regenstreif, 'The Liberal Party,' p. 186

62 BC, v. 60, Kidd to Fogo, 5 Jan. 1950; Regenstreif, 'The Liberal Party,' p. 193; NLF, v. 596, McLean to Fogo, 10 Nov. 1945

63 BC, v. 30, Kidd to MacTavish, 31 March 1953. By May the number of delinquent constituencies had been reduced to 51. BC, v. 50, memorandum, n.a. 5 May 1953

64 BC, v. 30, MacTavish to Claxton, 2 April 1953, with enclosed memo, Kidd, 'Re General Election,' 31 March 1953

65 NLF, v. 861, 1947 advisory council, pp. 11-12
66 BC, v. 30, Kidd to MacTavish, 31 March 1953. An independent venture in Toronto by a Liberal supporter to publish a *Canadian Liberal News* in the late 1940s died from lack of interest and funds. BC, v. 61, Kidd to Claxton, 31 March 1953. NLF, v. 618, Kidd to D.A. Emerson, 16 April 1953
67 NLF, v. 861, 1947 advisory council, p. 116
68 NLF, v. 629, minutes of meeting, 16 April 1954; v. 637, Kidd to Norman Ward, 2 Aug. 1955. Lafond survived the post-1958 purge which felled Kidd, and was later given a senatorship by the Trudeau government.
69 BC, v. 61, memorandum, Alan MacNaughton (Mount Royal), n.d.
70 NLF, v. 621, B.T. Richardson to Kidd, 13 Feb.; v. 634, Kidd to MacTavish, 19 March, Kidd, memo to Lafond, 27 April; v. 829, Beatrice Knowles to Kidd, 14 May, W.O. Hannah to Kidd, 6 May 1953
71 *Ibid.*, v. 632, Kidd to Walter Tucker, 10 March 1954
72 *Ibid.*, v. 631, J.L. MacDougall to St Laurent, 14 Oct., Tom Goode to St Laurent, 13 Oct.; v. 635, memo, MacTavish to Kidd, 25 Nov. 1955
73 LSTL, v. 224, file N-14-2, St Laurent, letters to ministers, 12 Dec. 1956, 19 March 1957
74 NLF, v. 623, Fogo to St Laurent, 18 March 1952. The results, even from those who replied, were sometimes appalling. Senator Rupert Davies, when asked what were the major political issues in the country, replied (from his summer home in Europe) that 'I and every other Senator have been struck by the fact that every time one goes up into the cafeteria, at any hour of the morning or afternoon, it is full of girls either drinking coffee or sucking down tea. I do not know what control there is over this constant tea-drinking and gossiping in the cafeteria.' NLF, v. 826, Davies to Kidd, 22 Aug. 1952. With political intelligence like that, the Liberals were obviously on top of the national situation.
75 *Ibid.*, v. 625, various files
76 For example, *ibid.*, v. 617, Kidd to N. Borse, 15 March and 18 April 1952, concerning a by-election in Victoria-Carleton, NB
77 *Ibid.*, v. 599, various files
78 *Ibid.*, v. 620, Kidd to Fogo, 11 March 1952
79 *Ibid.*, v. 618, Kidd to D.A. Emerson, 28 Nov. 1957; v. 619, McLean to Fogo, 8 March 1949
80 *Ibid.*, v. 595, E.T. Applewhaite to NLF, 18 Feb.; v. 601, McLean to W.M. Swan, 31 March; v. 598, McLean to W.J.F. Pratt, 23 April 1948; v. 597
81 Sometimes these matters could become highly complicated. An imbroglio concerning patronage for engraving companies, and involving the intervention of Howe on behalf of one supplier, was described by Kidd as an 'impasse.' NLF, v. 826, Kidd to Alan Woodrow, 18 May 1953

82 The Young Liberals held a summer school at McMaster University in 1948, which was attended by a number of academics, from W.A. Mackintosh, Arthur Lower, and J.-C. Falardeau to Etienne Gilson, the Catholic philosopher from France. NLF, v. 862, 1948 advisory council, p. 20. It was the closest the Liberals came to a 'thinkers conference' between Port Hope in 1933 and the renewal of such activity under Lester Pearson's leadership in the early 1960s.

83 *Ibid.*, v. 619, Kidd to Mrs Jeanne Embree, 21 May 1953. Copies were sent to Premier Smallwood and to Jack Pickersgill.

84 *Ibid.*, v. 621, Embree to Woodrow, 23 Sept., Woodrow to Embree, 3 Oct. 1952; MacTavish to Kidd, 5 Feb. 1953; v. 634, MacTavish to Kidd, 30 Jan. 1957

85 *Ibid.*, v. 861, 1947 advisory council, pp. 356-7, Mrs H. Walsh of Winnipeg

86 Margaret P. Hyndman in the *Canadian Liberal* (Summer 1952), p. 137

87 One recent discussion of this phenomenon is in Courtney, *The Selection of National Party Leaders*, pp. 137-60. Robert Jackson and Michael Atkinson, *The Canadian Legislative System* (Toronto, 1974), pp. 141-3, evaluate its effect on the functioning of Parliament.

88 MKR, III, p. 351. King prudently added that while he could 'manage all right' at present, 'it might be different once I found it necessary to retire.' When he did retire he was presented with $100,000 from the Rockefellers. Hutchison, *The Incredible Canadian*, p. 443

89 Denis Smith, *Gentle Patriot: A Political Biography of Walter Gordon* (Edmonton, 1973), p. 28

90 Douglas Fisher, 'Cabinet Split on Energy,' *Ottawa Citizen*, 4 Dec. 1973

91 For the controversy over the Pearson fund, see James Eayrs, 'Double-Standard: Three PMs Accepted Cash Gifts,' *Ottawa Citizen*, 28 Nov. 1973; letter to the editor, Alex Inglis and John Munro, 5 Dec., and reply by Eayrs, 12 Dec. 1973

92 Thomson, *Louis St. Laurent*, p. 213; WLMK, Diary, 21 Oct. 1947

93 *Ibid.*, p. 216. St Laurent appears to have been careful in the expenditure of public money for political purposes. For example, when he used government aircraft to campaign he sent the bills to the NLF for payment. NLF, v. 824, M.J. Deacey to Kidd, MacTavish, and Department of Transport, 24 Oct. 1953

94 Dunn was ambivalent about Howe and perhaps wished to back a candidate for the leadership who would hold Howe in line. In 1948 he first urged Power to run, and then, having extracted a promise from Howe to allow Dunn to export steel to Europe, he used the promise of a legal retainer and a directorship of Algoma to vainly induce Power to withdraw. Ward, ed., *A Party Politician*, pp. 394, 397. Then in 1951 he came back with the offer of two retainers of $2500 each for a period of five years to encourage Power to stay in active party politics, ready to replace St Laurent when he retired. Power told him that he was 'not a horse, not even a dark one' for the leadership, and that there was 'no chance' of his even

being taken back into the administration. 'I think,' Power noted, 'Dunn is scouting around for something in connection with Labrador.' CGP, 'Political Jottings,' v. 3, July and Aug. 1957. This strange affair seems to suggest more about the curiously naïve politics of Sir James Dunn than anything else.

95 K.Z. Paltiel and Jean Brown Van Loon, 'Financing the Liberal Party, 1867-1965,' in Committee on Election Expenses, *Studies in Canadian Party Finance* (Ottawa, 1966), p. 192

96 BC, v. 155, Claxton to A.R. Renaud, 18 May 1949, with attached lists; *ibid.*, list of defence suppliers, 1 April to 30 Dec. 1948. The largest supplier was Bell Canada, listed for $192 million, but its head office was apparently not in Claxton's riding. See also another list apparently of contributors to the 1953 campaign, in *ibid.*, v. 162. Here again defence suppliers figure very prominently.

97 NLF, v. 621, Kidd to Woodrow, 13 March 1951, 18 and 19 March 1952

98 *Ibid.*, v. 807, Abbott to V.C. Wansbrough and N.F. Parkinson, 12 May, Wansbrough to Abbott, 14 May; v. 806, Kidd to Anglin Johnson, 20 June 1949

99 *Ibid.*, v. 836, MacTavish to Kidd, 4 Feb. 1957. MacTavish asked Kidd to help 'keep our friends happy' by giving more NLF business to CP Telegraphs.

100 CDH, v. 109, file 75(8), Howe to J.F. Tobin, 8 March, Tobin to Howe, 3 May 1958

101 NLF, v. 620, memorandum, Paul Lafond to Kidd, 12 May 1949

102 *Ibid.*, v. 826, memorandum, 'D.A.M(acTavish),' n.d.

103 This was a point often emphasized by Chubby Power. CGP, 1968, box 1, 'Memorandum, Political Expenditures,' n.d.; v. 30, transcripts, file II, interview with John Meisel, 17 May 1960

104 See K.Z. Paltiel, *Political Party Financing in Canada* (Toronto, 1970), for a much fuller discussion of the phenomenon of campaign donations than is possible here.

105 LSTL, v. 61, file 0-20-4, Daigle to St Laurent, 16 Feb. 1949

106 Quoted in E.E. Harrill, 'The Structure of Organization and Power in Canadian Political Parties: A Study in Party Financing,' unpublished PHD thesis, University of North Carolina, 1958, p. 181

107 Cited in Lois Torrence, 'The National Party System in Canada, 1945-1960,' unpublished PHD thesis, American University, Washington, DC, 1961, p. 453

108 John Meisel, *The Canadian General Election of 1957* (Toronto, 1962), p. 173. It might be noted that Meisel prefaces his estimate with the disclaimer that it 'is no doubt safe but not greatly enlightening.'

109 For the 1953 election, see NLF, v. 826, Kidd, memorandum to MacTavish, 6 June; MacTavish, memorandum to Kidd, 10 June, v. 817, Kidd to MacTavish, 6 June 1953

110 NLF, v. 836, S. Denman to Kidd, 21 Jan. 1957; v. 616, Kidd to Claxton, 6 July 1953; see also Chapter 6, below

111 CDH, v. 109, file 75(8), Howe to MacTavish, 10 Jan. 1958. Howe declined the chairmanship of the Liberal finance committee, but agreed to give help in raising funds. *Ibid.*, Howe to W.L. Williamson, 24 Feb. 1958

112 NLF, v. 864, 1959 advisory council, report of finance committee, p. 134

113 *Ibid.*, v. 621, memorandum, Kidd to Woodrow, 8 Jan. 1952, indicates a surplus of almost $15,000 for the year 1951. Near the end of 1953, an election year, Kidd reported that a surplus of $16,000 would be possible. *Ibid.*, Kidd to Woodrow, 30 Oct. 1953

114 *Ibid.*, v. 861, 1945 advisory council, pp. 91-2

115 *Political Party Financing*, pp. 34-5

116 'The Liberal Party,' p. 175. Woodrow was in fact only acting president, for a brief interregnum between Fogo and MacTavish.

117 When Alan Woodrow began his activities as NLF treasurer, he complained to Fogo that he was finding some trouble in gaining acceptance from sources in certain areas of Ontario. An announcement was placed in the business pages of the press giving official notice of his status. NLF, v. 806, Woodrow to Fogo, 23 Feb., Fogo to Woodrow, 25 Feb., Kidd to A.W. Cooper, 5 and 21 March 1949. Later Woodrow was made acting president to further publicize his standing. See n. 55, above

118 *Ibid.*, v. 620 and 621, contain a number of files dealing with 1952 finances; v. 621, MacTavish to Kidd, 15 Dec., MacTavish to R.B. Brenan, 16 Dec. 1952

119 CDH, v. 109, file 75(8), 'Standing of Budget for year 1956' (*sic*, actually 1957), 14 Jan. 1958, shows that Ontario and Quebec fulfilled their quotas of $75,000 each, but British Columbia and Saskatchewan paid nothing, and still owed $35,000 and $10,000 respectively. In 1955 and 1956, British Columbia had filled only about half of its much smaller commitment. Both provinces were notorious in the party for failure to live up to financial obligations.

120 NLF, v. 835, B.F. McEnery to Kidd, 17 April; v. 627, memorandum, Lafond to MacTavish and Kidd, 19 April 1957

121 *Ibid.*, v. 611, Kidd to A. Archibald, 15 Sept. 1949; v. 802, F. Ryan, memorandum, 8 June 1945; v. 625, R.A. Batten to Kidd, 18 Jan., Kidd to Batten, 12 Feb., Archibald to Kidd, 8 March 1949. It is interesting to note that these two Liberal firms have since merged to form Bomac-Batten, and that this new company continues to receive government patronage.

122 *Ibid.*, v. 621; v. 826, R.G. Bartlett to S. Denman, 23 Oct. 1952

123 *Ibid.*, v. 811, W.A. Munro to Kidd, 16 June 1949; Ross Harkness, *J.E. Atkinson of the Star* (Toronto, 1963), p. 365

124 NLF, v. 827, Kidd to MacTavish, 1 June, MacTavish to Cooke, 10 July 1953

125 One striking example is radio station CFRA in Ottawa which provided free advertising worth $1424 to the Liberals in the 1948 provincial election, and $1658 to the party in the 1949 federal election. *Ibid.*, v. 600, Frank Ryan to McLean, 24 July 1948; v. 625, Ryan to Kidd, 30 Sept. 1949. CFRA's devotion to the Liberal cause may have had something to do with the fact the Liberal party had helped owner Frank Ryan gain a licence for his station from the CBC. *Ibid.*,

v. 596, McLean to Fogo, 10 Nov. 1945. Liberal connections were not helpful when CFRA unsuccessfully applied for a private television channel licence from the Board of Broadcast Governors set up by the Diefenbaker government.

126 *Ibid.*, v. 867, Nathanson to Kidd, 16 July 1948; v. 811, Kidd, memorandum of conversation, 9 Feb. 1949; v. 618, Kidd to Paul Martin, 5 Nov. 1952; v. 825, Kidd to MacTavish, 29 Dec. 1952, memorandum, 27 Jan. 1953, Nathanson to Kidd, 4 March, Kidd to Nathanson, 20 July 1953

127 Especially Part II, chaps. 4 to 9, pp. 63-197

128 NLF, v. 619, Alistair Fraser to Kidd, 23 Jan., MacTavish to D.C. Abbott, 18 June 1953; v. 616, Claxton to MacTavish and Kidd, 22 June 1953

129 Chubby Power complained to a correspondent during the 1949 campaign of the difficulties of running in a constituency adjacent to that of the prime minister. Looking after his own riding was 'not so easy owing to the close proximity of a powerful neighbour whose friends seem to be bent on overshadowing every one in an endeavour to show that he is not only the source of all wisdom but the fountain from whom all blessings flow.' CGP, v. 4, file 2(6), Power to Harry Butcher, 31 March 1949

130 NLF, v. 840, contains files on the 1958 campaign organization

131 CDH, v. 107, file 75(2), Howe to Jimmy Gardiner, 24 May 1958; NLF, v. 850, Connolly to Kidd, 16 April 1958

132 *In Defence of Canada*, III, p. 16

133 Pickersgill interview

134 *Diefenbaker Interlude*, p. 26

135 CDH, v. 107, file 75(2), Howe to Irvin Studer, 23 May 1958

136 'The Liberal and the Bureaucrat,' p. 183

137 LSTL, v. 138, file O-20-7, St Laurent to Gardiner, 26 Sept. 1951

138 BC, v. 61, executive committee meeting, 24 Feb. 1954

139 Regenstreif, 'The Liberal Party,' p. 202

140 Quoted in Wearing, 'Mutations in a Political Party,' p. 21

141 BC, v. 166. The authorship of this very interesting document is not clear. It is perspicacious enough to have come from Claxton's own able pen, but it might have originated elsewhere.

142 Smith, *Gentle Patriot*, pp. 51-133

CHAPTER SIX
The Liberal party and its advertising agencies

1 The best introduction into the history of political public relations is Stanley Kelley, Jr., *Professional Public Relations and Political Power* (Baltimore, 1956), pp. 9-38.

2 The difference between the patronage style of political campaign and the newer communications orientation which comes with advertising is well illustrated by the reaction of Angus L. Macdonald to observing a media-centred provincial campaign in Manitoba in 1932. Macdonald wrote to J.L. Ralston about the implications for Nova Scotia: 'Can it be that we could conduct a campaign in this Province with radio hire and other publicity as our major items of expense? Speed the day!' JLR, v. 12, Macdonald to Ralston, 12 Dec. 1932

3 For a recent empirical investigation of the effects of advertising on voting behaviour in Quebec, see Kristian S. Palda, 'Does Advertising Influence Votes? An Analysis of the 1966 and 1970 Quebec Elections,' *Canadian Journal of Political Science*, VI, 4 (Dec. 1973), pp. 638-53. Palda concludes that there is indeed a relationship between advertising and voting. A recent American study of the effects of television advertising in the 1972 presidential election came to similar conclusions regarding that medium. See Thomas E. Patterson and Robert D. McClure, 'Television News and Televised Political Advertising: Their Impact on the Voter,' paper delivered at the National Conference on Money and Politics, Washington, DC, 27-28 Feb. 1974

4 O.J. Firestone, *The Economic Implications of Advertising* (Toronto, 1967), pp. 49-57. Part, but clearly not all, of this difference may be attributed to the 'spill-over' effect of American advertising *via* television and magazines.

5 Dan Nimmo, *The Political Persuaders: The Techniques of Modern Election Campaigns* (Englewood Cliffs, NJ, 1970), app. A, pp. 201-7. Nimmo also lists no less than 76 political polling organizations in the United States (pp. 208-10).

6 General works touching on the phenomenon of 'campaign management' in the United States include Kelley, *Professional Public Relations*; Nimmo, *The Political Persuaders*; James M. Perry, *The New Politics: The Expanding Technology of Political Manipulation* (London, 1968); Richard D. McCarthy, *Elections for Sale* (Boston, 1972); articles in Reo Christenson and Robert McWilliams, eds., *Voice of the People* (New York, 2nd ed., 1967). On Nixon's advertising see the brilliantly funny insider's account by Joe McGinniss, *The Selling of the President, 1968* (New York, 1969). Two interesting attempts to look at advertising in a broader social context are Giancarlo Buzzi, *Advertising: Its Cultural and Political Effects* (Minneapolis, 1968), and Stuart Ewen, *Captains of Consciousness: Advertising and the Social Roots of the Consumer Culture* (New York, 1976).

7 *Political Party Financing in Canada* (Toronto, 1970), p. 77

8 'The Liberal Party of Canada: A Political Analysis,' unpublished PHD thesis, Cornell University, 1963, p. 197

9 *Gentlemen, Players and Politicians* (Toronto, 1970), p. 47

10 There is a meagre literature on advertising in Canada. O.J. Firestone in two books, *The Economic Implications of Advertising*, and *The Public Persuader: Government Advertising* (Toronto, 1970), has provided much basic data from an

economic point of view, although the fact that the former book was sponsored by the Institute of Canadian Advertising perhaps suggests some of Firestone's limitations as a critical analyst. H.E. Stephenson and Carlton McNaught in *The Story of Advertising in Canada: A Chronicle of Fifty Years* (Toronto, 1940), provides some historical perspective up to the Second World War. Unfortunately, the authors were loyal members of the Toronto agency of McKim; and while the latter agency was often referred to, the authors were unable to bring themselves to ever name a single competitor. The result is a curiously monomaniacal 'history.' Much more interesting from an analytical point of view, but narrower in scope, is Frederick Elkin's *Rebels and Colleagues: Advertising and Social Change in French Canada* (Montreal, 1973). Elkin's work is the first serious attempt at a sociology of advertising in Canada. There is also an unpublished thesis by Brian M. McFadzen, 'The Liberal Party and MacLaren Advertising Company, Ltd., 1957-65,' Queen's University, MA, 1971, which provides very useful information on the Pearson years.

11 The 15 + 2 per cent system was only established as late as 1935, which indicates the rudimentary nature of the advertising industry until the last few decades. *Marketing*, 12 Dec. 1958

12 *The Story of Advertising*, pp. 159-85, quotation from p. 174

13 *Political Party Financing*, p. 77

14 NPL, Diary, 1935, list of expenditures; 14 July 1939. WLMK, v. 270, Norman P. Lambert to King, 1 July (228963-4), A.D.P. Heeney to Lambert, 19 July 1939 (228965). Cockfield was again brought in for high-level consultations with Lambert on billboard, newspaper, and radio advertising for the wartime election of 1940. NPL, Diary, 25 Jan. 1940

15 *Marketing*, 3 Nov. 1945. Statistics from 1941 to the present can be found in Dominion Bureau of Statistics, *Advertising Agencies in Canada* (Ottawa, 1968).

16 The amount of government spending is calculated from figures in an unpublished Sessional Paper, no. 257 (12 Aug. 1946), Public Archives of Canada, v. 505. The proportion spent through ad agencies is estimated from figures in another unpublished Sessional Paper, no. 14B (19 May 1947), PAC, v. 515. The proportion is only a rough estimate, since the time periods are not exactly comparable in the two sets of figures, but it is no doubt generally accurate.

17 *Marketing*, 12 Dec. 1958

18 See H.S. Ferns and Bernard Ostry, *The Age of Mackenzie King: The Rise of the Leader* (London, 1955), and Bradley Rudin, 'Mackenzie King and the Writing of Canada's (Anti) Labour Laws,' *Canadian Dimension*, VIII, 4-5

19 PAC, Walsh Advertising Agency, *A Formula for Liberal Victory* (1948)

20 Camp, *Gentlemen, Players and Politicians*, pp. 78-9. The Liberals must have agreed; by the time of the next provincial election in 1956, the MacLaren's and Canadian agencies were in charge of the Liberal campaign (p. 198).

21 *Marketing* 12 Dec. 1958; see also 21 Nov.

22 NPL, Diary, 1935, list of contributions. There were personal connections as well. The head of a newly formed Toronto Liberal Businessman's Club in 1933 was a member of the Cockfield, Brown staff. WLMK, v. 198, H.R.L. Henry to W.R.P. Parker, 3 Jan. (168203); Parker to Henry, 4 Jan. 1933 (168212). Duncan Marshall, a minister in the Hepburn government and later a Liberal senator, was an executive of the firm from 1923 to 1934.

23 *Marketing*, 3 Feb. 1940, 12 Dec. 1958

24 'Charles Percy Stacey,' in M. Cross and R. Bothwell, eds., *Policy by Other Means: Essays in Honour of C.P. Stacey* (Toronto, 1972), p.10

25 BC, v. 155. Claxton to A.R. Renaud, 18 May 1949, includes list of contributors, either actual or potential, for the 1949 campaign. Another list in file 26 ('Broadcasts, Elections, 1949') contains a list of defence supplies 1 April to 30 Dec. 1948 with exact amounts of contracts. At least three-quarters of the names on the first list also appear on the second.

26 As Kidd reminded Pickersgill a decade later, 'It was largely you and Brooke, I believe, who brought into being the programmes of reform which, having Mr. King's acceptance, we were able successfully to develop as our principal appeal in the '45 election ... Brooke was a tower of strength in the party councils.' NLF, v. 633, Kidd to Pickersgill, 13 Aug. 1954. Pickersgill has described Claxton as 'the link between Mackenzie King and the political organization of the Liberal party.' MKR, II, pp. 5-6. He also wrote his own advertising copy for the Department of National Defence when he was minister. James Eayrs, *In Defence of Canada: Peacemaking and Deterrence* (Toronto, 1972), III, pp. 67, 121, 127

27 BC, v. 44, Kidd to Claxton, 16 March, 24 June 1943. Although born in Sweden, Kidd was of English parents.

28 BC, v. 28, Campbell Smart to A.M. Mitchell, 22 April, Mitchell to Smart, 23 April 1940; v. 44. Kidd to Claxton, 3 June, Claxton to Kidd, 4 June 1941

29 BC, v. 44, Kidd to Claxton, 16 March 1943. Kidd did not leave his client's own constituency unattended. A 'Hansard Club' was set up in 1940, with Kidd as secretary, to function for the 'greatest benefit of members as well as our party representative for St. Lawrence–St. George,' Kidd, notice, n.d., BC, v. 44

30 BC, v. 44, Kidd to Claxton, 15 July, Claxton to Kidd, 21 July 1943

31 BC, v. 44, Kidd to Claxton, 27 Nov. 1942, 1 Feb. 1943; Claxton to Kidd, 23 Dec. 1942, 28 Jan., 9 and 23 Feb. 1943

32 BC, v. 44, Cockfield, Brown memorandum, 25 April 1944, with attachments; report, 2 May 1944. BC, v. 28, 'Breakdown, Election Expenses,' 5 July 1945; v. 29 and 30 also include material on the various agencies involved, seven in all. *Ibid.*, Claxton to Anderson; BC, v. 44, Claxton to Kidd, 26 Dec. 1951

33 NLF, v. 602. Kidd to G.C. Hammond, 11 May, 1945. Almost all the information

available on the Liberal–Cockfield, Brown relationship comes from the National Liberal Federation files. It might be noted that a written inquiry from the author to the Montreal office of Cockfield, Brown and Company concerning access to any remaining records of the Liberal party account, elicited no response, not even an acknowledgment. Apparently the sensitive nature of the subject has not lessened appreciably in thirty years.

34 Task Force on Government Information, *To Know and Be Known: The Report of the Task Force on Government Information* (Ottawa, 1969), pp. 324-38. See also Firestone, *Public Persuader*, pp. 67-77, 182-6; interview with Hon. J.W. Pickersgill, 15 July 1974

35 NLF, v. 596, Fogo to A.G. McLean, 7 Feb. 1945. J.L. Granatstein, 'Financing the Liberal Party, 1935-1945,' in Cross and Bothwell, *Policy by Other Means*, p. 194. Granatstein's article is far and away the best piece on Liberal party organization in print – and the first to utilize the archival goldmine in the Norman Lambert diaries at Queen's University, except for Neil McKenty's biography of *Mitch Hepburn* (Toronto, 1967).

36 NLF, v. 599, McLean to Annis, 13 July 1948. The agency in question was R.C. Smith of Toronto.

37 Submission of J.S. Crosbie, president, the Magazine Advertising Bureau of Canada, to the Task Force on Government Information, 30 Jan. 1969; quoted in Task Force, *Report*, p. 335, and in Firestone, *Public Persuader*, p. 69

38 Firestone, *ibid.*, pp. 68-9

39 NLF, v. 629, Kidd to MacTavish, 8 Oct., Kidd to Archibald, 14 Oct. 1954

40 See, *inter alia*, NLF, v. 826, Cockfield, Brown memorandum, R.G. Bartlett to S.D. Denman, 23 Oct. 1952 ('I understand that our commission is added to the net price when we bill the National Liberal Federation'), and Kidd to Bartlett, 1 April 1953; v. 809, Bartlett to Paul Lafond, 3 Aug., and Lafond to Fogo, 5 Aug. 1949 ('All Cockfield, Brown invoices include full agency commission, and thus prices on individual invoices as well as on the total are boosted by some 17%').

41 NLF, v. 603, Kidd to Archibald, 8 June 1945. Granatstein, 'Financing the Liberal Party,' p. 194, writes that 'how this fact squared with Fogo's belief that Cockfield, Brown was working without profit is unclear.' Unclear indeed!

42 NLF, v. 621, G.C. Hammond to Alan Woodrow, 23 Dec. 1952; v. 868, Hammond to A.W. Cooper, 30 July 1948. A vice-president of the agency suggested to Kidd that 'you might like to draw this to the attention of Gordon [Fogo] at some convenient time.' Hammond to Kidd, 2 Aug. 1948

43 NLF, v. 815, Denman to Hammond, 2 April 1953; v. 617, Kidd to Walter Harris, 23 July 1952; v. 603, Kidd to H.R. Conway, 18 April 1945; v. 806, Conway to Kidd, 25 May 1949; v. 632, Kidd to MacTavish, 21 Nov. 1955. In 1954 a Claxton

radio speech was advertised and the agency pondered the cheque. If the party 'has any political funds,' the agency suggested, 'we should collect ... if not, then I think we should absorb the charge.' NLF, v. 629, Hammond to Kidd, 27 Aug. 1954. The federation paid, commission included. Kidd to Archibald, 29 Oct. 1954

44 NLF, v. 826, Kidd to Hammond, 2 April 1953. The agency had in fact already made Munro's status clear by committing to writing an undertaking for 'Cockfield, Brown to supply the services of Mr. Munro and secretary for the duration, with the understanding that some time might have to be spent on other Cockfield, Brown business.' Hammond to Kidd, 29 Jan. 1953

45 *Ibid.*, Howe to MacTavish, 8 April 1953

46 *Ibid.*, Hammond to Kidd, 29 Jan. 1953

47 *Gentlemen, Players and Politicians*, p. 226

48 NLF, v. 863, 1955 advisory council, proceedings, p. 69; BC, v. 44, Robertson to Claxton, 29 March 1944

49 J.L. Granatstein, *Canada's War: The Politics of the Mackenzie King Government, 1939-1945* (Toronto, 1975), pp. 385-7

50 NLF, v. 602, Kidd to MacLean, 1 Sept. 1944; v. 602, note in file on 'CCF Saskatchewan Election, 1944'; Hammond to Kidd, 25 July 1944. According to the note, the following amounts were spent by the various parties on advertising:

	1938	1944
Liberals	$10,462	$25,613
CCF	140	16,530
Conservatives	1070	5027
Social Credit		56

51 See Granatstein, 'Financing the Liberal Party,' pp. 194-5

52 NLF, v. 602, Cockfield, Brown account files; Kidd to Fogo, 2 Nov. 1944; v. 603, Cockfield, Brown estimate, 18 Dec. 1943. After its 1943 revival the NLF was budgetting for $100,000 per year and about $8000 per month – for all purposes. Yet by Aug. of 1944 the demands of Cockfield, Brown and of that traditional sinkhole of Liberal money, the Quebec organization, had pushed the federation 'beyond what was originally contemplated in our budget,' and the NLF president was fearful that the 'matter will get out of hand.' NLF, v. 620, Robertson to J.-A. Blanchette, MP, 1 Aug. 1944

53 NLF, v. 603, Kidd to T.L. Anderson, 26 Jan. 1945; v. 602, 1940 advertising budget, Cockfield, Brown, 'National Liberal Committee, Estimate for Advertising,' 24 April 1945, files on Cockfield, Brown account, invoices, statements, etc. *Marketing*, 21 April 1945

54 NPL, Diary, 2, 12, and 15 May 1945. Granatstein, 'Financing the Liberal Party,' p. 194

55 NLF, v. 602, Kidd to Hammond, 11 May, Kidd memorandum, 1 May 1945. This was a recurrent problem in the party-agency relationship as is well illustrated by a memorandum in the NLF files concerning the Ontario provincial election of 1945 detailing the shortfall of funds for projected publicity: ' ... because of the way in which campaign funds are raised and distributed, no long range advertising plans can be made ... If the entire amount that was eventually spent was on hand early in the campaign, a working plan could be put into effect. But, when moneys are made available for advertising in scattered amounts over a five week period, it is not possible to work out a plan, and there has to be a considerable degree of makeshift.' NLF, v. 632, memorandum, n.d., n.a.

56 19 May 1945

57 BC, v. 44, Claxton to C.D. Howe, 30 Nov. 1945; Claxton to King, 2 Dec. 1947

58 Ibid., Kidd to Claxton, 3 Aug. 1945

59 NLF, v. 806, Kidd to Brown, 25 May 1949

60 'The Liberal Party,' p. 197

61 Marketing, 24 Feb. 1956. It is not clear what this promotion actually signified. Dalton Camp was also promoted to a vice-presidency of his agency in the same year, but comments drily that 'advertising agencies proliferate executive titles; I looked upon my elevation ... much as I did on becoming a lance-corporal in the army – an assumption of greater responsibility without any apparent corresponding benefit.' Gentlemen, Players and Politicians, p. 256

62 NLF, v. 806, Kidd to J. McNab, 8 Feb., Kidd to Archibald, 9 March; v. 614, Kidd to Vernon Knowles, 25 July 1949

63 Interview with Hon. J.W. Pickersgill, 15 July 1974

64 Can. H. of C. Debates, 7 March 1951, p. 999

65 Both quoted in E.E. Harrill, 'The Structure of Organization and Power in Canadian Political Parties: A Study in Party Financing,' unpublished PHD thesis, University of North Carolina, 1958, pp. 209-10

66 CDH, v. 109, file 75(7), Howe to W.A. Fraser, 30 Jan. 1959

67 NLF, v. 826. E.T. Applewhaite to Kidd, 25 Aug. 1952. Sometimes the ad men caused hostility among others in Ottawa as well. In 1956 Kidd complained to his agency about expense account charges by Cockfield, Brown men working on a Liberal television series. He explained that 'sometimes the way advertising men spend money in Ottawa excites the envy and dislike of civil servants who don't have expense accounts ... That is the tradition of the business, I know, but it doesn't go down with people here ... ' NLF, v. 837, Kidd to D.R. McRobie, 16 Oct., Kidd to Archibald, 1 Nov. 1956

68 Camp, Gentlemen, Players and Politicians, p. 99

69 A strategy meeting of the Cockfield, Brown election group in early 1953 decided on the following copy approach: 'In all advertising, it is desirable to incorporate a St. Laurent picture, a quotation or both, as a major or secondary unit. With the possible exception of Mr. Howe, cabinet ministers will not be featured.' NLF, v. 826, C. Nelson, 'Notes on meeting at Ritz-Carleton,' 27 Feb. 1953. A Cockfield, Brown PR man usually accompanied the prime minister when he travelled about the campaign trail, and sometimes on trips in the inter-election period as well. See, for example, NLF, v. 811, files on prime minister's tours
70 *Gentlemen, Players and Politicians*, p. 137
71 NLF, v. 629, Kidd to Hammond, 17 June 1953
72 *Gentlemen, Players and Politicians*, pp. 213, 227
73 As one example, in 1953 Brooke Claxton wanted data on comparative GNP growth figures. Cockfield, Brown undertook 'rather extensive research,' and a tentative allocation of $3000 was set aside in the budget for such purposes. NLF, v. 826, Kidd to S.D. Denman, 16 March 1953; BC, v. 61, Kidd to Claxton, 27 March 1953. Civil servants often contributed their expertise to this process as well. NLF, v. 606, Mitchell Sharp to Kidd, 30 Oct. 1944
74 BC, v. 44, Kidd to Claxton, 13 July 1947. NLF, v. 614, Kidd to Fogo, 26 Feb. 1949, notes a summer conference billing from Cockfield, Brown of $1165. A twenty-fifth-anniversary dinner for Mackenzie King was held in 1944, with a PR campaign orchestrated around it. NLF, v. 597, Kidd to MacLean, 30 June 1944. A dinner for St Laurent in Quebec City excited some sarcastic press notice about the ubiquitous ad men in attendance.
75 NLF, v. 602, amounts were as follows:

Massey-Harris	$7500
Dominion Woollens	5000
Firestone Tire and Rubber	2750
G.H. Wood and Company	689.42
Total	$15,948.42

76 *Ibid.*, Kidd to Hammond, 4 Jan., Hammond to Kidd, 13 Jan. 1945. The practice was publicly alluded to during the 1972 federal campaign.
77 NLF, v. 631, contains minutes of committee meetings from 1954 to 1956; v. 838 has similar records for 1957. See also Regenstreif, 'The Liberal Party,' pp. 196-7
78 NLF, v. 815, Kidd to Denman, 16 March 1953; see also Kidd to Denman, 10 April. Fears about security were hardly groundless. Dalton Camp recalls that early in the 1956 Nova Scotia provincial election, an anonymous informant handed him a thick roll of Cockfield, Brown pamphlets 'in first-proof stage, uncut, the ink still damp.' *Gentlemen, Players and Politicians*, p. 214

79 NLF, v. 806, 'Notes re Organization,' n.d. (1949), n.a; v. 621. The agency, Tandy Advertising, was pulled into the Ontario campaign. NLF, v. 828, MacTavish to Kidd, 21 June 1953

80 NLF, v. 807, Phare to L.L. Leprohon, 18 May 1949. Phare was the inventor of the standard rate card in 1932. *Marketing*, 1 Dec. 1958. R.C. Smith and Son were campaign contributors ($1000 in 1940). NPL, Diary, 1940 list of contributors

81 BC, v. 29, Claxton to J.A. MacLaren, 28 June 1949. $1000 was contributed in late 1957, NLF, v. 620, Fogo to Kidd, 19 Nov. 1957. NLF, v. 826, W.G. Abel to Kidd, 13 Aug. 1953; BC, v. 61, Kidd to W.F. Harrison, 16 April 1953

82 NLF, v. 596, McLean to Fogo, 1 Feb., Fogo to McLean, 7 Feb. 1945

83 NLF, v. 808; BC, v. 30, Alan MacNaughton to Claxton, 4 June 1953

84 NLF, v. 831, Denman to P. Lafond, 14 March 1957: 'Historically, the reason has been that the local influences prevalent in Quebec do not obtain in other provinces and therefore the specific appeal to the Quebec voter would not in most cases apply to French speaking people outside the province.' But this was not always the case, in fact.

85 NLF, v. 802, G. Warren Brown to Robertson, 16 March 1944

86 BC, v. 155, notes on interview with Senators Beauregard and Gouin, 13 May 1949

87 NLF, v. 818, Lafond to Kidd, 16 April, L.M. Gouin to Lafond, 3 April, Lafond to Gouin, 7 April 1953; v. 635, Kidd to MacTavish, 11 Dec. 1956

88 A full discussion of the impact of the Quiet Revolution on advertising is in Elkin, *Rebels and Colleagues, passim*

89 NLF, v. 836, memo Denman to Kidd, n.d. (received in NLF office, 18 Dec. 1956). I have no idea what truth there is in this assertion. It might be noted that in the 1960s Cockfield, Brown was accommodating enough to the 'French fact' to provide steady employment for Pierre Maheu, a leading light of the *Parti Pris* group of left-wing separatists. See Malcolm Reid, *The Shouting Signpainters: A Literary and Political Account of Quebec Revolutionary Nationalism* (New York, 1972), p. 297

90 NLF, *ibid.*; v. 635, Kidd to MacTavish, 11 Dec. 1956

91 NLF, v. 846, 'Meeting in Montreal, Feb. 7, 1958'; Cockfield, Brown Contact Report no. 14, 24 March 1958

92 As late as 1948 R.C. Smith was put in charge of an unsuccessful federal by-election campaign in Oshawa. NLF, v. 601, G.F. Stiritt to MacLean, 18 Aug. 1948. But by the turn of the decade the agency had lost all its federal government patronage (see below).

93 Granatstein, *Canada's War*, p. 387. NPL, Diary, 28 Feb. and 2 March 1945. Lambert was told by Peter Campbell that the Walsh president had 'set up' $11,500 in unpaid bills.

94 BC, v. 50, 'Report of the Standing Committee on Publicity of the Ontario Liberal Association,' Dec. 1952

95 As Dalton Camp remembers the 1948 national convention, the Ontario Liberals were 'leaderless, poor-mouthing, and gauche ... so crudely inept, so preposterously vulgar.' *Gentlemen, Players and Politicians*, p. 2. Camp's disdainful words were no doubt echoed on more than one occasion by Ottawa.

96 NLF, v. 827, Kidd to T.L. Anderson, 10 April, MacTavish to Hamilton, 9 April, Kidd to MacTavish, 17 April 1953

97 The phrase is that of H.E. Kidd. NLF, v. 827, Kidd to Conway, 6 July 1953

98 *Marketing*, 6 July 1956. The authoritative *National List of Advertisers* lists Lovick as the Alberta Liberal agency in the mid-1950s.

99 NLF, v. 806, Kidd to A.D. Black, 25 March 1949. Kidd plaintively asked his agency's Vancouver office to phone the official in question and 'let me know what the score is in the Provincial office ... '

100 NLF, v.-807, Kidd to Black, 4 March (see also Chapter 9, below); v. 806, Black to Kidd, 14 April, 1949; v. 827, Kidd to H.R. Conway, 6 July 1953; v. 631, F.W. Ellis to Kidd, 30 May 1957

101 Paltiel, *Political Party Financing*, p. 38, and Paltiel, 'Party and Candidate Expenditures in the Canadian General Election of 1972,' *Canadian Journal of Political Science*, VII, 2 (June 1974), pp. 341-57

102 *Marketing*, 15 March 1957

103 NLF, v. 836, Denman to Kidd, 21 Jan. 1957. Kidd protested to Claxton the day after the meeting. NLF, v. 616, Kidd to Claxton, 6 July 1953. The secretary of the Nova Scotia Liberal Association complained about undue emphasis on 'organization and bringing in a vote on election day' and wanted more advertising. NLF, v. 621, Kidd to MacTavish, 3 July 1953

104 In 1949 the Cockfield, Brown radio man was employed 'full time' in Ottawa during the campaign, and the agency believed that the 'operation was most successful.' NFL, v. 826, Denman to Kidd *et al.*, 26 March 1953

105 21-22 Eliz. II, 1973, Bill C-203, s.99.3

106 NLF, v. 611, Kidd to R. Conway, 26 May 1952. The worst of it was that the weeklies, which were most prone to change 'political rates,' were highly thought of by the Liberals in terms of voter impact. As Kidd informed a member of the prime minister's staff, 'The weekly press ... is a much more important force than is commonly realized ... The weekly editors, of whom there are eight or nine hundred, have a good deal of influence in their communities and they are certainly in a position to promote a line of thought or to influence opinion if they want to.' NLF, v. 623, Kidd to W.R. Martin, 1 Oct. 1952

107 NLF, v. 826, Cockfield, Brown invoices; v. 601, J.W. Stebenne to I.B. Gardner, 16 Nov. , *Le Devoir* to Gardner, 10 Nov. 1948. For the general practice, see Blair Fraser, 'Our Illegal Federal Elections,' *Maclean's*, LXVI (17 April 1948), pp. 24-5; Harrill, 'The Structure of Organization and Power in Canadian Political Parties,' p. 209; Committee on Election Expenses, *Report* (Ottawa, 1966), p. 52

108 NLF, v. 800, cheques issued for years 1954, 1955, and 1956

109 McFadzen, 'The Liberal Party and MacLaren,' pp. 125-31, argues that MacLaren's was reluctantly, but inevitably, drawn into policy-making as well as image-making in the Pearson era.

110 NLF, v. 824, W.A. Munro to MacTavish, 23 June 1953; see also J.W. Pickersgill, *My Years with Louis St Laurent: A Political Memoir* (Toronto, 1975), p. 194

111 NLF, v. 826, files on television, Denman to Kidd, 6 April 1953; v. 836, Kidd to McRobie, 16 Nov. 1956; v. 837, Kidd to R.W. Harwood, 24 Feb. 1956, memo, Gordon Atkinson, 2 July 1957, Kidd to McRobie, 13 Feb., Kidd to Harwood, 1 March, Kidd to M. Wood, 25 Oct. 1956

112 NLF, v. 838, *Free Press*, 3 May 1957

113 NLF, v. 836, Kidd to Archibald, 25 May, Kidd to MacTavish, 15 May, 8 Aug. 1957. 'From a public relations standpoint,' Kidd suggested, 'it would be a mistake' for the Liberal Party to contest the billed cancellations. In the event, some Liberal broadcasters cancelled their charges as a campaign contribution. See NLF, v. 839, M.T. Brown to Kidd, 17 June 1958. Pressure was brought to bear on others to drop the charges. *Ibid.*, Kidd to Walter Harris, 23 Nov. 1957

114 NLF, v. 837, Kidd to MacTavish, 23 May 1957, Kidd to Miss Thurber, 25 Sept. 1958; v. 838, Kidd to MacTavish, 11 July, Caldwell to MacTavish, 27 Aug., MacTavish to Caldwell, 16 May, Kidd to MacTavish, 11 July 1957; MacTavish to Lafond, 25 March 1963

115 CDH, v. 108, file 75(5), Howe to H.A. Mackenzie, 27 Aug. 1957

116 NLF, v. 836, McRobie to Kidd, 9 Sept., Kidd to McRobie, 23 Oct. 1957. John Meisel reports that no less than 40 Cockfield, Brown employees worked on the election. *The Canadian General Election of 1957* (Toronto, 1962), p. 65

117 NLF, v. 843, P.C. Logan to Kidd, 11 Feb. 1958; BC, v. 79, Claxton to Kidd, 27 Nov. 1957; Claxton to Matthews, 30 Nov. 1959; Pickersgill interview. Background to the changeover is given in Denis Smith, *Gentle Patriot: A Political Biography of Walter Gordon* (Edmonton, 1973), pp. 57-9.

118 *Marketing*, 7 March, 2 May 1958, 27 Feb., 20 March, 17 July 1959; NLF, v. 876, McRobie to Kidd, 7 Jan. 1958; v. 846, 'Newspaper Advertising Copy Plan (for discussion),' n.d.; v. 850, advertising estimates, 6 Feb. 1958; v. 847, Connolly to W.A. Ellis, 31 March, Connolly to E.V. Rechnitzer, 31 March 1958; v. 875, G. Marler to MacTavish, 14 Dec., MacTavish to Marler, 20 Dec. 1957. McFadzen, 'The Liberal Party and MacLaren,' p. 57, suggests that Cockfield, Brown 'fell from favour,' resulting from the defeat of 1957-8 and the 'controversy created by apparent conflicts of interest involving the Trans-Canada Pipeline, the agency, and its government employer.'

119 *Gentlemen, Players and Politicians*, p. 93

120 Camp Associates has recently gained a certain notoriety in the press for their

close relationship with the government of Premier William Davis. See 'Ontario Ads Net $525,000 for Camp Agency,' *Globe and Mail*, 30 Nov. 1974

121 Elkin, *Rebels and Colleagues*, pp. 31, 121. Ironically, the Quebec Liberals 'had some trouble' finding an agency in 1960, finally settling on Collyer, of which former Liberal MP Roland Beaudry was vice-president and financial director. *Marketing*, 1 July 1960. It seems that ad agencies have been little better than either journalists or political scientists in predicting electoral transformations.

122 NPL, Diary, 31 Dec. 1936, 9 Jan. 1939, 7 Feb. 1937, 7 March 1938, 10 Nov. 1940

123 BC, v. 44, Kidd to Claxton, 2 Aug., Claxton to Kidd, 3 Aug. 1945

124 In 1951, MacLaren's indicated some discontent with their state. NLF, v. 613, H.S. Hamilton to Kidd, 22 Sept., Kidd to Hamilton, 22 Oct. 1951

125 'Public' is a somewhat ambiguous term in this context, in which data has been consolidated and compiled from very disparate sources. It should be emphasized that the raw data has actually been put together here for the first time. Sources from which the columns have been compiled in detail are as follows: 1940-6: PAC, *Sessional Papers*, v. 505, no. 257 (12 Aug. 1946); 1945-7: *ibid.*, v. 528, no. 149A (18 Feb. 1948); 1949-50: *ibid.*, v. 570, no. 175B (22 June 1951); 1952: *ibid.*, v. 601, no. 172 (26 Jan. 1953); 1953: *ibid.*, v. 612, no. 172 (12 Jan. 1954); 1954: *ibid.*, v. 625, no. 169A (8 Feb. 1955); 1955: *ibid.*, v. 641, no. 199 (1 March 1956) – also see NLF, v. 632, Kidd to Stuart Garson, 8 Nov. 1956; 1956: *Sessional Papers*, v. 650, no. 188 (27 Feb. 1957) – see also *Marketing*, 19 July 1957. All these figures have been cross-checked with the relevant sections of the *Public Accounts*, 1944-57, and in places supplemented by figures from the latter source. The years indicated in the columns sometimes overlap and for this reason have not been totalled for the entire period. Moreover, some indicate fiscal years and others calendar years, depending upon the nature of the information asked in Parliament. The data do not, therefore, give us a chronologically very coherent picture, but they do indicate the relative share of dollars earned by the various agencies at specific points in time.

126 *Marketing*, 8 Sept. 1945

127 R.C. Smith was a financial contributor to the party in 1940, donating $1000 to the bagman in Toronto. NPL, Diary, 1 March 1940

128 Canada, House of Commons, 1956, Sessional Committee on Railways and Shipping, *Minutes of Proceedings and Evidence*, 20 March 1956, pp. 198-9

129 *Marketing*, 16 and 23 March, 7 Sept. 1956. In answer to a question from Tory ad man William Hamilton in a committee hearing, Gordon replied: 'If you asked me how we chose between Cockfield, Brown, and the Canadian Advertising Agency, I do not think you should press that point ... I do not want to have this conversation create the idea, or let it get abroad, that we are critical of Cockfield, Brown or that we regard their services as inferior to some other

agency. I do not want that to go out of this room.' Committee on Railways and
Shipping, p. 200. It did, of course. See *Marketing*, 30 March 1956
130 *Marketing*, 19 July, 16 Aug. 1957, 18 April, 17 Oct. 1958, 28 Oct. 1960

CHAPTER SEVEN
Quebec

1 See, for instance, Donald Creighton's assault on the bicultural compact theory of
Confederation, 'The Myth of Biculturalism,' *Saturday Night*, Sept. 1966. See also
Donald Smiley, *The Canadian Political Nationality* (Toronto, 1967), pp. 22-31,
110-31. Nor should one forget the contumacious pen of Senator Eugene Forsey,
well represented in the collection of his writings, *Freedom and Order* (Toronto,
1974), especially Part IV, pp. 240-68.
2 The pathetic story of the Conservative failure in Quebec in this period has been
told in Marc LaTerreur, *Les Tribulations des conservateurs au Québec, de Bennett
à Diefenbaker* (Quebec, 1973).
3 *Mémoires: Le vent de l'oubli* (Montreal, 1970), II, p. 139
4 ER, v. 1, interviews with A. Savard, 6 July, Bert Perks, 12 July, Chubby Power, 14
July 1932; CGP, v. 4, transcript of interview of Chubby Power by John Meisel, 3
May 1960; WLMK, v. 179, Philippe Paradis to Miss E. O'Malley, 24 April 1930
(152794-7), also in CGP, 1968, box 1; Norman Ward, ed., *A Party Politician: The
Memoirs of Chubby Power* (Toronto, 1966), pp. 311-68. Even the apparent
informal structures could be misleading as well: Pierre Laporte reported in the
1950s that local organizers named by candidates might not be the real ones but
'organisateurs de paille' to confuse the enemy. 'La machine électorale,' *Cité
Libre*, XI, 3 (Dec. 1952), p. 42.
5 S.P. Regenstreif, 'The Liberal Party of Canada: A Political Analysis,'
unpublished PHD thesis, Cornell University, 1963, p. 153
6 For a fuller discussion of the kind of cabinet posts French-speaking Quebec
ministers have tended to receive – a distribution clearly reflecting the monopoly
over economic affairs enjoyed by English Canada until the 1960s – see F.W.
Gibson, ed., *Cabinet Formation and Bicultural Relations: Seven Case Studies*,
Study no. 6 of the Royal Commission on Bilingualism and Biculturalism
(Ottawa, 1970), and R.J. Van Loon, 'The Structure and Membership of the
Canadian Cabinet,' unpublished study of the same commission. With his usual
frankness, Chubby Power recalled that when he was postmaster-general, he led a
'free-lance' existence, and was able to absent himself for two months to direct the
provincial campaign of 1939 without worrying in the least about his department.
A Party Politician, pp. 184, 189

7 Regenstreif, 'The Liberal Party,' pp. 152-3; Ward, ed., *A Party Politician*, pp. 312-13

8 Gibson, *Cabinet Formation*, p. 74

9 Dale C. Thomson, *Louis St. Laurent: Canadian* (Toronto, 1967), p. 14. In this same connection it is interesting to note that one of the first *economic* posts in the federal cabinet to be held by a French Canadian was the northern affairs and natural resources portfolio held by Jean Lesage, from Quebec City, from 1953 to 1957.

10 For details, see Chapters 1 and 2, above

11 A list of Reform Club members in 1947 can be found in BC, v. 57. See also Power interview by Meisel, p. 7, in which Power recalled that there were strong feelings in Montreal against the 'coteries and cliques' of the Reform Club. In the seething cauldron of ethnic and linguistic suspicions which was Montreal, the domination of the Reform Club by French-language members excited some comment as well. WLMK, v. 197, D.A. MacDonald to King, 5 April 1933 (167396)

12 'The Liberal Party,' p. 251

13 *Ibid.*, p. 214

14 EL, v. 9, file 41; v. 22, file 68

15 *Ibid.*, v. 30, file 137

16 *Ibid.*, file 127, Lapointe to P. Corriveau, 16 Jan 1936

17 *A Party Politician*, p. 37

18 EL, v. 31, file 139, memorandum, A. Cardinal for L.-P. Picard, 28 Oct. 1936

19 *Ibid.*, O. Bouchard to Picard, 4 Oct. 1937

20 *Ibid.*, Cardinal to Picard, 28 Oct. 1936. There is a lengthy correspondence between Lapointe's patronage agents and the Harbour Commission in file 139 of this volume.

21 *Ibid.*, Cardinal to Picard, 9 Oct. 1936

22 *Ibid.*, v. 30, file 128, Lacroix to Lapointe, 27 March 1936, Lapointe to Mackenzie, 29 June 1938; WLMK, v. 257, J.A. Sharpe to R.L. Frendenburg, 8 Sept. 1938 (218982); EL, v. 30, file 128, Lacroix to King, 12 Sept. 1938

23 Jérôme Proulx, *Le Panier de crabes* (Montreal, 1971). Proulx's description of the carving up of the spoils following the Union Nationale victory in 1966 has a familiar ring to it.

24 To one group of clergymen who wrote a letter of protest, Lapointe replied curtly that they might better have protested in 1930 when the Conservatives were applying the axe. EL, v. 30, file 127, Lapointe to J.-A. Turmel, 13 Nov. 1935. But Power also reported that Lapointe often gave in to the 'tears, supplications, and protestations of the sweethearts, wives, and mothers of those marked for sacrifice on the altar of party devotion.' *A Party Politician*, p. 37

25 In late 1938 Lapointe told King that he 'personally could not stand meeting with

constituents; they got his nerves on edge. He had simply to keep away from Quebec altogether.' WLMK, Diary, 29 Nov. 1938

26 EL, v. 30, file 138, Bouchard to Picard, 27 Oct., Lapointe to J.-A. Belleville, 8 Dec. 1938

27 For somewhat divergent views of the same election, see *A Party Politician*, pp. 133-4, and Thomson, *Louis St. Laurent*, pp. 109-19.

28 See Harold Angell, 'The Evolution and Application of Quebec Election Expense Legislation, 1964-66,' Committee on Election Expenses, *Report* (Ottawa, 1966); and Herbert F. Quinn, *The Union Nationale: A Study in Quebec Nationalism* (Toronto, 1963), for details of how this system operated. The famous 'machine' of Maurice Duplessis was little more than a perfected version of the Liberal machine operated by Gouin and Taschereau. It might be noted here that one of Escott Reid's informants in the early 1930s told him that it was the general rule for Quebec parties in power to levy a 10 per cent tollgate on prospective government contractors. ER, v. 1, interview with Bert Perks, 12 July 1932. If this were so, it is evident that the provincial party far outdid the federal party, which, in the late 1930s was only levying 1½ to 2½ per cent on *successful* bidders (see Chapter 3, above).

29 Regenstreif, 'The Liberal Party,' p. 214

30 *A Party Politician*, pp. 311-27

31 Power was very clear on this point: financial considerations were more important than any others. *Ibid.*, p. 319

32 This was generally true across the country but more explicit in Quebec. As Brooke Claxton told a friend interested in a nomination many years later, the sitting member was a fixture: 'Unless he gets a long jail sentence, votes against the party too often or gets defeated, he generally gets the nod, and frequently without a nominating convention.' BC, v. 89, Claxton to Paul Paré, 19 March 1957. A formal statement endorsing renominations without conventions, even when called for, was issued by the provincial party in 1935. R. MacGregor Dawson, *The Government of Canada*, revised by Norman Ward (5th ed., Toronto, 1970), p. 443

33 H. M. Angell, 'Quebec Provincial Politics in the 1920s,' unpublished MA thesis, McGill University, 1960, p. 152

34 Goldwin Smith, *Canada and the Canadian Question* (new ed., Toronto, 1971), p. 172

35 Robert Rumilly, *Histoire de la province de Québec* (Montreal, 1940-69), XXVI, pp. 92, 149

36 For developments in the 1920s see H. Blair Neatby, *William Lyon Mackenzie King: The Lonely Heights, 1924-1932* (Toronto, 1963), II, and the correspondence between Montreal Liberal businessman Kirk Cameron and T.A. Crerar in the Cameron Papers (Public Archives of Canada).

37 WLMK, v. 179, Paradis to King, 29 April (152793), Paradis to O'Malley, 24 April 1930 (152794-7), also in CGP, 1968, box 1; WLMK, v. 180, Power to King, 24 April 1930 (153176-8), also in CGP, 1968, box 1

38 ER, v. 1, interview with Savard, 6 July 1932

39 NPL, v. 8, Lambert, memorandum regarding the NLF, May 1941; WLMK, Memoranda and Notes, v. 192, memorandum re meeting of executive committee of the NLF, 16 March 1937 (C135210-13). On another occasion, Lambert noted that Quebec Liberals 'have not in the past shown any warmth for the idea of participation in the National Liberal Federation.' *Ibid.*, memorandum, Lambert on NLF meeting, 10 Dec. 1936 (C135180-9)

40 Gibson, *Cabinet Formation*, pp. 116, 124, 130-2

41 Angell, 'Quebec Election Expense Legislation,' pp. 286-7

42 Lapointe himself had family and political connections with the ALN, through Roger Ouimet, his son-in-law, and Oscar Drouin, the provincial member for Lapointe's district. King's office calculated that twenty-two Union Nationale members elected in 1936 had 'definite' Liberal backgrounds. WLMK, Memoranda and Notes, v. 204, memorandum, W.B. Herbert, 28 Aug. 1936 (C140898-9)

43 *A Party Politician*, pp. 332-5, 340-2. Roger Ouimet assured Lambert that the ALN's activities would be confined to provincial politics. NPL, Diary, 14 March 1935. See also EL, v. 30, file 124, Fernand Choquette to Lapointe, 16 June 1936, for evidence of federal financial involvement in the provincial campaign. WLMK, Diary, 17 Aug. 1936; v. 220, King to E.M. MacDonald, 3 July 1936 (189356-7)

44 'Quebec Election Expense Legislation,' p. 286. The decentralization of power in the provincial party organization toward those with money and influence is illustrated by the fact that Quebec industrialist Jules Brillant was able to find jobs for young Liberal organizers displaced from provincial posts by Duplessis. EL, v. 30, Brillant to Lapointe, 22 Oct. 1937

45 EL, v. 30, file 124, F.-A. Monk to King, 16 April 1938, referred to Lapointe. Monk was the son of F.-D. Monk, Sir Robert Borden's Quebec lieutenant, but was himself a Liberal of ALN views. *Ibid.*, letters and memoranda of Philippe Brais, Godbout to Lapointe, 16 June, Bourdon to Brais, 1 Aug. 1938, minutes of meeting of Montreal Reform Club, 20 Sept. 1938; *ibid.*, file 123, Maurice Hartt to L.-P. Picard, 8 March 1939. WLMK, Memoranda and Notes, v. 193, memorandum, E.A. Pickering for King, 21 April, (C135699); v. 252, H.R.L. Henry to Lambert, 19 April, (215177); and D.A. Turgeon to King, 13 April 1938 (215178-9)

46 EL, v. 30, file 123, Lacroix to Lapointe, 26 July 1938

47 WLMK, Diary, 18 and 23 Nov. 1936, 3 and 9 May 1938, 29 Nov. 1938; CGP, 'Political Jottings,' v. 2, 'Memorandum of conversation with Mr. King, June 26, 1939,' 27 June 1939

48 See Chapter 3, above, and Chapter 8, below. WLMK, Diary, 6 July 1938

49 *Ibid.*, Memoranda and Notes, v. 192, 'Meeting of Executive Committee, NLF,' 16 March 1937
50 *Ibid.*, Diary, 6 July 1938
51 *Ibid.*, 31 March 1939
52 NPL, Diary, 25 Sept.; WLMK, Diary, 28 Sept. 1939. Brooke Claxton, soon to be a federal candidate in Montreal, laid out the logic of the federal response in a clear and clever memorandum circulated privately to the cabinet. EL, v. 49, file 33, memorandum, 27 Sept. 1939
53 EL, v. 30, file 124, Lapointe, press release, n.d. (1939)
54 *A Party Politician*, pp. 347-9
55 NPL, Diary, 26 Sept., 3 and 4 Oct. 1939; WLMK, Diary, 5 Oct. 1939
56 *A Party Politician*, pp. 128, 349. J.L. Granatstein, *The Politics of Survival: The Conservative Party of Canada, 1939-1945* (Toronto, 1967), p. 33, and 'Conservative Party Finances, 1939-1945,' in Committee on Election Expenses, *Studies in Canadian Party Finance* (Ottawa, 1966), p. 272
57 NPL, Diary, 26 Sept., 3-4, 10, 12-13, 18-19, 25-26 Oct., and 7 Dec. 1939
58 The accounts laying most stress on King's skills are R.M. Dawson, *The Conscription Crisis of 1944* (Toronto, 1961), and J.L. Granatstein, *Canada's War: The Politics of the Mackenzie King Government, 1939-45* (Toronto, 1975). See also the same author's *Conscription in the Second World War, 1939-1945* (Toronto, 1969). André Laurendeau's *La crise de la conscription* (Montreal, 1962), describes the anti-conscriptionist campaign. See also *A Party Politician*, pp. 97-180, and MKR, I and II.
59 On the island of Montreal, the Liberals took over 60 per cent of the vote in the six English-speaking ridings, but carried only 35 per cent in the seven French majority seats. See H.F. Quinn, 'The Quebec Provincial Election of 1944: An Analysis of the Role of the Election in the Democratic Process,' unpublished MA thesis, McGill University, 1945
60 CGP, 'Political Jottings,' v. 3, memorandum, 'Quebec: Political situation as of July 19th, 1944,' n.d.
61 See *A Party Politician*, pp. 173-6; CGP, 'Political Jottings,' v. 5, Feb. to April 1945, has original notes taken by Power during the period of negotiations and manoeuvrings of the factions.
62 Thomson, *Louis St. Laurent*, p. 161. St Laurent's only instructions to Jean were to try to find Liberal or Independent Liberal candidates for every riding.
63 *Ibid.*, pp. 233-4
64 *A Party Politician*, p. 393; see also CGP, 'Political Jottings,' v. 5, 26-27 Nov. 1947, 12, 14, 16, and 18 Feb. 1948. Alphonse Fournier, minister of public works, told St Laurent that 'nos partisans eux-mêmes avaient détruit monsieur Godbout.' LSTL, Fournier to St Laurent, 16 March 1949

65 BC, V. 63, H.E. Kidd to Claxton, 28 June 1948, suggests early evidence of deals between the federal Liberals and the Union Nationale organization.

66 Lapalme had built up a strong organization in his own constituency of Joliette, started a series of large and well-attended monthly dinner meetings featuring leading federal and provincial politicians, and founded a successful local newspaper to spread Liberal ideas. See *Mémoires*, I, pp. 309-10, 331-45

67 *Ibid.*, II, pp. 19-20, 21

68 Lapalme, speech at the 1958 Congress of the Fédération Libérale du Québec, quoted in Gérard Bergeron, 'Les partis libéraux du Canada et du Québec: 1955-1965,' unpublished study for the Royal Commission on Bilingualism and Biculturalism, p. 1

69 *Mémoires*, II, p. 139

70 Jean-Marie Nadeau, *Carnets politiques* (Montreal, 1966), p. 17. Lapalme, *ibid.*, p. 29, expresses faith in Bouffard's loyalty, but the appearance must have been disheartening enough in itself. As Nadeau wrote, 'Combien intéressant ce serait de connaître les dessous de ce voyage des deux compères! Quelles confidences ne se sont-ils pas faites, même s'ils n'ont pas frappé aux mêmes portes pour quêter de l'argent?'

71 Nadeau, *ibid.*, p. 56; Lapalme, *ibid.*, p. 138; NLF, V. 623, Paul Lafond to J.G. Fogo, 25 Feb. 1949

72 Lapalme, *ibid.*, p. 100, 71

73 In his series in *Le Devoir* in 1956, Pierre Laporte estimated that the Union Nationale in that year's election spent from $10 to $15 million. *Le Devoir*, 7 Dec. 1956. 1952 must have been comparable.

74 Angell, 'Quebec Election Expense Legislation,' p. 280. The estimate is by Chubby Power, who might be expected to know about such things.

75 *Mémoires*, II, p. 30. Just how much more could have gone to an opportunistic Liberal party was brought home to Lapalme when, during the election, two prominent Quebec persons approached him on behalf of American corporations offering him 'une mine d'or' if he promised preference for them in resource concessions. Lapalme turned them down, but he later wondered what those with less sense of propriety than himself might be getting away with. *Ibid.*, pp. 123-4

76 *Mémoires*, I, p. 346

77 LSTL, V. 61, Maurice Boisvert to St Laurent, 5 March, Jean to St Laurent, 17 March 1949; CGP, 1968, box 1, memorandum, 're: by-elections held in the province of Quebec,' etc. Power noted that such members of the Liberal caucus were 'beholden' to the Duplessis machine, and must count on it in future elections; they were thus unlikely to support the Liberals in provincial contests. In 1949, it might be noted, thirteen 'independent' Liberals contested seats. In 1953 seventeen such candidates received 58,000 votes, or over 6 per cent of the

total Liberal vote for seventy-five constituencies; two were elected. Of course, the lack of legitimate nominating procedures, together with the electoral supremacy of the Liberal label, had a certain tendency to turn elections into the equivalent of Democratic primaries in the us South.

78 Thomson, *Louis St. Laurent*, p. 330. Even the Liberal organization in Montmagny, Jean Lesage's constituency federally, was collaborating with the Union Nationale provincially in 1952. Lapalme was actually booed when he denounced Duplessis at a Liberal banquet in that constituency in late 1951. *Mémoires*, ii, pp. 122-3

79 Thomson, *ibid.*, p. 352; cgp, box 6 2(b), Power to Bruce Hutchison, 30 July 1953; nlf, v. 635, memorandum, Lafond to Duncan MacTavish, 17 April 1956

80 See Pierre Laporte, *Le Devoir*, 7-8 Jan. 1955. Some of the wealthier Liberals were forced to support Duplessis because of the arbitrary power he could wield over businesses in the province. For example, Jules Brillant became a reluctant collaborator with Duplessis to preserve his extensive business interests. Senator Jacob Nicol, a former provincial cabinet minister, legislative councillor, and Liberal fund-raiser, became an open Duplessis supporter through articles and editorials in the many newspapers he owned. There were many other ways in which Duplessis 'won over' federal Liberals. An especially grotesque story concerns the 'clown prince' of Parliament, Jean-François Pouliot, who became an ally as early as 1944 when the Duplessis government was so thoughtful as to purchase several thousand unsold copies of his learned treatise, *Le Droit paroissial*. See *Le Devoir*, 15 Aug. 1956

81 *The Diefenbaker Interlude: Parties and Voting in Canada* (Toronto, 1965), p. 112

82 Laporte, *Le Devoir*, 8 Jan. 1955

83 Thomson, *Louis St. Laurent*, p. 303

84 Quinn, *Union Nationale*, pp. 82-3

85 *Can. H. of C. Debates* (1951), p. 706; Lapalme, *Mémoires*, ii, pp. 85, 89-93

86 Thomson, *Louis St. Laurent*, p. 376

87 *Le fédéralisme canadien* (Quebec, 1954)

88 Thomson, *Louis St. Laurent*, pp. 380, 382

89 *Mémoires*, ii, pp. 174, 178; *Can. H. of C. Debates*, 14 April 1954

90 *Maclean's Magazine*, 5 March 1955

91 Thomson, *Louis St. Laurent*, p. 396. One internal party document examining the federal Liberal defeat in 1957 suggested that the Windsor Hotel incident was a disaster not only for the provincial but for the federal party as well. bc, v. 166, 'The reason why,' n.a., n.d.

92 *Mémoires*, ii, p. 176; Gérard Filion, *Le Devoir*, 14 Jan. 1961

93 'Les partis libéraux,' p. 3

94 *Le Devoir*, 2 Nov. 1955

95 'La transformation du parti libéral québécois,' *Canadian Journal of Economics and Political Science*, xxxi, 3 (Aug. 1965), p. 366

96 *Mémoires*, ii, p. 187

97 Comeau, 'La transformation,' p. 359; see this article and also the same author's unpublished MA thesis for Université de Montréal, 1964, 'L'organisation d'une parti politique dans un comté du Québec,' upon which the article is based.

98 See the articles in *Le Devoir* by 'Isocrate,' reprinted in Gérard Bergeron, *Du Duplessisme au Johnsonisme: 1956-1966* (Montreal, 1967), pp. 40-62

99 Bergeron, 'Les partis libéraux,' p. 7

100 6 March 1956

101 *The Canadian General Election of 1957* (Toronto, 1962), p. 176

102 *Le Soleil*, 19 June 1957, quoted in Bergeron, 'Les partis libéraux,' p. 17

103 Quebec, as indicated earlier, had been the only province which had never had a provincial affiliate of the NLF.

104 Quoted in Bergeron, 'Les partis libéraux,' p. 25

105 *Le Devoir*, 7 June 1958

106 Regenstreif cites narrow Conservative victories in Quebec City and in the rural constituencies on the south shore of the St Lawrence as examples of where the UN machine made the difference. 'The Liberal Party,' p. 64

107 Bergeron, 'Les partis libéraux,' pp. 32, 49

108 One Quebec Liberal who saw the developing dangers of the situation very early was Chubby Power. In a memorandum written in Dec. 1950 – but not circulated to the party leaders, who were unfriendly to Power after his challenge to St Laurent at the 1948 national convention – he argued that 'there appears to be no longer any moral or ideological appeal in Liberalism,' while at the same time the provincial government held control over almost all the 'material rewards' of politics in the form of patronage. Prophetically enough, Power concluded his gloomy analysis with the following *obiter dicta*: 'When Laurier disappeared, he left behind him popular leaders, his devoted followers and above all a tradition, a tradition of glory and martyrdom, of having sacrificed power for his race, of having been betrayed by his own people in 1911. There will be no such appeal, no such leaders, no such tradition in St. Laurent's case.' CGP, 1968, box 1, memorandum, 'Re: by-elections held in the Province of Quebec . . .' etc., Dec. 1950

109 'Federal Strains within a Canadian Party,' in H.G. Thorburn, ed., *Party Politics in Canada* (2nd ed., Toronto, 1967), p. 139

110 Comeau, 'La Transformation'

111 Information was extracted from J.K. Johnson, ed., *The Canadian Directory of Parliament, 1867-1967* (Ottawa, 1968)

CHAPTER EIGHT
Ontario

1 John Wilson and David Hoffman, 'Ontario: A Three-Party System in Transition,' in Martin Robin, ed., *Canadian Provincial Politics: The Party Systems of the Ten Provinces* (Scarborough, 1972), pp. 198-239; John Wilson, 'The Ontario Political Culture,' in Donald C. MacDonald, ed., *Government and Politics in Ontario* (Toronto, 1975), pp. 211-34

2 'The Sources of Ontario "Progressive" Conservatism, 1900-1914,' in *Historical Papers Presented to the Annual Meeting of the Canadian Historical Association, Ottawa, 1967*, p. 119

3 'The Liberal Party in Contemporary Ontario Politics,' *Canadian Journal of Political Science*, III, 2 (June 1970), p. 204. The three provincial elections held since this article was published have only strengthened this prognosis.

4 Neil McKenty, *Mitch Hepburn* (Toronto, 1967), pp. 30-3. One source informed Mackenzie King that the federal party had supplied the provincial party with all their funds for the election of 1929. WLMK, v. 182, Senator J.H. Spence to King, 28 Nov. 1930 (155351-2)

5 WLMK, v. 173, Dafoe to Grant Dexter, 12 Dec. 1930 (147281). A report on Liberal organization in Toronto prepared by some Young Liberals in 1930 painted the usual dreary picture of unsuccessful party organizations: small bickering cliques scrambling for crumbs of patronage, lack of leadership, and electoral inactivity. *Ibid.*, v. 183, J.L. Wilson to King, 7 March 1930 (156444-5), with enclosure, 'West Young Liberal Club of Toronto, Report of Survey Committee' (156446-51)

6 *Ibid.*, v. 179, W.R.P. Parker to King, 21 Nov. (152935-7), and 1 Dec. (152940-1), King to Alex Darrach, 27 Nov. (147344-6), King to Harry Johnson, 27 Nov. (149707-8), and 10 Dec. (149717-9); v. 176, King to B.H. McCreath, 9 Dec. (150589-90); Diary, 5 Nov., 11 and 17 Dec. 1930

7 *Ibid.*, v. 182, Sinclair to King, 30 Dec. 1930 (155090-1)

8 *Ibid.*, v. 175, King to Hepburn, 18 Dec. (149228-30), King to Johnson, 22 Dec. 1930 (149723); v. 185, King to Darrach, 5 Jan. 1931 (157485-6)

9 *Ibid.*, v. 186, Johnson to King, 28 July (158688-90), Senator A.C. Hardy to King, 25 July 1931 (158366); v. 187, W.H. Moore to Hardy, 27 July 1931 (159776-7); v. 193, Nelson Parliament to King, 5 Aug. 1932 (164121-3); v. 196, W.A. Fraser to King, 13 July (166284-5), 1 Nov. (166295), 20 Nov. 1933 (166309-10); v. 197, Vincent Massey to King, 30 Oct. 1933 (167940-1); v. 199, Fraser to King, 17 July 1934 (170642-3); v. 200, Hardy to King, 7 Aug. 1934 (170888-9); v. 201, Massey to King, 28 July 1934 (172351-5). NPL, Diary, 9 Feb., 17 May, 28-29 June, 10-14, 18-20, 26, and 30 July, 3-4 Nov. 1934; 23 April 1935

10 WLMK, v. 186, Johnson to King, 3 Nov. (158720-1), B.H. McCreath to King, 10

Nov. 1931 (159118-20); v. 191, Johnson to King, 5 Aug. 1932 (163130-1); v. 198, Parker to King, 13 Nov. (168221-2), Arthur Roebuck to King, 7 Dec. 1933 (168643-7). McKenty, *Mitch Hepburn*, is a gold mine (pun intended) of information on Hepburn's business associates. Richard Alway's unpublished MA thesis, University of Toronto, 1965, 'Mitchell F. Hepburn and the Liberal Party in the Province of Ontario, 1937-1943,' also has considerable information. See also Chapter 2, above, for details of provincial financial control in the early 1930s.

11 'The Canadian Mining Industry,' in H.A. Innis, *Essays in Canadian Economic History* (Toronto, 1956), pp. 317-18

12 Wilson and Hoffman conclude that in 1934 'Hepburn *was* the Liberal party.' 'Ontario: A Three Party System,' p. 214

13 WLMK, Diary, 20 June 1934. The spiritual crisis was more or less resolved when King concluded later that only God knew the future, that lesser spirits could be wrong, and that Sir Wilfrid had spoken in 'terms of fleshly wisdom, the limited French Canadian view.' *Ibid.*, 12 July and 30 Aug. 1934

14 Joseph Wearing, 'Ontario Political Parties: Fish or Fowl,' in MacDonald, *Government and Politics*, p. 335

15 WLMK, v. 199, King to Hardy, 16 Aug. 1934 (170892-5), Drury to King, 21 June (170424-7), King to Drury, 7 July 1934 (170428-9); Diary, 25 June 1934

16 *Ibid.*, v. 200, King to Hepburn, 11 Sept. 1934 (17002-5)

17 *Ibid.*, v. 206, Hepburn to King, 21 Oct. 1935 (177132-4); v. 210, Parker to King, 17 Oct. 1935

18 *Ibid.*, Diary, 19 Oct. 1935; F.W. Gibson, 'The Cabinet of 1935,' in Gibson, ed., *Cabinet Formation and Bicultural Relations: Seven Case Studies*, Study no. 6 of the Royal Commission on Bilingualism and Biculturalism (Ottawa, 1970), p. 121; McKenty, *Mitch Hepburn*, pp. 73-5

19 WLMK, v. 206, King to Hepburn, 22 Oct. 1935 (177136-40)

20 McKenty, *Mitch Hepburn*, p. 85; WLMK, Diary, 30 April 1936

21 NPL, v. 2, file 1936, Lambert to Hepburn, 5 Nov., Hepburn to Lambert, 12 Nov. 1936; also in WLMK, v. 218 (187622-3)

22 Alway, 'Hepburn,' pp. 210-11

23 *Ibid.*, p. 383

24 *The Politics of Development: Forests, Mines & Hydro-electric Power in Ontario, 1849-1941* (Toronto, 1974), pp. 486-7

25 'Hepburn,' pp. 103-6; McKenty, *Mitch Hepburn*, pp. 94-5; Nelles, *ibid.*, pp. 433-4

26 WLMK, Diary, 5 Jan. 1939

27 *The Politics of Development*, pp. 435-41

28 *Settlement and the Mining Frontier*, vol. IX in W.A. Mackintosh and W.L.G. Joerg, *Canadian Frontiers of Settlement* (Toronto, 1936)

29 Brian J. Young, 'C. George McCullagh and the Leadership League,' in Ramsay Cook, ed., *Politics of Discontent* (Toronto, 1967), pp. 78-81; McKenty, *Mitch Hepburn*, pp. 92-3

30 'Oshawa 1937,' in Abella, ed., *On Strike: Six Key Labour Struggles in Canada, 1919-1949* (Toronto, 1974), pp. 121, 124

31 WLMK, Diary, 13, 15 April 1937

32 *Ibid.*, 13 April 1937

33 See Irving Abella, *Nationalism, Communism, and Canadian Labour* (Toronto, 1973), *passim*

34 Abella, 'Oshawa 1937,' pp. 116-17; McKenty, *Mitch Hepburn*, pp. 112-13

35 Quoted in McKenty, *ibid.*, p. 117

36 One of King's aides broached this argument explicitly to the prime minister in a memorandum suggesting that the mining interests of both Ontario and Quebec were uniting around a 'Fascist programme under the spell-binders, Hepburn and Duplessis' to make a 'successful last ditch stand.' WLMK, Memoranda and Notes, v. 171, W.J. Turnbull to King, 4 June 1937 (C121378-9)

37 On the Leadership League, see Young, 'C. George McCullagh.' When King divulged his fears to the governor-general of McCullagh establishing a 'Fuehrer principle' in Canada to protect the big financial interests, the vice-regent was not very impressed: he 'did not think McCullagh had the brains to do much.' WLMK, Diary, 27 Feb. 1939. In this case at least, the cool judgment of the British outsider was sounder than the imaginative fears of his Canadian prime minister.

38 Abella, 'Oshawa 1937,' pp. 122-3; McKenty, *Mitch Hepburn*, pp. 119-25

39 *The Politics of Development*, pp. 464-87; quote is from p. 484

40 WLMK, Diary, 29 Nov. 1937

41 *Ibid.*, v. 247, Roebuck to King, 22 April 1937 (1207064-9)

42 *Ibid.*, v. 240, Elmore Philpott to King, 19 Dec. 1937 (206278-86). Even Norman Lambert passed on the information that the 'power ring was behind Mitch.' NPL, Diary, 3 Jan. 1939; see also WLMK, Diary, 5 Dec. 1938 and 18 Nov. 1939. There were other voices as well. In a speech at which King was present on the same platform in 1938, President Franklin D. Roosevelt issued a striking warning about a single American group ('with, of course, the usual surrounding penumbra of allies, affiliates, subsidiaries and satellites') which controlled all the central North American development of hydro-electric power – with the exception of Ontario Hydro, and which was attempting through control over the Great Lakes basin, to 'determine the economic fate of a large area, both in Canada and the United States.' See 'Address at Thousand Island Bridge,' 18 Aug. 1938, in E.H. Kavinsky and Julian Park, eds., *My Friends: 28 History Making Speeches by Franklin Delano Roosevelt* (Buffalo, NY, 1945), p. 57

43 McKenty, *Mitch Hepburn*, pp. 139-44; WLMK, v. 235, King to Hepburn, 8 Oct.

(202077), Hepburn to King, 12 Oct. (202078-9), and 18 Oct. 1937 (212080); v. 243, H.A. Bruce to Lord Tweedsmuir, 27 Oct. (209353-4), King to Tweedsmuir, 29 Oct. 1937 (209355-9); Diary, 14 and 19 Oct. 1937

44 WLMK, v. 237, Ian Mackenzie to King, 28 July 1937 (203801-4); NPL, Diary, 9 March 1935

45 WLMK, Diary, 6 Aug. 1932, 27 Nov. 1934, 28 July 1937, 6 Jan. 1938

46 Sir Anthony Jenkinson, 'The Premier at Home,' *Saturday Night*, 4 Dec. 1937

47 ER, v. 1, interview with Hepburn, 27 June 1932

48 NPL, Diary, 14 Jan. 1934

49 WLMK, Diary, 29 April, 27 Nov. 1934. King defined 'beggars on horseback' as 'men in positions of power and authority, but without tradition, education, and often any sense of responsibility and duty.'

50 McKenty, *Mitch Hepburn*, p. 184

51 WLMK, Memoranda and Notes, v. 171, W.P. Mulock, 'Memorandum re Hepburn's attitude and threats, etc.' 26 April 1938 (c121416-7); Diary, 26 April 1938; v. 254, V.C. McRuer to King, 13 Dec. 1938 (216508-9)

52 WLMK, v. 213, Thomas Ahearn to King, 6 Nov. 1936 (183385-8); Diary, 16 Oct. 1935; A.W. Rasporich, 'Faction and Class in Modern Lakehead Politics,' *Lakehead University Review*, VII (Summer 1974); WLMK, Memoranda and Notes, v. 152, memorandum, E.A. Pickering to King, 4 Feb. 1937 (c110200-1); v. 253, R.A. MacDougall to King, 11 Jan. 1938 (215789-90)

53 WLMK, Diary, 3 May, 21 Dec. 1938, 29 Nov. 1937; NPL, Diary, 12 March 1938

54 WLMK, Diary, 3 Oct. 1937, 21 Nov. 1938; McKenty, *Mitch Hepburn*, pp. 168-9; Alway, 'Hepburn,' pp. 215-16; NPL, Diary, 3 Dec. 1938

55 WLMK, Diary, 22 Oct. 1937

56 NPL, Diary, 13 Oct., 22 July 1938; McKenty, *Mitch Hepburn*, p. 168

57 J.L. Granatstein, 'Conservative Party Finance, 1939-1945,' in Committee on Election Expenses, *Studies in Canadian Party Finance* (Ottawa, 1966), p. 281. On Smith, see NLF, v. 826, memorandum, Duncan MacTavish to H.E. Kidd, 23 April 1953.

58 NPL, Diary, 6 April 1938. Of course the obverse of this equation was that the provincial party *did* have adequate funding. There is unfortunately little detailed information. We do know that in the 1937 provincial campaign, the Liberals spent at least $119,153 on province-wide advertising ($60,000 on print media, $25,000 on radio, $21,000 on outdoor displays, $8000 on literature, $5000 on other sundries). WLMK, v. 237, J.F. MacKay to King, 23 Oct. 1937 (203678-9). This amount was more than the national publicity budget in the federal campaign of 1935, and more than the federal spending on Ontario publicity, even with provincial financial help in that same election. See Table 2.6, Chapter 2, above

59 NPL, Diary, 15 Aug., 2 Dec. 1938; WLMK, Diary, 2 and 5 Dec. 1938; Memoranda and Notes, v. 171, memorandum, W.P. Mulock and S. Factor, 26 April 1938 (c121418). Raymond, in the course of a bitter attack on King at this time, spoke in friendly fashion of Hepburn. *Ibid.*, v. 252, Raymond to Ernest Lapointe, 3 Dec. 1938 (215318-9)

60 WLMK, Diary, 29 April, 3 May 1938; Alway, 'Hepburn,' pp. 267-8

61 WLMK, Diary, 15 Dec. 1938

62 *Ibid.*, 8, 10, and 13 Dec. 1938; Rasporich, 'Faction and Class,' pp. 49-50

63 WLMK, Diary, 12, 15, and 19 Dec. 1938, 18 Jan. 1939; Memoranda and Notes, v. 192, nos. c135110-35. Alway, 'Hepburn,' pp. 262-5; McKenty, *Mitch Hepburn*, pp. 170-2

64 NPL, Diary, 9 Sept., 20 Nov. 1936

65 WLMK, Diary, 19 June 1938, 5, 6, Jan., 5 June 1939; v. 235, Hardy to King, 20 July (201900), 7 Aug. (291901-2), and 20 Aug. 1937 (201903-5)

66 NPL, Diary, 8 and 9 Dec. 1938; WLMK, v. 273, Norman McLarty to King, 15 July 1939 (230796-804)

67 NPL, Diary, 17 Jan., 28 March, 15 April, 11 May 1939; WLMK, v. 270, Lambert to King, 24 July 1939 (228966-7)

68 WLMK, Diary, 20 July 1939; Alway, 'Hepburn,' pp. 257, 287-92

69 *Canada in Question: Federalism in the Seventies* (Toronto, 1972), pp. 12-14

70 McKenty, *Mitch Hepburn*, pp. 199-205; NPL, v. 2, H.C. Hindmarsh to Lambert, 6 Oct. 1939, with enclosures; MKR, I, pp. 36-7

71 WLMK, Diary, 10, 12, 15, and 28 Sept. 1939

72 *Ibid.*, 18 Jan. 1940; NPL, Diary, 3 March 1940; Alway, 'Hepburn,' pp. 298-307; McKenty, *Mitch Hepburn*, pp. 206-19. J.L. Granatstein, *Canada's War: The Politics of the Mackenzie King Government, 1939-45* (Toronto, 1975), pp. 72-93

73 NPL, Diary, 17 Sept. 1940; McKenty, *Mitch Hepburn*, pp. 236-57. On Hepburn's curious love affair with the Communists, see also Alway, 'Hepburn,' pp. 344-5, and Ivan Avakumovic, *The Communist Party in Canada: A History* (Toronto, 1975), p. 151. The friendship of these unlikely allies continued into 1945. NPL, Diary, 19 Feb. 1945

74 McKenty, *Mitch Hepburn*, pp. 258-66; Alway, 'Hepburn,' pp. 357-63; Wearing, 'Ontario Political Parties,' p. 335

75 MKR, I, pp. 492-3

76 *Ibid.*, pp. 570-1. One Manitoba MP assisted in the Ontario election and concluded that 'it has never been my unfortunate lot to witness a condition of greater disorganization or worse organization ... This was due largely to the Hepburn turmoil over several years.' Provincial Archives of Manitoba, Ralph Maybank Papers, Maybank to King, 13 Aug. 1943

77 NLF, v. 802, memorandum, Frank Ryan, 8 June 1945; Public Archives Library,

Ontario Liberal Association, 'Annual Meeting and Convention, May 15-16, 1947' (typescript record), pp. 11-12

78 NLF, v. 599, Caroline Crerar to Mrs S.C. Tweed, 8 June 1943; v. 632, memorandum, n.a., n.d. (probably from Walter Harris' office)

79 Wearing, 'Ontario Political Parties,' pp. 331-2. Jack Pickersgill describes Thompson as a 'disaster,' the worst in a whole 'series of disasters.' Interview with Hon. J.W. Pickersgill, Ottawa, 15 July 1974

80 NLF, v. 596, confidential memorandum, 29 May, George Bagwell to Arthur Roebuck, 12 April 1946

81 Canadian Liberal (Summer 1954), cited in Paul H. Heppe, 'The Liberal Party of Canada,' unpublished PHD thesis, University of Wisconsin, 1957, p. 103. NLF, v. 618, Kidd to federal cabinet ministers, 31 Jan. 1950; v. 828, MacTavish to Harry Hamilton, 30 March 1953

82 'The Liberal Party,' pp. 202-3

83 Henry Jacek et al., 'The Congruence of Federal-Provincial Campaign Activity in Party Organizations: The Influence of Recruitment Patterns in Three Hamilton Ridings,' Canadian Journal of Political Science, V, 2 (June 1972), p. 194

CHAPTER NINE
The West

1 T. Peterson, 'Ethnic and Class Politics in Manitoba,' in Martin Robin, ed., Canadian Provincial Politics: The Party Systems of the Ten Provinces (Scarborough, 1972), pp. 69-71. On class voting in Manitoba historically, see Nelson Wiseman and K.W. Taylor, 'Ethnic vs Class Voting: The Case of Winnipeg, 1945', Canadian Journal of Political Science, VII, 2 (June 1974), pp. 314-27.

2 M.S. Donnelly, The Government of Manitoba (Toronto, 1963), pp. 51-6

3 John Wilson, 'The Decline of the Liberal Party in Manitoba Politics,' Journal of Canadian Studies, X, 1 (Feb. 1975), pp. 24-41

4 Donnelly, The Government of Manitoba, pp. 63-4; ER, v. 1, interview with D.G. Mackenzie, 16 July 1931. One Liberal MP claimed that his party had always been behind the Bracken government from the first 'even though some of its members at least were blissfully unaware of it.' PAC, H.W. Winkler Papers, 'Political Memoirs of Howard Winkler,' Jan. 1965

5 NPL, Diary, 16 Sept. and 28 Dec. 1932, 19-23 Jan. 1933; WLMK, v. 191, King to F.C. Hamilton, 29 Nov. 1932 (102827-8)

6 WLMK, v. 195, Crerar to King, 30 June 1933 (165687-90); v. 197, W.J. Lindal to Lambert, 4 Nov. 1933 (167220-1); v. 199, Crerar to King, 16 Feb. 1934 (170119-

21); v. 205, J.C. Davis to Lambert, 23 Feb. (175682), Davis to Lambert, 28 Feb. 1935 (175683). Lambert's interventions included federal nominations, some of which, given the complexities of Manitoba politics, do not easily fall into the simple dichotomy of 'die-hard' *v.* 'co-operator.' See WLMK, v. 197, Lindal to King, 18 Jan. 1933 (167247-8); and Winkler, 'Political Memoirs'

7 Donnelly, *The Government of Manitoba*, pp. 66-9, 104

8 Winkler, 'Political Memoirs,' postscript, 13 Oct. 1969

9 David Smith, 'The Prairie Provinces,' in D.J. Bellamy, J.H. Pammett, and D.C. Rowat, eds., *The Provincial Political Systems: Comparative Essays* (Toronto, 1976), p. 58. By 1958 it was apparent to all that the once efficient Liberal organization in Manitoba had been 'run into the ground' and that a 'completely new organization must be created.' NLF, v. 881, 'Notes on Organization in Manitoba,' n.a., n.d. (prepared for 1958 National Liberal Convention). Jimmy Gardiner had no doubt as to who was to blame: it was the 'co-operators' who had sold out pure Liberalism, 'the group in Manitoba who ruined Liberalism in the West.' Gardiner also warned prophetically that 'our route back will be, so far as the West is concerned, a long one.' Twenty years later, that route has become more doubtful than ever. CDH, v. 107, file 75 (1), Gardiner to C.D. Howe, 11 Dec. 1958

10 *Prairie Liberalism: The Liberal Party in Saskatchewan, 1905-71* (Toronto, 1975), p. 324

11 See John C. Courtney and David E. Smith, 'Saskatchewan: Parties in a Politically Competitive Province,' in Robin, *Canadian Provincial Politics*, pp. 290-318

12 'The Saskatchewan Liberal Machine before 1929,' *Canadian Journal of Economics and Political Science*, II, 1 (Feb. 1936), pp. 27-40. Transcripts of the interviews which formed the basis of this article may be found in ER, v. 1.

13 Smith, *Prairie Liberalism*, pp. 220-3

14 See Chapter 2, above. Most of the information on this point is drawn from Norman Lambert's diaries from 1932 through 1935.

15 WLMK, v. 185, T.C. Davis to King, 13 Aug. 1931 (157593-5)

16 NPL, Diary, 4 Nov. 1935. It is not immediately apparent from the nature of Lambert's entry here whether Gardiner was referring to the public or to the party treasury. One must assume that either was *possible.*

17 Courtney and Smith, 'Saskatchewan,' p. 315. One man, T.C. Douglas, went from federal to provincial back to federal politics.

18 F.W. Gibson, 'The Cabinet of 1935,' in Gibson, ed., *Cabinet Formation and Bicultural Relations: Seven Case Studies*, Study no. 6 of the Royal Commission on Bilingualism and Biculturalism (Ottawa, 1970), p. 139

19 WLMK, Diary, 18-21 Oct. 1935

20 See Chapter 8, above; and WLMK, Memoranda and Notes, v. 192, memo, E.A. Pickering to King, 14 July 1938 (C134984), citing both financial and publicity support given the Saskatchewan provincial party by Hepburn's organization.

21 WLMK, Diary, 11 Aug. 1939

22 NLF, v. 632, Gardiner to H.E. Kidd, 21 Nov. 1955

23 Ibid., v. 596, memorandum, n.a., July 1944

24 See Chapter 5, above. A good barometer of Gardiner's standing in the party is the attitude of Jack Pickersgill. When interviewed, Pickersgill was rather critical of the Saskatchewan minister, whose vaunted machine, he noted caustically, had failed even to deliver King's own Prince Albert seat in 1945. Pickersgill interview, 15 July 1974. In his memoirs, Pickersgill's judgment is more muted, but still biting. My Years with Louis St Laurent: A Political Memoir (Toronto, 1975), p. 66. Gardiner himself has until now lacked an academic biographer, a gap which Norman Ward is about to fill. Ward has edited the publication of a previously unpublished novel written by Gardiner in 1910 which suggests some of his political philosophy. The Politician, or The Treason of Democracy (Saskatoon, 1975)

25 NLF, v. 826, Gardiner to Kidd, 8 Sept. 1952

26 Smith, Prairie Liberalism, pp. 259-60

27 Ibid., p. 262

28 Ibid., pp. 264-70; NLF, v. 635, memo, Kidd to Duncan MacTavish, 9 Nov. 1956

29 L.G. Thomas, The Liberal Party in Alberta: A History of Politics in the Province of Alberta, 1905-1921 (Toronto, 1959), pp. 172, 195-207

30 WLMK, v. 175, King to W.R. Howson, 7 Feb. 1930 (149353-4). On the lack of organization, see letter from R.A. Blatchford, defeated Liberal MP from Edmonton, to Miss O'Malley, 12 Sept. 1930, v. 172.

31 John J. Barr, The Dynasty: The Rise and Fall of Social Credit in Alberta (Toronto, 1974), pp. 35-6

32 WLMK, v. 197, J.B. McBride to King, 22 Aug. 1933 (167341-2), and submission by W.R. Howson to MacMillan Commission, 21 Aug. 1933 (167343-56)

33 Ibid., v. 200, exchange of correspondence between King and Howson, from Sept. through Dec. 1934 (171050-66); Alberta Liberal Association pamphlet (191708-11)

34 John A. Irving, The Social Credit Movement in Alberta (Toronto, 1959), p. 331

35 NPL, Diary, 23 March 1934, 4 June, 9 July 1935. According to the latter entry, almost $8500 had gone to Alberta from the federal party from 1934 through June 1935, the eve of the election. See also WLMK, Memoranda and Notes, v. 162, f. 1476, 'Private Report from Alberta,' 31 May 1935 (C116383-4), and CAD, v. 10, Charles Campbell to Charles Dunning, 5 July 1935

36 Norman Ward, 'Hon. James Gardiner and the Liberal Party of Alberta, 1935-40,'

Canadian Historical Review, LVI, 3 (Sept. 1975), p. 305. G. Anton, 'The Liberal Party in Alberta,' unpublished MA thesis, University of Calgary, 1972, cites the following areas of federal patronage in the post-Second World War period: (a) NHA mortgage lawyers; (b) 25 judges; (c) QC's; (d) Crown prosecutors; (e) other executive and administrative positions. All these tend, Anton suggests, to draw a lawyer-dominated provincial opposition party toward federal-provincial intra-party co-operation. MacKinnon suggested to King as early as 1936 that 'lawyer leadership' should be avoided, given the evident unpopularity in the province of lawyers who used Liberal politics as a 'stepping stone' to the Bench. WLMK, v. 220, MacKinnon to King, 4 June 1936 (190144-5)

37 Ward, 'Hon. James Gardiner,' p. 305; WLMK, v. 204, Buchanan to King, 26 Oct. 1935 (194857-8)

38 WLMK, v. 245, King to W.C. Barrie, 7 April 1938 (210144). This statement followed a Social Credit victory in an Edmonton by-election. See also Diary, 2 and 15 Dec. 1936

39 Ward, 'Hon. James Gardiner,' pp. 308-11; WLMK, Diary, 13 Nov. 1936

40 NPL, Diary, 3 and 13 April, 7 Oct. 1937. When Gray asked Lambert for funds in late 1938, Lambert replied 'that while my position re Alberta was clearly favourable to his independent action, I was bound to play the game with the policy of the federal Government as expressed by Gardiner.' *Ibid.*, 21 Nov. 1938. When Lambert had protested directly to King he was informed that Gardiner had been given full responsibility. WLMK, Memoranda and Notes, v. 192, memorandum for Mr Henry, 13 Sept. 1937, (c134991). There was also some cabinet opposition to the Gardiner move. *Ibid.*, Diary, 28 Oct. and 10 Sept. 1937

41 *Ibid.*, v. 250, Gray to Gardiner, 25 March (213442-3) and Gardiner to Gray, 28 March (213439-41); Diary, 21 March; v. 245, Barrie to King, 2 April (210145-6) and 17 June (210152-3); Memoranda and Notes, v. 152, 'Comment contained in correspondence received re Edmonton by-election, etc.,' 21 April (c110166-8); v. 247, memorandum, E.A. Pickering to King, 23 June (211260-2); v. 254, MacKinnon to King, 15 Aug. (216309-13), all 1938

42 The federal government was under intense pressure from finance capital to stamp out the offending legislation. See WLMK, v. 253, Leighton McCarthy to King, 10 May 1938 (215585-6). J.R. Mallory, *Social Credit and the Federal Power in Canada* (Toronto, 1954), indicates the extent of the pressure. On the other hand, Hepburn's Hydro repudiation also affected investors, including so eminent a personage as King Edward VIII who complained to the prime minister about Hepburn's 'communism.' Diary, 27 Oct. 1936. Despite such influential enemies, the government of Ontario was not to be treated in so cavalier a fashion as governments from the prairie hinterland. King was troubled by this double standard, even as he accepted it. 'I believe we should really have disallowed in

both cases, but a larger political issue of a party character would have been raised.' Diary, 6 Aug. 1937. The contrast between reservation of the Alberta Press Bill, limiting the freedom of the press, and the refusal to act against the 'Padlock Law' in Quebec was perhaps the most striking contradiction of all.

43 WLMK, v. 214, Buchanan to King, 6 July 1936 (184559)

44 The worsening background is detailed in Mallory, *Social Credit*, pp. 80-1, and the entire affair is recounted by Norman Ward, 'William Aberhart in the Year of the Tiger,' *Dalhousie Review*, LIV, 3 (Autumn 1974). See also J.C. Courtney, 'Prime Ministerial Character: An Examination of Mackenzie King's Political Leadership,' *Canadian Journal of Political Science*, IX, 1 (March 1976), p. 93

45 WLMK, v. 254, Bowen to MacKinnon, 6 May 1938 (216302); v. 250, Gray to King, 16 May 1938 (213870-1); Diary, 16 May 1938. As late as 1939, Bowen was still carrying on a form of guerilla warfare against Aberhart. During the royal tour of that year, King was surprised to discover that the lieutenant-governor had not invited the premier to the reception at the legislature, in order to 'limit the numbers'(!). King thoughtfully arranged to have Aberhart's children presented to the royal couple. H. Blair Neatby, *William Lyon Mackenzie King: The Prism of Unity, 1932-1939* (Toronto, 1976), III, pp. 311-12.

46 WLMK, v. 250, A.C. Grant to Gardiner, 4 April 1938 (213849-50); Diary, 21 Nov. 1938

47 Ward, 'Hon. James Gardiner,' pp. 319-20; J.A. Long and F.Q. Quo, 'Alberta: One Party Dominance,' in Robin, *Canadian Provincial Parties*, pp. 3, 6

48 LSTL, v. 61, T.H. Wood to C.D. Howe, 29 Sept. 1948, claiming that $40,000 had gone to Alberta through Saskatchewan from 1936-9, and A.J. McGowan to Gardiner, 3 March 1949. NPL, Diary, 21-22 May 1941. Anton, 'The Liberal Party in Alberta,' p. 41, declares that before the 1970s the federal Liberals collected funds for all the provincial election campaigns.

49 NLF, v. 861, 1945 advisory council, p. 54; v. 862, 1949 advisory council, p. 39

50 Joseph Wearing, 'Mutations in a Political Party: The Liberal Party of Canada in the Fifties and Sixties,' paper presented to the Canadian Political Science Association annual meeting, Edmonton, June 1975, p. 19

51 NLF, v. 635, Kidd to MacTavish, 9 Nov. 1956; LSTL, v. 225, J.H. Prowse to St Laurent, 20 Dec. 1956; Anton, 'The Liberal Party in Alberta, p. 26

52 Martin Robin, 'British Columbia: The Politics of Class Conflict,' in Robin, *Canadian Political Parties*, pp. 27-68. See also the same author's two-volume history of British Columbia, *The Company Province: The Rush for Spoils, 1871-1933* and *Pillars of Profit, 1934-1972* (Toronto, 1972 and 1973). Richard Simeon and David J. Elkins, 'Regional Political Cultures in Canada,' *Canadian Journal of Political Science*, VII, 3 (Sept. 1974), pp. 397-437, offer striking evidence of the divergence of British Columbia from the political attitudes of the rest of

the country. Particularly noteworthy is the high proportion of working class 'critics,' and the low proportion of 'deferentials' and 'disaffecteds' from the same class (Table XIII, p. 424).

53 ER, v. 1, interviews with General Odlum and J.E. Norcross, 31 Aug. 1931, give interesting background on the weakness of partisanship.

54 This volatility is a long-standing phenomenon, extending even to before the First World War. *Ibid.*, interview with R.L. Reid, 6 Sept. 1931

55 WLMK, Memoranda and Notes, v. 236, W.J. Turnbull to King, 26 March 1943 (C159815); IM, v. 23, Mackenzie to D. Cromie, 10 April 1943

56 Margaret Ormsby, *British Columbia: A History* (Toronto, 1958), p. 449

57 Robin, *The Company Province*, I, p. 249

58 Margaret A. Ormsby, 'T. Dufferin Pattullo and the Little New Deal,' *Canadian Historical Review*, XLIII, 4 (Dec. 1962), 277-97

59 WLMK, v. 171, Ralph Campney to King, 31 May 1930; NPL, Diary, 24-26 March, 26-27 April 1934, suggest intrigues in Vancouver too Byzantine to unravel. The Ian Mackenzie Papers, v. 15-22, bear ample evidence of his intimate connections with BC patronage and local projects such as post offices and dredging contracts in the Vancouver area. WLMK, Diary, 4 Oct. 1932; Neatby, *King*, III, pp. 14-15

60 Wealthy BC department store owner E.S. Woodward wrote King to complain about McGeer's 'half-baked and unscientific programme.' WLMK, v. 212, Woodward to King, 12 Jan. 1935 (193052). Woodward then followed with his own somewhat bizarre set of ideas which could only with great care be distinguished from those of McGeer in terms of unorthodoxy. British Columbia was fertile ground for free thinking.

61 Robin, *The Company Province*, II, pp. 11-12

62 IM, v. 15, McGeer to Mackenzie, 15 May 1942, explaining that he was 'not friendly' with the chief Liberal organizer in the province.

63 *The Incredible Canadian* (Toronto, 1952), p. 216

64 NPL, Diary, 23-24 Sept. 1932; *Ibid.*, v. 2, Tom Reid to Lambert, 22 Sept. 1935

65 WLMK, Diary, 19-23 Oct. 1935. King had had suspicions of 'what may have happened in B.C. in some deals there' two years earlier. *Ibid.*, 22 Jan. 1933. The alleged scandal *may* have been connected to campaign contributions surrounding the projected New Westminster bridge planned by Pattullo, but this is only speculation. See Chapter 2, above, and n. 68 below

66 *Ibid.*, 16 Jan., 7 April 1936, 26 Feb. 1937; v. 226, Pattullo to King, 18 May (193166), and 6 July 1936 (193181-2)

67 *Ibid.*, v. 239, Pattullo to King, 17 Dec. 1937 (206199-202)

68 Robin, *The Company Province*, II, pp. 19 and 43, notes some of the alleged scandals which surrounded the project.

69 WLMK, Diary, 4 Nov. 1937; v. 256, Pattullo to King, 6 June 1938 (218460-2)

70 Judith Barbara Ward, 'Federal-Provincial Relations within the Liberal Party of British Columbia,' unpublished MA thesis, University of British Columbia, 1966, pp. 43-8

71 Ormsby, *British Columbia*, p. 478

72 Robin, *The Company Province*, II, p. 107

73 *Ibid.*, pp. 50-5; IM, v. 23, letter from six BC Liberal MPs to W.J. Knox, president, Provincial Liberal Association, 8 March 1947; Ward, 'Federal-Provincial Relations,' p. 71

74 NLF, v. 861, 1947 advisory council, p. 32

75 *Ibid.*, v. 618, Sherwood Lett to Martin, 12 May 1949

76 *Ibid.*, v. 619, A.H. Sager to Kidd, 1 March, Kidd to Sager, 2 and 23 March 1949; BC-Ottawa conflicts on advertising are noted in Chapter 6, above

77 Robin, *The Company Province,* II, p. 107-37. NLF, v. 826, E.T. Applewhaite to Kidd, 25 Aug. 1952, suggested that both Liberals and Conservatives had 'asked for ruin. Each was split from top to bottom ... personal ambitions and personal prejudices.'

78 Ward, 'Federal-Provincial Relations,' pp. 90-9; Robin, *The Company Province,* II, II, p. 331 and n. 99

79 In the 1930s BC federal Liberals had been abjectly dependent upon eastern funds. WLMK, v. 197, Mackenzie to King, 28 Sept. (167622-3) and King to Mackenzie, 4 Oct. 1933 (167624-5). See also Chapter 2, above. Mackenzie tried to explain this on the following grounds: 'In our financing we are handicapped by the fact that all over British Columbia our industries are but local branches of Eastern concerns. This means that the local offices will not make contributions as they claim that the head offices have made contributions in the East.' *Ibid.*, v. 272, Mackenzie to King, 25 July 1939 (230384-6). Following the war this logic no longer held; Social Credit certainly was able to collect from local sources. Yet even if the BC Liberals were able to raise funds they were altogether unco-operative with the federal party, so much so that when funds became scarce in the 1958 election, Duncan MacTavish turned BC Liberals down flat when asked for funds and made it plain that they deserved such treatment for past behaviour. CDH, v. 107, John Aird to Howe, 2 Sept. 1958, and Howe to Senator S.J. Smith, 16 Sept. 1958

80 See Chapter 5, above

81 NLF, v. 619, Alistair Fraser to Kidd, 23 Jan., 9 May, 3 June 1953; v. 626, Senator Gray Turgeon to Kidd, 22 Oct. 1952; v. 632, Kidd to Campney, 22 Dec. 1954. BC, v. 61, Minutes of National Executive Committee, 24 Feb. 1954

82 NLF, v. 635, Kidd to MacTavish, 9 Nov. 1956

83 Ward, 'Federal-Provincial Relations,' p. 110

CHAPTER TEN
The Atlantic Provinces

1 On the 'development of underdevelopment' in the Maritimes, see T.W. Acheson, 'The National Policy and the Industrialization of the Maritimes, 1880-1919,' *Acadiensis*, I, 1 (Spring 1972); Tom Naylor, *The History of Canadian Business, 1867-1914*, 2 vols. (Toronto, 1975); and Bruce Archibald, 'Atlantic Regional Underdevelopment and Socialism,' in Laurier LaPierre *et al.*, eds., *Essays on the Left: Essays in Honour of T.C. Douglas* (Toronto, 1971), pp. 103-20.

2 See Ramsay Cook, *Provincial Autonomy, Minority Rights and the Compact Theory, 1867-1921*, Study no. 4 of the Royal Commission on Bilingualism and Biculturalism (Ottawa, 1969), pp. 9-12, and William H. Riker, *Federalism: Origin, Operation, Significance* (Boston, 1964)

3 In five general elections from 1935 to 1953, Liberal candidates received the highest popular vote in each of the Atlantic provinces without exception. With only three exceptions (out of eighteen cases) they polled over 50 per cent of the vote. In Newfoundland's first Canadian federal election in 1949, the Liberal vote reached 71.9 per cent – a higher percentage than the party had ever received in one province since the First World War. Figures from H. Scarrow, *Canada Votes* (New Orleans, 1962)

4 JLR, v. 12, Macdonald to Ralston, 10 Dec. 1931; NLF, v. 619, Murray Veinotte to R.L. Winters, 4 April 1953

5 In the 1920 Nova Scotia provincial election a Farmer-Labour group briefly replaced the Conservatives as the major opposition in the legislature, but disappeared as quickly as it had arisen. A Maritime bloc movement, inspired by Atlantic business interests, attempted to make an impact on federal policies through co-operation between Liberal and Conservative MPs from the region in the 1921 to 1925 Parliament. Partisan loyalties and party discipline were too strong for such a movement to succeed. ER, v. 1, interview with John Baxter, Conservative premier of New Brunswick, 1925-31. The Maritimes Rights movement, also inspired by Atlantic business interests, did succeed in gaining some rare concessions from Ottawa, but it too avoided any attempt to circumvent traditional party lines, utilizing the Conservative party in Nova Scotia as one of its instruments. See Royal Commission on Dominion-Provincial Relations, *Report* (Ottawa, 1941), I, p. 134. Graphic representation of popular vote statistics in provincial elections, demonstrating the low level of third-party support in the Maritime provinces, may be found in John Wilson, 'The Canadian Political Cultures: Towards a Redefinition of the Nature of the Canadian Political System,' *Canadian Journal of Political Science*, VII, 3 (Sept. 1974), pp. 465-6.

6 Committee on Election Expenses, *Report* (Ottawa, 1966)

7 *The Rise of a Third Party* (Englewood Cliffs, NJ, 1971), and 'Third Parties in Canada Revisited: A Rejoinder and Elaboration of the Theory of One-Party Dominance,' *Canadian Journal of Political Science*, VI, 3 (Sept. 1973), 439-60

8 'Regional Political Cultures in Canada,' *Canadian Journal of Political Science*, VII, 3 (Sept. 1974), pp. 397-437; see also Mildred A. Schwartz, *Politics and Territory: The Sociology of Regional Persistence in Canada* (Montreal, 1974), especially pp. 243-6

9 ER, v. 1, interview with Sinclair, 13 Oct. 1931

10 *Ibid.* A series of articles by Robert Campbell in the *Globe and Mail*, 19-22 Jan. 1972, on New Brunswick indicates that the importance of patronage has scarcely diminished over the years.

11 WLMK, v. 204, Thane Campbell to King, 26 July 1935 (175055-6); NLF, v. 826, Angus Elderkin to H.E. Kidd, 4 Sept. 1952. Of course the federal merit system could cut against either party, but it was the Liberals very success at Ottawa which tended to focus the problem on them. For the Conservatives' difficulties when in office nationally see WLMK, v. 177, E.M. Macdonald to King, 12 Dec. 1930 (150638)

12 ER, v. 1, interview with J.B. McNair, Sept. 1931

13 See, for example, James M. Cameron, *Political Pictonians* (Ottawa, n.d.), p. 148. Mr Cameron writes: 'The loose form of organization has been fertile soil for the cultivation of cliques, jealousies and quarrels. The party in office, with patronage to dispense, generally has been able to preserve unity.'

14 Cited by J. Murray Beck, 'The Party System in Nova Scotia: Tradition and Conservatism,' in Martin Robin, ed., *Canadian Provincial Politics: The Party Systems of the Ten Provinces* (Scarborough, 1972), p. 196

15 P.J. Fitzpatrick, 'New Brunswick: The Politics of Pragmatism,' in Robin, *ibid.*, pp. 117-19

16 *Politics in New Brunswick* (Toronto, 1961)

17 WLMK, v. 183, King to Veniot, 31 May (156131-4), Veniot to King, 3 June 1930 (156137-9)

18 NLF, v. 871, H.R. Emmerson to J.-A. Blanchette, 24 July 1948; 'Liberal Party Organization' (NLF document), 23 Oct. 1948

19 Thorburn, *Politics in New Brunswick*, pp. 100-2; BC, v. 61, minutes of national executive committee, NLF, 24 Feb. 1954

20 Beck, 'The Party System in Nova Scotia, p. 191; see also Beck, *The Government of Nova Scotia* (Toronto, 1957).

21 See Chapter 6, above

22 'The Party System in Nova Scotia,' pp. 183-4

23 Wayne E. MacKinnon, *The Life of the Party: A History of the Liberal Party in Prince Edward Island* (Summerside, 1973), p. 132. NLF, v. 862, 1950 advisory

council, pp. 46, 48, 1951, p. 95; v. 621, 1952 advisory council, and Kidd to Schurman, 19 Nov. 1952; LSTL, v. 137, folder 0-20-1, Robert Winters to J.G. Fogo, 13 March 1952. On PEI politics in general, see Frank MacKinnon, *The Government of Prince Edward Island* (Toronto, 1951), especially pp. 249-58, and MacKinnon, 'Prince Edward Island: Big Engine, Little Body,' in Robin, *Canadian Provincial Politics*, pp. 240-61.

24 MacKinnon, *Life of the Party*, pp. 117, 127-9

25 See, for example, Peter Neary, 'Democracy in Newfoundland: A Comment,' *Journal of Canadian Studies*, IV, 1 (Feb. 1969), pp. 43-4; D.J. Bellamy, 'The Atlantic Provinces,' in Bellamy, J.H. Pammett, and D.C. Rowat, eds., *The Provincial Political Systems: Comparative Essays* (Toronto, 1976), p. 5

26 See S.J.R. Noel's study, *Politics in Newfoundland* (Toronto, 1971) which covers the pre-Confederation period, but includes a suggestive final chapter on the post-1949 period. Anthony P. Cohen's *The Management of Myths: The Politics of Legitimation in a Newfoundland Community* (Manchester, 1975) is a book-length exploration of the Newfoundland political culture. Richard Gwyn's *Smallwood: The Unlikely Revolutionary* (Toronto, 1972) is a journalistic approach of uncommonly high quality. Articles include Susan McCorquordale, 'The Only Living Father's Realm,' in Robin, *Canadian Political Parties*, pp. 134-67; Neary, 'Democracy in Newfoundland,' and 'Party Politics in Newfoundland, 1949-71: A Survey and Analysis,' *Journal of Canadian Studies*, VI, 4 (Nov. 1971) and VII, 1 (Feb. 1972); George Perlin, 'Patronage and Paternalism: Politics in Newfoundland,' in Ioan Davies and Kathleen Herman, eds., *Social Space: Canadian Perspectives* (Toronto, 1971), pp. 190-5. There is also an important unpublished paper by Steven B. Wolinetz, 'Party Organization in Newfoundland,' paper presented to the Canadian Political Science Association annual meeting, Edmonton, June 1975. Joey Smallwood's own volume of memoirs, *I Chose Canada: The Memoirs of the Honourable Joseph R. 'Joey' Smallwood* (Toronto, 1973), not surprisingly proves to be of limited value.

27 See Pickersgill's memoir, *My Years with Louis St Laurent* (Toronto, 1975), pp. 76-85

28 Horwood, 'Newfoundland and Confederation, 1948-49,' in Mason Wade, ed., *Regionalism in the Canadian Community, 1867-1967* (Toronto, 1969), pp. 249-57; Gwyn, *Smallwood*, p. 100

29 Horwood, *ibid.*, pp. 247, 249

30 On one occasion, Smallwood's deputy minister of fisheries left the province owing a substantial amount of money to the premier, which the national party had to make up. Gwyn, *Smallwood*, p. 173; BC, v. 50, confidential memorandum 'Newfoundland Politics,' 4 Nov. 1952, no author

31 *Parliamentary Debates on the Subject of the Confederation of the British North American Provinces, 1865*, (new ed., Ottawa, 1951), p. 519

32 *Smallwood*, p. 125
33 'Party Politics,' part 1, p. 5
34 *Politics in Newfoundland*, p. 282
35 Neary, 'Party Politics,' p. 14; the phrase is Smallwood's own.
36 Much later, in the 1970s, after Pickersgill had retired from politics and Smallwood had been defeated, the former minister intervened against Smallwood's attempt to win back the provincial Liberal leadership, provoking a somewhat petulant comment from Smallwood that he had made Pickersgill all that he was. By this stage, Smallwood's political sense was obviously less than that of Pickersgill.
37 'Democracy in Newfoundland,' p. 44
38 Alan Kornberg, 'Parliament in Canadian Society,' in Kornberg and Lloyd D. Mosolf, eds., *Legislatures in Developmental Perspective* (New York, 1970), p. 118, cites figures from Roman March indicating that the proportion of MPs with provincial experience was never higher than 24 per cent from the 1870s on, and by the period 1954-8 had dropped to 4 per cent.

CONCLUSION
Party and state in the Liberal era

1 *The Real World of Democracy* (Toronto, 1965), and *Democratic Theory: Essays in Retrieval* (London, 1973)
2 Siegfried, *The Race Question in Canada* (1906; new ed., Toronto, 1966); James Bryce, *Canada: An Actual Democracy* (Toronto, 1921)
3 R.J. Van Loon, 'Political Participation in Canada: The 1965 Election,' *Canadian Journal of Political Science*, III, 3 (Sept. 1970), pp. 376-99; Robert Presthus, *Elite Accommodation in Canadian Politics* (Toronto, 1973)
4 D.V. Smiley, *Canada in Question: Federalism in the Seventies* (2nd ed., Toronto, 1976)
5 'Federal Strains within a Canadian Party,' in H.G. Thorburn, ed., *Party Politics in Canada* (3rd ed., Scarborough, 1972), pp. 129-30
6 *Industry and Humanity* (1918; new ed., Toronto, 1973), p. 246

Index